Syon Abbey Book of Hours (15th Cent.)
*Courtesy of Special Collections, University of Exeter.*

# Daily Office of Our Lady

*According to the usage of*
*The Order of the Most Holy Saviour*
*(The Bridgettines)*

*Frontispiece from the 1697 Landshut edition of The Bridgettine Breviary. An engraving of Saint Bridget depicting her receiving divine inspiration from the Holy Spirit about the composition of the Breviary, accompanied by her daughter Saint Katharine. Reprinted in the 1908 Tournai edition.*

# Daily Office of Our Lady

## The Syon Breviary

*Syon Abbey*

# Daily Office of Our Lady
## *The Syon Breviary*

Published by The Bridgettine Sisters
(Order of the Most Holy Saviour)
Nazareth House, Durnford Street, Plymouth, Devon PL1 3QR



A CIP catalogue record of this book is available from The British Library.
ISBN 978-0-9930346-0-2



Ninth edition & first publication in English with music.
*First published in Latin in Lübeck, 1512; Champs, 1544; Arras, 1610; Cologne, 1628; Wilna, 1684; Landshut, 1697; Lublin, 1748 and Tournay, 1908.*
Concordat cum originali: *Very Rev. Leo Smith, O.S.B., Prior of Buckfast Abbey, 1967.*
Cum approbatio Ordinarii 'ad usum privatim': *Rt. Rev. Charles Graham, 1906; Rt. Rev. Cyril Restieaux, 1967; Rt. Rev. Christopher Budd, 2001; Rt. Rev. Mark O'Toole, 2015, Bishops of Plymouth.*
***Published for private prayer only. Not for public worship or recitation.***

Translated from Latin and set to music by *Rev. Brian Foley*. Psalm tones by *Dom Gregory Murray, O.S.B.* Music pages typeset by *Theo Keller*. Edited and produced by *Adrian Wardle*. Printed & bound in the UK by CPI Books Ltd, Croydon CR0 3YY www.cpibooks.co.uk FSC Certificate TT-COC-002231. Printed on chlorine bleach-free paper from sustainable sources.

---

*The Syon Breviary*

# TABLE OF CONTENTS


FOREWORD

by the *Rt. Rev. Christopher Budd*, eighth Bishop of Plymouth. ........ 9.

PREFACE

by *Sister Anne Smyth, O.Ss.S.*, Abbess of Syon, 1976 – 2011. ........ 11.

STRUCTURE OF THE DAILY OFFICE

a guide to the order of service of each of the Hours. ........ 19.

RUBRICS IN CURRENT USE

essential notes and guidance for the correct use of the Breviary. ........ 25.

SUNDAY

*Introduction to Lauds* ........ 33.
Lauds *(Morning Prayer)* ........ 39.
Terce & Sext ........ 48.
*Before None* ........ 55.
None ........ 57.
*Before the Office of Readings* ........ 67.
Office of Readings *(Matins)* ........ 68.
*Before Vespers* ........ 77.
Vespers *(Evening Prayer)* ........ 79.
*Hymn in honour of Saint Bridget* ........ 93.
Compline ........ 95.

MONDAY

Lauds *(Morning Prayer)* ........ 109.
Terce & Sext ........ 111.
None ........ 119.
Office of Readings *(Matins)* ........ 127.
Vespers *(Evening Prayer)* ........ 134.
Compline ........ 147.

**TUESDAY**

Lauds *(Morning Prayer)* ... ... ... 155.
Terce & Sext ... ... ... 157.
None ... ... ... 166.
Office of Readings *(Matins)* ... ... ... 174.
Vespers *(Evening Prayer)* ... ... ... 182.
Compline ... ... ... 194.

**WEDNESDAY**

Lauds *(Morning Prayer)* ... ... ... 201.
Terce & Sext ... ... ... 203.
None ... ... ... 214.
Office of Readings *(Matins)* ... ... ... 222.
Vespers *(Evening Prayer)* ... ... ... 230.
Compline ... ... ... 241.

**THURSDAY**

Lauds *(Morning Prayer)* ... ... ... 248.
Terce & Sext ... ... ... 250.
None ... ... ... 258.
Office of Readings *(Matins)* ... ... ... 266.
Vespers *(Evening Prayer)* ... ... ... 274.
Compline ... ... ... 283.

**FRIDAY**

Lauds *(Morning Prayer)* ... ... ... 291.
*Canticles at Lauds* ... ... ... 294.
Terce & Sext ... ... ... 301.
None ... ... ... 311.
Office of Readings *(Matins)* ... ... ... 321.
Vespers *(Evening Prayer)* ... ... ... 332.
Compline ... ... ... 344.

**SATURDAY**

Lauds *(Morning Prayer)* ... ... ... 353.
Terce & Sext ... ... ... 356.
None ... ... ... 362.
Office of Readings *(Matins)* ... ... ... 369.
Vespers *(Evening Prayer)* ... ... ... 377.
Compline ... ... ... 389.

## Proper of the Seasons

*Liturgical Calendar* ... ... ... 405.
Feasts of the Lord ... ... ... 407.
Feasts of Our Lady ... ... ... 422.
Saints & Martyrs of The Bridgettine Order ... ... ... 440.
Responsories at First Vespers ... ... ... 451
Melodies for Advent ... ... ... 467.
Melodies for Lent ... ... ... 486.
Compline during Lent ... ... ... 494.
Readings in Passiontide ... ... ... 499.
Terce at Pentecost ... ... ... 501.

## Readings

Readings at Matins *for Week Two* ... ... ... 509.
Readings at Matins *for Week Three* ... ... ... 528.

## Appendices

*Appendix 1* ~ Abbesses of Syon 1420 - 2011 ... ... ... 549.
*Appendix 2* ~ Map of the travels of the sisters of Syon ... ... ... 551.
*Appendix 3* ~ Biography of Fr Brian Foley, translator of this breviary ... ... 552.
*Appendix 4* ~ Websites with links to Syon ... ... ... 554.
*Appendix 5* ~ The Bridgettines world-wide (*Vocations contacts*) ... ... ... 555.
*Appendix 6* ~ Acknowledgements ... ... ... 557.
*Appendix 7* ~ Bibliography ... ... ... 559.

**OUR LADY OF SYON.** *This large painting is one of many copies of the picture of the Madonna ascribed to St Luke. It used to hang in the chapel of Syon Abbey and was left in the care of 'the English nuns' nearly 400 years ago. The community was living in Lisbon, in exile, when a pilgrim returning to the shrine of St James in Compostela told them that a voice came to him from the picture saying, "Take me to the English nuns". Yet he knew of no English nuns until he asked a passer-by who gave him directions. He never returned from his pilgrimage and so it appears that our Blessed Lady chose her own resting place in the home of those dedicated to her service.*
*Similarly, this painting now has a home in the care of the Benedictine monks of Buckfast Abbey.*

## *Foreword by*
# BISHOP CHRISTOPHER BUDD

*"Dear Lord, we pray that what we sing with our lips we may believe in our hearts; and what we believe in our hearts we may show forth in our lives. We ask this through Jesus Christ, our Lord. Amen."*

**Dear brothers and sisters in Christ,**

It is nearly one hundred years since my predecessor, the *Right Reverend Charles Graham*, the third Bishop of Plymouth, gave his approbation for the publication of the Breviary of the Order of the Most Holy Saviour (the Bridgettines) primarily for the use of the sisters of Syon Abbey in our Diocese.

*The Right Reverend Christopher Budd, 8th Bishop of Plymouth.*

The ancient rite of this Daily Office of Our Lady has its roots in the foundation of the Order in about 1370 by Saint Bridget of Sweden, who in recent years has been adopted as a Patron Saint of Europe. It was she who instructed the sisters to pray the solemn Hours every day 'in reverence of the Blessed Virgin Mary'.[1]

In those days, Europe had been decimated by the Great Plague and many of those in holy orders had lost their lives tending the sick and dying. It was a time of trial and a great challenge to our faith. St Bridget knew that if Christianity was to survive it would need men and women of prayer and devotion. The same is true today.

Daily prayer is the foundation of our vocation, whether we are clergy, religious or laity. It is through prayer that we express our love of God and experience his love of us and the deep joy which that brings. It brings us into close contact with Our Lord and his Blessed Mother and all the faithful departed. It is the power of prayer that drives away all our anxieties, confirms us in our faith and brings us deep into the comfort of the family of God.

Prayer fortifies us in our consecrated endeavours and protects us from evil. It brings hope and banishes despair, it drives out fear and replaces it with courage and determination. People of prayer are enabled to serve God in ways that otherwise they may not have thought possible. Enclosed communities of prayer such as the Bridgettines are the powerhouses from which all of us benefit. It is their prayers, for example, which have supported countless souls through Purgatory to the eternal happiness of heaven: it is part of their 'work'. The Church commends prayer and penance undertaken on behalf of the dead. "Let us not hesitate to help those who have died and offer our prayers for them," said St John Chrysostom.

So it is that for nearly six hundred years, this Daily Office was recited and sung in Latin. In more recent times it is said in English, thanks to the translation, about forty years ago, by Father Brian Foley of the Archdiocese of Liverpool. There has not been an opportunity to publish the English version until now and most of the copies of the 1908 Latin edition perished in the World Wars of the last century. Sadly, Father Foley will not see this edition as he died a few years ago.

Bishop Graham, writing in 1906, urged the Sisters, "that kindled with the desire for Divine Love, so may they exercise themselves in the use of this Breviary that what they sing with their mouths, they may likewise pray profoundly in mind and spirit, so that day by day they may endeavour to receive from God the most abundant fruits of their devotion." *

So I pray that the love of God – Father, Son and Holy Spirit – and the intercession of His blessed mother Mary, ever virgin, together with Saint Bridget and all the saints and martyrs of this holy Order may sanctify and protect all those who, with sincerity and devotion, use this *'Office of Our Lady'* for their personal worship, prayer and praise.

✠ **Rt. Rev. Christopher Budd**
*Eighth Bishop of Plymouth (Retired in 2014)*
Feast of St Bridget of Sweden:
23rd July, 2001.

** 'Ut Divinae Charitatis studio incensae, ita se in hujus Breviarii usu exerceant, ut quod ore psallunt mente spirituque idem intime psallant, sicque toto animo suae pietatis fructus in dies uberrimos a Deo percipere studeant.'*

✳ ✳ ✳ ✳ ✳ ✳ ✳ ✳ ✳ ✳

***Permission is granted for the publication of this Office book for private use only. All public Office books need the*** Recognitio ***of the Holy See and the approval of the relevant Bishops' Conference or Religious Order.***

[1] *Rule of Our Saviour, Chap. IV: The Divine Office of the Sisters. See online at http://www.forgottenbooks.org/readbook_text/Rule_of_Our_Most_Holy_Saviour_1000707394/107*

*Preface*

# INTRODUCING THE DAILY OFFICE

***The life and visions of Saint Bridget ~ She receives the Rule of the Order of The Most Holy Saviour ~ The Daily Office of Our Lady comes into use ~ The foundation of the Bridgettine community in England.***

Bridget (*Birgitta*, meaning 'bright') was one of three surviving children of Birger Persson and Ingeborg Bengstdotter, and is believed to have been born at Finsta in Sweden in 1303. Little is known of her childhood but at the age of seven she received her first vision: a lady appeared to her one night, holding a precious crown in her hands. The lady said "Come" and Bridget rose from her bed and went to the altar in her room where the lady was seated. Then Bridget was asked, "Will you have this crown?" Bridget assented and felt the crown placed on her head.

Saint Bridget's vision of Christ holding a model of Vadstena monastery (from Syon Abbey).

Bridget was married in 1316 to Ulf Gudmarsson, an eminent nobleman. She had wealth, broad domains, tenants, dependants and a circle of rich friends. Her home at Ulfasa was one of the wood-built castles of Sweden, with moat and drawbridge, which her husband later rebuilt in stone. She became the mother of eight children – four girls and four boys – and was widowed in 1344.

Early in the year 1346 King Magnus bequeathed to Bridget his palace at Vadstena for conversion to a monastery. It is at this time that her life as an 'apostle and prophet' begins. It is thought that it was also at this time that she received the call to found a religious order – a new vineyard of which she is to be the 'new vine'. This became Bridget's vocation, as she understood it, and the thought of a new vineyard of Christ's own planting would never leave her.

Bridget received many revelations over the years, about 700 in all, which were collected into eight books by her confessor Alfonso of Jaén.[1] These 'visions' came from Our Lord – who called her 'Bride of Christ' – from the Virgin Mary and sometimes other saints. The revelation which contains the Rule to be observed by the sisters of this new order opens with the following: 'This Order, to the honour of my most beloved Mother, I shall have instituted chiefly for wo-men, and the Rule and statutes I shall, by my own mouth, most fully declare.'[2]

The Rule is based on the usual three vows, expressed as 'true humility, pure chastity and voluntary poverty'. The strictness of the poverty is declared at the outset: the religious must not even touch gold or silver without the permission of the abbess. The treasure of the monastery must consist in 'the grace of God, continual study, devout prayer and divine praise.'[3] Bridget's devotion to the Passion and Cross and to the wounds of her Saviour were to be the special mark of her Order. The grey habit signifying penance, the crown, worn by the sisters, of white linen with five red 'spots', signifying both constancy and chastity: these were to be the constant reminders of the five wounds of Christ to their wearers. The maximum number of sisters in any community would be 60.

But this 'planting' of a new vineyard was to include men as well as women, each with their separate monastery and choir but worshipping God under one roof and governed in temporal things by the abbess, who would represent the Virgin Mary. The maximum number of men was to be 25, of whom 13 would be priests to act as chaplains for the sisters. One priest, chosen by the community of broth-ers and sisters, would be named as confessor-general. He would be the head of the brothers, and govern on all spiritual matters for both communities.[4] The life of both communities was to be contemplative, each living within their own en-closure. The Rule linked this enclosure with the practice of silence, allowing the communities to 'listen to God'.[5] But the priests were to preach on Sundays and feast days, in the vernacular, to those who attended the monastery church. The Divine Office of the brothers (in the local rite) and sisters was to alternate, the men singing from their choir behind the high altar while the sisters sang theirs from a choir high above the nave. The sisters' Office was to be a special one in honour of Our Lady, whose Votive Mass they were to sing daily.[6]

*A fragment of manuscript of the Revelations said to be in Saint Bridget's hand-writing. (Revelations Mss, Royal Library, Stockholm, Sweden)*

What was the 'genesis' of this Office, which became known as the *'Cantus Sororum'*? We must follow Bridget to Rome in 1349 to celebrate the Holy Year of 1350. In fact, Bridget was told in a vision to go to Rome and her response was to obey without question or doubt.

It was particularly courageous of Bridget to travel to Rome in 1349. The Black Death (bubonic plague) was at its height in 1348 and in 1349 had reached Norway. The devastation was so great that by 1350 one in every three people had perished. Her request for the approval of the new Order had received no encouragement from Pope Clement VI, and she had everything to discourage her as she set out from her country at the end of 1349.

It was early in 1354, while Bridget was living in Rome next to the Church of San Lorenzo in Damaso, that she began to receive the revelations known as the *'Sermo Angelicus'* containing the daily readings for Matins which were to be used at Vadstena and later by the Order.

She could see the altar of the church from her house and would sit daily 'with pen, paper and tablet' ready to receive the text, dictated in sections by an angel. Her Swedish version was then given to Master Peter Olafsson of Skänninge, a secular priest who was her chaplain, confessor and spiritual adviser, to be translated into Latin. It became a major part of the liturgy for the sisters and is devoted to the Virgin Mary.

The readings for each day describe a particular aspect of Mary's life. These Lessons, three of which were to be read at Matins each day, were the basis of the weekly Office of the sisters. In them we read of the part played by Our Lady in salvation history.

Master Peter devoted much time and effort in the formation of what was to become the Daily Office of the sisters: the *'Cantus Sororum'*. In part, he composed the texts and supplied some of the music. He also borrowed or adapted parts from existing sources, basing all his work on the 'theme' for each day as given in the 21 daily Lessons or Readings. Ultimately, he became the superior of the monks at Vadstena and the Order's first confessor-general.

Master Peter died in 1378 so it would be reasonable to deduce that the Breviary was completed by this date. Perhaps it would be equally reasonable to think that it had been completed before Bridget's death in 1373. There is some evidence [7] to show that it had been sent to the nearby Cistercian monastery at Alvastra for safe keeping until the monastery at Vadstena was ready for occupation, perhaps as early as 1365.

Bridget made many pilgrimages away from Rome from her arrival in 1349 until her death in 1373. Her final pilgrimage was to the Holy Land where, in a series of visions she experienced the birth, the passion and death of Jesus. Leaving Rome in November 1371 with three of her children as well as several chaplains and others, including Master Peter, Bridget returned to Rome in the early months of 1373 and died there on 23rd July. In December of that year her last journey began when her body was returned to Sweden, accompanied by her daughter Katherine and son Birger, arriving at Vadstena on 4th July 1374.

The original (1370) *Rule of Our Saviour* was ratified by Pope Urban VI in 1378 and Bridget was canonised on 7th October 1391; the only woman canonised in the 14th century. On 1st October 1999, *Pope John Paul II* proclaimed Bridget to be one of the patron saints of Europe, saying that after she was widowed, she "travelled through Europe from north to south", working tirelessly for the return of the Holy Father to Rome. Her daughter, Katherine, who had followed her mother to Rome in 1350 and had brought Bridget's body home, was able to give great guidance to the burgeoning community assembled at Vadstena until her own death in 1381. The Vadstena community was enclosed in 1384; the official beginning of the Bridgettine way of life. The first foundation from Vadstena was made at Florence in 1394 and over the following years foundations were made in other northern European countries.

A foundation in England was first suggested in 1406 when Philippa, the daughter of King Henry IV married Eric of Pomerania, King of Sweden and Denmark. The English delegation to the royal wedding visited Vadstena and while they were there, Sir Henry (later Lord) FitzHugh made a grant of his own property with

*The monastery and abbey church at Vadstena in Sweden. The first Bridgettine community was enclosed here in 1384.*

the aim of setting up a Bridgettine house in England. This eventually came to fruition when King Henry V (1386 – 1422) arranged for the foundation of Syon Abbey at Twickenham near London in 1415 with the first English members of the community making their professions on 21st April 1420. The elections of the first abbess and the first confessor-general were ratified by the Bishop of London in 1421. But Twickenham proved to be unsuitable and so a new monastery was begun at Isleworth on the banks of the Thames, on 5th February 1426.

When Syon Abbey was founded in 1415, four professed sisters, two brothers and three novices were sent to England from Vadstena to assist in the formation of the new community. We know that they brought copies of the *'Cantus Sororum'* with them and taught and explained its use to those who were to make their first professions in April 1420. It was soon apparent that a guide or handbook for the correct use of the Breviary was needed, written in English. This was *'The Myroure of oure Ladye'*.

A. J. Collins argues most cogently that the anonymous author of *'The Myroure of oure Ladye'* was probably Thomas Fishbourne, the first confessor-general of Syon. It was written for the Syon sisters to explain their Breviary to those whose knowledge of Latin would more than likely be minimal, and so they could understand not only what they were reading but also the rite of ceremonial involved. If indeed Thomas Fishbourne was the author, he must have completed *'The Myroure of oure Ladye'* by 13th September 1428, the day of his death.

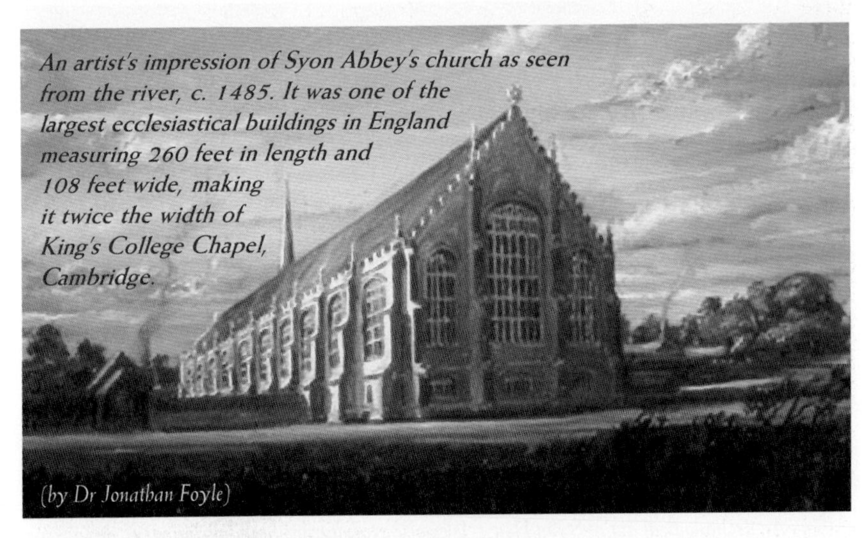

*An artist's impression of Syon Abbey's church as seen from the river, c. 1485. It was one of the largest ecclesiastical buildings in England measuring 260 feet in length and 108 feet wide, making it twice the width of King's College Chapel, Cambridge.*

*(by Dr Jonathan Foyle)*

'The Breviaries for the Syon nuns,' writes Christopher de Hamel,[8] 'followed a quite different routine [from (say) the common Use of Sarum]. The liturgy is unique and completely distinctive. It is an arrangement of psalms and anthems with specific Bridgettine readings and hymns, varying according to the eight liturgical hours and according to the day of the week. Otherwise the offices never vary. Every week is the same, month after month, following the same unvarying praise of the Virgin Mary.'

This unique rite of daily prayer and praise by the English Bridgettine community has survived for 600 years, despite the hardships suffered by us at our suppression and closure in 1539 and subsequent exile and displacement abroad.[9]
We are the only English Catholic religious community to have survived the Reformation: having never surrendered our monastery to the Crown or yielded up our keys or our royal seal.

The first sisters had to copy their own Daily Office by hand and the earliest copy attributed to Syon was a little Swedish Bridgettine prayer book with the text in Swedish and Latin and bearing the owner's very prominent calligraphic initials: 'AK'. It is very possible that this is Anna Kaarlsdottir who had made her profession at Vadstena in 1400, came to England in 1415, was recorded among the nuns of Syon in 1428 and who died at Syon, probably before 1447. As she never returned to Sweden, any books which were her property presumably remained at Syon.[10] Her prayer book, which she composed while in England, is now in the Royal Library in Stockholm.

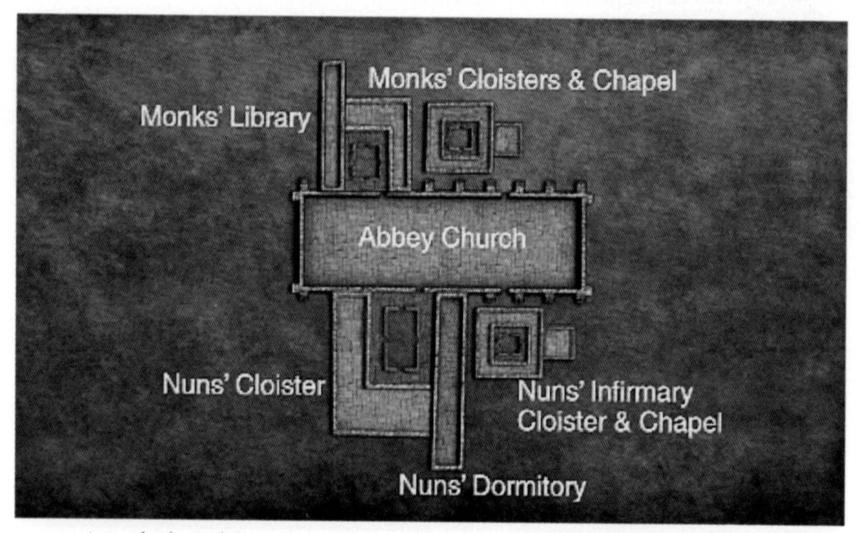


*An archeological dig at Syon House, Isleworth revealed this probable layout of the pre-Reformation Syon Abbey. (Courtesy of Channel 4's Time Team)*

By the end of the fifteenth century, books began to be printed. The *"Breviarium Sacrarum Virginum Ordinis Sanctissimi Salvatoris"* (The Breviary of the Blessed Virgin of the Order of the Most Holy Saviour) was first printed at Lübeck in 1512 and most recently at Tournay in 1908 by Desclée & Soc.[11] Until now, each of our preceding eight editions has always been in Latin.

The Second Vatican Council of 1962 *(Vatican II)* sanctioned the use of English in the liturgy of the Church and those who have seen previous editions will notice some omissions since Vatican II. Bishop Cyril Restieaux (the seventh Bishop of Plymouth) appointed Abbot Placid Hooper of Buckfast (1957-1968) to help us revise our Breviary in accordance with Vatican decrees.[12] At the same time it was translated from the Latin by Father Brian Foley (1919-2000).[13]

So, with this unique Book of Hours now printed in English for the first time since its inception six centuries ago, we can share our traditional and historic daily prayer and praise with you. And even though our community of Syon is finally dispersed, may these daily devotions continue to fortify you and those you love in your Christian faith. I hope and pray that these prayers and revelations of our foundress, Saint Bridget, will help you to discover a way of life dedicated to Our Most Holy Saviour through the love and intercession of his Blessed Mother.

***Sister Anne Smyth, O.Ss.S.***
*Abbess of Syon, 1976 – 2011.*

1. *There is a comprehensive, critical publication in English: 'The Revelations of St Birgitta of Sweden' (Liber Caelestis), translated by Denis Searby with Introductions and Notes by Bridget Morris (4th Vol. due 2015), Oxford University Press. Syon's first MS edition of the Revelations dates from about 1440 and is in the British Library. The first printed edition was made at Lübeck in 1492.*
2. *'God's Ambassadress, St Bridget of Sweden', by Helen M. D. Redpath, (1947) p.49.*
3. *Ibid. p. 50.*
4. *Ibid. p.51.*
5. *'Studies in St Birgitta and the Brigittine Order', Vol 2, p. 218. (Essay) by Dr Ann M. Hutchison.*
6. *'God's Ambassadress, St Bridget of Sweden', by Helen M. D. Redpath, (1947) p. 51.*
7. *'The Bridgettine Breviary of Syon Abbey', by A. J. Collins, (1963) Publ. by Stanbrook Abbey for the Henry Bradshaw Society.*
8. *'The medieval manuscripts of Syon Abbey and their dispersal' (Essay) by Christopher de Hamel, (1991) for The Roxburghe Club. (600th Anniversary of the canonisation of Saint Bridget).*
9. *England was briefly reconciled to the Holy See under Queen Mary who restored Syon Abbey to the community by means of the 'restoration charter' [Lettters Patent] of 1st March 1557. The sisters were enclosed in their former home the following August and stayed there until1559 after the accession of Queen Elizabeth I when Syon was again suppressed.*
10. *Christopher de Hamel (1991) as above.*
11. *Lübeck, 1512; Champs, 1544; Arras, 1610; Cologne, 1628; Wilna, 1684; Landshut, 1697; Lublin, 1748. Shortly after the exiled 'English Sisters' arrived in Lisbon in 1594, the Pope prohibited the use of our Breviary, possibly at the request of the Bishop of Lisbon. So we used the local rite instead until after our return to England in 1861 whereupon the 'Office of Our Lady' was resumed in 1897. There soon followed the fine Tournay edition of 1908 which was based on the 1697 edition, but all spare copies held by Desclée & Soc. were destroyed by fire when Belgium was invaded in 1914.*
12. *See 'Rubrics in current use', page 25.*
13. *See biography on page 552.*

*Guide to the structure of*

# EACH OFFICE OF THE DAY

| *The first Office of the day begins with the Prayer...*<br>'Open my mouth, O Lord...'<br>Opening Prayers<br>Antiphon in full<br>INVITATORY PSALM<br>Antiphon in full |
|---|
| LAUDS (Morning Prayer) |
| *For LAUDS continue as below* but if starting the day with the OFFICE OF READINGS (Matins) *see page 21.* |
| PSALMODY<br>Antiphon (short)<br>PSALMS 92 & 99<br>PSALM 62 *(omit 'Glory be...')*<br>PSALM 66<br>CANTICLE of the Three Children *(Daniel 3:57-88,56)*<br>*or Canticle as noted on ferial Fridays through the year and in Lent. All ferial days in Passiontide.*<br>PSALMS 148 & 149 *(omit 'Glory be...' for both)*<br>PSALM 150<br>Antiphon in full |
| READING and ℟. |
| HYMN followed by ℣. & ℟. |
| Antiphon for Canticle (short)<br>CANTICLE of Zechariah *(Benedictus) (Luke 1: 68-79)*<br>Antiphon in full |
| ℣. & ℟. and Prayer |
| Antiphon in honour of SAINT BRIDGET *(1 or 2)*<br>with ℣. & ℟. and Prayer<br>*On Bridgettine feasts and memorials the Antiphon, ℣. & ℟. and Prayer for the feast precedes that of St Bridget.* |
| ℣. Lord, hear my prayer. ℟. Lord, grant my prayer.<br>℣. & ℟. *(Thanksgiving)* & Closing Prayers for Lauds. |

| TERCE |
| --- |
| Opening Prayers |
| HYMN |
| Antiphon (short)<br>Three PSALMS<br>Antiphon in full |
| READING and ℟. |
| Short Responsory<br>Closing Prayers for Small Hours. |

| SEXT and NONE |
| --- |
| *NOTE: There is an option for SEXT & NONE to be observed at separate times (See Rubrics, page 26.)* |
| SEXT: As at TERCE until<br>end of Short Responsory, then... |
| NONE: Antiphon (short)<br>Three PSALMS<br>Antiphon in full |
| READING and ℟. |
| Short Responsory<br>Closing Prayers for Small Hours but before<br>'May the souls...' add |
| LAUDS OF OUR LADY<br>for the day, season or feast |
| with ℣. & ℟. and Prayer, then |
| 'May the souls...' |
| 'Out of the depths...' *(De Profundis)*<br>with ℣. & ℟. and Prayers. |

## OFFICE OF READINGS

(Matins)

*Can be said at any time of day.*

*But if this is the first Office of the day, begin with the Prayer…*

'Open my mouth, O Lord…'

Opening Prayers

Antiphon in full

INVITATORY PSALM

Antiphon in full

*Otherwise start with…* Opening Prayers

omitting the Invitatory Psalm & Antiphon.

HYMN

PSALMODY

Antiphon 1 (short)

PSALM 1

Antiphon 1 in full

Antiphon 2 (short)

PSALM 2

Antiphon 2 in full

Antiphon 3 (short)

PSALM 3

Antiphon 3 in full

℣. & ℟. and

'OUR FATHER…'

ABSOLUTION

Ask for Blessing

BLESSING

READING (Lesson of the day)

*Cycle of Weeks 1/2/3.*

℣. & ℟.

Responsory

*'Te Deum'* (or Psalm 50)

℣. & ℟.

Closing Prayers for Office of Readings

*But if first Office of the day and followed immediately by Lauds, omit Closing Prayers and begin LAUDS with…*

℣. & ℟.

'Come to us…'

| VESPERS<br>(Evening Prayer) |
|---|
| *Preparation for Vespers:*<br>'Hail Mary…' with ℣. & ℟.<br>HYMN *'Ave Maris Stella'* repeating<br>the 4th verse as shown.<br>℣. & ℟. and Prayers followed by<br>'Hail Mary' (short form) and<br>Prayer for forgiveness: *'Indulgete'* *(See Rubrics, page 27)*. |
| Opening Prayers |
| PSALMODY<br>Antiphon (short)<br>Five PSALMS with Psalm 147 always the 5th Psalm.<br>Antiphon in full |
| READING and ℟. |
| Responsory *(if First Vespers)*<br>HYMN |
| ℣. & ℟. |
| Antiphon for Canticle (short)<br>MAGNIFICAT Canticle *(Luke 1: 46 - 55)*<br>Antiphon in full |
| ℣. & ℟. and Prayer |
| Antiphon in honour of<br>SAINT BRIDGET *(1 or 2)*<br><br>*On Bridgettine feasts and memorials*<br>*the Antiphon, ℣. & ℟. and Prayer for the feast*<br>*precedes that of St Bridget.*<br>℣. & ℟. and Prayer |
| ℣. Lord, hear my prayer. ℟. Lord, grant my prayer. |
| ℣. & ℟. *(Thanksgiving)* and<br>Closing Prayers for Vespers. |
| HYMN in honour of Saint Bridget<br>with ℣. & ℟. and Prayer |

| COMPLINE<br>(Night Prayer) |
|---|
| Opening Prayers |
| PSALMODY<br>Antiphon (short)<br>PSALMS 131, 132, 133<br>*These Psalms are said at Compline every day without exception.*<br>Antiphon in full |
| READING and ℟. |
| Short Responsory<br>*for the day, season or feast.* |
| HYMN<br>℣. & ℟. |
| Antiphon for Canticle (short)<br><br>CANTICLE OF SIMEON *(Nunc Dimittis)*<br>*(Luke 2: 29 - 32)*<br><br>Antiphon in full |
| ℣. & ℟. and Prayer |
| ℣. & ℟.<br>℣. *(Thanksgiving)* Glory, honour and praise… & ℟.<br>then 'Mary, you are full of grace…' |
| LAUDS OF OUR LADY<br>*for the day, season or feast.*<br>℣. & ℟. and Prayer |
| 'Mary, rejoice in God…'<br>*Sung twice.*<br>Closing Prayer for Compline. |

| DAILY TIMETABLE<br><br>*Times of the Divine Office currently in use by the Sisters of Syon Abbey.* |
|---|
| LAUDS at 7.00 a.m.<br>(Breakfast at 7.30 a.m.) |
| HOLY MASS at 9.00 a.m.<br>followed by TERCE. |
| SEXT & NONE at 11.30 a.m.<br>(Lunch at 12 noon) |
| MATINS at 3.30 p.m.<br>(Office of Readings) |
| VESPERS at 6.00 p.m.<br>(Followed by recreation and Supper at 7.00 p.m.) |
| COMPLINE at 8.00 p.m. |

*Notes and guidance*

# RUBRICS IN CURRENT USE

*'The constant praise of God by women, with and through the Virgin-Mother' that, before all else, was the mission of Saint Bridget.*[1]

This mission was achieved through the daily liturgy of the Sisters of the Bridgettine Order, based on the 21 Lessons read at Matins (now the Office of Readings).

Those who have seen or studied earlier editions of our Syon Breviary will notice several alterations in this edition. The modifications of daily worship which have enabled the Syon nuns to share in the solemnities, feasts and memorials of the Church's Calendar began in 1906 when the community adopted the Roman Calendar in place of the antiquated version prefixed to the Breviary then in circulation.[2]

However, without the diligent work of Abbess M. Teresa Jocelyn, Sister M. Dominic Redpath and other Sisters starting in the 1890s, our unique Daily Office may not have been revived at all, as A. J. Collins writes: "Within two or three years of their arrival in Lisbon (May 1594), the Sisters ceased to use their Bridgettine Office and adopted the Roman Breviary. It is impossible to say whether a Brief from Pope Clement VIII ordered the change or whether the undoubted lack of service-books of their own had left the Sisters no alternative. Not until May 1897 did Syon receive leave to revert to their former Breviary."[3]

Further modifications took place after the Second Vatican Council (Vatican II: 1962 – 1965) which, by the 1963 constitution *'Sacrosanctum Concilium'*, suppressed Prime and gave permission for Matins (the Office of Readings) to be recited at any convenient time of the day. With the permission of the competent superior, use of the vernacular instead of Latin was also sanctioned.[4]

About this time Barbara Hunt, one of Father Brian Foley's parishioners, was staying at Syon and it was at her suggestion that he accepted the task of translating the Sisters' daily Office into English.[5] While this work was in progress, the then Bishop of Plymouth, the Rt. Rev. Cyril Restieaux, asked the Rt. Rev. Placid Hooper, OSB, Abbot of St Mary's Abbey of Buckfast – in whose parish we were living – to assist the community in adapting our Divine Office in accordance with the norms of *'Sacrosanctum Concilium'*. The following adaptations were agreed between our community and the bishop:

1. The use of the English language was permitted.

2. The re-organisation of the 21 Lessons at Matins into a three-weekly cycle of seven Lessons, each divided into three parts, using the first Lesson of each day for week one and the second and third Lessons for weeks two and three.

3. Sext and None to form one Office with the Hymn used once, the psalms, readings and short responsory for Sext followed by the psalms etc. for None, ending with the closing prayers at the end of None. *Since Fr Foley had already completed the work on Sext and None, they are printed in full to give the user the option of a longer or shorter version.*

4. The Litany of Our Lady to be prayed in Choir on Saturdays only.

5. The Penitential Psalms and Litany of the Saints to be prayed in Choir on Ash Wednesday and Good Friday only.

6. Other Offices previously prayed privately by the Sisters, that is: the Office of the Holy Spirit on Sundays; the Office of the Dead on Mondays, Tuesdays and Wednesdays as well as extra psalms on Thursdays and Saturdays, to be omitted.

❀❀❀❀❀❀❀❀

***The rubrics which follow are those used by the Sisters from the late 1960s to the present time.***

Every day, before the Opening Prayers for Vespers, the Sisters pray the 'Hail Mary' with ℣. & ℟. and then sing the Hymn 'Star of Ocean, lead us' (*Ave, Maris Stella, page 77*) as St Bridget herself did, with her companions while living in Rome, asking for Our Lady's protection. The Hymn is followed by two Versicles and Responses which, as shown, have an Alleluia added during Easter only. Two prayers follow and then the right-hand side of the Choir, bowing to the left side, say the 'Hail Mary' and the request for forgiveness: 'Forgive us, for the love of God...' known as the *Indulgete*. The left side of the Choir then, bowing to the right side, repeat the 'Hail Mary' and the *Indulgete*. This brief liturgical rite is unique to the Bridgettines.[6]

Beginning at Vespers on Saturday, one Sister is *Hebdomadary* (leader) for a week *[Hebdomadas: Greek – 'seven days']*. She begins the opening prayers of each Office, sings or recites the Reading, intones the first short antiphon (**bold type**) and says the prayer(s). Another Sister is *Cantor* for the week. She intones the first lines of all hymns and psalms and says the short responsory – the choir (the rest of the Sisters) replying with the ℣ & ℟ as given. The *Cantor* also sings or recites the longer responsory at Vespers and the Versicles after the *Salve Regina* at Compline, where it is indicated on Solemnities.

Each day the Office begins with the Introduction to Lauds *(page 33)* even if the first Office is Matins (Office of Readings) – although it has been the Sisters custom to pray Matins mid-afternoon. After the second prayer ending 'especially...' particular intentions are mentioned, for example: a Sister's Profession anniversary, feast day or birthday, the deaths of her parents or the anniversary of a Sister's death. Requests for prayer from individuals or groups would also be mentioned here.

The Invitatory antiphon for the day, season or feast follows together with Psalm 94. The psalm is said by the Cantor, the antiphon repeated in whole or in part by the Choir. If Lauds is to follow, begin with the short form of the antiphon for the day, season or feast. If the Office of Readings (Matins) is to follow, begin with the Hymn. The Readings for Matins follow a three-weekly cycle thus: Sunday, Week One; next Sunday, Week Two; next Sunday, Week Three; with the exception of the season of Christmas when the Office is that of Thursday only. At the end of the Christmas and Easter seasons begin a new cycle with Week One. On feasts and other celebrations, the Reading at Matins comes from the current Week, unless a particular Reading is indicated. However, during Passiontide, the Readings for Friday only are used.

It should be noted that the psalms for Lauds and Compline are the same for every day and do not vary; with the exception that, on a ferial Friday and in Passiontide, the Canticle of the Three Children at Lauds is replaced by one of four alternative Old Testament canticles used in rotation *(pages 294 - 300)*.

At all other Hours, the psalms appointed for each day of the week are always used at that Hour and on that day; even if the Antiphons, Readings and Hymns are of a particular feast or season.

As a general guide, THE STRUCTURE of each Office of the day is set out on *pages 19 to 24*.

## NOTES FOR SEASONS OF THE YEAR AND FEAST DAYS:

**Advent**: The Office for Advent begins with Vespers on the evening before the 1st Sunday of Advent. On Sundays and ferial days, use Psalm 50 in place of the *'Te Deum'* at Matins. Always begin the Readings at Matins at Week One at the beginning of Advent. Except on solemnities or feasts such as The Immaculate Conception on 8th December, the Readings, Prayer and most Hymn tones are proper to Advent *(see page 467 for music)*. After None and Compline each day, unless noted, use the Advent Lauds of Our Lady with its ℣. & ℟. and Prayer, up to and including Compline on Christmas Eve *(page 484)*.

**Christmas**: The Office for Christmas begins at First Vespers on Christmas Eve. Use the Office for Thursday for all Hours each day, with Alleluias. All psalms are as usual and the *'Te Deum'* is said each day. After None and Compline, except on Christmas Eve (see **Advent** above) the Christmas Lauds of Our Lady is sung with its ℣. & ℟. and Prayer *(page 288)*. Thursday's Office continues each day until Compline on the feast of the Baptism of the Lord. Please note that at First Vespers of the following: Christmas Day; the Solemnity of Mary, Mother of God; the Epiphany of the Lord and the Baptism of the Lord a Responsory will be said or sung *(pages 451 ff)*. See also paragraph below on **Responsories**.

**Lent**: Lent begins on Ash Wednesday. Alleluia is not said until Easter and is replaced in the Opening Prayers by, 'We praise you, Lord, the King of Glory.' On Sundays and ferial days, the *'Te Deum'* at Matins is replaced by Psalm 50. There are Lenten hymn tones for the Small Hours every day *(pages 490ff)* and for Vespers on Sunday, Monday, Tuesday and Friday *(pages 486ff)*. At Compline *(pages 494ff)* – unless a Solemnity or Feast occurs, for example, the Annunciation of the Lord *(page 408)* – Friday's Office is used until Passiontide, with Lenten Short Responsory and Lenten Versicles after the Antiphon following the Canticle of Simeon *(Nunc Dimittis – page 497)*. The Lauds of Our Lady at None and Compline is of the day occurring.

**Passiontide:** From the First Vespers on the eve of Passion Sunday (the fifth Sunday of Lent) to Compline on Wednesday of Holy Week, Friday's Office is used at all Hours every day but always with the psalms proper to each day and with special Readings and Prayer *(pages 499 - 500)*. Continue to use Lenten Hymn tones *(page 486)*. From Thursday in Holy Week to Compline on Easter Sunday inclusive, the Divine Office of the Church is used.

**Easter:** From Lauds on Easter Monday, the Daily Office of Our Lady is resumed. Alleluia is added to each ℣. & ℟., at the end of 'Mary, rejoice in God', in the Closing Prayers and elsewhere as shown until Compline of Pentecost inclusive. The *'Te Deum'* is used at Matins every day and the Readings will be for Week One. The Easter Lauds of Our Lady *(Regina Coeli)* [7] is used at None and Compline with ℣. & ℟. and Prayer. In this Lauds of Our Lady, until the Ascension, there is a Versicle added before the ℣. & ℟. and Prayer. There are different forms of this Versicle for Easter, for the feast of the Ascension and for the feast of Pentecost itself *(page 402)*.

**Pentecost:** Versions of Terce, with musical notation for Pentecost Sunday, Monday and Tuesday, celebrating the coming of the Holy Spirit to the apostles, have been included *(pages 501ff)*. "During the singing of Terce at Pentecost and the two following days, the Sisters shall hold lighted candles in their right hands and with inward devotion they shall seek comfort and grace of the Holy Spirit while they sing the hymn *'Veni, Creator Spiritus'*." [8]

**Responsories:** *(See pages 451ff)* Responsories are sung or said on Solemnities at First Vespers and on Feasts of the Lord which occur on a Sunday and so have First Vespers (e.g. The Baptism of the Lord). They are placed after the Reading and before the Hymn. As indicated, some Responsories are used on particular days, namely:

| | |
|---|---|
| • Christmas Day | 2nd of Thursday |
| • Mary, Mother of God | 1st of Thursday *(1st January)* |
| • The Epiphany of the Lord | 3rd of Thursday |
| • The Ascension of the Lord | 3rd of Tuesday |
| • Pentecost | 3rd of Sunday |
| • Trinity Sunday | 1st of Sunday |
| • The Body & Blood of Christ | 1st of Sunday *(Corpus Christi)* |
| • The Assumption of Our Lady | 3rd of Saturday *(15th August)* |

Unless otherwise indicated, use the 3rd Responsory of the day occurring. If no music version is available use the Responsory from the Office of Readings (Matins).

**Solemnities – Lauds of Our Lady at Compline:**
At Compline on the eve of all Solemnities of Our Lord and Our Lady (except those falling in the Advent, Christmas and Easter seasons), on Trinity Sunday and the Solemnity of Holy Mother Saint Bridget, the *Salve Regina* *(page 394)* is sung with the long Versicles *(page 399)*. On all other Solemnities the same Lauds of Our Lady is sung but with the short Versicles *(page 397)* unless another Lauds of Our Lady is indicated. These Versicles are never added to the Lauds of Our Lady at None.

**Solemnities & Feasts of Our Lord:** *(See pages 407 ff)* The celebrations of the Feast of the Presentation of the Lord and the Annunciation of the Lord which were both formerly Marian celebrations, retain in our Office their original form, while omitting the Canticle of the Three Children at Vespers. On the Ascension of the Lord, the Office is of Thursday or Sunday since, according to local custom, this Solemnity may be kept on either day. The celebration of the Transfiguration of the Lord on 6th August – the patronal feast of our Order – is of the day occurring. When it falls on a Sunday, the Responsory at First Vespers is the 3rd Responsory from Saturday Matins.

**Solemnities & Feasts of Our Lady:** *(See pages 422 ff)* On all Solemnities, Feasts, Memorials and Optional Memorials of Our Lady, the Office of Wednesday is used unless otherwise indicated for particular celebrations; with Alleluias and always with the psalms of the day occurring. The Canticle of the Three Children is said or sung at Vespers immediately after the Thanksgiving ℣. & ℟. and before the Closing Prayers. The Readings with the Responsory at Matins will be from the weekly cycle then in use, unless otherwise indicated.

**Solemnities & Feasts of our Order:** *(See pages 440 ff)* On the Solemnity of Holy Mother St Bridget the Office is of the day occurring. Beginning at First Vespers, Alleluias are added to all ℣. & ℟. as for feasts of Our Lady. After the Reading at First Vespers a Responsory is inserted before the Hymn, taken from Matins of the day. Music versions for some Responsories will be found at *pages 451ff.* The Antiphons and Prayers proper to the Memorials of St Richards Reynolds; St Katherine; St Anne & St Joachim and Blessed Anne Mary & Mary Frances are sung or said at Lauds and Vespers immediately before the Antiphon to St Bridget. The Office for each is of the day occurring, with Alleluias as indicated. For the feast of the Transfiguration of Our Lord (our patronal feast) see above. On the feast of the Archangels (29th September) the Office is of Monday, with Alleluias. For the memorial of the Holy Guardian Angels (2nd October) Monday's Office is also used but without Alleluias.

---

[1] *'The Bridgettine Breviary of Syon Abbey', by A. J. Collins, (1963), Introduction, page ix.*
[2] *Ibid. page xxii.*
[3] *Ibid. page vii.*
[4] *'Sacrosanctum Concilium', Chap. 1: III, C Para. 36.3*
[5] *See Father Brian Foley's biography, by Barbara Hunt (page 554).*
[6] *Rule of Our Saviour, Chap. IV: The Divine Office of the Sisters. See online at http://www.forgottenbooks.org/readbook_text/Rule_of_Our_Most_Holy_Saviour_1000707394/107*
[7] *The 'Regina Coeli' is still sung in Latin. Father Foley felt it was too traditional to translate.*
[8] *'The Syon Additions' (to the Rule of Our Saviour) page 82.*

**MEMORIAL TO A SAINT.** *This section of the old gateway from Syon Abbey, Isleworth, is said to have borne part of the body of St Richard Reynolds after his execution. It was so revered by the sisters that they carried it with them throughout their exile and upon returning to England gave it a prominent place in their chapel. St Richard Reynolds, a Bridgettine monk of Syon, was martyred at Tyburn on 4th May, 1535 and canonised by Pope Paul VI on 25th October, 1970.* *(see page 441)*
*It is now at the Blessed Sacrament Church, Heavitree, Exeter.*

*Introduction to*

# LAUDS

***The first prayer of the day.***

Open my mouth, O Lord, to bless your holy name. Cleanse my heart also from all vain, perverse and distracting thoughts; enlighten my understanding, inflame my affections, that I may recite this Office with worthy attention and devotion, and may deserve to be heard in the sight of your divine Majesty; through Christ our Lord. Amen.

O Lord, we offer these Hours to you in union with that divine intention with which you offered praises to God while you were on earth. We also offer them for our benefactors and associates living and dead, and all for whom we have promised to pray, especially...

**OPENING PRAYERS** *For all Hours except Compline.*

℣. Mary, help me to praise you.
℟. Guard me from all that displeases you.
℣. Mary, you are full of grace, the Lord is with you.
℟. Mary, you are most blessed of all women, for Jesus Christ is your Son.
℣. Grant Lord, that the prayer we now say together.
℟. May be truly a prayer of praise and pleasing to you. } *Only if first Office of the day.*
℣. Come to us, Lord God, to help us.
℟. Come to us and save us.

Glory to God, Father, Son and Holy Spirit, now and always. Amen. (Alleluia)
*(During Lent)* We praise you Lord, the King of glory.

## INVITATORY ANTIPHON *(Sunday)*

*(Daily antiphons are at the end of the psalm)*

God who is Three in One must be the adoration of our hearts.
† Mary who is Mother yet ever Virgin
must be our praise and joy.

**Psalm 94**

Come, ring out our joy to the Lord; hail the rock who saves us.
Let us come before him giving thanks, with songs let us hail the Lord.
℟. *Whole antiphon.*

A mighty God is the Lord, a great king above all gods.
In his hand are the depths of the earth; the heights of the mountains are his.
℟. *Part antiphon from †.*

To him belongs the sea, for he made it, and the dry land shaped by his hands.
Come in; let us bow and bend low;
let us kneel before the God who made us for he is our God
and we the people who belong to his pasture, the flock that is led by his hand.
℟. *Whole antiphon.*

O that today you would listen to his voice! Harden not your hearts as at
Meribah, as on that day at Massah in the desert
when your fathers put me to the test; when they tried me though they
saw my work.
℟. *Part antiphon from †.*

For forty years I was wearied of these people and I said: "their hearts are astray,
these people do not know my ways."
Then I took an oath in my anger: "never shall they enter my rest."
℟. *Whole antiphon.*

*Glory be to the Father...*
℟. *Part antiphon from †.*

℟. *Whole antiphon.*

## Invitatory Antiphons

*(During the week...)*

### *Monday*

Christ who is Lord and King must be the adoration of our hearts.
† With the angels we rejoice in Christ, the Son of Mary,
and ever adore him.

### *Tuesday*

The Son of God, born of a Virgin, must be the adoration of our hearts.
The prophets rejoiced, foretelling the coming of Christ, and
† he must ever be our praise and joy.

### *Wednesday*

The birth of Mary, Virgin-Mother to be, *(on Feasts of Mary:*
This feast of Mary, ever Virgin-Mother) must be our praise and joy.
† Christ her Son and Lord must be the adoration of our hearts.

### *Thursday*

Mary, you are full of grace;
† the Lord is with you.

### *Friday*

Christ the Virgin's son; the eternal King,
was crucified to save us.
† He († Christ) must ever be the adoration of our hearts.

### *Saturday*

The Virgin Mary, assumed by God to heaven, must be our praise and joy:
† he who has crowned her with glory
must be the adoration of our hearts.

# PROPER OF THE SEASONS

## PRAYERS

### *Through the year:*

Grant us, your servants, we pray you, Lord God, to enjoy perpetual health of mind and body. By the glorious intercession of blessed Mary ever Virgin, may we be delivered from present sorrows and enjoy everlasting happiness: through our Lord Jesus Christ your Son, who lives and reigns with you in the unity of the Holy Spirit, God for ever and ever. ℟. Amen.

### *During Advent:*

O Lord, you have willed that your Word should take flesh in the womb of the Blessed Virgin Mary at the message of an angel. We, your suppliants, believe her to be truly the Mother of God. Grant to us that we may be helped by her intercession with you: through our Lord Jesus Christ your Son, who lives and reigns with you in the unity of the Holy Spirit, God, for ever and ever. ℟. Amen,

### *Christmas:*

O God, through the fruitful virginity of the blessed Mary, you have given the treasure of salvation to mankind. Grant, we ask you, that we may be blessed by the prayers of her through whom it was possible for us to receive the source of life, our Lord Jesus Christ your Son, who lives and reigns with you in the unity of the Holy Spirit, for ever and ever. ℟. Amen.

### *Passiontide:*

The most holy soul of your Mother, Mary, O Lord Jesus Christ, was pierced with a sword at the time of your Passion. May this blessed Virgin, we pray you, intercede for us with your mercy, now and at the hour of our death, you who are God, living and reigning with the Father, in the unity of the Holy Spirit, for ever and ever. ℟. Amen.

### *Easter:*

Favourably regard at all times, Almighty Father, but especially when we celebrate the Paschal solemnities of your Son, our continual remembrance of Mary, the Virgin Mother of God. When your Son, Jesus Christ our Lord was hanging on the Cross, his loving Mother stood by, suffering too. Now she sits at his right hand as Queen of heaven, where he lives and reigns with you in the unity of the Holy Spirit, for ever and ever. ℟. Amen.

---

## CLOSING PRAYERS FOR LAUDS AND VESPERS

℣. Mary, rejoice in God, and in his grace to you, for he is with you. Mary, rejoice in him, most blest among all women, most blest to bear the child whose name is Jesus Christ, (now and for ever). *or* (Alleluia). ℣. Let us pray.

### Prayer

Almighty, everlasting God, who for us chose to be born of a most pure Virgin, we ask you to make us worthy to serve you with a pure body and to please you with a humble spirit. We pray also, loving Virgin Mary, Queen of this world and of angels, that you may obtain relief for those suffering the fires of purgatory, forgiveness for sinners, perseverance in goodness for the just, and defend us in our weakness from present perils.
Through Jesus Christ our Lord. ℟. Amen.

May the souls of our founders, of our brothers and sisters and of all the faithful departed, through the mercy of Jesus Christ rest in peace. ℟. Amen.

## CLOSING PRAYERS FOR OFFICE OF READINGS *(Matins)* and for *Terce & Sext.*

℣. Lord, hear my prayer.
℟. Lord, grant my prayer. ℣. Let us pray.

**PRAYER** *For Proper of the Seasons, see pages 36 ff.*

Grant us, your servants we pray you, Lord God, to enjoy perpetual health of mind and body. By the glorious intercession of blessed Mary ever Virgin, may we be delivered from present sorrows and enjoy everlasting happiness; through our Lord Jesus Christ your Son, who lives and reigns with you in the unity of the Holy Spirit, God for ever and ever.
℟. Amen.

℣. Lord, hear my prayer.
℟. Lord, grant my prayer.
℣. Glory, honour and praise to God. (Alleluia)
℟. And our thanks to him. (Alleluia)

℣. Mary, rejoice in God, and in his grace to you, for he is with you. Mary, rejoice in him, most blest among all women, most blest to bear the child whose name is Jesus Christ, (now and for ever). *or* (Alleluia).
℣. Let us pray.

**PRAYER**

Almighty, everlasting God, who for us, chose to be born of a most pure Virgin, we ask you to make us worthy to serve you with a pure body and to please you with a humble spirit. We pray also, loving Virgin Mary, Queen of this world and of angels, that you may obtain relief for those suffering the fires of purgatory, forgiveness for sinners, perseverance in goodness for the just, and defend us, in our weakness, from present perils.
Through Jesus Christ, our Lord. ℟. Amen.

May the souls of our founders, of our brothers and sisters, and of all the faithful departed, through the mercy of Jesus Christ, rest in peace. ℟. Amen.

*Sunday*

# LAUDS

## OPENING PRAYERS

***(The first prayer of the day...)*** *(page 33)*

Open my mouth, O Lord ... *including Invitatory psalm (Ps. 94)*

## ANTIPHON

Lord Jesus Christ.

**Psalm 92**

The Lord is king, with majesty enrobed;
the Lord has robed himself with might, he has girded himself with power.

The world you made firm, not to be moved;
your throne has stood firm from of old. From all eternity, O Lord, you are.

The waters have lifted up, O Lord,
the waters have lifted up their voice, the waters have lifted up their thunder.

Greater than the roar of mighty waters more glorious than the surgings
of the sea,
the Lord is glorious on high.

Truly your decrees are to be trusted.
Holiness is fitting to your house, O Lord, until the end of time.

*Glory be to the Father and to the Son and to the Holy Spirit,*
*as it was in the beginning, is now, and ever shall be, world without end. Amen.*

**Psalm 99**

Cry out with joy to the Lord, all the earth.
Serve the Lord with gladness. Come before him, singing for joy.

Know that he, the Lord, is God.
He made us, we belong to him, we are his people, the sheep of his flock.

Go within his gates, giving thanks.
Enter his courts with songs of praise. Give thanks to him and bless his name.

Indeed, how good is the Lord, eternal his merciful love.
He is faithful from age to age.

*Glory be...*

**Psalm 62**

O God, you are my God, for you I long; for you my soul is thirsting.
My body pines for you like a dry, weary land without water.

So I gaze on you in the sanctuary to see your strength and your glory.
For your love is better than life, my lips will speak your praise.

So I will bless you all my life, in your name I will lift up my hands.
My soul shall be filled as with a banquet, my mouth shall praise you with joy.

On my bed I remember you. On you I muse through the night
for you have been my help; in the shadow of your wings I rejoice.

My soul clings to you; your right hand holds me fast.
Those who seek to destroy my life shall go down to the depths of the earth.

They shall be put into the power of the sword
and left as the prey of the jackals.

But the king shall rejoice in God;
(all that swear by him shall be blessed) for the mouth of liars shall be silenced.

(No *Glory be... straight into ...*)

**Psalm 66**

O God, be gracious and bless us and let your face shed its light upon us.
So will your ways be known upon earth and all nations learn your saving help.

Let the peoples praise you, O God;
let all the peoples praise you.

Let the nations be glad and exult for you rule the world with justice.
With fairness you rule the peoples, you guide the nations on earth.

Let the peoples praise you, O God;
let all the peoples praise you.

The earth has yielded its fruit for God, our God, has blessed us.
May God still give us his blessing till the ends of the earth revere him.

Let the peoples praise you, O God;
let all the peoples praise you.

*Glory be...*

## Canticle of the Three Children

*(Daniel* 3:57-88,56)

O all you works of the Lord, bless the Lord: praise and exalt him for ever.
You angels of the Lord, bless the Lord: and you the heavens, bless the Lord.

All you waters above the heavens, bless the Lord: all you powers of God,
bless the Lord.
Sun and moon, bless the Lord: stars of the sky, bless the Lord.

All rain and dew, bless the Lord: all winds of God, bless the Lord.
Fire and heat, bless the Lord: cold and heat, bless the Lord.

Mists and frost, bless the Lord: ice and cold, bless the Lord.
Ice and snow, bless the Lord: nights and days, bless the Lord.

Light and darkness, bless the Lord: thunderclouds and lightning,
bless the Lord.
O let the earth, bless the Lord: praise and exalt him for ever.

You mountains and hills, bless the Lord: all things that grow in the earth,
bless the Lord.
You fountains, bless the Lord: you seas and rivers, bless the Lord.

Great fish, and all that move in the waters, bless the Lord: all the birds of heaven, bless the Lord.
All beasts wild and tame, bless the Lord: O children of men, bless the Lord.

Let Israel bless the Lord: praise and exalt him for ever.
You priests of the Lord, bless the Lord: you servants of the Lord, bless the Lord.

You spirits and souls of the just, bless the Lord: you holy and humble of heart, bless the Lord.
Ananias, Azarias, Misael, bless the Lord: praise and exalt him for ever.

Let us praise the Father, Son, and Holy Spirit: let us praise and exalt him for ever.
May you be blessed, O Lord, in the heavens: to you be highest glory and praise for ever.

(No *Glory be...* or *Amen*)

**Psalm 148**

Praise the Lord from the heavens, praise him in the heights.
Praise him, all his angels, praise him, all his host.

Praise him, sun and moon, praise him, shining stars.
Praise him, highest heavens and the waters above the heavens.

Let them praise the name of the Lord. He commanded: they were made.
He fixed them for ever, gave a law which shall not pass away.

Praise the Lord from the earth, sea creatures and all oceans,
fire and hail, snow and mist, stormy winds that obey his word;

all mountains and hills, all fruit trees and cedars,
beasts, wild and tame, reptiles and birds on the wing;

all earth's kings and peoples, earth's princes and rulers;
young men and maidens, old men together with children.

Let them praise the name of the Lord for he alone is exalted.
The splendour of his name reaches beyond heaven and earth.

He exalts the strength of his people. He is the praise of all his saints,
of the sons of Israel, of the people to whom he comes close.

(No *Glory be..*)

**Psalm 149**

Sing a new song to the Lord,
his praise in the assembly of the faithful.

Let Israel rejoice in its Maker, let Sion's sons exult in their king.
Let them praise his name with dancing and make music with timbrel and harp.

For the Lord takes delight in his people. He crowns the poor with salvation.
Let the faithful rejoice in their glory, shout for joy and take their rest.

Let the praise of God be on their lips and a two-edged sword in their hand,
to deal out vengeance to the nations and punishment on all the peoples;

to bind their kings in chains and their nobles in fetters of iron;
to carry out the sentence pre-ordained: this honour is for all his faithful.

(No *Glory be...*)

**Psalm 150**

Praise God in his holy place, praise him in his mighty heavens.
Praise him for his powerful deeds, praise his surpassing greatness.

O praise him with sound of trumpet, praise him with lute and harp.
Praise him with timbrel and dance, praise him with strings and pipes.

O praise him with resounding cymbals, praise him with clashing of cymbals.
Let everything that lives and that breathes give praise to the Lord.

*Glory be...*

## Antiphon

**Lord Jesus Christ,** we have loved your house as you commanded, and reverenced it as the house of God, so we may reverence the Virgin Mary, truly a house of God, from whence you came, clothed in strength and beauty.

## Reading *(Eccles 24: 7, 8)*

I have sought a dwelling among men, but it is in the Lord's house alone that I shall find my rest. The Lord, the creator of all, has taught me; he alone is my peace and joy. ℟. Our thanks to God.

## Hymn

Lord God and Father, in your love for us
you willed that Christ your only Son should come
into this world of ours to be our joy,
born from the ever-virgin Mother's womb.

Your Son makes known to us your will, your way;
through him, and through the Virgin, we must learn
that holiness and purity of life
with which to live and love you in return.

This is your way to everlasting joy;
keep, Lord, our hearts from sin and sinfulness,
lest we, surprised by death, should lose for ever
our promised joy, your glory's blessedness.

Spirit of Father and of Son, we pray:
come with those gifts of love you love to give,
that we, once cleansed by water and your power,
filled now with grace may love and ever live.

Pray Mary Virgin-Mother, full of grace,
pray in your love for all for all we need;
protect us from all sin and sinful ways,
and at our dying hour intercede.

Christ Jesus, Son of God, we pray to you
and praise you, naming you the Virgin's Son;

we ever praise the Father, God with you
and with the Holy Spirit, Three in One. Amen.

℣. Christ who dwelt in the Virgin's womb. (Alleluia)
℟. Is the eternal Word of God the Father. (Alleluia)

## ANTIPHON

**Bless God.**

## THE CANTICLE OF ZECHARIAH

*(Luke 1:68-79)*

Blessed be the Lord, the God of Israel!
He has visited his people and redeemed them.

He has raised up for us a mighty saviour in the house of David his servant,
as he promised by the lips of holy men, those who were his prophets
from of old.

A saviour who would free us from our foes, from the hands of all who hate us.
So his love for our fathers is fulfilled, and his holy covenant remembered.

He swore to Abraham our father to grant us, that free from fear, and saved from
the hands of our foes,
we might serve him in holiness and justice, all the days of our life,
in his presence.

As for you, little child, you shall be called a prophet of God, the Most High.
You shall go ahead of the Lord, to prepare his ways before him.

To make known to his people their salvation through forgiveness of
all their sins,
the loving-kindness of the heart of our God who visits us like the dawn
from on high.

He will give light to those in darkness, those who dwell in the
shadow of death,
and guide us into the way of peace.

*Glory be...*

## ANTIPHON

**Bless God**; may he be blessed by all, he who was known as Lord and God of Israel, whom we know and name Father, Son and Holy Spirit, our God and Lord. For he who once spoke from heaven through the prophets, has come himself to us on earth, through the Virgin predestined by his eternal decree to be the sinless Virgin-Mother. So we may truly claim, it is through her that he has redeemed his people.

℣. Lord hear my prayer. ℟. Lord grant my prayer. ℣. Let us pray.

## PRAYER

*For Proper of the Seasons, see pages 36 ff.*

**Grant us**, your servants, we pray you, Lord God, to enjoy perpetual health of mind and body. By the glorious intercession of blessed Mary ever Virgin, may we be delivered from present sorrows and enjoy everlasting happiness: through our Lord Jesus Christ your Son, who lives and reigns with you in the unity of the Holy Spirit, God for ever and ever. ℟. Amen.

## ANTIPHON *to Holy Mother Saint Bridget on Sundays, Feasts & Memorials.*

**Bridget, loving servant of God,** heavenly bride of Christ, we hear in your words the voice of Christ: and we who call you foundress and loving mother, pray as your daughters that in your holy Rule we may ever live as you have lived – the way and will of God our way and will, the truth of Christ, the love of Christ our light, our love. Bridget, Saint and Patron, pray for us that we may follow you as lovers of Christ, with all who love him on earth and in heaven.

## ANTIPHON *on ferial days.*

**Bridget, Saint and Patron,** whose honour and praise we sing,
pray for us in our sorrow and weakness,
that we may come to share in your heavenly joy.

℣. Mother and Patron, Bridget, heavenly bride of Christ, make known to us the ways of Christ. (Alleluia)
℟. Pray for us that Christ himself may be ever our way to heaven. (Alleluia)

℣. Let us pray.

## Prayer

**Lord Jesus Christ**, you were pleased to call blessed Bridget your bride; and inspired her with many of your secrets and adorned her with remarkable virtues. Grant, we pray, that we may become like her in our life and ways, and freed from the allurements of this world we may enjoy with her the joys of heaven. You, who live and reign with the Father and Holy Spirit, for ever and ever. ℟. Amen.

℣. Lord hear my prayer. ℟. Lord grant my prayer.

## Thanksgiving

℣. Glory, honour and praise, to Christ the Virgin's Son, God with the Father and the Holy Spirit, ever Three in One. (Alleluia, alleluia, alleluia)

℟. Our thanks to God. (Alleluia, alleluia, alleluia)

## Closing Prayers *(page 37)*

Mary, rejoice in God …

*Early woodcut from a medieval illustration of St Bridget.*

*Sunday*

# TERCE

## OPENING PRAYERS *(page 33)*

*On Pentecost Sunday Terce is sung (pages 501 ff).*

## HYMN

God, One in Three, your light reveals
yourself to all men everywhere;
this light is Christ, the Virgin's Son,
hear now the Virgin-Mother's prayer.

For she who came by your decree
first sign of dawn in our dark night,
holds out to all men everywhere
her Son, your all-revealing Light.

Pray Mary Mother, full of grace,
pray in your love for all we need;
protect us from all danger now,
and at our dying intercede.

Christ, Son of God, we pray to you,
and honour you, the Virgin's Son.
We praise the Father, God with you,
and with the Spirit, Three in One. Amen.

## ANTIPHON

Mary, Mother.

**Psalm 118** *(vv. 33 – 48)*

Teach me the demands of your statutes and I will keep them to the end.
Train me to observe your law, to keep it with my heart.

Guide me in the path of your commands; for there is my delight.
Bend my heart to your will and not to love of gain.

Keep my eyes from what is false: by your word, give me life.
Keep the promise you have made to the servant who fears you.

Keep me from the scorn I dread, for your decrees are good.
See, I long for your precepts: then in your justice, give me life.

Lord, let your love come upon me, the saving help of your promise.
And I shall answer those who taunt me for I trust in your word.

Do not take the word of truth from my mouth for I trust in your decrees.
I shall always keep your law for ever and ever.

I shall walk in the path of freedom for I seek your precepts.
I will speak of your will before kings and not be abashed.

Your commands have been my delight; these I have loved.
I will worship your commands and love them and ponder your statutes.

*Glory be...*

**Psalm 118** *(vv. 49 – 64)*

Remember your word to your servant by which you gave me hope.
This is my comfort in sorrow that your promise gives me life.

Though the proud may utterly deride me I keep to your law.
I remember your decrees of old and these, Lord, console me.

I am seized with indignation at the wicked who forsake your law.
Your statutes have become my song in the land of exile.

I think of your name in the night-time and I keep your law.
This has been my blessing, the keeping of your precepts.

My part, I have resolved, O Lord, is to obey your word.
With all my heart I implore your favour; show the mercy of your promise.

I have pondered over my ways and returned to your will.
I made haste and did not delay to obey your commands.

Though the nets of the wicked ensnared me I remembered your law.
At midnight I will rise and thank you for your just decrees.

I am a friend of all who revere you, who obey your precepts.
Lord, your love fills the earth. Teach me your statutes.

*Glory be...*

**Psalm 118** *(vv. 65 – 80)*

Lord, you have been good to your servant according to your word.
Teach me discernment and knowledge for I trust in your commands.

Before I was afflicted I went astray but now I keep your word.
You are good and your deeds are good; teach me your statutes.

Though proud men smear me with lies yet I keep your precepts.
Their minds are closed to good but your law is my delight.

It was good for me to be afflicted, to learn your statutes.
The law from your mouth means more to me than silver and gold.

It was your hands that made me and shaped me: help me to learn
your commands.
Your faithful will see me and rejoice for I trust in your word.

Lord, I know that your decrees are right, that you afflicted me justly.
Let your love be ready to console me by your promise to your servant.

Let your love come to me and I shall live for your law is my delight.
Shame the proud who harm me with lies while I ponder your precepts.

Let your faithful turn to me, those who know your will.
Let my heart be blameless in your statutes lest I be ashamed.

*Glory be...*

## ANTIPHON

**Mary, Mother,** help us to resist the attraction of foolish things, and look only for the things of God. Make us strong in Christ, to will as you willed, the things for which he made us.

## READING *(Eccles. 24: 9)* [1]

In the eternal decree of God, I was present before his creating, and I shall be for ever with him, in the holiness of his heaven. ℟. Our thanks to God.

## SHORT RESPONSORY

***1) … Throughout the year.***

℣. Queen of heaven, we who pray to you know the power of your prayer.

℟. *Repeat.*

℣. Mary, your Son, who is truly God, obeyed you, and your word was powerful with him.

℟. We who pray to you know the power of your prayer.

℣. Glory to God, Father, Son and Holy Spirit.

℟. Queen of heaven, we who pray to you know the power of your prayer.

℣. Mary, Queen of heaven, do not leave us unprotected.

℟. Look on us in mercy and love.

***2) …During Easter and on other special days where shown.***

℣. Queen of heaven, we who pray to you know the power of your prayer. Alleluia, Alleluia. ℟. *Repeat.*

℣. Mary, your Son, who is truly God, obeyed you, and your word was powerful with him.

℟. Alleluia, Alleluia.

℣. Glory to God, Father, Son and Holy Spirit.

℟. Queen of heaven, we who pray to you know the power of your prayer. Alleluia, Alleluia.

℣. Mary, Queen of heaven, do not leave us unprotected. Alleluia.

℟. Look on us in mercy and love. Alleluia.

## CLOSING PRAYERS *(page 38)*

[1] READING: (*Capitulum* or 'Little Chapter') usually from Ecclesiasticus (or Sirach).

*Sunday*
# SEXT

## OPENING PRAYERS *(page 33)*

## HYMN

God, One in Three... *see Sunday Terce, page 48.*

## ANTIPHON

**Christ, Lord and God.**

**Psalm 118** *(vv. 81 - 96)*

I yearn for your saving help; I hope in your word.
My eyes yearn to see your promise. When will you console me?

Though parched and exhausted with waiting I remember your statutes.
How long must your servant suffer? When will you sentence my oppressors?

For me the proud have dug pitfalls, against your law.
Your commands are all true; then help me when lies oppress me.

They almost made an end of me on earth but I kept your precepts.
Because of your love give me life and I will do your will.

Your word, O Lord, for ever stands firm in the heavens:
your truth lasts from age to age, like the earth you created.

By your decree it endures to this day; for all things serve you.
Had your law not been my delight I would have died in my affliction.

I will never forget your precepts for with them you give me life.
Save me, for I am yours since I seek your precepts.

Though the wicked lie in wait to destroy me yet I ponder on your will.
I have seen that all perfection has an end but your command is boundless.

*Glory be...*

**Psalm 118** *(vv. 97 - 112)*

Lord, how I love your law! It is ever in my mind.
Your command makes me wiser than my foes; for it is mine for ever.

I have more insight than all who teach me for I ponder your will.
I have more understanding than the old for I keep your precepts.

I turn my feet from evil paths to obey your word.
I have not turned away from your decrees; you yourself have taught me.

Your promise is sweeter to my taste than honey in the mouth.
I gain understanding from your precepts and so I hate false ways.

Your word is a lamp for my steps and a light for my path.
I have sworn and have determined to obey your decrees.

Lord, I am deeply afflicted: by your word give me life.
Accept, Lord, the homage of my lips and teach me your decrees.

Though I carry my life in my hands, I remember your law.
Though the wicked try to ensnare me I do not stray from your precepts.

Your will is my heritage for ever, the joy of my heart.
I set myself to carry out your statutes in fullness, for ever.

*Glory be...*

**Psalm 118** *(vv. 113 - 128)*

I have no love for half-hearted men: my love is for your law.
You are my shelter, my shield; I hope in your word.

Leave me, you who do evil; I will keep God's command.
If you uphold me by your promise I shall live; let my hopes not be in vain.

Sustain me and I shall be saved and ever observe your statutes.
You spurn all who swerve from your statutes; their cunning is in vain.

You throw away the wicked like dross: so I love your will.
I tremble before you in terror; I fear your decrees.

I have done what is right and just: let me not be oppressed.
Vouch for the welfare of your servant lest the proud oppress me.

My eyes yearn for your saving help and the promise of your justice.
Treat your servant with love and teach me your statutes.

I am your servant, make me understand; then I shall know your will.
It is time for the Lord to act for your law has been broken.

That is why I love your commands more than finest gold.
That is why I rule my life by your precepts: I hate false ways.

*Glory be...*

## ANTIPHON

C**hrist, Lord and God,** true life comes only by obedience to your commandments, for they are guiding lights on our way to you. Guide us in this way, followed so faithfully by Mary, your Mother, who ever prays for us that we may obey and live.

## READING *(Eccles. 24: 11)*

Jerusalem has been my dwelling and my resting-place:
there in the holy city, I have taken up my rule and my reign.
℟. Our thanks to God.

## SHORT RESPONSORY

℣. Christ is the Word, the eternal Word of God the Father. (Alleluia, Alleluia)
℟. *Repeat.*
℣. He who dwelt in the Virgin's womb
℟. Is the eternal Word of God the Father. († ℟. Alleluia, Alleluia)
℣. Glory to God, Father, Son and Holy Spirit.
℟. Christ is the Word, the eternal Word of God the Father. (Alleluia, Alleluia)

℣. Mary, Virgin-Mother and Queen, we pray to you. (Alleluia)
℟. That nothing we think or do may displease the Son of your pure virginity. (Alleluia)

*NOTE: If continuing immediately with None, omit the Opening Prayers and Hymn for None and start with the (short) Antiphon before the Psalms: as detailed in the Rubrics, page 26.*

**CLOSING PRAYERS** *(page 38)*

---

† ***Response during Easter and on other special days where shown, as well as in brackets thus: (Alleluia). For style, see Sunday Terce on page 51.***

---

*Before*

# NONE

## OPENING PRAYERS

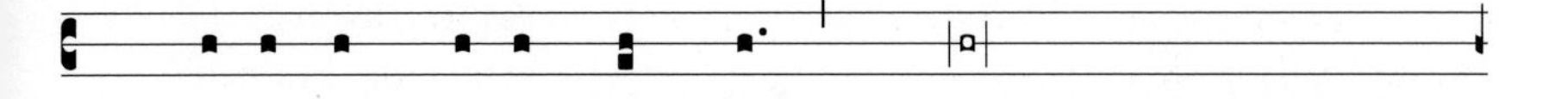

℣. Ma-ry, help me to praise you, ℟. Guard me from all that

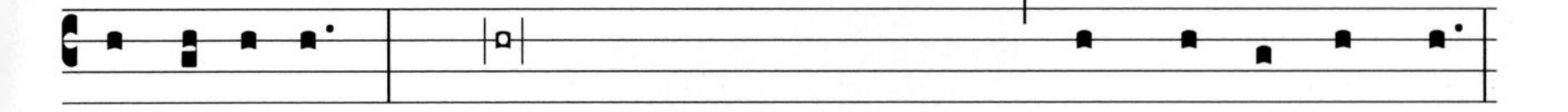

displeases you. ℣. Mary, you are full of grace, the Lord is with you.

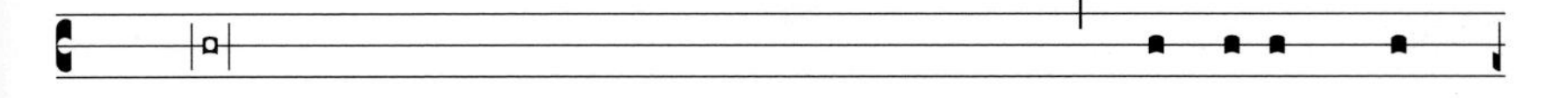

℟. Ma-ry, you are most blessed of all women, for Jesus Christ

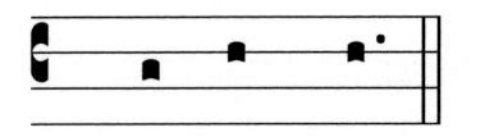

is your Son.

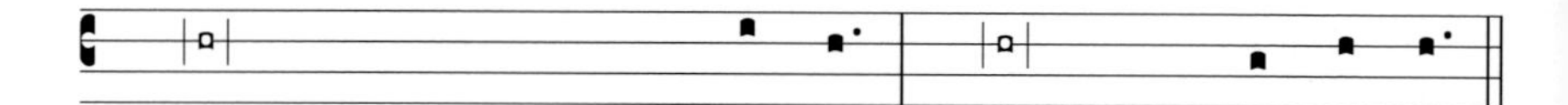

℣. Come to us, Lord God, to help us. ℟. Come to us, and save us.

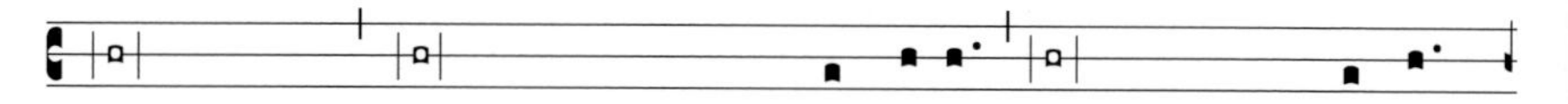

Glory to God, Father, Son and Holy Spirit, now & always. Amen.

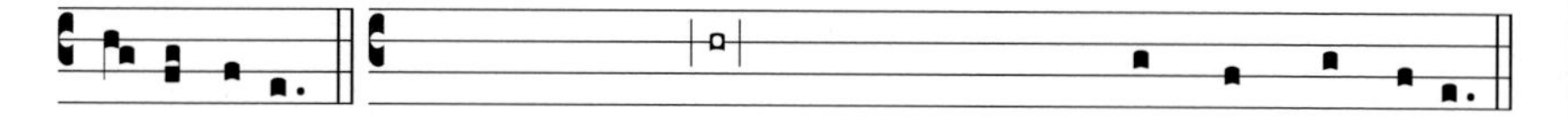

Al-le-lu-ia. *(or during Lent)* We praise you Lord, the King of glory.

*Sunday*

# NONE

## HYMN

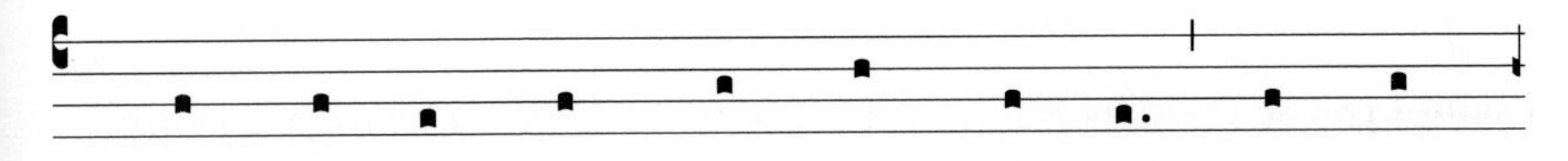

1. God, One in Three, your light re - veals your - self
2. For she who came by your de - cree first sign
3. Pray Ma - ry Mo - ther full of grace, pray in
4. Christ Son of God we pray to you, and ho-

1. to all men ev' ry - where; this light is Christ, the
2. of dawn in our dark night holds out to all men
3. your love for all we need, pro - tect us from all
4. nour you the Vir-gin's Son; we praise the Fa - ther,

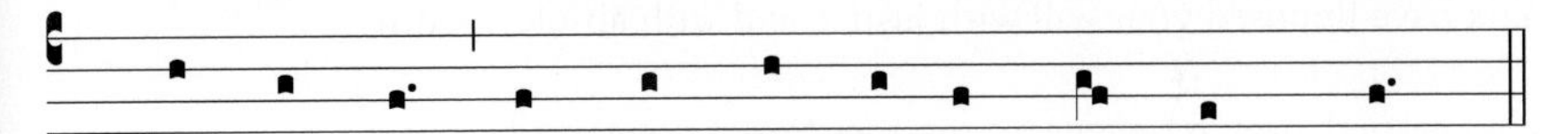

1. Vir - gin's Son hear now the Vir-gin Mo-ther's prayer.
2. ev' - ry - where her Son, your all- re - veal - ing light.
3. dan - ger now, and at our dy-ing in - ter - cede.
4. God with you and with the Spi-rit, Three in One.

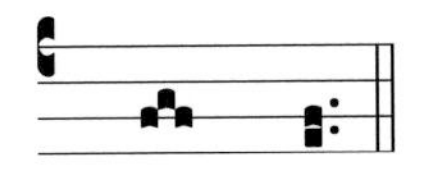

4. A - men.

ANTIPHON

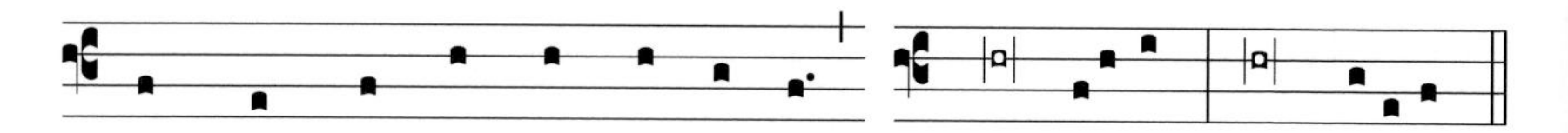

Vir - gin Mo-ther we pray to you, TONE II

**Psalm 118** *(vv. 129 – 144.)*

Your will is wonderful indeed; therefore I obey it.
The unfolding of your word gives light and teaches the simple.

I open my mouth and I sigh as I yearn for your commands.
Turn and show me your mercy; show justice to your friends.

Let my steps be guided by your promise; let no evil rule me.
Redeem me from man's oppression and I will keep your precepts.

Let your face shine on your servant and teach me your decrees.
Tears stream from my eyes because your law is disobeyed.

Lord, you are just indeed; your decrees are right.
You have imposed your will with justice and with absolute truth.

I am carried away by anger for my foes forget your word.
Your promise is tried in the fire, the delight of your servant.

Although I am weak and despised, I remember your precepts.
Your justice is eternal justice and your law is truth.

Though anguish and distress have seized me, I delight in your commands.
The justice of your will is eternal: if you teach me, I shall live.

*Glory be...*

**Psalm 118** *(vv. 145 – 160.)*

I call with all my heart; Lord, hear me, I will keep your statutes.
I call upon you, save me and I will do your will.

I rise before dawn and cry for help, I hope in your word.
My eyes watch through the night to ponder your promise.

In your love hear my voice, O Lord; give me life by your decrees.
Those who harm me unjustly draw near; they are far from your law.

But you, O Lord, are close, your commands are truth.
Long have I known that your will is established for ever.

See my affliction and save me for I remember your law.
Uphold my cause and defend me; by your promise, give me life.

Salvation is far from the wicked who are heedless of your statutes.
Numberless, Lord, are your mercies; with your decrees give me life.

Though my foes and oppressors are countless I have not swerved from your will.
I look at the faithless with disgust; they ignore your promise.

See how I love your precepts; in your mercy give me life.
Your word is founded on truth, your decrees are eternal.

*Glory be...*

**Psalm 118** *(vv. 161 – 176.)*

Though princes oppress me without cause I stand in awe of your word.
I take delight in your promise like one who finds a treasure.

Lies I hate and detest but your law is my love.
Seven times a day I praise you for your just decrees.

The lovers of your law have great peace; they never stumble.
I await your saving help, O Lord, I fulfill your commands.

My soul obeys your will and loves it dearly.
I obey your precepts and your will; all that I do is before you.

Lord, let my cry come before you: teach me by your word.
Let my pleading come before you: save me by your promise.

Let my lips proclaim your praise because you teach me your statutes.
Let my tongue sing your promise for your commands are just.
Let your hand be ready to help me, since I have chosen your precepts.

Lord, I long for your saving help and your law is my delight.

Give life to my soul that I may praise you. Let your decrees give me help.
I am lost like a sheep; seek your servant for I remember your commands.

*Glory be...*

## ANTIPHON

V**ir - gin Mo-ther we pray to you,** that you may pray to Christ,

your Son, to pardon us and not demand in justice what we

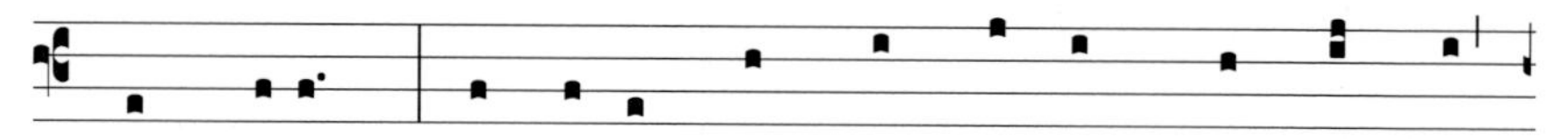

have deserved. For we like sheep have wandered from safe paths

to die in desert lands. Pray and he will come, Christ who is

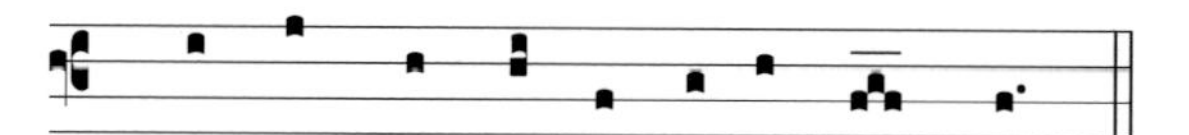

Shepherd and Saviour in his mer - cy.

## READING *(Eccles. 24:12)*

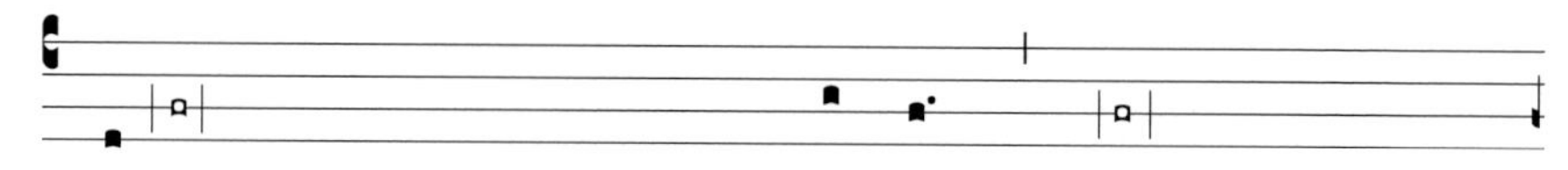

I have grown up among God's peo-ple: I will live for

## SHORT RESPONSORY

Shepherd and Saviour.

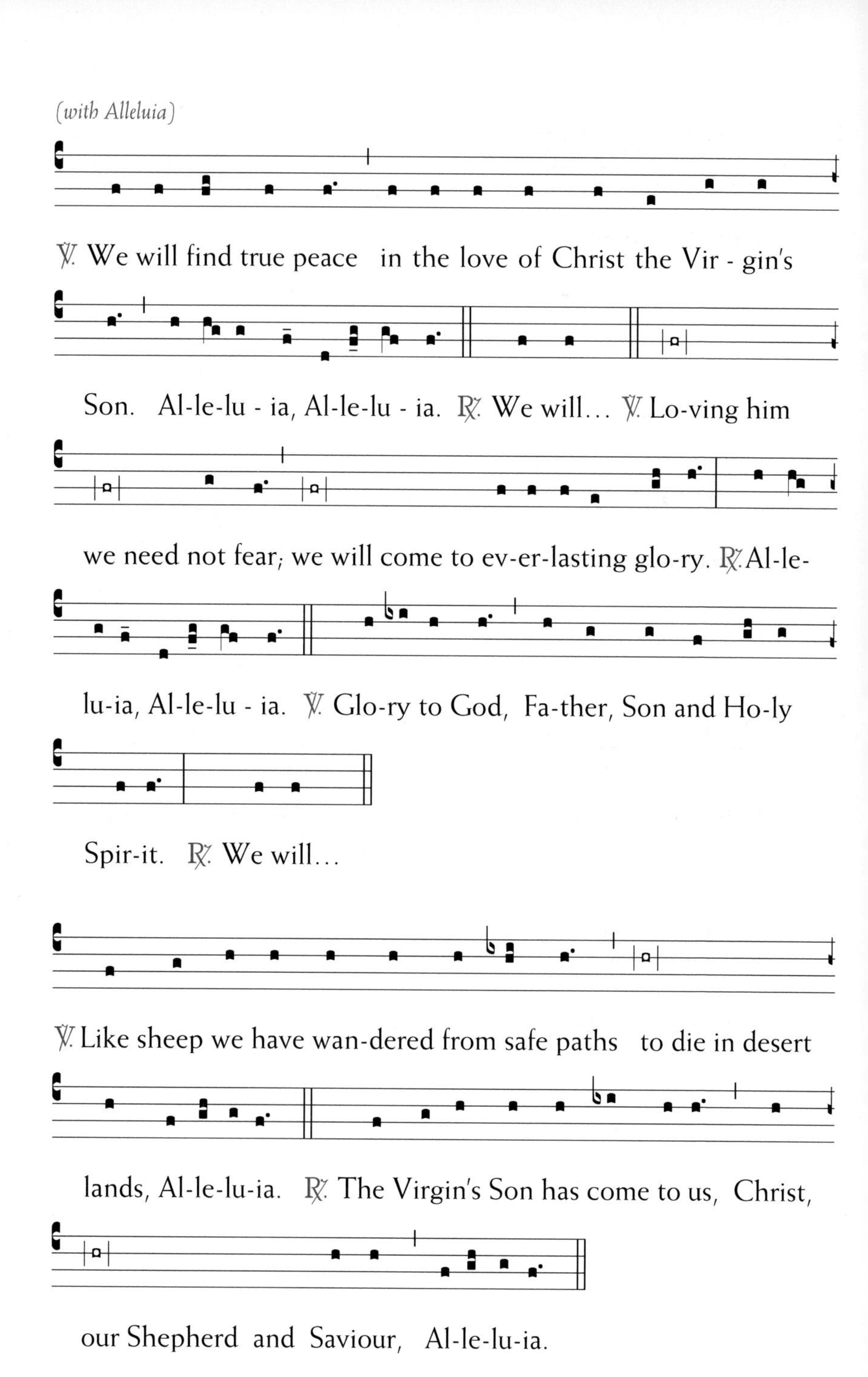
(with Alleluia)
℣. We will find true peace in the love of Christ the Vir - gin's
Son. Al-le-lu - ia, Al-le-lu - ia. ℟. We will… ℣. Lo-ving him
we need not fear; we will come to ev-er-lasting glo-ry. ℟. Al-le-
lu-ia, Al-le-lu - ia. ℣. Glo-ry to God, Fa-ther, Son and Ho-ly
Spir-it. ℟. We will…
℣. Like sheep we have wan-dered from safe paths to die in desert
lands, Al-le-lu-ia. ℟. The Virgin's Son has come to us, Christ,
our Shepherd and Saviour, Al-le-lu-ia.

℣. Lord, hear my prayer. ℟. Lord, grant my prayer. ℣. Let us pray.

**PRAYER** *(pages 36 - 37)*

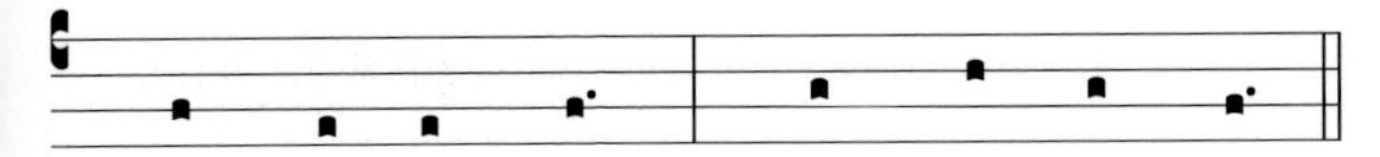

℣. Lord, hear my prayer. ℟. Lord, grant my prayer.

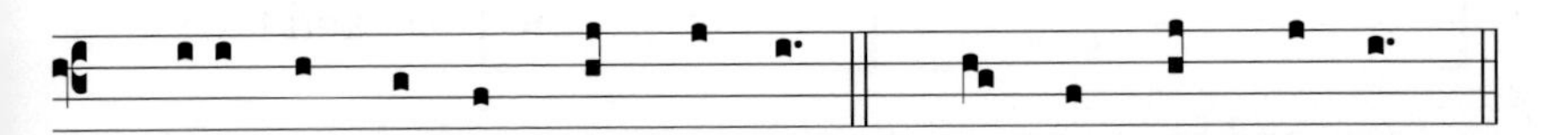

℣. Glory hon-our and praise to God. ℟. And our thanks to him.

*(with Alleluia)*

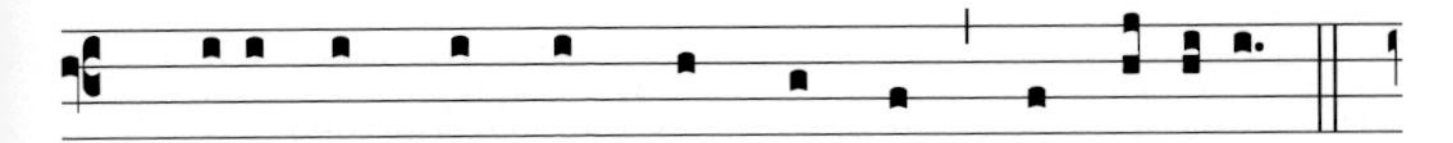

℣. Glory hon-our and praise to God, Al - le-lu-ia.

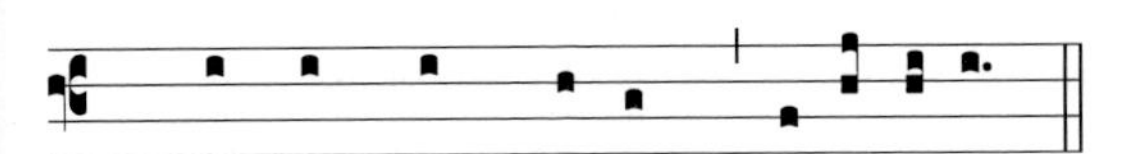

℟. And our thanks to him, Al-le-lu-ia.

## Closing Prayers

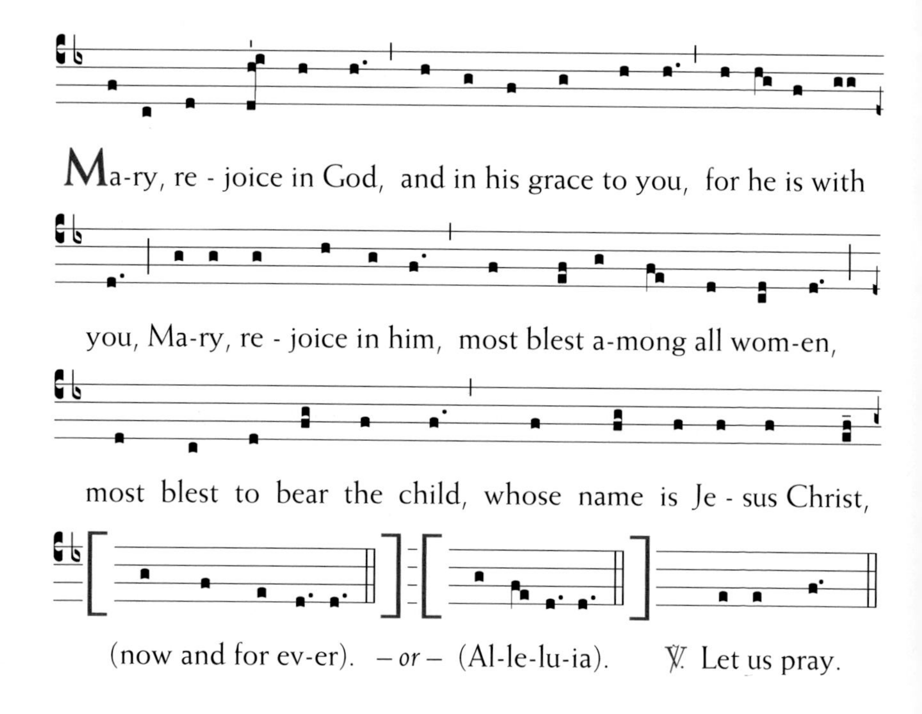


## Prayer

Almighty, everlasting God, who for us chose to be born of a most pure Virgin, we ask you to make us worthy to serve you with a pure body and to please you with a humble spirit. We pray also, loving Virgin Mary, Queen of this world and of angels, that you may obtain relief for those suffering the fires of purgatory, forgiveness for sinners, perseverance in goodness for the just, and defend us in our weakness from present perils.
Through Jesus Christ Our Lord. Amen.

## Lauds of Our Lady

*Every day, the Lauds of our Lady (of the day, season or feast) is now said or sung with the prayer; as shown daily after Compline.*

℣. May the souls of our founders, of our brothers and sisters and of all the faithful departed through the mercy of Jesus Christ rest in peace. ℟. Amen.
*None concludes with the following psalm together with two prayers or three after the death of a Sister or Pope or Bishop.*

**Psalm 129**

Out of the depths I cry to you, O Lord, Lord, hear my voice!
O let your ears be attentive to the voice of my pleading.

If you, O Lord, should mark our guilt, Lord, who would survive?
But with you is found forgiveness: for this we revere you.

My soul is waiting for the Lord. I count on his word.
My soul is longing for the Lord more than watchman for daybreak.

Let the watchman count on daybreak
and Israel on the Lord.

Because with the Lord there is mercy and fullness of redemption,
Israel indeed he will redeem from all its iniquity.

Eternal rest grant to them, O Lord. And let perpetual light shine upon them.
May they rest in peace. Amen.

℣. Lord, have mercy. ℟. Christ have mercy. Lord have mercy.
℣. Our Father…
℣. From the gates of hell ℟. Deliver their souls, O Lord.
℣. May they rest in peace. ℟. Amen.
℣. Lord, hear my prayer. ℟. Lord, grant my prayer.
℣. Let us pray.

## Prayer

O God, to whose bounty and love man owes his pardon and salvation, we beg of your mercy that, through the intercession of Blessed Mary, ever Virgin, and all your saints, (the soul of N… ) the souls of the brothers, sisters, relatives and benefactors of our congregation, and also our parents, who have departed this life, may be admitted into the fellowship of everlasting bliss.

*(Insert here the Prayer for a deceased Sister, Pope or Bishop when needed. They are said for 30 days after death, as below…)*

O God, Creator and Redeemer of all the faithful, grant to the souls of your departed servants the forgiveness of all their sins. Let our loving prayers obtain for them the pardon they have always desired, you who live and reign for ever and ever. ℟. Amen.

℣. Eternal rest give to them, O Lord,
℟. And let perpetual light shine upon them.
℣. May they rest in peace. ℟. Amen.

---

PRAYER FOR A DECEASED SISTER

We pray you, O Lord, in your mercy, have pity on the soul of your servant, our Sister, N… You have freed her from the perils of this mortal life; grant her to be numbered for evermore among the saved.

PRAYER FOR A DECEASED POPE

God our Father, you reward all who believe in you. May your servant, N… our Pope, Vicar of Peter and shepherd of your Church, who faithfully administered the mysteries of your forgiveness and love on earth, rejoice with you for ever in heaven.

PRAYER FOR OUR DIOCESAN BISHOP, DECEASED

God our Father, may your servant, N… who was our Bishop, rejoice in the fellowship of the successors of the apostles whose office he shared in this life.

*Before*

# THE OFFICE OF READINGS (MATINS)

The Office of Readings (Matins) may be said at any time of the day. However, if it is the first Office of the day, begin with the Introductory prayers before Lauds *(Introduction to Lauds, page 33)* and the Invitatory Psalm *(Psalm 94)* with its associated Antiphon and Responses; as shown for the day of the week.

---

## OPENING PRAYERS

℣. Mary help me to praise you.
℟. Guard me from all that displeases you.

℣. Mary, you are full of grace the Lord is with you.
℟. Mary, you are most blessed of all women, for Jesus Christ is your Son.

℣. Come to us, Lord God, to help us.
℟. Come to us and save us.

*Glory to God, Father, Son and Holy Spirit, now and always. Amen. (Alleluia)*
*(**During Lent** – We praise you Lord, the King of Glory.)*

*Sunday*

# OFFICE OF READINGS (MATINS)

**OPENING PRAYERS** *as on preceding page.*

## HYMN

Mary, you ever magnify the Lord,
and glorify your God in everything,
as heavenly bride, as Mother of God's Son,
as heavenly Queen of the eternal King.

Before all years, your years were known to God,
willed by his will and his divine decree,
that you should come and reign, creation's Queen,
when all creation's years should come to be.

All heavens, all lands and seas, all living things,
each in their way praise you, their crown and Queen;
speak then for all, commend us to your Son,
who comes through you to save and to redeem.

Pray Mary Virgin-Mother full of grace,
pray in your love for all, for all we need;
protect us from all sin and sinful ways,
and at our dying hour intercede.

Christ Jesus, Son of God, we pray to you
and praise you, naming you the Virgin's Son;
we ever praise the Father, God with you,
and with the Holy Spirit, Three in One. Amen.

## ANTIPHON 1

**Virgin, you draw all hearts to love you.**

## Psalm 2

Why this tumult among nations, among peoples this useless murmuring?
They arise, the kings of the earth, princes plot against the Lord and
his Anointed.

"Come, let us break their fetters, come, let us cast off their yoke."
He who sits in the heavens laughs; the Lord is laughing them to scorn.

Then he will speak in his anger, his rage will strike them with terror.
"It is I who have set up my king on Sion, my holy mountain."

(I will announce the decree of the Lord:)
The Lord said to me: "You are my Son. It is I who have begotten you this day.

Ask and I shall bequeath you the nations, put the ends of the earth
in your possession.
With a rod of iron you will break them, shatter them like a potter's jar."

Now, O kings, understand,
take warning, rulers of the earth;

serve the Lord with awe and trembling, pay him your homage
lest he be angry and you perish; for suddenly his anger will blaze.

Blessed are they
who put their trust in God.

*Glory be to the Father and to the Son and to the Holy Spirit,*
*As it was in the beginning, is now and ever shall be, world without end. Amen.*

## ANTIPHON 1

V**irgin, you draw all hearts to love you.** Crowned now by God as Queen, enthroned on Syon his holy mountain, you draw us to love you not less, but more; and loving you we love your Son. Teach us to serve him in holy fear; to praise him in our love and helplessness.

## ANTIPHON 2

**Father, you have glorified the Virgin Mary.**

**Psalm 3**

How many are my foes, O Lord! How many are rising up against me!
How many are saying about me: "There is no help for him in God."

But you, Lord, are a shield about me, my glory, who lift up my head.
I cry aloud to the Lord. He answers from his holy mountain.

I lie down to rest, and I sleep. I wake, for the Lord upholds me.
I will not fear even thousands of people who are ranged on every side
against me.

Arise, Lord; save me, my God, you who strike my foes on the mouth,
you who break the teeth of the wicked! O Lord of salvation, bless your people!

*Glory be...*

## ANTIPHON 2

**Father, you have glorified the Virgin Mary,** and she has ever glorified you in return. Strengthen your people that we may not fall; bless your people that we may live in your blessing.

## ANTIPHON 3

**Pray for us, Mary, Mother of God.**

**Psalm 4**

When I call, answer me, O God of justice; from anguish you released me,
have mercy and hear me!

O men, how long will your hearts be closed, will you love what is futile
and seek what is false?

It is the Lord who grants favours to those whom he loves; the Lord hears me
whenever I call him.
Fear him; do not sin: ponder on your bed and be still. Make justice your
sacrifice and trust in the Lord.

"What can bring us happiness?" many say.
Lift up the light of your face on us, O Lord.

You have put into my heart a greater joy than they have from abundance
of corn and new wine.
I will lie down in peace and sleep comes at once for you alone, Lord, make me
dwell in safety.

*Glory be...*

## ANTIPHON 3

P**ray for us, Mary, Mother of God,** that we may receive the blessing of God; that he may accept the adoration we owe him, and our love – that love his love has made known.

℣. Mary, your Son who is truly God, obeyed you, and your word was powerful with him. (Alleluia)
℟. Queen of heaven, we who pray to you know the power of your prayer. (Alleluia)

Our Father...

## ABSOLUTION

God and father, holy and merciful Lord, take into account the prayer and holiness of Mary, the Virgin-Mother of God, and of all the saints and bring us back from death to life. ℟. Amen.

*These daily readings, revealed to St Bridget by an angel, are arranged for reading in a three-week cycle. Now one reading a day, there were formerly three.* *Those for Week Two start on page 509, and Week Three on page 528.* *Before the Reading, the reader says...*
Lord, we ask for your blessing.

Week One

## Blessing

May the Virgin Mary, so dear to Father, Son and Holy Spirit, protect us with her prayer. ℟. Amen.

## Reading

When John in his Gospel speaks of the Word,
that Word is he who is, and has ever been,
with the Father and the Holy Spirit, one God.
In this one God, there are truly three Persons;
yet not three Gods,
for in the three Persons is only one Divinity,
the one, perfect Godhead,
belonging equally to each;
and in the three Persons,
only one will,
one wisdom, one power,
one beauty, one strength,
one love, one joy.
The Word, then,
being for ever one with the Father and the Holy Spirit,
is truly God.

A familiar word like ONE can help us, perhaps, to understand,
for each of the three letters is necessary to the whole,
and we cannot take away one letter without destroying the meaning.
So in God,
there must ever be the three Persons,
equal in all things,
with all things equally in each,
for there can be no dividing of God.

There was no dividing when the Word, the Son of God,
took a human nature;
he was not separated, by this, from the Father and the Holy Spirit.
He took our human nature,
yet remained ever the Word of God.
His human nature was necessary for him

to achieve our salvation.
It can help us to understand this
if we consider how our thoughts and our words
are not things we can see or touch,
except in so far as writing gives them a more material existence.

The Word of God, the Son of God,
could not have come as one of us,
or lived with us, for our salvation,
unless he had taken on our human nature.
A written word can be seen and read,
then understood, then spoken.
The Son of God can be seen, in that flesh he took to himself,
and so we can understand and have no doubt
that he is one with the Father and the Holy Spirit.
Truly then, there are three Persons,
undivided,
unchanging and unchangeable,
eternally in all things equal,
three, yet but one God.

Since God is eternal and timeless,
all things were eternally known to him,
before their existence in time.
Then, when he willed them to be,
they came to be
with that exact perfection which suited their purpose.
The divine wisdom of God willed all things to be what they are
for his own honour and glory.
He had no need of them;
it was not to make up for any deficiency in himself –
something wanting to his goodness or joy –
there can be no defect or deficiency in God.
It was his love,
and his love alone,
which led him to create;
that there might be beings, apart from himself,
whose existence should be an existence of joy,
deriving from his own being and joy.
All things, then,
foreseen by God,
and present to him eternally, though as yet uncreated,

had already that design and perfection which they would possess
when his creating brought them to be.

One thing excelled all others,
designed and perfected by God with a special joy.
This was Mary,
the Virgin who was a Mother,
the Mother who was ever a Virgin.

It has been said that all created things are made up of four elements –
fire, air, water and earth.
If so, then in Mary's pure body,
these elements were to have a special perfection:
the air should be fittingly an image of the Holy Spirit;
the earth should be rich and fruitful,
for the growth of useful things, to supply every need;
the water should be calm and unmenacing,
unruffled by every wind;
and the fire so strong and bright
that all the earth should be warmed by it,
and the heavens themselves.
Virgin Mary,
we know that in you the design and perfection willed by God
have come to be.
As he foresaw you,
so he has perfectly created you.
And of all his creation,
you most please him.

The Father rejoiced that he would do so much through you:
the Son rejoiced in your holiness and love:
the Holy Spirit rejoiced in your lowliness and obedience.

The Father's joy is that of the Son and the Holy Spirit:
the Son's joy is that of the Father and Spirit:
and the Holy Spirit's joy is that of the Father and the Son.

Father, Son and Holy Spirit rejoice in you,
the one joy of Three who are One.
Father, Son and Holy Spirit love you, Mary,
the love of the Three Persons, One God.

*(After the reading)*

℣. Have mercy, Lord, and help our understanding. ℟. Our thanks to God.

## RESPONSORY

**Glory to God who is,** who alone must be, eternal Father, Son and Holy Spirit, one God, yet ever Three in equal glory. Glory to God, who holds all things in being.
℣. Glory to God who has looked on you, Mary, with love, and willed your coming by his eternal decree. May he look on us and love us, he who is and who alone must be, Trinity and Unity, Trinity in Unity.
℟. Who holds all things in being.
℣. Glory to God, glory to Father, Son and Holy Spirit.
℟. Who holds all things in being.

## TE DEUM

*(or PSALM 50 on Sundays and ferial days in Advent and Lent; ferias in Passiontide and ferial Fridays throughout the year, except in Eastertide – as on Friday, page 330)*

We praise you O God, we acknowledge you to be the Lord.
All the earth worships you,
the Father everlasting.

To you all angels cry aloud, the heavens and all the powers therein.
To you cherubim and seraphim continually cry: Holy, Holy, Holy,
Lord God of hosts.

Heaven and earth are full of the majesty of your glory.
The glorious choir of the apostles praise you,

The admirable company of the prophets, the white-robed army
of martyrs praise you,
the holy Church throughout all the world acknowledges you.

The Father of infinite majesty; your adorable, true, and only Son.
The Holy Spirit also, the Comforter.

You are the King of glory, O Christ, you are the everlasting Son of the Father.
When you took upon yourself to deliver man, you humbled yourself to be
born of a virgin.

When you had overcome the sting of death, you opened the kingdom of heaven to all believers.
Now you sit at the right hand of God in the glory of the Father.

We believe that you will come to be our judge.
We therefore pray you to help your servants, whom you have redeemed with your precious blood.

Make them to be numbered with your saints in everlasting glory.
O Lord save your people and bless your inheritance.

Govern them and lift them up forever.
Day by day we praise you, and we glorify your name for ever: yes, for ever and ever.

Be pleased, O Lord, this day, to keep us free from sin.
Have mercy upon us, O Lord, have mercy upon us.

O Lord, let your mercy be shown to us, as we have hoped in you.
In you, have I hoped, O Lord: I shall not be confounded for ever.

---

℣. Mary, Queen of heaven, do not leave us unprotected. (Alleluia)
℟. Look on us in mercy and love. (Alleluia)

**CLOSING PRAYERS** *(page 38)*

*Before*
# VESPERS

Hail Mary, full of grace, the Lord is with thee. Blessed art thou among women, and blessed is the fruit of thy womb, Jesus. Holy Mary, Mother of God, pray for us sinners, now and at the hour of our death. Amen.

℣. Our Lady, Help of Christians, ℟. Pray for us.

## HYMN

7. A - men.

1. Star of ocean, lead us, God for Mother claims thee,
   ever-virgin names thee; Gate of heaven, speed us.
2. Ave to thee crying, Gabriel went before us;
   peace do thou restore us, Eva's knot untying.
3. Loose the bonds that chain us, darkened eyes enlighten,
   clouded prospects brighten, heav'nly mercies gain us.
4. For thy sons thou carest; offer Christ our praying,
   still thy word obeying whom on earth thou barest. *(Repeat this verse twice)*
5. Purer, kinder maiden God did never fashion;
   pureness and compassion grant to hearts sin-laden.
6. From that sin release us, shield us heaven-ward faring;
   heav'n, that is but sharing in thy joy with Jesus.
7. Honour, praise and merit to our God address we;
   Three in One confess we, Father, Son and Spirit. Amen.

*(9th Century: translated by R. A. Knox.)*

*(with Alleluia during Easter only)*

℣. Pray for us, holy Virgin Mary, Mother of God. (Alleluia)

℟. That we may be made worthy of the promises of Jesus Christ. (Alleluia)

℣. May peace be in thy strength. (Alleluia)

℟. And abundance in thy towers. (Alleluia)

℣. Let us pray.

## Prayer

Protect your servants, O Lord, with the blessings of peace, and keep safe from their enemies and from every danger, those who trust in the patronage of blessed Mary, ever a Virgin.

O God, from whom come all holy desires, all right resolves and all good deeds, grant to your servants that peace which the world cannot give; that our hearts being devoted to the keeping of your commandments, and the fear of enemies being removed, our times, by your protection, may be peaceful. Through Christ our Lord. ℟. Amen.

*The following two prayers are said to ask forgiveness for daily faults.*
Hail Mary, full of grace, the Lord is with thee, blessed art thou among women, and blessed is the fruit of thy womb, Jesus Christ.

Forgive us, for the love of God, and of his most piteous Mother, Mary, if we have offended you in word or deed, by sign or token; for likewise, if there be any default in you against us, we forgive it gladly.

*Sunday*

# VESPERS

**OPENING PRAYERS** – with music – *as at None, pages 55 - 56.*

## ANTIPHON

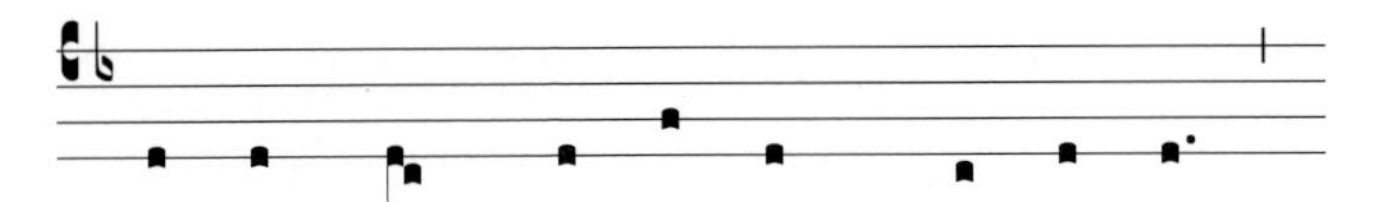

**Blest are those who hon-our Christ as Lord,**

TONE I

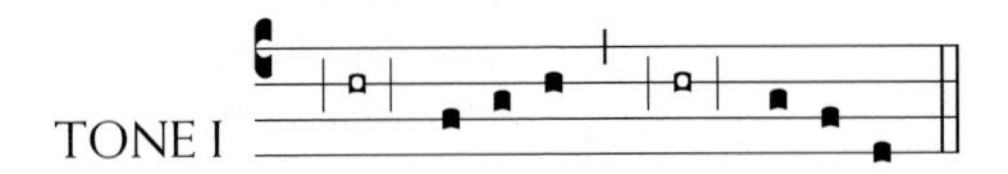

### Psalm 109

The Lord's revelation to my Master: "Sit on my right:
I will put your foes beneath your feet."

The Lord will send from Sion your sceptre of power:
rule in the midst of all your foes.

A prince from the day of your birth on the holy mountains;
from the womb before the daybreak I begot you.

The Lord has sworn an oath he will not change. "You are a priest for ever,
a priest like Melchizedek of old."

The Master standing at your right hand
will shatter kings in the day of his great wrath.

He, the Judge of the nations, will heap high the bodies;
heads shall be shattered far and wide.

He shall drink from the stream by the wayside
and therefore he shall lift up his head.

*Glory be...*

**Psalm 110**

I will thank the Lord with all my heart in the meeting of the just
and their assembly.
Great are the works of the Lord, to be pondered by all who love them.

Majestic and glorious his work, his justice stands firm for ever.
He makes us remember his wonders. The Lord is compassion and love.

He gives food to those who fear him; keeps his covenant ever in mind.
He has shown his might to his people by giving them the lands of the nations.

His works are justice and truth, his precepts are all of them sure,
standing firm for ever and ever; they are made in uprightness and truth.

He has sent deliverance to his people and established his covenant for ever.
Holy his name, to be feared.

To fear the Lord is the beginning of wisdom; all who do so prove
themselves wise.
His praise shall last for ever!

*Glory be...*

**Psalm 111**

Happy the man who fears the Lord, who takes delight in his commands.
His sons will be powerful on earth; the children of the upright are blessed.

Riches and wealth are in his house; his justice stands firm for ever.
He is a light in the darkness for the upright: he is generous,
merciful and just.

The good man takes pity and lends, he conducts his affairs with honour.
The just man will never waver: he will be remembered for ever.

He has no fear of evil news; with a firm heart he trusts in the Lord.
With a steadfast heart he will not fear; he will see the downfall of his foes.

Open-handed, he gives to the poor; his justice stands firm for ever.
His head will be raised in glory.

The wicked man sees and is angry, gnashes his teeth and pines away;
the desire of the wicked leads to doom.

*Glory be...*

**Psalm 112**

Praise, O servants of the Lord, praise the name of the Lord!
May the name of the Lord be blessed both now and for evermore!

From the rising of the sun to its setting praised be the name of the Lord!
High above all nations is the Lord, above the heavens his glory.

Who is like the Lord, our God, who has risen on high to his throne
yet stoops from the heights to look down, to look down upon
heaven and earth?

From the dust he lifts up the lowly, from the dungheap he raises the poor
to set him in the company of princes, yes, with the princes of his people.

To the childless wife he gives a home
and gladdens her heart with children.

*Glory be...*

**Psalm 147**

O praise the Lord, Jerusalem!
Sion, praise your God!

He has strengthened the bars of your gates, he has blessed the
children within you.
He established peace on your borders, he feeds you with finest
wheat.

He sends out his word to the earth and swiftly runs his command.
He showers down snow white as wool, he scatters hoar-frost like
ashes.

He hurls down hailstones like crumbs. The waters are frozen at his touch;
he sends forth his word and it melts them: at the breath of his mouth the waters flow.

He makes his word known to Jacob, to Israel his laws and decrees.
He has not dealt thus with other nations; he has not taught them his decrees.

*Glory be…*

## ANTIPHON

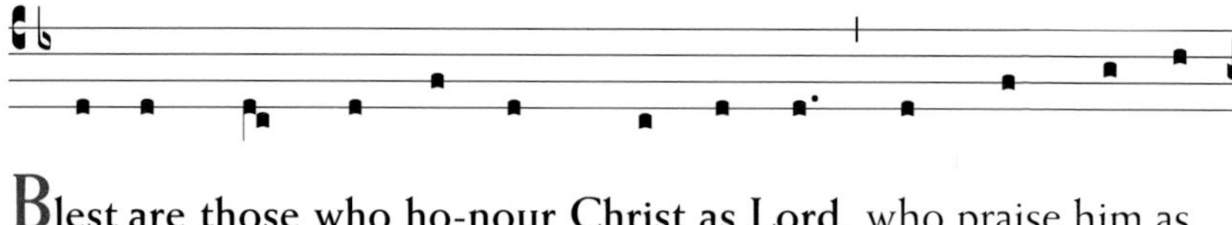

**Blest are those who ho-nour Christ as Lord,** who praise him as

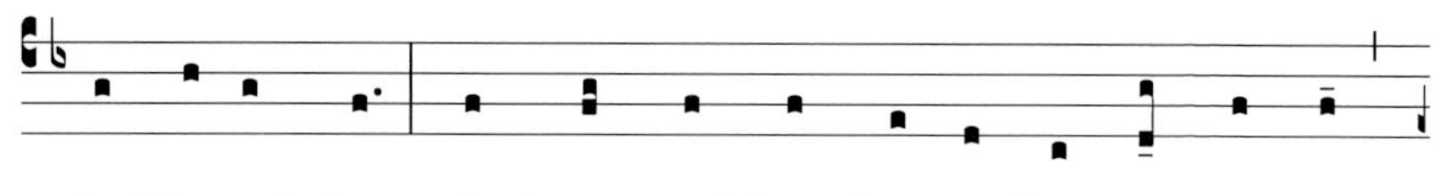

the Virgin's Son, who know and hear him as the Word of God,

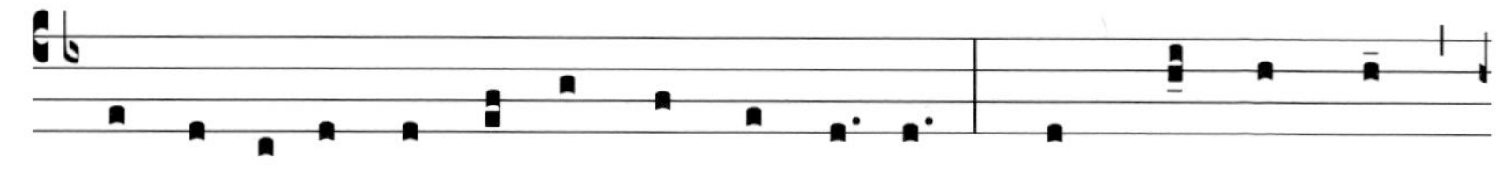

and the e-ter-nal Son of God the Father. Most blest are they,

for he will say to them – Come to me, all you my Father loves;

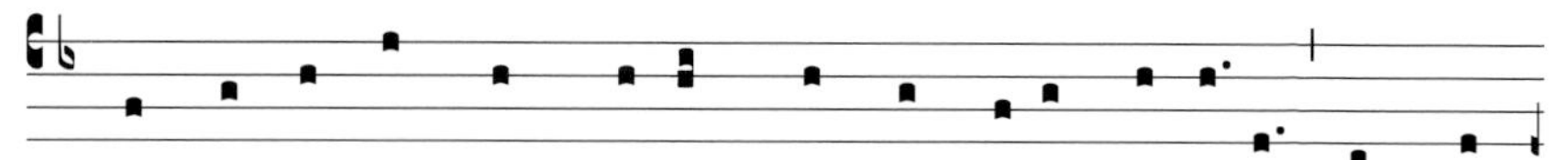

come to the kingdom prepared for you before all ages, come to

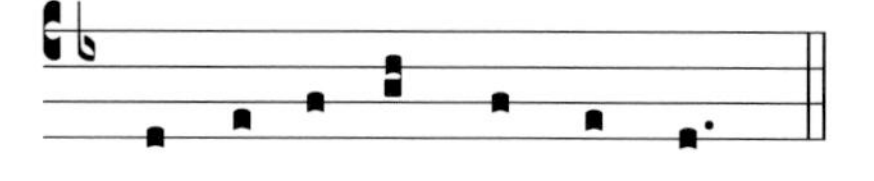

your ev-er-last-ing re-ward.

## Reading

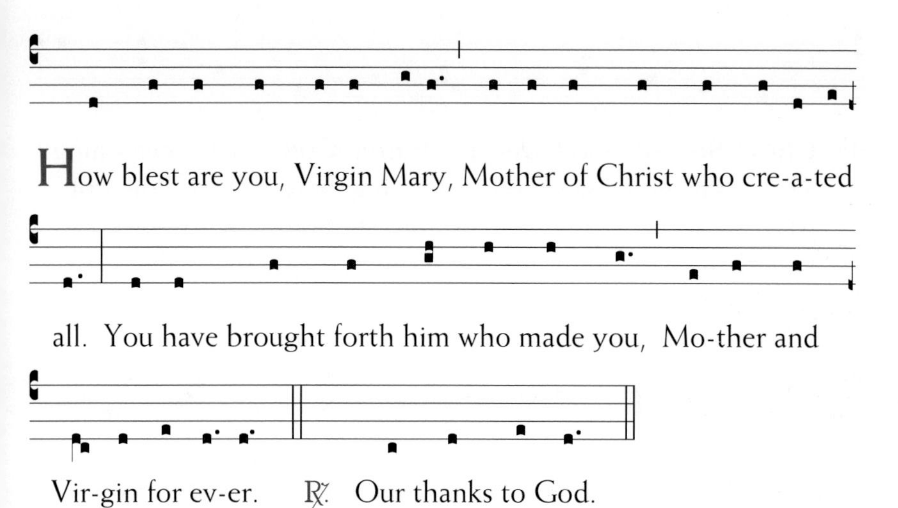
How blest are you, Virgin Mary, Mother of Christ who cre-a-ted
all. You have brought forth him who made you, Mo-ther and
Vir-gin for ev-er. ℟. Our thanks to God.

## HYMN

1. Christ, Son of God, true light from God, as eve - ning
2. We saw you, knew you, liv - ing here, Christ, Son of
3. Ma - ry we name you, bright-est Star, of Christ the
4. Guard us by night to rest in Christ, by day in
5. Pray Ma - ry Mo - ther full of grace, pray in your
6. Christ Son of God, we pray to you, and hon - our

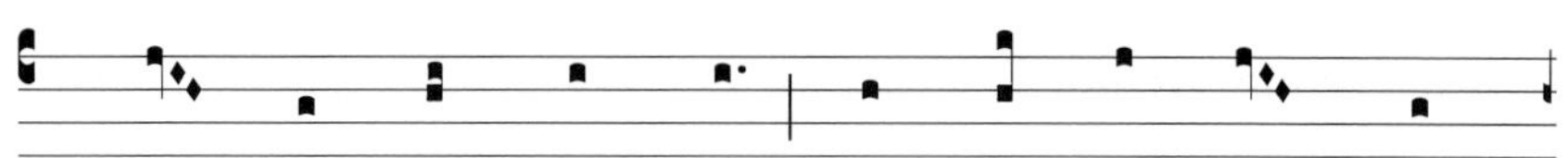

1. comes to end our day, guard now our dark - ness
2. God, the Vir - gin's Son, as light from heav'n to
3. Sun, the light of light, shine now pro - claim the
4. ac - tion, thought and word, to do the will of
5. love for all we need, pro - tect us from all
6. you, the Vir - gin's Son; we praise the Fa - ther,

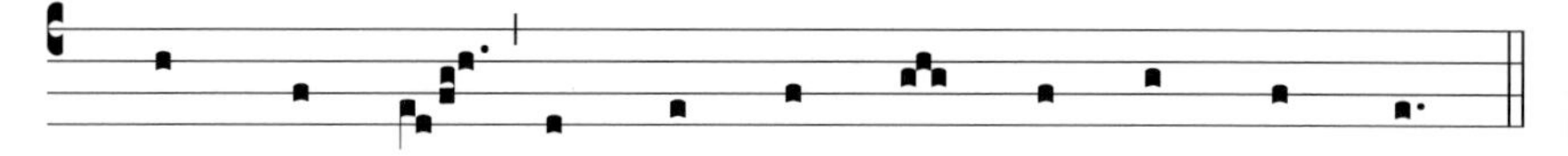

1. and our night, and guide our minds in love we pray.
2. be our life, as truth from God, to make God known.
3 dawn of day, pier - cing the clouds of sin's dark night.
4. Christ your Son, plea - sing to him who is our Lord.
5 dan - ger now and at our dy - ing in - ter - cede.
6. God with you and with the Spi - rit, Three in One.

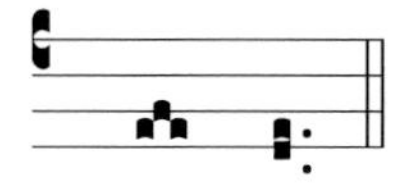

6. A - men.

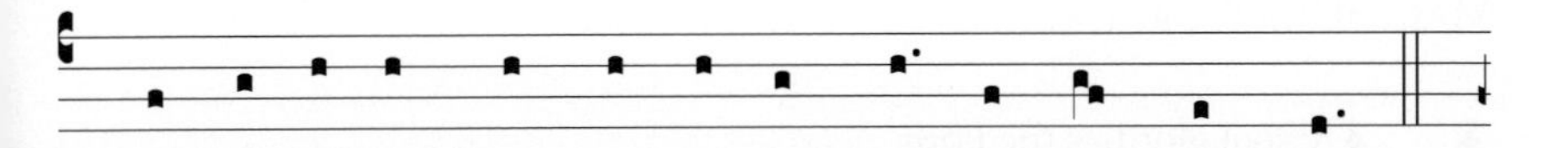

℣. In the love of Christ the Vir-gin's Son, we find true peace.

(Al-le-lu-ia)

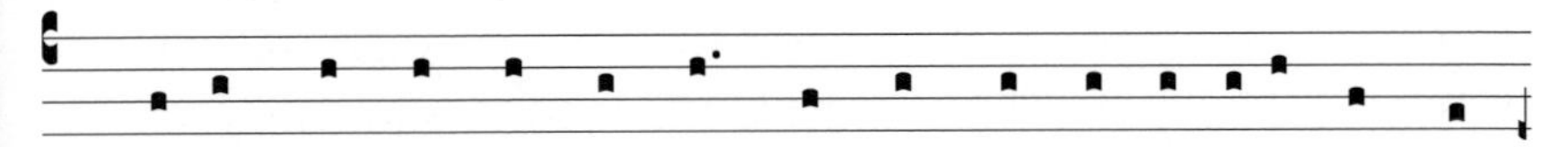

℟. Loving him we need not fear, his love will be our ever-last-ing

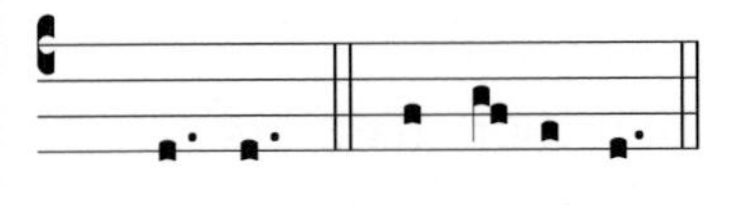

glo-ry. (Al-le-lu-ia)

---

ANTIPHON

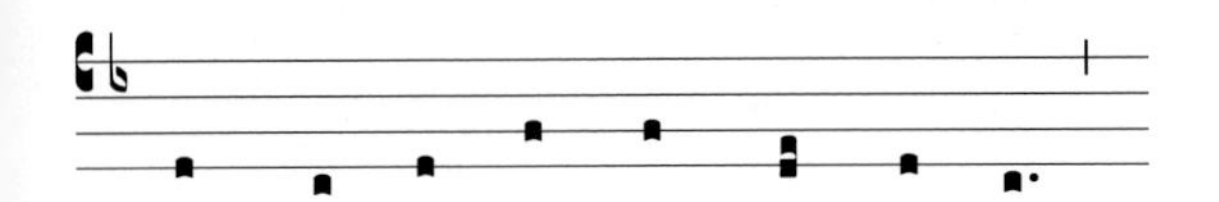

Glo - ry, hon-our and praise to God,

TONE I

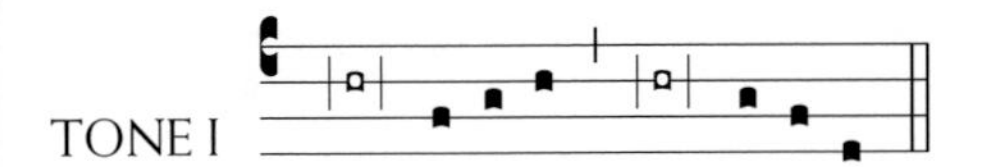

## MAGNIFICAT *(Luke 1: 46 - 55)*

My soul glorifies the Lord,
my spirit rejoices in God,
my Saviour.

He looks on his servant in her nothingness; henceforth all ages
will call me blessed.
The Almighty works marvels for me. Holy his name!

His mercy is from age to age, on those who fear him.
He puts forth his arm in strength and scatters the proud-
hearted.

He casts the mighty from their thrones and raises the lowly.
He fills the starving with good things, sends the rich away empty.

He protects Israel, his servant, remembering his mercy,
the mercy promised to our fathers, to Abraham and his sons
for ever.

Praise the Father, the Son and the Holy Spirit,
both now and for ever, world without end.

## ANTIPHON

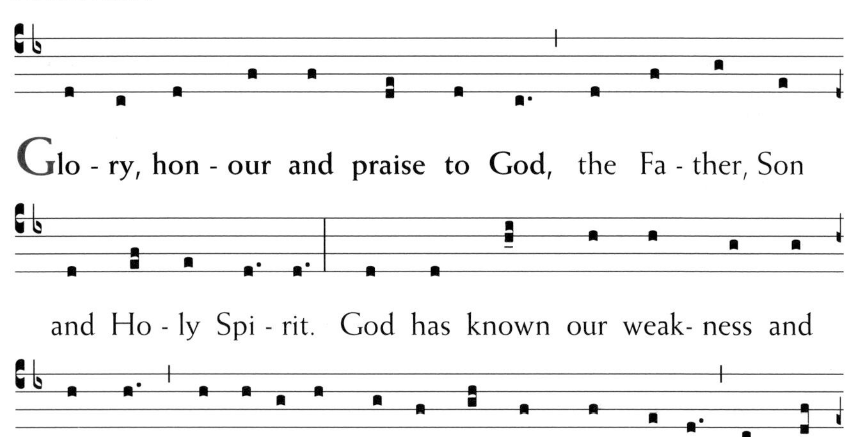

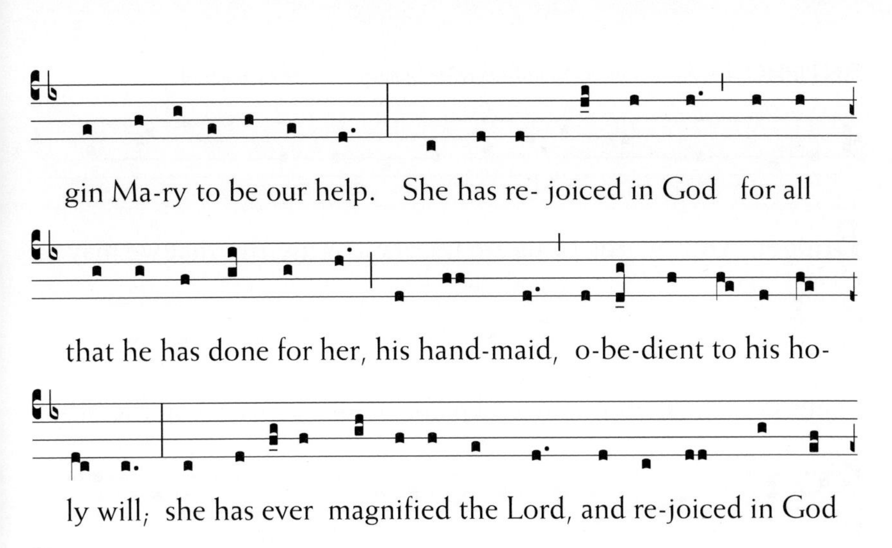


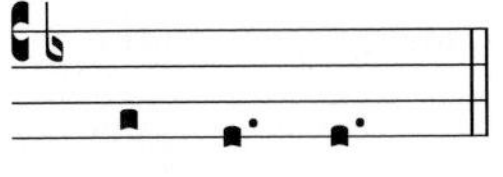

her Sav-iour.

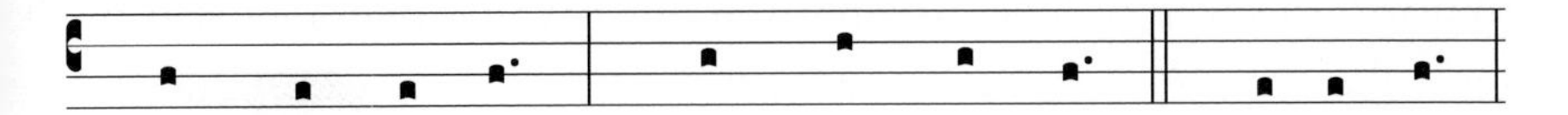

℣. Lord, hear my prayer. ℟. Lord, grant my prayer. ℣. Let us pray.

**PRAYER** *According to the season, day or feast.* *See pages 36 - 37 or...*

G**rant us,** your servants, we pray you, Lord God, to enjoy perpetual health of mind and body. By the glorious intercession of blessed Mary ever Virgin, may we be delivered from present sorrows and enjoy everlasting happiness: through our Lord Jesus Christ your Son, who lives and reigns with you in the unity of the Holy Spirit, God for ever and ever. ℟. Amen.

**ANTIPHON** *to Holy Mother, Saint Bridget, on Sundays, Feasts & Memorials.*

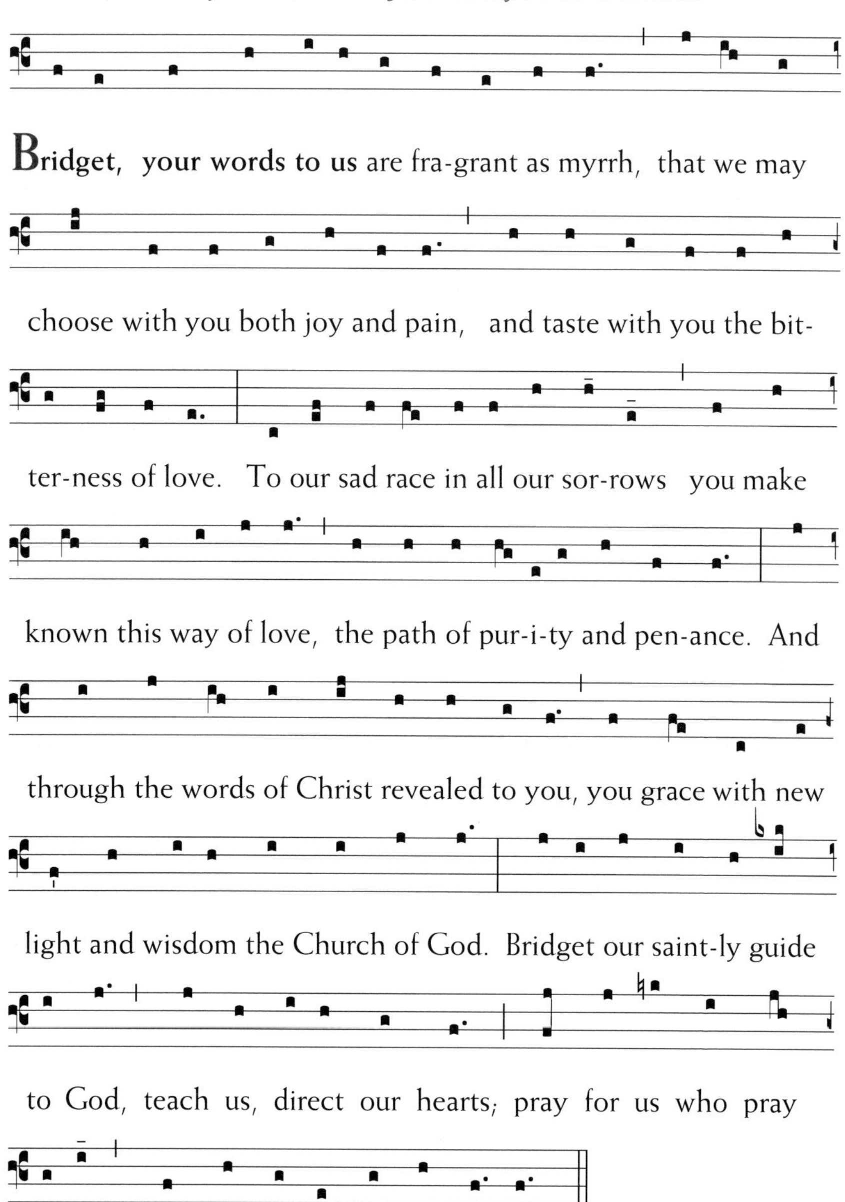


to you, our Mo-ther and lov-ing Pat-ron.

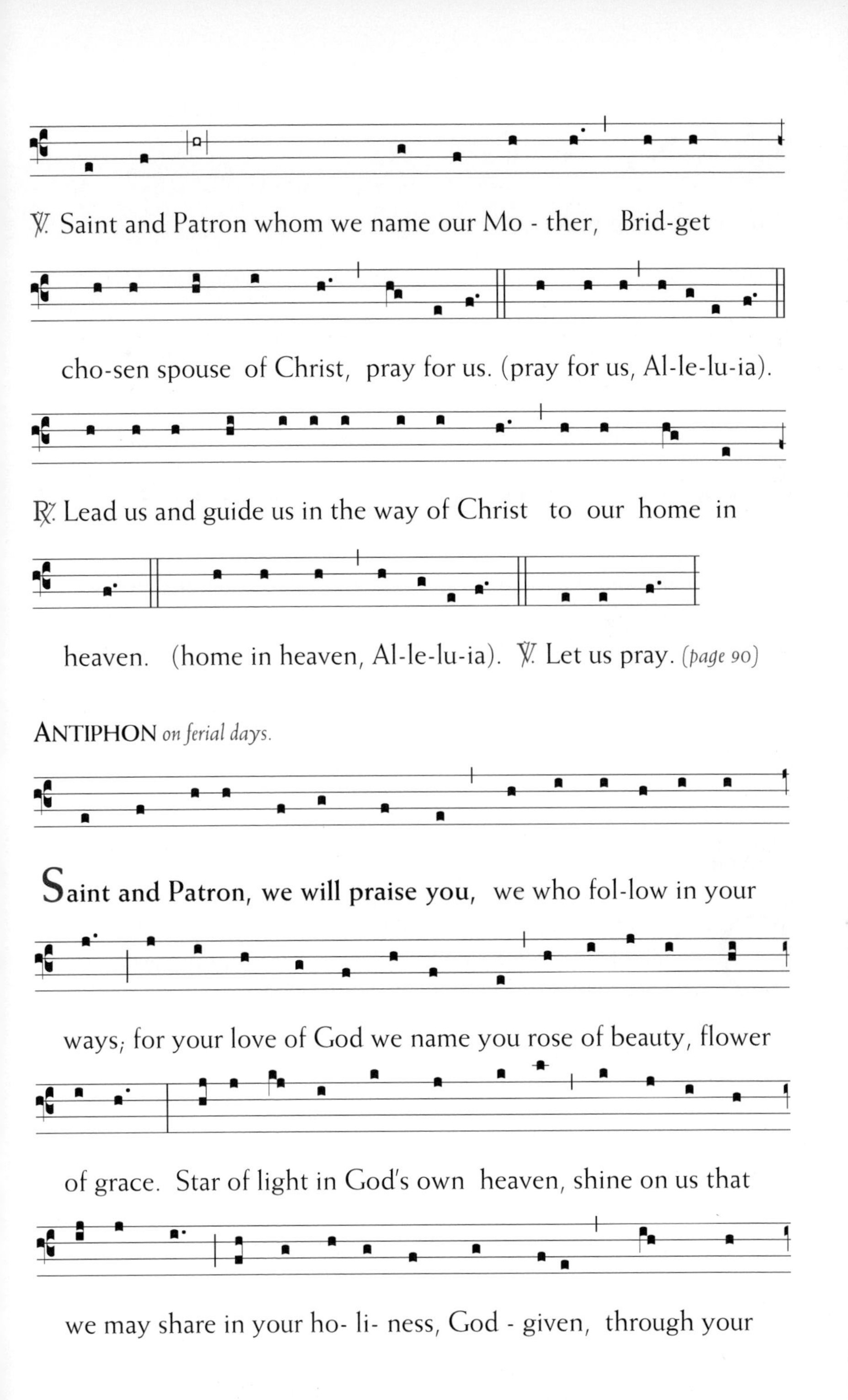
℣. Saint and Patron whom we name our Mo - ther, Brid-get
cho-sen spouse of Christ, pray for us. (pray for us, Al-le-lu-ia).
℟. Lead us and guide us in the way of Christ to our home in
heaven. (home in heaven, Al-le-lu-ia). ℣. Let us pray. (page 90)
ANTIPHON on ferial days.
Saint and Patron, we will praise you, we who fol-low in your
ways; for your love of God we name you rose of beauty, flower
of grace. Star of light in God's own heaven, shine on us that
we may share in your ho- li- ness, God - given, through your

in-ter-ced-ing prayer.

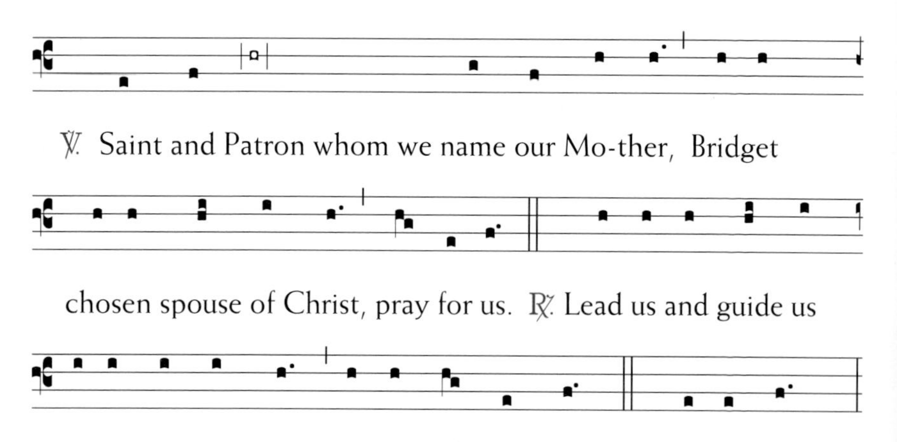


## Prayer

O God, you chose to enlighten your Church with the holy teaching and example of blessed Bridget. Mercifully grant, that by her prayer, we may faithfully do those things necessary for the forgiveness of our sins, which of your goodness you revealed to her. Through our Lord Jesus Christ your Son, who lives and reigns with you in the unity of the Holy Spirit for ever and ever. ℟. Amen.

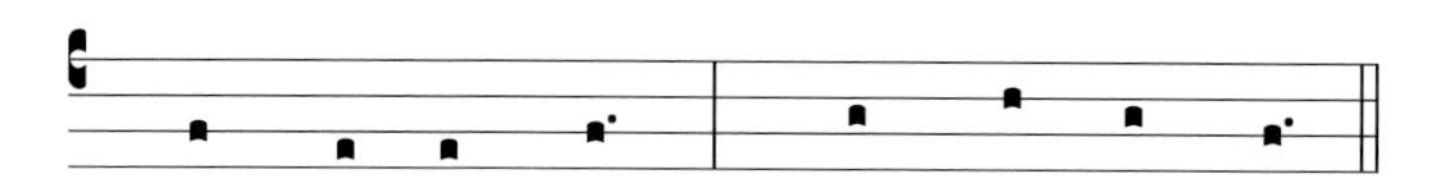

℣. Lord, hear my prayer. ℟. Lord, grant my prayer.

## Thanksgiving

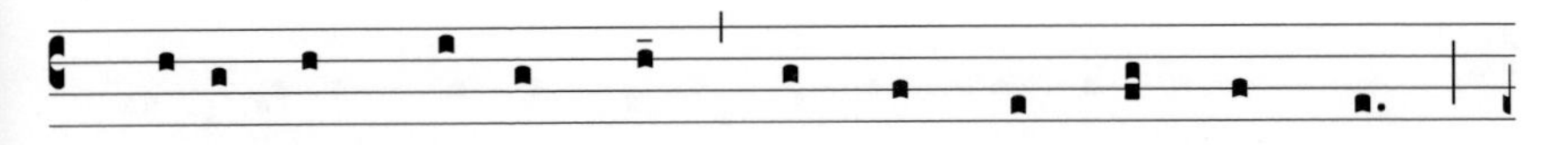

℣. Glory, hon - our and praise to Christ the Vir - gin's Son,

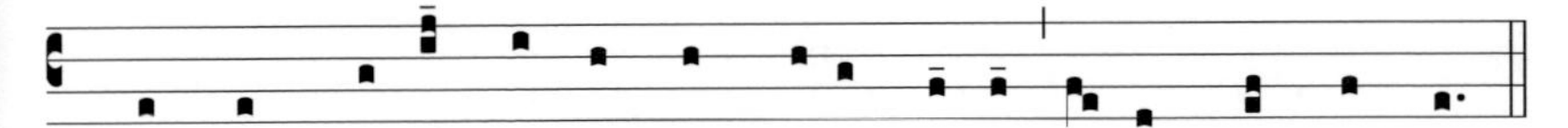

God with the Father and the Holy Spi-rit ev-er Three in One.

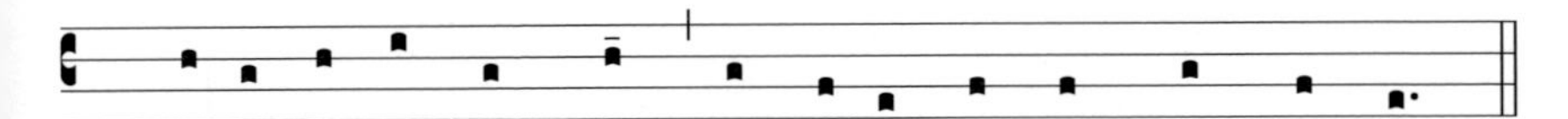

℟. Glory, honour and praise, and ne-ver-end-ing thanks to God.

*(with Alleluia)*

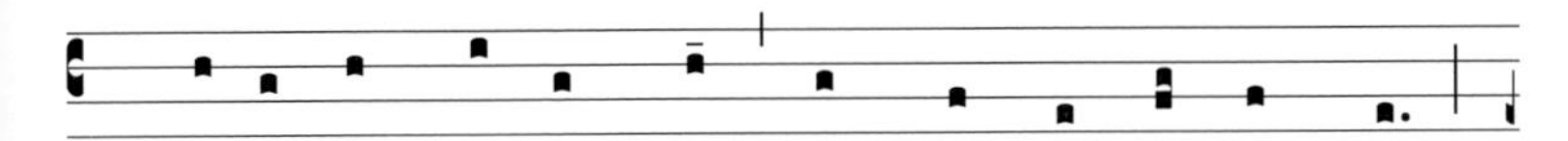

℣. Glo-ry, hon-our and praise to Christ the Vir-gin's Son,

Al-le-lu-ia, Al-le-lu-ia, Al-le-lu-ia.

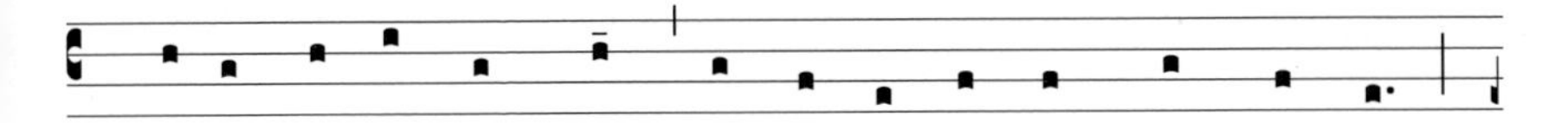

℟. Glory, honour and praise, and ne-ver-end-ing thanks to God,

Al-le-lu-ia, Al-le-lu-ia, Al-le-lu-ia.

## Closing Prayers

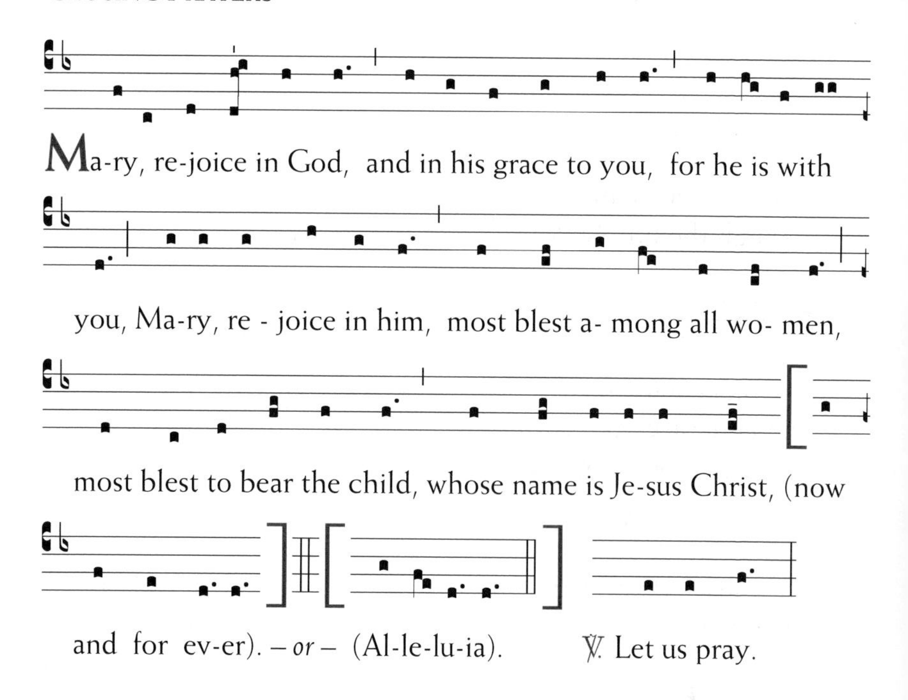


## Prayer

Almighty, everlasting God, who for us chose to be born of a most pure Virgin, we ask you to make us worthy to serve you with a pure body and to please you with a humble spirit. We pray also, loving Virgin Mary, Queen of this world and of angels, that you may obtain relief for those suffering the fires of purgatory, forgiveness for sinners, perseverance in goodness for the just, and defend us in our weakness from present perils.
Through Jesus Christ our Lord. ℟. Amen.

May the souls of our founders, of our brothers and sisters and of all the faithful departed, through the mercy of Jesus Christ rest in peace. ℟. Amen.

## HYMN TO HOLY MOTHER SAINT BRIDGET AFTER VESPERS

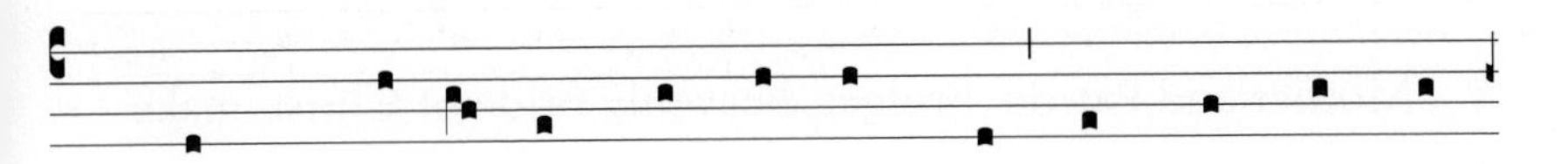

1. Brid - get we may tru - ly name you Saint and Pa - tron,
2. Through the ho - ly Rule you gave us, heaven- ly guide to

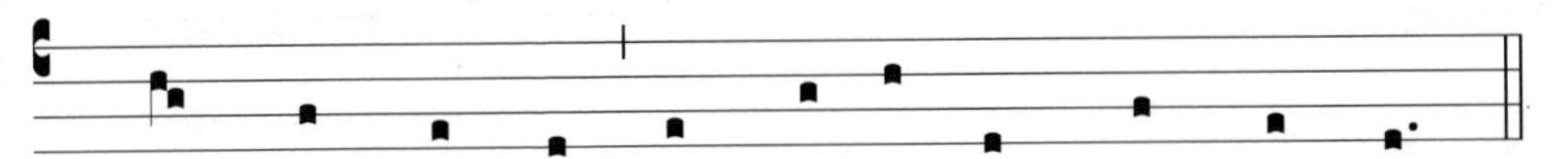

1. and ac- claim you Mo-ther of our earth - ly days.
2. teach and save us, path-way to God's love and praise.

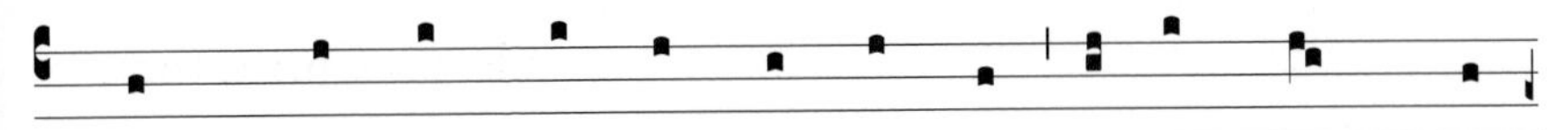

3. In the storms of dark temp-ta - tion, be our strength and
4. Christ will hear your in - ter - ced - ing, he will spare us

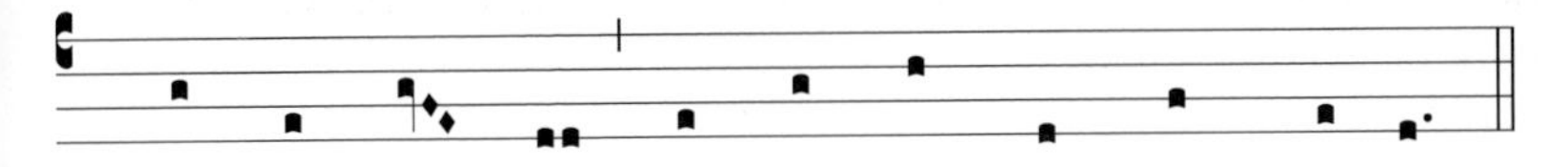

3. con - so - la - tion, pray that grace may change our sin.
4. at your plead-ing, for your life of love for him.

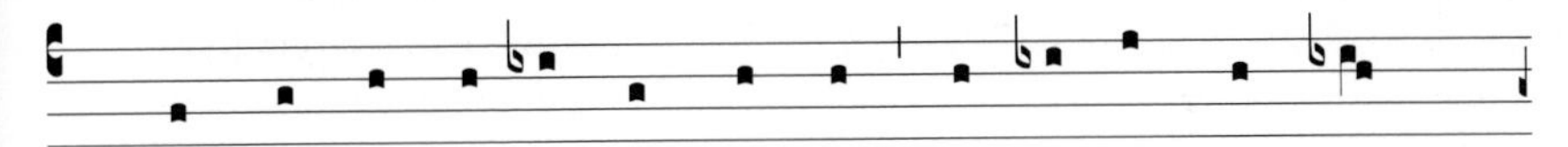

5. Pray that with a love in-creas-ing, pur - i - ty and prayer
6. Till with you in con-tem-pla-tion, we may live in a-

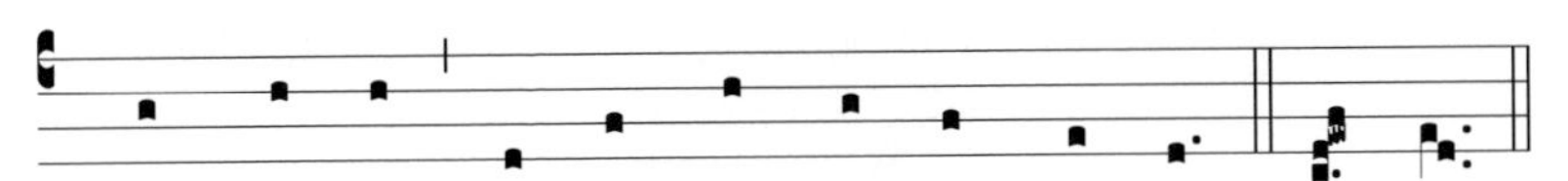

5. un - ceas-ing we may learn the ways of God.
6. do - ra-tion and e - ter - nal praise of God. A - men.

*(Followed by the ℣. and ℟. and prayer on the next page)*

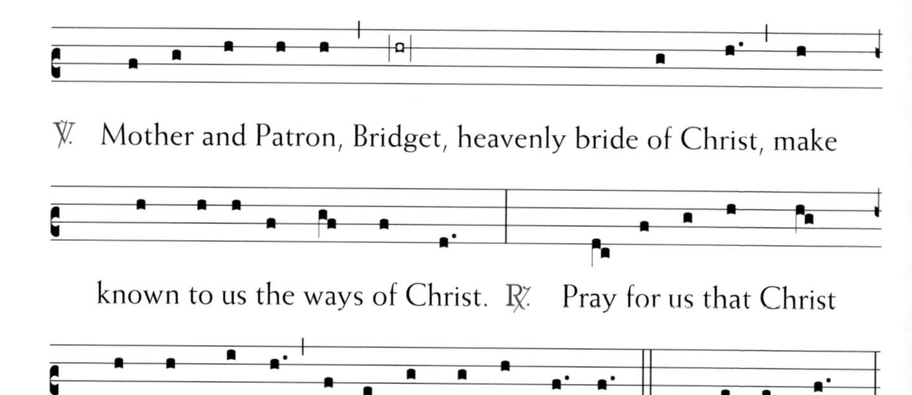


## Prayer

Lord Jesus Christ, you were pleased to call blessed Bridget your bride, and inspired her with many of your secrets and adorned her with remarkable virtues. Grant we pray, that we may become like her in our life and ways, and freed from the allurements of this world, we may enjoy with her the joys of heaven. You who live and reign with the Father and Holy Spirit,
for ever and ever. ℟. Amen.

*Sunday*

# COMPLINE

## OPENING PRAYERS

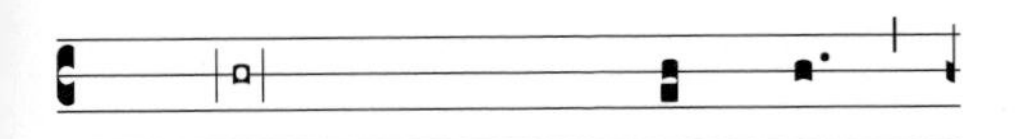

℣. Ma-ry, help me to praise you,

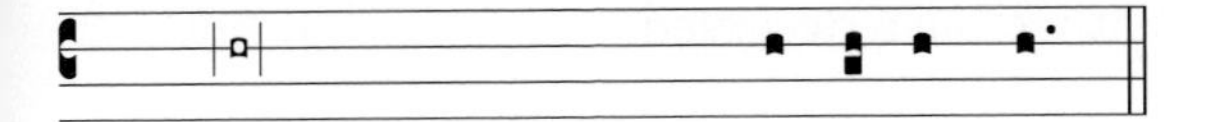

℟. Guard me from all that displeases you.

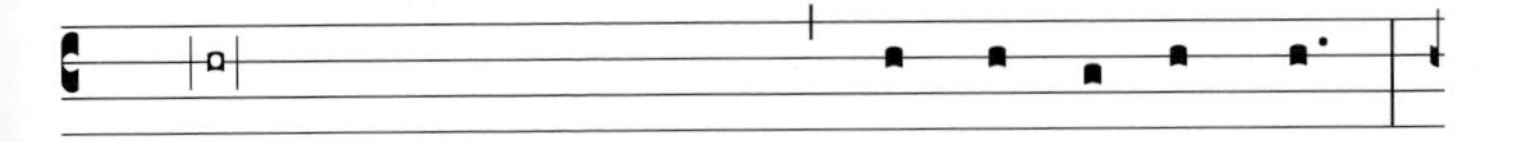

℣. Ma-ry, you are full of grace, the Lord is with you.

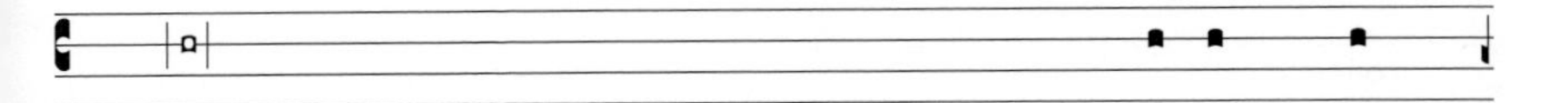

℟. Ma-ry, you are most blessed of all women, for Je-sus Christ

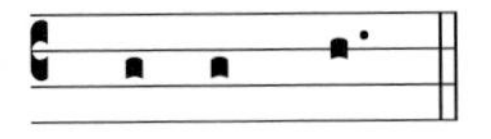

is your Son.

We praise you Lord, the King of glo-ry.

ANTIPHON

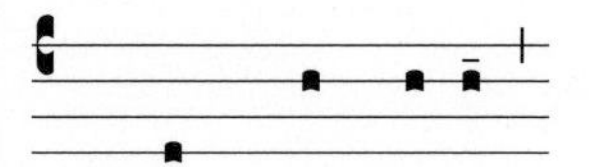

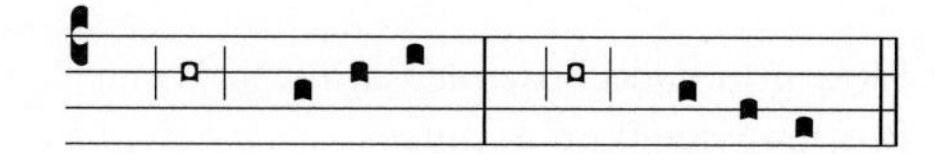

How good it is

TONE IV

**Psalm 131**

O Lord, remember David and all the hardships he endured,
the oath he swore to the Lord, his vow to the Strong One of Jacob.

"I will not enter the house where I live nor go to the bed where I rest.
I will give no sleep to my eyes, to my eyelids will give no slumber

till I find a place for the Lord, a dwelling for the Strong One of Jacob."
At Ephrata we heard of the ark; we found it in the plains of Yearim.

"Let us go to the place of his dwelling; let us go to kneel at his footstool."
Go up, Lord, to the place of your rest, you and the ark of your strength.

Your priests shall be clothed with holiness; your faithful shall ring
out their joy.
For the sake of David your servant do not reject your anointed.

The Lord swore an oath to David; he will not go back on his word:
"A son, the fruit of your body, will I set upon your throne.

If they keep my covenant in truth and my laws that I have taught them,
their sons also shall rule on your throne from age to age."

For the Lord has chosen Sion; he has desired it for his dwelling:
"This is my resting-place for ever; here have I chosen to live.

I will greatly bless her produce, I will fill her poor with bread.
I will clothe her priests with salvation and her faithful shall ring out their joy.

There the stock of David will flower; I will prepare a lamp for my anointed.
I will cover his enemies with shame but on him my crown shall shine."

*Glory be...*

## Psalm 132

How good and how pleasant it is,
brothers dwelling in unity!

It is like precious oil upon the head running down upon the beard,
running down upon Aaron's beard, upon the collar of his robes.

It is like the dew of Hermon which falls on the heights of Sion.
For there the Lord gives his blessing, life for ever.

*Glory be...*

## Psalm 133

O come, bless the Lord, all you who serve the Lord,
who stand in the house of the Lord, in the courts of the house of our God.

Lift up your hands to the holy place and bless the Lord through the night.
May the Lord bless you from Sion, he who made both heaven and earth.

*Glory be...*

### ANTIPHON

**How good it is** for us to be to-gether in lo-ving praise of

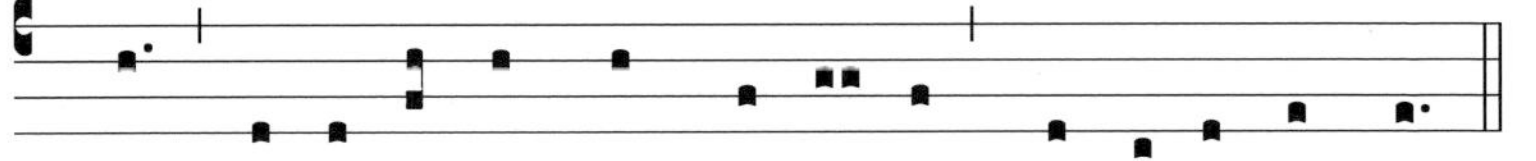

God, and in lov-ing praise of Ma-ry Mother of his Son.

## READING *(Proverbs 31: 29)*

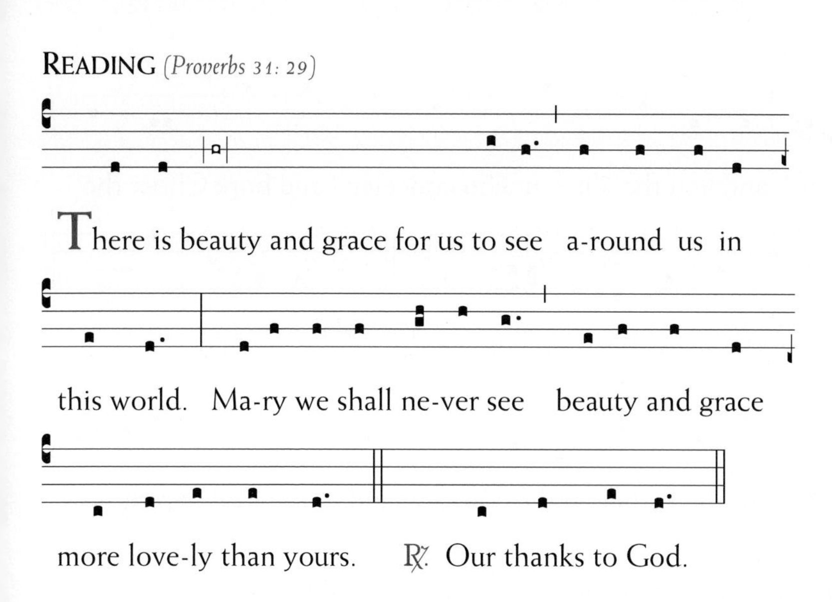


---

## SHORT RESPONSORY

Lord, and you the Vir-gin who conceived and bore Christ the

Son of God and his revealing word. ℟. for we may pray...

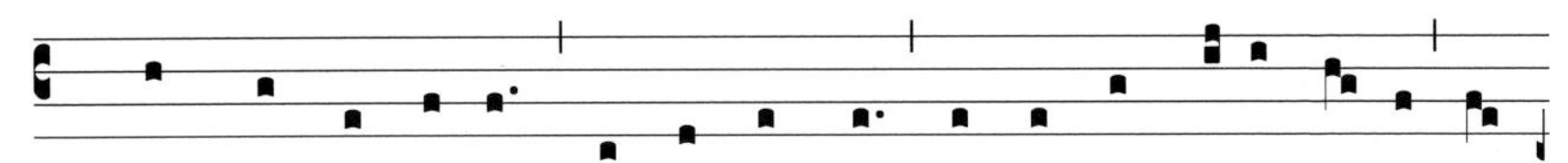

℣. Praise to the Father, and to the Son and to the Holy Spirit now

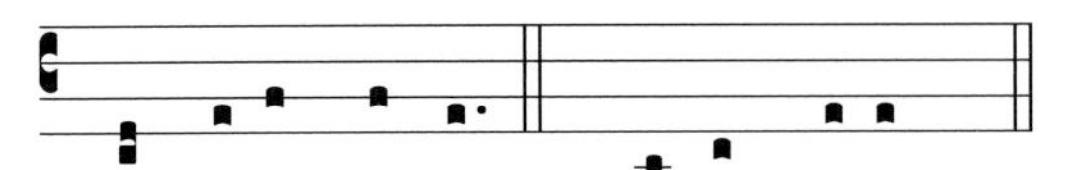

and ever. Amen. ℟. Virgin Ma-ry...

SHORT RESPONSORY *on ferial days.*

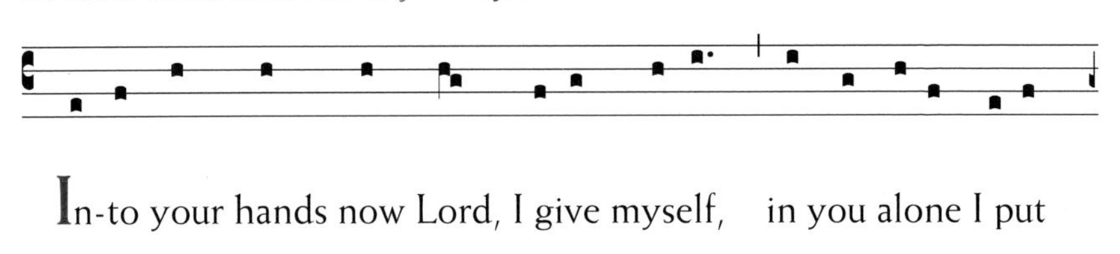

In-to your hands now Lord, I give myself, in you alone I put

my trust. ℟. *Repeat.* ℣. You are my God and my redeeming Lord.

℟. in you alone… ℣. Glory to Father and Son, and to Holy Spirit.

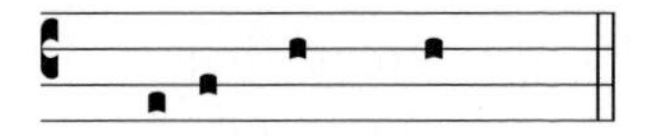

℟. Into your hands…

## Short Responsory

*During Easter and on Solemnities and Feasts where Alleluia is used.*

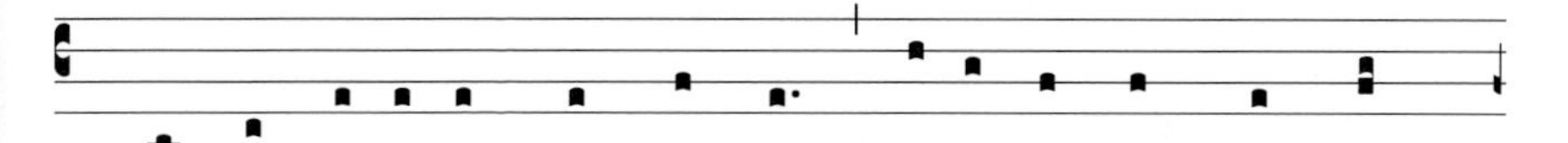

Vir - gin Ma-ry commend our souls into the hands of Christ

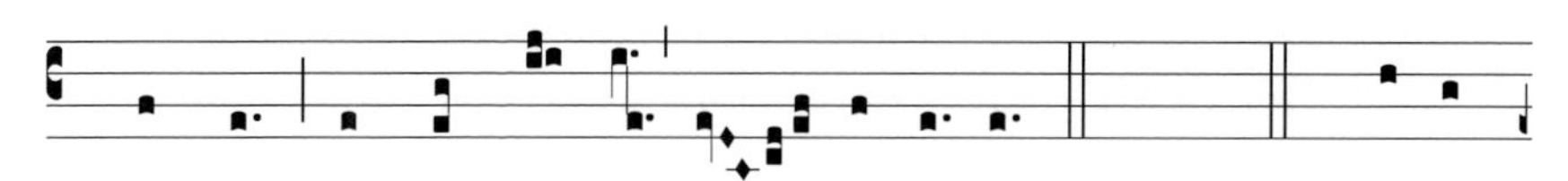

your Son Al - le - lu - ia, Al - le- lu- ia. ℟. *Repeat.* ℣. He is

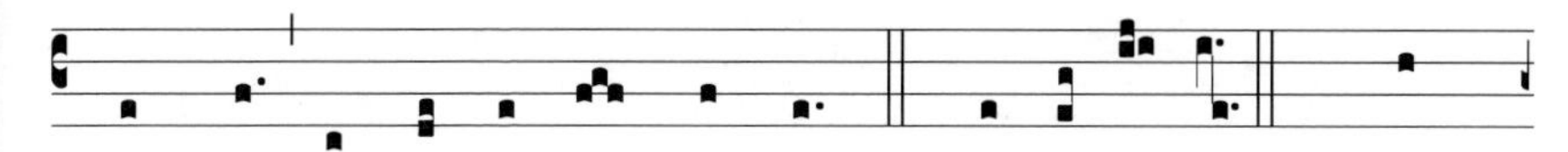

our God and our re-deem-ing Lord. ℟. Al- le- lu- ia… ℣. Praise

to the Father, and to the Son and to the Ho-ly Spi- rit now and

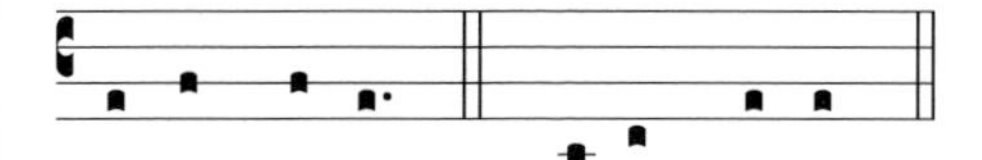

e-ver. Amen. ℟. Virgin Ma-ry…

## Hymn

1. The Fa - ther, who be - gets the Son, gives him the
2. The Fa - ther's one e - ter - nal will de - crees that
3. In Fa - ther, Son and Spi - rit God is U - ni -
4. True God, true man, the Son has come as man to
5. To you, both God and man we pray, true God from
6. Pray Ma - ry Mo - ther full of grace, pray in your
7. Christ Son of God we pray to you, and ho - nour

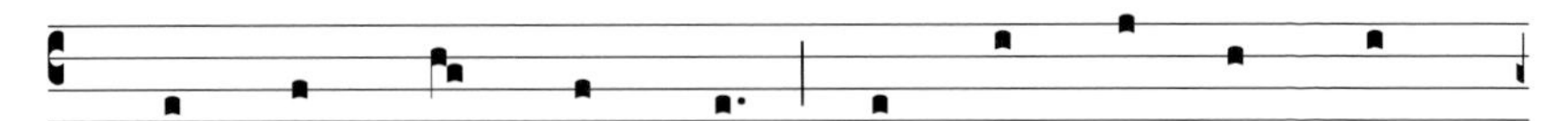

1. be - ing that is his; the Son and Fa - ther
2. Ma - ry should be - come made rea - dy by his
3. ty in Tri - ni - ty; in Ma - ry is true
4. men to make God known; the Vir - gin Mo - ther
5. God, God with us here; look on us, guide us
6. love for all we need, pro - tect us from all
7. you the Vir - gin's Son; we praise the Fa - ther,

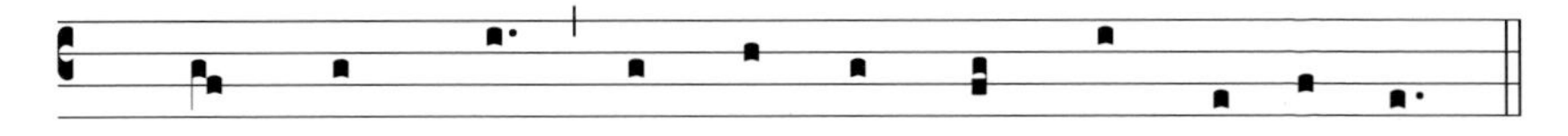

1. each in each, love with the love the Spi - rit is.
2. Spi - rit's power the Vir - gin Mo - ther of his Son.
3. Moth- er - hood and yet most pure vir - gi - ni - ty.
4. bears God's Son, the Son of God is hers a - lone.
5. in God's way and take from us all sin and fear.
6. dan - ger now, and at our dy - ing in - ter- cede.
7. God with you and with the Spi - rit, Three in One.

7. A - men

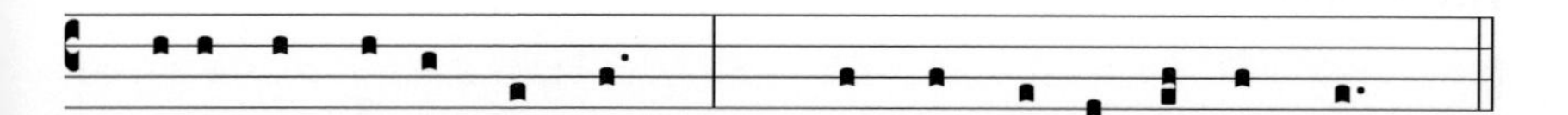

℣. I am the servant of God. ℟. To hear and o-bey his word.

*During Easter and on Solemnities and Feasts where Alleluia is used.*

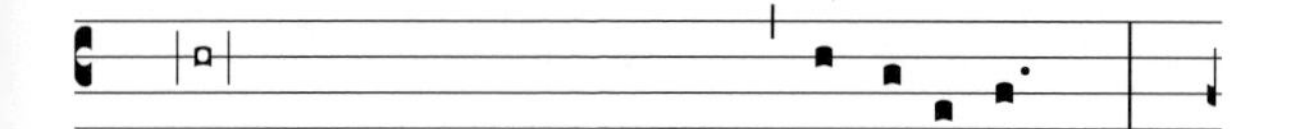

℣. I am the servant of God, Al-le-lu-ia.

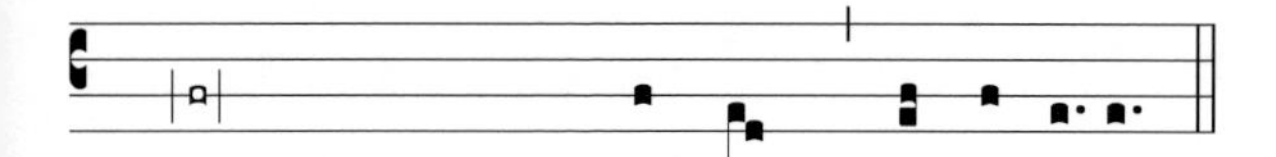

℟. To hear and obey his word, Al -le-lu-ia.

## Antiphon

**Vir - gin Mary to you we pray,** TONE IV

## Canticle of Simeon *(Luke 2: 29 - 32)*

At last, all powerful Master you give leave
to your servant to go in peace,
according to your promise.

For my eyes have seen your salvation which you have prepared
for all nations.
The light to enlighten the gentiles and give glory to Israel,
your people.

Give praise to the Father Almighty: to his Son, Jesus Christ,
the Lord;
to the Spirit who dwells in our hearts, both now and forever. Amen.

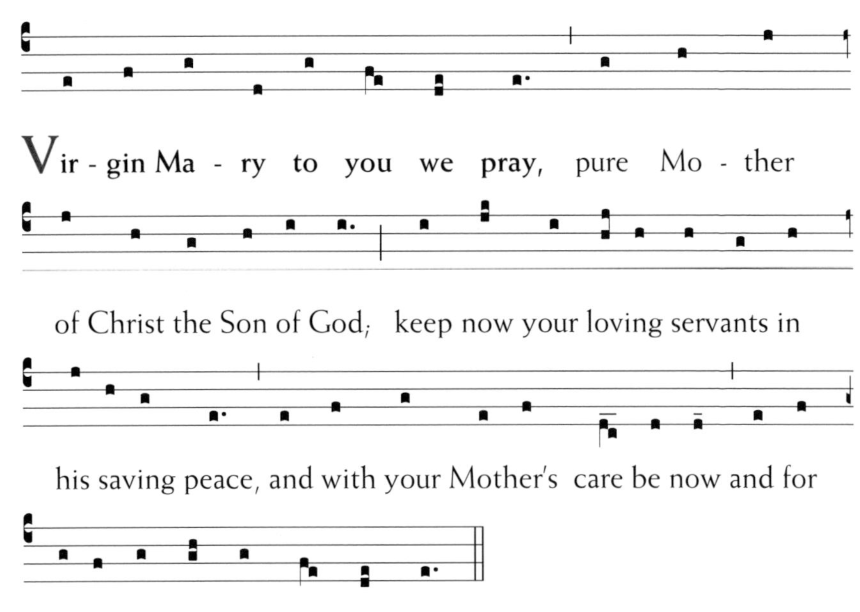


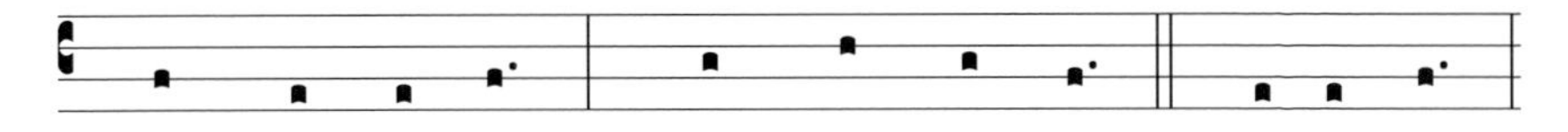

℣. Lord, hear my prayer. ℟. Lord, grant my prayer. ℣. Let us pray.

## Prayer

Come to us, Lord God, come with your grace; we have learned through your holy angel, of the birth of Christ your Son; through his Passion and Cross, bring us to the glory of his Resurrection. We ask through Jesus Christ your Son, who lives and reigns with you and with the Holy Spirit, one God, for ever. ℟. Amen.

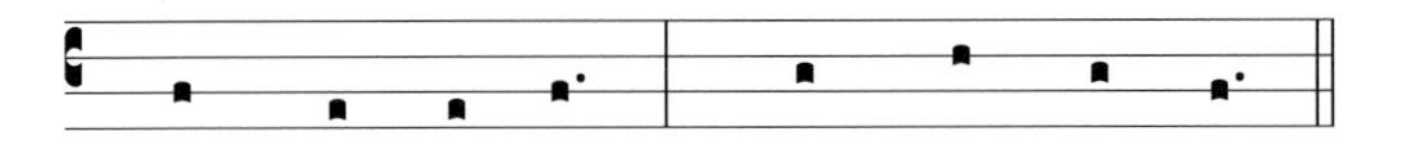

℣. Lord, hear my prayer. ℟. Lord, grant my prayer.

## Thanksgiving

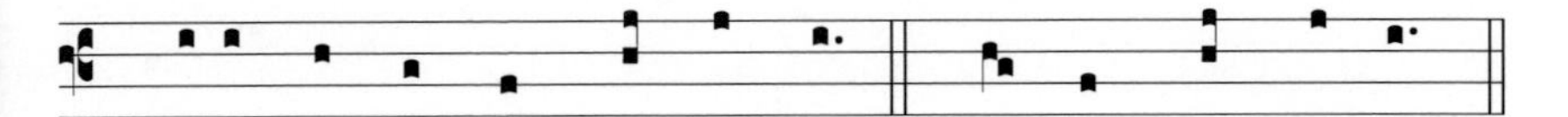

℣. Glory, hon-our and praise to God. ℟. And our thanks to him.

*(During Easter and on Solemnities and Feasts where Alleluia is used)*

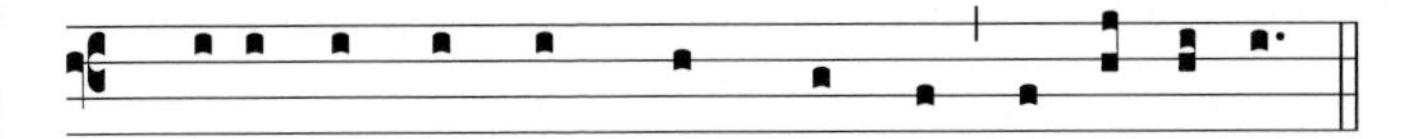

℣. Glory hon-our and praise to God, Al- le- lu- ia.

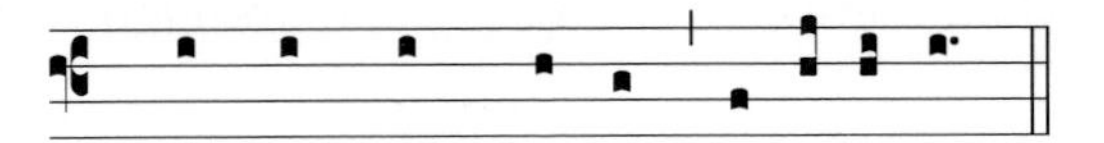

℟. And our thanks to him, Al-le-lu-ia.

℣. Mary, you are full of grace, the Lord is with you.
℟. Mary, you are most blessed of all women, for Jesus Christ is your Son. (Alleluia)

## Lauds of Our Lady

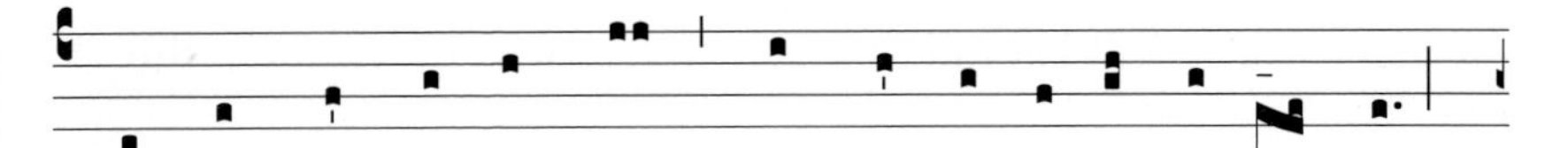

**Vir - gin Mother of Christ,** sweet Mother of our Re-dee-mer,

Ma-ry, we name you gate of heav'n through you a-lone we may

en-ter in-to the pro-mised joys of heav'n and the glo-ry of God.

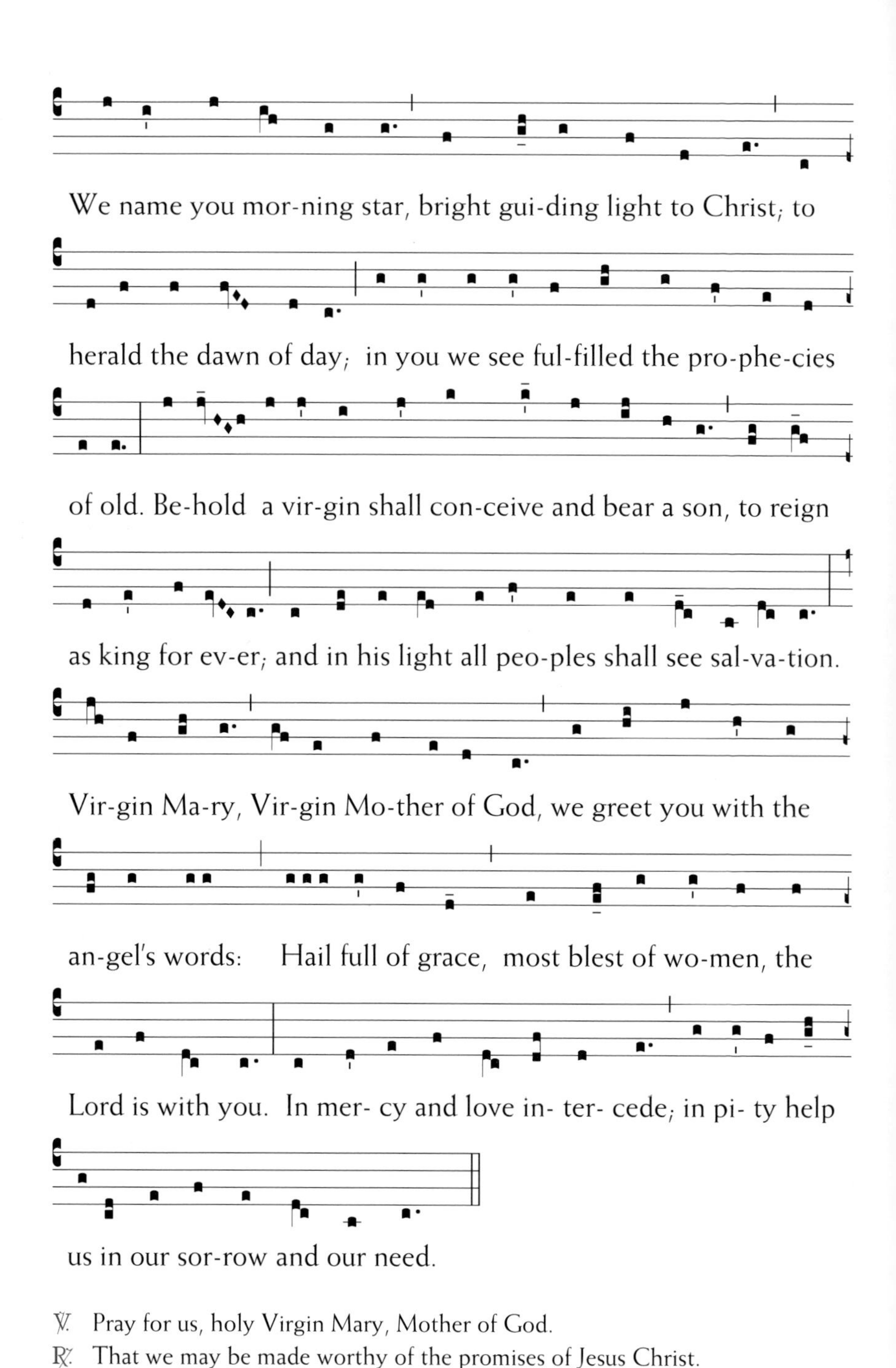


℣. Pray for us, holy Virgin Mary, Mother of God.

℟. That we may be made worthy of the promises of Jesus Christ.

℣. Let us pray.

Forgive, we ask you Lord, the sins of your servants: and may we who of ourselves are unable to please you, be saved by the prayers of the Mother of your Son, Jesus Christ our Lord. ℟. Amen.

## MARY, REJOICE IN GOD *(sung twice)*

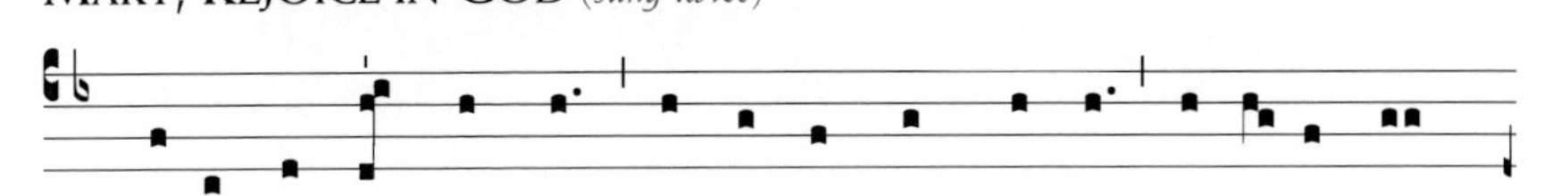

Ma-ry, re-joice in God, and in his grace to you, for he is with

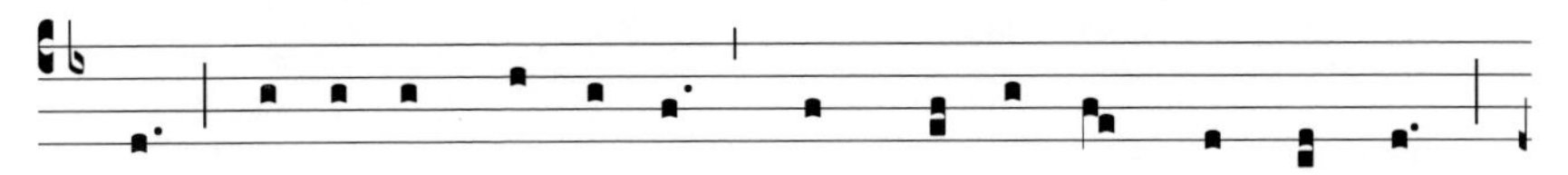

you, Ma-ry, re-joice in him, most blest a-mong all wom-en,

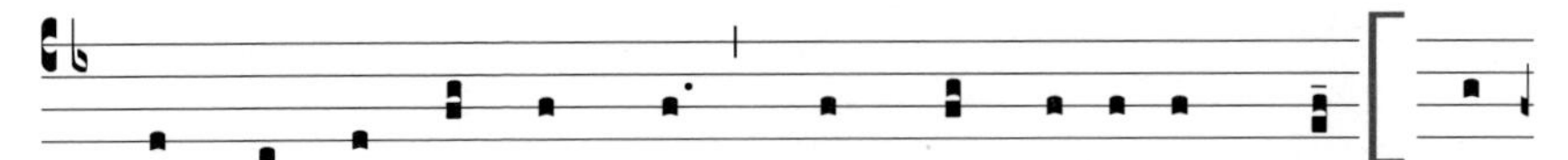

most blest to bear the Child, whose name is Je-sus Christ, (now

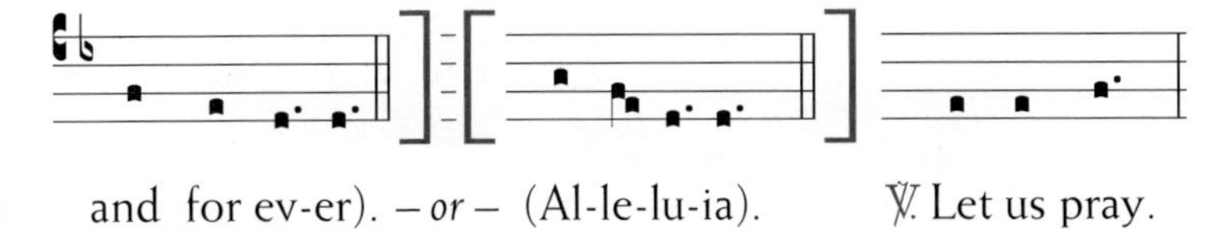

and for ev-er). – *or* – (Al-le-lu-ia). ℣. Let us pray.

## PRAYER

Almighty, everlasting God, who for us chose to be born of a most pure Virgin, we ask you to make us worthy to serve you with a pure body and to please you with a humble spirit. We pray also, loving Virgin Mary, Queen of this world and of angels, that you may obtain relief for those suffering the fires of purgatory, forgiveness for sinners, perseverance in goodness for the just, and defend us in our weakness from present perils.
Through Jesus Christ our Lord. Amen.

May the souls of our founders, of our brothers and sisters and of all the faithful departed, through the mercy of Jesus Christ rest in peace. ℟. Amen.

*Illustration from the 1697 Landshut edition of The Bridgettine Breviary.*

*Inspired by God, Saint Bridget was able to fully understand the fall of our first parents, the conception of the Blessed Virgin Mary free from original sin and how the Archangel Michael cast the devil and his angels into hell.*
*(Sermo Angelicus, Chapter 10)*
*Reprinted in the 1908 Tournai edition.*

*Monday*

# LAUDS

## OPENING PRAYERS

***(The first prayer of the day...)*** *(page 33)*
Open my mouth, O Lord ... *including Invitatory psalm (Ps. 94)*

## ANTIPHON

**Angels of God.**

Psalms and Canticle as for Sunday Lauds *(pages 39ff)*

**Angels of God**, praise Christ, your Creator and King; praise him for Mary, predestined by eternal decree to be Queen of heaven. Pray for us, angels of God; pray for us who pray to be worthy to praise Christ as King, and to bless Mary for ever as Queen.

**READING** *as on Sunday, page 44.*

## HYMN

God is, and he alone must ever be,
eternal being – his and his alone:
yet he has willed creation for his sake,
making his glory and his goodness known.

So by their very being and their choice,
orders of angels and our human race
show forth and worship their Creator's will
and offer him creation's highest praise.

Higher than highest angels in God's heaven,
highest of all creation at God's throne,
Mary is praised by all creation's praise,
she whose pure womb enthroned on earth God's Son.

Pray Mary Virgin-Mother, ... *Last two verses as on Sunday, page 44.*

℣. Let all children of holy Church rejoice in Mary. (Alleluia)
℟. With all the angels of God we rejoice in her and in all the wonders God has done. (Alleluia)

## ANTIPHON

L**ord and God.**

## CANTICLE

Blessed be the Lord, the God of Israel! ... *as on Sunday, page 45.*

L**ord and God**, Father and Creator of all, we pray to praise you, and pray that you may be ever praised, for the everlasting glory you have given to Mary, truly Mother of God. The angels of heaven rejoice in her, and the evil of sin is crushed beneath her heel. And we who are surrounded by sorrow and sin find hope in her. Glory, honour and praise to you, Father in heaven.

℣. Lord hear my prayer. ℟. Lord grant my prayer. ℣. Let us pray.

## PRAYER

Grant us, your servants, ...
*As on Sunday page 46 or according to the time of year. See pages 36ff.*

**ANTIPHON** to holy Mother Saint Bridget *as on Sunday, page 46.*
Bridget, loving servant of God, ... *or on ferial days:* Bridget, Saint and Patron, ...

℣. and ℟. with Prayer *(page 47).*

℣. Lord hear my prayer. ℟. Lord grant my prayer.

## THANKSGIVING

℣. Glory, honour and praise to Christ, whose angel made known that he who is Lord and creator of angels would come to us, a Virgin's Child. (Alleluia, alleluia, alleluia)
℟. Our thanks to God. (Alleluia, alleluia, alleluia)

**CLOSING PRAYERS** 'Mary, rejoice in God,' ... *(page 37).*

*Monday*

# TERCE

## OPENING PRAYERS *(page 33).*

*On Pentecost Monday Terce is sung (pages 504ff).*

## HYMN

God made you, Mary in his grace,
creation's crown most blessed of all:
so we are blessed who find in you
strength and protection when we call.

Strength and correction when we fall,
and grace to drive all sin away,
new love to win God's love again,
your love and mercy as we pray.

Pray Mary Mother, full of grace,
pray in your love for all we need;
protect us from all danger now,
and at our dying intercede.

Christ, Son of God, we pray to you,
and honour you, the Virgin's Son.
We praise the Father, God with you,
and with the Spirit, Three in One. Amen.

## ANTIPHON

**Mary, your coming.**

### Psalm 13

The fool has said in his heart: "There is no God above."
Their deeds are corrupt, depraved; not a good man is left.

From heaven the Lord looks down on the sons of men
to see if any are wise, if any seek God.

All have left the right path, depraved, every one:
there is not a good man left, no, not even one.

Will the evil-doers not understand?
They eat up my people as though they ate bread: they never pray to the Lord.

See how they tremble with fear without cause for fear:
for God is with the just.

You may mock the poor man's hope,
but his refuge is the Lord.

O that Israel's salvation might come from Sion!
When the Lord delivers his people from bondage, then Jacob will be glad
and Israel rejoice.

*Glory be...*

**Psalm 15**

Preserve me, God, I take refuge in you.
I say to the Lord: "You are my God. My happiness lies in you alone."

He has put into my heart a marvellous love
for the faithful ones who dwell in his land.

Those who choose other gods increase their sorrows.
Never will I offer their offerings of blood. Never will I take their name
upon my lips.

O Lord, it is you who are my portion and cup; it is you yourself who are
my prize.
The lot marked out for me is my delight: welcome indeed the heritage
that falls to me!

I will bless the Lord who gives me counsel, who even at night directs my heart.
I keep the Lord ever in my sight: since he is at my right hand,
I shall stand firm.

And so my heart rejoices, my soul is glad; even my body shall rest in safety.
For you will not leave my soul among the dead, nor let your beloved
know decay.

You will show me the path of life,
the fullness of joy in your presence, at your right hand happiness
for ever.

*Glory be...*

**Psalm 16**

Lord, hear a cause that is just, pay heed to my cry.
Turn your ear to my prayer: no deceit is on my lips.

From you may my judgment come forth.
Your eyes discern the truth.

You search my heart, you visit me by night.
You test me and you find in me no wrong. My words are not sinful
as are men's words.

I kept from violence because of your word,
I kept my feet firmly in your paths; there was no faltering in my steps.

I am here and I call, you will hear me, O God. Turn your ear to me;
hear my words.
Display your great love, you whose right hand saves your friends from those
who rebel against them.

Guard me as the apple of your eye.
Hide me in the shadow of your wings from the violent attack of the wicked.

My foes encircle me with deadly intent.
Their hearts tight shut, their mouths speak proudly. They advance against me,
and now they surround me.

Their eyes are watching to strike me to the ground
as though they were lions ready to claw or like some young lion crouched
in hiding.

Lord, arise, confront them, strike them down! Let your sword rescue my soul from the wicked;
let your hand, O Lord, rescue me from men, from men whose reward is in this present life.

You give them their fill of your treasures;
they rejoice in abundance of offspring and leave their wealth to their children.

As for me, in my justice I shall see your face
and be filled, when I awake, with the sight of your glory.

*Glory be...*

## ANTIPHON

M**ary, your coming** has brought to nothing the evil of Satan;
for you have crushed the Serpent's head
and restored us to grace.

## READING *as on Sunday, page 51.*

## SHORT RESPONSORY

℣. Mary, Queen of angels, holiest and highest of all in heaven, pray for us in our need. (Alleluia, Alleluia) ℟. *Repeat.*
℣. Protect us from sin and the snares of Satan.
℟. Pray for us in our need. († ℟. Alleluia, Alleluia)
℣. Glory to God, Father, Son and Holy Spirit.
℟. Mary, Queen of angels, holiest and highest of all in heaven, pray for us in our need. (Alleluia, Alleluia)
℣. Praise God, as all in heaven praise him. (Alleluia)
℟. For the holiness and glory of Mary the Mother of God. (Alleluia)

## CLOSING PRAYERS *(page 38).*

---

† ***Response during Easter and on other special days where shown, as well as in brackets thus: (Alleluia). For style, see Sunday Terce*** *on page 51.*

*Monday*

# SEXT

## OPENING PRAYERS *(page 33).*

## HYMN

God made you, Mary in his grace... *as at Monday Terce, page 111.*

## ANTIPHON

**Mary, your loving prayer for us.**

**Psalm 19**

May the Lord answer in time of trial; may the name of Jacob's God
protect you.
May he send you help from his shrine and give you support from Sion.

May he remember all your offerings and receive your sacrifice with favour.
May he give you your heart's desire and fulfil every one of your plans.

May we ring out our joy at your victory and rejoice in the name of our God.
May the Lord grant all your prayers.

I am sure now that the Lord will give victory to his anointed,
will reply from his holy heaven with the mighty victory of his hand.

Some trust in chariots or horses, but we in the name of the Lord.
They will collapse and fall, but we shall hold and stand firm.

Give victory to the king, O Lord,
give answer on the day we call.

*Glory be...*

## Psalm 20

O Lord, your strength gives joy to the king; how your saving help makes him glad!
You have granted him his heart's desire; you have not refused the prayer of his lips.

You came to meet him with the blessings of success, you have set on his head a crown of pure gold.
He asked you for life and this you have given, days that will last from age to age.

Your saving help has given him glory. You have laid upon him majesty and splendour,
you have granted your blessings to him forever. You have made him rejoice with the joy of your presence.

The king has put his trust in the Lord: through the mercy of the Most High he shall stand firm.
His hand will seek and find all his foes, his right hand find out those that hate him.

You will burn them like a blazing furnace on the day when you appear.
And the Lord shall destroy them in his anger; fire will swallow them up.

You will wipe out their race from the earth and their children from the sons of men.
Though they plan evil against you, though they plot, they shall not prevail.

For you will force them to retreat; at them you will aim with your bow.
O Lord, arise in your strength; we shall sing and praise your power.

*Glory be...*

## Psalm 24

To you, O Lord, I lift up my soul.
I trust you, let me not be disappointed; do not let my enemies triumph.

Those who hope in you shall not be disappointed, but only those who wantonly break faith.
Lord, make me know your ways. Lord, teach me your paths.

Make me walk in your truth, and teach me: for you are God my saviour.
In you I hope all the day long because of your goodness, O Lord.

Remember your mercy, Lord, and the love you have shown from of old.
Do not remember the sins of my youth. In your love remember me.

The Lord is good and upright. He shows the path to those who stray,
he guides the humble in the right path; he teaches his way to the poor.

His ways are faithfulness and love for those who keep his covenant and will.
Lord, for the sake of your name forgive my guilt; for it is great.

If anyone fears the Lord he will show him the path he should choose.
His soul shall live in happiness and his children shall possess the land.

The Lord's friendship is for those who revere him;
to them he reveals his covenant.

My eyes are always on the Lord; for he rescues my feet from the snare.
Turn to me and have mercy for I am lonely and poor.

Relieve the anguish of my heart and set me free from my distress.
See my affliction and my toil and take all my sins away.

See how many are my foes; how violent their hatred for me.
Preserve my life and rescue me. Do not disappoint me, you are my refuge.

May innocence and uprightness protect me: for my hope is in you, O Lord.
Redeem Israel, O God, from all its distress.

*Glory be...*

## ANTIPHON

**Mary, your loving prayer for us** is most pleasing to Christ,
and for your sake
he will pardon our foolishness and sin.

## READING *(Eccles. 24: 11)*

Jerusalem has been my dwelling and my resting-place:
there in the holy city, I have taken up my rule and reign.

℟. Our thanks to God.

## Short Responsory

℣. Praise God, as all in heaven praise him. (Alleluia, Alleluia) ℟. *Repeat.*
℣. Praise him for the holiness and glory of Mary the Mother of God,
℟. As all in heaven praise him. († ℟. Alleluia, Alleluia)
℣. Glory to God, Father, Son and Holy Spirit.
℟. Praise God, as all in heaven praise him. (Alleluia, Alleluia)
℣. Let all children of holy church rejoice in Mary. (Alleluia)
℟. With all the angels of God we rejoice in her, and in all the wonders God has done. (Alleluia)

*NOTE: If continuing immediately with None, omit the Opening Prayers and Hymn for None and start with the (short) Antiphon before the Psalms: as detailed in the Structure, page 26.*

## Closing Prayers *(page 38)*.

---

† ***Response during Easter and on other special days where shown, as well as in brackets thus: (Alleluia). For style, see Sunday Terce*** *on page 51.*

*Monday*

# None

**Opening Prayers** *as before Sunday None, pages 55 - 56.*

## Hymn

1. God made you, Ma - ry in his grace, cre - a - tion's
2. Strength and cor - rec - tion when we fall and grace to
3. Pray Ma - ry Mo-ther full of grace, pray in your
4. Christ Son of God we pray to you, and hon - our

1. crown most blessed of all: so we are blessed who find
2. drive all sin a - way, new love to win God's love
3. love for all we need, pro-tect us from all dan-
4. you, the Vir - gin's Son; we praise the Fa - ther, God

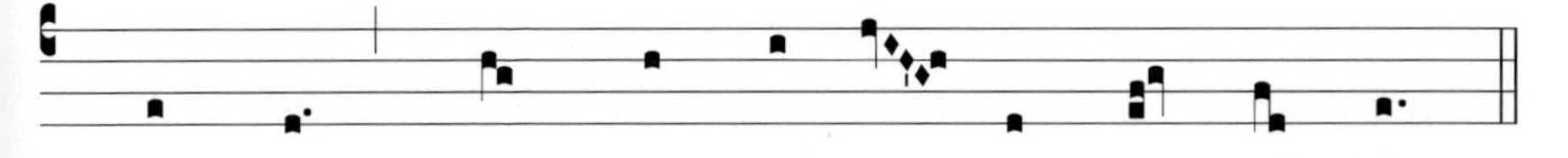

1. in you strength and pro - tec - tion when we call.
2. a - gain, your love and mer - cy as we pray.
3 ger now, and at our dy - ing in - ter - cede.
4. with you and with the Spi - rit, Three in One.

4. A - men.

ANTIPHON

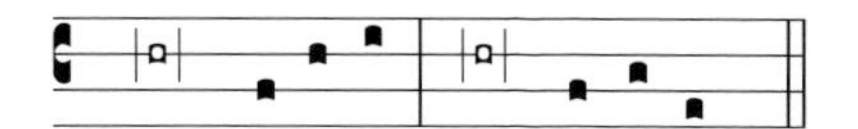

Heav'n - ly Bride of God,     TONE VIII

**Psalm 25**

Give judgment for me, O Lord: for I walk the path of perfection.
I trust in the Lord; I have not wavered.

Examine me, Lord, and try me; O test my heart and my mind,
for your love is before my eyes and I walk according to your truth.

I never take my place with liars and with hypocrites I shall not go.
I hate the evil-doer's company: I will not take my place with the wicked.

To prove my innocence I wash my hands and take my place around your altar,
singing a song of thanksgiving, proclaiming all your wonders.

O Lord, I love the house where you dwell,
the place where your glory abides.

Do not sweep me away with sinners, nor my life with bloodthirsty men
in whose hands are evil plots, whose right hands are filled with gold.

As for me, I walk the path of perfection. Redeem me and show me your mercy.
My foot stands on level ground: I will bless the Lord in the assembly.

*Glory be...*

**Psalm 30** *(vv. 2 – 16.)*

In you, O Lord, I take refuge. Let me never be put to shame.
In your justice, set me free, hear me and speedily rescue me.

Be a rock of refuge for me, a mighty stronghold to save me,
for you are my rock, my stronghold. For your name's sake, lead me
and guide me.

Release me from the snares they have hidden for you are my refuge, Lord.
Into your hands I commend my spirit. It is you who will redeem me, Lord.

O God of truth, you detest those who worship false and empty gods.
As for me, I trust in the Lord: let me be glad and rejoice in your love.

You who have seen my affliction and taken heed of my soul's distress,
have not handed me over to the enemy, but set my feet at large.

Have mercy on me, O Lord, for I am in distress.
Tears have wasted my eyes, my throat and my heart.

For my life is spent with sorrow and my years with sighs.
Affliction has broken down my strength and my bones waste away.

In the face of all my foes I am a reproach,
an object of scorn to my neighbours and of fear to my friends.

Those who see me in the street run far away from me.
I am like a dead man, forgotten in men's hearts, like a thing thrown away.

I have heard the slander of the crowd, fear is all around me,
as they plot together against me, as they plan to take my life.

But as for me, I trust in you, Lord; I say: "You are my God.
My life is in your hands, deliver me from the hands of those who hate me."

*Glory be...*

**Psalm 30** *(vv. 17 - 25)*

"Let your face shine on your servant. Save me in your love.
Let me not be put to shame for I call you, but let the wicked be put to shame!

Let them be silenced in the grave, let lying lips be dumb,
that speak haughtily against the just with pride and contempt."

How great is the goodness, Lord, that you keep for those who fear you,
that you show to those who trust you in the sight of men.

You hide them in the shelter of your presence from the plotting of men;
you keep them safe within your tent from disputing tongues.

Blessed be the Lord who has shown me the wonders of his love
in a fortified city.

"I am far removed from your sight," I said in my alarm.
Yet you heard the voice of my plea when I cried for help.

Love the Lord, all you saints. He guards his faithful
but the Lord will repay to the full those who act with pride.

Be strong, let your heart take courage,
all who hope in the Lord.

*Glory be...*

---

## Antiphon

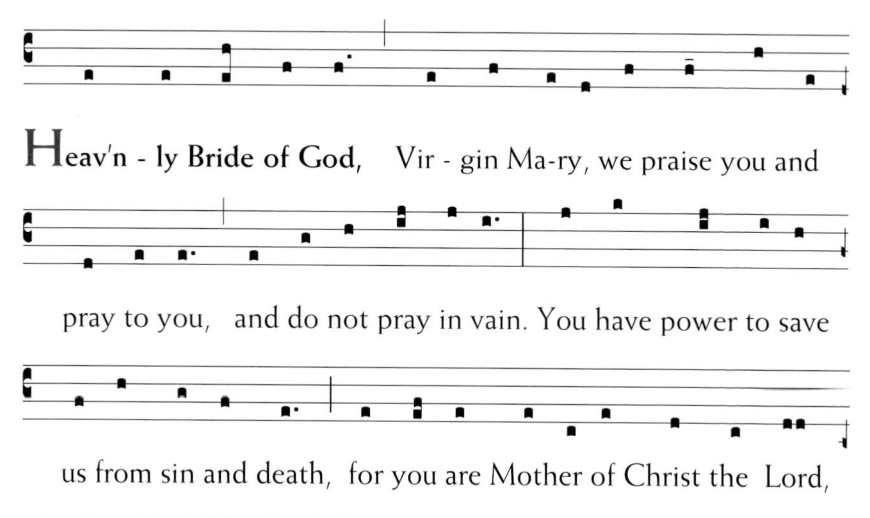


our Saviour and sal-va-tion.

**READING** *(Eccles. 24:12)*

---

**SHORT RESPONSORY**

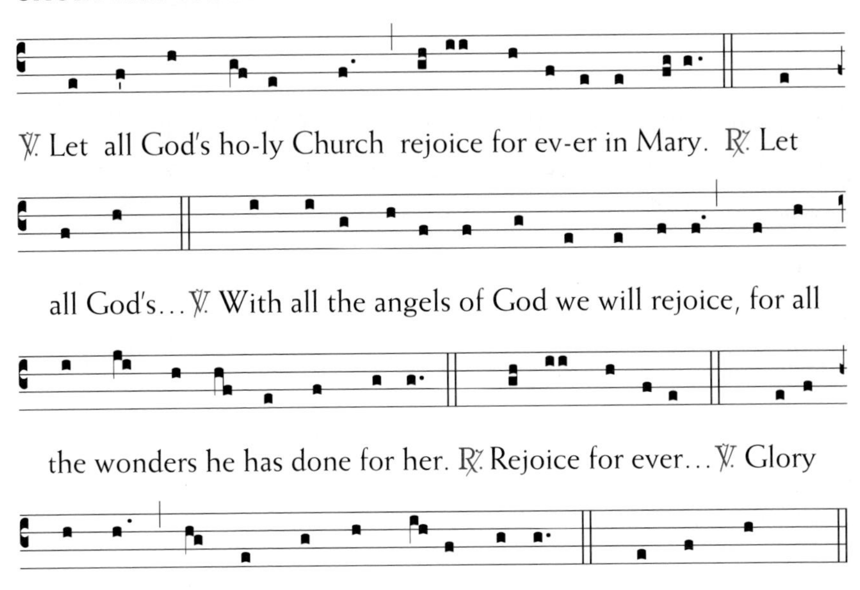

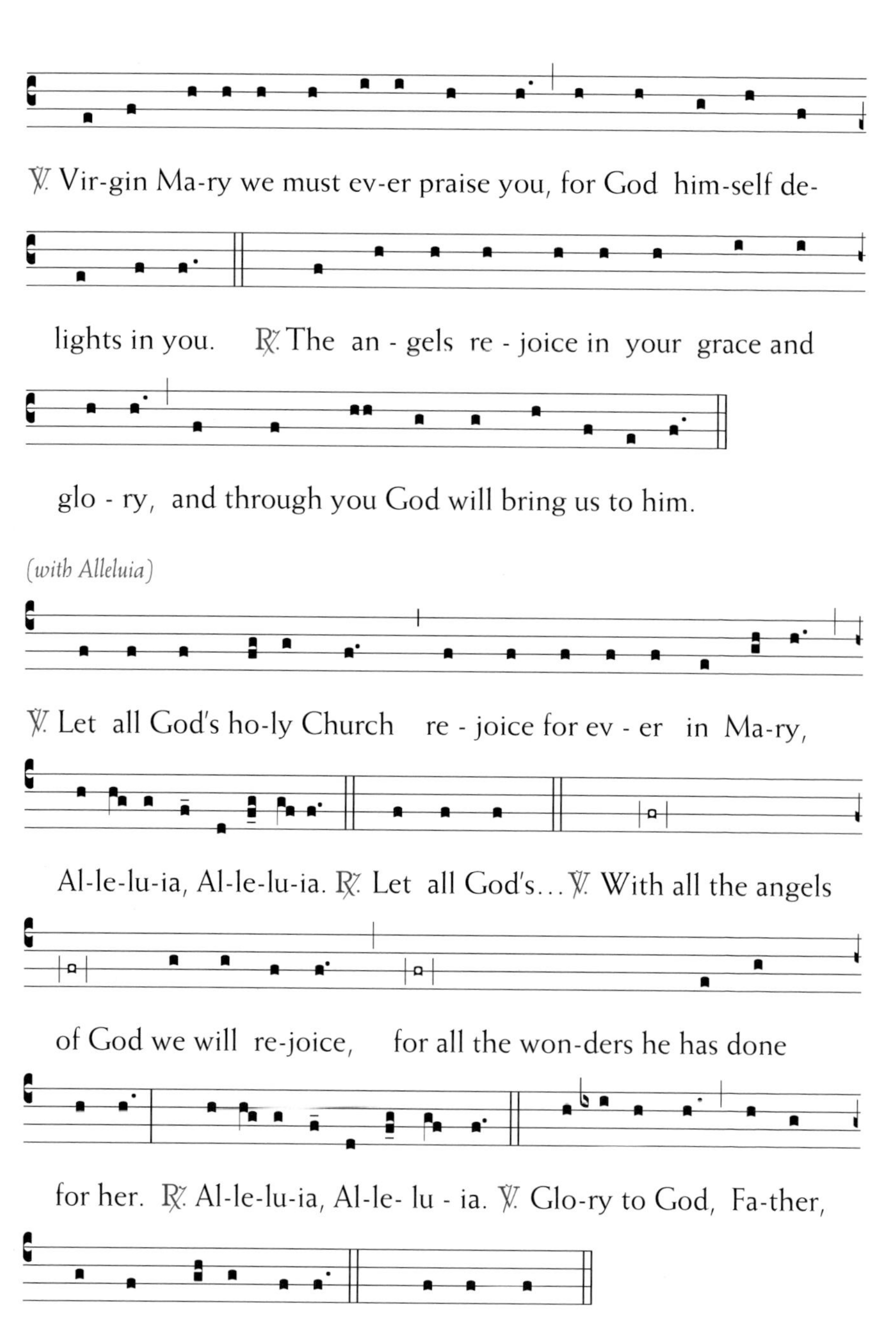
℣. Vir-gin Ma-ry we must ev-er praise you, for God him-self de-
lights in you. ℟. The an - gels re - joice in your grace and
glo - ry, and through you God will bring us to him.
(with Alleluia)
℣. Let all God's ho-ly Church re - joice for ev - er in Ma-ry,
Al-le-lu-ia, Al-le-lu-ia. ℟. Let all God's... ℣. With all the angels
of God we will re-joice, for all the won-ders he has done
for her. ℟. Al-le-lu-ia, Al-le- lu - ia. ℣. Glo-ry to God, Fa-ther,
Son and Ho-ly Spir-it. ℟. Let all God's...

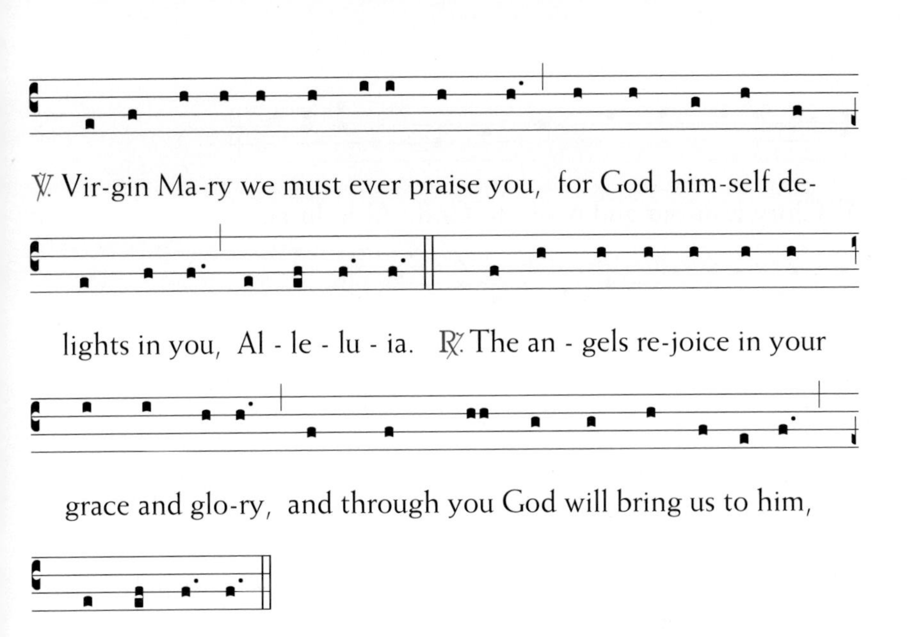


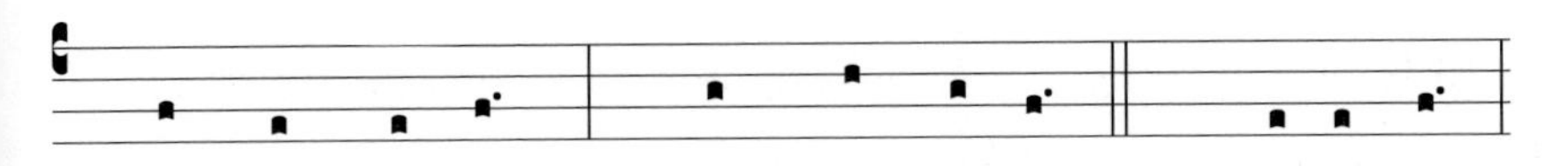

℣. Lord, hear my prayer. ℟. Lord, grant my prayer. ℣. Let us pray.

**PRAYER** *(pages 36 - 37)*

℣. Lord, hear my prayer. ℟. Lord, grant my prayer.

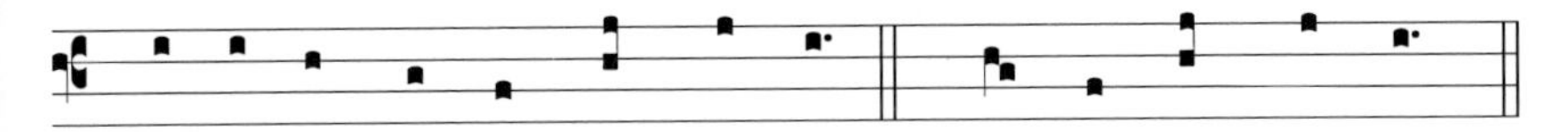

℣. Glo-ry hon-our and praise to God. ℟. And our thanks to him.

*(with Alleluia)*

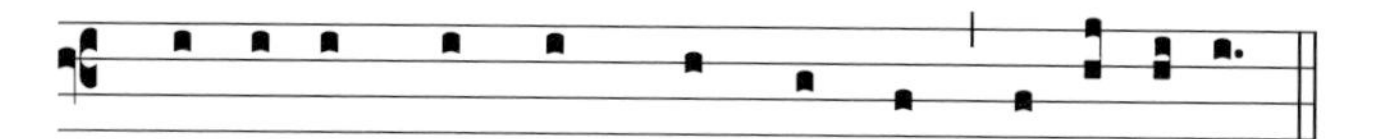

℣. Glory hon-our and praise to God, Al-le-lu-ia.

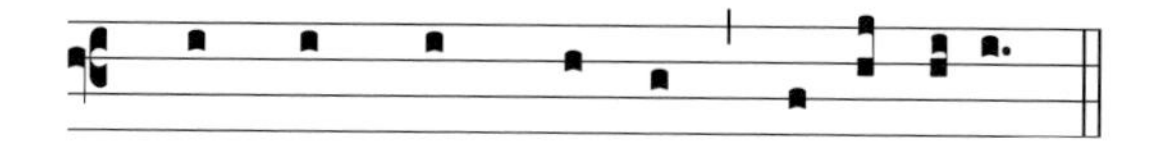

℟. And our thanks to him, Al-le-lu-ia.

## Closing Prayers

'Mary, rejoice...' *as on Sunday,* *pages 64ff.*

**Lauds of Our Lady** *of the day, season or feast. (See daily after Compline)*
*With* ℣. & ℟. *and Prayer. Then* 'May the souls of our founders...' *and...*

**Psalm 129** 'Out of the depths...' *and two or three memorial prayers for the souls of the departed, as on Sunday,* *page 65 - 66.*

*Monday*

# OFFICE OF READINGS (MATINS)

## OPENING PRAYERS (*page 67*)

## HYMN

No earthly jewels of themselves are bright,
no lovely things have beauty all their own;
all earthly glory mirrors God's true light,
all loveliness comes forth from God alone.

He is, and he alone must ever be,
for he alone is ever he who is;
all else that comes to be, comes at his will –
creation and creation's plan are his.

The angels, heaven itself, all earthly things,
eternal ages and time's passing days,
bear in themselves some image of their God,
to tell his goodness and declare his praise.

Nearest to God in being and in power,
yet angels chose to turn from him in pride,
his praise withheld by many and refused,
his all-creating power and love denied.

But not all fell, and angels still adored,
singing the praise of God eternally,
foreseeing Christ's salvation and his reign,
awaiting Mary, Queen of heaven to be.

Pray Mary Virgin-Mother full of grace,
pray in your love for all, for all we need;
protect us from all sin and sinful ways,
and at our dying hour intercede.

Christ Jesus, Son of God, we pray to you
and praise you, naming you the Virgin's Son;

we ever praise the Father, God with you
and with the Holy Spirit, Three in One. Amen.

## ANTIPHON 1

**Praise to Christ.**

### Psalm 27

To you, O Lord, I call, my rock, hear me.
If you do not heed I shall become like those in the grave.

Hear the voice of my pleading as I call for help,
as I lift up my hands in prayer to your holy place.

Do not drag me away with the wicked, with the evil-doers,
who speak words of peace to their neighbours but with evil in their hearts.

Repay them as their actions deserve and the malice of their deeds.
Repay them for the works of their hands; give them their deserts.

For they ignore the deeds of the Lord and the work of his hands.
(May he ruin them and never rebuild them.)

Blessed be the Lord for he has heard my cry, my appeal.
The Lord is my strength and my shield; in him my heart trusts.

I was helped, my heart rejoices
and I praise him with my song.

The Lord is the strength of his people, the stronghold where his anointed
find salvation.
Save your people; bless Israel your heritage. Be their shepherd and carry
them for ever.

*Glory be...*

## ANTIPHON 1

P**raise to Christ,** that we may pray to him and hope;
praise to Christ, that as we pray to him,
the Virgin Mary intercedes.

## ANTIPHON 2

C**all to all people of earth.**

### Psalm 28

O give the Lord you sons of God, give the Lord glory and power;
give the Lord the glory of his name. Adore the Lord in his holy court.

The Lord's voice resounding on the waters, the Lord on the immensity
of waters;
the voice of the Lord, full of power, the voice of the Lord, full of splendour.

The Lord's voice shattering the cedars, the Lord shatters the cedars
of Lebanon;
he makes Lebanon leap like a calf and Sirion like a young wild-ox.

(The Lord's voice flashes flames of fire.)
The Lord's voice shaking the wilderness, the Lord shakes the wilderness
of Kadesh;

the Lord's voice rending the oak tree
and stripping the forest bare.

The God of glory thunders. In his temple they all cry: "Glory!"
The Lord sat enthroned over the flood; the Lord sits as king for ever.

The Lord will give strength to his people,
the Lord will bless his people with peace.

*Glory be...*

## ANTIPHON 2

**Call to all people of earth**: honour Christ, the Virgin's Son;
for in this praise, we become
the people of God.

## ANTIPHON 3

**Mary, your joy in Christ.**

### Psalm 29

I will praise you, Lord, you have rescued me
and have not let my enemies rejoice over me.

O Lord, I cried to you for help and you, my God, have healed me.
O Lord, you have raised my soul from the dead, restored me to life from those who sink into the grave.

Sing psalms to the Lord, you who love him, give thanks to his holy name.
His anger lasts but a moment; his favour through life. At night there are tears, but joy comes with dawn.

I said to myself in my good fortune: "Nothing will ever disturb me."
Your favour had set me on a mountain fastness, then you hid your face and I was put to confusion.

To you, Lord, I cried, to my God I made appeal:
"What profit would my death be, my going to the grave? Can dust give you praise or proclaim your truth?"

The Lord listened and had pity. The Lord came to my help.
For me you have changed my mourning into dancing, you removed my sackcloth and girdled me with joy.

So my soul sings psalms to you unceasingly.
O Lord my God, I will thank you for ever.

*Glory be...*

## ANTIPHON 3

**Mary, your joy in Christ,** has taken away our sorrow;
that we may make known with joy
the truth of God.

℣. Mary, Queen of angels, holiest and highest of all in heaven, pray for us in our need. (Alleluia)
℟. Protect us from sin and the snares of Satan. (Alleluia)

Our Father ...

## ABSOLUTION

God and father, holy and merciful Lord, take into account the prayer and holiness of Mary, the Virgin-Mother of God, and of all the saints and bring us back from death to life. ℟. Amen.
*Reader:* Lord, we ask for your blessing.

**Week One**
*Blessing, Reading and Response for Mondays in Week Two start on page 511, and for Week Three on page 530.*

## BLESSING

May Mary, Queen of angels, bring us to the blessedness of heaven. ℟. Amen.

## READING

It was love that led God to create.
There could be nothing lacking in God,
nothing wanting to his goodness or his joy.
It was out of love alone that he willed creation,
that there might be beings, apart from himself,
who would partake of his infinite goodness and joy.
So the angels came to be,
created by God in countless numbers.
To them he gave free will,
freedom to act, in accordance with their nature,
as they willed.

As he himself is under no necessity
but has created out of love alone,
he willed that the angels,
whom he designed for eternal happiness with him,
should likewise be under no necessity.
He looked for love in response to his love,
obedience in response to his offer of eternal joy.

Yet in the first moment of their creation,
there were angels who chose, freely and deliberately,
against their Creator,
in spite of his infinite love, which called them to love in return.
Justly they fell, fixed in their evil will,
from an eternal joy into an eternal misery.
But not all fell.
To those angels who chose love for love,
there was given the contemplation of God
in all his glory, power and holiness.
From this contemplation, they came to know the eternity of God,
that he has no beginning and no end;
they learnt what it meant to have him for their Creator;
and they saw most clearly
how everything they possessed had come to them from his love
and his power.
They learnt too that his wisdom had given them a wisdom of their own,
by which he allowed them to foresee the future.
And it was a joy and consolation to them
to know that God in his mercy and love
wished to replace, in his own way,
those angels who had forfeited by pride and envy
their place in heaven.

In their contemplation of God,
the angels saw with wonder
a throne placed next to that of God himself.
They knew that the one for whom this throne had been prepared
had not yet been created.
Yet already they loved this chosen one,
and rejoiced as they waited.
Their love for God their Creator was their greatest love.
Their love for each other was born of their love for God.
But between these two loves they saw one who was more lovable

than themselves,
one whom God loved with great joy
more than all his other creatures.

Virgin Mary, you were the chosen one,
destined for that throne near to the throne of God.
It was you whom the angels loved, after God,
from the first moment of their creation,
seeing in the contemplation of God
how beautiful he had made themselves,
but how much more beautiful he would make you.
They saw that in you there would be a love and a joy far greater
than their own.
They saw too the crown that awaited you,
a crown of glory and beauty surpassed only by the majesty of God.
They knew how God their Creator was glorified by themselves and
they rejoiced.
They knew how much more he would be glorified by you,
and they rejoiced still more.
Before ever you were created, Mary,
God and angels together rejoiced in you.

℣. Have mercy, Lord, and help our understanding. ℟. Our thanks to God.

## RESPONSORY

**All holy God and Lord,** all honour and praise must be ever yours.
The angels adore you, saying:
"All honour and praise to you, all holy God and Lord."
℣. Mary, all the angels of God's creating, rejoice in your grace and your glory, in all that God has done for you, and ever adore him, saying:
℟. "All honour and praise to you, all holy God and Lord."
℣. Glory to God, glory to Father, Son and Holy Spirit.
℟. "All honour and praise to you, all holy God and Lord."

## TE DEUM *as on Sunday, page 75* or PSALM 50 *as on Friday, page 330.*

℣. Praise God, as all in heaven praise him. (Alleluia)
℟. For the holiness and glory of Mary the Mother of God. (Alleluia)

## CLOSING PRAYERS *(page 38).*

*Monday*

# VESPERS

**PRAYERS** before Vespers, *(pages 77 - 78)* and
**OPENING PRAYERS** – with music – *as at None, pages 55 - 56.*

**ANTIPHON**

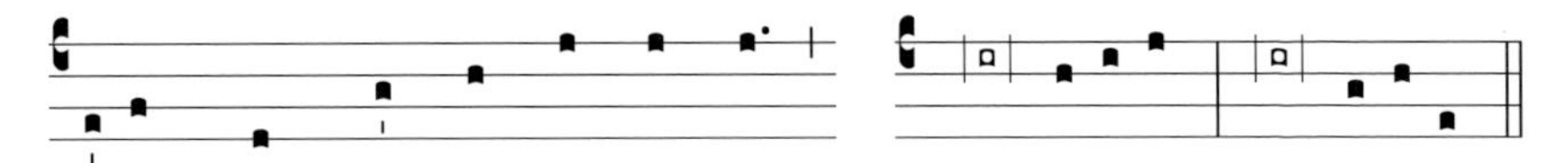

**Jesus, true God, the Vir-gin's Son,** TONE III

**Psalm 113**

When Israel came forth from Egypt, Jacob's sons from an
alien people,
Judah became the Lord's temple, Israel became his kingdom.

The sea fled at the sight: the Jordan turned back on its course,
the mountains leapt like rams and the hills like yearling sheep.

Why was it, sea, that you fled, that you turned back, Jordan,
on your course?
Mountains, that you leapt like rams; hills, like yearling sheep?

Tremble, O earth, before the Lord, in the presence of the God of Jacob,
who turns the rock into a pool and flint into a spring of water.

Not to us, Lord, not to us, but to your name give the glory
for the sake of your love and your truth, lest the heathen say:
"Where is their God?"

But our God is in the heavens; he does whatever he wills.
Their idols are silver and gold, the work of human hands.

They have mouths but they cannot speak; they have eyes but they
cannot see;

they have ears but they cannot hear; they have nostrils but they
cannot smell.

With their hands they cannot feel; with their feet they cannot walk.
No sound comes from their throats.

Their makers will come to be like them and so will all who
trust in them.
Sons of Israel, trust in the Lord; he is their help and their shield.

Sons of Aaron, trust in the Lord; he is their help and their shield.
You who fear him, trust in the Lord; he is their help
and their shield.

He remembers us, will give us his blessing; he will bless the
sons of Israel.
He will bless the sons of Aaron.

The Lord will bless those who fear him, the little no less
than the great:
to you may the Lord grant increase, to you and all your children.

May you be blessed by the Lord, the maker of heaven and earth.
The heavens belong to the Lord but the earth he has given to men.

The dead shall not praise the Lord, nor those who go down into
the silence.
But we who live bless the Lord now and for ever. Amen.

*Glory be...*

**Psalm 114**

I love the Lord for he has heard the cry of my appeal;
for he turned his ear to me in the day when I called him.

They surrounded me, the snares of death, with the anguish
of the tomb;
they caught me, sorrow and distress.

I called on the Lord's name. O Lord my God, deliver me!
How gracious is the Lord, and just; our God has compassion.

The Lord protects the simple hearts; I was helpless so he saved me.
Turn back, my soul, to your rest for the Lord has been good;

he has kept my soul from death, my eyes from tears
and my feet from stumbling.

I will walk in the presence of the Lord
in the land of the living.

*Glory be...*

**Psalm 115**

I trusted, even when I said: "I am sorely afflicted,"
and when I said in my alarm: "No man can be trusted."

How can I repay the Lord for his goodness to me?
The cup of salvation I will raise; I will call on the Lord's name.

My vows to the Lord I will fulfil before all his people.
O precious in the eyes of the Lord is the death of his faithful.

Your servant, Lord, your servant am I; you have loosened my bonds.
A thanksgiving sacrifice I make; I will call on the Lord's name.

My vows to the Lord I will fulfil before all his people,
in the courts of the house of the Lord, in your midst, O Jerusalem.

*Glory be...*

**Psalm 117**

Give thanks to the Lord for he is good,
for his love has no end.

Let the sons of Israel say: "His love has no end."
Let the sons of Aaron say: "His love has no end."

Let those who fear the Lord say: "His love has no end."
I called to the Lord in my distress; he answered and freed me.

The Lord is at my side; I do not fear. What can man do against me?
The Lord is at my side as my helper; I shall look down on my foes.

It is better to take refuge in the Lord than to trust in men:
it is better to take refuge in the Lord than to trust in princes.

The nations all encompassed me; in the Lord's name
I crushed them.
They compassed me, compassed me about; in the Lord's name
I crushed them.

They compassed me about like bees; they blazed like a fire
among thorns.
In the Lord's name I crushed them.

I was thrust, thrust down and falling, but the Lord
was my helper.
The Lord is my strength and my song; he was my saviour.

There are shouts of joy and victory
in the tents of the just.

The Lord's right hand has triumphed; his right hand raised me up.
The Lord's right hand has triumphed;

I shall not die, I shall live and recount his deeds.
I was punished, I was punished by the Lord, but not doomed to die.

Open to me the gates of holiness: I will enter and give thanks.
This is the Lord's own gate where the just may enter.

I will thank you for you have given answer and you are my saviour.
The stone which the builders rejected has become the corner stone.

This is the work of the Lord, a marvel in our eyes.
This day was made by the Lord; we rejoice and are glad.

O Lord, grant us salvation; O Lord, grant success.
Blessed in the name of the Lord is he who comes.

We bless you from the house of the Lord; the Lord God
is our light.
Go forward in procession with branches even to the altar.

You are my God, I thank you. My God, I praise you.
Give thanks to the Lord for he is good; for his love has no end.

*Glory be…*

**Psalm 147**

O praise the Lord, Jerusalem!
Sion, praise your God!

He has strengthened the bars of your gates, he has blessed the
children within you.
He established peace on your borders, he feeds you with
finest wheat.

He sends out his word to the earth and swiftly runs his command.
He showers down snow white as wool, he scatters hoar-frost
like ashes.

He hurls down hailstones like crumbs. The waters are frozen
at his touch;
he sends forth his word and it melts them: at the breath of his
mouth the waters flow.

He makes his word known to Jacob, to Israel his laws and decrees.
He has not dealt thus with other nations; he has not taught them
his decrees.

*Glory be…*

ANTIPHON

**Jesus, true God, the Vir-gin's Son,** set in our hearts the light of

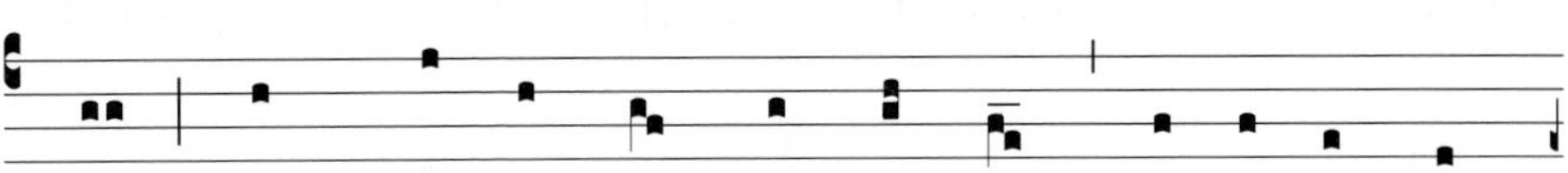

faith, strength-en our hearts with firm hope, light in our hearts

a fire of love. Mo-ther of Christ in all your grace come to us,

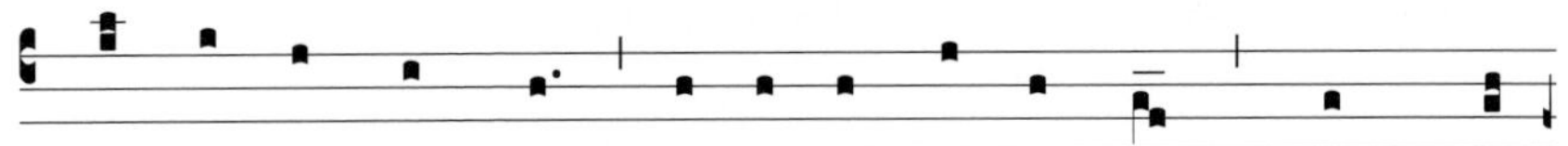

help us with your grace, you are the gate of heav'n, through you

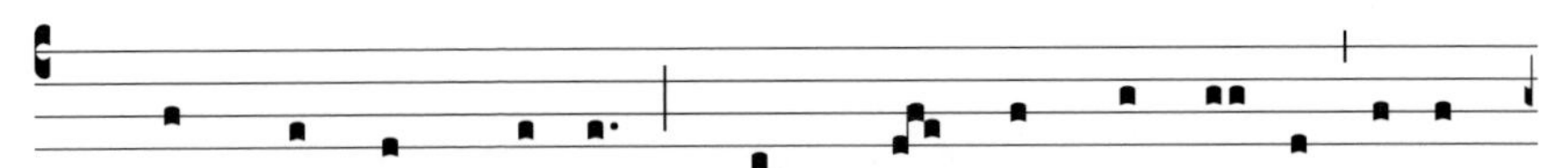

Christ has come to us, through you we may en-ter in-to

e-ter-nal glo-ry.

## Reading

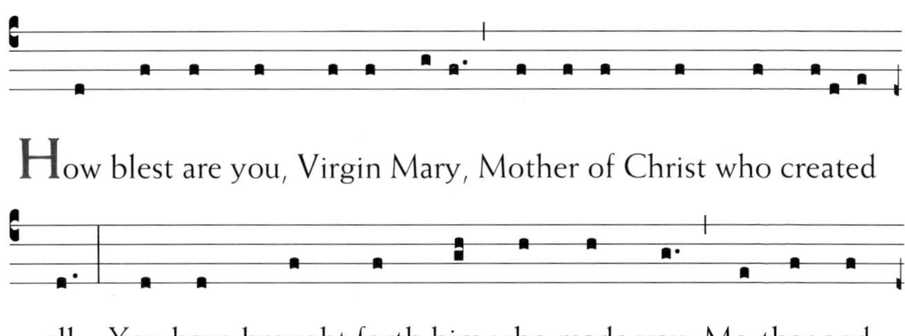

How blest are you, Virgin Mary, Mother of Christ who created all. You have brought forth him who made you, Mo-ther and

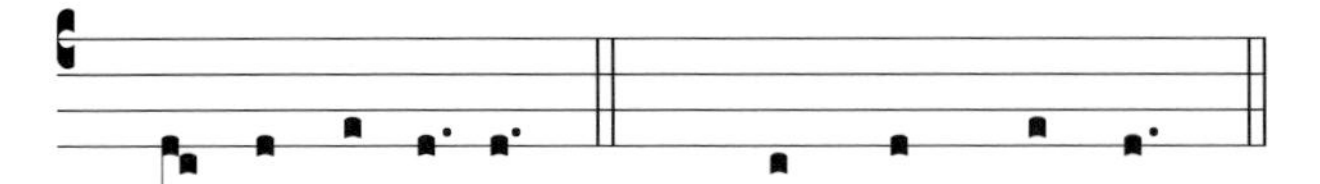

Vir-gin for ev-er. ℟. Our thanks to God.

## Hymn

1. Christ, Lord Cre - a - tor, vir - gin born you
2. The an - gels and our - selves in pride a-
3. Re - pent - ant hearts you wel - come back, from
4. To all who do your ho - ly will, your
5. Grant, Lord, that we may come to you when
6. Pray Ma - ry Mo - ther full of grace, pray
7. Christ Son of God we pray to you, and

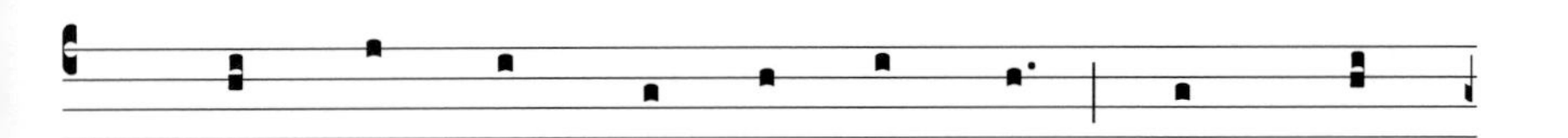

1. willed all things that are to be, you see
2. gainst your will and clear com-mands, ab - used
3. hard - ened hearts you turn a - way, you look
4. own true life is ours to share; make us
5. love is set a - part from pride, through Ma-
6. in your love for all we need; pro - tect
7. hon - our you, the Vir - gin's Son; we praise

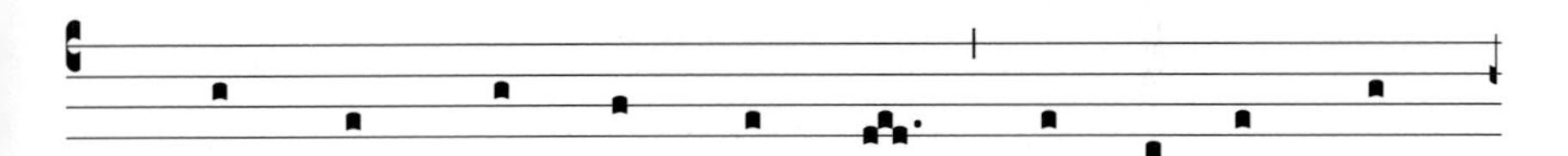

1. all things our hearts will choose yet in all things
2. your gift and so must bear the bur - den of
3 on those who look to you but not on those
4. o - bed - ient, quick to choose your will in all
5. ry's in - ter - ced - ing prayer call us for ev
6. us from all dan - ger now and at our dy-
7. the Fa - ther, God with you and with the Spi-

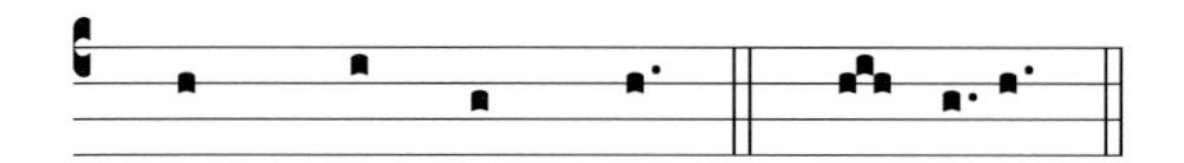

1. you leave us free.
2. your just de - mands.
3 who dis - o - bey.
4. things ev' - ry - where
5. er to your side.
6. ing in - ter - cede.
7. rit, Three in One. A - men.

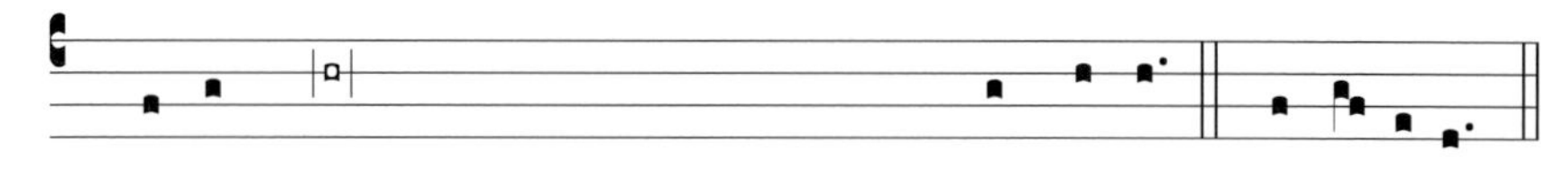

℣. Let all children of holy church rejoice in Ma-ry; (Al-le-lu-ia)

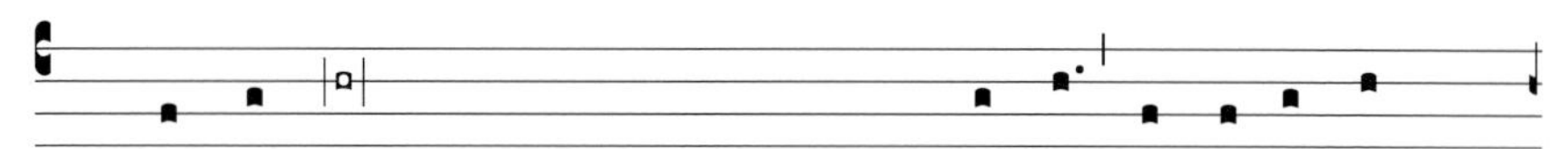

℟. With all the angels of God we rejoice in her, and in all the

wonders God has done. (Al - le - lu – ia)

ANTIPHON

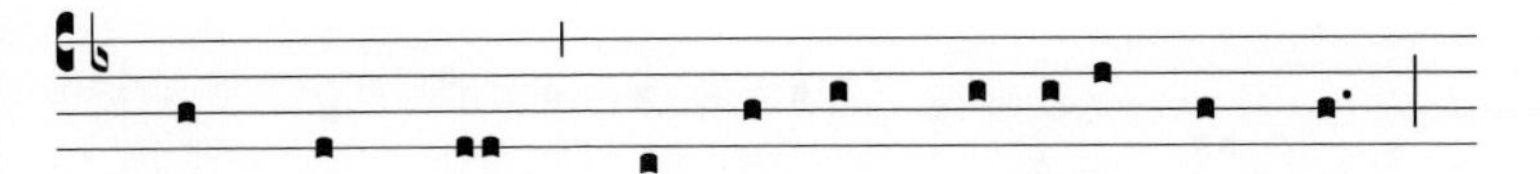

Praise to Christ, the ang-els' Cre-ator and King.

TONE VI 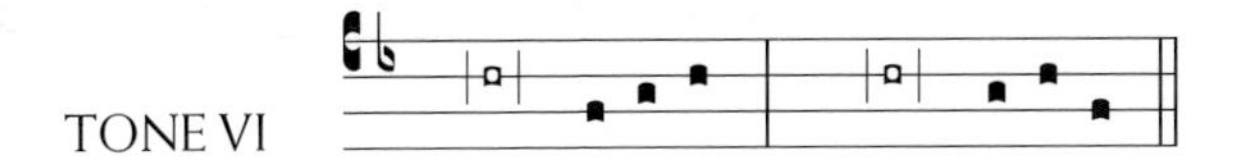

MAGNIFICAT *(Luke 1: 46 - 55)*

My soul glorifies the Lord,
my spirit rejoices in God,
my Saviour.

He looks on his servant in her nothingness; henceforth all ages
will call me blessed.
The Almighty works marvels for me. Holy his name!

His mercy is from age to age, on those who fear him.
He puts forth his arm in strength and scatters the proud-
hearted.

He casts the mighty from their thrones and raises the lowly.
He fills the starving with good things, sends the rich away empty.

He protects Israel, his servant, remembering his mercy,
the mercy promised to our fathers, to Abraham and his sons
for ever.

Praise the Father, the Son and the Holy Spirit,
both now and for ever, world without end.

ANTIPHON

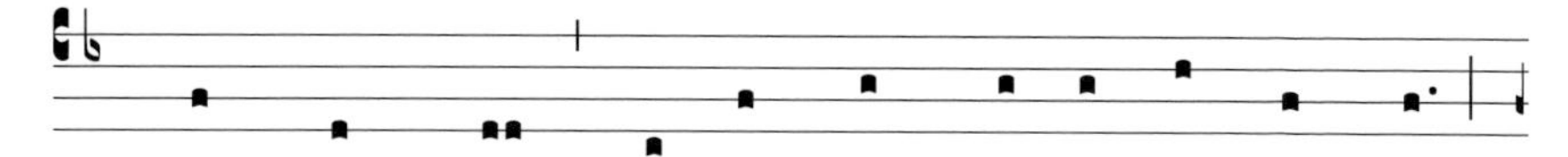

Praise to Christ, the an - gels' Cre - a - tor and King.

He has cho-sen the Vir-gin Ma-ry in her low-li-ness, and in his

love has made her love-lier than all. Praise to Christ whose

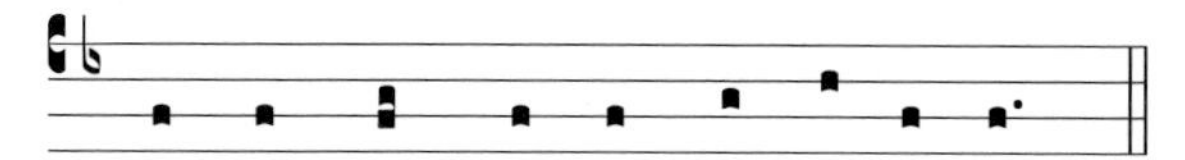

love has made her our Mo-ther of love.

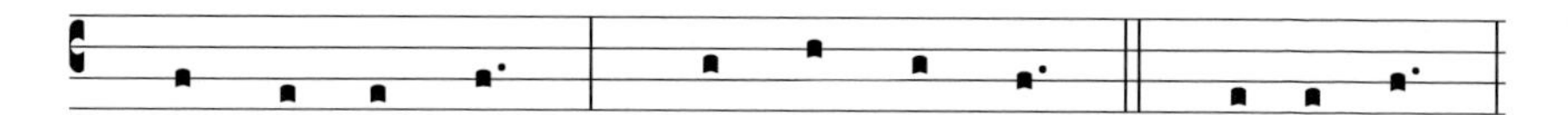

℣. Lord hear my prayer. ℟. Lord grant my prayer. ℣. Let us pray.

PRAYER *(pages 36 - 37).*

ANTIPHON TO ST. BRIDGET & PRAYER *(pages 88 - 90).*

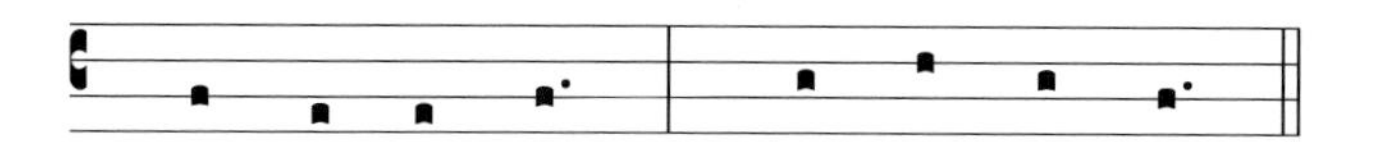

℣. Lord hear my prayer. ℟. Lord grant my prayer.

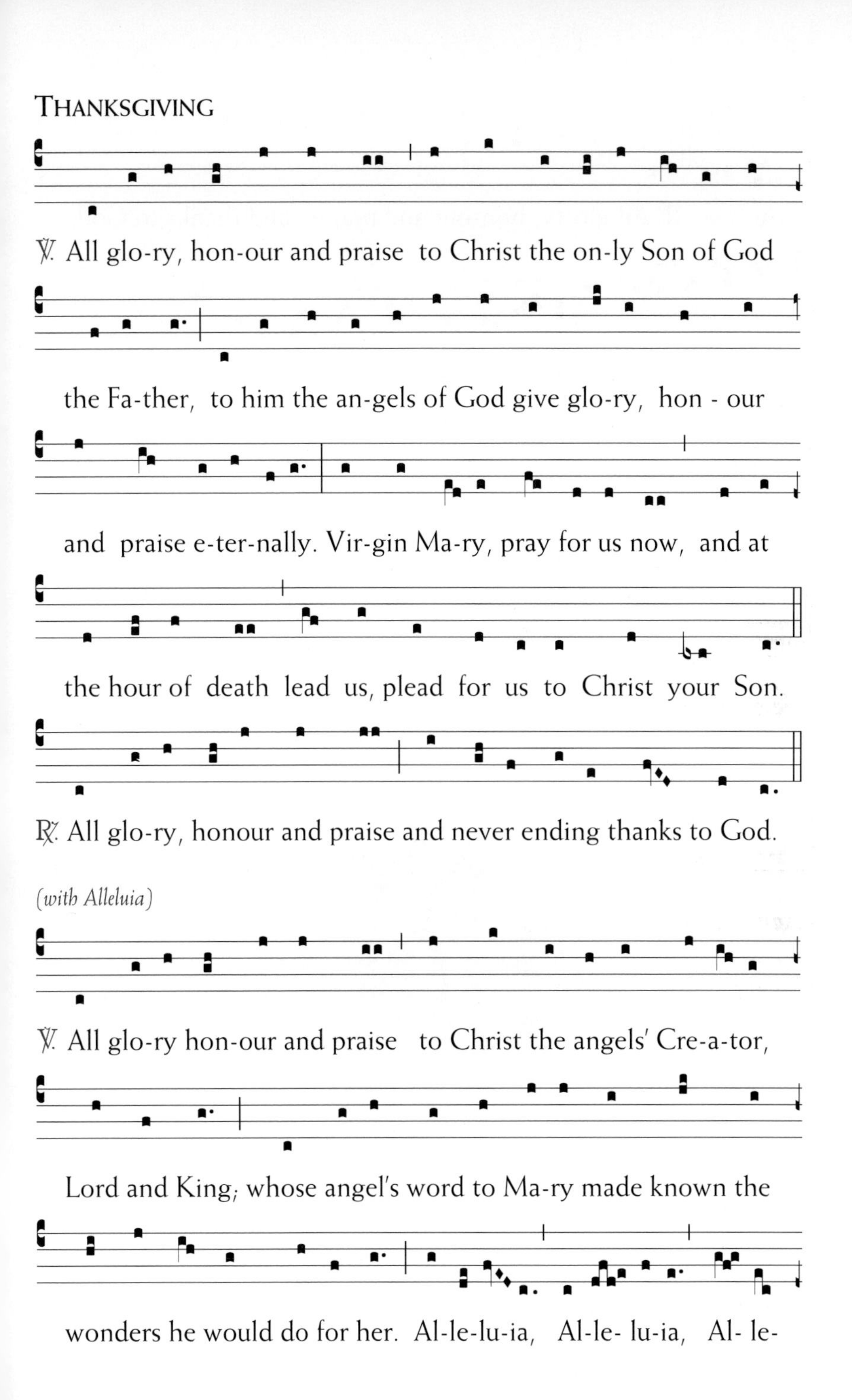
THANKSGIVING
℣. All glo-ry, hon-our and praise to Christ the on-ly Son of God
the Fa-ther, to him the an-gels of God give glo-ry, hon - our
and praise e-ter-nally. Vir-gin Ma-ry, pray for us now, and at
the hour of death lead us, plead for us to Christ your Son.
℟. All glo-ry, honour and praise and never ending thanks to God.
(with Alleluia)
℣. All glo-ry hon-our and praise to Christ the angels' Cre-a-tor,
Lord and King; whose angel's word to Ma-ry made known the
wonders he would do for her. Al-le-lu-ia, Al-le- lu-ia, Al- le-

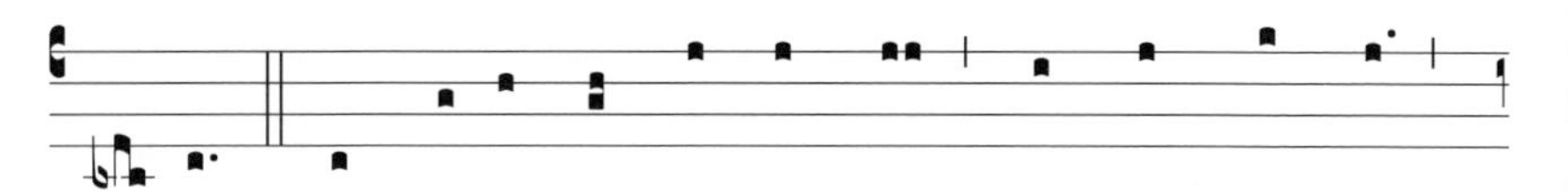

lu - ia. ℟. All glo-ry, hon-our and praise and thanks to God,

Al-le-lu - ia, Al-le-lu - ia, Al- le - lu - ia.

## Closing Prayers

'Mary, rejoice in God,' ... *with music (page 92) followed by...*

**Hymn** *to Holy Mother St. Bridget, (pages 93 - 94).*

*Monday*

# COMPLINE

**OPENING PRAYERS** *as before Sunday Compline,* *pages 95 - 96.*

ANTIPHON

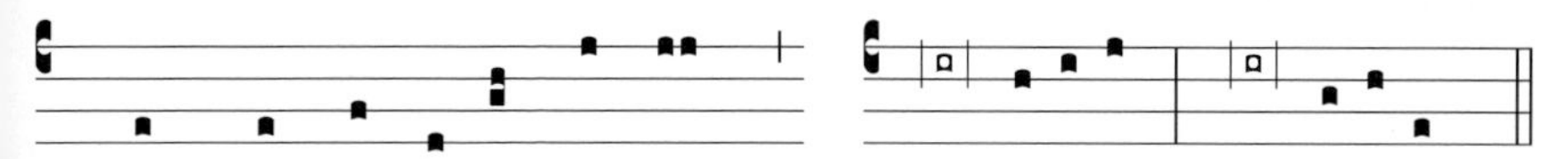

God's peo-ple of old re-joiced TONE III

**Psalms 131, 132 & 133** *as on Sunday* *pages 97 - 98.*

ANTIPHON

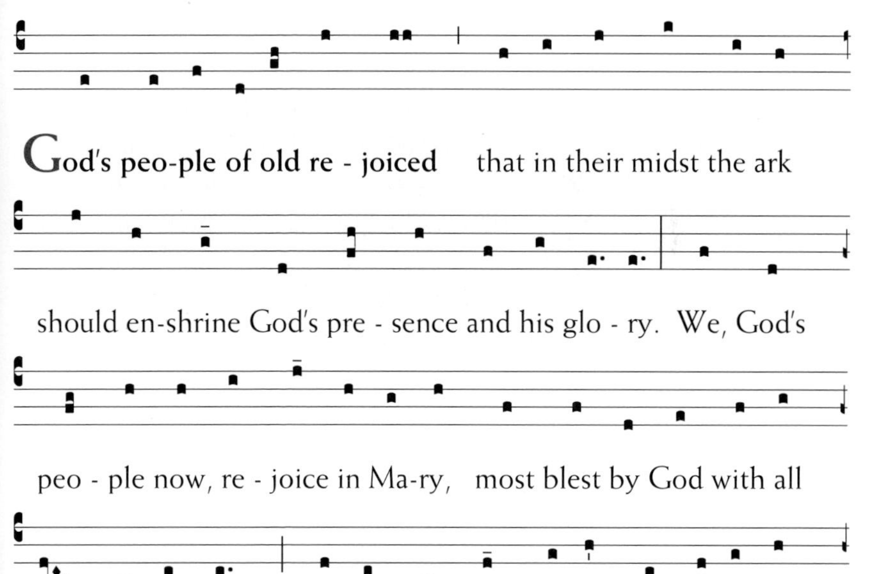

treasures of God, to help and save us.

**READING** *as on Sunday, page 99.*

**SHORT RESPONSORY** *as on Sunday, pages 99 ff.*

---

**HYMN**

1. God's heaven is God him - self, who wills cre - a-
2. This, this is heaven, to be with God, in ev-
3. Yet in God's time there came to earth a gent-
4. We found a li - ly gro - wing here, a low-
5. Christ, seed of Ma - ry, flower of grace, grow in
6. Pray Ma - ry Mo - ther full of grace, pray in
7. Christ Son of God we pray to you, and ho-

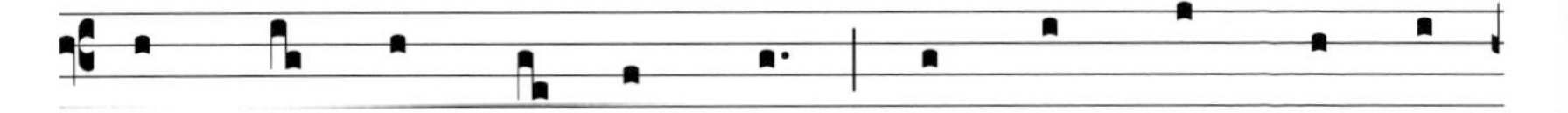

1. tion and cre - a - tion's praise, who brings forth beau-ty
2. er - las - ting joy with him, where flowers of grace and
3. ler breath, a sa - ving dew, to wa - ter and re-
4. ly plant, to bloom a - lone, but not to die – to
5. earth's gar - den ev' - ry - where, grow in our hearts, bring
6. your love for all we need, pro - tect us from all
7. nour you the Vir - gin's Son; we praise the Fa - ther,

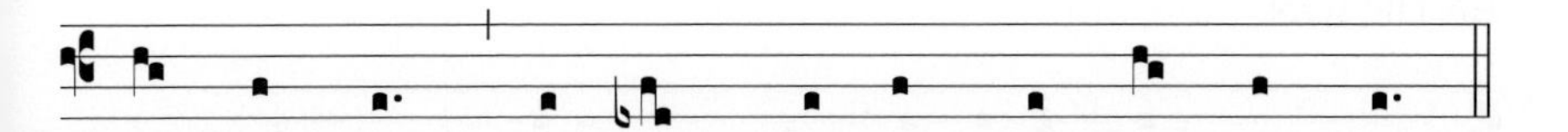

1. from his thought, and makes all ho - ly in his grace.
2. good-ness grow, not touched by earth's cold winds of sin.
3. fresh all lands and make with sweet-ness all things new.
4. live and bear the pre - cious seed which God had sown.
5. forth in us, the fruits you look to us to bear.
6. dan - ger now, and at our dy - ing in - ter - cede.
7. God with you and with the Spi - rit, Three in One.

7. A - men

℣. I am the ser-vant of God, ℟. To hear and o-bey his word.

*(with Alleluia)*

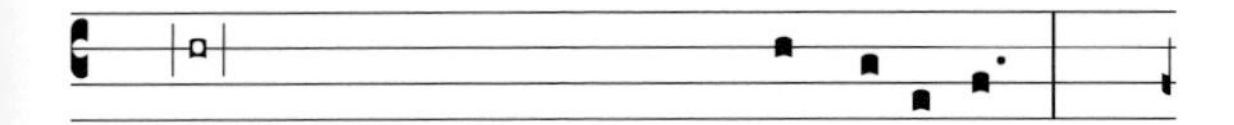

℣. I am the servant of God, Al-le-lu-ia.

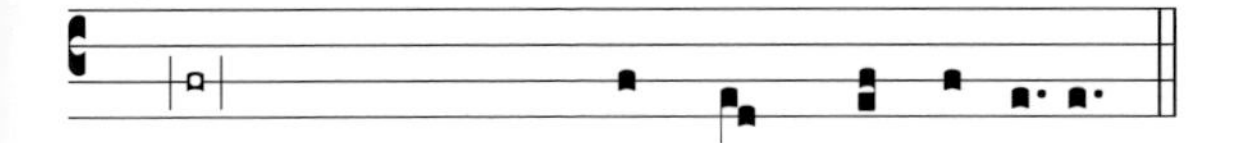

℟. To hear and obey his word, Al -le-lu-ia.

## ANTIPHON

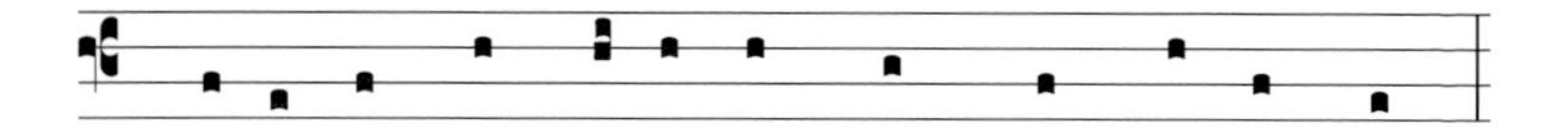

Mary, we may tru- ly name you Queen of an - gels,

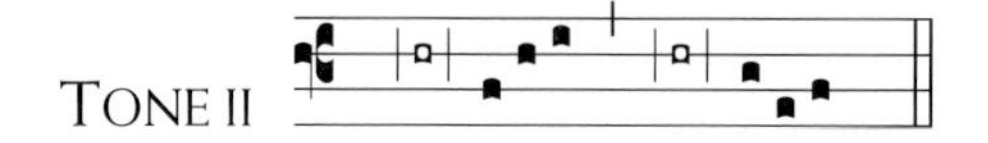


## CANTICLE OF SIMEON *(Luke 2: 29 - 32)*

At last, all powerful Master you give leave
to your servant to go in peace,
according to your promise.

For my eyes have seen your salvation which you have prepared
for all nations.
The light to enlighten the gentiles and give glory to Israel, your people.

Give praise to the Father Almighty: to his Son, Jesus Christ, the Lord;
to the Spirit who dwells in our hearts, both now and forever. Amen.

## ANTIPHON

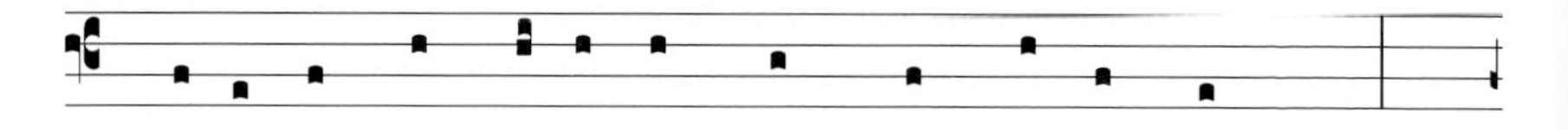

Mary, we may tru- ly name you Queen of an - gels,

Mo-ther of Christ through whom all heav'n - ly spi - rits

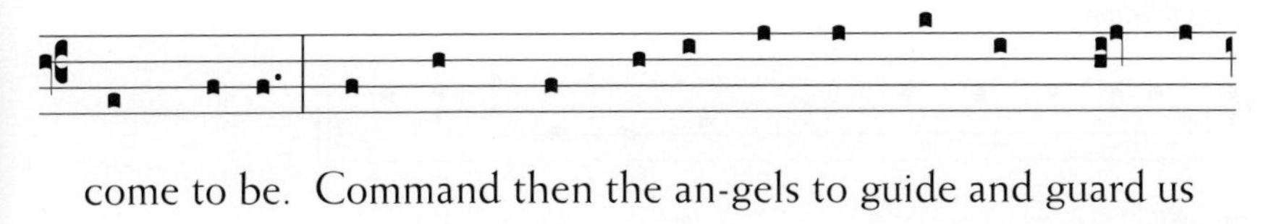

come to be. Command then the an-gels to guide and guard us

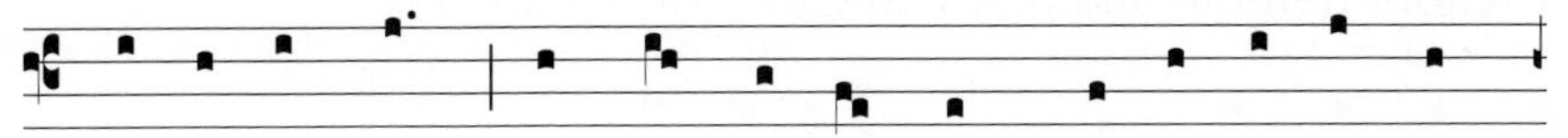

this coming night; and drive a-way those who like li-ons would

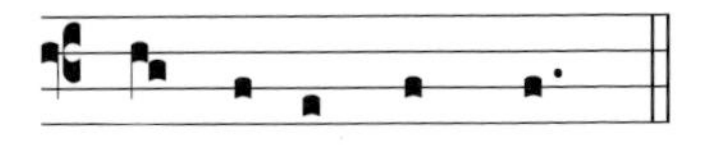

seek us as their prey.

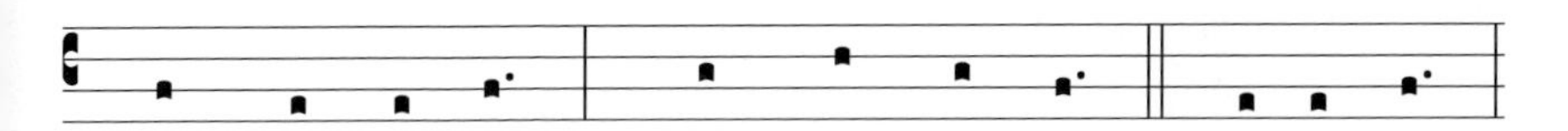

℣. Lord, hear my prayer. ℟. Lord, grant my prayer. ℣. Let us pray.

**Prayer** *as on Sunday,* *page 104.*

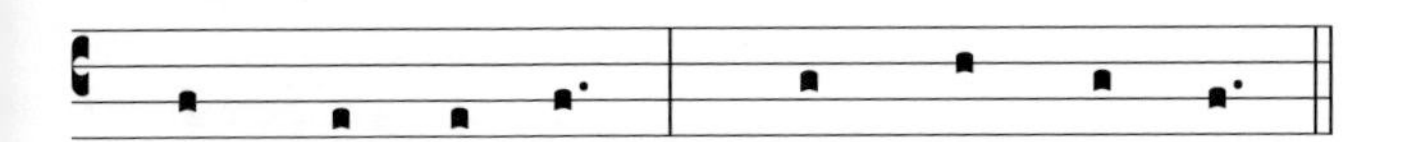

℣. Lord, hear my prayer. ℟. Lord, grant my prayer.

**Thanksgiving**

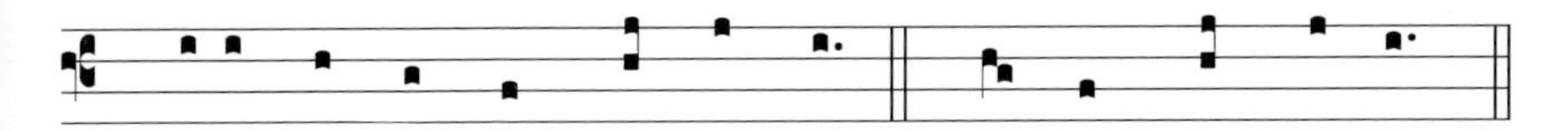

℣. Glory, hon-our and praise to God. ℟. And our thanks to him.

*(with Alleluia)*

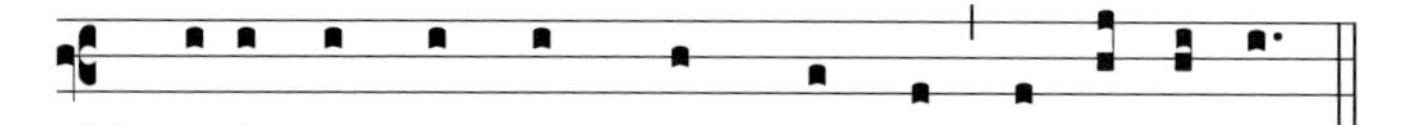

℣. Glory hon-our and praise to God, Al- le- lu- ia.

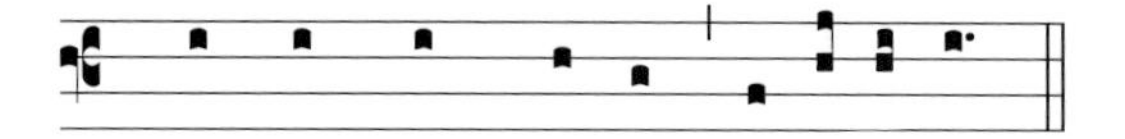

℟. And our thanks to him, Al-le-lu-ia.

℣. Mary, you are full of grace, the Lord is with you.
℟. Mary, you are most blessed of all women, for Jesus Christ is your Son. (Alleluia)

## Lauds of Our Lady

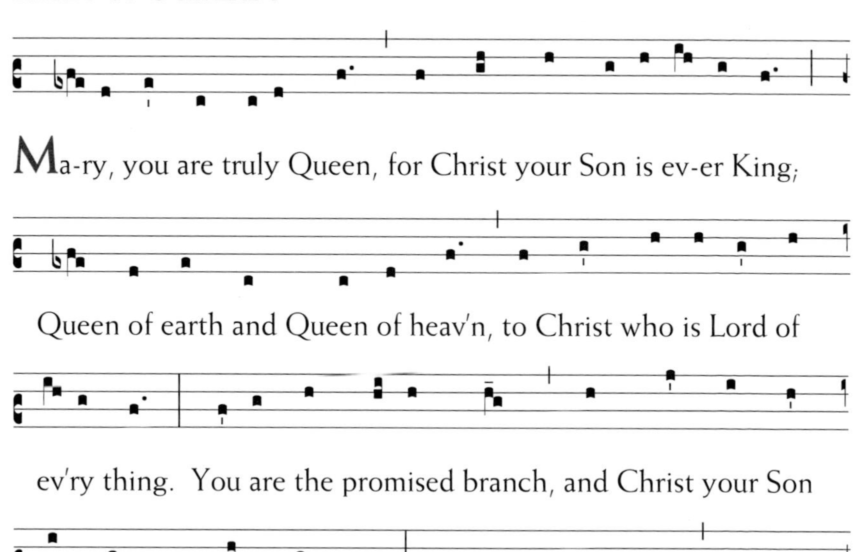

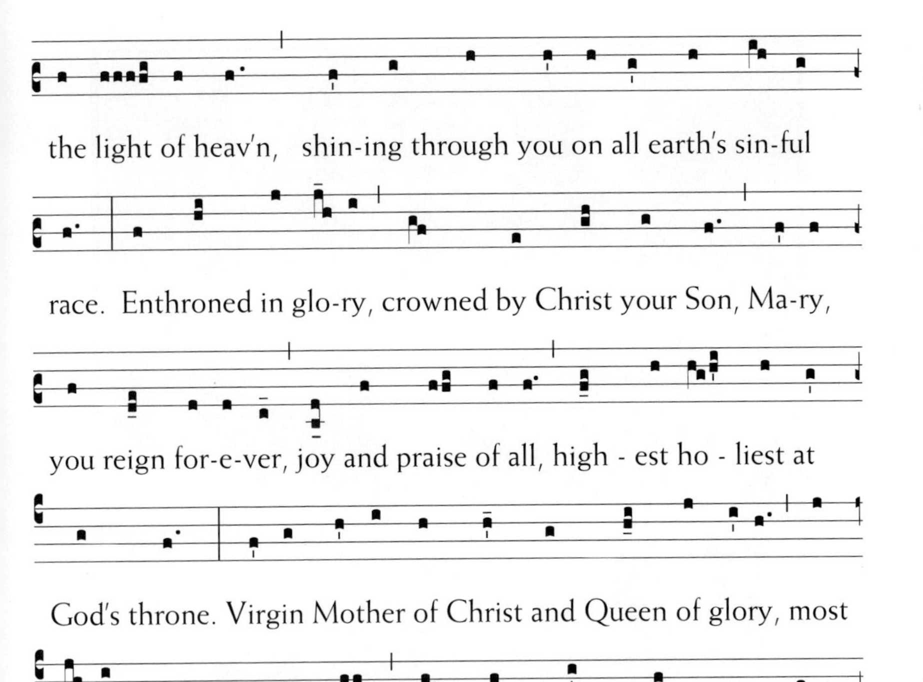


ho-ly Ma-ry, we may claim none who sought your prayer with

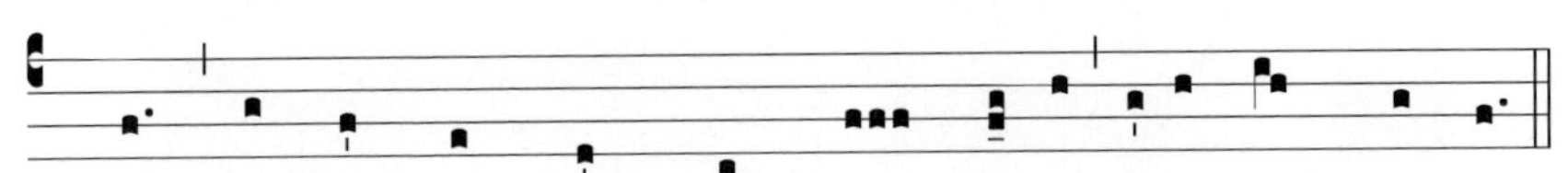

Christ, or prayed to Christ through you, Mary, ever prayed in vain.

℣. Pray for us, holy Virgin Mary, Mother of God.
℟. That we may be made worthy of the promises of Jesus Christ.

℣. Let us pray.

Forgive, we ask you Lord, the sins of your servants: and may we who of ourselves are unable to please you, be saved by the prayers of the Mother of your Son, Jesus Christ our Lord. ℟. Amen.

## Closing Prayers

'Mary, rejoice in God,' … *as on Sunday,* *page 107.*

*Illustration from the 1697 Landshut edition of The Bridgettine Breviary.*

*Saint Bridget receiving instruction from an angel: how the Blessed Virgin was conceived body and soul free from original sin by her most worthy parents Anne and Joachim. (Sermo Angelicus, chapter 10 and Book 6, chapter 49.)*

*Tuesday*

# LAUDS

## OPENING PRAYERS

***(The first prayer of the day...)*** *(page 33)*

Open my mouth, O Lord ... *including Invitatory psalm (Ps. 94)*

## ANTIPHON

**Make known to all men everywhere.**

Psalms and Canticle as for Sunday Lauds *(pages 39ff)*

**Make known to all men everywhere,** that the Virgin's Son, foretold and long desired by holy men of old, is truly God, our Creator, come to us with mercy for all.

## READING *as on Sunday, page 44.*

## HYMN

In bitter sorrow Adam knew his sin,
Eve's weakness and the Serpent's lying voice,
yet sorrow bore a hope to change despair,
that he and all mankind might still rejoice.

A second Adam, sent to sinful men,
with mercy and salvation to reveal,
a second Eve, a Virgin free from sin
to crush the Serpent's head beneath her heel.

A second Adam to obey and save
and take away the pride and sin of men,
a second Eve in lowliness and grace
to open wide the gates of heaven again.

Pray Mary Virgin-Mother, ... *Last two verses as on Sunday, page 44.*

℣. Here is a daughter of Eve, truly a child of grace to bring not death but life to all. (Alleluia)
℟. This is she who came, Mary, new Eve to be. (Alleluia)

## ANTIPHON

**Father, we praise you.**

## CANTICLE

Blessed be the Lord, the God of Israel! ... *as on Sunday, page 45.*

**Father, we praise you** with highest praise, for you are the Sower, Christ the Seed. He is that grain of purest wheat, planted in the rich soil which was Mary, watered with the dew of your Holy Spirit, not remaining alone, a single grain, but dying, bringing forth a rich harvest, food of angels, life-giving nourishment for the lifeless, sweetness for the sick, strength for the strong, and refreshment for all.

℣. Lord hear my prayer. ℟. Lord grant my prayer. ℣. Let us pray.

## PRAYER

Grant us, your servants, ...
*As on Sunday page 46 or according to the time of year. See pages 36ff.*

**ANTIPHON** to holy Mother Saint Bridget *as on Sunday, page 46.*
Bridget, loving servant of God, ... *or on ferial days:* Bridget, Saint and Patron, ...
℣. and ℟. with Prayer *(page 47).*
℣. Lord hear my prayer. ℟. Lord grant my prayer.

## THANKSGIVING

℣. Glory, honour and praise to Christ, whose coming fulfilled the prophecies of old – that he would be born of a Mother free from sin.
℟. Our thanks to God.
*(with Alleluia)*
℣. Glory, honour and praise to Christ, whose coming fulfilled the prophecies of old – that he would be born of the house of David. Alleluia, Alleluia, Alleluia. ℟. Our thanks to God. Alleluia, Alleluia, Alleluia.

**CLOSING PRAYERS** 'Mary, rejoice in God,' ... *(page 37).*

*Tuesday*

# TERCE

## OPENING PRAYERS *(page 33).*

*On Pentecost Tuesday Terce is sung (pages 506ff)*

## HYMN

Come, Lord Creator Spirit, come,
inspire our hearts to tell again
that news your prophets once foretold,
God virgin-born and peace to men.

Come in our need as Advocate,
Consoler of our troubled days;
come for her sake whom you have made
Virgin and Mother by your grace.

Pray Mary Mother, full of grace,
pray in your love for all we need;
protect us from all danger now,
and at our dying intercede.

Christ, Son of God, we pray to you,
and honour you, the Virgin's Son.
We praise the Father, God with you,
and with the Spirit, Three in One. Amen.

## ANTIPHON

**We know you, Lord.**

**Psalm 35**

Sin speaks to the sinner in the depths of his heart.
There is no fear of God before his eyes.

He so flatters himself in his mind that he knows not his guilt.
In his mouth are mischief and deceit. All wisdom is gone.

He plots the defeat of goodness as he lies on his bed.
He has set his foot on evil ways, he clings to what is evil.

Your love, Lord, reaches to heaven; your truth to the skies.
Your justice is like God's mountain, your judgments like the deep.

To both man and beast you give protection. O Lord, how precious is
your love.
My God, the sons of men find refuge in the shelter of your wings.

They feast on the riches of your house; they drink from the stream of
your delight.
In you is the source of life and in your light we see light.

Keep on loving those who know you, doing justice for upright hearts.
Let the foot of the proud not crush me nor the hand of the wicked cast me out.

See how the evil-doers have fallen!
Flung down, they shall never arise.

*Glory be...*

**Psalm 36** *(vv. 1 – 15)*

Do not fret because of the wicked; do not envy those who do evil:
for they wither quickly like grass and fade like the green of the fields.

If you trust in the Lord and do good, then you will live in the land and
be secure.
If you find your delight in the Lord, he will grant your heart's desire.

Commit your life to the Lord, trust in him and he will act,
so that your justice breaks forth like the light, your cause like the
noon-day sun.

Be still before the Lord and wait in patience; do not fret at the man
who prospers;
a man who makes evil plots to bring down the needy and the poor.

Calm your anger and forget your rage; do not fret, it only leads to evil.
For those who do evil shall perish; the patient shall inherit the land.

A little longer – and the wicked shall have gone. Look at his place,
he is not there.
But the humble shall own the land and enjoy the fullness of peace.

The wicked man plots against the just and gnashes his teeth against him;
but the Lord laughs at the wicked for he sees that his day is at hand.

The sword of the wicked is drawn, his bow is bent to slaughter the upright.
Their sword shall pierce their own hearts and their bows shall be
broken to pieces.

*Glory be...*

**Psalm 36** *(vv. 16 – 40)*

The just man's few possessions are better than the wicked man's wealth;
for the power of the wicked shall be broken and the Lord will support the just.

He protects the lives of the upright, their heritage will last for ever.
They shall not be put to shame in evil days, in time of famine their food
shall not fail.

But all the wicked shall perish and all the enemies of the Lord.
They are like the beauty of the meadows, they shall vanish, they shall
vanish like smoke.

The wicked man borrows and cannot repay, but the just man is generous
and gives.
Those blessed by the Lord shall own the land, but those he has cursed
shall be destroyed.

The Lord guides the steps of a man and makes safe the path of one he loves.
Though he stumble he shall never fall for the Lord holds him by the hand.

I was young and now I am old,
but I have never seen the just man forsaken nor his children begging for bread.

All the day he is generous and lends
and his children become a blessing.

Then turn away from evil and do good and you shall have a home for ever;
for the Lord loves justice and will never forsake his friends.

The unjust shall be wiped out for ever and the children of the wicked
destroyed.
The just shall inherit the land; there they shall live for ever.

The just man's mouth utters wisdom and his lips speak what is right;
the law of his God is in his heart, his steps shall be saved from stumbling.

The wicked man watches for the just and seeks occasion to kill him.
The Lord will not leave him in his power nor let him be condemned
when he is judged.

Then wait for the Lord, keep to his way. It is he who will free you
from the wicked,
raise you up to possess the land and see the wicked destroyed.

I have seen the wicked triumphant, towering like a cedar of Lebanon.
I passed by again; he was gone. I searched; he was nowhere to be found.

See the just man, mark the upright, for the man of peace a future lies in store,
but sinners shall all be destroyed. No future lies in store for the wicked.

The salvation of the just comes from the Lord, their stronghold in time
of distress.
The Lord helps them and delivers them and saves them: for their
refuge is in him.

*Glory be...*

## ANTIPHON

W**e know you, Lord,** and pray to know you; we know your mercy and pray for mercy. We know that those who seek you will find you. The Virgin Mary sought you with all her heart, and you have given yourself to her to be her everlasting joy.

## READING *(Eccles. 24: 9)*

In the eternal decree of God, I was present before his creating, and I shall be for ever with him, in the holiness of his heaven. ℟. Our thanks to God.

## Short Responsory

℣. He who brought death into the world was driven out into a world of death. (Alleluia, Alleluia) ℟. *Repeat..*

℣. Man was ensnared into an exile without end.

℟. He was driven out into a world of death. († ℟. Alleluia, Alleluia)

℣. Glory to God, Father, Son and Holy Spirit.

℟. He who brought death into the world was driven out into a world of death. (Alleluia, Alleluia)

℣. She who was mother of all the living, the woman named Eve. (Alleluia)

℟. Enticed by the lying voice of Satan, subjected her children yet to be to sin and death. (Alleluia)

## Closing Prayers *(page 38)*.

---

† *Response during Easter and on other special days where shown, as well as in brackets thus: (Alleluia). For style, see Sunday Terce* *on page 51.*

*Tuesday*

# SEXT

## OPENING PRAYERS (*page 33*)

## HYMN

Come, Lord Creator Spirit, come… *as at Tuesday Terce, page 157.*

## ANTIPHON

Mary,

**Psalm 45**

God is for us a refuge and strength, a helper close at hand, in time of distress:
so we shall not fear though the earth should rock, though the mountains fall
into the depths of the sea,

even though its waters rage and foam, even though the mountains be shaken
by its waves.
The Lord of hosts is with us: the God of Jacob is our stronghold.

The waters of a river give joy to God's city, the holy place where the
Most High dwells.
God is within, it cannot be shaken; God will help it at the dawning of the day.

Nations are in tumult, kingdoms are shaken: he lifts his voice, the earth
shrinks away.
The Lord of hosts is with us: the God of Jacob is our stronghold.

Come, consider the works of the Lord the redoubtable deeds he has done
on the earth.
He puts an end to wars over all the earth; the bow he breaks, the spear
he snaps.

He burns the shields with fire.
"Be still and know that I am God, supreme among the nations, supreme
on the earth!"

The Lord of hosts is with us:
the God of Jacob is our stronghold.

*Glory be...*

**Psalm 46**

All peoples, clap your hands, cry to God with shouts of joy!
For the Lord, the Most High, we must fear, great king over all the earth.

He subdues peoples under us and nations under our feet.
Our inheritance, our glory, is from him, given to Jacob out of love.

God goes up with shouts of joy; the Lord goes up with trumpet blast.
Sing praise for God, sing praise, sing praise to our king, sing praise.

God is king of all the earth. Sing praise with all your skill.
God is king over the nations; God reigns on his holy throne.

The princes of the people are assembled with the people of Abraham's God.
The rulers of the earth belong to God, to God who reigns over all.

*Glory be...*

**Psalm 47**

The Lord is great and worthy to be praised in the city of our God.
His holy mountain rises in beauty, the joy of all the earth.

Mount Sion, true pole of the earth, the Great King's city!
God, in the midst of its citadels, has shown himself its stronghold.

For the kings assembled together, together they advanced.
They saw; at once they were astounded; dismayed, they fled in fear.

A trembling seized them there, like the pangs of birth,
or as the east wind destroys the ships of Tarshish.

As we have heard, so we have seen in the city of our God,
in the city of the Lord of hosts which God upholds for ever.

O God, we ponder your love within your temple.
Your praise, O God, like your name reaches to the ends of the earth.

With justice your right hand is filled. Mount Sion rejoices;
the people of Judah rejoice at the sight of your judgments.

Walk through Sion, walk all round it; count the number of its towers.
Review all its ramparts, examine its castles,

that you may tell the next generation that such is our God,
our God for ever and always. It is he who leads us.

*Glory be...*

## Antiphon

**Mary,** there could be no resting-place so pleasing, no temple more fitting for the King of glory than your chaste womb. You were truly the house of God, the temple of his mercy to men.

## Reading *(Eccles. 24: 11)*

Jerusalem has been my dwelling and my resting-place:
there in the holy city, I have taken up my rule and my reign.
℟. Our thanks to God.

## Short Responsory

℣. She who was mother of all the living, the woman named Eve, was enticed by the lying voice of Satan. (Alleluia, Alleluia) ℟. *Repeat.*
℣. She subjected her children yet to be, to sin and death.
℟. Enticed by the lying voice of Satan. († ℟. Alleluia, Alleluia)
℣. Glory to God, Father, Son and Holy Spirit.
℟. She who was mother of all the living, the woman named Eve, was enticed by the lying voice of Satan. (Alleluia, Alleluia)
℣. Here is a daughter of Eve truly a child of grace to bring not death but life to all. (Alleluia)
℟. This is she who came, Mary, new Eve to be. (Alleluia)

*NOTE: If continuing immediately with None, omit the Opening Prayers and Hymn for None and start with the (short) Antiphon before the Psalms: as detailed in the Structure, page 26.*

CLOSING PRAYERS *(page 38).*

---

† ***Response during Easter and on other special days where shown, as well as in brackets thus: (Alleluia). For style, see Sunday Terce on page 51.***

# NONE

**OPENING PRAYERS** *as before Sunday None, pages 55 - 56.*

## HYMN

1. Come, Lord Cre - a - tor Spir - it, come; in - spire our
2. Come in our need as Ad - vo - cate, Con- sol - er
3. Pray Ma - ry Mo - ther full of grace, pray in your
4. Christ Son of God, we pray to you, and hon- our

1. hearts to tell a - gain: that news your pro-phets once
2. of our troub- led days; come for her sake whom you
3. love for all we need; pro-tect us from all dan-
4. you, the Vir - gin's Son; we praise the Fa - ther, God

1. fore- told God vir- gin born and peace to men.
2. have made Vir - gin and Mo - ther by your grace.
3 ger now, and at our dy - ing in - ter - cede.
4. with you, and with the Spi - rit, Three in One.

4. A - men.

ANTIPHON

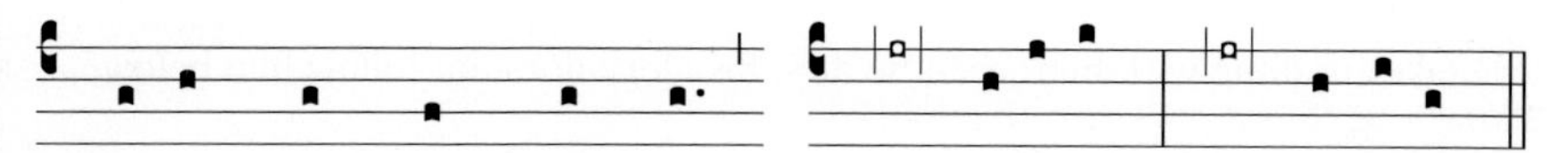

Ma-ry, when Christ your Son TONE VIII

**Psalm 48**

Hear this, all you peoples, give heed, all who dwell in the world,
men both low and high, rich and poor alike!

My lips will speak words of wisdom. My heart is full of insight.
I will turn my mind to a parable, with the harp I will solve my problem.

Why should I fear in evil days the malice of the foes who surround me,
men who trust in their wealth, and boast of the vastness of their riches?

For no man can buy his own ransom,
or pay a price to God for his life.

The ransom of his soul is beyond him.
He cannot buy life without end, nor avoid coming to the grave.

He knows that wise men and fools must both perish
and leave their wealth to others.

Their graves are their homes for ever, their dwelling place from age to age,
though their names spread wide through the land.

In his riches, man lacks wisdom; he is like the beasts that are destroyed.
This is the lot of the self-confident, who have others at their beck and call.

Like sheep they are driven to the grave, where death shall be their shepherd
and the just shall become their rulers.

With the morning their outward show vanishes and the grave
becomes their home
But God will ransom me from death and take my soul to himself.

Then do not fear when a man grows rich, when the glory of his house
increases.
He takes nothing with him when he dies, his glory does not follow him below.

Though he flattered himself while he lived: "Men will praise me for
doing well for myself,"
yet he will go to join his fathers, who will never see the light any more.

In his riches, man lacks wisdom;
he is like the beasts that are destroyed.

*Glory be...*

**Psalm 49**

The God of gods, the Lord, has spoken and summoned the earth,
from the rising of the sun to its setting. Out of Sion's perfect beauty he shines.

(Our God comes, he keeps silence no longer.)
Before him fire devours, around him tempest rages.

He calls on the heavens and the earth
to witness his judgment of his people.

"Summon before me my people who made covenant with me by sacrifice."
The heavens proclaim his justice, for he, God, is the judge.

"Listen, my people, I will speak; Israel, I will testify against you,
for I am God, your God. I accuse you, lay the charge before you.

I find no fault with your sacrifices, your offerings are always before me.
I do not ask more bullocks from your farms, nor goats from among your herds.

For I own all the beasts of the forest, beasts in their thousands on my hills.
I know all the birds in the sky, all that moves in the field belongs to me.

Were I hungry, I would not tell you, for I own the world and all it holds.
Do you think I eat the flesh of bulls, or drink the blood of goats?

Pay your sacrifice of thanksgiving to God and render him your votive offerings.
Call on me in the day of distress. I will free you and you shall honour me."

(But God says to the wicked:)
"But how can you recite my commandments and take my covenant
on your lips,

you who despise my law
and throw my words to the winds,

you who see a thief and go with him; who throw in your lot with adulterers,
who unbridle your mouth for evil and whose tongue is plotting crime,

you who sit and malign your brother and slander your own mother's son.
You do this, and should I keep silence? Do you think that I am like you?

Mark this, you who never think of God, lest I seize you and you cannot escape;
a sacrifice of thanksgiving honours me and I will show God's
salvation to the upright."

*Glory be...*

**Psalm 51**

Why do you boast of your wickedness,
you champion of evil?

Why plan ruin all day long,
(your tongue like a sharpened razor,) you master of deceit?

You love evil more than good, lies more than truth.
You love the destructive word, you tongue of deceit.

For this God will destroy you and remove you for ever.
He will snatch you from your tent and uproot you from the land of the living.

The just shall see and fear.
They shall laugh and say:

"So this is the man who refused to take God as his stronghold,
but trusted in the greatness of his wealth and grew powerful by his crimes."

But I am like a growing olive tree in the house of God.
I trust in the goodness of God for ever and ever.

I will thank you for evermore; for this is your doing.
I will proclaim that your name is good, in the presence of your friends.

*Glory be...*

## ANTIPHON

**Ma-ry, when Christ your Son** comes in his Fa-ther's name as

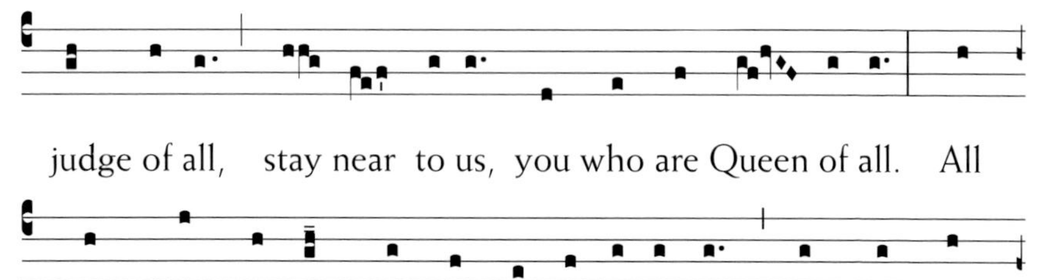

judge of all, stay near to us, you who are Queen of all. All

heav'n will pro-claim the justness of his judging; the great ones

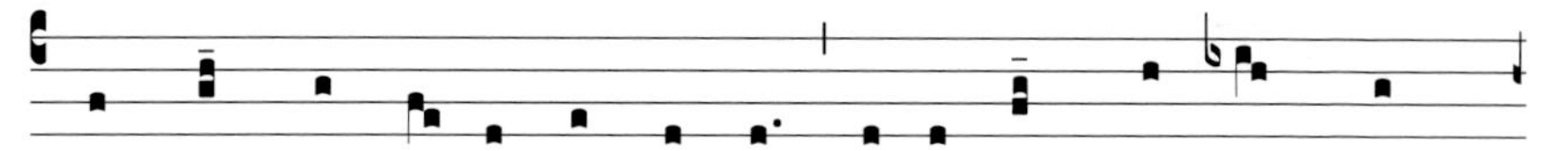

of earth will fear to look on him, as he comes to search the

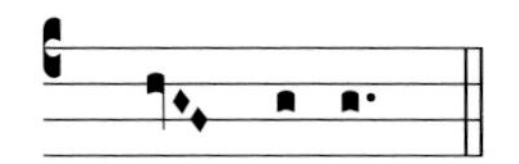

hearts of all.

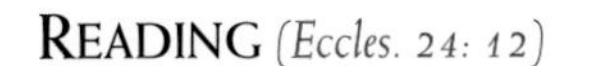

## READING *(Eccles. 24: 12)*

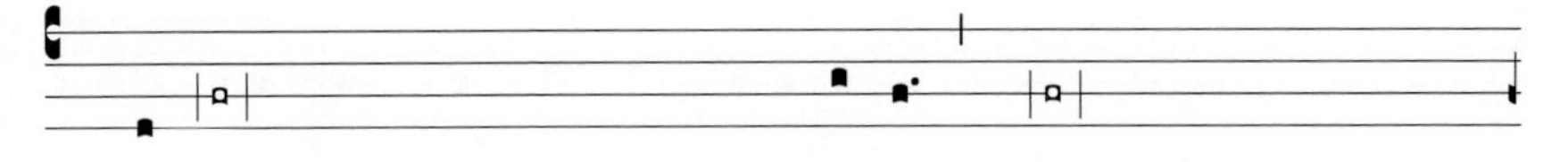

I have grown up among God's people: I will live for ever

in the land of the Lord. ℟. Our thanks to God.

## SHORT RESPONSORY

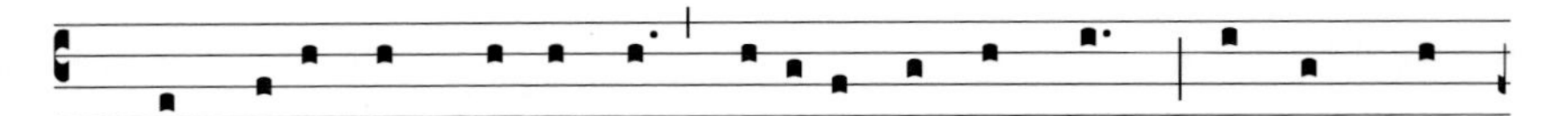

℣. Here is a daughter of Eve, truly a child of grace to bring not

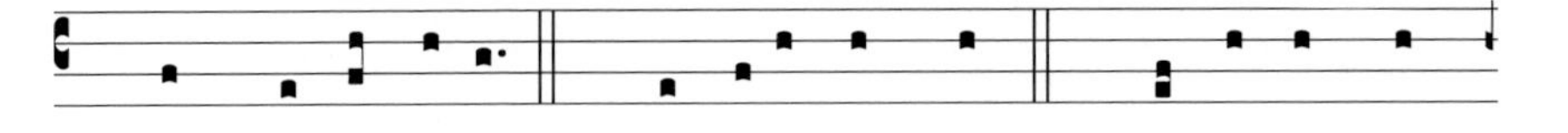

death but life to all. ℟. Here is a daughter… ℣. This is she who

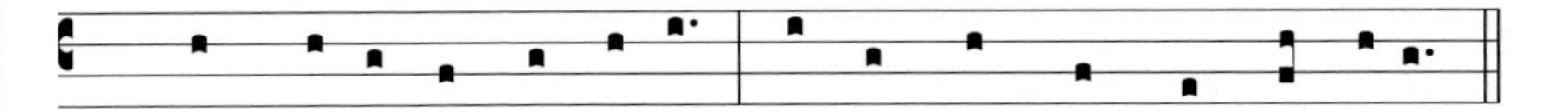

came, Mary new Eve to be ℟. to bring not death but life to all.

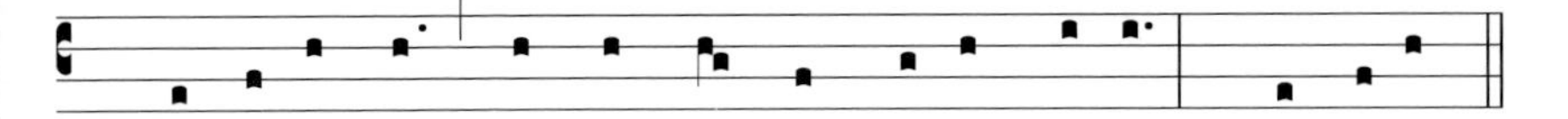

℣. Glo-ry to God, Fa-ther, Son and Ho-ly Spir-it. ℟. Here is a…

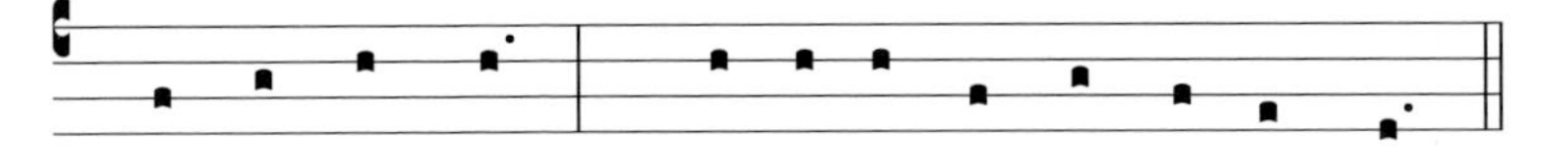

℣. Ma-ry most blest, ℟. Win for us the blessing of Christ.

*(with Alleluia)*

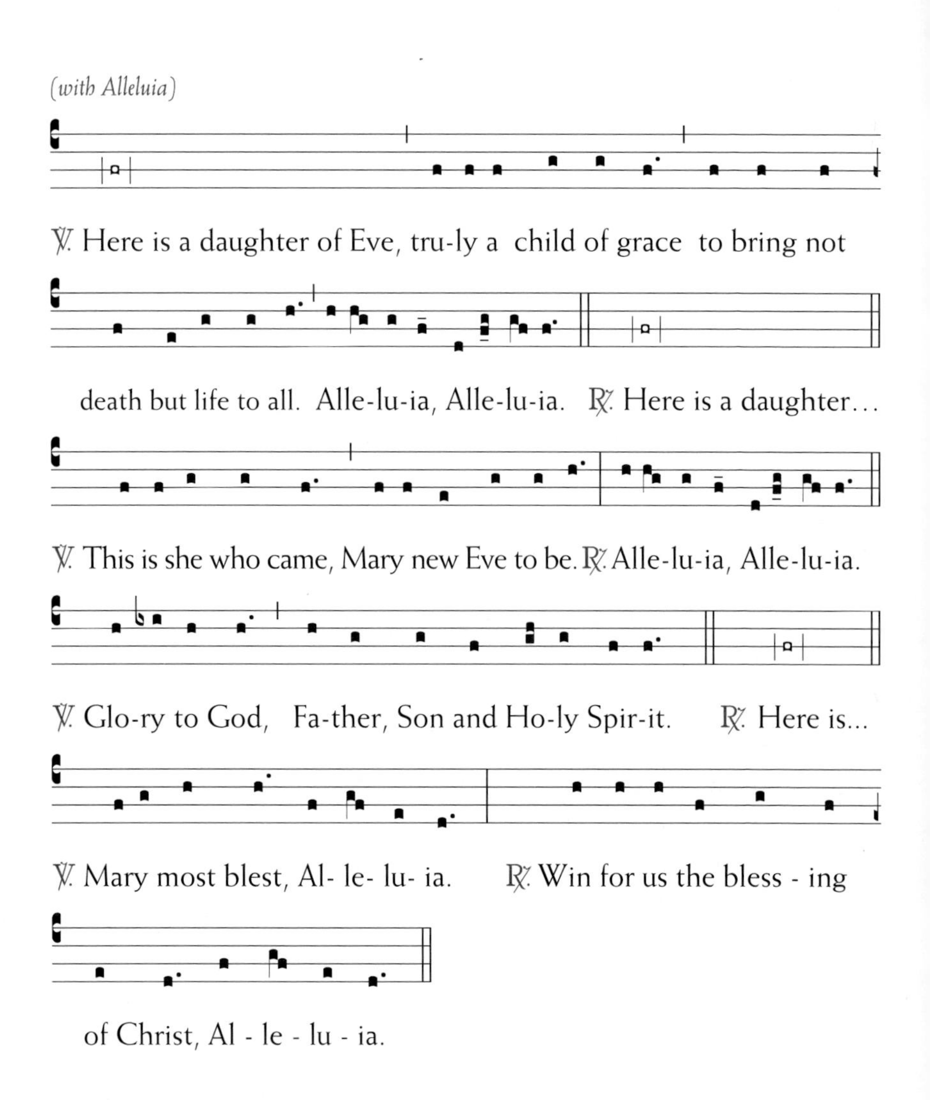


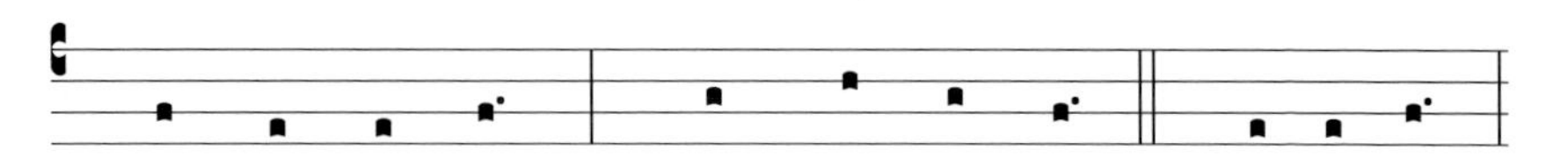

**PRAYER** *(pages 36 - 37)*

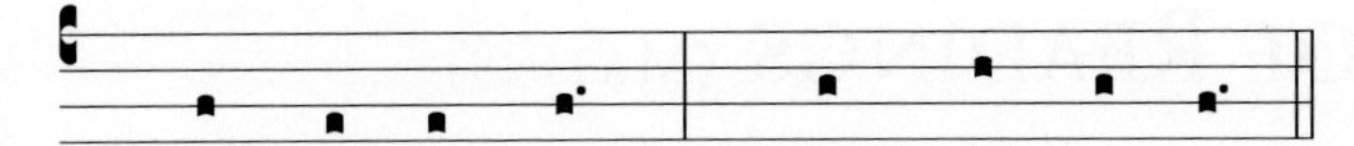

℣. Lord, hear my prayer. ℟. Lord, grant my prayer.

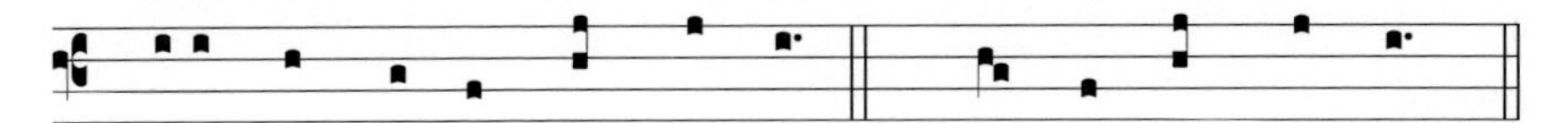

℣. Glory hon-our and praise to God. ℟. And our thanks to him.

*(with Alleluia)*

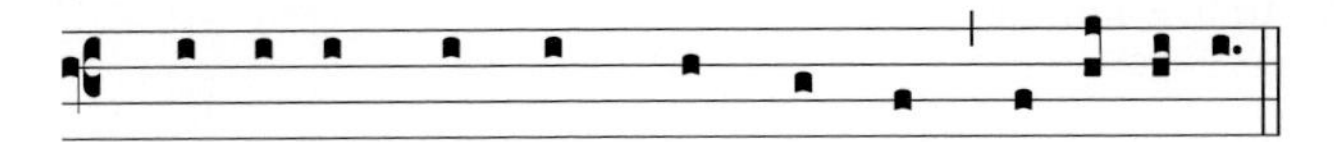

℣. Glory hon-our and praise to God, Al-le-lu-ia.

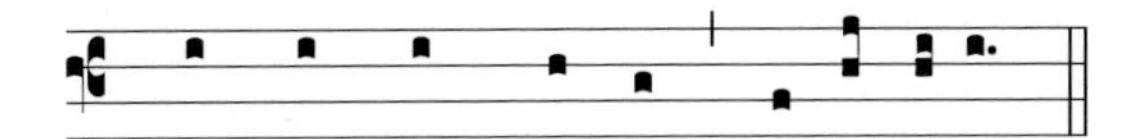

℟. And our thanks to him, Al-le-lu-ia.

**CLOSING PRAYERS**
'Mary, rejoice…' *as on Sunday, pages 64ff.*

**LAUDS OF OUR LADY** *of the day, season or feast (See daily after Compline). With ℣. & ℟. and Prayer. There are two given for Tuesday, to be said on alternate weeks. See pages 198 - 199. Then* 'May the souls of our founders…' *and…*

**Psalm 129** 'Out of the depths…' *and two or three memorial prayers for the souls of the departed, as on Sunday, page 65 - 66.*

*Tuesday*

# OFFICE OF READINGS (MATINS)

## OPENING PRAYERS *(page 67)*.

## HYMN

Man's first self-seeking spurned the will of God,
lured by the woman's word, the Serpent's lie,
and brought him earthly exile and disgrace
in sorrow and despair to live and die;

to live with lesser creatures and grow old,
to die and know the darkness of the grave,
to lose the gifts of God, his grace, his love,
no more like angels, earthly and earth's slave.

Yet God's great mercy took away despair,
for man's deep sorrow promising reprieve –
his Son to come as man to save all men,
an ever-sinless Virgin to conceive.

Pray Mary Virgin-Mother full of grace,
pray in your love for all, for all we need;
protect us from all sin and sinful ways,
and at our dying hour intercede.

Christ Jesus, Son of God, we pray to you
and praise you, naming you the Virgin's Son;
we ever praise the Father, God with you
and with the Holy Spirit, Three in One. Amen.

## ANTIPHON 1

**Mary, our Queen.**

**Psalm 38**

I said: "I will be watchful of my ways for fear I should sin with my tongue.
I will put a curb on my lips when the wicked man stands before me."

I was dumb, silent and still.
His prosperity stirred my grief.

My heart was burning within me.
At the thought of it, the fire blazed up and my tongue burst into speech:

"O Lord, you have shown me my end, how short is the length of my days.
Now I know how fleeting is my life.

You have given me a short span of days;
my life is as nothing in your sight.

A mere breath, the man who stood so firm, a mere shadow,
the man passing by;
a mere breath the riches he hoards, not knowing who will have them."

And now, Lord, what is there to wait for? In you rests all my hope.
Set me free from all my sins, do not make me the taunt of the fool.

I was silent, not opening my lips, because this was all your doing.
Take away your scourge from me. I am crushed by the blows of your hand.

You punish man's sins and correct him; like the moth you devour
all he treasures.
Mortal man is no more than a breath; O Lord, hear my prayer.

O Lord, turn your ear to my cry. Do not be deaf to my tears.
In your house I am a passing guest, a pilgrim, like all my fathers.

Look away that I may breathe again
before I depart to be no more.

*Glory be...*

## ANTIPHON 1

M**ary, our Queen,** free us from sin and self-seeking;
pray for us to your Son, that he may not demand in justice
what we have deserved.

## ANTIPHON 2

S**on of God.**

### Psalm 42

Defend me, O God, and plead my cause against a godless nation.
From deceitful and cunning men rescue me, O God.

Since you, O God, are my stronghold, why have you rejected me?
Why do I go mourning oppressed by the foe?

O send forth your light and your truth; let these be my guide.
Let them bring me to your holy mountain, to the place where you dwell.

And I will come to the altar of God, the God of my joy.
My redeemer, I will thank you on the harp, O God, my God.

Why are you cast down my soul, why groan within me?
Hope in God; I will praise him still, my saviour and my God.

*Glory be...*

## ANTIPHON 2

S**on of God**, make us see all things in the light of your truth,
that nothing may keep us
from the merciful arms of your holy Mother.

ANTIPHON 3

Mary, Mother of life and salvation.

**Psalm 43**

We heard with our own ears, O God, our fathers have told us the story
of the things you did in their days, you yourself, in days long ago.

To plant them you uprooted the nations;
to let them spread you laid peoples low.

No sword of their own won the land; no arm of their own brought them
victory.
It was your right hand, your arm and the light of your face; for you loved them.

It is you, my king, my God, who granted victories to Jacob.
Through you we beat down our foes; in your name we trampled our aggressors.

For it was not in my bow that I trusted nor yet was I saved by my sword:
it was you who saved us from our foes, it was you who put our foes to shame.

All the day long our boast was in God
and we praised your name without ceasing.

Yet now you have rejected us, disgraced us; you no longer go forth
with our armies.
You make us retreat from the foe and our enemies plunder us at will.

You make us like sheep for the slaughter and scatter us among the nations.
You sell your own people for nothing and make no profit by the sale.

You make us the taunt of our neighbours, the mockery and scorn of all
who are near.
Among the nations, you make us a byword, among the peoples a thing
of derision.

All the day long my disgrace is before me; my face is covered with shame
at the voice of the taunter, the scoffer, at the sight of the foe and avenger.

This befell us though we had not forgotten you, though we had not been false to your covenant,
though we had not withdrawn our hearts; though our feet had not strayed from your path.

Yet you have crushed us in a place of sorrows
and covered us with the shadow of death.

Had we forgotten the name of our God, or stretched out our hands to another god
would not God have found this out, he who knows the secrets of the heart?

It is for you that we face death all the day long
and are counted as sheep for the slaughter.

Awake, O Lord, why do you sleep? Arise, do not reject us for ever!
Why do you hide your face and forget our oppression and misery?

For we are brought down low to the dust; our body lies prostrate on the earth.
Stand up and come to our help! Redeem us because of your love!

*Glory be...*

## ANTIPHON 3

**Mary, Mother of life and salvation,** save us from all that is sinful.
In the shadow of death we look to your Son,
knowing that he is truly God.

℣. He who brought death into the world, was driven out into a world of death. (Alleluia)
℟. Man was ensnared into an exile without end. (Alleluia)

Our Father...

## ABSOLUTION

God and father, holy and merciful Lord, take into account the prayer and holiness of Mary, the Virgin-Mother of God, and of all the saints and bring us back from death to life. ℟. Amen.

*Reader:* Lord, we ask for your blessing.

**Week One**

*Blessing, Reading and Response for Tuesdays in Week Two start on page 514, and for Week Three on page 533.*

## Blessing

May the Virgin Mary in her love, ever defend us from sin and temptation.
℟. Amen.

## Reading

We read in the Bible of Adam's original state of happiness.
Then of his disobedience to God,
which brought so much suffering and sorrow.
We are not told that he continued in disobedience.
From his conduct after Cain had killed Abel,
his refraining from intercourse with Eve
until he knew that this was no longer the will of God,
we may judge that the love and service of God was his first thought.
His sorrow was not so much the unhappiness he had brought on himself,
but rather the offence he had committed against God.
Created by God, owing his existence and his happiness to God,
he had turned against God,
and so justly deserved God's anger.
This was true sorrow,
bringing with it repentance and humility.
And with this true sorrow came also consolation from God.

One thing, and one thing only, could have fully consoled him,
the promise that God himself should come as man,
of Adam's own race,
and by love and humility redeem that race which his pride
had deprived of life.

That God should be born as men are born was unthinkable.
Adam and Eve owed their beginning in some way to a special creation by God.
Even this would not be fitting for the coming of God to earth.

It would seem that Adam understood from God's words
something of what was to be.
At least, we may picture him foreseeing the future,
foreseeing a woman, like Eve in womanhood,
but lovelier and holier than all of his race,
a virgin and mother,
bringing God himself to this world.

We may think of him grieving at the words spoken to Eve by the Devil.
But rejoicing, his sorrow turned to joy,
at the thought, Mary, of your words to the angel.
We may think of him grieving that Eve his wife,
created by God from his body,
had deceived him and drawn him on to eternal death.
But rejoicing that you, Virgin Mary, would bear in all purity
Christ, the Son of God, to restore man to life.
Grieving that Eve's first act was of disobedience;
rejoicing that you, Mary, would be a daughter of God,
most dear to him in all things,
ever obedient to his will.

Grieving that Eve had been tempted,
in the sight of God and all the angels,
by the false promise of being made like to God;
rejoicing that in the sight of God and the angels,
you, Mary, would acknowledge yourself the handmaid of God.
Grieving that Eve had offended God,
and brought about the condemnation of man;
rejoicing that your word to God should bring such joy
to yourself and to all men.
Grieving that Eve had closed to man the gate of heaven;
rejoicing that your word had opened that gate again
to yourself and to all who sought to enter.

So we may think of Adam rejoicing with great joy
at the thought, Mary, of your coming,
as we know the angels rejoiced,
before the creation of the world,
foreseeing your creation by God.

℣. Have mercy, Lord, and help our understanding. ℟. Our thanks to God.

## RESPONSORY

**Deceived by the Serpent's lie,** the woman named Eve brought shame to man and woman, sorrow in place of happiness, death instead of life. Mary with joy obeyed the word of God, crushing the Serpent's head beneath her heel, to change our sadness into joy, our death to life, our shame to glory.

℣. Glory to God for Mary, whom we name the second Eve, who in sinlessness and virginity brought forth her Creator into this world,

℟. Crushing the Serpent's head beneath her heel, to change our sadness into joy, our death to life, our shame to glory.

℣. Glory to God, glory to Father, Son and Holy Spirit.

℟. Crushing the Serpent's head beneath her heel, to change our sadness into joy, our death to life, our shame to glory.

## TE DEUM *as on Sunday, page 75* or PSALM 50 *as on Friday, page 330.*

℣. She who was Mother of all the living, the woman named Eve. (Alleluia)

℟. Enticed by the lying voice of Satan, subjected her children yet to be to sin and death. (Alleluia)

## CLOSING PRAYERS *(page 38).*

*Adam and Eve were banished from the Garden of Eden for their original sin.*

*Tuesday*

# VESPERS

**PRAYERS** before Vespers, *(pages 77 - 78)* and
**OPENING PRAYERS** – with music – *as at None, pages 55 - 56.*

ANTIPHON

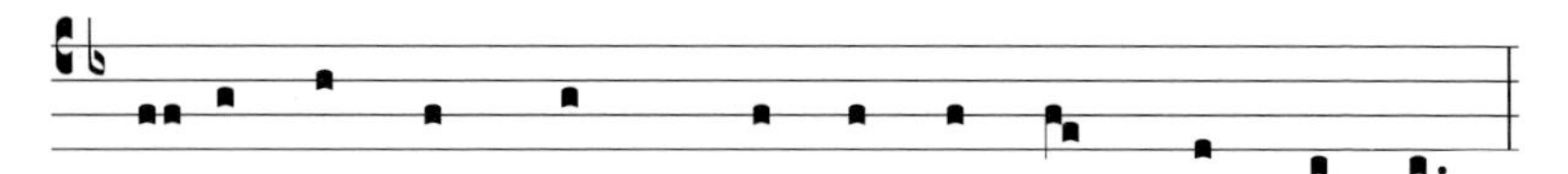

**Ma-ry, you have named yourself the hand-maid of God;**

TONE VI

**Psalm 134**

Praise the name of the Lord, praise him, servants of the Lord,
who stand in the house of the Lord in the courts of the house of our God.

Praise the Lord for the Lord is good. Sing a psalm to his name for he is loving.
For the Lord has chosen Jacob for himself and Israel for his own possession.

For I know the Lord is great, that our Lord is high above all gods.
The Lord does whatever he wills, in heaven, on earth, in the seas.

He summons clouds from the ends of the earth; makes lightning produce
the rain;
from his treasuries he sends forth the wind.

The first-born of the Egyptians he smote,
of man and beast alike.

Signs and wonders he worked in the midst of your land, O Egypt,
against Pharaoh and all his servants.

Nations in their greatness he struck
and kings in their splendour he slew.

Sihon, king of the Amorites, Og, the king of Bashan,
and all the kingdoms of Canaan.

He let Israel inherit their land;
on his people their land he bestowed.

Lord, your name stands for ever, unforgotten from age to age,
for the Lord does justice for his people; the Lord takes pity on his servants.

Pagan idols are silver and gold, the work of human hands.
They have mouths but they cannot speak; they have eyes but they cannot see.

They have ears but they cannot hear; there is never a breath on their lips.
Their makers will come to be like them and so will all who trust in them!

Sons of Israel, bless the Lord! Sons of Aaron, bless the Lord!
Sons of Levi, bless the Lord! You who fear him, bless the Lord!

From Sion may the Lord be blessed,
he who dwells in Jerusalem!

*Glory be...*

**Psalm 135**

O give thanks to the Lord for he is good, for his great love
is without end.
Give thanks to the God of gods, for his great love is without end.

Give thanks to the Lord of lords, for his great love is without end;
who alone has wrought marvellous works, for his great love is without end;

whose wisdom it was made the skies, for his great love is without end;
who fixed the earth firmly on the seas, for his great love is without end.

It was he who made the great lights, for his great love is without end;
the sun to rule in the day, for his great love is without end;

the moon and the stars in the night, for his great love is without end.

The first-born of the Egyptians he smote, for his great love is without end.

He brought Israel out from their midst, for his great love is without end;
arm outstretched, with power in his hand, for his great love is without end.

He divided the Red Sea in two, for his great love is without end;
he made Israel pass through the midst, for his great love is without end;

he flung Pharaoh and his force in the sea, for his great love is without end.
Through the desert his people he led, for his great love is without end.

Nations in their greatness he struck, for his great love is without end.
Kings in their splendour he slew, for his great love is without end.

Sihon, king of the Amorites, for his great love is without end;
and Og, the king of Bashan, for his great love is without end.

He let Israel inherit their land, for his great love is without end.
On his servant their land he bestowed, for his great love is without end.

He remembered us in our distress, for his great love is without end.
And he snatched us away from our foes, for his great love is without end.

He gives food to all living things, for his great love is without end.
To the God of heaven give thanks, for his great love is without end.

*Glory be...*

**Psalm 136**

By the rivers of Babylon there we sat and wept, remembering Sion;
on the poplars that grew there we hung up our harps.

For it was there that they asked us, our captors, for songs, our oppressors,
for joy.
"Sing to us," they said, "one of Sion's songs."

O how could we sing the song of the Lord on alien soil?
If I forget you, Jerusalem, let my right hand wither!

O let my tongue cleave to my mouth if I remember you not,
if I prize not Jerusalem above all my joys!

Remember, O Lord, against the sons of Edom the day of Jerusalem;
when they said: "Tear it down! Tear it down to its foundations!"

O Babylon, destroyer, he is happy who repays you the ills you brought on us.
He shall seize and shall dash your children on the rock!

*Glory be...*

**Psalm 137**

I thank you, Lord, with all my heart, you have heard the words of my mouth.
In the presence of the angels I will bless you. I will adore before your
holy temple.

I thank you for your faithfulness and love which excel all we ever knew of you.
On the day I called, you answered; you increased the strength of my soul.

All earth's kings shall thank you when they hear the words of your mouth.
They shall sing of the Lord's ways: "How great is the glory of the Lord!"

The Lord is high yet he looks on the lowly and the haughty he knows
from afar.
Though I walk in the midst of affliction you give me life and frustrate my foes.

You stretch out your hand and save me, your hand will do all things for me.
Your love, O Lord, is eternal, discard not the work of your hands.

*Glory be...*

**Psalm 147**

O praise the Lord, Jerusalem!
Sion praise your God!

He has strengthened the bars of your gates, he has blessed the children
within you.
He established peace on your borders, he feeds you with finest wheat.

He sends out his word to the earth and swiftly runs his command.
He showers down snow white as wool, he scatters hoar-frost like ashes.

He hurls down hailstones like crumbs. The waters are frozen at his touch;

he sends forth his word and it melts them: at the breath of his mouth
the waters flow.

He makes his word known to Jacob, to Israel his laws and decrees.
He has not dealt thus with other nations; he has not taught them his decrees.

*Glory be...*

### ANTIPHON

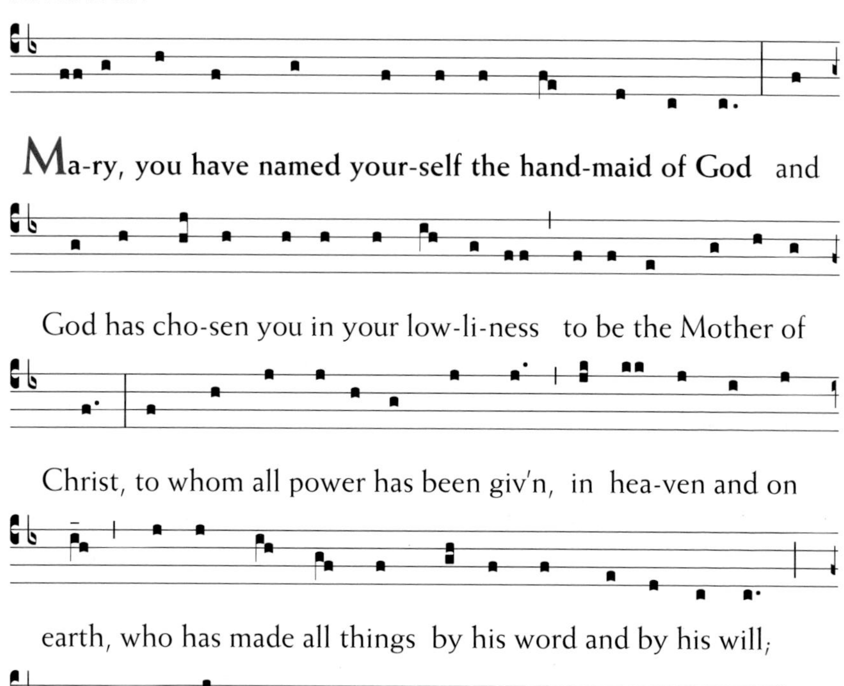

## Reading

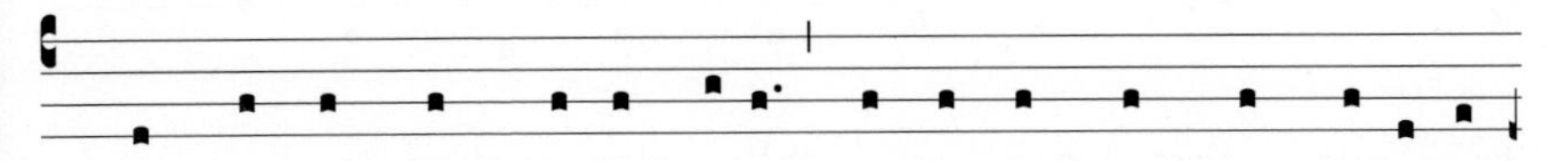

How blest are you, Virgin Mary, Mother of Christ who cre-a-ted

all. You have brought forth him who made you, Mo - ther and

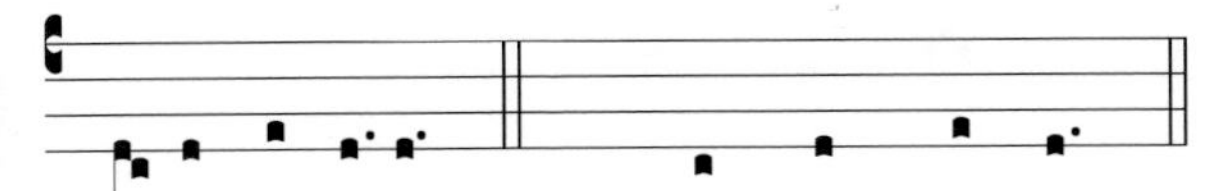

Virgin for ever. ℟. Our thanks to God.

## Hymn

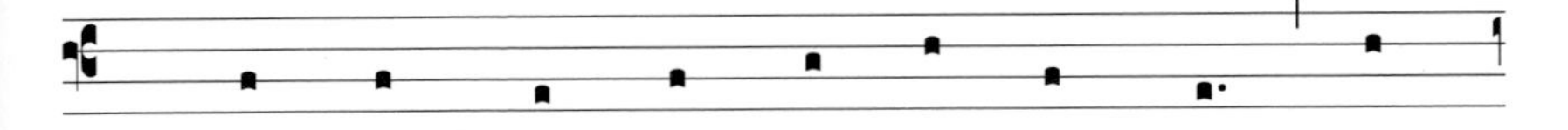

1. Ma - ry, in you God took de - light, the
2. Pro - phets and pa - tri - archs made known your
3. Great joy to all that cho - sen race great
4. God's love which chose you for his Son, will
5. Pray Ma - ry Mo - ther full of grace, pray
6. Christ Son of God, we pray to you, and

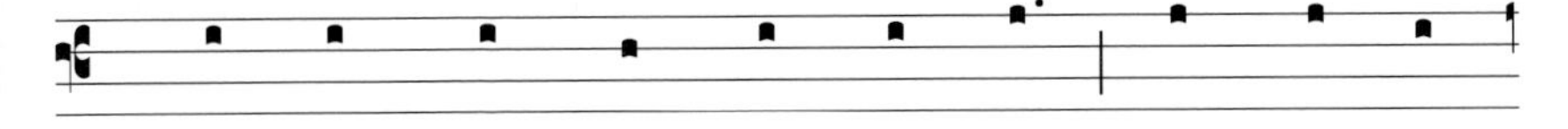

1. an - gels praised you, yet to be, fore - told at
2. com - ing to God's cho - sen race, great joy to
3. joy to ev' - ry race to see the word of
4. ev - er Ma - ry, be our praise, your love for
5. in your love for all we need, pro - tect us
6. hon- our you, the Vir - gin's Son; we praise the

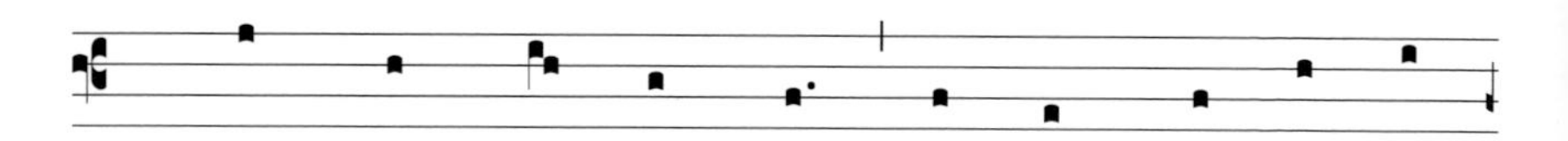

| | | | | | | | | | | | | |
|---|---|---|---|---|---|---|---|---|---|---|---|---|
| 1. | our | first | par - | ents' | fall | man | looked | to | you | to |
| 2. | those | whose | child | you | were, | to | know | and | won-der |
| 3 | God | ful - | filled | in | you, | God's | Vir - | gin | Mo- ther |
| 4. | us, | your | prayer | for | us, | will | save | us | from | our |
| 5. | from | all | dan - | ger | now, | and | at | our | dy - ing |
| 6. | Fa - | ther | God | with | you | and | with | the | Spi - rit |

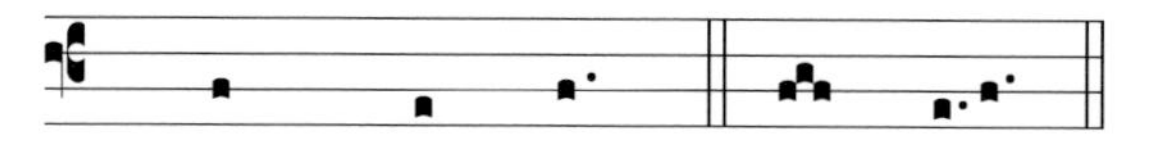

1. set man free.
2. at God's grace.
3 soon to be.
4. sin - ful ways.
5. in - ter - cede.
6. Three in One. A - men.

---

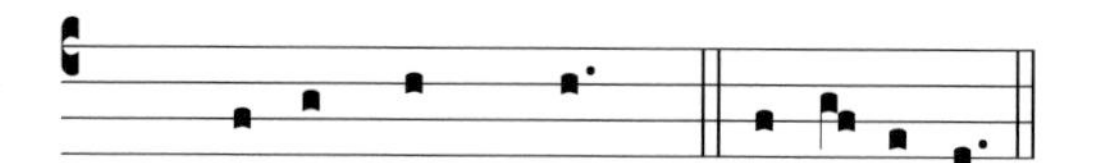

℣. Ma-ry most blessed, (Al-le-lu-ia)

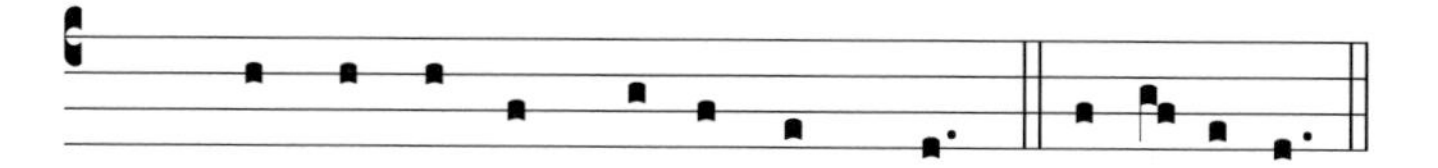

℟. Win for us the blessing of Christ. (Al-le-lu-ia)

## ANTIPHON

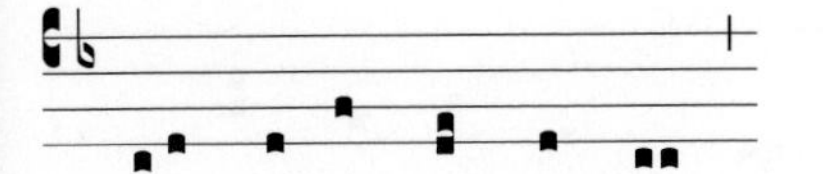

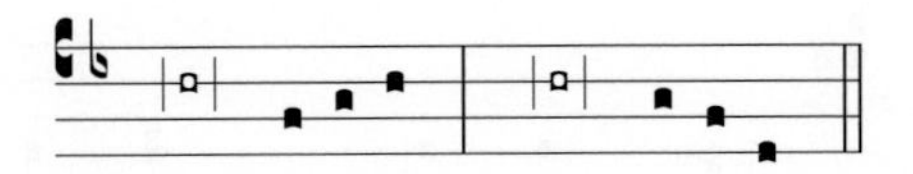

Holy Ma-ry, pray for all,

TONE I

## MAGNIFICAT *(Luke 1: 46 - 55)*

My soul glorifies the Lord,
my spirit rejoices in God,
my Saviour.

He looks on his servant in her nothingness; henceforth all ages
will call me blessed.
The Almighty works marvels for me. Holy his name!

His mercy is from age to age, on those who fear him.
He puts forth his arm in strength and scatters the proud-
hearted.

He casts the mighty from their thrones and raises the lowly.
He fills the starving with good things, sends the rich away empty.

He protects Israel, his servant, remembering his mercy,
the mercy promised to our fathers, to Abraham and his sons
for ever.

Praise the Father, the Son and the Holy Spirit,
both now and for ever, world without end.

## ANTIPHON

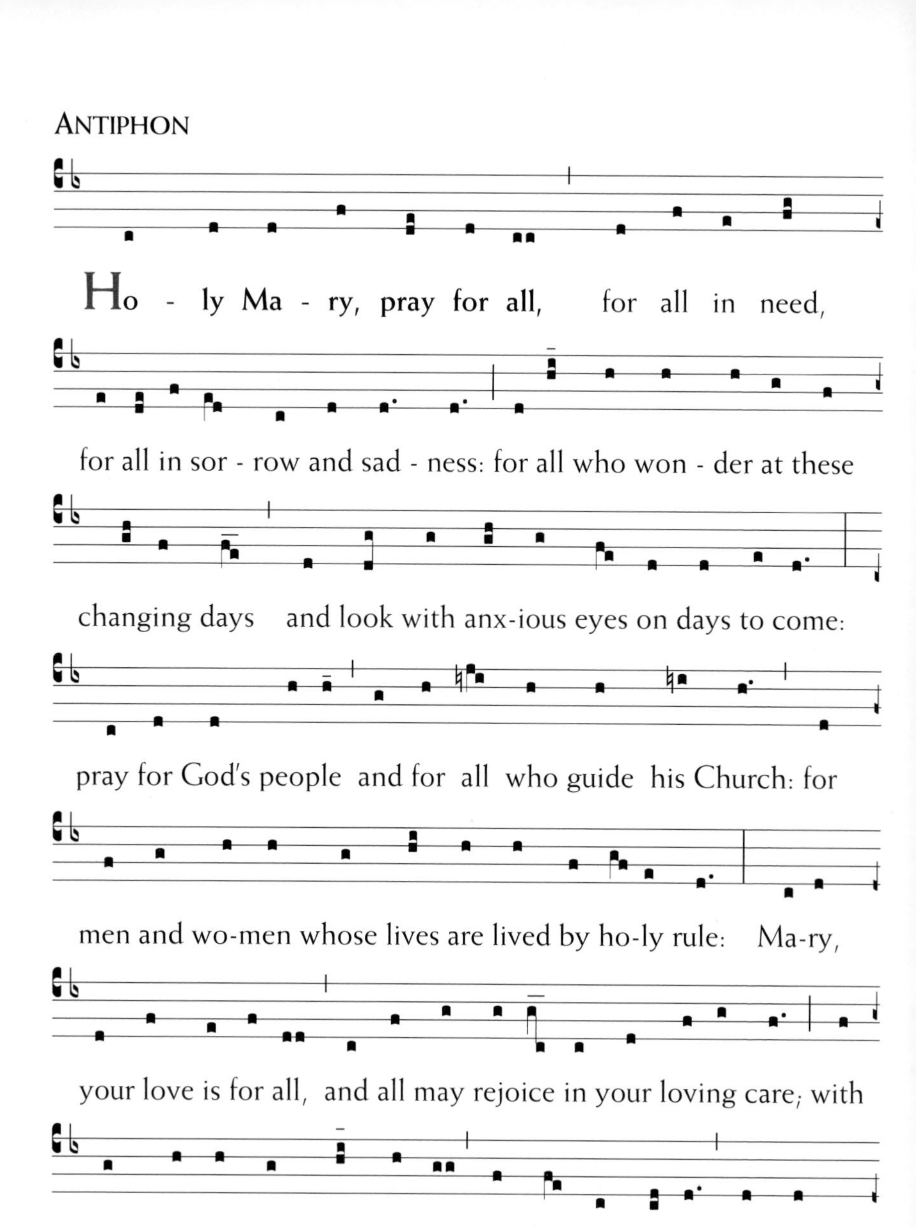
Ho - ly Ma - ry, pray for all, for all in need,
for all in sor - row and sad - ness: for all who won - der at these
changing days and look with anx-ious eyes on days to come:
pray for God's people and for all who guide his Church: for
men and wo-men whose lives are lived by ho-ly rule: Ma-ry,
your love is for all, and all may rejoice in your loving care; with
prayer to you and praise of you, the Vir-gin Ma-ry, con-ceived

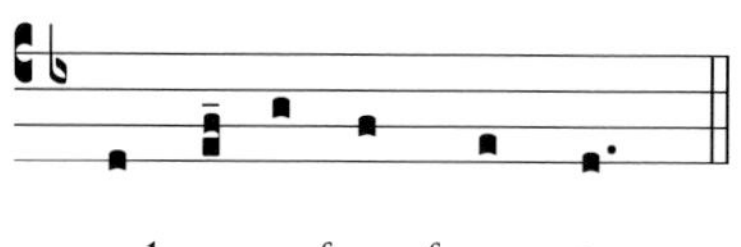
and ev-er free from sin.

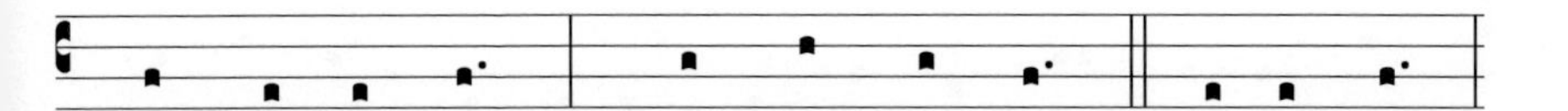

℣. Lord hear my prayer. ℟. Lord grant my prayer. ℣. Let us pray.

**PRAYER** *(page 36 - 37)*

**ANTIPHON TO ST. BRIDGET & PRAYER** *(pages 88 - 90).*

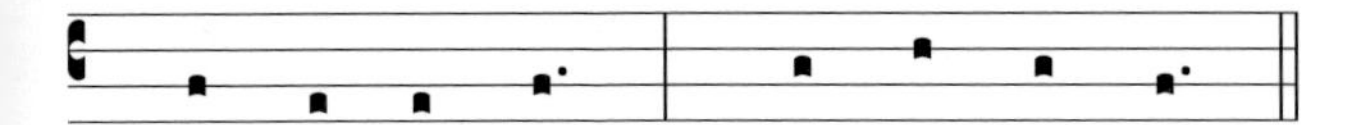

℣. Lord hear my prayer. ℟. Lord grant my prayer.

**THANKSGIVING**

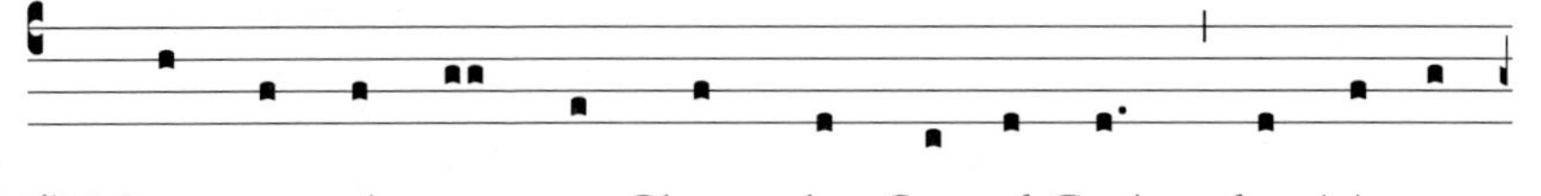

℣. Hon-our and praise to Christ the Son of God, for Ma-ry

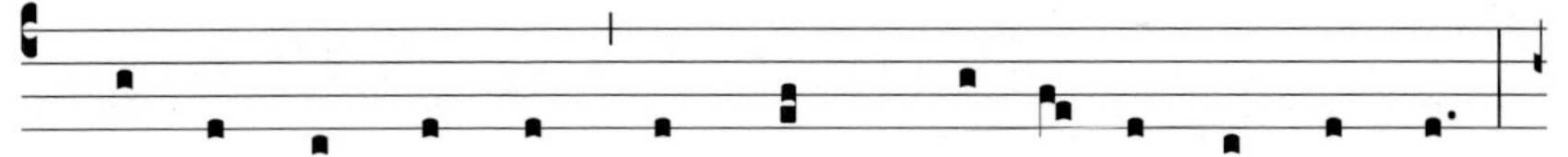

his Vir - gin Mo - ther, con - ceived and ev - er free from sin.

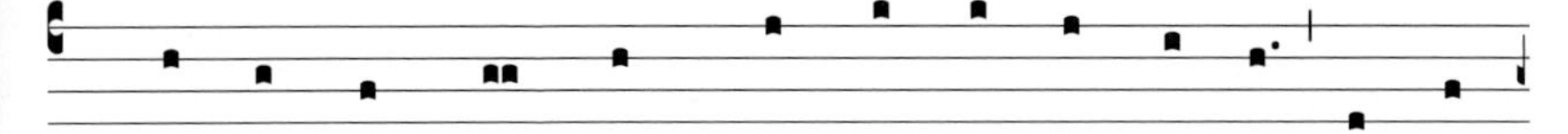

Hon-our and praise to Christ who is Lord of all, to whom

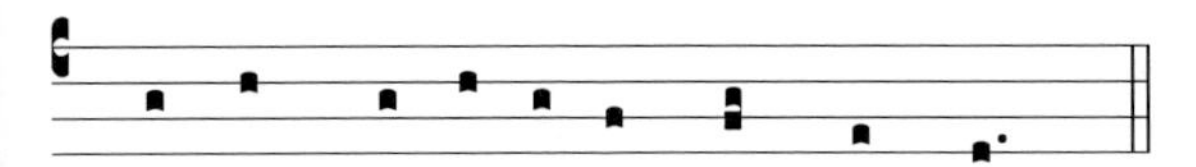

all power is giv-en in heav'n and earth.

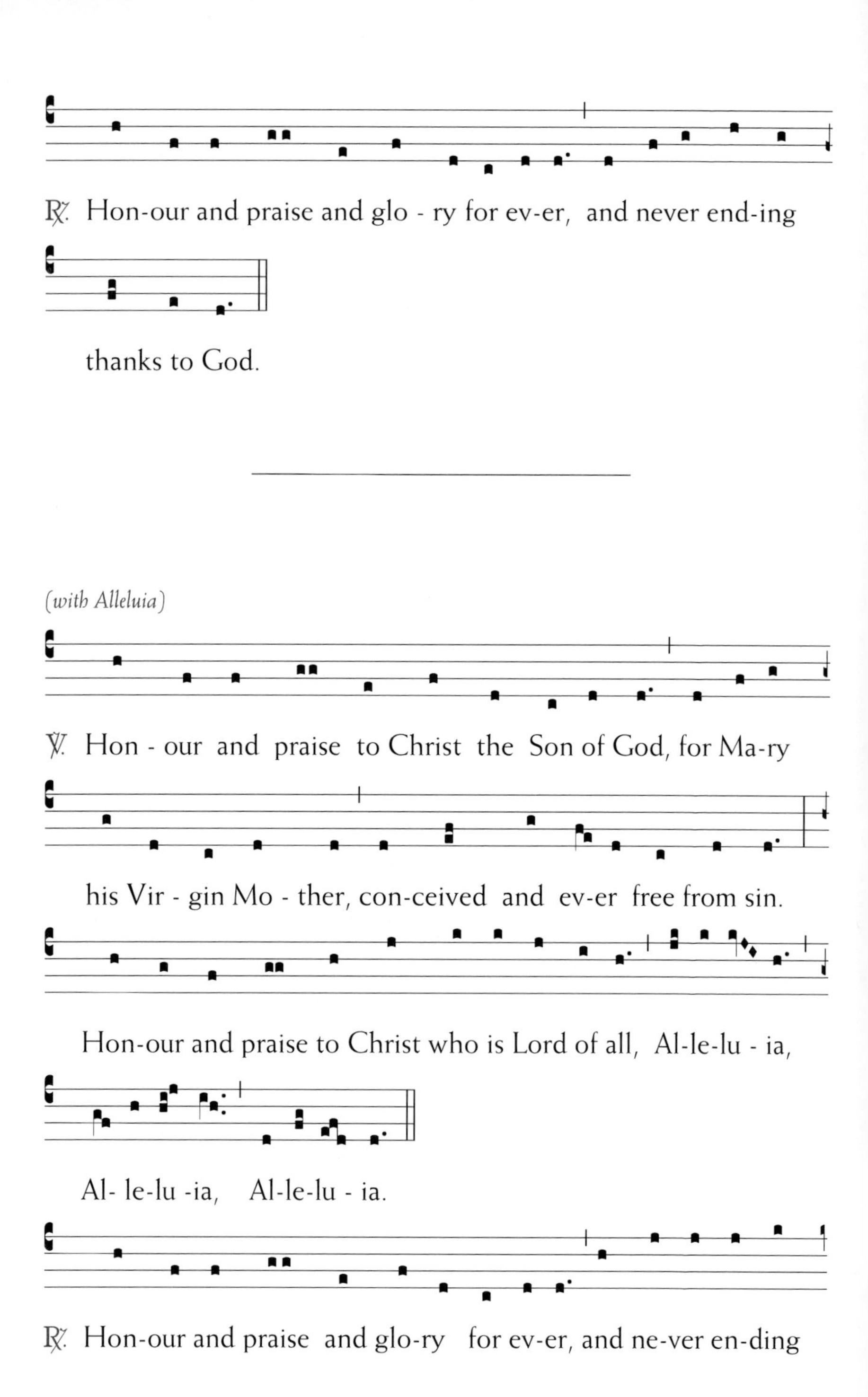
℟. Hon-our and praise and glo - ry for ev-er, and never end-ing
thanks to God.
(with Alleluia)
℣. Hon - our and praise to Christ the Son of God, for Ma-ry
his Vir - gin Mo - ther, con-ceived and ev-er free from sin.
Hon-our and praise to Christ who is Lord of all, Al-le-lu - ia,
Al- le-lu -ia, Al-le-lu - ia.
℟. Hon-our and praise and glo-ry for ev-er, and ne-ver en-ding

## Closing Prayers

'Mary, rejoice in God,' ... *with music (page 92) followed by...*

**Hymn** *to Holy Mother St. Bridget, (pages 93 - 94).*

*Tuesday*

# COMPLINE

**OPENING PRAYERS** *as before Sunday Compline, pages 95 - 96.*

**ANTIPHON**

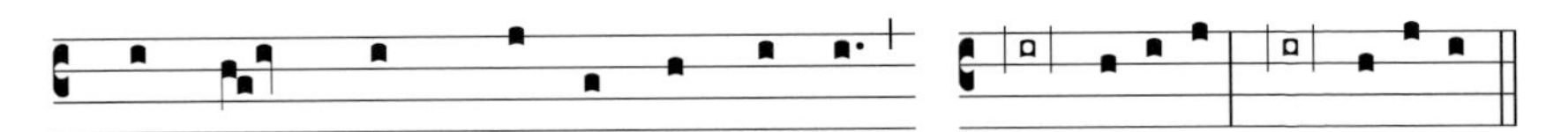

The Lord looked on her low-li-ness, TONE VII

**Psalms 131, 132 & 133** *as on Sunday, page 97 - 98.*

**ANTIPHON**

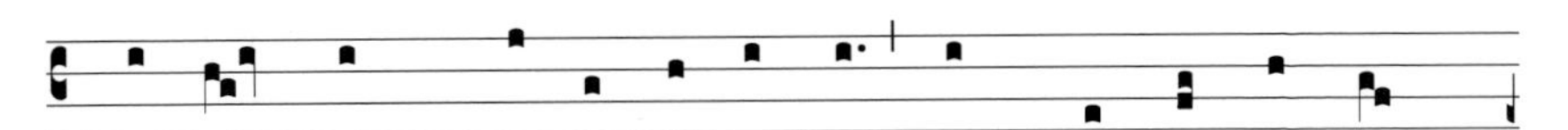

The Lord looked on her lowli-ness, looked on her and loved

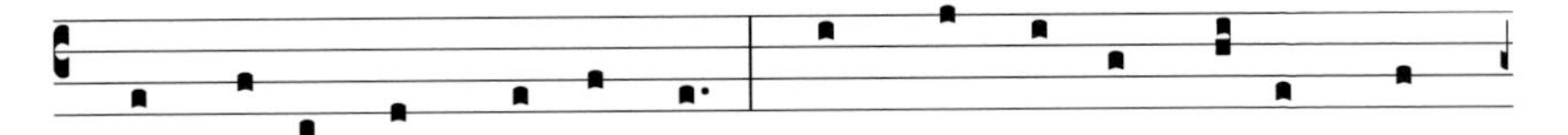

her, Ma-ry, handmaid of God. This shall be his dwelling-place,

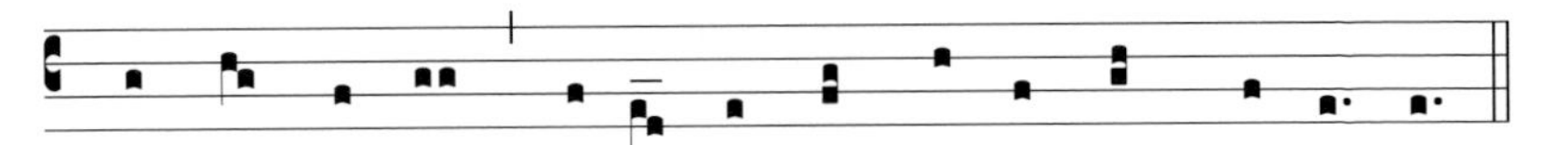

the house of God; in her the Lord will de - light for ev - er.

**READING** *as on Sunday, page 99.*

**SHORT RESPONSORY** *as on Sunday, pages 99 ff.*

Hymn

1. The tree of life God in his love pro - vi - ded
2. The hearts of pro-phets then were filled with sweet and
3. As Aa - ron's rod sent forth its bud, this mai - den
4. O Je - sus, you the ve - ry truth, stay with us
5. Pray Ma - ry Mo - ther full of grace, pray in your
6. Christ Son of God, we pray to you, and ho - nour

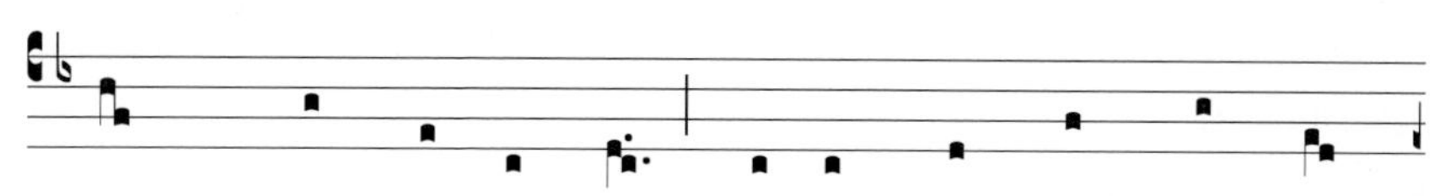

1. for the hu-man race, the en - e - my by ly-
2. sac - red flame to tell the mar - vel that was yet
3. should bring forth a fruit, and he would bring a draught
4. now and e - ver-more, lest that same fierce and ly-
5. love for all we need, pro-tect us from all dan -
6. you the Vir- gin's Son; we praise the Fa - ther, God,

1. ing words spread dead-ly poi - son in its place.
2. to come, a Vir - gin who would all ex - cel.
3. of life to those the e - ne - my had hurt.
4. ing foe en - snare us by his craf - ty lore.
5. ger now and at our dy - ing in - ter - cede.
6. with you and with the Spi - rit, Three in One. A-men.

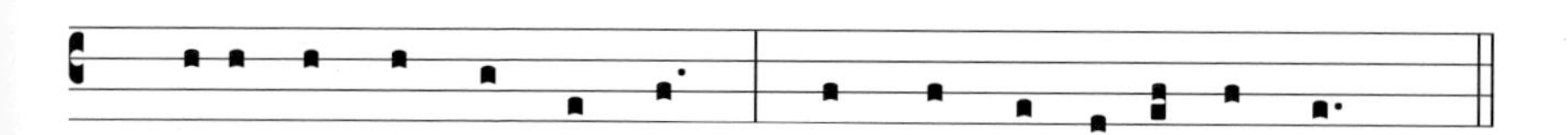

℣. I am the ser-vant of God, ℟. To hear and o-bey his word.

*(with Alleluia)*

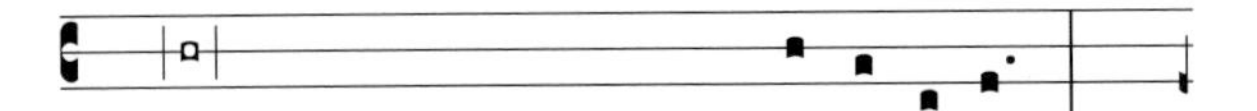

℣. I am the servant of God, Al-le-lu-ia.

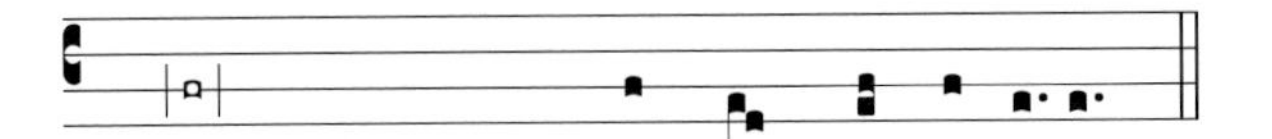

℟. To hear and obey his word, Al -le-lu-ia.

## ANTIPHON

**Like the morn-ing star,** TONE III

## CANTICLE OF SIMEON *(Luke 2: 29 - 32)*

At last, all powerful Master you give leave
to your servant to go in peace,
according to your promise.

For my eyes have seen your salvation which you have prepared
for all nations.
The light to enlighten the gentiles and give glory to Israel, your people.

Give praise to the Father Almighty: to his Son, Jesus Christ, the Lord;
to the Spirit who dwells in our hearts, both now and forever. Amen.

## ANTIPHON

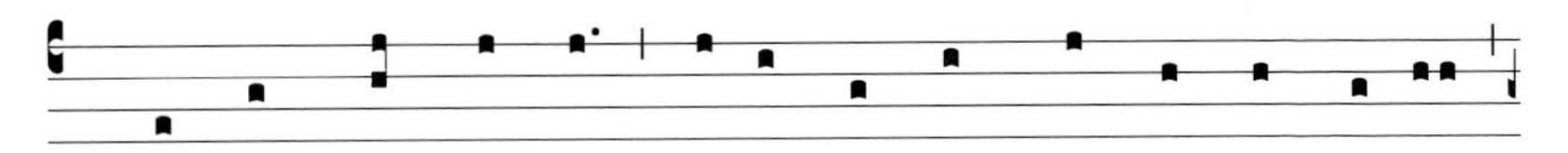

**Like the morn-ing star**, Ma-ry, you her - ald the dawn of day,

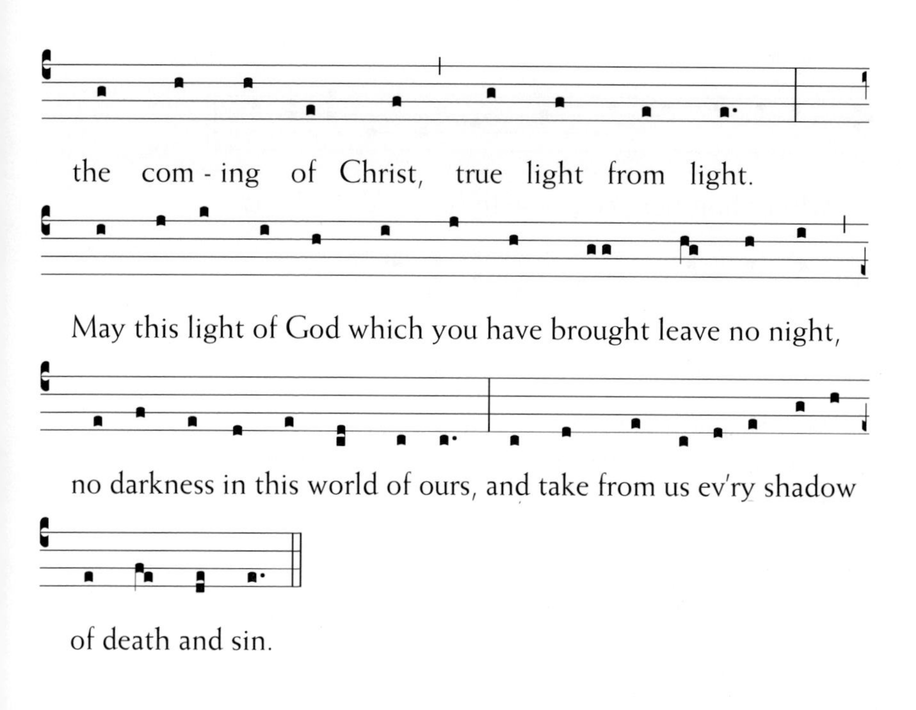


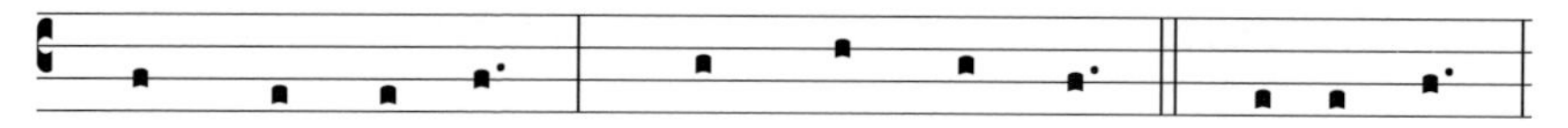

℣. Lord, hear my prayer. ℟. Lord, grant my prayer. ℣. Let us pray.

**Prayer** *as on Sunday, page 104.*

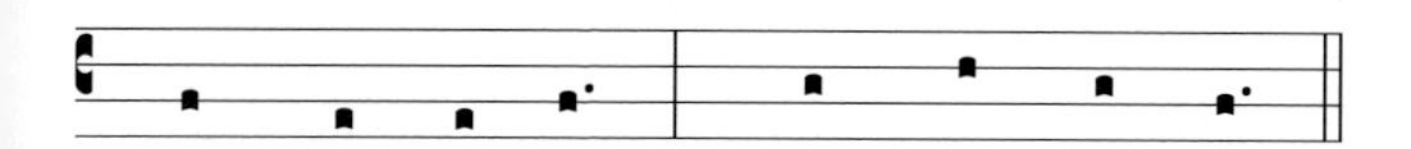

℣. Lord, hear my prayer. ℟. Lord, grant my prayer.

### Thanksgiving

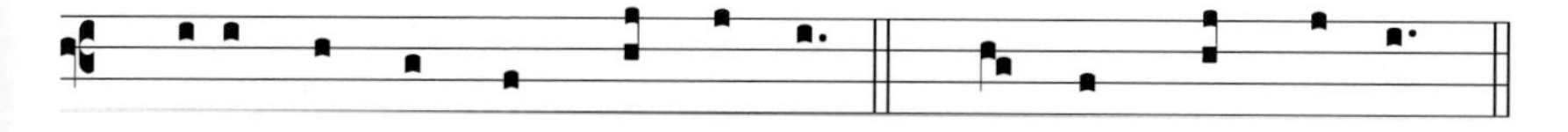

℣. Glory, hon-our and praise to God. ℟. And our thanks to him.

*(with Alleluia)*

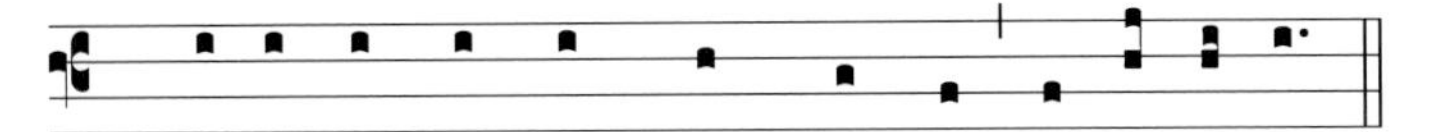

℣. Glo-ry hon-our and praise to God, Al- le- lu- ia.

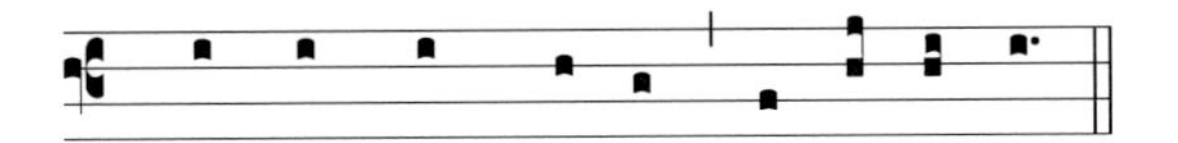

℟. And our thanks to him, Al- le- lu- ia.

℣. Mary, you are full of grace, the Lord is with you.
℟. Mary, you are most blessed of all women, for Jesus Christ is your Son. (Alleluia)

## LAUDS OF OUR LADY *(Tuesday – 'A')*

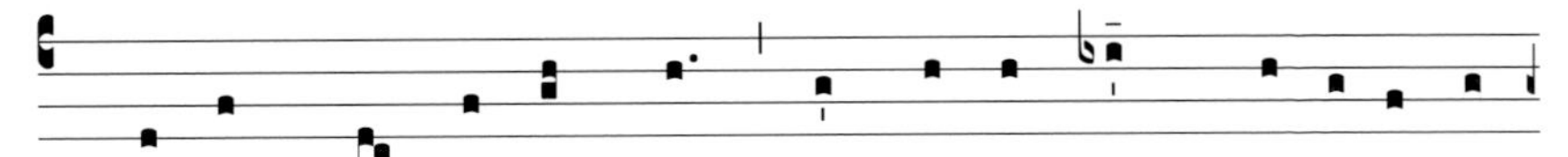

**Ma - ry, Queen of hea - ven,** Mo-ther of Christ, Cre-a-tor and

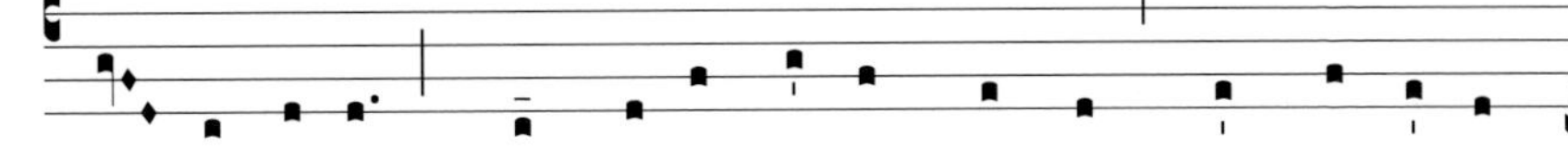

King of angels; Queen ev-er Vir-gin Mo-ther, Queen of all as

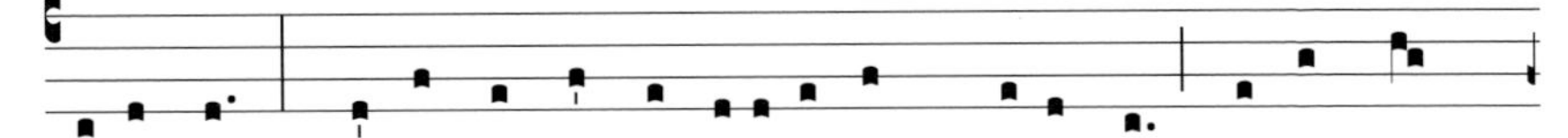

he is King. Ma-ry, no rose or lily is love - ly as you; fair-est flow'r

of God in heav'n where all are fair to see. Pray for all who pray to

live in love of Christ; pray for all who pray to find their joy in him.

## LAUDS OF OUR LADY *(Tuesday – 'B')*

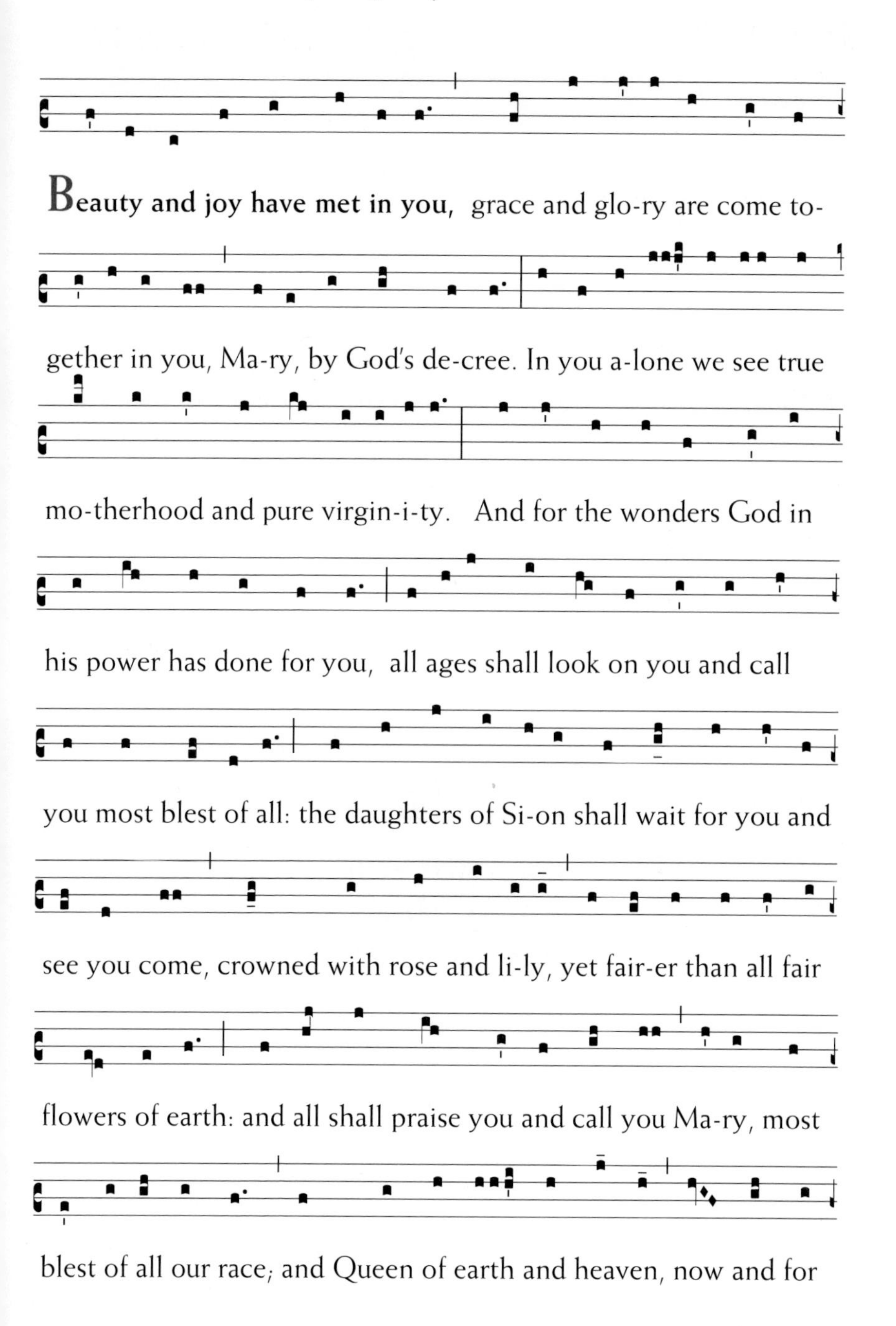

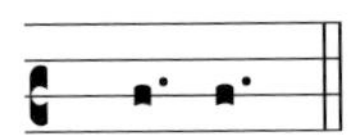

ev-er.

℣. Pray for us, holy Virgin Mary, Mother of God.
℟. That we may be made worthy of the promises of Jesus Christ.

℣. Let us pray.

## PRAYER

Forgive, we ask you Lord, the sins of your servants: and may we who of ourselves are unable to please you, be saved by the prayers of the Mother of your Son, Jesus Christ our Lord. ℟. Amen.

## CLOSING PRAYERS

'Mary, rejoice in God,' … *as on Sunday, page 107.*

*Wednesday*

# LAUDS

## OPENING PRAYERS

***(The first prayer of the day…)*** *(page 33).*
Open my mouth, O Lord … *including Invitatory psalm (Ps. 94)*

## ANTIPHON

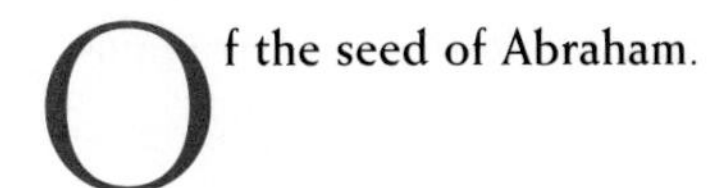


Psalms and Canticle as for Sunday Lauds *(pages 39 ff)*

**Of the seed of Abraham,** of the tribe of Judah,
of the royal house of David, the Virgin Mary is born,
to the joy of all heaven and earth.

## READING *as on Sunday, page 44.*

## HYMN

Mary, we name you by that shining star
which points the way to those who sail the sea,
for by your light we see the way to God
through life, through death, to joy eternally.

We name you with the names of fairest things,
yet earthly beauty fades before your grace;
draw us from earthly things, as God himself
was drawn to make with you his dwelling-place.

Pray Mary Virgin-Mother, … *Last two verses as on Sunday, page 44.*

℣. Mary we see you as a star of beauty, heralding the sun at dawn. (Alleluia)
℟. How lovely this morning star, in whose light all the heavens rejoice. (Alleluia)

## Antiphon

**Virgin-Mother of God**.

## Canticle

Blessed be the Lord, the God of Israel! ... *as on Sunday, page 45.*

**Virgin-Mother of God**, your birth was news of great gladness for all this world, for soon would come, by your motherhood, Christ, the Light of light, the Truth of God, and God himself; to change our evil to good, our damnation to redemption, our hate to love, our curse to blessing, and by opposing death, our death to everlasting life.

℣. Lord hear my prayer. ℟. Lord grant my prayer. ℣. Let us pray.

## Prayer

Grant us, your servants, ...
*As on Sunday page 46 or according to the time of year. See pages 36ff.*

**Antiphon** to holy Mother Saint Bridget *as on Sunday, page 46.*
Bridget, loving servant of God, ...
*or on ferial days:* Bridget, Saint and Patron, ...

℣. and ℟. with Prayer *(page 47).*

℣. Lord hear my prayer. ℟. Lord grant my prayer.

## Thanksgiving

℣. Glory, honour and praise to God, for the coming of Mary to be Mother of Christ, his Son, who is Lord of all, ruler of heaven and earth, judge over good and evil, Creator, and King for ever.
℟. Our thanks to God.
*(with Alleluia)*
℣. Glory, honour and praise to God, for the coming of Mary to be Mother of Christ, his Son. Alleluia, alleluia, alleluia.
℟. Our thanks to God. Alleluia, alleluia, alleluia.

**Closing Prayers** 'Mary, rejoice in God,' ... *(page 37).*

*Wednesday*

# TERCE

## OPENING PRAYERS

*(page 33)*

## HYMN

See how fierce flames of three-fold fire,
have wilted all fair things of earth;
see how a fountain springs on high,
and with fresh flowers the land gives birth.

O Virgin fountain of delights,
water our withered hearts and bless;
that they bedewed with heaven's grace,
may bring forth flowers of holiness.

Pray Mary Mother full of grace,
pray in your love for all we need;
protect us from all danger now,
and at our dying intercede.

Christ, Son of God, we pray to you,
and honour you, the Virgin's Son.
We praise the Father, God with you,
and with the Spirit, Three in One. Amen.

## ANTIPHON

**From a kingly line she came,**

### Psalm 63

Hear my voice, O God, as I complain, guard my life from dread of the foe.
Hide me from the band of the wicked, from the throng of those who do evil.

They sharpen their tongues like swords; they aim bitter words like arrows
to shoot at the innocent from ambush, shooting suddenly and recklessly.

They scheme their evil course; they conspire to lay secret snares.
They say: "Who will see us? Who can search out our crimes?"

He will search who searches the mind
and knows the depths of the heart.

God has shot an arrow at them and dealt them sudden wounds.
Their own tongue has brought them to ruin and all who see them mock.

Then all men will fear; they will tell what God has done.
They will understand God's deeds.

The just will rejoice in the Lord and fly to him for refuge.
All the upright hearts will glory.

*Glory be...*

**Psalm 65**

Cry out with joy to God all the earth, O sing to the glory of his name.
O render him glorious praise. Say to God: "How tremendous your deeds!

Because of the greatness of your strength your enemies cringe before you.
Before you all the earth shall bow; shall sing to you, sing to your name!"

Come and see the works of God, tremendous his deeds among men.
He turned the sea into dry land, they passed through the river dry-shod.

Let our joy then be in him; he rules for ever by his might.
His eyes keep watch over the nations: let rebels not rise against him.

O peoples, bless our God, let the voice of his praise resound,
of the God who gave life to our souls and kept our feet from stumbling.

For you, O God, have tested us, you have tried us as silver is tried:
you led us, God, into the snare; you laid a heavy burden on our backs.

You let men ride over our heads;
we went through fire and through water but then you brought us relief.

Burnt offering I bring to your house; to you I will pay my vows,
the vows which my lips have uttered, which my mouth spoke in my distress.

I will offer burnt offerings of fatlings with the smoke of burning rams.
I will offer bullocks and goats.

Come and hear, all who fear God. I will tell what he did for my soul:
to him I cried aloud, with high praise ready on my tongue.

If there had been evil in my heart, the Lord would not have listened.
But truly God has listened; he has heeded the voice of my prayer.

Blessed be God who did not reject my prayer
nor withhold his love from me.

*Glory be...*

**Psalm 67**

Let God arise, let his foes be scattered.
Let those who hate him flee before him.

As smoke is blown away so will they be blown away;
like wax that melts before the fire, so the wicked shall perish at the
presence of God.

But the just shall rejoice at the presence of God,
they shall exult and dance for joy.

O sing to the Lord, make music to his name; make a highway for him
who rides on the clouds.
Rejoice in the Lord, exult at his presence.

Father of the orphan, defender of the widow,
such is God in his holy place.

God gives the lonely a home to live in; he leads the prisoners forth
into freedom:
but rebels must dwell in a parched land.

When you went forth, O God, at the head of your people, when you marched
across the desert, the earth trembled:

the heavens melted at the presence of God, at the presence of God,
Israel's God.

You poured down, O God, a generous rain: when your people were starved
you gave them new life.
It was there that your people found a home, prepared in your goodness,
O God, for the poor.

The Lord gives the word to the bearers of good tidings: "The Almighty has
defeated a numberless army
and kings and armies are in flight, in flight while you were at rest among
the sheepfolds."

At home the women already share the spoil. They are covered with silver
as the wings of a dove,
its feathers brilliant with shining gold and jewels flashing like snow
on Mount Zalmon.

The mountains of Bashan are mighty mountains;
high-ridged mountains are the mountains of Bashan.

Why look with envy, you high-ridged mountains, at the mountain where God
has chosen to dwell?
It is there that the Lord shall dwell for ever.

The chariots of God are thousands upon thousands.
The Lord has come from Sinai to the holy place.

You have gone up on high; you have taken captives, receiving men in tribute,
O God,
even those who rebel, into your dwelling, O Lord.

May the Lord be blessed day after day.
He bears our burdens, God our saviour.

This God of ours is a God who saves. The Lord our God holds the keys
of death.
And God will smite the head of his foes, the crown of those who persist
in their sins.

The Lord said: "I will bring them back from Bashan; I will bring them back
from the depth of the sea.

Then your feet will tread in their blood and the tongues of your dogs take their share of the foe."

They see your solemn procession, O God, the procession of my God, of my king, to the sanctuary:
the singers in the forefront, the musicians coming last, between them, maidens sounding their timbrels.

"In festive gatherings, bless the Lord;
bless God, O you who are Israel's sons."

There is Benjamin, least of the tribes, at the head, Judah's princes, a mighty throng,
Zebulun's princes, Naphtali's princes.

Show forth, O God, show forth your might, your might, O God, which you have shown for us.
For the sake of your temple high in Jerusalem may kings come to you bringing their tribute.

Threaten the wild beast that dwells in the reeds,
the bands of the mighty and lords of the peoples.

Let them bow down offering silver. Scatter the peoples who delight in war.
Princes will make their way from Egypt: Ethiopia will stretch out her hands to God.

Kingdoms of the earth, sing to God, praise the Lord who rides on the heavens, the ancient heavens.
He thunders his voice, his mighty voice. Come, acknowledge the power of God.

His glory is over Israel; his might is in the skies.
God is to be feared in his holy place.

He is the Lord, Israel's God. He gives strength and power to his people.
Blessed be God!

*Glory be...*

## Antiphon

**From a kingly line she came**, Mary, truly a Queen,
our joy to think of, our happiness to love,
our sure help to pray to.

## Reading *(Eccles. 24: 9)*

In the eternal decree of God, I was present before his creating, and I shall be for ever with him, in the holiness of his heaven. ℟. Our thanks to God.

## Short Responsory

℣. By eternal decree, Mary is Mother of God. (Alleluia, Alleluia) ℟. *Repeat.*
℣. If we would measure the love of her heart, say only
℟. Mary is Mother of God. († ℟. Alleluia, Alleluia)
℣. Glory to God, Father, Son and Holy Spirit.
℟. By eternal decree, Mary is Mother of God. (Alleluia, Alleluia)
℣. The prophets of God made known to us (Alleluia)
℟. The Virgin who would come of a kingly line. (Alleluia)

## Closing Prayers *(page 38)*.

---

† ***Response during Easter and on other special days where shown, as well as in brackets thus: (Alleluia). For style, see Sunday Terce** on page 51.*

# SEXT

## OPENING PRAYERS *(page 33).*

## HYMN

See how fierce flames of three-fold fire... *as at Wednesday Terce, page 203.*

## ANTIPHON

**Glory, glory to Christ.**

**Psalm 72**

How good God is to Israel, to those who are pure of heart.
Yet my feet came close to stumbling, my steps had almost slipped

for I was filled with envy of the proud when I saw how the wicked prosper.
For them there are no pains; their bodies are sound and sleek.

They have no share in men's sorrows; they are not stricken like others.
So they wear their pride like a necklace, they clothe themselves with violence.

Their hearts overflow with malice, their minds seethe with plots.
They scoff; they speak with malice; from on high they plan oppression.

They have set their mouths in the heavens and their tongues dictate
to the earth.
So the people turn to follow them and drink in all their words.

They say: "How can God know? Does the Most High take any notice?"
Look at them, such are the wicked, but untroubled, they grow in wealth.

How useless to keep my heart pure and wash my hands in innocence,
when I was stricken all day long, suffered punishment day after day.

Then I said: "If I should speak like that,
I should betray the race of your sons."

I strove to fathom this problem, too hard for my mind to understand,
until I pierced the mysteries of God and understood what becomes
of the wicked.

How slippery the paths on which you set them; you make them slide
to destruction.
How suddenly they come to their ruin, wiped out, destroyed by terrors.

Like a dream one wakes from, O Lord,
when you wake you dismiss them as phantoms.

And so when my heart grew embittered and when I was cut to the quick,
I was stupid and did not understand, no better than a beast in your sight.

Yet I was always in your presence; you were holding me by my right hand.
You will guide me by your counsel and so you will lead me to glory.

What else have I in heaven but you? Apart from you I want nothing on earth.
My body and my heart faint for joy; God is my possession for ever.

All those who abandon you shall perish; you will destroy all those
who are faithless.
To be near God is my happiness. I have made the Lord God my refuge.

I will tell of your works
at the gates of the city of Sion.

*Glory be...*

**Psalm 73**

Why, O God, have you cast us off for ever?
Why blaze with anger against the sheep of your pasture?

Remember your people whom who chose long ago,
the tribe you redeemed to be your own possession, the mountain of Sion
where you made your dwelling.

Turn your steps to these places that are utterly ruined!

The enemy has laid waste the whole of the sanctuary.

Your foes have made uproar in your house of prayer:
they have set up their emblems, their foreign emblems, high above the entrance to the sanctuary.

Their axes have battered the wood of its doors. They have struck together with hatchet and pickaxe.
O God, they have set your sanctuary on fire: they have razed and profaned the place where you dwell.

They said in their hearts: "Let us utterly crush them: let us burn every shrine of God in the land."
There is no sign from God, nor have we a prophet, we have no one to tell us how long it will last.

How long, O God, is the enemy to scoff? Is the foe to insult your name for ever?
Why, O Lord, do you hold back your hand? Why do you keep your right hand hidden?

Yet God is our king from time past, the giver of help through all the land.
It was you who divided the sea by your might, who shattered the heads of the monsters in the sea.

It was you who crushed Leviathan's heads and gave him as food to the untamed beasts.
It was you who opened springs and torrents; it was you who dried up ever-flowing rivers.

Yours is the day and yours is the night. It was you who appointed the light and the sun:
it was you who fixed the bounds of the earth: you who made both summer and winter.

Remember this, Lord, and see the enemy scoffing; a senseless people insults your name.
Do not give Israel, your dove, to the hawk nor forget the life of your poor servants for ever.

Remember your covenant; every cave in the land is a place where violence makes its home.

Do not let the oppressed return disappointed; let the poor and the needy
bless your name.

Arise, O God, and defend your cause! Remember how the senseless revile
you all the day.
Do not forget the clamour of your foes, the daily increasing uproar of
your foes.

*Glory be...*

**Psalm 74**

We give thanks to you, O God, we give thanks and call upon your name.
We recount your wonderful deeds.

"When I reach the appointed time, then I will judge with justice.
Though the earth and all who dwell in it may rock, it is I who uphold
its pillars.

I say to the boastful: 'Do not boast,' to the wicked: 'Do not flaunt
your strength,
do not flaunt your strength on high. Do not speak with insolent pride.' "

For neither from the east nor from the west, nor from desert or mountains
comes judgment,
but God himself is the judge. One he humbles, another he exalts.

The Lord holds a cup in his hand, full of wine, foaming and spiced.
He pours it; they drink it to the dregs: all the wicked on the earth must
drain it.

As for me, I will rejoice for ever and sing psalms to Jacob's God.
He shall break the power of the wicked, while the strength of the just
shall be exalted.

*Glory be...*

## Antiphon

**Glory, glory to Christ,**
for the coming of (for this feast of) Mary his Mother,
truly Mother of God.

## Reading *(Eccles. 24: 11)*

Jerusalem has been my dwelling and my resting-place:
there in the holy city, I have taken up my rule and my reign.
℟. Our thanks to God.

## Short Responsory

℣. The prophets of God made known to us the Virgin to come.
(Alleluia, Alleluia) ℟. *Repeat.*
℣. Foretelling, from the line of David
℟. The Virgin to come. († ℟. Alleluia, Alleluia)
℣. Glory to God, Father, Son and Holy Spirit.
℟. The prophets of God made known to us the Virgin to come.
(Alleluia, Alleluia)
℣. Mary, we see you as a star of beauty, heralding the sun at dawn. (Alleluia)
℟. How lovely this morning star, in whose light all the heavens rejoice.
(Alleluia)

*NOTE: If continuing immediately with None, omit the Opening Prayers and Hymn for None and start with the (short) Antiphon before the Psalms: as detailed in the Structure,* *page 26.*

## Closing Prayers *(page 38).*

---

† ***Response during Easter and on other special days where shown, as well as in brackets thus: (Alleluia). For style, see Sunday Terce on page 51.***

*Wednesday*

# NONE

**OPENING PRAYERS** *as before Sunday None,* *pages 55 - 56.*

## HYMN

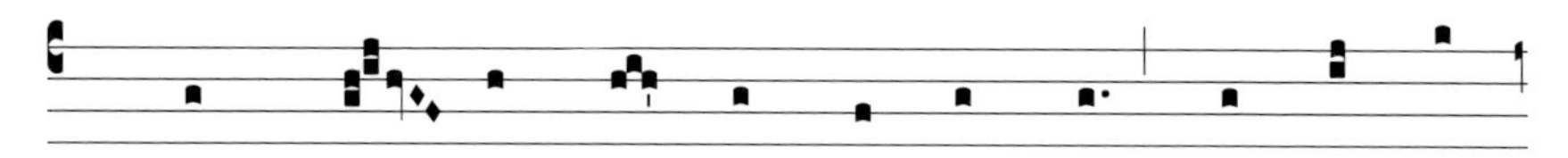

1. See how fierce flames of three-fold fire, have wil - ted
2. O vir - gin fount-ain of de- lights, wa - ter our
3. Pray Ma - ry Mo- ther full of grace, pray in your
4. Christ Son of God we pray to you, and hon - our

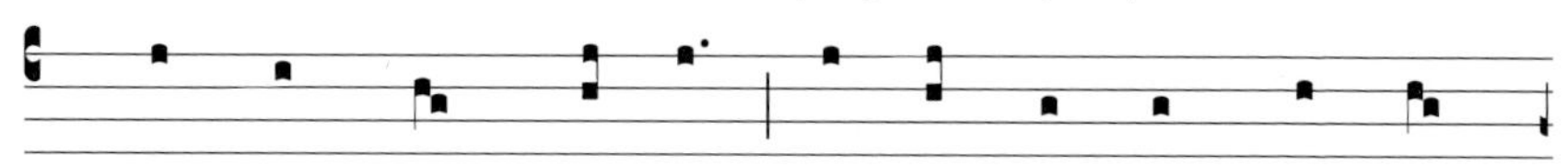

1. all fair things of earth; see how a fount - ain springs
2. with-ered hearts and bless; that they be-dewed with hea-
3. love for all we need, pro-tect us from all dan-
4. you, the Vir - gin's Son; we praise the Fa - ther, God

1. on high, and with fresh flowers the land gives birth.
2. ven's grace, may bring forth flowers of ho - li - ness.
3 ger now and at our dy - ing in - ter - cede.
4. with you and with the Spi - rit, Three in One.

4. A - men.

ANTIPHON

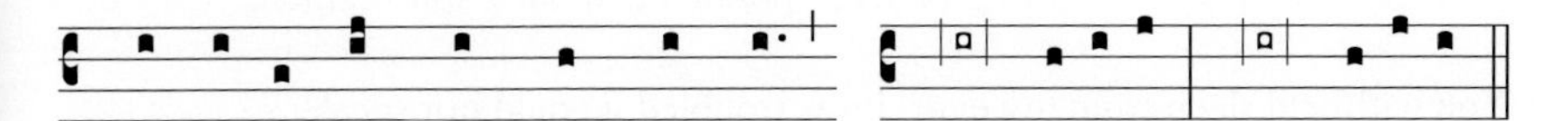

Ma-ry, in you God took de-light TONE VII

**Psalm 75**

God, is made known in Judah; in Israel his name is great.
He set up his tent in Jerusalem and his dwelling place in Sion.

It was there he broke the flashing arrows, the shield, the sword, the armour.
You Lord, are resplendent, more majestic than the everlasting mountains.

The warriors, despoiled, slept in death; the hands of the soldiers
were powerless.
At your threat, O God of Jacob, horse and rider lay stunned.

You, you alone, strike terror.
Who shall stand when your anger is roused?

You uttered your sentence from the heavens; the earth in terror was still
when God arose to judge, to save the humble of the earth.

Men's anger will serve to praise you;
its survivors surround you with joy.

Make vows to your God and fulfill them. Let all pay tribute to him
who strikes terror,
who cuts short the breath of princes, who strikes terror in the kings
of the earth.

*Glory be...*

**Psalm 76**

I cry aloud to God, cry aloud to God that he may hear me.
In the day of my distress I sought the Lord.

My hands were raised at night without ceasing; my soul refused to be consoled.
I remembered my God and I groaned. I pondered and my spirit fainted.

You withheld sleep from my eyes. I was troubled, I could not speak.
I thought of the days of long ago and remembered the years long past.

At night I mused within my heart. I pondered and my spirit questioned.
"Will the Lord reject us for ever? Will he show us his favour no more?

Has his love vanished for ever? Has his promise come to an end?
Does God forget his mercy or in anger withhold his compassion?"

I said: "This is what causes my grief; that the way of the Most High
has changed."
I remember the deeds of the Lord, I remember your wonders of old,

I muse on all your works and ponder your mighty deeds.
Your ways, O God, are holy. What god is great as our God?

You are the God who works wonders. You showed your power among
the peoples.
Your strong arm redeemed your people, the sons of Jacob and Joseph.

The waters saw you, O God,
the waters saw you and trembled; the depths were moved with terror.

The clouds poured down rain, the skies sent forth their voice;
your arrows flashed to and fro.

Your thunder rolled round the sky,
your flashes lighted up the world.

The earth was moved and trembled when your way led through the sea,
your path through the mighty waters and no one saw your footprints.

You guided your people like a flock
by the hand of Moses and Aaron.

*Glory be...*

**Psalm 78**

O God, the nations have invaded your land, they have profaned
your holy temple.
They have made Jerusalem a heap of ruins.

They have handed over the bodies of your servants as food to feed
the birds of heaven
and the flesh of your faithful to the beasts of the earth.

They have poured out blood like water in Jerusalem; no one is left to
bury the dead.
We have become the taunt of our neighbours, the mockery and scorn
of those who surround us.

How long, O Lord? Will you be angry for ever; how long will your anger
burn like fire?
Pour out your rage on the nations, the nations that do not know you.

Pour out your rage on the kingdoms that do not call on your name,
for they have devoured Jacob and laid waste the land where he dwells.

Do not hold the guilt of our fathers against us.
Let your compassion hasten to meet us; for we are in the depths of distress.

O God our saviour, come to our help, come for the sake of the glory
of your name.
O Lord our God, forgive us our sins; rescue us for the sake of your name.

Why should the nations say: "Where is their God?"
Let us see the nations around us repaid with vengeance for the blood
of your servants that was shed!

Let the groans of the prisoners come before you; let your strong arm
reprieve those condemned to die.
Pay back to our neighbours seven times over the taunts with which
they taunted you, O Lord.

But we, your people, the flock of your pasture, will give you thanks for
ever and ever.
We will tell your praise from age to age.

*Glory be...*

## ANTIPHON

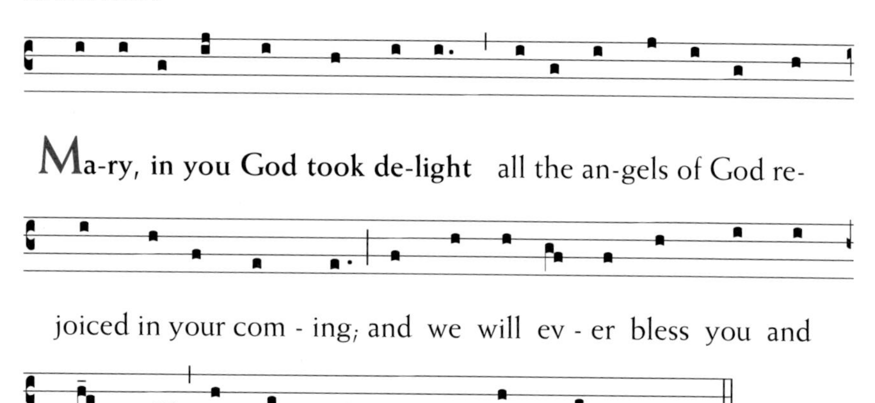


praise you, and name you Ma-ry most blessed of all.

## READING *(Eccles. 24: 12)*

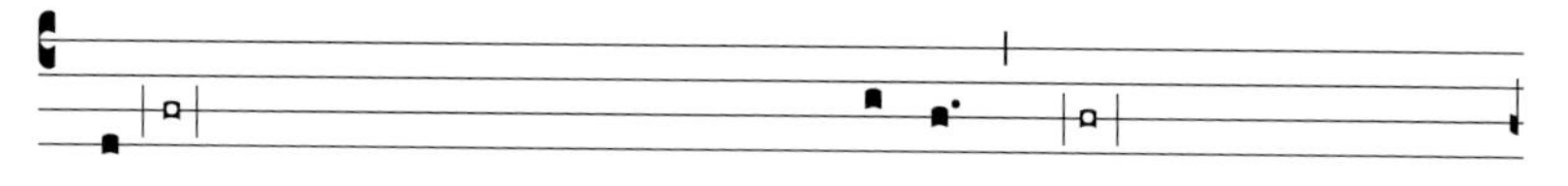

I have grown up among God's people: I will live for ever

in the land of the Lord. ℟. Our thanks to God.

## SHORT RESPONSORY

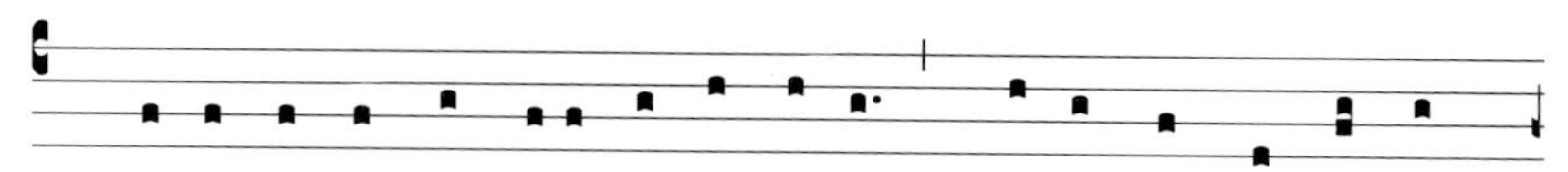

℣. Ma-ry we see you as a star of beauty, herald-ing the sun at

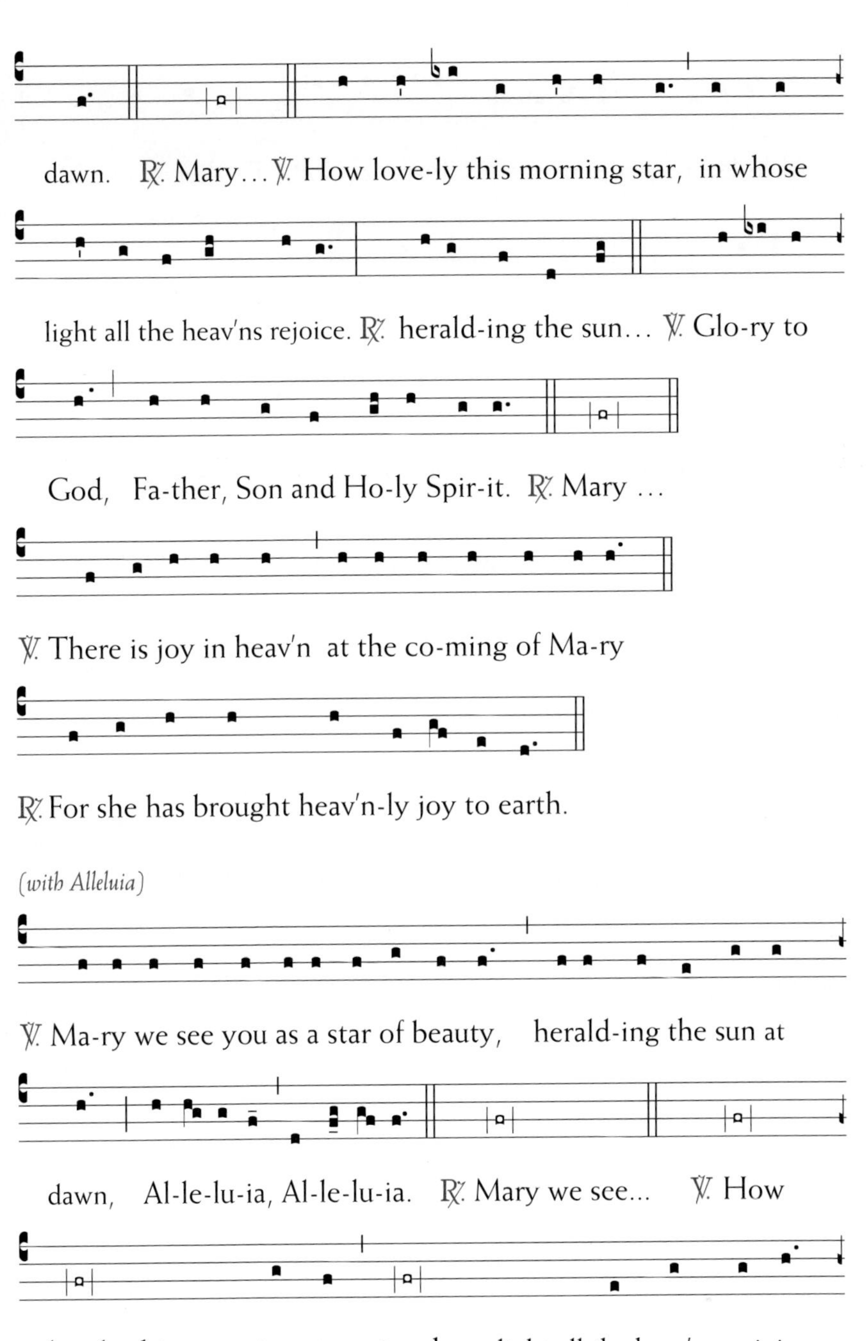
dawn. ℟. Mary… ℣. How love-ly this morning star, in whose
light all the heav'ns rejoice. ℟. herald-ing the sun… ℣. Glo-ry to
God, Fa-ther, Son and Ho-ly Spir-it. ℟. Mary …
℣. There is joy in heav'n at the co-ming of Ma-ry
℟. For she has brought heav'n-ly joy to earth.
(with Alleluia)
℣. Ma-ry we see you as a star of beauty, herald-ing the sun at
dawn, Al-le-lu-ia, Al-le-lu-ia. ℟. Mary we see... ℣. How
lovely this morn-ing star, in whose light all the heav'ns re-joice.

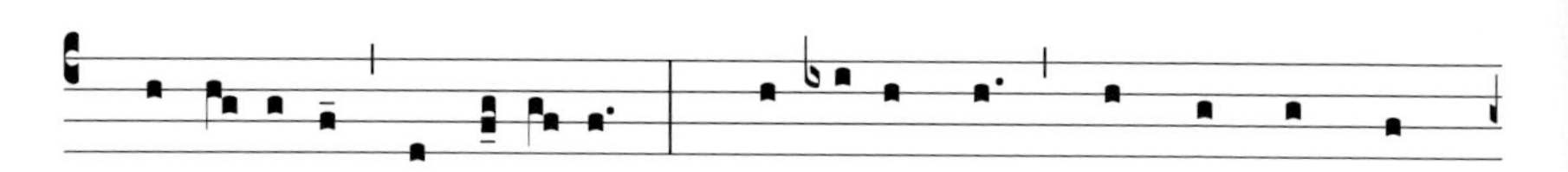

Al-le-lu-ia, Al-le-lu –ia. ℣. Glo-ry to God, Fa-ther, Son and

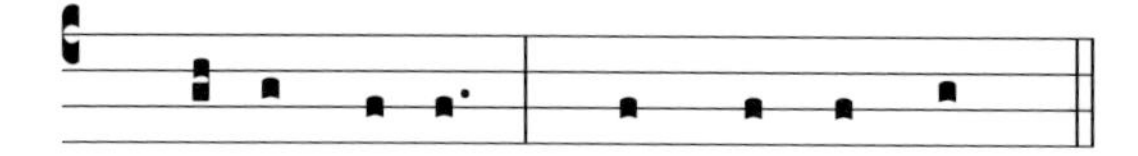

Ho-ly Spir-it. ℟. Mary we see you…

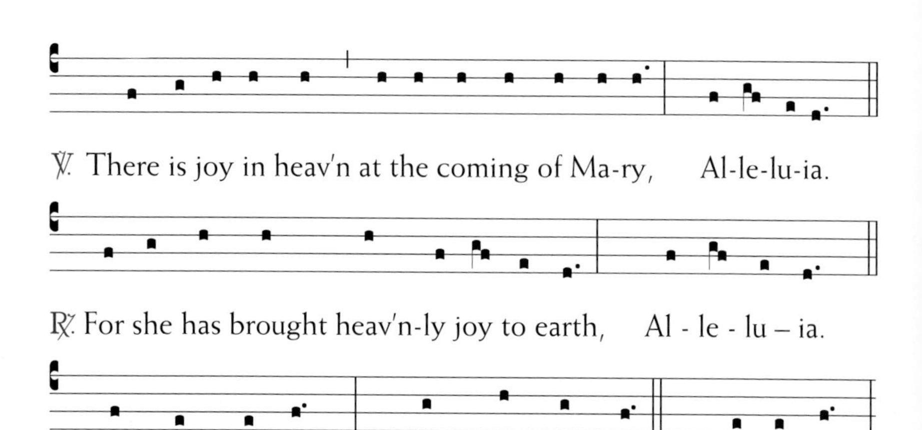


℣. Lord, hear my prayer. ℟. Lord, grant my prayer. ℣. Let us pray.

**Prayer** *(pages 36 - 37)*

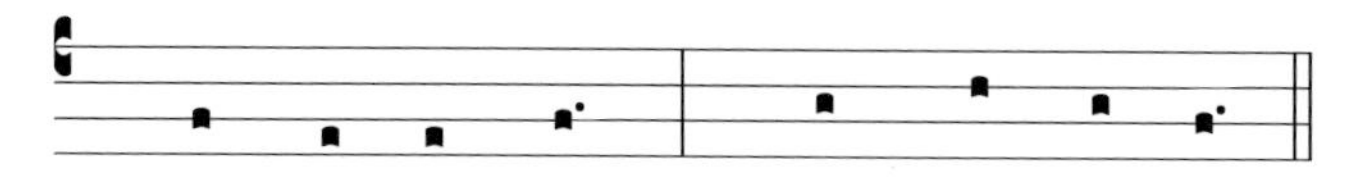

℣. Lord, hear my prayer. ℟. Lord, grant my prayer.

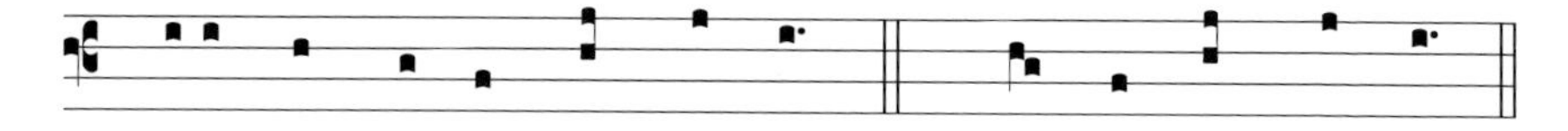

℣. Glory hon-our and praise to God. ℟. And our thanks to him.

*(with Alleluia)*

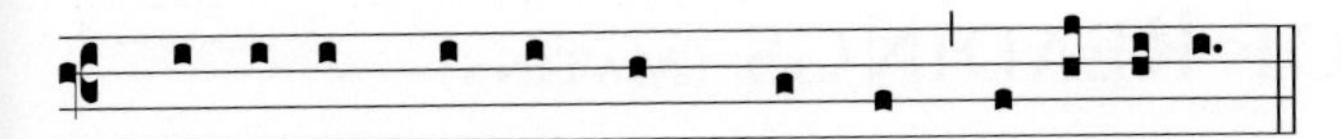

℣. Glory hon-our and praise to God, Al-le-lu-ia.

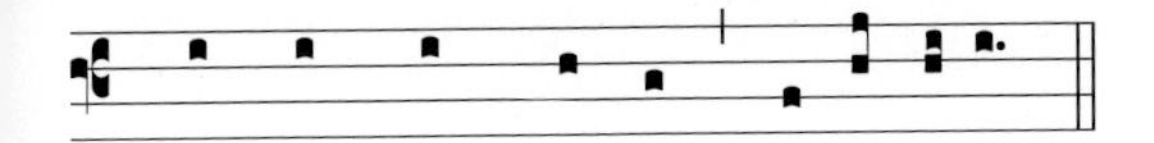

℟. And our thanks to him, Al-le-lu-ia.

## Closing Prayers

'Mary, rejoice...' *as on Sunday, pages 64ff.*

**Lauds of Our Lady** *of the day, season or feast. (See daily after Compline)* *With* ℣. & ℟. *and Prayer. Then* 'May the souls of our founders...' *and...*

**Psalm 129** 'Out of the depths...' *and two or three memorial prayers for the souls of the departed, as on Sunday, page 65 - 66.*

# OFFICE OF READINGS (MATINS)

## OPENING PRAYERS *(page 67)*.

## HYMN

Like light to darkness, like the day to night,
unlooked-for hope for man's despairing mind,
Mary came forth, with news of joy for all –
new life, new grace, which all could hope to find.

Like purest crystal filled with purest light,
Mary came forth in holiness, to bring
an end to man's long darkness and despair,
bearing to man his Saviour and his King.

Pray Mary Virgin-Mother full of grace,
pray in your love for all, for all we need;
protect us from all sin and sinful ways,
and at our dying hour intercede.

Christ Jesus, Son of God, we pray to you
and praise you, naming you the Virgin's Son;
we ever praise the Father, God with you
and with the Holy Spirit, Three in One. Amen.

## ANTIPHON 1

Virgin Mary.

### Psalm 52

The fool has said in his heart: "There is no God above."
Their deeds are corrupt, depraved, not a good man is left.

God looks down from heaven on the sons of men,
to see if any are wise, if any seek God.

All have left the right path; depraved, every one.
There is not a good man left, no, not even one.

Will the evil-doers not understand?
They eat up my people as though they were eating bread; they never
pray to God.

See how they tremble with fear without cause for fear:
for God scatters the bones of the wicked. They are shamed, rejected by God.

O that Israel's salvation might come from Sion!
When God delivers his people from bondage, then Jacob will be glad
and Israel rejoice.

*Glory be...*

## ANTIPHON 1

**Virgin Mary,** take from our hearts all attachment to foolish things;
make us wise as you were wise,
seeking ever the will of Christ in the ways of Christ.

## ANTIPHON 2

**Mary, let no evil come near us.**

### Psalm 54

O God, listen to my prayer, do not hide from my pleading,
attend to me and reply; with my cares, I cannot rest.

I tremble at the shouts of the foe, at the cries of the wicked;
for they bring down evil upon me. They assail me with fury.

My heart is stricken within me, death's terror is on me,
trembling and fear fall upon me and horror overwhelms me.

O that I had wings like a dove to fly away and be at rest.
So I would escape far away and take refuge in the desert.

I would hasten to find a shelter from the raging wind,
from the destructive storm, O Lord, and from their plotting tongues.

For I can see nothing but violence and strife in the city.
Night and day they patrol high on the city walls.

It is full of wickedness and evil; it is full of sin.
Its streets are never free from tyranny and deceit.

If this had been done by an enemy I could bear his taunts.
If a rival had risen against me, I could hide from him.

But it is you, my own companion, my intimate friend!
(How close was the friendship between us).

We walked together in harmony
in the house of God.

May death fall suddenly upon them! Let them go to the grave:
for wickedness dwells in their homes and deep in their hearts.

As for me, I will cry to God and the Lord will save me.
Evening, morning and at noon I will cry and lament.

He will deliver my soul in peace in the attack against me:
for those who fight me are many, but he hears my voice.

God will hear and will humble them, the eternal judge:
for they will not amend their ways. They have no fear of God.

The traitor has turned against his friends;
he has broken his word.

His speech is softer than butter, but war is in his heart.
His words are smoother than oil, but they are naked swords.

Entrust your cares to the Lord and he will support you.
He will never allow the just man to stumble.

But you, O God, will bring them down
to the pit of death.

Deceitful and bloodthirsty men shall not live half their days.
O Lord, I will trust in you.

*Glory be...*

## ANTIPHON 2

M**ary, let no evil come near us**; let nothing sinful enter in.
We are safe in your care,
and unafraid when we pray to you.

## ANTIPHON 3

T**he grace and holiness of Mary.**

### Psalm 55

Have mercy on me, God, men crush me; they fight me all day long
and oppress me.
My foes crush me all day long, for many fight proudly against me.

When I fear I will trust in you, in God, whose word I praise.
In God I trust, I shall not fear: what can mortal man do to me?

All day long they distort my words, all their thought is to harm me.
They band together in ambush, track me down and seek my life.

Repay them, God, for their crimes;
in your anger, cast down the peoples.

You have kept an account of my wanderings; you have kept a record
of my tears;
(are they not written in your book?)

Then my foes will be put to flight on the day that I call to you.
This I know, that God is on my side.

In God, whose word I praise, in the Lord, whose word I praise,
in God I trust; I shall not fear: what can mortal man do to me?

I am bound by the vows I have made you. O God, I will offer you praise
for you rescued my soul from death, you kept my feet from stumbling

that I may walk in the presence of God
in the light of the living.

*Glory be...*

## ANTIPHON 3

**The grace and holiness of Mary,** which fitted her to be Mother of God,
can rescue us from death, and lead us back from sinful paths
into the light and life of God.

℣. By eternal decree, Mary is Mother of God. (Alleluia)
℟. And only he can know how great her love. (Alleluia)

Our Father ...

## ABSOLUTION

God and father, holy and merciful Lord, take into account the prayer and holiness of Mary, the Virgin-Mother of God, and of all the saints and bring us back from death to life. ℟. Amen.

*Reader:* Lord, we ask for your blessing.

**Week One**
*Blessing, Reading and Response for Wednesdays in Week Two start on page 517, and for Week Three on page 536.*

## BLESSING

May Mary, the Virgin-Mother, come as light to the darkness of our minds, to make us wise as she is wise. ℟. Amen.

## Reading

Before God made known his law to Moses,
man had to live without a rule of life.
Those who loved God, did what they thought was God's will.
Those who rejected his love, and did not fear to do so,
acted as they chose.
To dispel their ignorance,
God in his goodness made known his law,
teaching first the love of God,
then love for others,
then his will concerning marriage,
its holiness and binding force,
its purpose in his plan, the growth of his people.

The union of man and woman in a holy marriage was most pleasing to God,
for he willed to choose the child of such a union
as the Mother of Christ.

The eagle, flying above the earth, looks down at the trees,
and choosing with its sharp eyes the tallest tree,
one firmly rooted to withstand the storms,
one that cannot be climbed,
one that nothing can fall on,
builds there its nest.
God sees, with penetrating gaze, all things, both present and future.

He looked therefore among all men and women,
from the beginning to the end of time,
for a husband and wife fit for the bearing of the child of his choice.
He found none so worthy as Joachim and Anne,
who lived together in holiness
and a love for each other born of their love for him.
It was to them he entrusted the one who was to be Mother of his Son.
She was to be, as it were, the eagle's nest,
in which he could find protection and shelter.
Joachim and Anne were the tall tree in which this nest would be built,
firmly rooted in a union based on the love and honour of God;
the branches of this tree their lifelong thought for the will of God,
and their desire for a child, not for their own sake,
but to beget one who would grow to love God and serve him
as they themselves did.

The tallness of this tree,
beyond the reach of the winds, and higher than all around,
was the height of holiness which Joachim and Anne had attained,
beyond the attacks of Satan,
untroubled, except by the thought that God's honour
was many times assailed by the sins of many,
with no thought of honour or worldly possessions,
no pride or ambition to move them from their selfless love of God.

God knew that for the birth of the Mother of Christ,
none holier could be found
than Joachim and Anne.

What a treasure you held, bless-ed Anne,
while she who was to be Mother of God rested in your womb.
How precious to God that seed of Mary's life in your womb,
more precious than the offspring of all men on earth.

Anne became God's treasure-house,
keeping safe this most precious thing,
the seed of so precious a life.
God saw it and watched over it,
for as his Son was to say,
where one's treasure is, there is one's heart.
The angels looked on this treasure with joy,
knowing how precious it was to God their Creator.

It was a holy and bless-ed day,
to be honoured by all,
the day when this precious seed was first sown.
God himself and the angels greeted that day
with great rejoicing.

℣. Have mercy, Lord, and help our understanding. ℟. Our thanks to God.

## Responsory

**Anne was blessed by God** to hold, as did the Ark of God's Covenant, a treasure most precious to him; for from this treasure came forth riches for all in need, the ransom of captive slaves, the price of redemption, Christ, the Son of God.
℣. She will ever rejoice, and we will ever praise her for her holiness and her joy; and for her child, holiest of daughters, destined to be the Virgin-Mother of her Creator,
℟. Christ, the Son of God.
℣. Glory to God, glory to Father, Son and Holy Spirit.
℟. Christ, the Son of God.

## Te Deum *as on Sunday, page 75* or Psalm 50 *as on Friday, page 330.*

℣. The prophets of God made known to us. (Alleluia)
℟. The Virgin who would come of a kingly line. (Alleluia)

## Closing Prayers *(page 38).*

*Wednesday*

# VESPERS

**PRAYERS** before Vespers, *(pages 77 - 78)* and
**OPENING PRAYERS** – with music – *as at None, pages 55 - 56.*

## ANTIPHON

**We re-joice to-day in prayer and praise**

TONE I

**Psalm 138**

O Lord, you search me and you know me, you know my resting and my rising,
you discern my purpose from afar.

You mark when I walk or lie down, all my ways lie open to you.
Before ever a word is on my tongue you know it, O Lord,
through and through.

Behind and before you besiege me, your hand ever laid upon me.
Too wonderful for me this knowledge, too high, beyond my reach.

O where can I go from your spirit, or where can I flee from your face?
If I climb the heavens, you are there. If I lie in the grave, you are there.

If I take the wings of the dawn and dwell at the sea's furthest end,
even there your hand would lead me, your right hand would hold me fast.

If I say: "Let the darkness hide me and the light around me be night,"
even darkness is not dark for you and the night is as clear as the day.

For it was you who created my being, knit me together in my mother's womb.
I thank you for the wonder of my being, for the wonders of all your creation.

Already you knew my soul, my body held no secret from you
when I was being fashioned in secret and moulded in the depths of the earth.

Your eyes saw all my actions, they were all of them written in your book;
every one of my days was decreed before one of them came into being.

To me, how mysterious your thoughts, the sum of them not to be numbered!
If I count them, they are more than the sand; to finish, I must be eternal,
like you.

O God, that you would slay the wicked! Men of blood, keep far away
from me!
With deceit they rebel against you and set your designs at naught.

Do I not hate those who hate you, abhor those who rise against you?
I hate them with a perfect hate and they are foes to me.

O search me, God, and know my heart. O test me and know my thoughts.
See that I follow not the wrong path and lead me in the path of life eternal.

*Glory be...*

**Psalm 139**

Rescue me, Lord, from evil men;
from the violent keep me safe,

from those who plan evil in their hearts and stir up strife every day;
who sharpen their tongue like an adder's, with the poison of viper on their lips.

Lord, guard me from the hands of the wicked; from the violent keep me safe;
they plan to make me stumble.

The proud have hidden a trap, have spread out lines in a net,
set snares across my path.

I have said to the Lord: "You are my God." Lord, hear the cry of my appeal!
Lord my God, my mighty help, you shield my head in the battle.

Do not grant the wicked their desire nor let their plots succeed.
Those surrounding me lift up their heads. Let the malice of their speech
overwhelm them.

Let coals of fire rain upon them. Let them be flung in the abyss,
no more to rise.
Let the slanderer not endure upon the earth. Let evil hunt the violent man
to death!

I know that the Lord will avenge the poor, that he will do justice for the needy.
Truly the just will praise your name; the upright shall live in your presence.

*Glory be...*

**Psalm 140**

I have called to you, Lord; hasten to help me! Hear my voice
when I cry to you.
Let my prayer come before you like incense, the raising of my hands
like an evening oblation.

Lord, set a guard over my mouth; keep watch at the door of my lips!
Do not turn my heart to things that are wrong, to evil deeds with men
who are sinners.

Never allow me to share in their feasting. If a good man strikes or reproves me
it is kindness
but let the oil of the wicked not anoint my head. Let my prayer be ever
against their malice.

Their princes were thrown down by the side of the rock; then they understood
that my words were kind.
As a millstone is shattered to pieces on the ground, so their bones were strewn
at the mouth of the grave.

To you, Lord God, my eyes are turned: in you I take refuge; spare my soul!
From the trap they have laid for me keep me safe: keep me from the snares
of those who do evil.

Let the wicked fall into the traps they have set
while I pursue my way unharmed.

*Glory be...*

**Psalm 141**

With all my voice I cry to the Lord, with all my voice I entreat the Lord.
I pour out my trouble before him; I tell him all my distress

while my spirit faints within me. But you, O Lord, know my path.
On the way where I shall walk they have hidden a snare to entrap me.

Look on my right and see: there is not one who takes my part.
I have no means of escape, not one who cares for my soul.

I cry to you, O Lord. I have said: "You are my refuge
all I have in the land of the living."

Listen, then, to my cry for I am in the depths of distress.
Rescue me from those who pursue me for they are stronger than I.

Bring my soul out of this prison and then I shall praise your name.
Around me the just will assemble because of your goodness to me.

*Glory be...*

**Psalm 147**

O praise the Lord, Jerusalem!
Sion praise your God!

He has strengthened the bars of your gates, he has blessed the children
within you.
He established peace on your borders, he feeds you with finest wheat.

He sends out his word to the earth and swiftly runs his command.
He showers down snow white as wool, he scatters hoar-frost like ashes.

He hurls down hailstones like crumbs. The waters are frozen at his touch;
he sends forth his word and it melts them: at the breath of his mouth
the waters flow.

He makes his word known to Jacob, to Israel his laws and decrees.
He has not dealt thus with other nations; he has not taught them his decrees.

*Glory be...*

## Antiphon

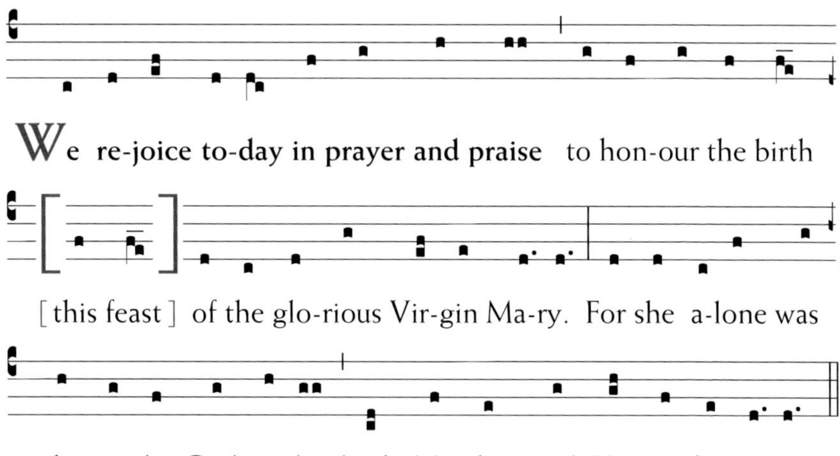


---

## Reading

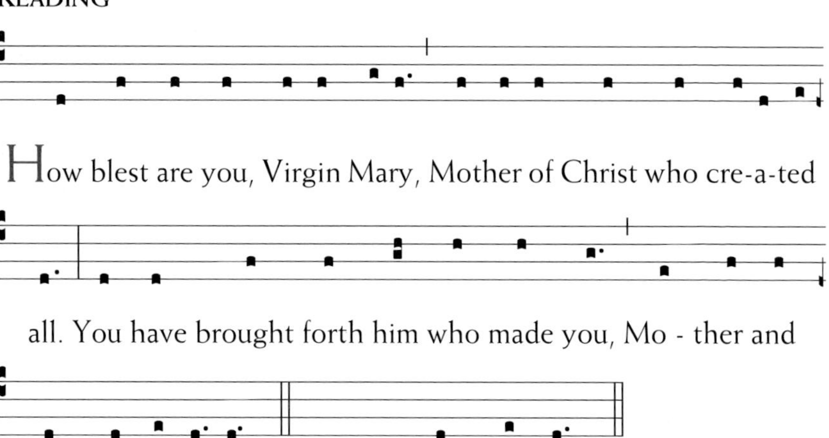

Hymn

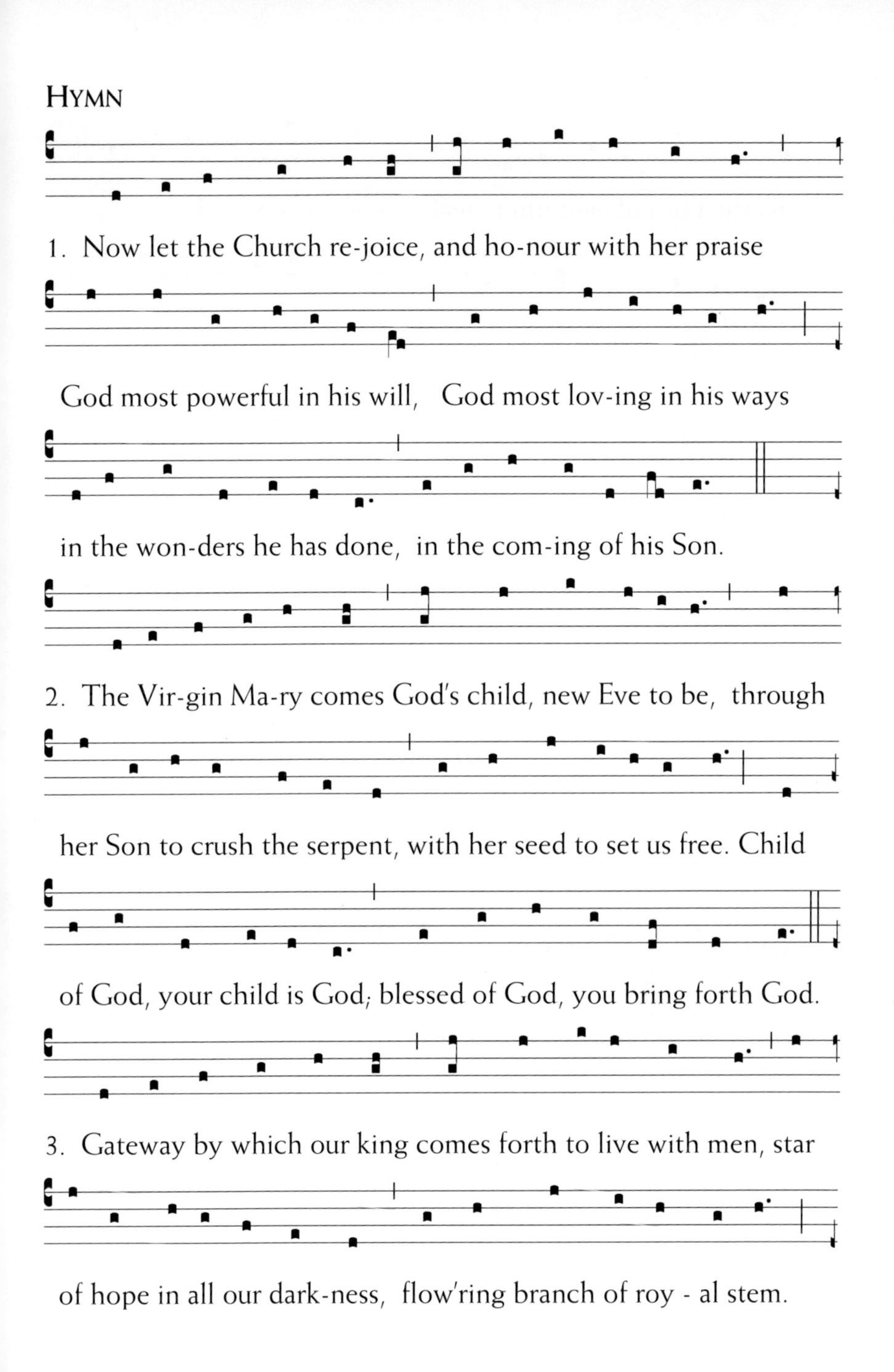
1. Now let the Church re-joice, and ho-nour with her praise
God most powerful in his will, God most lov-ing in his ways
in the won-ders he has done, in the com-ing of his Son.
2. The Vir-gin Ma-ry comes God's child, new Eve to be, through
her Son to crush the serpent, with her seed to set us free. Child
of God, your child is God; blessed of God, you bring forth God.
3. Gateway by which our king comes forth to live with men, star
of hope in all our dark-ness, flow'ring branch of roy - al stem.

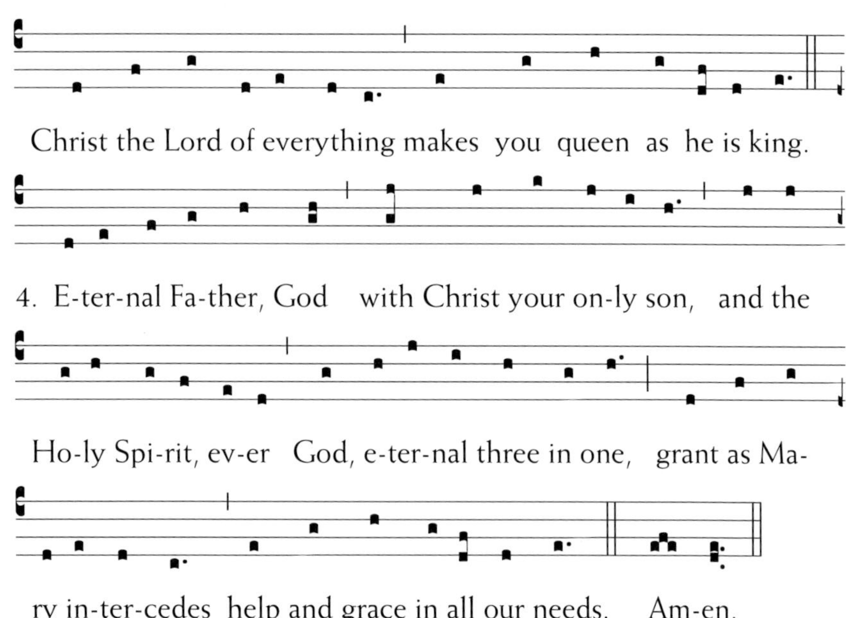

Christ the Lord of everything makes you queen as he is king.
4. E-ter-nal Fa-ther, God with Christ your on-ly son, and the
Ho-ly Spi-rit, ev-er God, e-ter-nal three in one, grant as Mary in-ter-cedes help and grace in all our needs. Am-en.


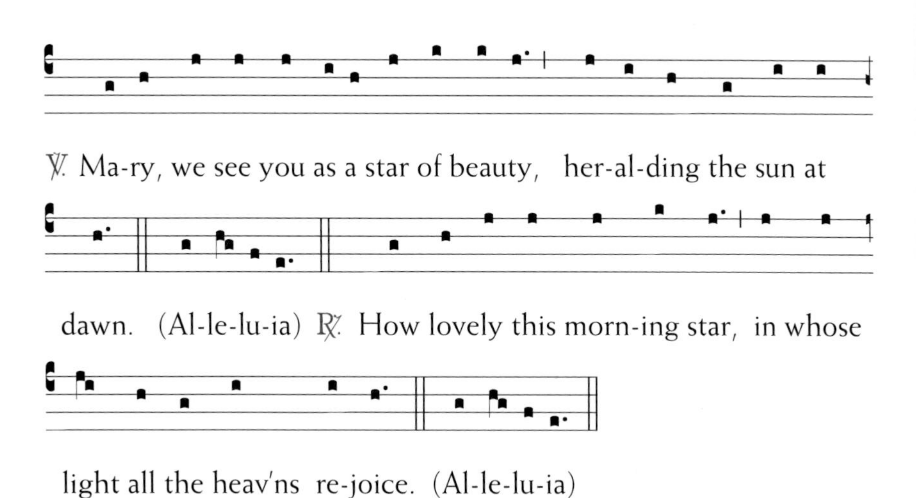

℣. Ma-ry, we see you as a star of beauty, her-al-ding the sun at
dawn. (Al-le-lu-ia) ℟. How lovely this morn-ing star, in whose
light all the heav'ns re-joice. (Al-le-lu-ia)

ANTIPHON

**Most ho-ly Vir-gin,** TONE III

MAGNIFICAT *(Luke 1: 46 - 55)*

My soul glorifies the Lord,
my spirit rejoices in God,
my Saviour.

He looks on his servant in her nothingness; henceforth all ages
will call me blessed.
The Almighty works marvels for me. Holy his name!

His mercy is from age to age, on those who fear him.
He puts forth his arm in strength and scatters the proud-
hearted.

He casts the mighty from their thrones and raises the lowly.
He fills the starving with good things, sends the rich away empty.

He protects Israel, his servant, remembering his mercy,
the mercy promised to our fathers, to Abraham and his sons
for ever.

Praise the Father, the Son and the Holy Spirit,
both now and for ever, world without end.

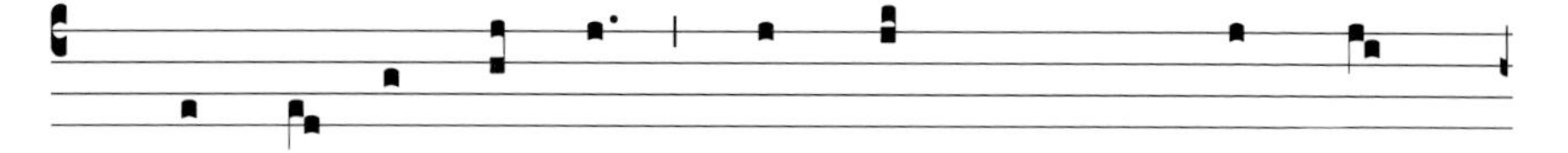

**M**ost ho - ly Vir - gin, [ your birth (feast) brings joy

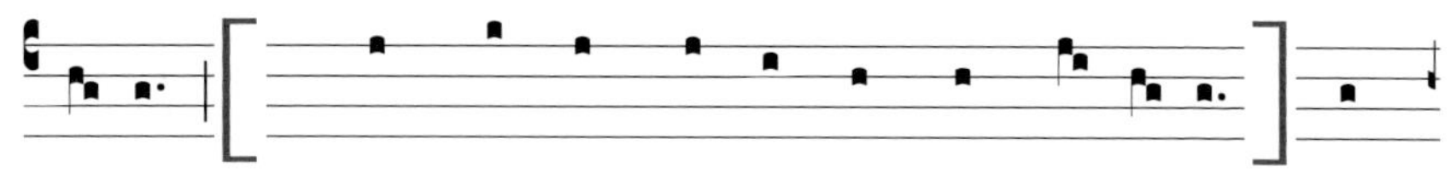

to all ] *or* [ brought to God's temple you bring joy to all *] and

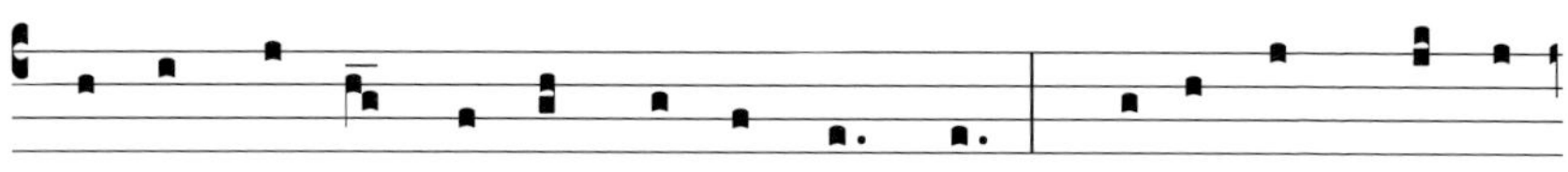

the light of hope to shine in our dark-ness. Ma-ry most bles-sed

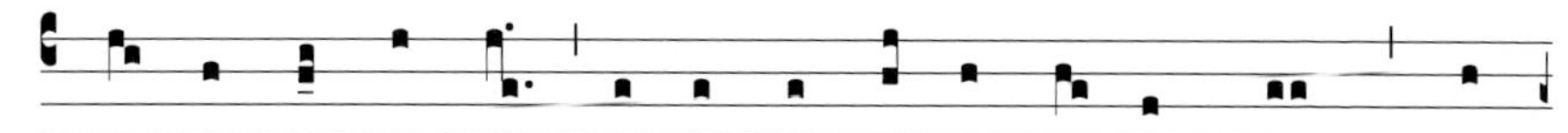

child of bless-ed line; you are the flow-er bearing branch, whose

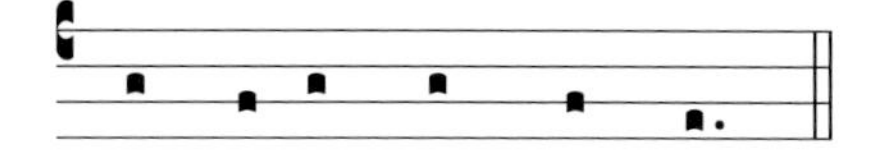

flow-er is Christ your Son.

* *Used only on 21st November, the feast of The Presentation of Our Lady.*

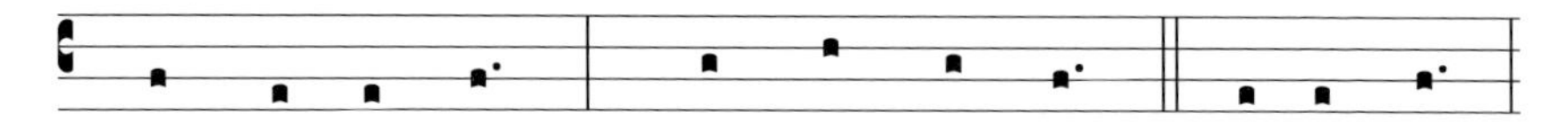

℣. Lord hear my prayer. ℟. Lord grant my prayer. ℣. Let us pray.

PRAYER *(page 36 - 37)*

ANTIPHON TO ST. BRIDGET & PRAYER *(pages 88 - 90).*

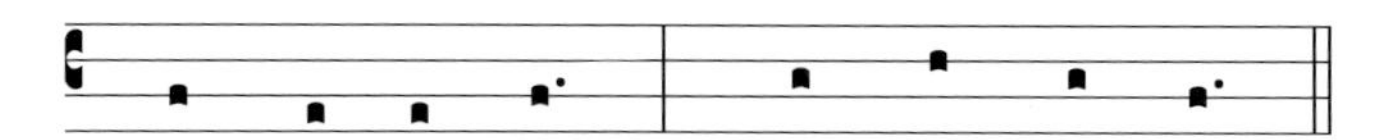

℣. Lord hear my prayer. ℟. Lord grant my prayer.

## Thanksgiving

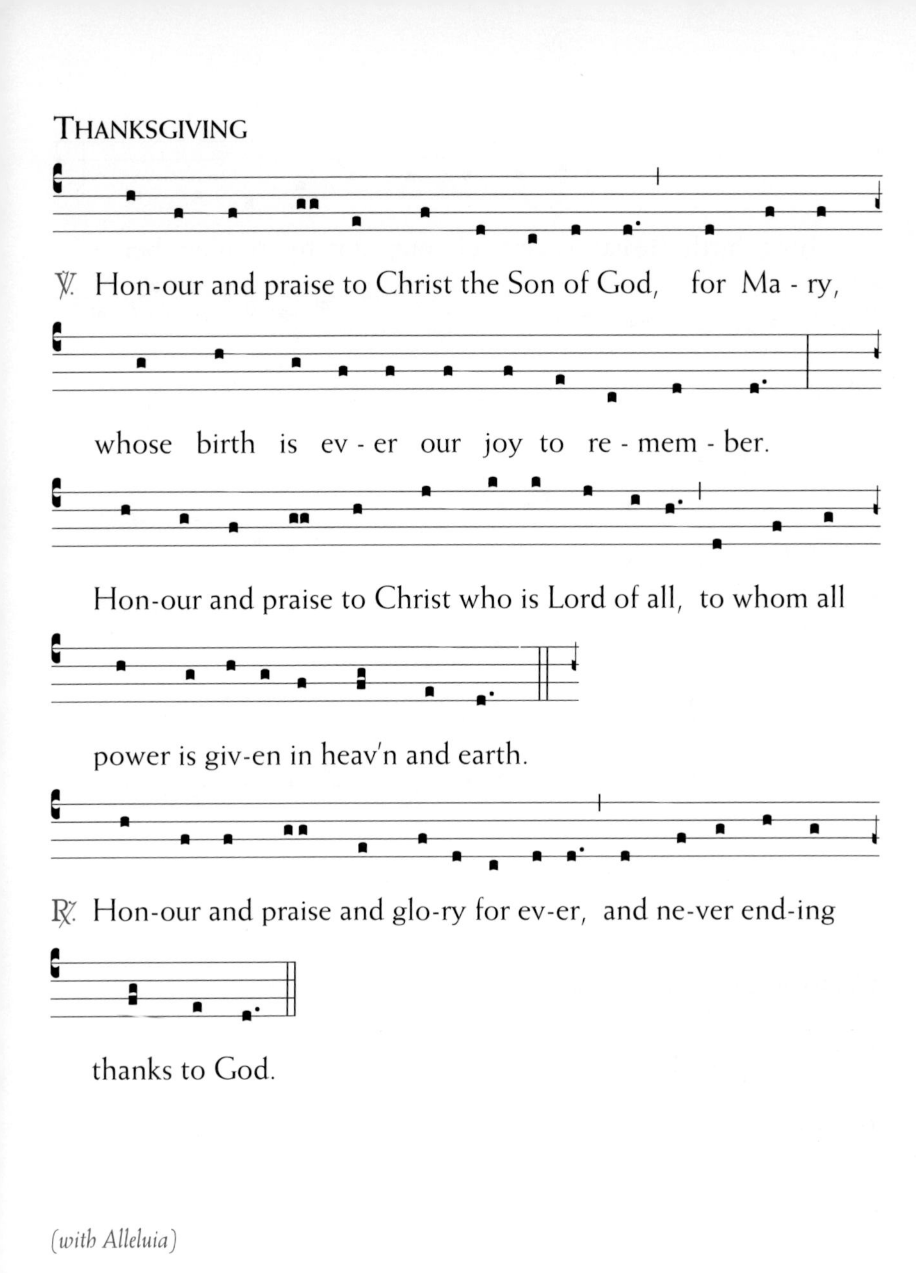


*(with Alleluia)*

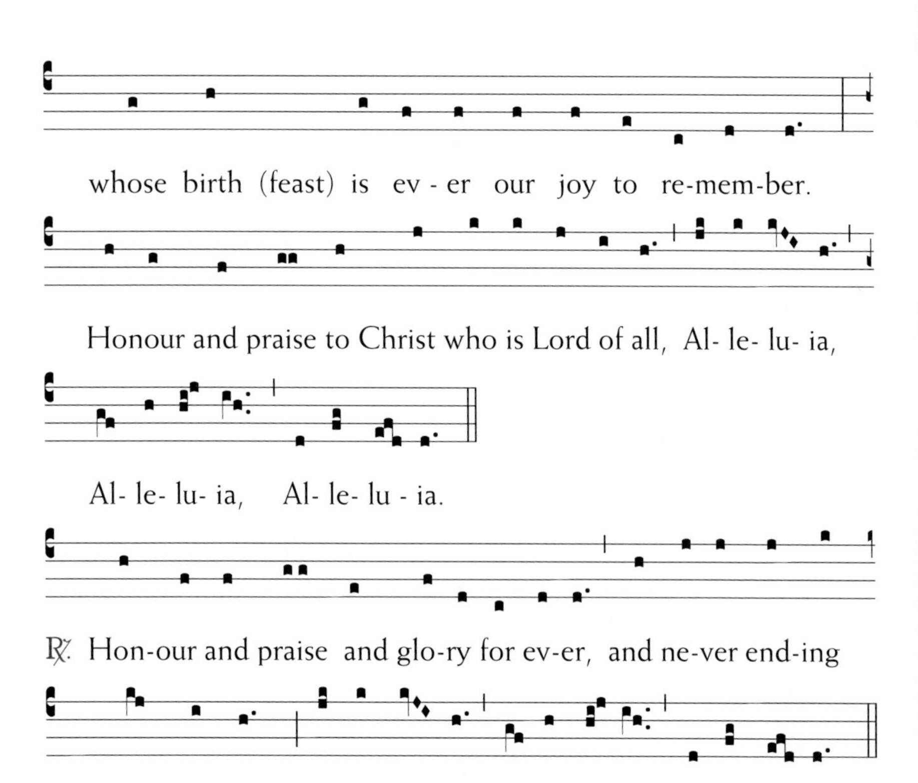


## Closing Prayers

'Mary, rejoice in God,' … *with music (page 92) followed by…*

**HYMN** *to Holy Mother St. Bridget, (pages 93 - 94).*

*Wednesday*
# COMPLINE

**OPENING PRAYERS** *as before Sunday Compline, pages 95 - 96.*

ANTIPHON

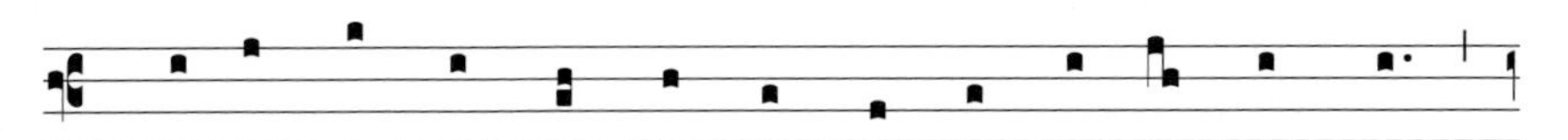

To her God and Lord the Vir - gin Ma - ry gave her - self,

TONE VII 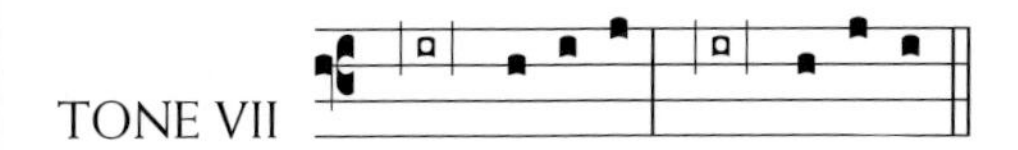

**Psalms 131, 132 & 133** *as on Sunday, pages 97 - 98.*

---

ANTIPHON

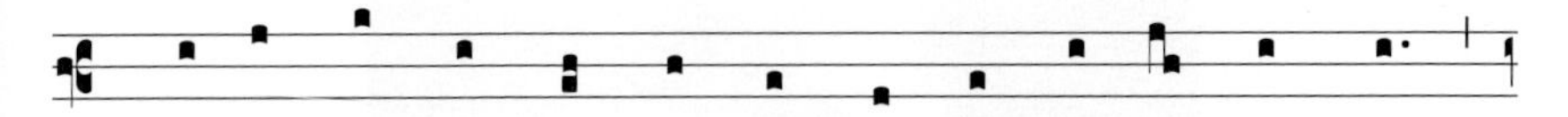

To her God and Lord the Vir - gin Ma - ry gave her - self,

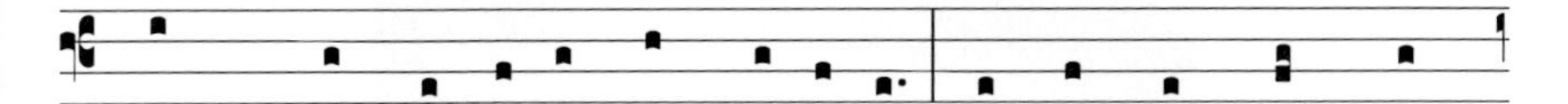

hand - maid and ev-er Vir - gin to be. Un-seen, un-known the

fav-our of God which graced her soul; concealed in Mo-ther-

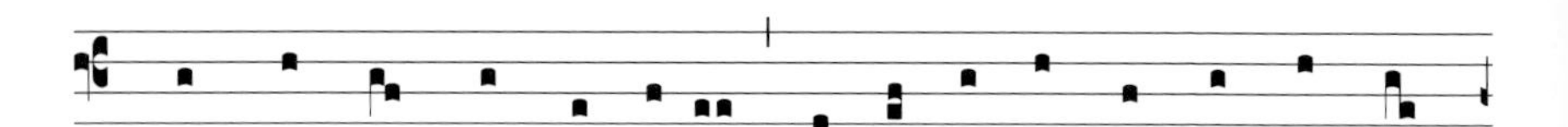

hood her pure Vir- gin- i- ty; and in her low- li- ness the won-

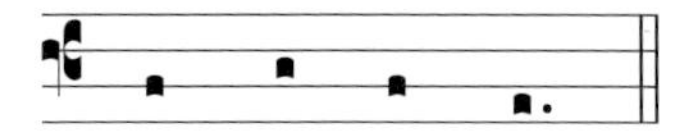

ders God had done.

**READING** *as on Sunday, page 99.*

**SHORT RESPONSORY** *as on Sunday, pages 99 ff.*

*Virgin and Child (c. 1454) by Rogier van der Weyden.*
*(Museum of Fine Arts, Houston.)*

## Hymn

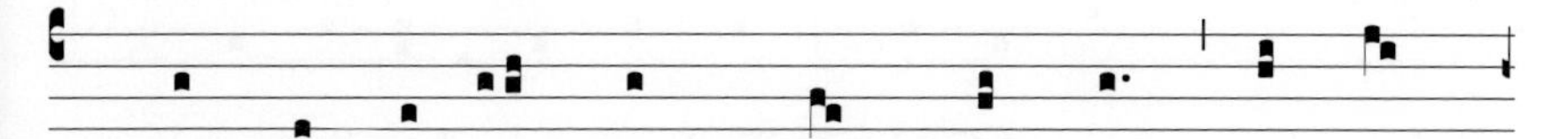

1. This is the gate through which Christ comes, the Vir-
2. This is the gate through which Christ comes, in - to
3. This is the gate through which Christ comes, to die
4. To all who hear him and be - lieve, Christ is
5. Pray, Ma -ry, Mo -ther full of grace, pray in
6. Christ Son of God we pray to you, and ho-

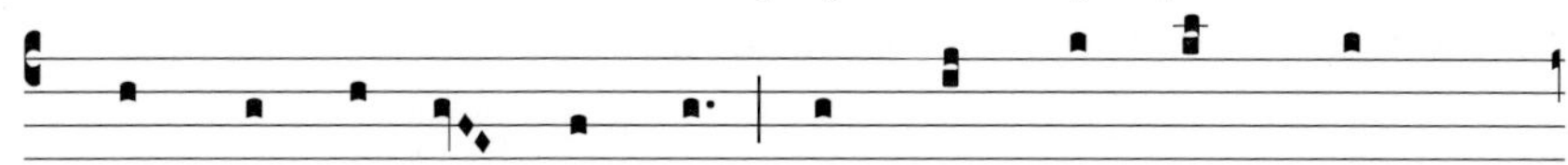

1. gin in her low - li - ness, made Vir-gin Mo - ther
2. this sin -ful world of men, and he a - lone of
3. and rise as King and Lord, and call to all to
4. the hope of life and rest, to her the gate through
5. your love for all we need, pro -tect us from all
6. nour you the Vir - gin's Son; we praise the Fa - ther,

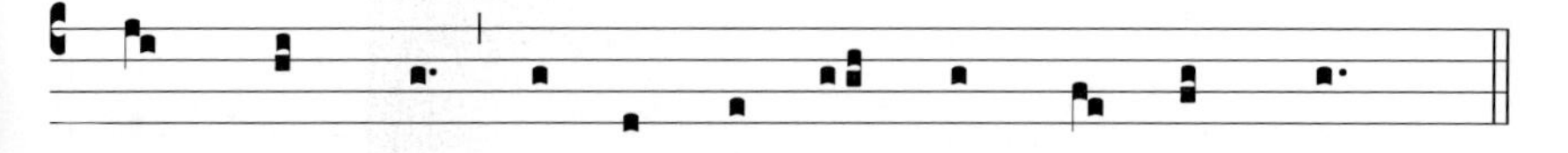

1. by God's will, in full - est grace and ho - li - ness.
2. men has right to op -en and to close a - gain.
3. en -ter in to his new king-dom and re - ward.
4. which he comes her glo - ry and her joy most blessed.
5. dan - ger now and at our dy - ing in - ter - cede.
6. God with you and with the Spi - rit, Three in One.

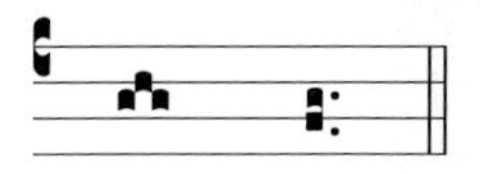

6. A - men.

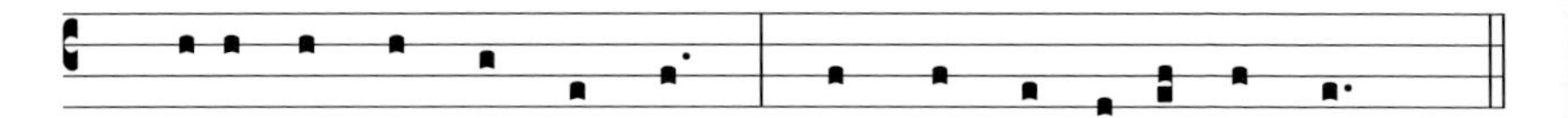

℣. I am the ser-vant of God. ℟. To hear and o-bey his word.

*(with Alleluia)*

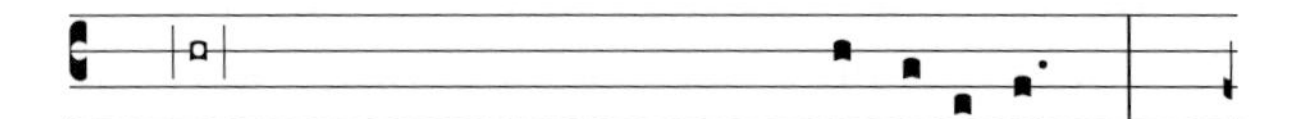

℣. I am the servant of God, Al-le-lu-ia.

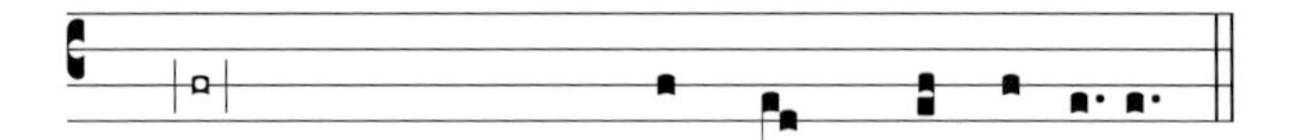

℟. To hear and obey his word, Al -le-lu-ia.

## ANTIPHON

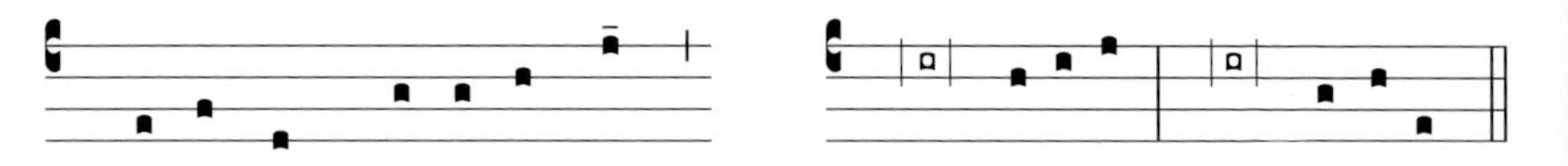

**Ma-ry your glo-ry and joy,** TONE III

## CANTICLE OF SIMEON *(Luke 2: 29 - 32)*

At last, all powerful Master you give leave
to your servant to go in peace,
according to your promise.

For my eyes have seen your salvation which you have prepared
for all nations.
The light to enlighten the gentiles and give glory to Israel, your people.

Give praise to the Father Almighty: to his Son, Jesus Christ, the Lord;
to the Spirit who dwells in our hearts, both now and forever. Amen.

**ANTIPHON**

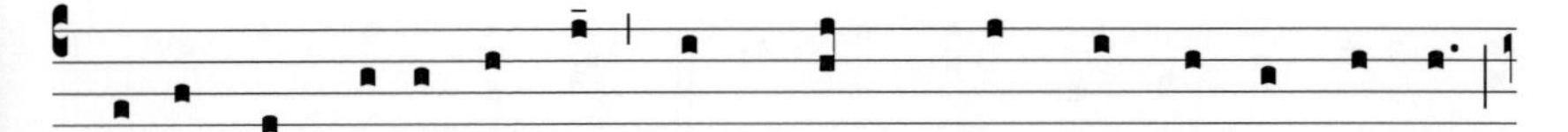

**Mary your glory and joy**, have brought new hope to our despair;

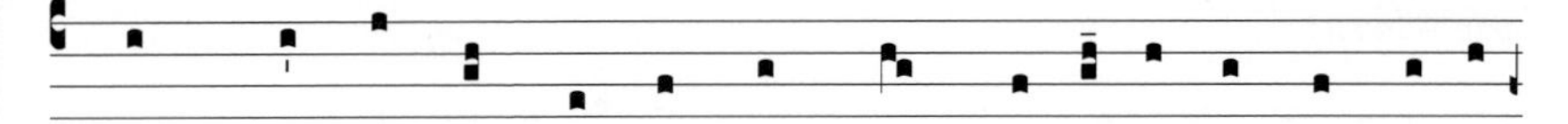

through you the grace of God has dawned on us to save this sin-ful

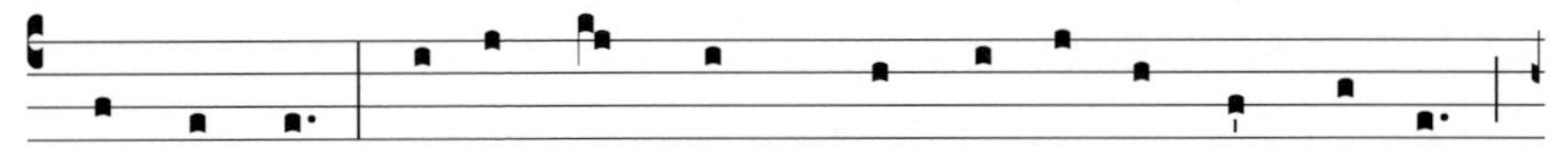

world of ours. In-ter-cede with Christ to save us from our sins;

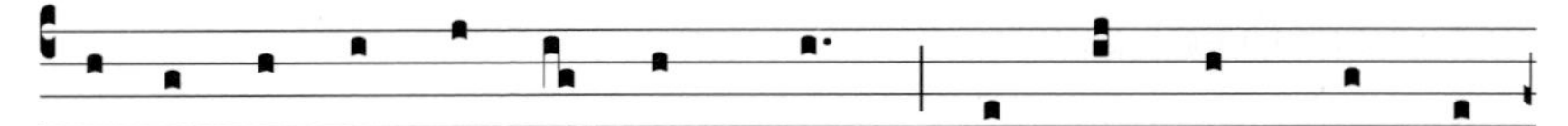

ligh-ten our bur-den by your prayer; for you have borne a

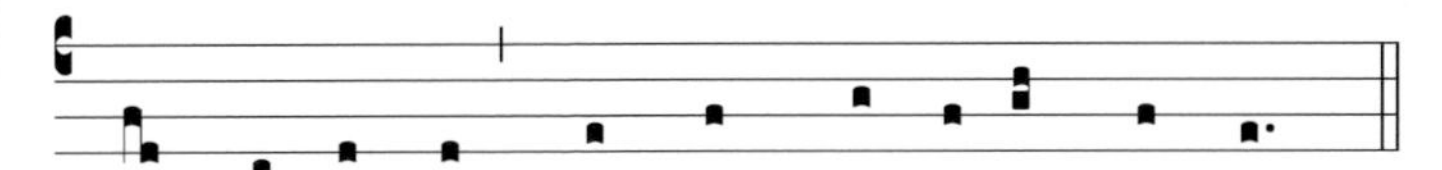

heav'n-ly bur-den: Christ your glo- ry and your joy.

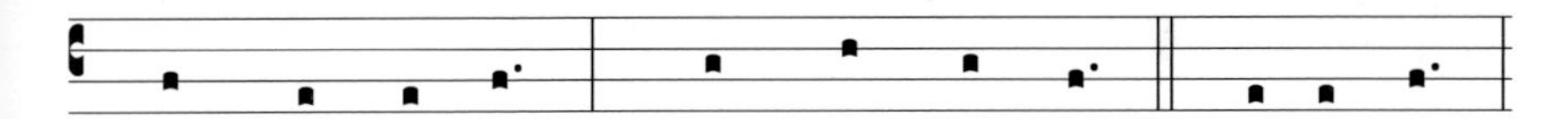

℣. Lord, hear my prayer. ℟. Lord, grant my prayer. ℣. Let us pray.

**PRAYER** *as on Sunday, page 104.*

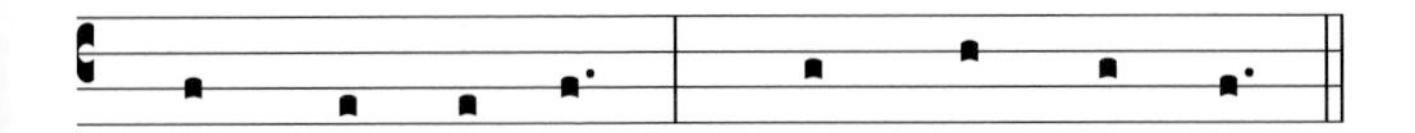

℣. Lord, hear my prayer. ℟. Lord, grant my prayer.

## THANKSGIVING

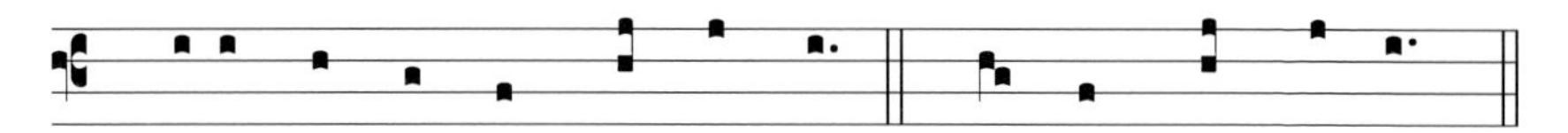

℣. Glory, hon-our and praise to God. ℟. And our thanks to him.

*(with Alleluia)*

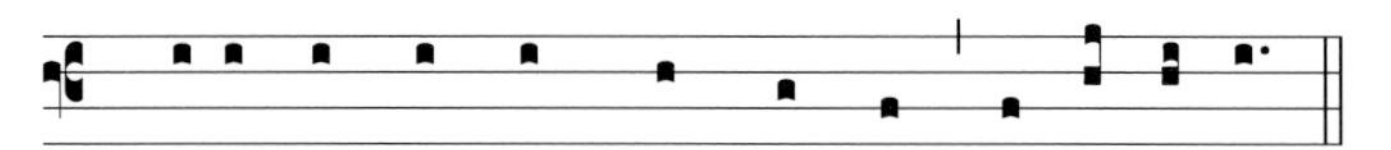

℣. Glory hon-our and praise to God, Al- le- lu- ia.

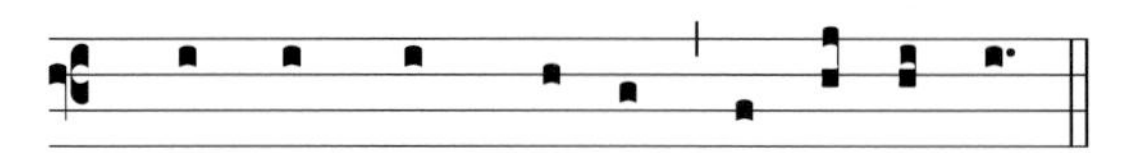

℟. And our thanks to him, Al- le- lu- ia.

℣. Mary, you are full of grace, the Lord is with you.
℟. Mary, you are most blessed of all women, for Jesus Christ is your Son. (Alleluia)

## LAUDS OF OUR LADY

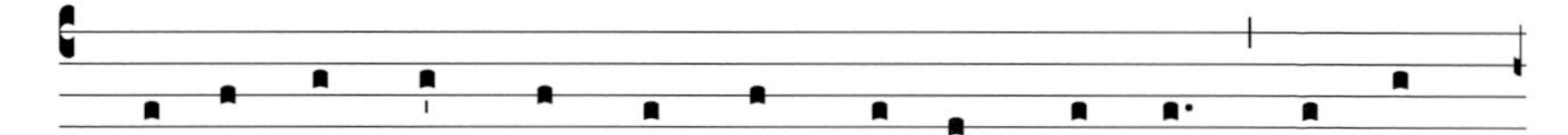

**Ma - ry, we name you** with names of love - ly things, and call

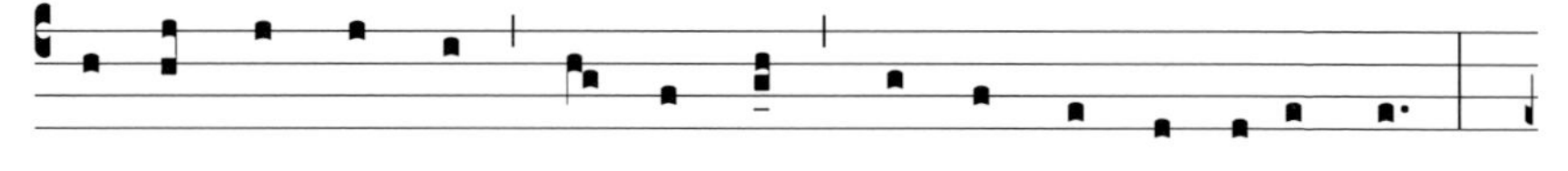

you rose of beau-ty, fruit-ful vine, and sun-rise of purest light.

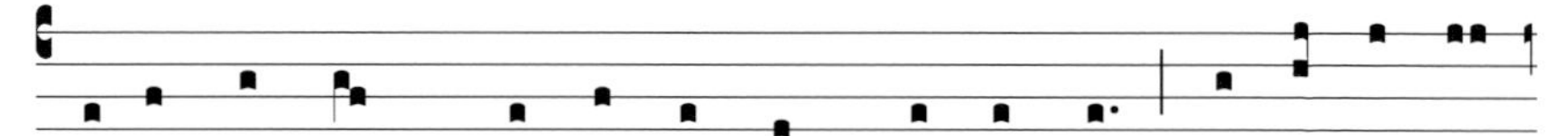

Ma-ry, you named yourself the handmaid of God, but we ac-claim

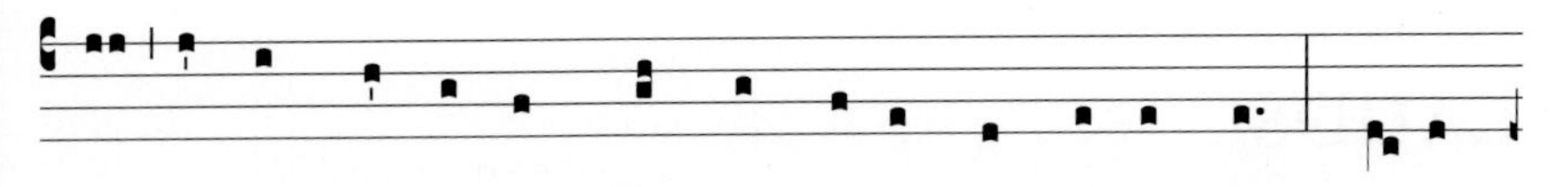

you Vir-gin Mother of Christ and tru-ly Mo-ther of God. Ma-ry,

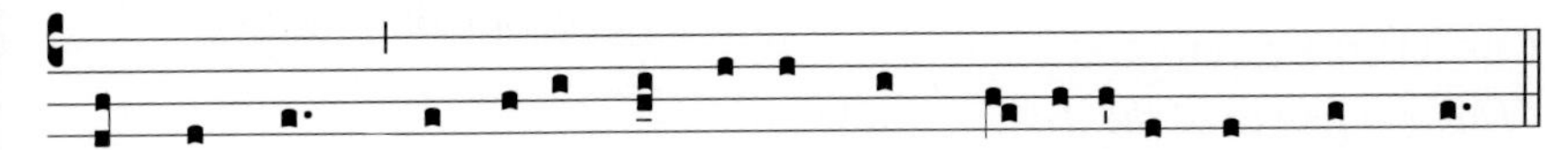

hear our prayer; and ever pray for us whose joy it is to sing your praise.

℣. Pray for us, holy Virgin Mary, Mother of God.
℟. That we may be made worthy of the promises of Jesus Christ.

℣. Let us pray.

## Prayer

Forgive, we ask you Lord, the sins of your servants: and may we who of ourselves are unable to please you, be saved by the prayers of the Mother of your Son, Jesus Christ our Lord. ℟. Amen.

**Closing Prayers** 'Mary, rejoice in God,' … *as on Sunday, page 107.*

*Thursday*

# LAUDS

## OPENING PRAYERS

***(The first prayer of the day…)*** *(page 33).*

Open my mouth, O Lord … *including Invitatory psalm (Ps. 94)*

## ANTIPHON

**See what God has done.**

Psalms and Canticle as for Sunday Lauds *(pages 39 ff).*

**See what God has done** – the Creator of man has came as man, born of a Virgin; not by the will of man, but by his eternal will,
to show and share his divinity with man.

## READING *as on Sunday, page 44.*

## HYMN

A virgin shall conceive, the prophet said,
Hail, Virgin full of grace, the angel's word;
God with her, through his Holy Spirit's power,
Mary in faith and love conceived her Lord.

This Virgin is the flower-bearing branch;
the flower is Christ the Lord of everything;
Virgin and Mother, in a crib she laid
her Son, her Lord-Creator and her King.

Pray Mary Virgin-Mother, … *Last two verses as on Sunday, page 44.*

℣. From the Virgin's womb, Christ has come in joy. (Alleluia)
℟. And we have seen him coming as a bridegroom to his bride. (Alleluia)

## ANTIPHON

**The evil of Satan came to us.**

## CANTICLE

Blessed be the Lord, the God of Israel! … *as on Sunday, page 45.*

**The evil of Satan came to us** in the lying of the serpent's tongue, to deceive us and win us to his ways. The infinity of God lay hidden, in the helplessness of a new-born child, to win us again to God. The virginity of the Mother was unseen by men, who looked with human eyes and saw only a mother and father and their child. So too was Satan led astray, and he who first practised deceit was himself deceived. Glory and praise, then, to this Son with his Mother, and to this Mother with her Son. Glory and praise from all on earth, with the eternal glory and praise of the angels in heaven.

℣. Lord hear my prayer. ℟. Lord grant my prayer. ℣. Let us pray.

## PRAYER

Grant us, your servants, …
*As on Sunday page 46 or according to the time of year. See pages 36ff.*

**ANTIPHON** to holy Mother Saint Bridget *as on Sunday, page 46.*
Bridget, loving servant of God, …
*or on ferial days:* Bridget, Saint and Patron, …

℣. and ℟. with Prayer *(page 47).*

℣. Lord hear my prayer. ℟. Lord grant my prayer.

## THANKSGIVING

℣. Glory, honour and praise to Christ, who to win our love, humbled himself, hiding his Godhead from our sight in the helplessness of a child, born of a lowly Virgin and nourished at her breast. (Alleluia, alleluia, alleluia)
℟. Our thanks to God. (Alleluia, alleluia, alleluia)

**CLOSING PRAYERS** 'Mary, rejoice in God,' … *(page 37).*

*Thursday*

# TERCE

## OPENING PRAYERS

(*page 33*).

## HYMN

Christ, Lord and King, in mercy come,
come, take our hearts to be your own;
to love and serve you in all things,
to praise you for yourself alone.

Remember, Lord, that for our sake,
a sinless Virgin's Child you came
as man to men to save all men,
salvation we your own may claim.

Pray Mary Mother full of grace,
pray in your love for all we need;
protect us from all danger now,
and at our dying intercede.

Christ, Son of God, we pray to you,
and honour you, the Virgin's Son.
We praise the Father, God with you,
and with the Spirit, Three in One. Amen.

## ANTIPHON

**The bush which Moses saw.**

**Psalm 82**

O God, do not keep silent, do not be dumb and unmoved, O God,
for your enemies raise a tumult. Those who hate you lift up their heads.

They plot against your people,
conspire against those you love.

They say: "Come, let us destroy them as a nation; let the name of Israel
be forgotten."
They conspire with a single mind, they make common alliance against you,

the camps of Edom and of Ishmael, the camps of Moab and Hagar,
the land of Ammon and Amalek, Philistia, with the people of Tyre.

Assyria, too, is their ally
and joins hands with the sons of Lot.

Treat them like Midian, like Sisera, like Jabin at the River Kishon,
the men who were destroyed at Endor, whose bodies rotted on the ground.

Make their captains like Oreb and Zeëb, all their princes like Zebah
and Zalmunna,
the men who said: "Let us take the fields of God for ourselves."

My God, scatter them like chaff,
drive them like straw in the wind!

As fire that burns away the forest, as the flame that sets the mountains ablaze,
drive them away with your tempest and fill them with terror at your storm.

Cover their faces with shame,
till they seek your name, O Lord.

Shame and terror be theirs for ever, let them be disgraced, let them perish!
Let them know that your name is the Lord, the Most High over all the earth.

*Glory be...*

**Psalm 83**

How lovely is your dwelling place,
Lord, God of hosts.

My soul is longing and yearning, is yearning for the courts of the Lord.
My heart and my soul ring out their joy to God, the living God.

The sparrow herself finds a home and the swallow a nest for her brood;
she lays her young by your altars, Lord of hosts, my king and my God.

They are happy, who dwell in your house, for ever singing your praise.
They are happy, whose strength is in you, in whose hearts are the
roads to Sion.

As they go through the Bitter Valley they make it a place of springs,
the autumn rain covers it with blessings.

They walk with ever growing strength,
they will see the God of gods in Sion.

O Lord God of hosts, hear my prayer, give ear, O God of Jacob.
Turn your eyes, O God, our shield, look on the face of your anointed.

One day within your courts is better than a thousand elsewhere.
The threshold of the house of God I prefer to the dwellings of the wicked.

For the Lord God is a rampart, a shield; he will give us his favour and glory.
The Lord will not refuse any good to those who walk without blame.

Lord, God of hosts,
happy the man who trusts in you!

*Glory be...*

**Psalm 84**

O Lord, you once favoured your land and revived the fortunes of Jacob,
you forgave the guilt of your people and covered all their sins.

You averted all your rage,
you calmed the heat of your anger.

Revive us now, God, our helper! Put an end to your grievance against us.
Will you be angry with us for ever, will your anger never cease?

Will you not restore again our life that your people may rejoice in you?
Let us see, O Lord, your mercy and give us your saving help.

I will hear what the Lord God has to say, a voice that speaks of peace,
peace for his people and his friends and those who turn to him in their hearts.

His help is near for those who fear him
and his glory will dwell in our land.

Mercy and faithfulness have met; justice and peace have embraced.
Faithfulness shall spring from the earth and justice look down from heaven.

The Lord will make us prosper and our earth shall yield its fruit.
Justice shall march before him and peace shall follow his steps.

*Glory be...*

## ANTIPHON

T**he bush which Moses saw**, burned but was not consumed by the fire.
Mary, your glorious motherhood is ever pure virginity.
Pray for us, Mother of God.

## READING *(Eccles. 24: 9)*

In the eternal decree of God, I was present before his creating, and I shall be for ever with him, in the holiness of his heaven. ℟. Our thanks to God.

## SHORT RESPONSORY

℣. God has entered this world of ours through the Virgin Mary.
(Alleluia, Alleluia) ℟. *Repeat.*
℣. To bring to heaven our fallen race.
℟. Through the Virgin Mary. (†℟. Alleluia, Alleluia)
℣. Glory to God, Father, Son and Holy Spirit.
℟. God has entered this world of ours through the Virgin Mary.
(Alleluia, Alleluia)
℣. God himself has come down to the Virgin's womb. (Alleluia)
℟. There to clothe himself as man, with flesh to offer for us, and blood to shed for us. (Alleluia)

## CLOSING PRAYERS *(page 38).*

---

† ***Response during Easter and on other special days where shown, as well as in brackets thus: (Alleluia). For style, see Sunday Terce on page 51.***

*Thursday*

# SEXT

## OPENING PRAYERS *(page 33)*

## HYMN

Christ, Lord and King, in mercy come… *as at Thursday Terce, page 250.*

## ANTIPHON

**Now is the flower seen.**

### Psalm 85

Turn your ear, O Lord, and give answer for I am poor and needy.
Preserve my life, for I am faithful: save the servant who trusts in you.

You are my God, have mercy on me, Lord, for I cry to you all the day long.
Give joy to your servant, O Lord, for to you I lift up my soul.

O Lord, you are good and forgiving, full of love to all who call.
Give heed, O Lord, to my prayer and attend to the sound of my voice.

In the day of distress I will call and surely you will reply.
Among the gods there is none like you, O Lord; nor work to compare
with yours.

All the nations shall come to adore you and glorify your name, O Lord:
for you are great and do marvellous deeds, you who alone are God.

Show me, Lord, your way so that I may walk in your truth.
Guide my heart to fear your name.

I will praise you, Lord my God, with all my heart and glorify your name
for ever;

for your love to me has been great: you have saved me from the depths
of the grave.

The proud have risen against me; ruthless men seek my life:
to you they pay no heed.

But you, God of mercy and compassion, slow to anger, O Lord,
abounding in love and truth, turn and take pity on me.

O give your strength to your servant
and save your handmaid's son.

Show me a sign of your favour that my foes may see to their shame
that you console me and give me your help.

*Glory be...*

**Psalm 87**

Lord my God, I call for help by day; I cry at night before you.
Let my prayer come into your presence. O turn your ear to my cry.

For my soul is filled with evils; my life is on the brink of the grave.
I am reckoned as one in the tomb: I have reached the end of my strength,

like one alone among the dead; like the slain lying in their graves;
like those you remember no more, cut off, as they are, from your hand.

You have laid me in the depths of the tomb, in places that are dark,
in the depths.
Your anger weighs down upon me: I am drowned beneath your waves.

You have taken away my friends and made me hateful in their sight.
Imprisoned, I cannot escape; my eyes are sunken with grief.

I call to you, Lord, all the day long; to you I stretch out my hands.
Will you work your wonders for the dead? Will the shades stand and
praise you?

Will your love be told in the grave or your faithfulness among the dead?
Will your wonders be known in the dark or your justice in the land of oblivion?

As for me, Lord, I call to you for help: in the morning my prayer comes
before you.
Lord, why do you reject me? Why do you hide your face?

Wretched, close to death from my youth, I have borne your trials; I am numb.
Your fury has swept down upon me; your terrors have utterly destroyed me.

They surround me all the day like a flood, they assail me all together.
Friend and neighbour you have taken away: my one companion is darkness.

*Glory be...*

**Psalm 89**

O Lord, you have been our refuge
from one generation to the next.

Before the mountains were born or the earth or the world brought forth,
you are God, without beginning or end.

You turn men back into dust
and say: "Go back, sons of men."

To your eyes a thousand years are like yesterday, come and gone,
no more than a watch in the night.

You sweep men away like a dream, like the grass which springs up
in the morning.
In the morning it springs up and flowers: by evening it withers and fades.

So we are destroyed in your anger struck with terror in your fury.
Our guilt lies open before you; our secrets in the light of your face.

All our days pass away in your anger. Our life is over like a sigh.
Our span is seventy years or eighty for those who are strong.

And most of these are emptiness and pain. They pass swiftly and we are gone.
Who understands the power of your anger and fears the strength of your fury?

Make us know the shortness of our life that we may gain wisdom of heart.
Lord, relent! Is your anger for ever? Show pity to your servants.

In the morning, fill us with your love; we shall exult and rejoice all our days.
Give us joy to balance our affliction for the years when we knew misfortune.

Show forth your work to your servants; let your glory shine on their children.
Let the favour of the Lord be upon us: give success to the work of our hands.

*Glory be...*

## ANTIPHON

**Now is the flower seen,** on that sweet branch. Now are the heavens bright with that promised star. Now has the Virgin brought forth her Son, the Saviour. Glory and praise for ever, to you, our Lord and our God.

## READING *(Eccles. 24: 11)*

Jerusalem has been my dwelling and my resting-place:
there in the holy city, I have taken up my rule and my reign.
℟. Our thanks to God.

## SHORT RESPONSORY

℣. God himself has come down to the Virgin's womb there to clothe himself as man. (Alleluia, Alleluia) ℟. *Repeat.*
℣. With flesh to offer for us, and blood to shed for us
℟. To clothe himself as man. († ℟. Alleluia, Alleluia)
℣. Glory to God, Father, Son and Holy Spirit.
℟. God himself has come down to the Virgin's womb there to clothe himself as man. (Alleluia, Alleluia)
℣. From the Virgin's womb, Christ has come in joy; (Alleluia)
℟. And we have seen him, coming as a bridegroom to his bride. (Alleluia)

*NOTE: If continuing immediately with None, omit the Opening Prayers and Hymn for None and start with the (short) Antiphon before the Psalms: as detailed in the Structure, page 26.*

## CLOSING PRAYERS *(page 38)*.

---

† ***Response during Easter and on other special days where shown, as well as in brackets thus: (Alleluia). For style, see Sunday Terce on page 51.***

*Thursday*

# NONE

**OPENING PRAYERS** *as before Sunday None, pages 55 - 56.*

## HYMN

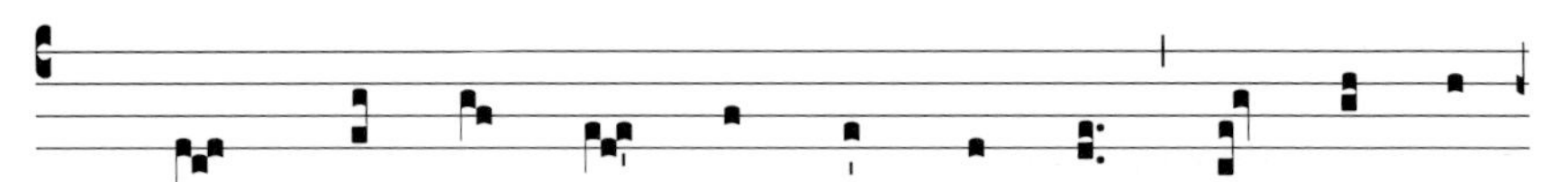

1. Christ, Lord and King, in mer - cy come, come take our
2. Re - mem- ber Lord, that for our sake, a sin- less
3. Pray Ma - ry Mo - ther full of grace, pray in your
4. Christ Son of God we pray to you, and hon-our

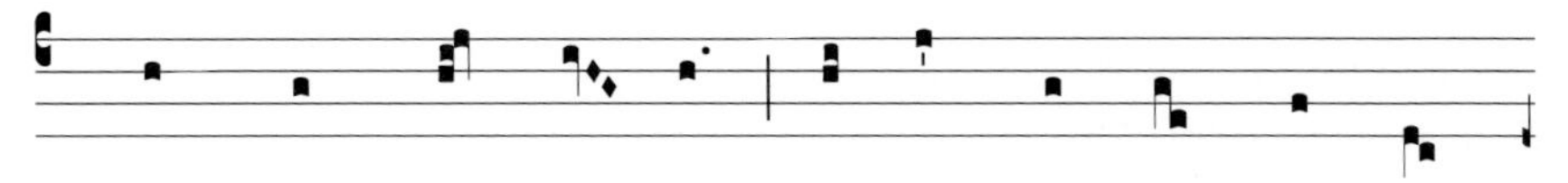

1 hearts to be your own to love and serve you in
2. Vir - gin's Child you came as man to men to save
3. love for all we need, pro-tect us from all dan-
4. you, the Vir - gin's Son; we praise the Fa - ther, God

1. all things, to praise you for your- self a - lone.
2. all men, sal - va - tion we your own may claim.
3 ger now and at our dy - ing in - ter - cede.
4. with you and with the Spi - rit, Three in One.

4. A - men.

ANTIPHON

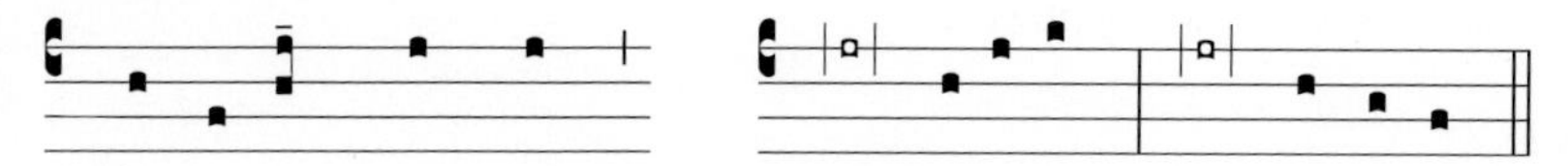

This is he who comes TONE V

**Psalm 90**

He who dwells in the shelter of the Most High and abides in the
shade of the Almighty
says to the Lord: "My refuge, my stronghold, my God in whom I trust!"

It is he who will free you from the snare of the fowler who seeks to
destroy you;
he will conceal you with his pinions and under his wings you will find refuge.

You will not fear the terror of the night nor the arrow that flies by day,
nor the plague that prowls in the darkness nor the scourge that
lays waste at noon.

A thousand may fall at your side, ten thousand fall at your right,
you, it will never approach; his faithfulness is buckler and shield.

Your eyes have only to look to see how the wicked are repaid,
you who have said: "Lord, my refuge!" and have made the Most High
your dwelling.

Upon you no evil shall fall, no plague approach where you dwell.
For you has he commanded his angels, to keep you in all your ways.

They shall bear you upon their hands lest you strike your foot against a stone.
On the lion and the viper you will tread and trample the young lion
and the dragon.

His love he set on me, so I will rescue him; protect him for he knows my name.
When he calls I shall answer: "I am with you," I will save him in distress
and give him glory.

With length of life I will content him;
I shall let him see my saving power.

*Glory be...*

**Psalm 91**

It is good to give thanks to the Lord, to make music to your name,
O Most High,
to proclaim your love in the morning and your truth in the watches
of the night,

on the ten-stringed lyre and the lute, with the murmuring sound of the harp.
Your deeds, O Lord, have made me glad; for the work of your hands
I shout with joy.

O Lord, how great are your works! How deep are your designs!
The foolish man cannot know this and the fool cannot understand.

Though the wicked spring up like grass and all who do evil thrive,
they are doomed to be eternally destroyed.

But you, Lord, are eternally on high.
See how your enemies perish; all doers of evil are scattered.

To me you give the wild ox's strength; you anoint me with the purest oil.
My eyes looked in triumph on my foes; my ears heard gladly of their fall.

The just will flourish like the palm tree and grow like a Lebanon cedar.
Planted in the house of the Lord they will flourish in the courts of our God,

still bearing fruit when they are old, still full of sap, still green,
to proclaim that the Lord is just. In him, my rock, there is no wrong.

*Glory be...*

**Psalm 93**

O Lord, avenging God, avenging God, appear!
Judge of the earth, arise, give the proud what they deserve!

How long, O Lord, shall the wicked, how long shall the wicked triumph?
They bluster with arrogant speech; the evil-doers boast to each other.

They crush your people, Lord, they afflict the ones you have chosen.
They kill the widow and the stranger and murder the fatherless child.

And they say: "The Lord does not see; the God of Jacob pays no heed."
Mark this, most senseless of people; fools, when will you understand?

Can he who made the ear, not hear? Can he who formed the eye, not see?
Will he who trains nations not punish? Will he who teaches men,
not have knowledge?

(The Lord knows the thoughts of men.
He knows they are no more than a breath.)

Happy the man whom you teach, O Lord, whom you train by means
of your law;
to him you give peace in evil days while the pit is being dug for the wicked.

The Lord will not abandon his people nor forsake those who are his own;
for judgment shall again be just and all true hearts shall uphold it.

Who will stand up for me against the wicked? Who will defend me from those
who do evil?
If the Lord were not to help me, I would soon go down into the silence.

When I think: "I have lost my foothold"; your mercy, Lord, holds me up.
When cares increase in my heart your consolation calms my soul.

Can judges who do evil be your friends? They do injustice under cover of law;
they attack the life of the just and condemn innocent blood.

As for me, the Lord will be a stronghold;
my God will be the rock where I take refuge.

He will repay them for their wickedness, destroy them for their evil deeds.
The Lord, our God, will destroy them.

*Glory be...*

## ANTIPHON

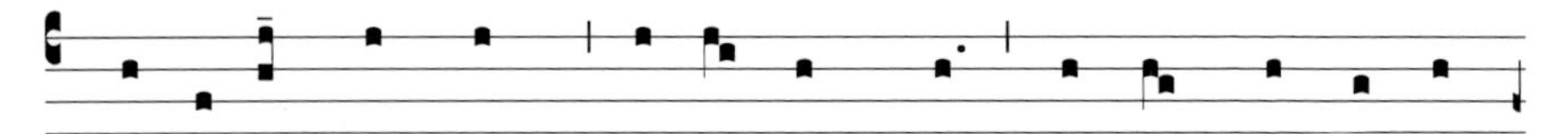

**This is he who comes,** a Vir-gin's child, the Sav - iour of his

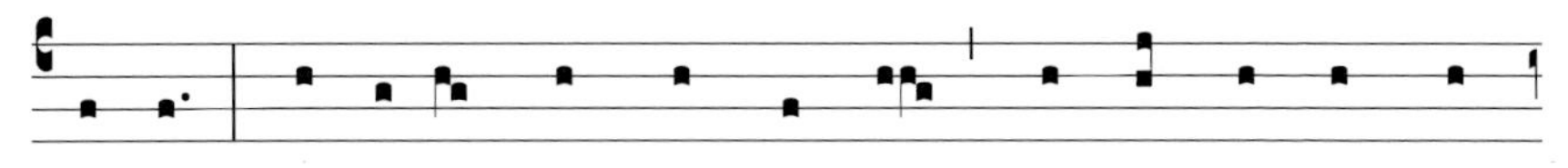

people. This is he whom John fore-tells – pre-pare his way, make

straight his paths. See the Lamb of God, for this is he who will

take a - way the sins of the world.

## READING *(Eccles. 24: 12)*

I have grown up among God's people: I will live for ever

in the land of the Lord. ℟. Our thanks to God.

## Short Responsory

℣. From the Virgin's womb Christ has come in joy. ℟. From the...

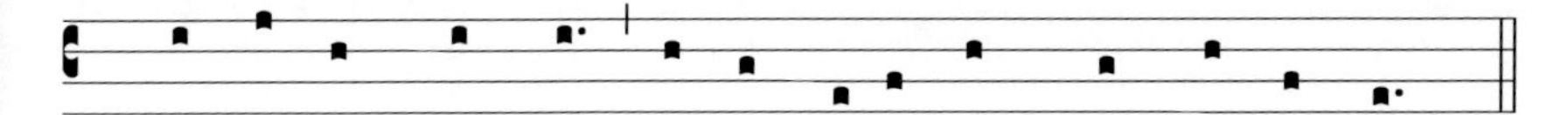

℣. And we have seen him co-ming as a bridegroom to his bride.

℟. Christ has come... ℣. Glo-ry to God, Fa-ther, Son and Ho-ly

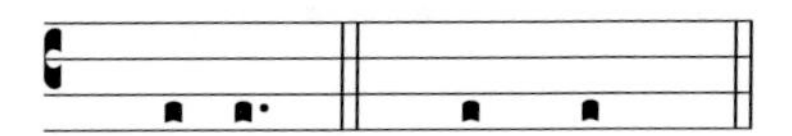

Spir-it. ℟. From the...

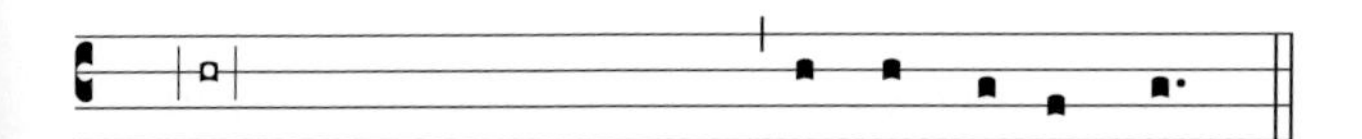

℣. By choosing for himself a Mother on earth,

℟. The Son of God makes known to all – his Father in heaven.

*(with Alleluia)*

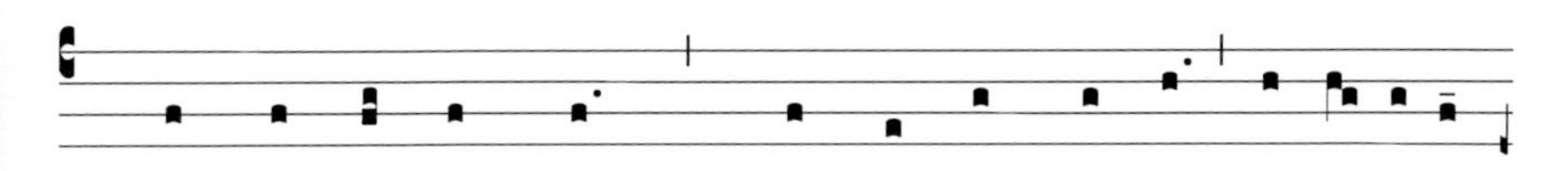

℣. From the Vir-gin's womb Christ has come in joy. Al-le-lu-ia,

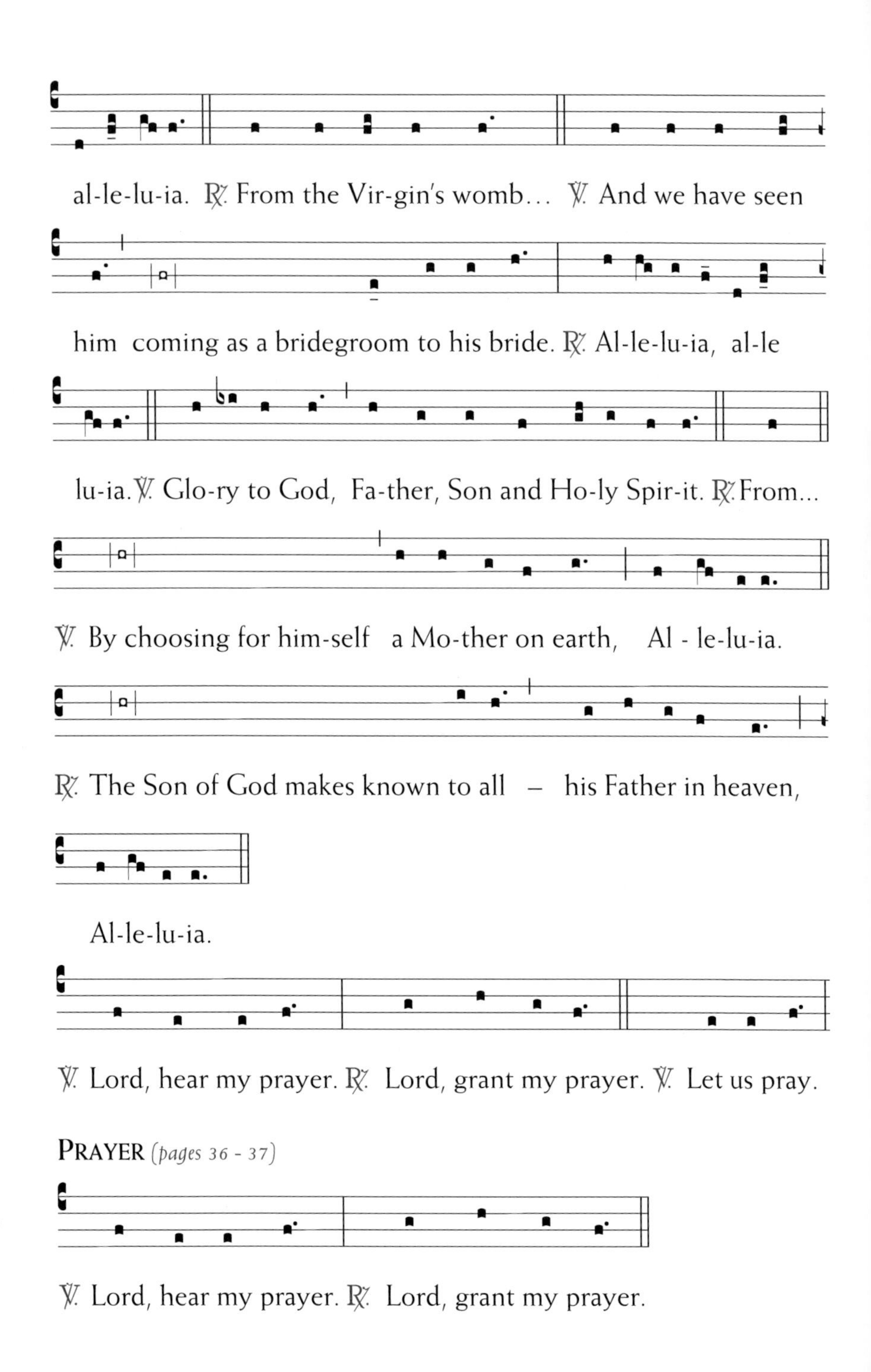
al-le-lu-ia. ℟. From the Vir-gin's womb… ℣. And we have seen
him coming as a bridegroom to his bride. ℟. Al-le-lu-ia, al-le
lu-ia. ℣. Glo-ry to God, Fa-ther, Son and Ho-ly Spir-it. ℟. From…
℣. By choosing for him-self a Mo-ther on earth, Al - le-lu-ia.
℟. The Son of God makes known to all – his Father in heaven,
Al-le-lu-ia.
℣. Lord, hear my prayer. ℟. Lord, grant my prayer. ℣. Let us pray.
PRAYER (pages 36 - 37)
℣. Lord, hear my prayer. ℟. Lord, grant my prayer.

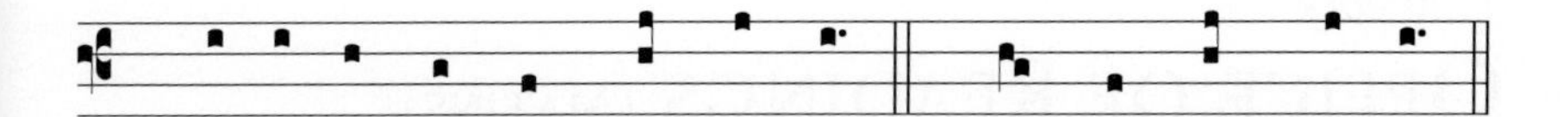

℣. Glo-ry hon-our and praise to God. ℟. And our thanks to him.

*(with Alleluia)*

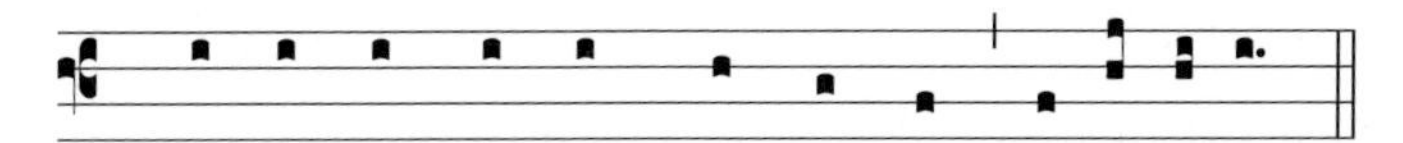

℣. Glo-ry hon-our and praise to God, Al-le-lu-ia.

℟. And our thanks to him, Al-le-lu-ia.

## Closing Prayers

'Mary, rejoice…' *as on Sunday, pages 64 ff.*

**Lauds of Our Lady** *of the day, season or feast. (See daily after Compline) With ℣. & ℟. and Prayer. Then* 'May the souls of our founders…' *and…*

**Psalm 129** 'Out of the depths…' *and two or three memorial prayers for the souls of the departed, as on Sunday, page 65 - 66.*

*Thursday*

# OFFICE OF READINGS (MATINS)

## OPENING PRAYERS (*page 67*).

## HYMN

The God whom earth and sea and sky
adore and praise and magnify,
who o'er their three fold fabric reigns,
the Virgin's spotless womb contains.

The God whom sun and moon obey,
whom all things serve from day to day,
is borne upon a Maiden's breast,
by fullest heavenly grace possessed.

How blest that Mother, in whose shrine
the world's Creator, Lord divine,
whose hand contains the earth and sky,
once deigned as in his ark to lie.

Blest in the message Gabriel brought,
blest by the work the Spirit wrought,
from whom the great desire of earth
took human flesh and human birth.

Pray Mary Mother full of grace,
pray in your love for all we need;
protect us from all danger now,
and at our dying intercede.

Christ, Son of God, we pray to you,
and honour you, the Virgin's Son;
we praise the Father, God with you
and with the Spirit, Three in One. Amen.

## ANTIPHON 1

**God in his goodness has heard our prayer.**

### Psalm 56

Have mercy on me, God, have mercy for in you my soul has taken refuge.
In the shadow of your wings I take refuge till the storms of destruction pass by.

I call to God the Most High,
to God who has always been my help.

May he send from heaven and save me and shame those who assail me.
May God send his truth and his love.

My soul lies down among lions, who would devour the sons of men.
Their teeth are spears and arrows, their tongue a sharpened sword.

O God, arise above the heavens;
may your glory shine on earth!

They laid a snare for my steps, my soul was bowed down.
They dug a pit in my path but fell in it themselves.

My heart is ready, O God, my heart is ready.
I will sing, I will sing your praise.

Awake, my soul, awake, lyre and harp,
I will awake the dawn.

I will thank you Lord among the peoples, praise you among the nations;
for your love reaches to the heavens and your truth to the skies.

O God, arise above the heavens;
may your glory shine on earth!

*Glory be...*

## ANTIPHON 1

G**od in his goodness has heard our prayer**; and Mary has come to us, in the fullness of his grace, beautiful as a bride, to bring forth to this world the truth of God. And in this light of truth, we see the hidden dangers of falsehood and the foolishness of sin.

## ANTIPHON 2

P**eople of God, praise and honour the Son of God.**

### Psalm 57

Do you truly speak justice, you who hold divine power? Do you mete out fair judgment to the sons of men?
No, in your hearts you devise injustice; your hands deal out violence to the land.

In their wickedness they have gone astray from their birth:
they wandered among lies as soon as they were born.

Their venom is like the venom of the snake; they are heedless as the adder that turns a deaf ear
for fear it should hear the snake-charmer's voice, the voice of the skilful dealer in spells.

O God, break the teeth in their mouths,
tear out the fangs of these wild beasts, O Lord!

Let them vanish like water that runs away: let them wither like grass that is trodden underfoot:
let them be like the snail that melts into nothing; perish like the untimely birth that never sees the sun.

Before they put forth thorns, like a bramble,
let them be swept away, green wood or dry!

The just shall rejoice at the sight of vengeance; they shall bathe their feet in the blood of the wicked.

"Truly", men shall say, "the just are rewarded. Truly, there is a God who does justice on the earth."

*Glory be...*

## ANTIPHON 2

P**eople of God, praise and honour the Son of God**; rejoice as the angels rejoiced, that he has come to us, the Virgin's Son, to save and protect us from those who like lions would seek us as their prey.

## ANTIPHON 3

J**esus, we pray that all men may bless you and praise you.**

**Psalm 58**

Rescue me, God, from my foes; protect me from those who attack me.
O rescue me from those who do evil and save me from blood-thirsty men.

See, they lie in wait for my life; powerful men band together against me.
For no offence, no sin of mine, Lord, for no guilt of mine they rush to take their stand.

Awake, come to my aid and see! Lord of hosts, you are Israel's God.
Rouse yourself and punish the nations; show no mercy to evil traitors.

Each evening they come back like dogs. They howl and roam about the city,
they prowl in search of food, they snarl till they have their fill.

See how they gabble open-mouthed; their lips are filled with insults.
"For who," they say, "will hear us?"

But you, Lord, will laugh them to scorn.
You make light of all the nations.

O my strength, it is you to whom I turn, for you, O God, are my stronghold,
the God who shows me love.

O God, come to my aid and let me look in triumph on my foes.
God, kill them lest my people be seduced; rout them by your power,
lay them low.

It is you, O Lord, who are our shield. For the sins of their mouths and
their lips,
for the curses and lies that they speak let them be caught in their pride.

Destroy them, Lord, in your anger. Destroy them till they are no more.
Let men know that God is the ruler over Jacob and the ends of the earth.

Each evening they come back like dogs. They howl and roam about the city,
they prowl in search of food, they snarl till they have their fill.

As for me, I will sing of your strength and each morning acclaim your love
for you have been my stronghold, a refuge in the day of my distress.

O my Strength, it is you to whom I turn, for you, O God, are my stronghold,
the God who shows me love.

*Glory be...*

## ANTIPHON 3

**Jesus, we pray that all men may bless you and praise you**; and adore that divine decree by which a Virgin became a Mother and God became Man, that all men might come by faith to inherit the joys of heaven.

℣. God has entered this world of ours through the Virgin Mary. (Alleluia)
℟. To bring to heaven our fallen race. (Alleluia)

Our Father ...

## ABSOLUTION

God and father, holy and merciful Lord, take into account the prayer and holiness of Mary, the Virgin-Mother of God, and of all the saints and bring us back from death to life.
℟. Amen.

*Reader:* Lord, we ask for your blessing.

**Week One**

*Blessing, Reading and Response for Thursdays in Week Two start on page 519, and for Week Three on page 538.*

## Blessing

May the Virgin Mary, holiest, most blest of all, intercede for us with God.
℟. Amen.

## Reading

Speaking of the beauty of Mary, we think of lovely things:
her sacred body is like a vase of purest crystal;
her soul like a lantern of clearest light;
her mind like a fountain of water rising up into the air,
then falling in cool streams to the deep valley.

Passing from infancy to childhood,
to the age when she was able to understand,
she began to think of the existence of God,
and how he had made all things,
and especially man,
for his own eternal glory,
and how his justice embraces all things.
Her thoughts reached out to God,
as the waters of the fountain rise into the air;
then, like those waters flowing down to the valley,
her thoughts returned to herself
and brought her a most profound humility.

The Church sings of Christ leaving and returning to the Father,
though he was ever with the Father
and the Father ever with him.
Mary's thoughts reached up to heaven in contemplation
and grasped God by faith.
Then in the love with which God possessed her,
she turned her mind again to earth and to herself,
never losing her thought of God.
Together with hope and trust, and with holy fear,
the fire of this love inflamed her heart,
as the flame is the brightness of the lantern.

She understood the perfect subjection of body to soul,
and no discord ever troubled her,
so that in body she was purer than purest crystal.

How soon she learnt to appreciate God's love,
and treasure it with all her being!

Think of this love as a lily which God had planted,
with a threefold root,
bearing three flowers of great beauty.
The three roots are three most powerful virtues, protecting her body.
The three flowers, three adornments of her soul,
which gave great joy to God and the angels.

The first of the three virtues was her abstinence,
her right use of God's gifts of food and drink:
no over-indulgence to make her slow in the service of God,
no unwise austerity to impair her health.
The second was her wakefulness,
so that she rested no longer than necessary:
not wasting God's time in laziness,
but not fatiguing herself to the detriment of her work.
The third was her command over her will,
so that she was not easily wearied in body,
and never over-anxious or over-excited.

The first adornment of her soul was her love for the things of God
rather than the things of earth,
no matter how beautiful these might seem to be.
The things men so often prize,
possessions and wealth,
were utterly distasteful to her.
The second adornment was her appreciation of the infinite distance
between worldly honours and spiritual glory.
This world's praises were as abhorrent to her as the poisoning air of corruption.
The third adornment was her love for all that God loves,
her repugnance for all that was hateful and displeasing to him.
She sought in all things the true sweetness of God,
and no taste of bitterness was permitted to endure in her after her death.

With such beauty of soul,
Mary surpassed all other created things.
God willed that only through her should his promises be fulfilled.
Her love left no blemish or defect, not even the smallest.
In nothing could the enemy claim victory over her.
If then she was so pleasing in the sight of God and the angels,
may we not think that she had also great earthly beauty?
Those who saw her looked with delight,
and knew that her loveliness was born of her love for God.
They saw her, and loved to see her,
and were led to a new love for God.
They watched her, and loved to be with her,
and knew that no evil could touch them,
nothing sinful attract them,
in the presence of her beauty and holiness.

℣. Have mercy, Lord, and help our understanding. ℟. Our thanks to God.

## Responsory

**Mary**, there is no holiness, no purity, no virginity like yours; for your holiness is fullness of grace, your purity is love of God, your Virginity true Motherhood, Mary, Mother of God. No land, no world, no sun or moon, no stars of heaven, not heaven itself could hold him; yet you, Mary, have held him and borne him in your womb.
℣. Virgin Mary, you are most blest of all, for Jesus Christ is your Son.
℟. No land, no world, no sun or moon, no stars of heaven, not heaven itself could hold him; yet you, Mary, have held him and borne him in your womb.
℣. Glory to God, glory to Father, Son and Holy Spirit.
℟. No land, no world, no sun or moon, no stars of heaven, not heaven itself could hold him; yet you, Mary, have held him and borne him in your womb.

## Te Deum *as on Sunday, page 75* or Psalm 50 *as on Friday, page 330.*

℣. God himself came down to the Virgin's womb. (Alleluia)
℟. There to clothe himself as Man, with flesh to offer for us and blood to shed for us. (Alleluia)

## Closing Prayers *(page 38).*

# VESPERS

**PRAYERS** before Vespers, *(pages 77 - 78)* and
**OPENING PRAYERS** – with music – *as at None, pages 55 - 56.*

## ANTIPHON

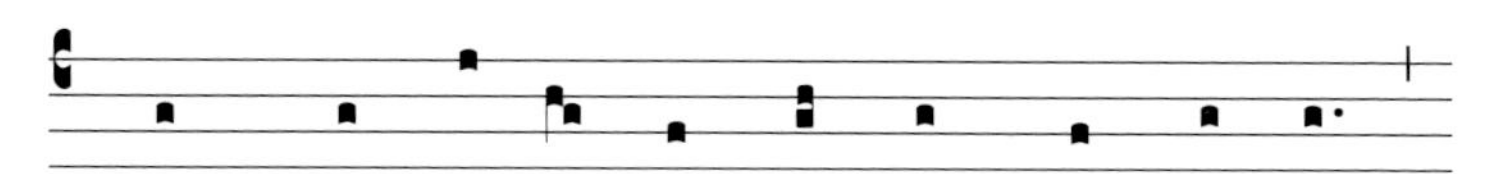

**How blessed are all who wor-ship Christ as Lord,**

TONE VIII

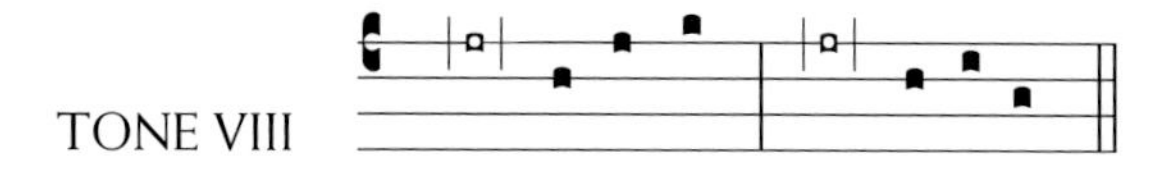

**Psalm 112**

Praise, O servants of the Lord, praise the name of the Lord!
May the name of the Lord be blessed both now and for evermore!

From the rising of the sun to its setting praised be the name of the Lord!
High above all nations is the Lord, above the heavens his glory.

Who is like the Lord, our God, who has risen on high to his throne
yet stoops from the heights to look down, to look down upon
heaven and earth?

From the dust he lifts up the lowly, from the dungheap he raises the poor
to set him in the company of princes, yes, with the princes of his people.

To the childless wife he gives a home
and gladdens her heart with children.

*Glory be...*

**Psalm 116**

O praise the Lord, all you nations, acclaim him all you peoples!
Strong is his love for us; he is faithful for ever.

*Glory be...*

**Psalm 121**

I rejoiced when I heard them say: "Let us go to God's house."
And now our feet are standing within your gates, O Jerusalem.

Jerusalem is built as a city strongly compact.
It is there that the tribes go up, the tribes of the Lord.

For Israel's law it is, there to praise the Lord's name.
There were set the thrones of judgment of the house of David.

For the peace of Jerusalem pray: "Peace be to your homes!
May peace reign in your walls, in your palaces, peace!"

For love of my brethren and friends I say: "Peace upon you!"
For love of the house of the Lord I will ask for your good.

*Glory be...*

**Psalm 126**

If the Lord does not build the house, in vain do its builders labour;
if the Lord does not watch over the city, in vain does the watchman keep vigil.

In vain is your earlier rising, your going later to rest,
you who toil for the bread you eat, when he pours gifts on his beloved
while they slumber.

Truly sons are a gift from the Lord, a blessing, the fruit of the womb.
Indeed the sons of youth are like arrows in the hand of a warrior.

O the happiness of the man who has filled his quiver with these arrows!
He will have no cause for shame when he disputes with his foes in the gateways.

*Glory be...*

**Psalm 147**

O praise the Lord, Jerusalem!
Sion praise your God!

He has strengthened the bars of your gates, he has blessed the children
within you.
He established peace on your borders, he feeds you with finest wheat.

He sends out his word to the earth and swiftly runs his command.
He showers down snow white as wool, he scatters hoar-frost like ashes.

He hurls down hailstones like crumbs. The waters are frozen at his touch;
he sends forth his word and it melts them: at the breath of his mouth
the waters flow.

He makes his word known to Jacob, to Israel his laws and decrees.
He has not dealt thus with other nations; he has not taught them his decrees.

*Glory be...*

ANTIPHON

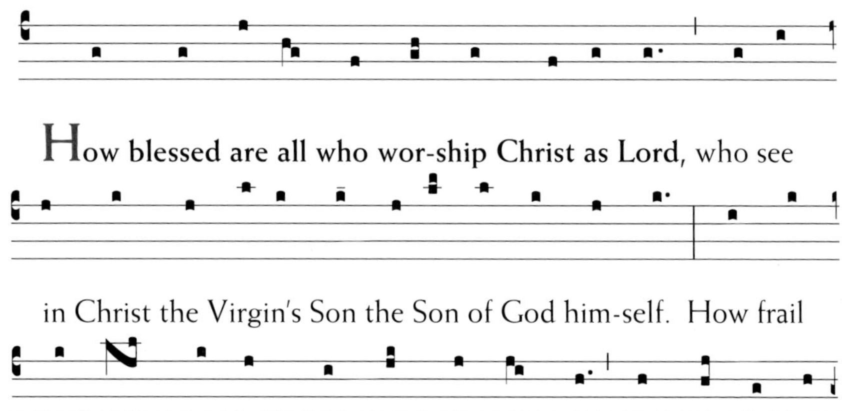

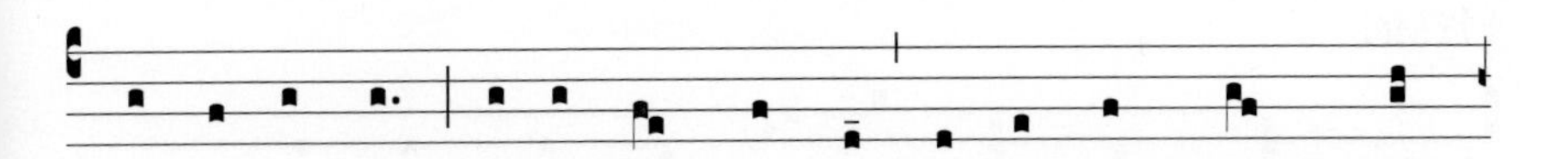

ly trust in men; for in none but God can we find strength and

sal-va-tion.

READING

How blest are you, Virgin Mary, Mother of Christ who created

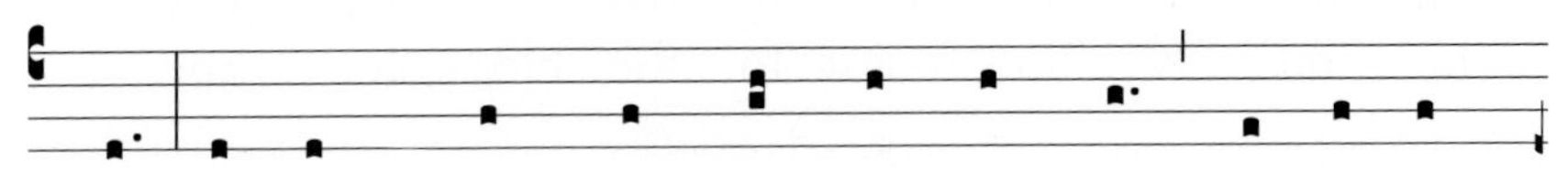

all. You have brought forth him who made you, Mo-ther and

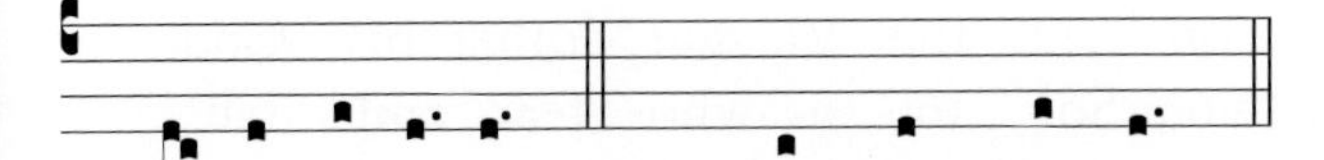

Vir-gin for e-ver. ℟. Our thanks to God.

HYMN

1. We name you, Ma - ry, Morn-ing Star, Gate of heav'n
2. "Re - joice, fear not," the an - gel said, "full of grace,
3. From sin and blind-ness make us free, show for each
4. Pure Vir - gin, make us pure of heart, keep our liv-
5. Praise to the Fa - ther, Lord and God, praise to Christ

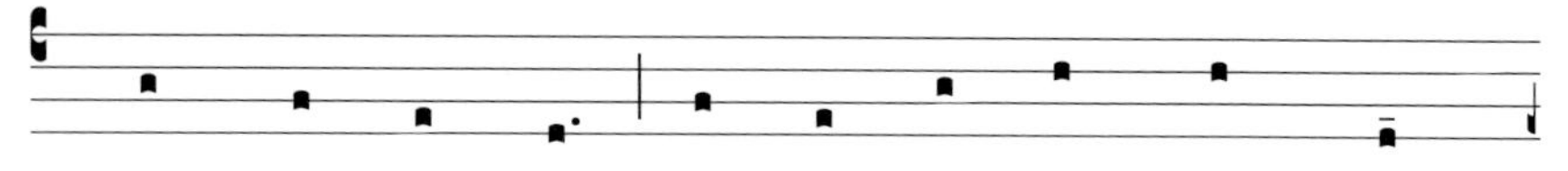

1. our way to God, but with a name more blessed
2. most blessed of all": Ma - ry, new Eve, bring joy
3. a mo - ther's care, pro - tect us, win from Christ
4. ing free from sin, and at our dy - ing pray
5. his on - ly Son, praise to the Ho - ly Spi-

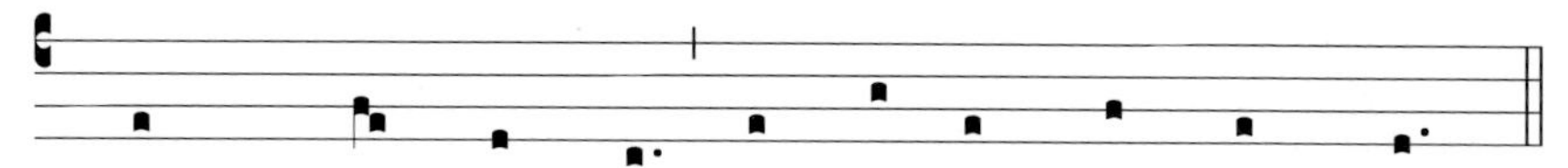

1. we call on you, the Vir -gin Mother of God.
2. through Christ your Son, to us who fear and fall.
3. the help we need, pray with a mo - ther's prayer.
4. that Christ may give e - ter-nal joy with him.
5. rit; praise to God e - ter-nal Three in One.

5. A – men.

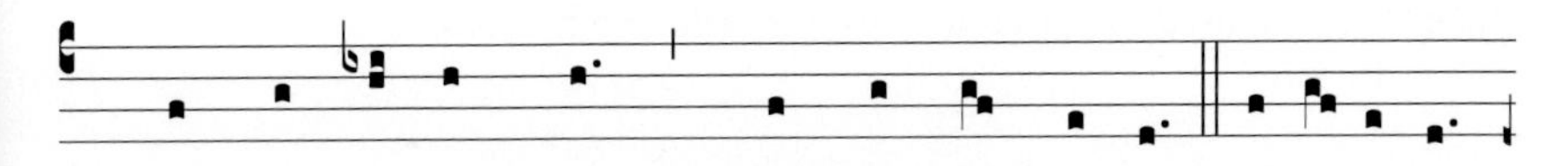

℣. From the Vir-gin's womb, Christ has come in joy. (Al-le-lu-ia)

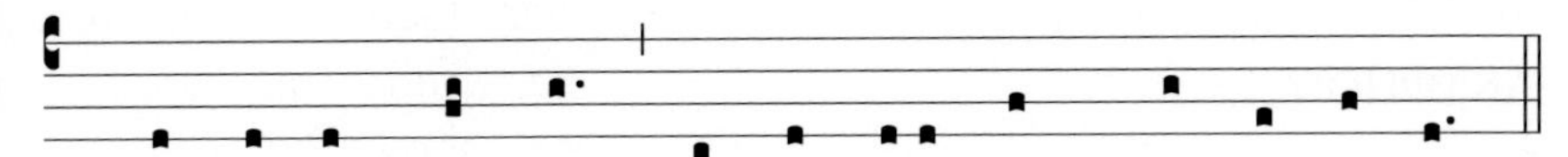

℟. And we have seen him, co-ming as a bride-groom to his bride.

(Al-le-lu-ia)

**ANTIPHON**

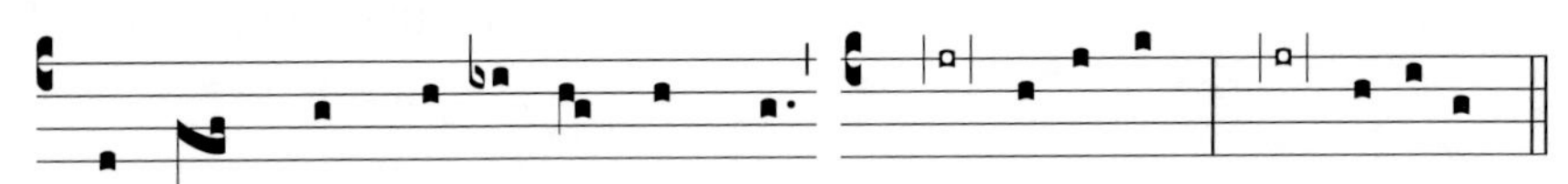

**Rejoice with nev-er ending joy,** TONE VIII

**MAGNIFICAT** *(Luke 1: 46 - 55)*

My soul glorifies the Lord,
my spirit rejoices in God,
my Saviour.

He looks on his servant in her nothingness; henceforth all ages
will call me blessed.
The Almighty works marvels for me. Holy his name!

His mercy is from age to age, on those who fear him.
He puts forth his arm in strength and scatters the proud-
hearted.

He casts the mighty from their thrones and raises the lowly.
He fills the starving with good things, sends the rich away empty.

He protects Israel, his servant, remembering his mercy,

the mercy promised to our fathers, to Abraham and his sons
for ever.

Praise the Father, the Son and the Holy Spirit,
both now and for ever, world without end.

ANTIPHON

in all our good you lead and guide; in our sin-ful-ness you plead

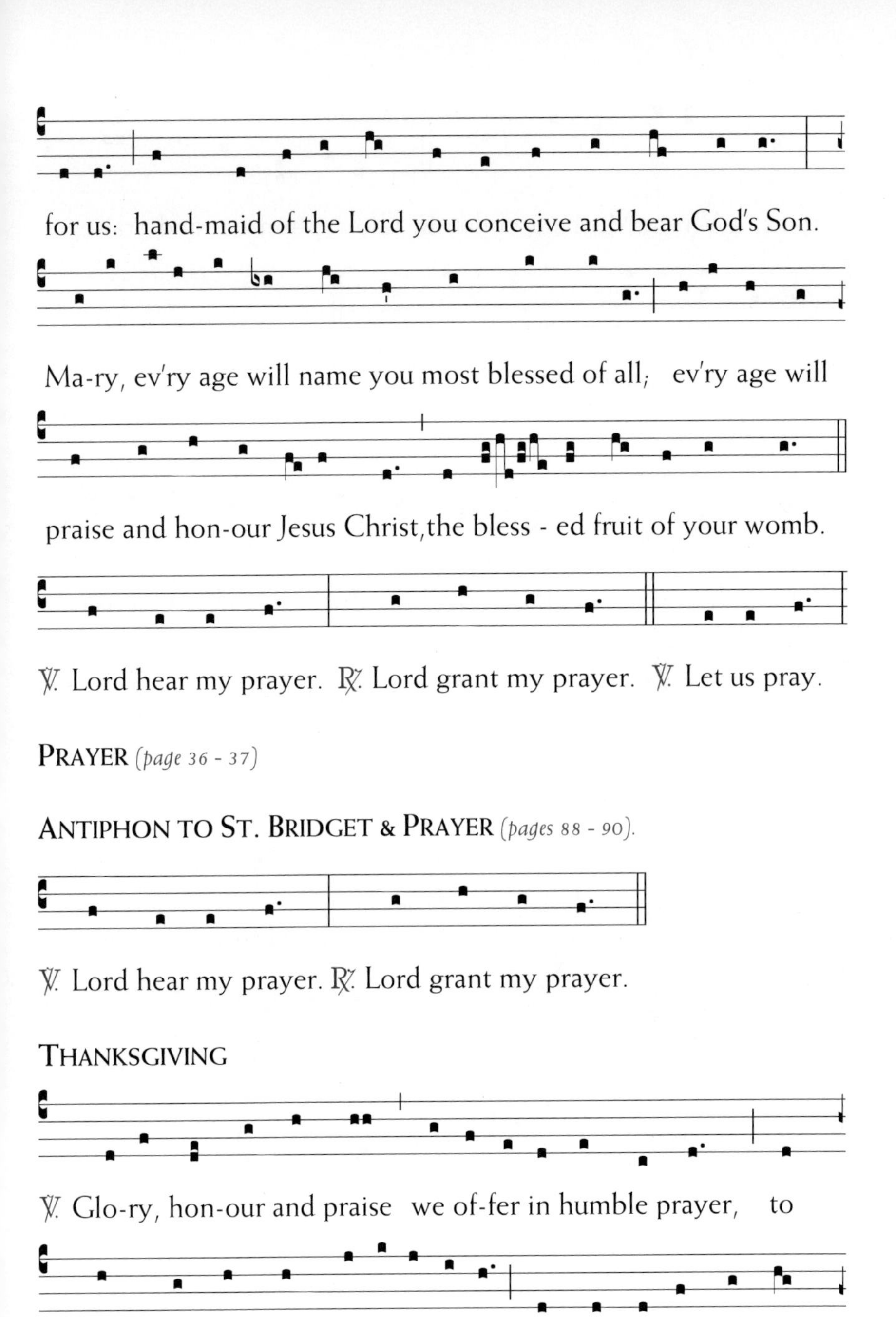


Christ the Lord and Cre-a-tor of all, who was content to come

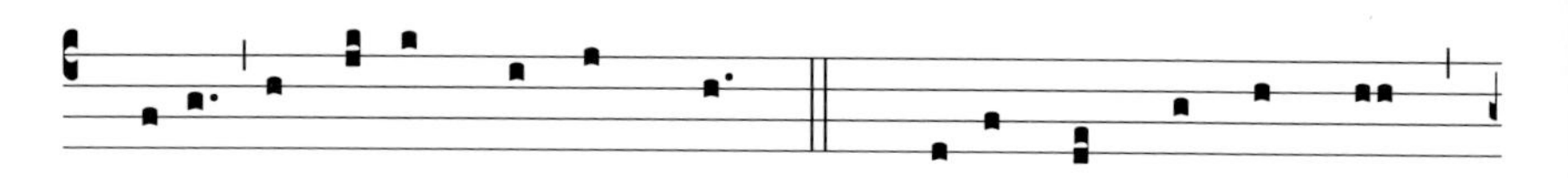

to us, a Virgin-Mother's child. ℟. Glo-ry, hon-our and praise,

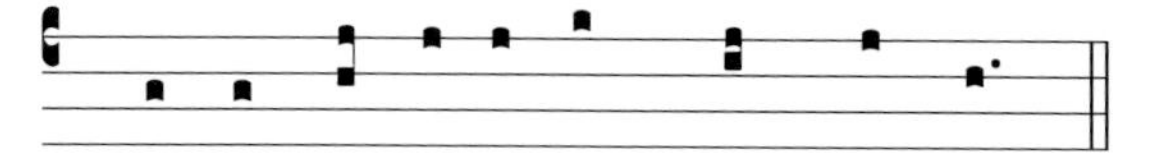

and our nev-er ending thanks to God.

*(with Alleluia)*

℣. Glo-ry, hon-our and praise to Christ the Lord and Cre- a- tor,

who was content to come to us, a Virgin-Mother's child.

Al-le - lu - ia, Al-le-lu- ia, Al-le- lu - ia.

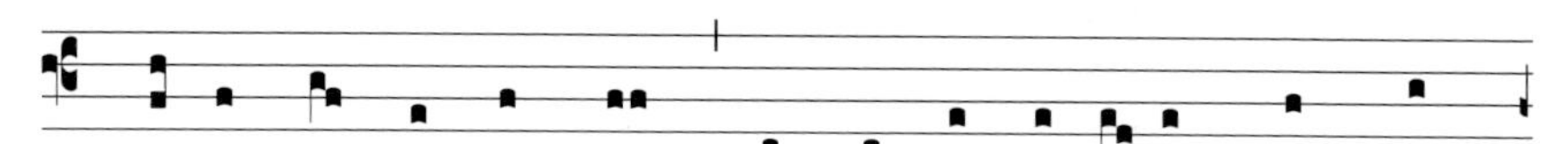

℟. Glo-ry, hon-our and praise, and our nev-er ending thanks to

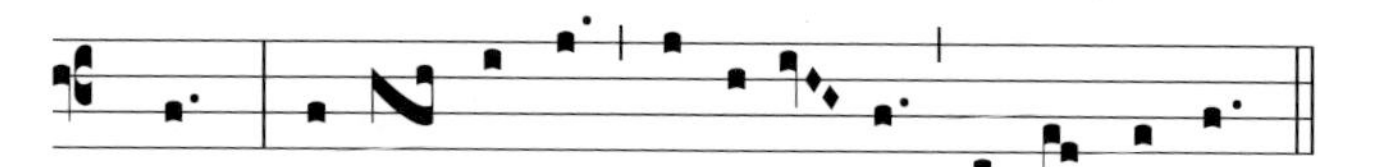

God. Al-le - lu- ia, Al-le-lu- ia, Al-le- lu- ia.

## CLOSING PRAYERS

'Mary, rejoice in God,' ... *with music* *(page 92)* *followed by...*

**HYMN** *to Holy Mother St. Bridget,* *(pages 93 - 94).*

*Thursday*
# COMPLINE

**OPENING PRAYERS** *as before Sunday Compline, pages 95 - 96.*

**ANTIPHON**

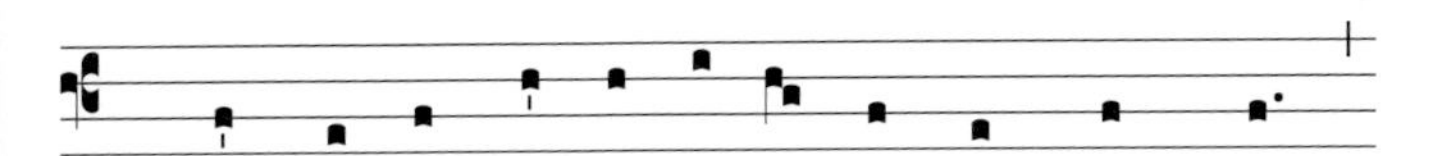

Praise of the Vir-gin is ev - er praise of Christ,

TONE II 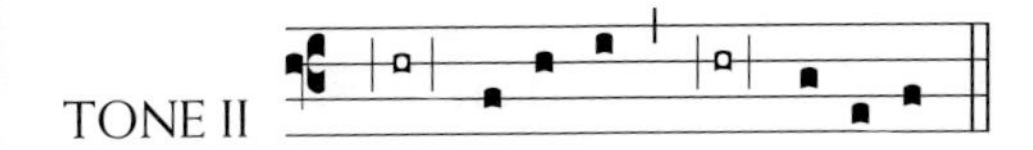

**Psalms 131, 132 & 133** *as on Sunday, pages 97 - 98.*

**ANTIPHON**

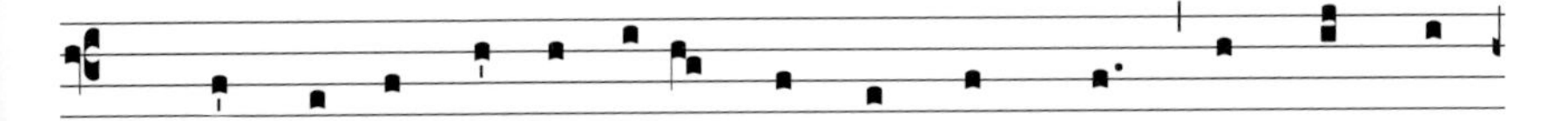

Praise of the Vir-gin is ev - er praise of Christ, as prayer to

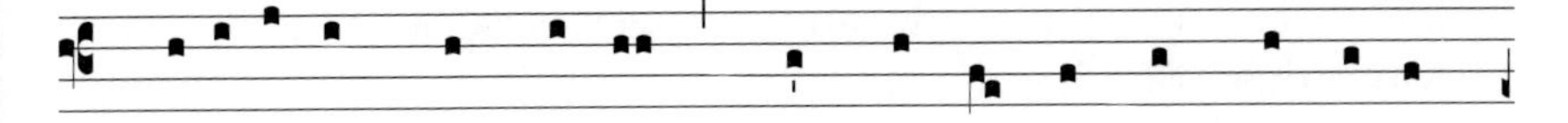

her is ev-er prayer to him, Christ the Son of God, her glo-ry

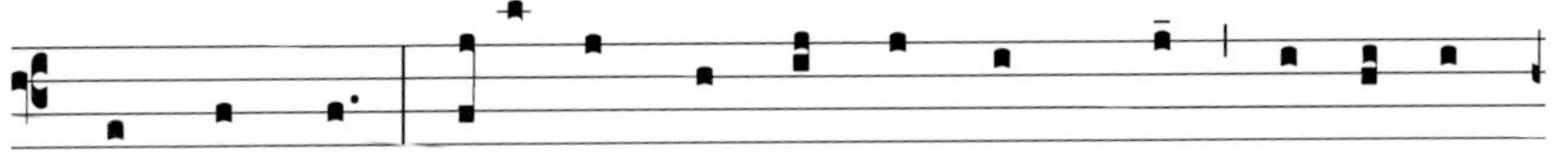

and her grace. Ev'ry age shall call her most blessed for all the

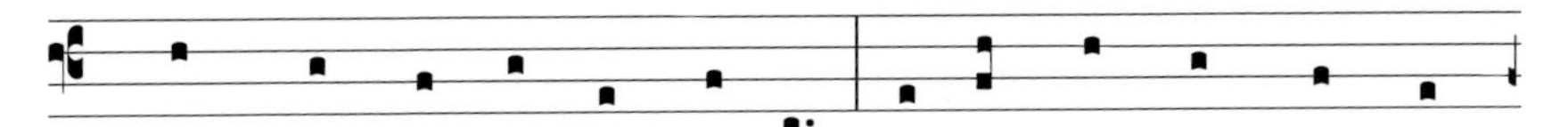

things that God has done for her; and all who praise and pray

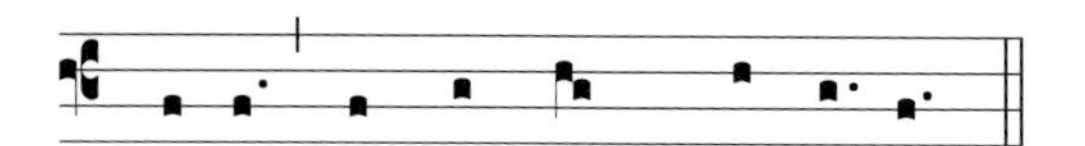

to her shall be blessed for ev-er.

**Reading** *as on Sunday, page 99.*

**Short Responsory** *as on Sunday, pages 99 ff.*

---

**Hymn**

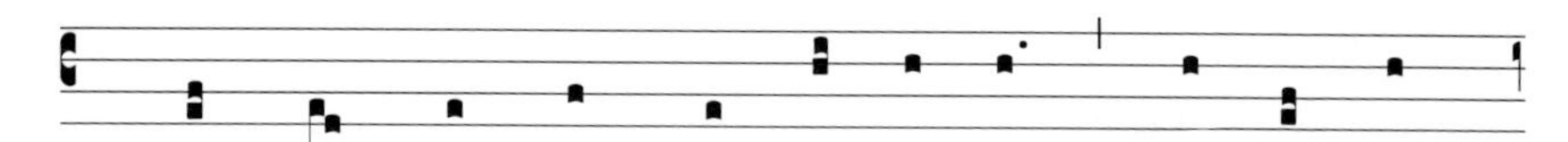

1. The Fa - ther's Son will make on earth the Vir - gin's
2. Here Christ will clothe him-self as man, his God-head's
3. The Vir - gin will be e - ver blessed as Vir - gin
4. Pray Ma - ry Mo - ther full of grace, pray in your
5. Christ Son of God we pray to you, and ho - nour

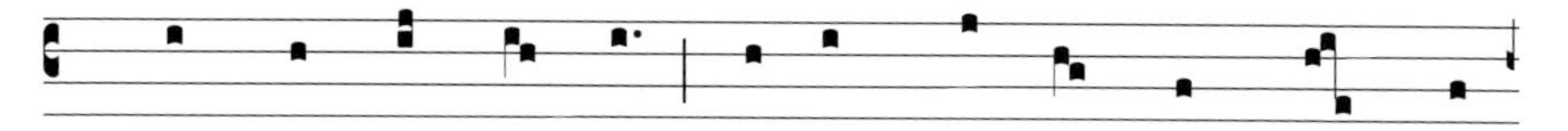

1. womb his dwel -ling place, the Fa - ther and the Spi - rit
2. glo - ry set a - side, and an - gels see him and ac-
3. Mo - ther of her Lord, and as his heaven-ly bride bring
4. love for all we need, pro-tect us from all dan - ger
5. you the Vir - gin's Son; we praise the Fa - ther, God with

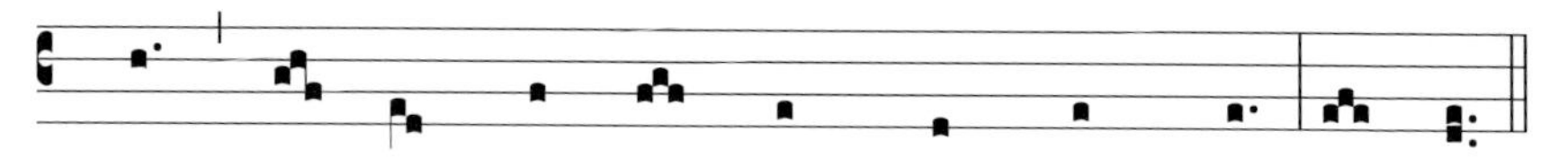

1. too will ev - er be with her in grace.
2. claim the bride-groom co - ming to his bride.
3. forth child -ren of grace to heaven's re - ward.
4. now and at our dy - ing in - ter - cede.
5. you and with the Spi - rit, Three in One. A - men.

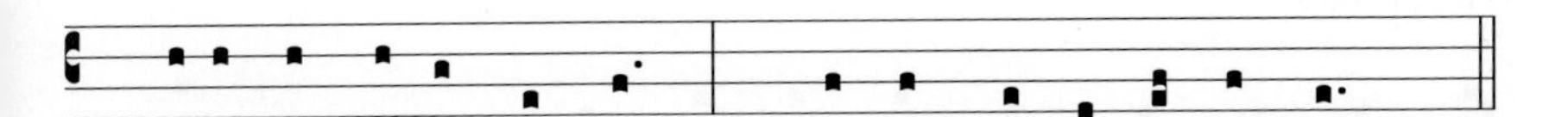

℣. I am the servant of God, ℟. To hear and o-bey his word.

*(with Alleluia)*

℣. I am the ser-vant of God, Al-le-lu-ia.

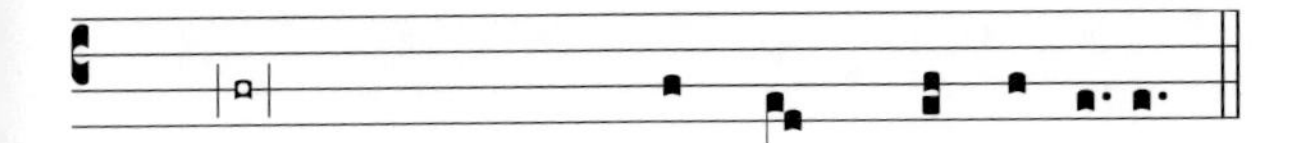

℟. To hear and obey his word, Al -le-lu-ia.

## ANTIPHON

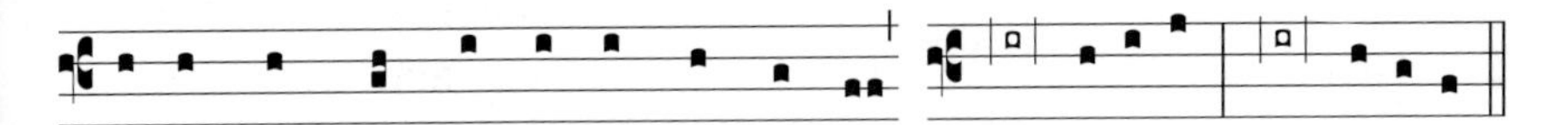

**Ma-ry, our praise of you is praise of God** TONE IV

## CANTICLE OF SIMEON *(Luke 2: 29 - 32)*

At last, all powerful Master you give leave
to your servant to go in peace,
according to your promise.

For my eyes have seen your salvation which you have prepared
for all nations.
The light to enlighten the gentiles and give glory to Israel, your people.

Give praise to the Father Almighty: to his Son, Jesus Christ, the Lord;
to the Spirit who dwells in our hearts, both now and forever. Amen.

ANTIPHON

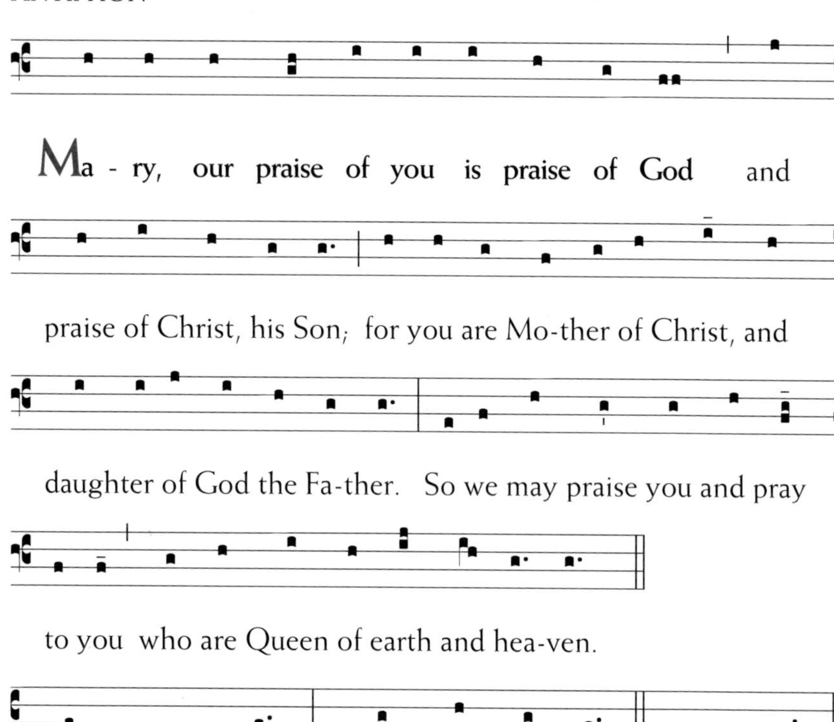


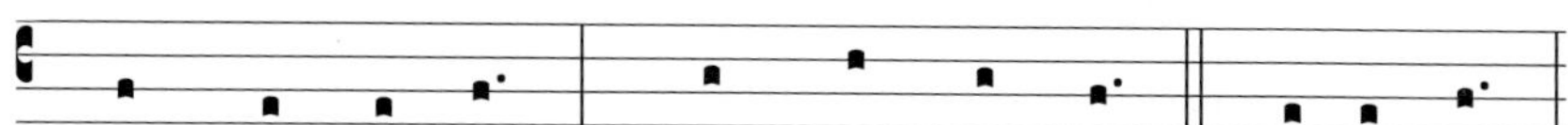

℣. Lord, hear my prayer. ℟. Lord, grant my prayer. ℣. Let us pray.

PRAYER *as on Sunday, page 104.*

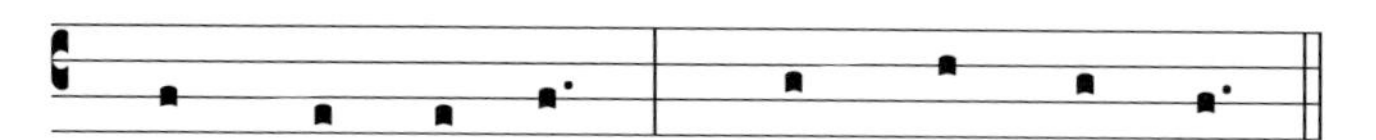

℣. Lord, hear my prayer. ℟. Lord, grant my prayer.

THANKSGIVING

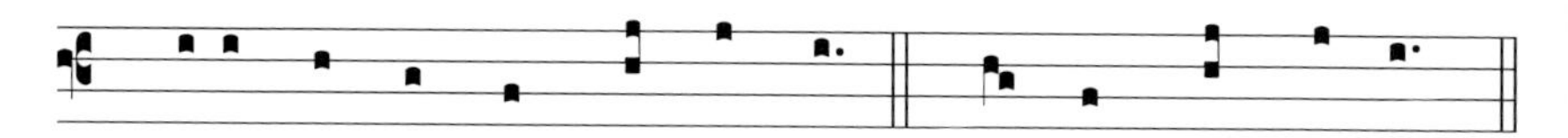

℣. Glory, hon-our and praise to God. ℟. And our thanks to him.

*(with Alleluia)*

℣. Glory hon-our and praise to God, Al- le- lu- ia.

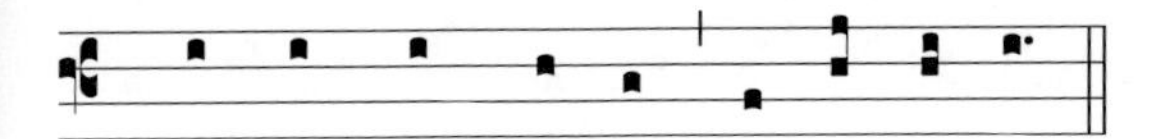

℟. And our thanks to him, Al- le- lu- ia.

℣. Mary, you are full of grace, the Lord is with you.
℟. Mary, you are most blessed of all women, for Jesus Christ is your Son.
(Alleluia)

## Lauds of Our Lady

*Except during the Christmas season: see following pages.*

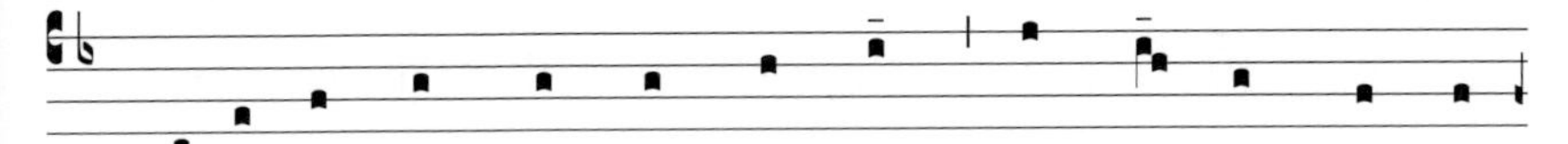

**Ma-ry, we name you morn-ing Star,** bright gui-ding light to

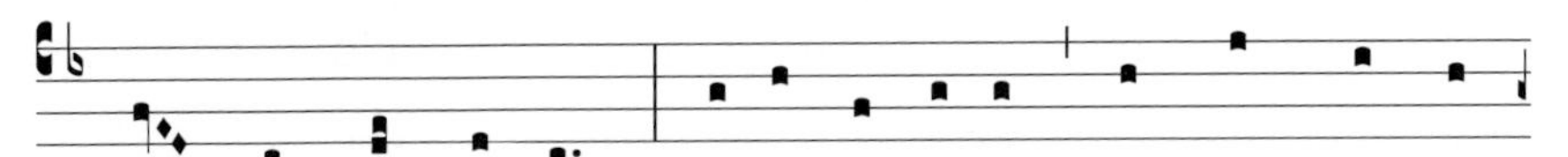

Christ the Light of light; Refuge of sinners, new hope and com-

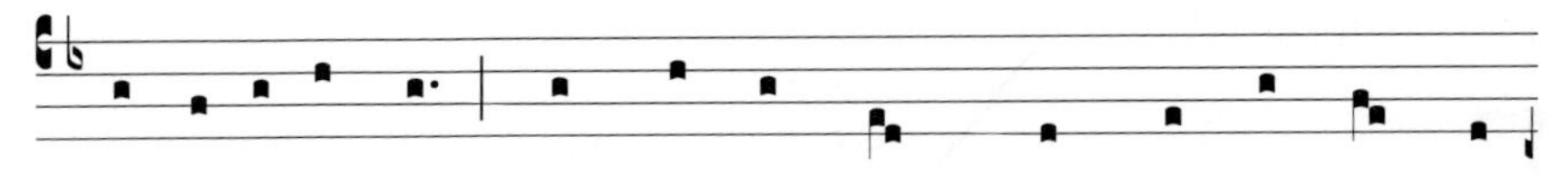

fort to all in need; guard-ian and guide through all our world-ly

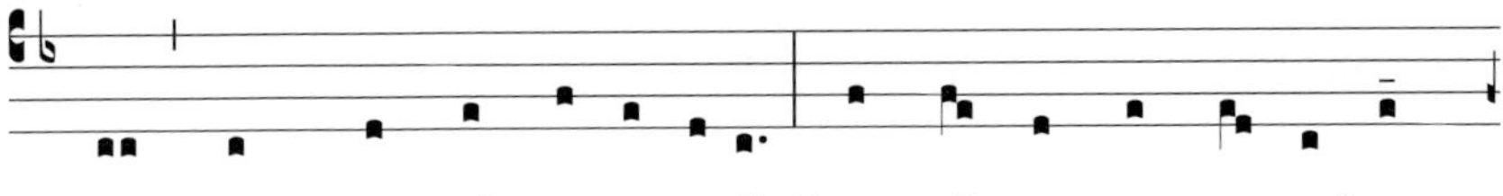

ways, and Queen of mercy to all. From all wo-men you a-lone

were worthy of Christ, and you a - lone, in sin-less-ness have

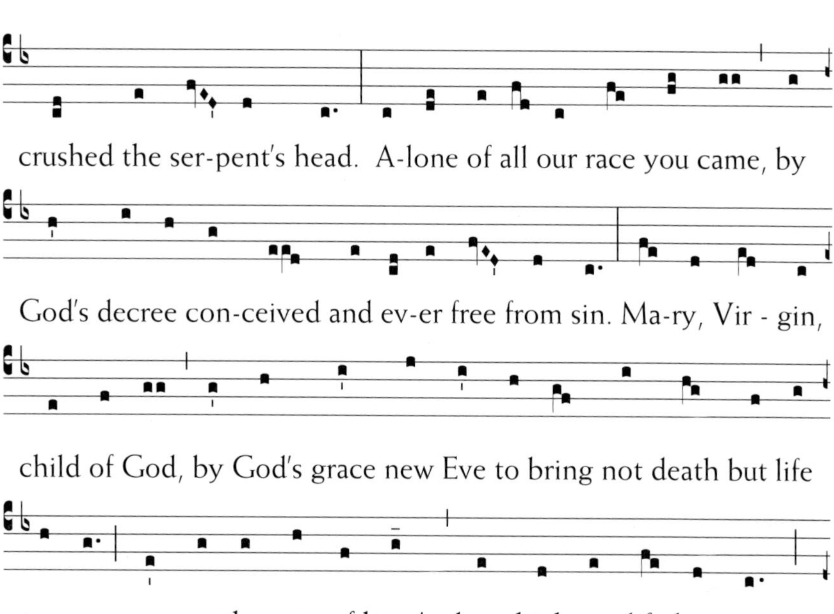


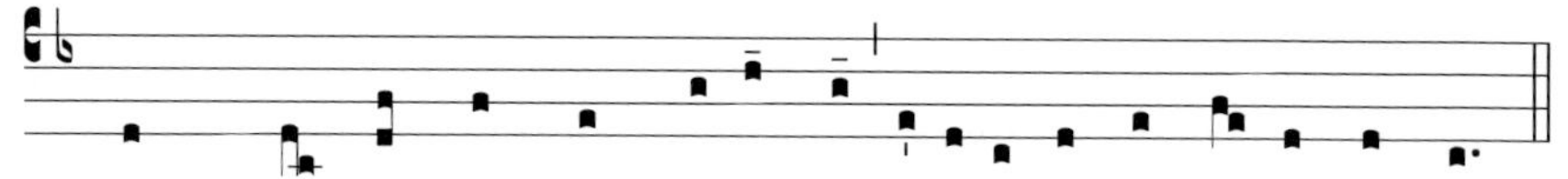


℣. Pray for us, holy Virgin Mary, Mother of God.
℟. That we may be made worthy of the promises of Jesus Christ.

℣. Let us pray.

Forgive, we ask you Lord, the sins of your servants: and may we who of ourselves are unable to please you, be saved by the prayers of the Mother of your Son, Jesus Christ our Lord. ℟. Amen.

**CLOSING PRAYERS** 'Mary, rejoice in God,' … *as on Sunday, page 107.*

**LAUDS OF OUR LADY** *During the Christmas season.*

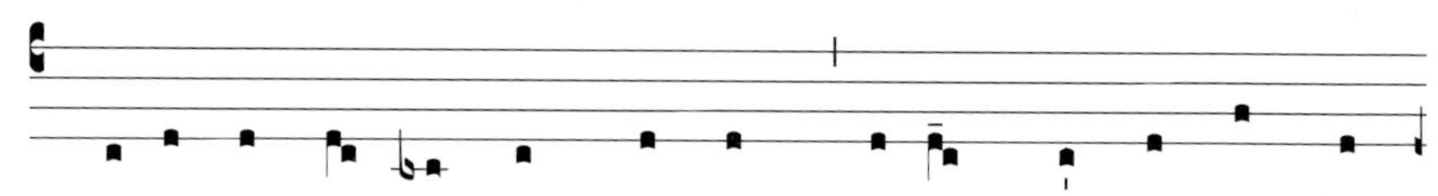

**Glory, to God and peace to men** – re-joice with the an - gels

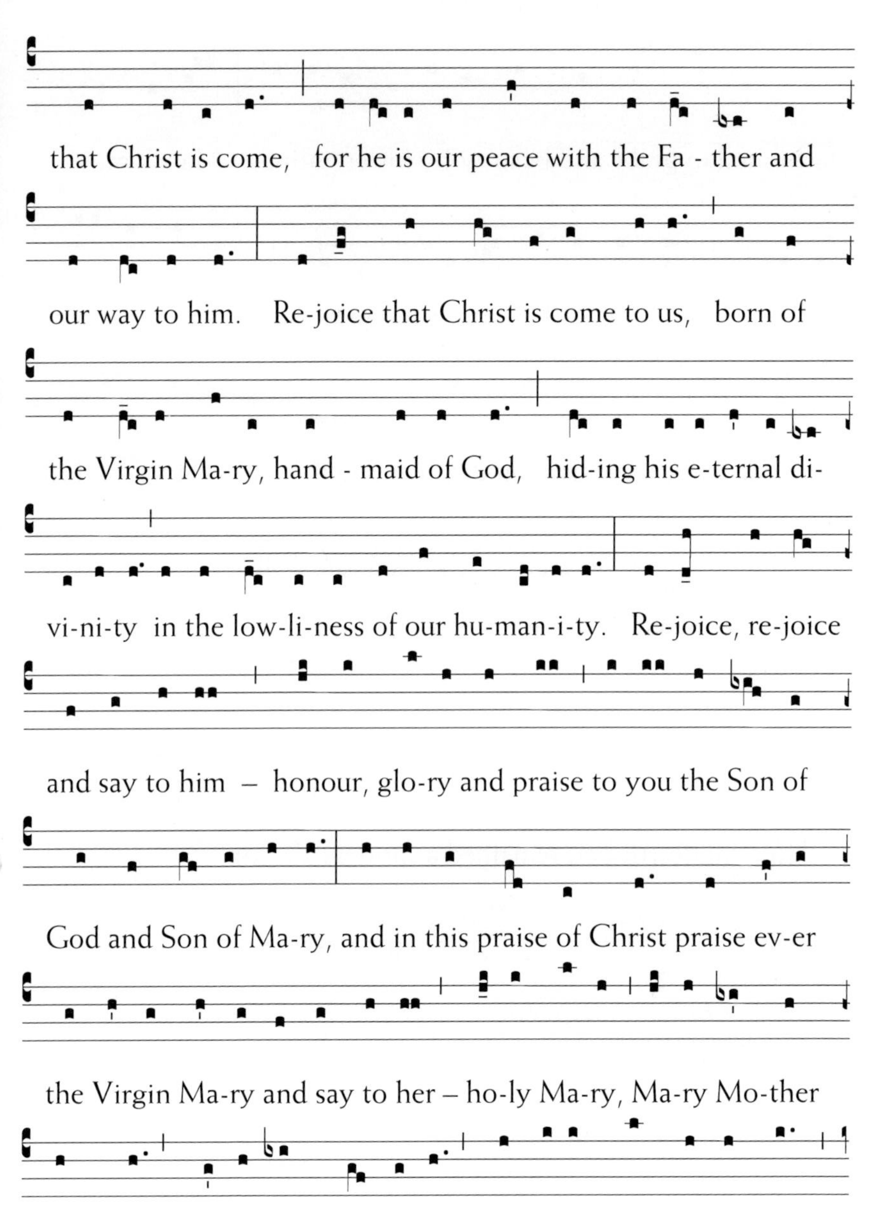
that Christ is come, for he is our peace with the Fa - ther and
our way to him. Re-joice that Christ is come to us, born of
the Virgin Ma-ry, hand - maid of God, hid-ing his e-ternal di-
vi-ni-ty in the low-li-ness of our hu-man-i-ty. Re-joice, re-joice
and say to him – honour, glo-ry and praise to you the Son of
God and Son of Ma-ry, and in this praise of Christ praise ev-er
the Virgin Ma-ry and say to her – ho-ly Ma-ry, Ma-ry Mo-ther
of Christ, Ma-ry most blest of all, love-li-est trea-sure of God

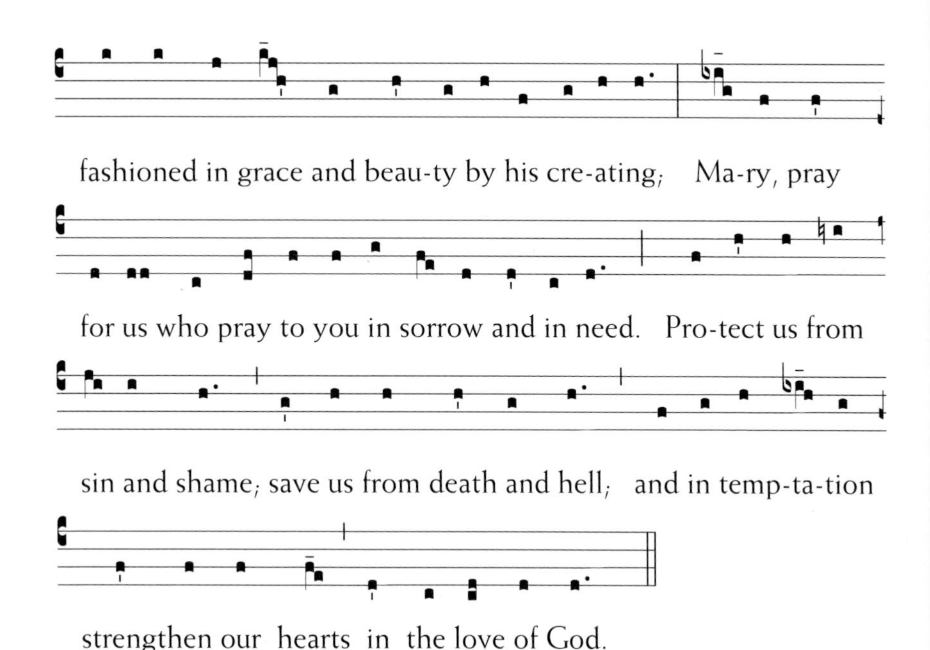


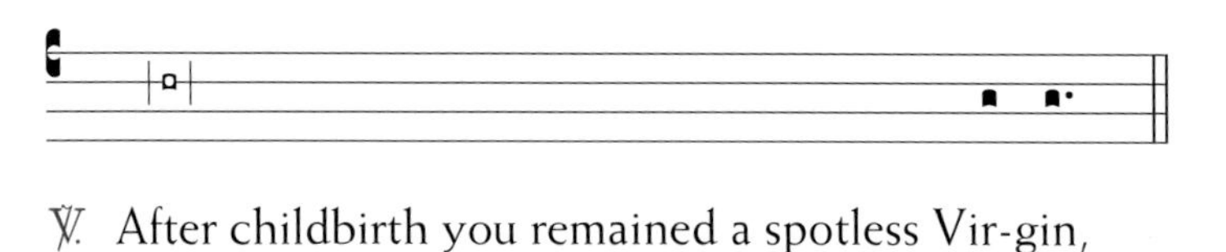


℟. Mother of God, intercede for us. ℣. Let us pray.

## Prayer

O God, through the fruitful virginity of the Blessed Mary, you have given the treasure of salvation to mankind. Grant, we ask you, that we may be blessed by the prayers of her, through whom it was possible for us to receive the source of life, Jesus Christ our Lord. ℟. Amen.

**Closing Prayers** 'Mary, rejoice in God,' … *as on Sunday, page 107.*

*Friday*

# LAUDS

## OPENING PRAYERS

***(The first prayer of the day...)*** *(page 33).*
Open my mouth, O Lord ... *including Invitatory psalm (Ps. 94)*

## ANTIPHON

**Mary, Mother of Christ our life.**

Psalms and Canticles *as on Sunday, (pages 39 ff), EXCEPT on ferial Fridays and ferial days in Passiontide when the* Canticle of the Three Children *is not said.*
*See page 294 for CANTICLES for ferial Fridays throughout the year and in Passiontide. Not to be used during Easter.*

**Mary, Mother of Christ our life**, we pray for God's mercy, trusting the power of your prayer. Think how Christ humbled himself, and came to men, made one of us by your Motherhood. Think what a death he underwent for us, watched by your love.

## READING *as on Sunday, page 44.*

## HYMN

Foretold and long desired, time's fullness came,
and Christ in joy came forth from heaven to earth,
as man to men, to seek and save all men,
like us in all but sin, by virgin birth.

Yet see the suffering Christ must undergo,
the scorn, the thanklessness, the hate of men,
the wounds of scourge and thorn, of nail and spear,
to die and win us to his love again.

Look on the cross of shame where Christ was nailed,
condemned with thieves to die in agony,

hated, despised, rejected by his own,
mocked and blasphemed by those who stood to see.

But Mary by the cross of Christ her Son,
shared with her love the bitter pain he bore.
Jesus, keep ever in our hearts and minds
your pain and love, that we may love you more.

Pray Mary Virgin-Mother, ... *Last two verses as on Sunday, page 44.*

℣. How deep were the sorrows of Mary, to stand and see. (Alleluia)
℟. Christ our life, crucified to death. (Alleluia)

## ANTIPHON

V**irgin Mary**.

## CANTICLE

Blessed be the Lord, the God of Israel! ... *as on Sunday, page 45.*

V**irgin Mary**, it has pleased God to make you our consolation in sorrow; for you have brought to our lifeless darkness the living light of Christ. Mary, we pray to you for the light of Christ your Son, to take from our hearts all shadow of sin. In this light of truth, we know the foolishness and vanity of earthly things and see, in the price of our redemption, the depths of God's love.

℣. Lord hear my prayer. ℟. Lord grant my prayer. ℣. Let us pray.

## PRAYER

Grant us, your servants, ...
*As on Sunday page 46 or according to the time of year. See pages 36ff.*

**ANTIPHON** to holy Mother Saint Bridget *as on Sunday, page 46.*
Bridget, loving servant of God, ...
*or on ferial days:* Bridget, Saint and Patron, ...

℣. and ℟. with Prayer *(page 47).*

℣. Lord hear my prayer. ℟. Lord grant my prayer.

## Thanksgiving

℣. Glory, honour and praise to Christ the Virgin's Son, the ever-living Lord, who died a victim for sin. (Alleluia, alleluia, alleluia)
℟. For this redemption from sin and death which opened to us the way to life and joy, our eternal thanks to God. (Alleluia, alleluia, alleluia)

## Closing Prayers (*page* 37).

'Mary, rejoice in God,' ...

*Visitors to Syon Abbey in Devon were greeted by this statue of St Bridget.*

*For ferial Fridays & during Passiontide**

# CANTICLES AT LAUDS

* One is said in place of the *Canticle of the Three Children* at Lauds on ferial Fridays throughout the year: one each Friday in rotation. They are also used similarly in Passiontide on ferial days from Monday after Passion Sunday to Wednesday of Holy Week inclusive. They are not used during the seasons of Christmas or Easter.

## 1. CANTICLE OF MOSES *(Exodus, 15: 1-19)*

I will sing to the Lord, glorious his triumph
Horse and rider he has thrown into the sea.

The Lord is my strength, my song; he is my salvation.
This is my God, I extol him, my Father's God, I give him praise.

The Lord is a warrior, the Lord is his name.
The chariots of Pharaoh he hurled into the sea.

The deeps hid them, they sank like a stone.
Your right hand, Lord, glorious in power, your right hand has shattered the enemy.

Before the greatness of your majesty they rose – but to fall.
The breath of your anger burnt them like stubble.

In the blast of your anger the waters piled high.
The waves were still; the deeps came together.

The enemy said, "I will pursue and overtake them, divide the spoil and have my fill.
I will draw my sword, my hand shall slay them."

One breath of yours and the sea closed over them;
they sank like lead into the mighty waters.

Who is like you, O Lord among the strong?
Who like you in majesty, glorious in deeds, in holiness?

You stretched out your hand;
the earth swallowed them.

In pity you led your own people whom you had saved.
Your strong arm guided them to your holy place.

The heathens raged, the Philistines were in dread;
Edom was dismayed, the princes of Moab trembled; Canaan melted away.

On them fall terror and dread; through the power of your arm they are
still as stone
as your people pass, O Lord, as the people pass whom you purchased.

You will bring them and plant them on your holy mountain,
the place you have made your dwelling, Lord, the sanctuary prepared
by your hands.

The Lord will reign
for ever and ever.

When the army of Pharaoh went forward the Lord released the waters.
But the people of Israel marched on, dry-shod in the midst of the sea.

*Glory be...*

## 2. CANTICLE OF HABAKKUK *(Habakkuk, 3: 2-19)*

Lord, I have heard of your renown,
your work, Lord, inspires me with dread.

Repeat it again in our time, reveal it in our own time;
for all your wrath, remember to be merciful.

God comes forth from Teman, and the Holy One from Mount Paran.
His majesty veils the heavens, the earth is filled with his glory.

His brightness is like the day, rays flash from his hands,
that is where his power lies hidden.

Plague goes in front of him, fever follows on his heels.
When he stands up the earth trembles; at his glance the nations quake.

Then the ancient mountains are dislodged, the everlasting hills sink down,
the hills where he walked from of old.

I have seen the tents of Cushan terrified,
the pavilions of the land of Midian shuddering.

Lord, is your anger blazing against the rivers, or your fury against the sea,
that you come mounted on your horses, on your victorious chariots?

You uncover your bow, you ply its string with arrows.
You cleave the earth with rivers; the mountains tremble at your coming;

great floods sweep on their way, the abyss roars aloud,
the waves lift high their hands.

Sun and moon stay in their houses, avoiding the flash of your arrows,
the gleam of your glittering spear.

Raging, you stride the earth,
in anger you trample the nations.

You have marched to save your people, to save your own anointed;
you have beaten down the wicked man's house, bared its foundations
to the rock.

Your shafts have pierced the warriors, who stormed out in triumph
to scatter us,
as if to devour the poor in secret.

You have trampled the sea with your horses,
and the mighty waters foamed.

I have heard. My whole body trembles, my lips quiver at the sound;
decay creeps into my bones, my feet stumble beneath me.

Calmly I await the day of anguish
which is dawning on those who attack us.

Even though the fig trees have no fruit, and no grapes grow on the vines;
even though the olive crop fails, and the fields produce no corn;

even though the sheep all die, and the cattle stalls are empty:

I will still be joyful and glad, I will exult in God my saviour.

The Lord my God is my strength;
he makes me sure-footed as a deer, and keeps me safe on the mountains.

*Glory be…*

### 3. CANTICLE OF MOSES Part 1 *(Deuteronomy, 32: 1-21)*

Listen, heavens, while I speak;
earth, hear the words I am saying.

May my teaching fall like the rain, may my word drop down like dew,
like showers on fresh grass and light rain on the turf.

For I proclaim the name of the Lord, O, tell the greatness of our God!
He is the Rock, his work is perfect, for all his ways are just.

Your God is faithful and true; he does what is right and fair.
But you are unfaithful, unworthy to be his people, a sinful and deceitful nation.

Is this the return you make to the Lord? O foolish, unwise people !
Is not this your Father, who gave you being, who made you, by whom you subsist?

Think back on the days of old, think over the years, down the ages.
Ask of your father, let him teach you; of your elders, let them enlighten you.

When the Most High gave the nations their inheritance, when he divided the sons of men,
he determined where people should live.

But the Lord's portion was his people,
Jacob's descendants he chose for himself.

In the waste lands he adopts him, in the howling desert of the wilderness.
He protects him, rears him, guards him as the pupil of his eye.

Like an eagle watching its nest, hovering over its young,
he spreads out his wings to hold him, he supports him on his pinions.

The Lord alone is his guide, with him is no alien god.
He gives him the heights of the land, he feeds him on the yield
of the mountains,

he gives him honey from the rock, and oil from the flinty crag;
curds from the cattle, milk from the flock, with rich food of the pastures,

rams of Bashan's breed, and goats, rich food of finest wheat,
and blood of the fermenting grape for drink.

Jacob ate and had his fill, he grew sleek and fat, turned restive.
He disowned the God who made him, dishonoured the Rock, his salvation.

They roused him to jealousy with alien gods,
the evil they did made him angry.

They sacrificed to demons who are not God, to gods they had never known,
new gods that Israel had never obeyed.

They forgot their God, their mighty Saviour, the one who had given them life.
When the Lord saw this he was angry; he cast off his sons and his daughters.

He said "I shall hide my face from them, and see what becomes of them.
For they are a stubborn people, children with no loyalty in them.

They have roused me to jealousy with their idols, they have angered me with
what is no god;
so I will anger them with what is no people, I will make them jealous with a
nation of fools."

*Glory be...*

## 4. CANTICLE OF MOSES Part 2 *(Deuteronomy, 32: 22-43)*

Yes, a fire has blazed from my anger, it will burn to the depths of Sheol;
it will devour the earth and all its produce, it will set fire to the foundations
of the mountains.

I will hurl disasters on them, and on them I will spend all my arrows.
For weapons I shall have empty barns, fever and consumption for poison.

I will send wild animals to attack them, and poisonous snakes to bite them.
War will bring death in the streets; terrors will strike in the homes.

Young men and young women will die;
neither babies nor old men will be spared.

I said, "I should crush them to dust, I should wipe out their memory
among men,"
did I not fear the boasting of the enemy.

But let not their foes be mistaken!
Let them not say: our own power wins the victory, the Lord plays no
part in this.

What a short-sighted nation this is; in them there is no understanding.
Were they wise, they would succeed, they would be able to read their destiny.

How else could one man rout a thousand, how could two put ten thousand
to flight,
were it not that their Rock has sold them, that their Lord has
delivered them up?

But their gods are not like our God; our enemies' prayers are useless.
For their stock springs from the vines of Sodom, and from the olive-groves
of Gomorrah:

their vines yield poisonous grapes, their clusters are bitter as gall;
their wine is the poison of serpents, made from the venom of snakes.

But Jacob, is he not something precious to me,
sealed inside my treasury?

Vengeance is mine, and recompense, for the time when they make a false step.
For it is close, the day of their ruin; their doom comes at speed.

For the Lord will see his people righted, he will take pity on his servants.
For he will see to it that their power fails, that, slave or freeman,
there is not one remaining.

Where are their gods? he will ask then, the rock where they thought
to take refuge,
who ate the fat of their sacrifices and drank the wine of their libations?

Let these arise and help you, let these be the shelter above you.
See now that I alone am he, and beside me there is no other god.

It is I who deal death and life; when I have wounded, it is I who heal
and none can deliver from my hand.

As surely as I am the living God, I raise my hand and I vow
that I will sharpen my flashing sword and take up the cause of Right.

I will take revenge on my enemies,
and punish those who hate me.

My arrows will drip with their blood, and my sword will kill all
who oppose me.
I will spare no-one who fights against me; even the wounded and
prisoners will die.

Praise his people, O you nations, for he avenges the blood of his servants;
he takes revenge on his enemies, and forgives the sins of his people.

*Glory be...*

*Friday*

# TERCE

## OPENING PRAYERS

*(page 33).*

## HYMN

Could there be joy so great as hers,
to be the Mother of God's Son?
Could there be sorrow deep as hers,
to see the evil men have done?

Mary, keep ever in our minds
your share in Christ's most bitter pain;
and through your sufferings make us know
how earth and earthly things are vain.

Jesus, keep ever in our hearts
your bitter death, that we may learn
the depths of your great love for men,
and ever love you in return.

Pray Mary Mother, full of grace,
pray in your love for all we need;
protect us from all danger now,
and at our dying intercede.

Christ, Son of God, we pray to you,
and honour you, the Virgin's Son.
We praise the Father, God with you,
and with the Spirit, Three in One. Amen.

## ANTIPHON

**Jesus, by your obedience.**

**Psalm 98**

The Lord is king; the peoples tremble.
He is throned on the cherubim; earth quakes. The Lord is great in Sion.

He is supreme over all the peoples.
Let them praise his name, so terrible and great. He is holy, full of power.

You are a king who loves what is right;
you have established equity, justice and right; you have established them
in Jacob.

Exalt the Lord our God;
bow down before Sion, his footstool. He the Lord is holy.

Among his priests were Aaron and Moses, among those who invoked his name
was Samuel.
They invoked the Lord and he answered.

To them he spoke in the pillar of cloud.
They did his will; they kept the law, which he, the Lord, had given.

O Lord our God, you answered them.
For them you were a God who forgives; yet you punished all their offences.

Exalt the Lord our God;
bow down before his holy mountain for the Lord our God is holy.

*Glory be...*

**Psalm 100**

My song is of mercy and justice; I sing to you, O Lord.
I will walk in the way of perfection. O when, Lord, will you come?

I will walk with blameless heart within my house;
I will not set before my eyes whatever is base.

I will hate the ways of the crooked; they shall not be my friends.
The false-hearted must keep far away; the wicked I disown.

The man who slanders his neighbour in secret I will bring to silence.

The man of proud looks and haughty heart I will never endure.

I look to the faithful in the land that they may dwell with me.
He who walks in the way of perfection shall be my friend.

No man who practices deceit shall live within my house.
No man who utters lies shall stand before my eyes.

Morning by morning I will silence all the wicked in the land,
uprooting from the Lord's city all who do evil.

*Glory be...*

**Psalm 102**

My soul, give thanks to the Lord, all my being, bless his holy name.
My soul, give thanks to the Lord and never forget all his blessings.

It is he who forgives all your guilt, who heals every one of your ills,
who redeems your life from the grave, who crowns you with
love and compassion,

who fills your life with good things, renewing your youth like an eagle's.
The Lord does deeds of justice, gives judgment for all who are oppressed.

He made known his ways to Moses and his deeds to Israel's sons.
The Lord is compassion and love, slow to anger and rich in mercy.

His wrath will come to an end; he will not be angry for ever.
He does not treat us according to our sins nor repay us according to our faults.

For as the heavens are high above the earth so strong is his love for
those who fear him.
As far as the east is from the west so far does he remove our sins.

As a father has compassion on his sons, the Lord has pity on those
who fear him;
for he knows of what we are made, he remembers that we are dust.

As for man, his days are like grass; he flowers like the flower of the field;
the wind blows and he is gone and his place never sees him again.

But the love of the Lord is everlasting
upon those who hold him in fear;

his justice reaches out to children's children when they keep his covenant
in truth,
when they keep his will in their mind.

The Lord has set his sway in heaven
and his kingdom is ruling over all.

Give thanks to the Lord, all his angels, mighty in power, fulfilling his word,
who heed the voice of his word.

Give thanks to the Lord, all his hosts,
his servants who do his will.

Give thanks to the Lord, all his works, in every place where he rules.
My soul, give thanks to the Lord!

*Glory be...*

## ANTIPHON

**Jesus, by your obedience** to your Father, by your suffering and death, you are truly our Redeemer, and our Redemption, our Saviour from sin.
Hear now our prayer which your Mother prays: draw us to you, that we may not be drawn away from you by sight, or sense, or self.

## READING *(Eccles. 24: 9)*

In the eternal decree of God, I was present before his creating, and I shall be for ever with him, in the holiness of his heaven.
℟. Our thanks to God.

## SHORT RESPONSORY

℣. Christ was crowned with a crown of thorns, who is King of kings.
(Alleluia, Alleluia) ℟. *Repeat.*
℣. This crown of shame has won for us the eternal reward of Christ:
℟. The King of kings. († ℟. Alleluia, Alleluia)
℣. Glory to God, Father, Son and Holy Spirit.
℟. Christ was crowned with a crown of thorns, who is King of kings.
(Alleluia, Alleluia)

℣. There by the cross of Christ she stood in deepest sorrow. Could there be sorrow so deep as hers? (Alleluia)

℟. To see how men could spit on him, and shed in hatred his precious blood. (Alleluia)

CLOSING PRAYERS *(page 38)*.

---

† ***Response during Easter and on other special days where shown, as well as in brackets thus: (Alleluia). For style, see Sunday Terce on** page 51.*

*Friday*

# SEXT

## OPENING PRAYERS *(page 33).*

## HYMN

Could there be joy so great as hers...? *as at Friday Terce, page 301.*

## ANTIPHON

**The rending of rocks.**

### Psalm 103

Bless the Lord, my soul! Lord God, how great you are,
clothed in majesty and glory, wrapped in light as in a robe!

You stretch out the heavens like a tent. Above the rains you build
your dwelling.
You make the clouds your chariot, you walk on the wings of the wind,

you make the winds your messengers and flashing fire your servants.
You founded the earth on its base, to stand firm from age to age.

You wrapped it with the ocean like a cloak:
the waters stood higher than the mountains.

At your threat they took to flight; at the voice of your thunder they fled.
They rose over the mountains and flowed down to the place which you
had appointed.

You set limits they might not pass lest they return to cover the earth.
You make springs gush forth in the valleys: they flow in between the hills.

They give drink to all the beasts of the field; the wild-asses quench their thirst.
On their banks dwell the birds of heaven; from the branches they sing
their song.

From your dwelling you water the hills; earth drinks its fill of your gift.
You make the grass grow for the cattle and the plants to serve man's needs,

That he may bring forth bread from the earth and wine, to cheer man's heart;
oil, to make his face shine and bread to strengthen man's heart.

The trees of the Lord drink their fill, the cedars he planted on Lebanon;
there the birds build their nests: on the tree-top the stork has her home.

The goats find a home on the mountains and rabbits hide in the rocks.
You made the moon to mark the months; the sun knows the time for
its setting.

When you spread the darkness it is night and all the beasts of the forest
creep forth.
The young lions roar for their prey and ask their food from God.

At the rising of the sun they steal away and go to rest in their dens.
Man goes forth to his work, to labour till evening falls.

How many are your works, O Lord!
In wisdom you have made them all. The earth is full of your riches.

There is the sea, vast and wide, with its moving swarms past counting,
living things great and small.

The ships are moving there
and the monsters you made to play with.

All of these look to you to give them their food in due season.
You give it, they gather it up: you open your hand, they have their fill.

You hide your face, they are dismayed;
you take back your spirit, they die, returning to the dust from which
they came.

You send forth your spirit, they are created; and you renew the face
of the earth.

May the glory of the Lord last for ever! May the Lord rejoice in his works!

He looks on the earth and it trembles; the mountains send forth smoke
at his touch.
I will sing to the Lord all my life, make music to my God while I live.

May my thoughts be pleasing to him.
I find my joy in the Lord.

Let sinners vanish from the earth and the wicked exist no more.
Bless the Lord, my soul.

*Glory be...*

**Psalm 104** *(vv. 1 - 22)*

Give thanks to the Lord, tell his name,
make known his deeds among the peoples.

O sing to him, sing his praise; tell all his wonderful works!
Be proud of his holy name, let the hearts that seek the Lord rejoice.

Consider the Lord and his strength; constantly seek his face.
Remember the wonders he has done, his miracles, the judgments he spoke.

O children of Abraham, his servant, O sons of the Jacob he chose.
He, the Lord, is our God: his judgments prevail in all the earth.

He remembers his covenant for ever, his promise for a thousand generations,
the covenant he made with Abraham, the oath he swore to Isaac.

He confirmed it for Jacob as a law, for Israel as a covenant for ever.
He said: "I am giving you a land, Canaan, your appointed heritage."

When they were few in number, a handful of strangers in the land,
when they wandered from country to country and from one kingdom
to another,

he allowed no one to oppress them; he admonished kings on their account:
"Do not touch my anointed; do no harm to any of my prophets."

But he called down a famine on the land; he broke the staff that
supported them.

He had sent a man before them, Joseph, sold as a slave.

His feet were put in chains, his neck was bound with iron,
until what he said came to pass and the Lord's word proved him true.

Then the king sent and released him; the ruler of the people set him free,
making him master of his house and ruler of all he possessed,

to instruct his princes as he pleased
and to teach his elders wisdom.

*Glory be...*

**Psalm 104** *(vv. 23 - 45)*

So Israel came into Egypt,
Jacob lived in the country of Ham.

He gave his people increase; he made them stronger than their foes,
whose hearts he turned to hate his people and to deal deceitfully with
his servants.

Then he sent Moses his servant and Aaron the man he had chosen.
Through them he showed his marvels and his wonders in the country of Ham.

He sent darkness, and dark was made but Egypt resisted his words.
He turned the waters into blood and caused their fish to die.

Their land was alive with frogs, even in the halls of their kings.
He spoke; the dog-fly came and gnats covered the land.

He sent hail-stones in place of the rain and flashing fire in their land.
He struck their vines and fig-trees; he shattered the trees through their land.

He spoke; the locusts came, young locusts, too many to be counted.
They ate up every blade in the land; they ate up all the fruit of their fields.

He struck all the first-born in their land, the finest flower of their sons.
He led out Israel with silver and gold. In his tribes were none who fell behind.

Egypt rejoiced when they left for dread had fallen upon them.
He spread a cloud as a screen and fire to give light in the darkness.

When they asked for food he sent quails; he filled them with bread
from heaven.
He pierced the rock to give them water; it gushed forth in the desert
like a river.

For he remembered his holy word, which he gave to Abraham his servant.
So he brought out his people with joy, his chosen ones with shouts of rejoicing.

And he gave them the land of the nations. They took the fruit of
other men's toil,
that thus they might keep his precepts, that thus they might observe his laws.

*Glory be...*

## ANTIPHON

T**he rending of rocks** which shook the earth, in the darkness of that day, marked the death of Christ, the Virgin's Son, the Creator of all things. The rending of our hearts by sorrow for the sinful darkness of our ways – this must be our prayer; that through his grace we may avail ourselves of the redemption of Christ.

## READING *(Eccles. 24: 11)*

Jerusalem has been my dwelling and my resting-place: there in the holy city, I have taken up my rule and my reign. ℟. Our thanks to God.

## SHORT RESPONSORY

℣. There by the cross of Christ she stood in deepest sorrow, to see how men could spit on him and shed in hatred his precious blood. (Alleluia, Alleluia)
℟. *Repeat.* ℣. Could there be sorrow so deep as hers?
℟. To see how men could spit on him and shed in hatred his precious blood.
(† ℟. Alleluia, Alleluia) ℣. Glory to God, Father, Son and Holy Spirit.
℟. There by the cross of Christ she stood in deepest sorrow, to see how men could spit on him and shed in hatred his precious blood. (Alleluia, Alleluia)
℣. How deep were the sorrows of Mary, to stand and see (Alleluia)
℟. Christ, our life, crucified to death. (Alleluia)

*NOTE: If continuing immediately with None, see instructions in the Rubrics, page 26.*

## CLOSING PRAYERS *(page 38).*

---

† ***Response during Easter and on other special days where shown, as well as in brackets thus: (Alleluia). For style, see Sunday Terce on page 51.***

*Friday*

# NONE

**OPENING PRAYERS** *as before Sunday None, pages 55 - 56.*

## HYMN

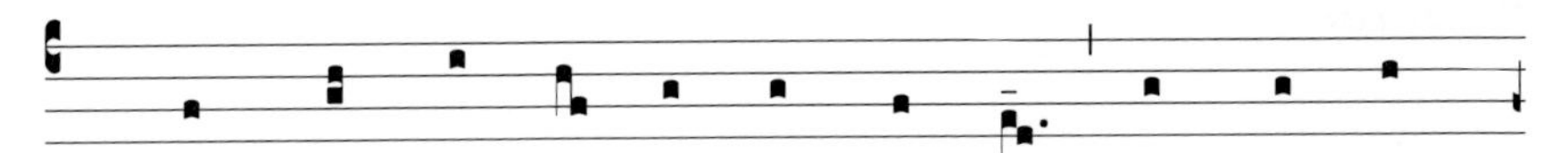

1. Could there be joy so great as hers to be the
2. Ma - ry, keep ev - er in our minds your share in
3. Je - sus keep ev - er in our hearts your bit - ter
4. Pray Ma - ry Mo - ther full of grace, pray in your
5. Christ Son of God, we pray to you, and hon - our

1 Mo - ther of God's Son? Could there be sor-row
2. Christ's most bit - ter pain, and through your suff'rings
3. death, that we may learn the depths of your great
4. love for all we need, pro - tect us from all
5. you, the Vir - gin's Son; we praise the Fa - ther,

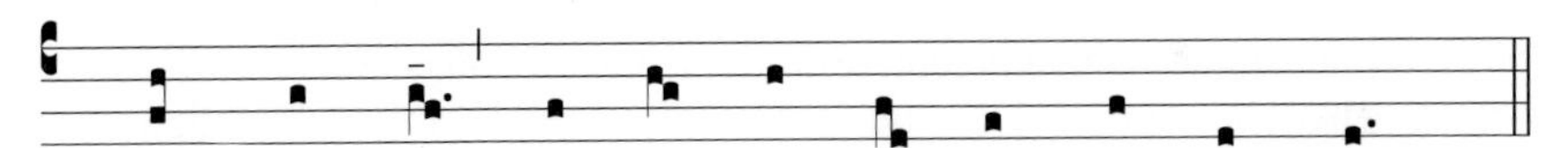

1. deep as hers to see the ev - il men have done?
2. make us know how earth and earth -ly things are vain.
3. love for men, and ev - er love you in re - turn.
4 dan - ger now and at our dy - ing in - ter - cede.
5. God with you and with the Spi - rit, Three in One.

5. A - men.

ANTIPHON

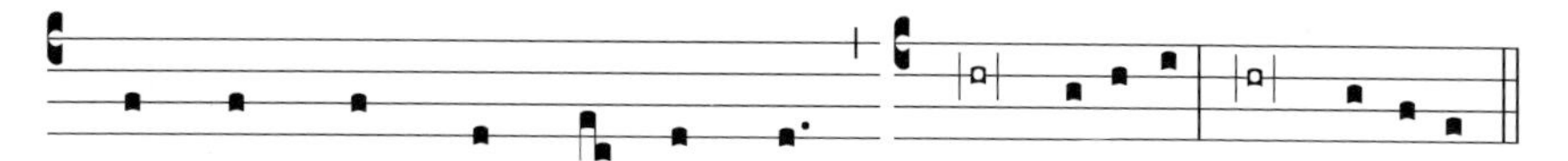

Praise to Christ, the King of heav'n TONE IV

**Psalm 106**

"O give thanks to the Lord for he is good;
for his great love is without end."

Let them say this, the Lord's redeemed, whom he redeemed from
the hand of the foe
and gathered from far-off lands, from east and west, north and south.

Some wandered in the desert, in the wilderness, finding no way to a city
they could dwell in.
Hungry they were and thirsty; their soul was fainting within them.

Then they cried to the Lord in their need and he rescued them
from their distress
and he led them along the right way, to reach a city they could dwell in.

Let them thank the Lord for his love, for the wonders he does for men:
for he satisfies the thirsty soul; he fills the hungry with good things.

Some lay in darkness and in gloom, prisoners in misery and chains,
having defied the words of God and spurned the counsels of the Most High.

He crushed their spirit with toil;
they stumbled; there was no one to help.

Then they cried to the Lord in their need and he rescued them from
their distress.
He led them forth from darkness and gloom and broke their chains to pieces.

Let them thank the Lord for his goodness, for the wonders he does for men:
for he bursts the gates of bronze and shatters the iron bars.

Some were sick on account of their sins and afflicted on account of their guilt.
They had a loathing for every food; they came close to the gates of death.

Then they cried to the Lord in their need and he rescued them from
their distress.
He sent forth his word to heal them and saved their life from the grave.

Let them thank the Lord for his love, for the wonders he does for men.
Let them offer a sacrifice of thanks and tell of his deeds with rejoicing.

Some sailed to the sea in ships to trade on the mighty waters.
These men have seen the Lord's deeds, the wonders he does in the deep.

For he spoke; he summoned the gale, tossing the waves of the sea
up to heaven and back into the deep; their souls melted away in their distress.

They staggered, reeled like drunken men, for all their skill was gone.
Then they cried to the Lord in their need and he rescued them from
their distress.

He stilled the storm to a whisper: all the waves of the sea were hushed.
They rejoiced because of the calm and he led them to the haven they desired.

Let them thank the Lord for his love, the wonders he does for men.
Let them exalt him in the gathering of the people and praise him in
the meeting of the elders.

He changes streams into a desert, springs of water into thirsty ground,
a fruitful land into a salt waste, for the wickedness of those who live there.

But he changes desert into streams, thirsty ground into springs of water.
There he settles the hungry and they build a city to dwell in.

They sow fields and plant their vines; these yield crops for the harvest.
He blesses them; they grow in numbers. He does not let their herds decrease.

He pours contempt upon princes, makes them wander in trackless wastes.
They diminish, are reduced to nothing by oppression, evil and sorrow.

But he raises the needy from distress; makes families numerous as a flock.
The upright see it and rejoice but all who do wrong are silenced.

Whoever is wise, let him heed these things.
And consider the love of the Lord.

*Glory be...*

**Psalm 107**

My heart is ready, O God; I will sing, sing your praise.
Awake, my soul; awake, lyre and harp, I will awake the dawn.

I will thank you, Lord, among the peoples, praise you among the nations;
for your love reaches to the heavens and your truth to the skies.

O God, arise above the heavens; may your glory shine on earth!
O come and deliver your friends; help with your right hand and reply.

From his holy place God has made this promise;
"I will triumph and divide the land of Shechem, I will measure out the
valley of Succoth.

Gilead is mine and Manasseh, Ephraim I take for my helmet,
Judah for my commander's staff.

Moab I will use for my washbowl, on Edom I will plant my shoe.
Over the Philistines I will shout in triumph."

But who will lead me to conquer the fortress? Who will bring me face to face
with Edom?
Will you utterly reject us, O God, and no longer march with our armies?

Give us help against the foe, for the help of man is vain.
With God we shall do bravely and he will trample down our foes.

*Glory be...*

**Psalm 108**

O God whom I praise, do not be silent:
for the mouths of deceit and wickedness are opened against me.

They speak to me with lying tongues;
they beset me with words of hate and attack me without cause.

In return for my love they accuse me while I pray for them.
They repay me evil for good, hatred for love.

Appoint a wicked man as his judge; let an accuser stand at his right.

When he is judged let him come out condemned; let his prayer be
considered as sin.

Let the days of his life be few; let another man take his office.
Let his children be fatherless orphans and his wife become a widow.

Let his children be wanderers and beggars driven from the ruins of their home.
Let the creditor seize all his goods; let strangers take the fruit of his work.

Let no one show him any mercy nor pity his fatherless children.
Let all his sons be destroyed and with them their name be blotted out.

Let his father's guilt be remembered, his mother's sin be retained.
Let it always stand before the Lord, that their memory may be cut off
from the earth.

For he did not think of showing mercy but pursued the poor and the needy,
hounding the wretched to death.

He loved cursing; let curses fall upon him.
He scorned blessing; let blessing pass him by.

He put on cursing like his coat;
let it soak into his body like water; let it sink like oil into his bones;

let it be like the clothes that cover him,
like a girdle he cannot take off!

Let the Lord thus repay my accusers, all those who speak evil against me.
For your name's sake act in my defence; in the goodness of your love
be my rescuer.

For I am poor and needy and my heart is pierced within me.
I fade like an evening shadow; I am shaken off like a locust.

My knees are weak from fasting; my body is thin and gaunt.
I have become an object of scorn, all who see me toss their heads.

Help me, Lord my God; save me because of your love.
Let them know that this is your work, that this is your doing, O Lord.

They may curse but you will bless.

Let my attackers be put to shame, but let your servant rejoice.

Let my accusers be clothed with dishonour,
covered with shame as with a cloak.

Loud thanks to the Lord are on my lips. I will praise him in the midst
of the throng,
for he stands at the poor man's side to save him from those who
condemn him.

*Glory be...*

## Antiphon

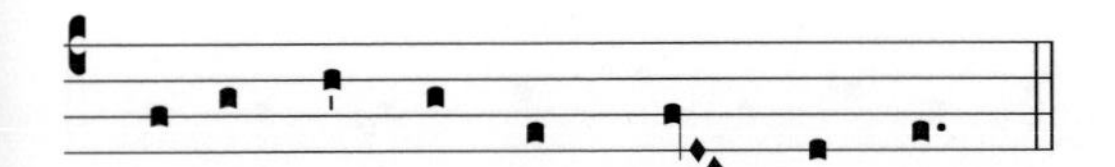

ho-ly Mo-ther, com-mend our souls.

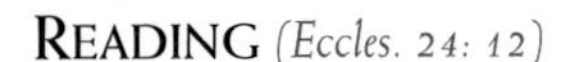

## READING *(Eccles. 24: 12)*

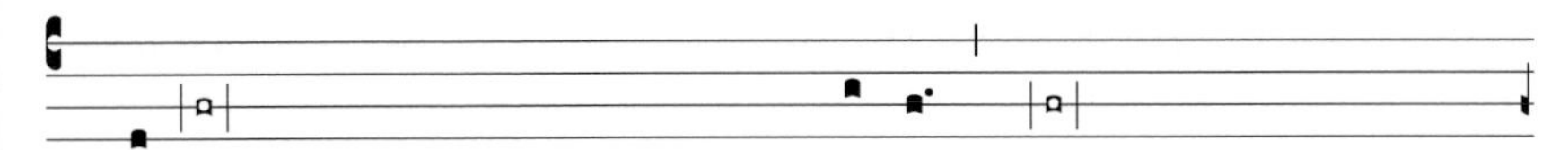

I have grown up among God's people: I will live for ever

in the land of the Lord. ℟. Our thanks to God.

## SHORT RESPONSORY

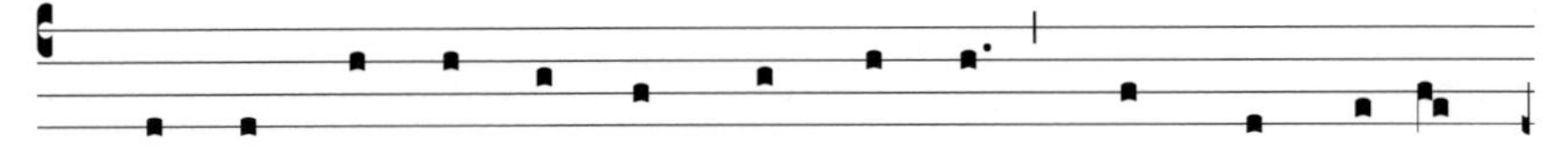

℣. To stand by the Cross of Christ her Son could there be sor-

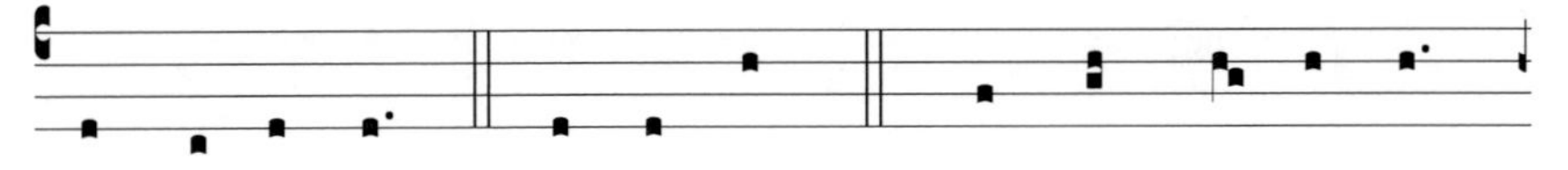

row deep as hers? ℟. To stand by… ℣. And see Christ our life

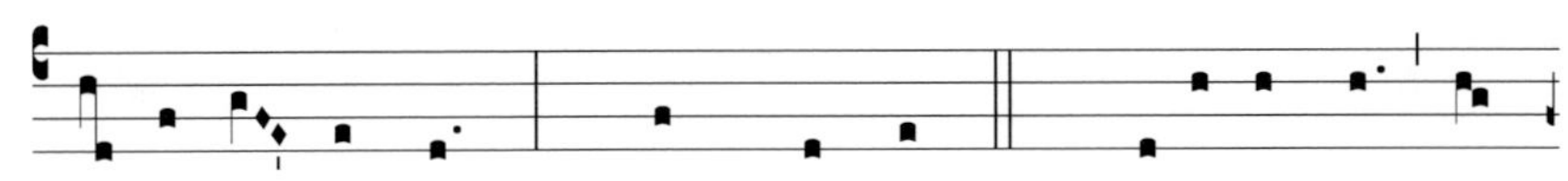

cru- ci- fied to death. ℟. Could there be… ℣. Glo-ry to God, Fa-

ther, Son and Ho-ly Spir-it. ℟. To stand by the Cross…

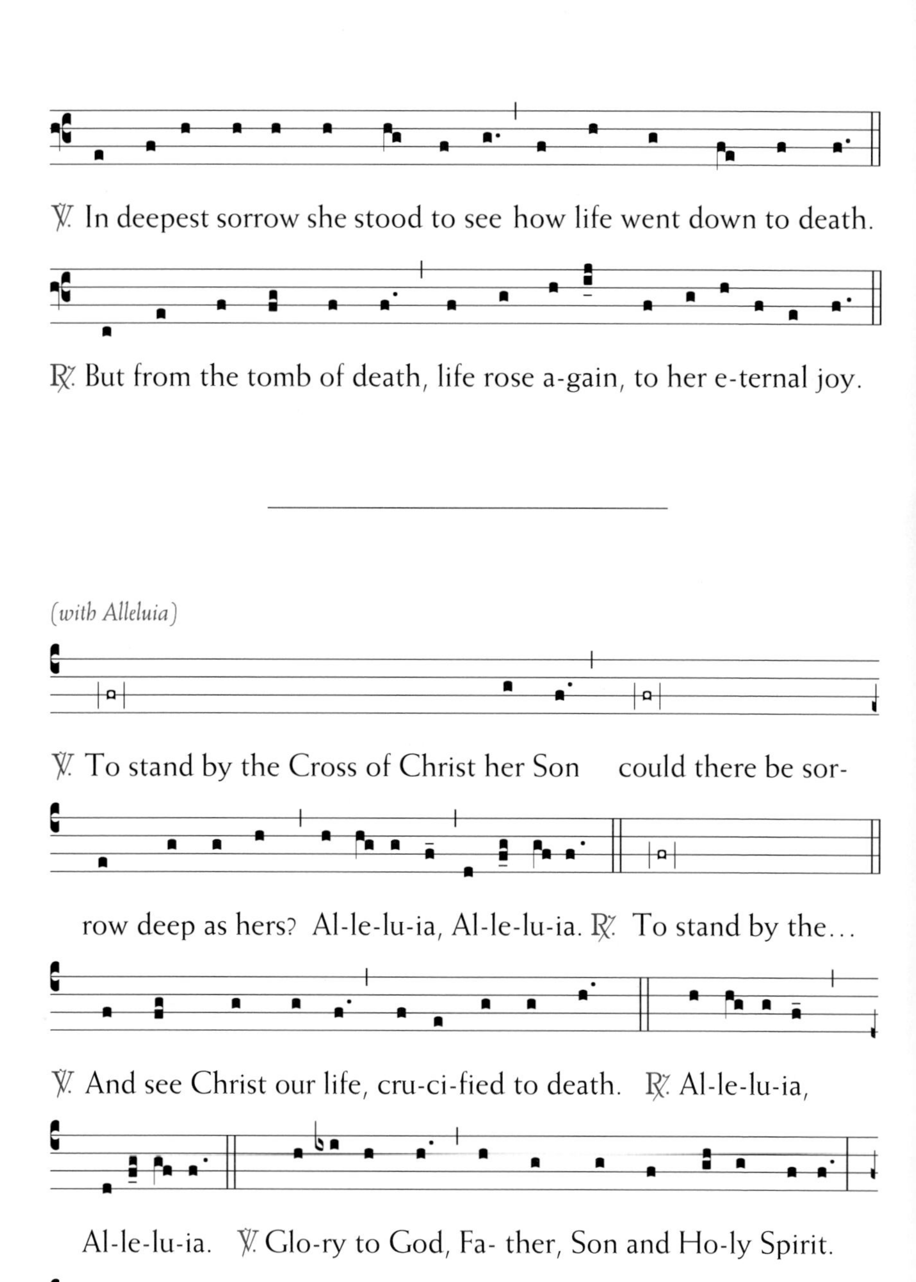


℟. To stand by the Cross…

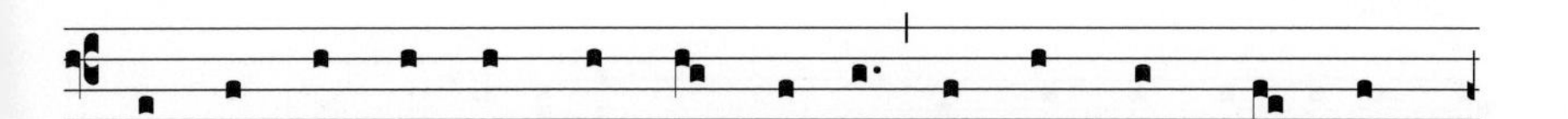

℣. In deep-est sor-row she stood to see how life went down to

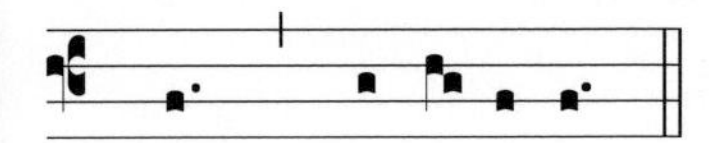

death, Al-le-lu-ia.

℟. But from the tomb of death, life rose a-gain, to her e-ternal joy,

Al-le-lu-ia.

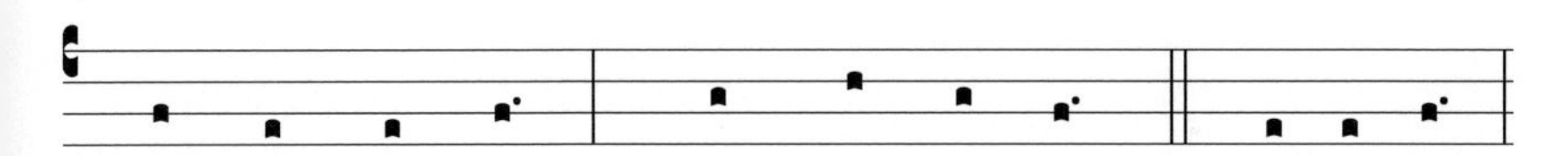

℣. Lord, hear my prayer. ℟. Lord, grant my prayer. ℣. Let us pray.

**PRAYER** *(pages 36 - 37)*

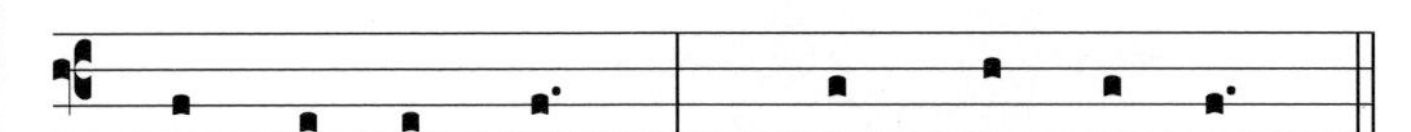

℣. Lord, hear my prayer. ℟. Lord, grant my prayer.

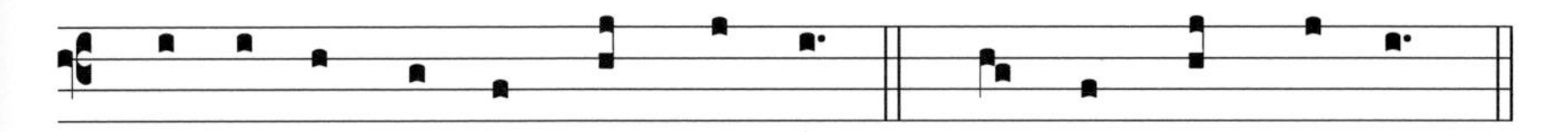

℣. Glo-ry hon-our and praise to God. ℟. And our thanks to him.

*(with Alleluia)*

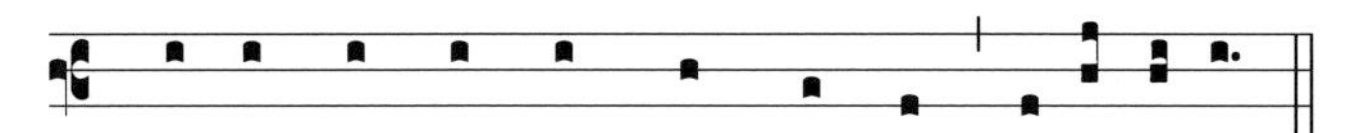

℣. Glo-ry hon-our and praise to God, Al-le-lu-ia.

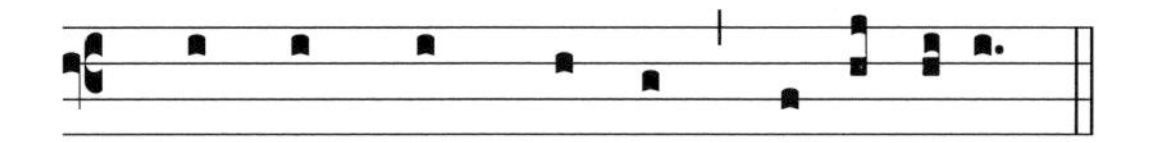

℟. And our thanks to him, Al-le-lu-ia.

## Closing Prayers

'Mary, rejoice...' *as on Sunday, pages 64 ff.*

**Lauds of Our Lady** *of the day, season or feast. (See daily after Compline)*
*With* ℣. & ℟. *and Prayer. Then* 'May the souls of our founders...' *and...*

**Psalm 129** 'Out of the depths...' *and two or three memorial prayers for the souls of the departed, as on Sunday, page 65 - 66.*

# OFFICE OF READINGS (MATINS)

## OPENING PRAYERS *(page 67)*.

## HYMN

Turn from all earthly thoughts, forget earth's joys,
think of the sufferings of the Virgin's Son,
his sweat of blood, the scourge, the crown of thorn,
his cross of shame – and our salvation won.

Think of the piercing nails, the soldier's spear,
the hate and scorn of men who stood to see,
the bitter anguish of those hours of death
of life itself, his death man's life to be.

Think how the Mother's sufferings and her love
made still more deep the bitter pain he bore.
Jesus, keep ever in our hearts and minds
your pain and love, that we may love you more.

Pray Mary Virgin-Mother full of grace,
pray in your love for all, for all we need;
protect us from all sin and sinful ways,
and at our dying hour intercede.

Christ Jesus, Son of God, we pray to you
and praise you, naming you the Virgin's Son;
we ever praise the Father, God with you
and with the Holy Spirit, Three in One. Amen.

## ANTIPHON 1

**Free us, Lord, from sin and sinfulness.**

**Psalm 68**

Save me, O God,
for the waters have risen to my neck.

I have sunk into the mud of the deep and there is no foothold.
I have entered the waters of the deep and the waves overwhelm me.

I am wearied with all my crying, my throat is parched.
My eyes are wasted away from looking for my God.

More numerous than the hairs on my head are those who hate me
without cause.
Those who attack me with lies are too much for my strength.

How can I restore what I have never stolen?
O God, you know my sinful folly; my sins you can see.

Let not those who hope in you be put to shame through me, Lord of hosts:
let not those who seek you be dismayed through me, God of Israel.

It is for you that I suffer taunts, that shame covers my face,
that I have become a stranger to my brothers, an alien to my own
mother's sons.

I burn with zeal for your house and taunts against you fall on me.
When I afflict my soul with fasting they make it a taunt against me.

When I put on sackcloth in mourning then they make me a byword,
the gossip of men at the gates, the subject of drunkards' songs.

This is my prayer to you,
my prayer for your favour.

In your great love, answer me, O God, with your help that never fails:
rescue me from sinking in the mud; save me from my foes.

Save me from the waters of the deep lest the waves overwhelm me.
Do not let the deep engulf me nor death close its mouth on me.

Lord, answer, for your love is kind; in your compassion, turn towards me.
Do not hide your face from your servant; answer quickly for I am in distress.

Come close to my soul and redeem me; ransom me pressed by my foes.
You know how they taunt and deride me; my oppressors are all before you.

Taunts have broken my heart; I have reached the end of my strength.
I looked in vain for compassion, for consolers; not one could I find.

For food they gave me poison; in my thirst they gave me vinegar to drink.
Let their table be a snare to them and their festive banquets a trap.

Let their eyes grow dim and blind; let their limbs tremble and shake.
Pour out your anger upon them, let the heat of your fury overtake them.

Let their camp be left desolate; let no one dwell in their tents:
for they persecute one whom you struck; they increase the pain of him
you wounded.

Charge them with guilt upon guilt; let them never be found just in your sight.
Blot them out from the book of the living; do not enrol them among the just.

As for me in my poverty and pain
let your help, O God, lift me up.

I will praise God's name with a song; I will glorify him with thanksgiving.
A gift pleasing God more than oxen, more than beasts prepared for sacrifice.

The poor when they see it will be glad and God-seeking hearts will revive;
for the Lord listens to the needy and does not spurn his servants
in their chains.

Let the heavens and the earth give him praise,
the sea and all its living creatures.

For God will bring help to Sion and rebuild the cities of Judah
and men shall dwell there in possession.

The sons of his servants shall inherit it;
those who love his name shall dwell there.

*Glory be...*

## ANTIPHON 1

F**ree us, Lord, from sin and sinfulness**; save us, Christ our Saviour, from the pit of hell. Hear how the Virgin, your holy Mother, prays and pleads for us, that your coming to us, your grievous suffering and the shame of the Cross may not be in vain.

## ANTIPHON 2

S**tay near us, Virgin Mary.**

### Psalm 70

In you, O Lord, I take refuge; let me never be put to shame.
In your justice rescue me, free me: pay heed to me and save me.

Be a rock where I can take refuge, a mighty stronghold to save me;
for you are my rock, my stronghold.

Free me from the hand of the wicked, from the grip of the unjust,
of the oppressor.
It is you, O Lord, who are my hope, my trust, O Lord, since my youth.

On you I have leaned from my birth, from my mother's womb you have
been my help.
My hope has always been in you.

My fate has filled many with awe but you are my strong refuge.
My lips are filled with your praise, with your glory all the day long.

Do not reject me now that I am old;
when my strength fails do not forsake me.

For my enemies are speaking about me; those who watch me
take counsel together
saying: "God has forsaken him; follow him, seize him; there is no one
to save him."

O God, do not stay far off: my God, make haste to help me!
Let them be put to shame and destroyed, all those who seek my life.

Let them be covered with shame and confusion, all those who seek
to harm me.
But as for me, I will always hope and praise you more and more.

My lips will tell of your justice and day by day of your help
(though I can never tell it all).

I will declare the Lord's mighty deeds proclaiming your justice, yours alone.
O God, you have taught me from my youth and I proclaim your wonders still.

Now that I am old and grey-headed,
do not forsake me, God.

Let me tell of your power to all ages, praise your strength and justice
to the skies,
tell of you who have worked such wonders. O God, who is like you?

You have burdened me with bitter troubles but you will give me back my life.
You will raise me from the depths of the earth; you will exalt me and
console me again.

So I will give you thanks on the lyre for your faithful love, my God.
To you will I sing with the harp; to you, the Holy One of Israel.

When I sing to you my lips shall rejoice
and my soul, which you have redeemed.

And all the day long my tongue shall tell the tale of your justice:
for they are put to shame and disgraced, all those who seek to harm me.

*Glory be...*

## ANTIPHON 2

S**tay near us, Virgin Mary,** pleading, interceding for us, that our hearts may ever thirst for the love of Jesus, your Son, who died to save us from our sin with the bitter taste of gall on his lips.

## ANTIPHON 3

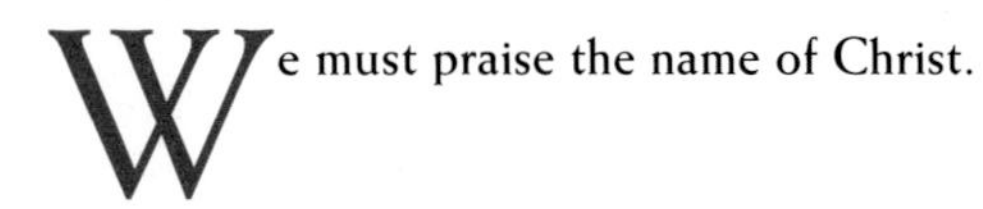

We must praise the name of Christ.

**Psalm 71**

O God, give your judgment to the king, to a king's son your justice,
that he may judge your people in justice and your poor in right judgment.

May the mountains bring forth peace for the people
and the hills, justice.

May he defend the poor of the people and save the children of the needy
(and crush the oppressor).

He shall endure like the sun and the moon from age to age.
He shall descend like rain on the meadow, like raindrops on the earth.

In his days justice shall flourish and peace till the moon fails.
He shall rule from sea to sea, from the Great River to earth's bounds.

Before him his enemies shall fall, his foes lick the dust.
The kings of Tarshish and the sea coasts shall pay him tribute.

The kings of Sheba and Seba shall bring him gifts.
Before him all kings shall fall prostrate, all nations shall serve him.

For he shall save the poor when they cry and the needy who are helpless.
He will have pity on the weak and save the lives of the poor.

From oppression he will rescue their lives, to him their blood is dear.
(Long may he live, may the gold of Sheba be given him).

They shall pray for him without ceasing
and bless him all the day.

May corn be abundant in the land
to the peaks of the mountains.

May its fruit rustle like Lebanon;
may men flourish in the cities like grass on the earth.

May his name be blessed for ever and endure like the sun.
Every tribe shall be blessed in him, all nations bless his name.

Blessed be the Lord, God of Israel, who alone works wonders,
ever blessed his glorious name. Let his glory fill the earth. Amen! Amen!

*Glory be...*

## ANTIPHON 3

We **must praise the name of Christ,** the Son of the Virgin Mary, for he is Lord of all. And by his death he has won us life.
We pray that all creation may praise him, saying: glory, honour and praise to Christ. Amen.

℣. Christ was crowned with a crown of thorns, who is King of kings. (Alleluia)
℟. This crown of shame has won for us the eternal reward of Christ. (Alleluia)

Our Father ...

## ABSOLUTION

God and father, holy and merciful Lord, take into account the prayer and holiness of Mary, the Virgin-Mother of God, and of all the saints and bring us back from death to life. ℟. Amen.

*Reader:* Lord, we ask for your blessing.

**Week One**
*Blessing, Reading and Response for Fridays in Week Two start on page 522, and for Week Three on page 542.*

## BLESSING

May the Virgin Mary lead us to her Son who redeemed us, drawing our hearts from sin to Christ who paid for us the price of sin. ℟. Amen.

## Reading

We are told that Mary was afraid
when the angel appeared and spoke to her.
It was not fear of any bodily harm to herself,
but dismay at the thought that this might be a trick of Satan,
to lead her into sin.

At the moment when her mind first knew God and his holy will,
she had chosen for herself a life of love,
and this brought with it a wise and holy fear of God.

It is our delight to call Mary a rose of great beauty.
We know that the lovelier and healthier the rose,
the stronger and sharper are the thorns which surround it.
If Mary is a rose of beauty,
she will not be untouched by the sharp thorns of trial and sorrow.
Indeed, as the days of her life went by,
her sorrows increased in bitterness and pressed more heavily upon her.
Her first sorrow was that fear of God which her knowledge
of his existence and his will had brought her.
It was a sorrow to her
that in all she did, she must keep in mind
the thought and the threat of sin.
She directed each thought, word and work to God,
but there was always the fear
that some defect might creep in
to lessen its value in his eyes.

How foolish are those who deliberately and without fear
throw themselves into all kinds of sin,
bringing on themselves suffering and sorrow.

Mary was sinless, and immune from sin.
Everything she did pleased God.
In every way she was entirely pleasing to him.
Yet she never allowed herself to be free from the fear of displeasing him.
A greater sorrow still was in her heart,
for she knew from the writings of the prophets
that God willed to come as man,
and suffer as man.

In her love for God, this caused her great grief,
though she did not yet know that she was to be the Mother of God.
When that moment arrived,
the moment when she knew that the Son of God had become her Son,
to take in her womb that human body
which was to suffer as the prophets had foretold.
Who could measure her joy? Who could measure her sorrow?
Like the rose, she had grown in beauty,
but the thorns had grown too,
stronger and sharper and more piercing.

To Mary, it was joy beyond words
that her Son should come in humility to lead man to heaven,
saving him from the penalty which Adam's pride had incurred,
the misery of hell.

It was great sorrow
that the sin of Adam by which man rebelled in both body and soul
should require the redeeming death of her Son
in such agony of body and soul.

It was great joy to her
to conceive her Son in sinlessness and purity.
It was great sorrow to her
that this so loved Son was born to suffer a shameful death,
and that she herself would be there to stand and see.
Great joy to know that he would rise from death,
and win in return for his Passion
an everlasting honour and glory;
great sorrow to know that this glory would not be won
except by the agony and shame of the Cross.

The perfect rose blooms in beauty on its stem,
and our delight is not spoiled by the sharp thorns around it.
The sharp thorns of Mary's sorrow piercing her heart
could not change her or weaken her will,
and in her suffering
she accepted whatever God's will should demand of her.

We call her a rose of Jericho,
for men say that nowhere else can so lovely a rose be found.

In her holiness,
Mary is more beautiful than all mankind,
surpassed only by her Son.

To God and the angels in heaven,
her patience and willing endurance brought joy.
To all on earth, it must be a joy
to meditate on her sufferings so willingly accepted,
and on that consolation she had ever in her heart,
that all was the will of God.

℣. Have mercy, Lord, and help our understanding. ℟. Our thanks to God.

## RESPONSORY

**The beauty and fragrance of the rose** are not spoiled by its thorns. Your faithfulness, Mother of Christ, was not overcome by your deep sorrow; for the piercing thorns of grief increased the sweetness of your holiness. Mary, we call you 'our hope', knowing your readiness to intercede, we pray that in prosperity we may live wisely and in time of suffering and sorrow, may think of your faithfulness,

℟. For the piercing thorns of grief increased the sweetness of your holiness.

℣. Glory to God, glory to Father, Son and Holy Spirit.

℟. For the piercing thorns of grief increased the sweetness of your holiness.

## TE DEUM *as on Sunday,* *page 75,* or PSALM 50 as follows:

*Use **Psalm 50** for Sundays and ferial days in Advent and Lent; ferial days in Passiontide and ferial Fridays throughout the year, except during Easter* *(see Rubrics, page 28).*

### Psalm 50

Have mercy on me, God, in your kindness. In your compassion
blot out my offence.
O wash me more and more from my guilt and cleanse me from my sin.

My offences truly I know them; my sin is always before me.
Against you, you alone, have I sinned; what is evil in your sight I have done.

That you may be justified when you give sentence and be without reproach
when you judge,
O see, in guilt I was born, a sinner was I conceived.

Indeed you love truth in the heart; then in the secret of my heart teach
me wisdom.
O purify me, then I shall be clean; O wash me, I shall be whiter than snow.

Make me hear rejoicing and gladness, that the bones you have crushed
may thrill.
From my sins turn away your face and blot out all my guilt.

A pure heart create for me, O God, put a steadfast spirit within me.
Do not cast me away from your presence, nor deprive me of your holy spirit.

Give me again the joy of your help; with a spirit of fervour sustain me,
that I may teach transgressors your ways and sinners may return to you.

O rescue me, God, my helper, and my tongue shall ring out your goodness.
O Lord, open my lips and my mouth shall declare your praise.

For in sacrifice you take no delight, burnt offering from me you would refuse,
my sacrifice, a contrite spirit, a humbled, contrite heart you will not spurn.

In your goodness, show favour to Sion:
rebuild the walls of Jerusalem.

Then you will be pleased with lawful sacrifice, (burnt offerings wholly
consumed),
then you will be offered young bulls on your altar.

*Glory be...*

℣. There by the Cross of Christ she stood in deepest sorrow. (Alleluia)
℟. To see how men could spit on him and shed in hatred his Precious Blood.
(Alleluia)

**CLOSING PRAYERS** *(page 38)*.

*Friday*

# VESPERS

**PRAYERS** before Vespers, *(pages 77 - 78)* and
**OPENING PRAYERS** – with music – *as at None, pages 55 - 56.*

## ANTIPHON

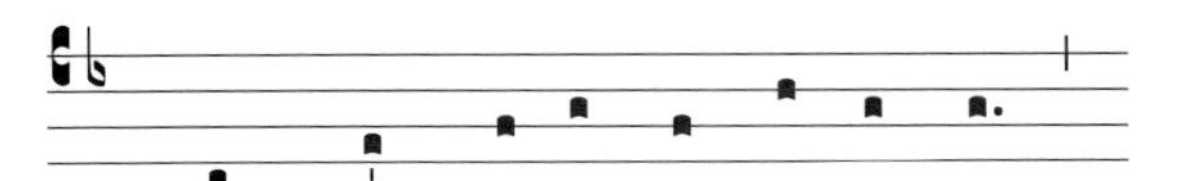

Make known to all men everywhere,

TONE VII 

**Canticle of Isaiah** *(Isaiah 12: 1-6)*

That day you will say: I give thanks to you, O Lord,
You were angry with me.

But your anger is appeased and you have given me consolation.
See now, he is the God of my salvation; I trust now and have no fear.

For the Lord is my strength, my song, he is my salvation.
And you will draw water joyfully, from the springs of salvation.

That day you will say: Give thanks to the Lord.
Call his name aloud.

Proclaim his deeds to the people, declare his name sublime.
Sing of the Lord, for he has done marvellous things, let them be known to
the whole world.

Cry out for joy and gladness, you dwellers in Sion,
For great in the midst of you is the Holy One of Israel.

*Glory be...*

**Psalm 6**

Lord, do not reprove me in your anger;
punish me not in your rage.

Have mercy on me, Lord, I have no strength; Lord, heal me,
my body is racked;
my soul is racked with pain. But you, O Lord ... how long?

Return, Lord, rescue my soul. Save me in your merciful love;
for in death no one remembers you; from the grave, who can give you praise?

I am exhausted with my groaning; every night I drench my pillow with tears;
I bedew my bed with weeping.

My eye wastes away with grief; I have grown old surrounded by my foes.
Leave me, all you who do evil; for the Lord has heard my weeping.

The Lord has heard my plea; the Lord will accept my prayer.
All my foes will retire in confusion, foiled and suddenly confounded.

*Glory be...*

**Canticle of Anna** (*1 Samuel* 2: 1 - 10)

My heart exults in the Lord, my horn is exalted in my God.
My mouth derides my foes, for I rejoice in your power of saving.

There is none as holy as the Lord, indeed there is no one but you:
no rock like our God.

Do not speak and speak with haughty words, let not arrogance come
from your mouth.
For the Lord is an all-knowing God, and his is the weighing of deeds.

The bow of the mighty is broken, but the feeble have girded themselves
with strength.
The sated hire themselves out for bread, but the famished cease from labour.

The barren woman bears sevenfold, but the mother of many is desolate.
The Lord gives death and life, brings down to Sheol and draws up.

The Lord makes poor and rich, he humbles and also exalts.
He raises the poor from the dust, he lifts the needy from the dunghill.

To give them a place with princes, and to assign them a seat of honour;
for to the Lord the props of the earth belong, on these he has
poised the world.

He safeguards the steps of his faithful, but the wicked vanish in darkness,
for it is not by strength that man triumphs.

The enemies of the Lord are scattered:
the Most High thunders in the heavens.

The Lord judges the ends of the earth, he endows his king with power,
he exalts the horn of his Anointed.

*Glory be…*

**Psalm 7**

Lord God, I take refuge in you. From my pursuer save me and rescue me,
lest he tear me to pieces like a lion and drag me off with no one to rescue me.

Lord God, if my hands have done wrong, if I have paid back evil for good,
I who saved my unjust oppressor:

then let my foe pursue me and seize me, let him trample my life to the ground
and lay my soul in the dust.

Lord, rise up in your anger, rise against the fury of my foes;
my God, awake! You will give judgment.

Let the company of nations gather round you,
taking your seat above them on high.

(The Lord is judge of the peoples.)
Give judgment for me, Lord; I am just and innocent of heart.

Put an end to the evil of the wicked! Make the just stand firm,
you who test mind and heart, O just God!

God is the shield that protects me, who saves the upright of heart.
God is a just judge, slow to anger;

but he threatens the wicked every day, men who will not repent.
God will sharpen his sword; he has braced his bow and taken aim.

For them he has prepared deadly weapons; he barbs his arrows with fire.
Here is one who is pregnant with malice, who conceives evil and
brings forth lies.

He digs a pitfall, digs it deep; and in the trap he has made he will fall.
His malice will recoil on himself; on his own head his violence will fall.

I will thank the Lord for his justice:
I will sing to the Lord, the Most High.

*Glory be...*

**Psalm 147**

O praise the Lord, Jerusalem!
Sion praise your God!

He has strengthened the bars of your gates, he has blessed the children
within you.
He established peace on your borders, he feeds you with finest wheat.

He sends out his word to the earth and swiftly runs his command.
He showers down snow, white as wool, he scatters hoar-frost like ashes.

He hurls down hailstones like crumbs. The waters are frozen at his touch;
he sends forth his word and it melts them: at the breath of his mouth
the waters flow.

He makes his word known to Jacob, to Israel his laws and decrees.
He has not dealt thus with other nations; he has not taught them his
decrees.

*Glory be...*

**ANTIPHON** *(Next page...)*

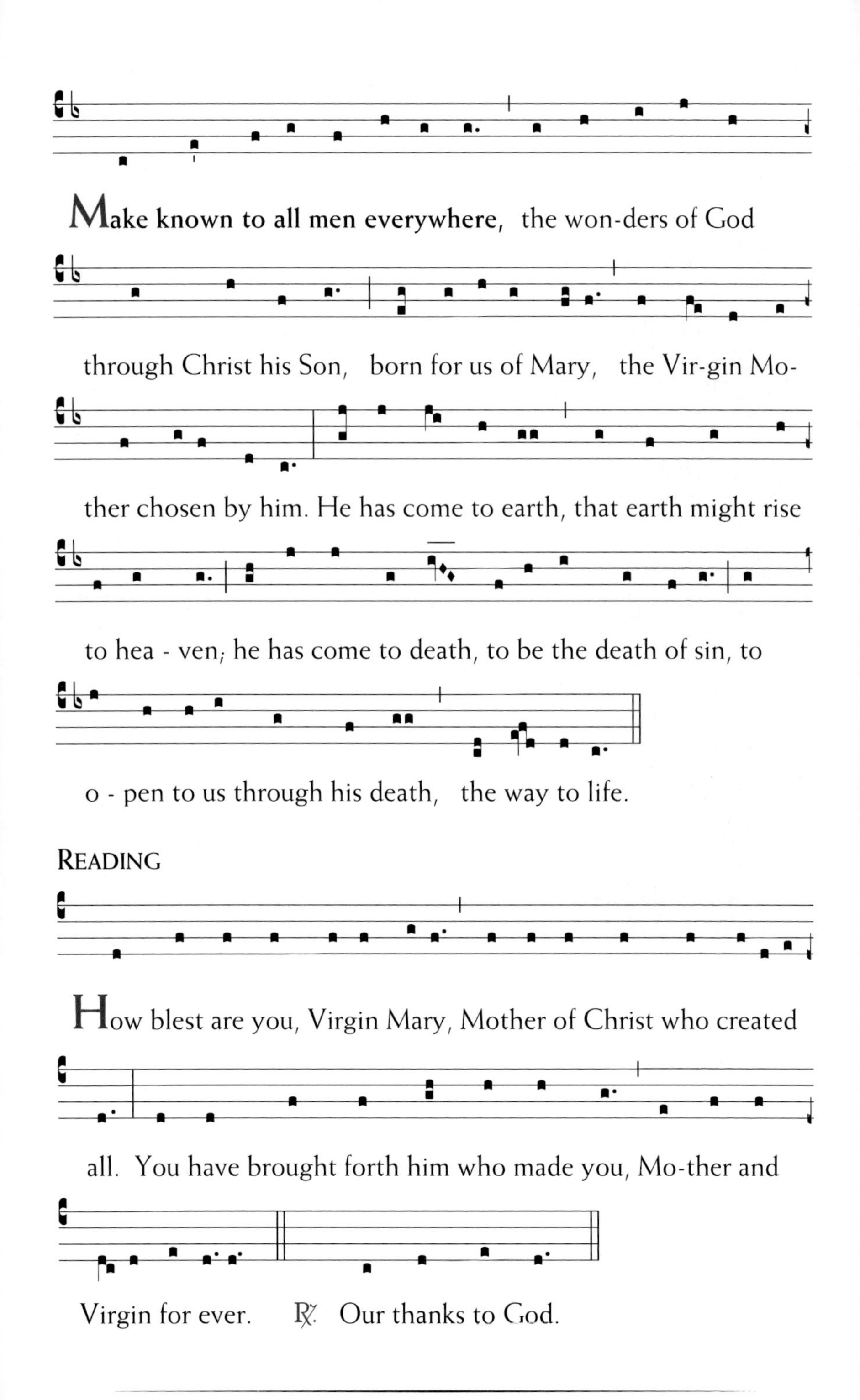
Make known to all men everywhere, the won-ders of God
through Christ his Son, born for us of Mary, the Vir-gin Mother chosen by him. He has come to earth, that earth might rise
to hea - ven; he has come to death, to be the death of sin, to
o - pen to us through his death, the way to life.
READING
How blest are you, Virgin Mary, Mother of Christ who created
all. You have brought forth him who made you, Mo-ther and
Virgin for ever. ℟. Our thanks to God.

*When in Jerusalem, on 14th May, 1372, in the Chapel of Mount Calvary within the Church of the Holy Sepulchre, Saint Bridget, in ecstasy, saw in detail the whole Passion of Our Lord. (Revelations, Book 7, chapter 15). Lithograph from the 1908 Tournai edition.*

## Hymn

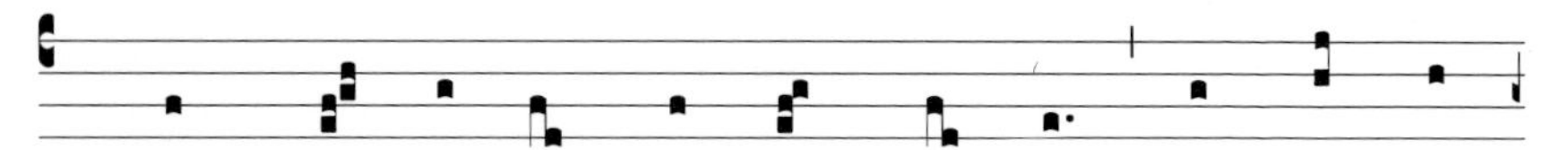

1. The Sun of right-eous-ness goes down, the stars of
2. But see how light from dark - ness comes, and hell is
3. The Vir - gin Ma - ry bears for God, the ar - row
4. The dart the Fa - ther sent is Christ, to strike the
5. O Ma - ry, Mo - ther filled with joy, deep joy your
6. Pray Ma - ry Mo - ther full of grace, pray in your
7. Christ, Son of God, we pray to you, and hon- our

1. heav'n give out no light, the har - dest rocks are
2. cheat - ed of its prey, the Vir - gin's Son re-
3. sharp to pierce the foe, to wound and end his
4. en - e - my of death, which slain, he gave us
5. dear Son's death has brought, pray that our hearts made
6. love for all we need; pro - tect us from all
7. you, the Vir - gin's Son; we praise the Fa - ther,

1. rent a - part, the world's found - a - tions fail and
2. turns once more, with tro - phy won by his own
3. e - vil sway, which ev - er troub - les all the
4. his own life, and liv - ing to his Fa - ther
5. free from sin, may flow - er with all vir - tues'
6. dan - ger now, and at our dy - ing in - ter -
7. God with you, and with the Spi - rit, Three in

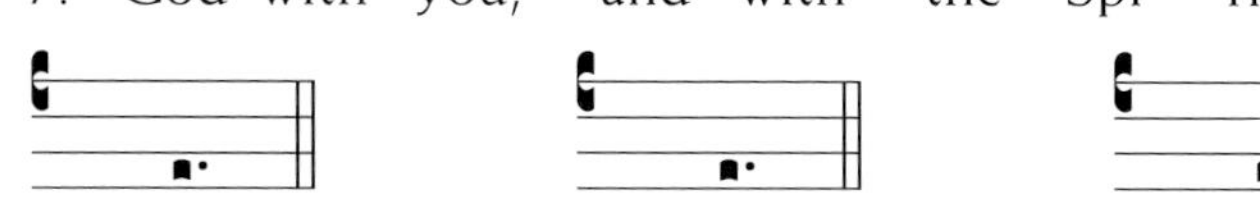

1. shake.
2. blood.
3. world.
4. went.
5. grace.
6. cede.
7. One. A - men.

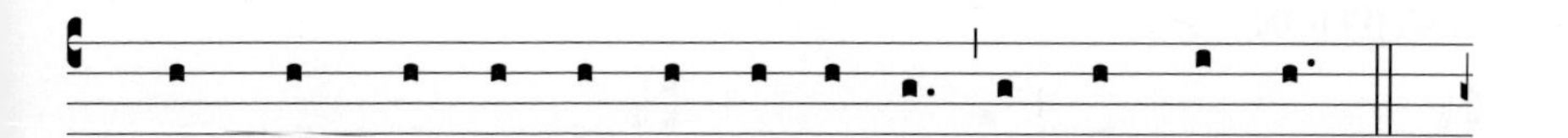

℣. How deep were the sor-rows of Ma-ry, to stand and see

(Al-le- lu - ia)

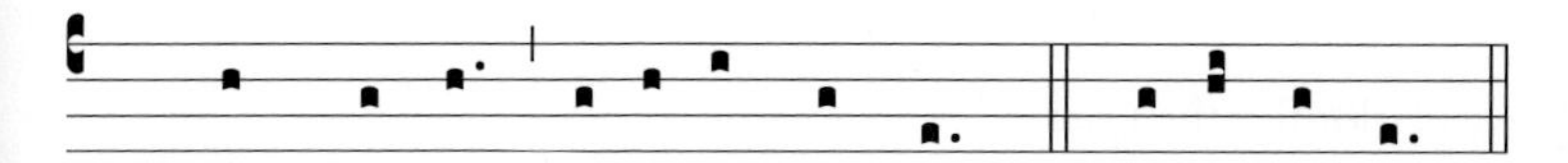

℟. Christ, our life, cru-ci-fied to death. (Al-le- lu - ia)

## Antiphon

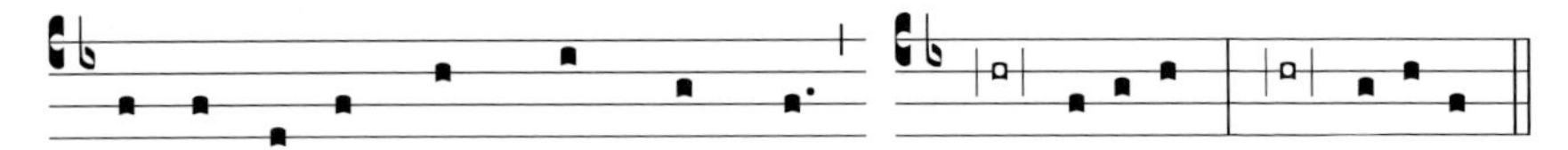

**Ma-ry, rejoice in Christ your Son,** TONE VI

## Magnificat *(Luke 1: 46 - 55)*

My soul glorifies the Lord,
my spirit rejoices in God,
my Saviour.

He looks on his servant in her nothingness; henceforth all ages
will call me blessed.
The Almighty works marvels for me. Holy his name!

His mercy is from age to age, on those who fear him.
He puts forth his arm in strength and scatters the proud-
hearted.

He casts the mighty from their thrones and raises the lowly.
He fills the starving with good things, sends the rich away empty.

He protects Israel, his servant, remembering his mercy,
the mercy promised to our fathers, to Abraham and his sons
for ever.

Praise the Father, the Son and the Holy Spirit,
both now and for ever, world without end.

## Antiphon

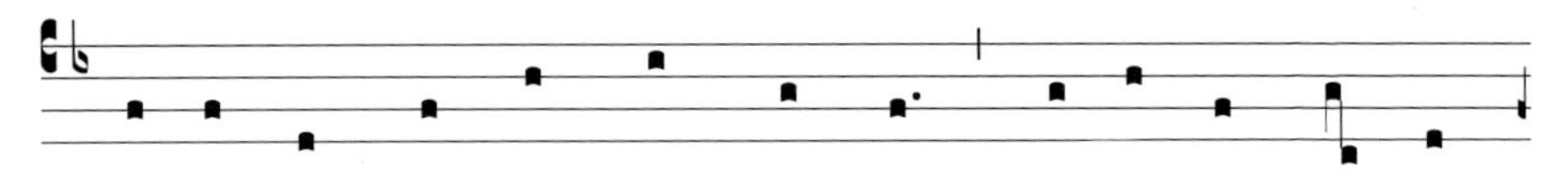

**Ma - ry, re - joice in Christ your Son,** for all the won-ders

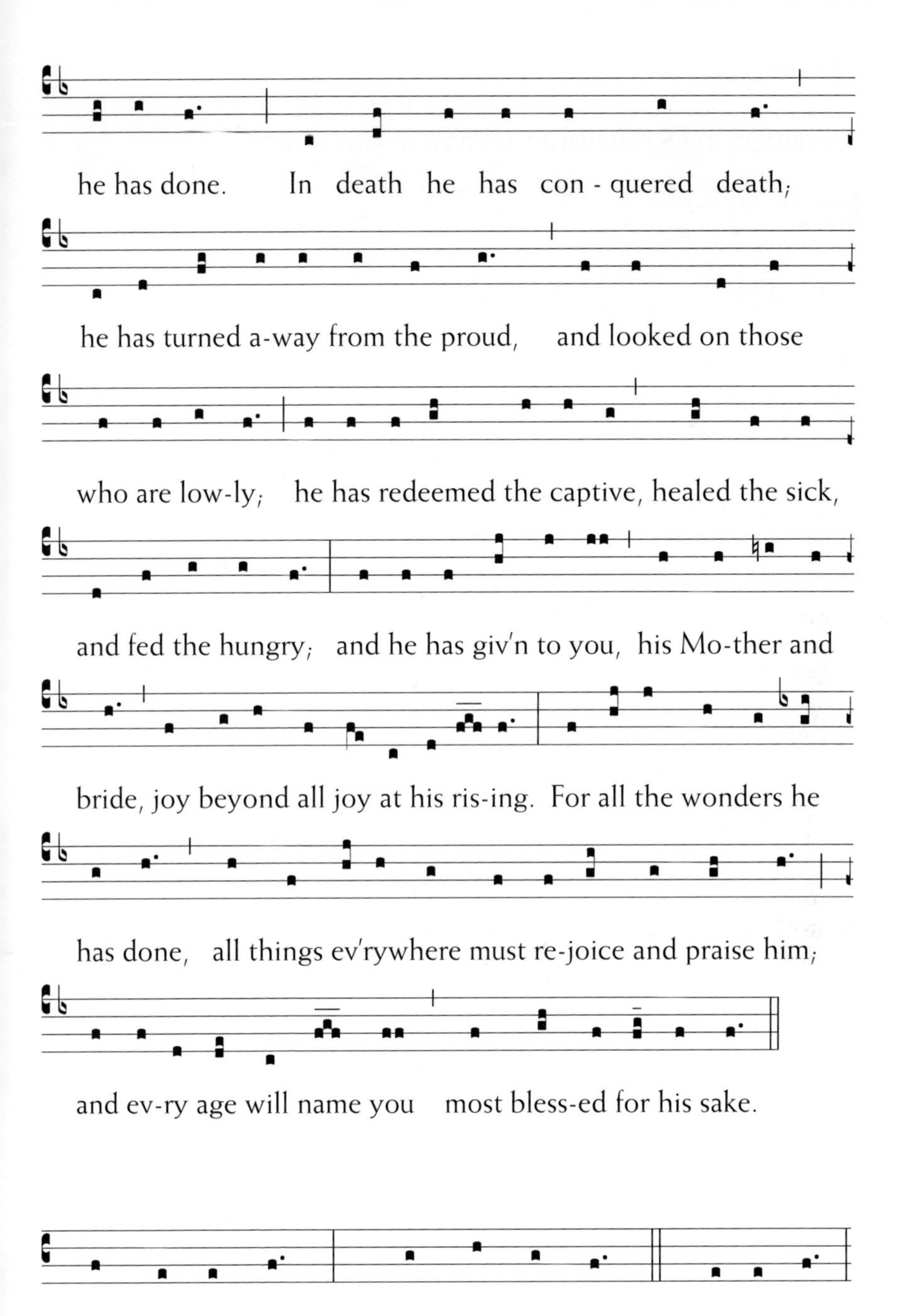


℣. Lord hear my prayer. ℟. Lord grant my prayer. ℣. Let us pray.

**PRAYER** *(page 36 - 37)*

**ANTIPHON TO ST. BRIDGET & PRAYER** *(pages 88 - 90).*

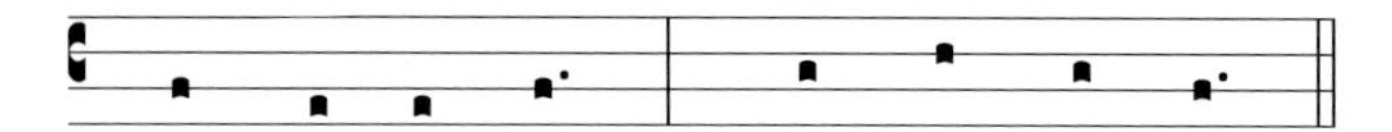

℣. Lord hear my prayer. ℟. Lord grant my prayer.

**THANKSGIVING**

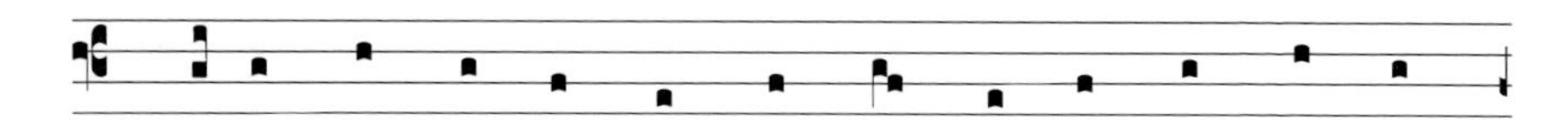

℣. Glo-ry, hon - our and praise to Christ the Vir - gin's Son, the

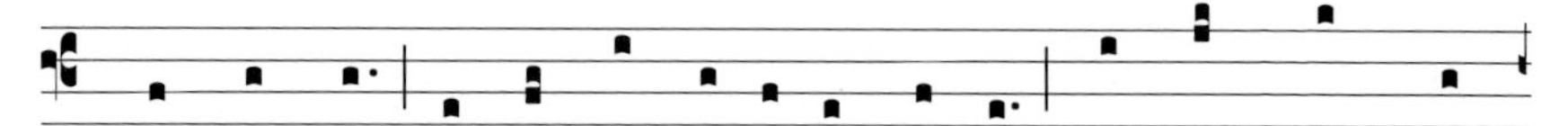

Lamb of God, the sin-less sacri-fice for sin, who rose from death

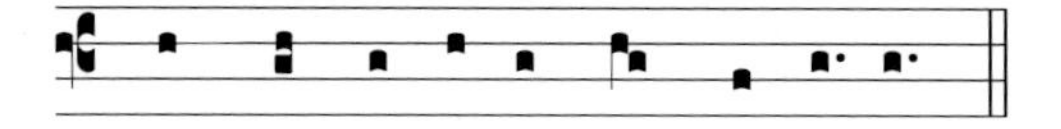

and lives to in-ter-cede for ev-er.

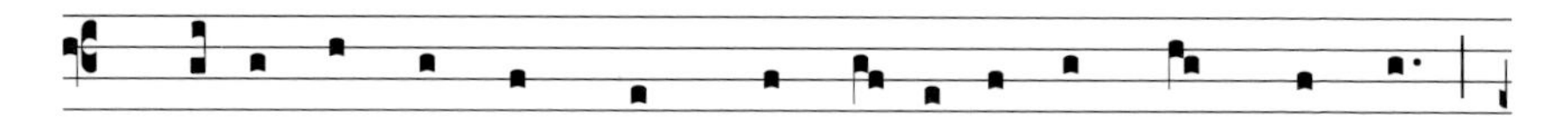

℟. Glo-ry, hon-our and praise, and nev-er ending thanks to God,

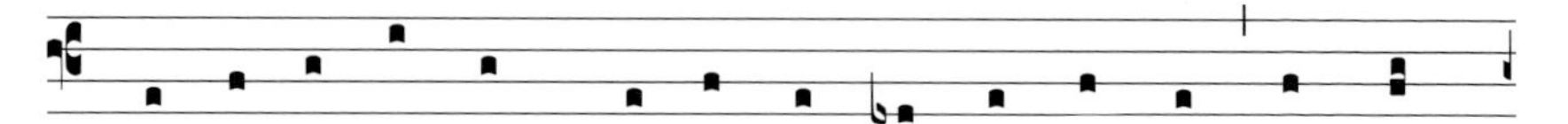

that we are re-deemed by his Son from sin and hell, and called

to share the joys of hea-ven.

*(with Alleluia)*

℣. Glo - ry, hon - our and praise to Christ the Vir - gin's Son, the

Lamb of God, the sin-less sacri-fice for sin, who rose from death

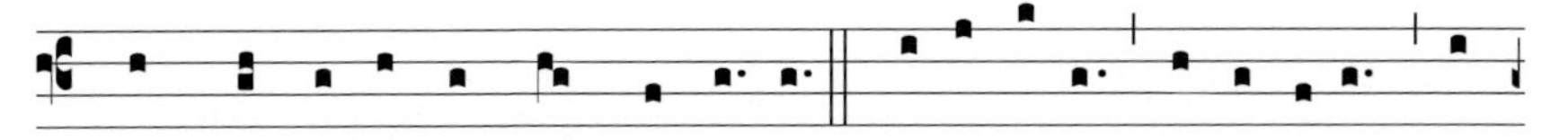

and lives to in-ter-cede for ev-er. Al-le-lu-ia, Al-le-lu-ia, Al-

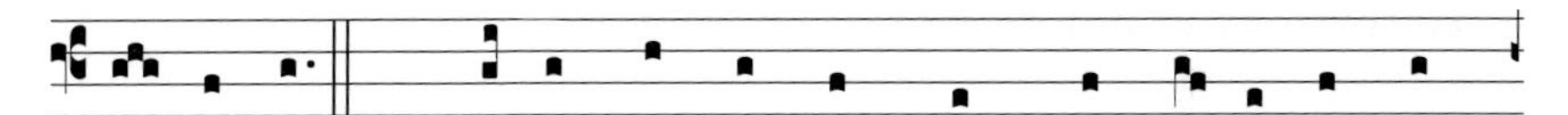

le- lu- ia ℟. Glo-ry, hon-our and praise, and nev-er end-ing

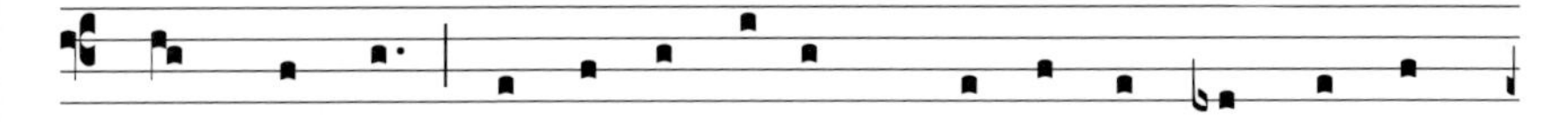

thanks to God, that we are redeemed by his Son from sin and

hell, and called to share the joys of heaven. Al-le-lu-ia, Al-le-

lu-ia, Al - le- lu- ia.

## Closing Prayers

'Mary, rejoice in God,' ... *with music* *(page 92)* *followed by...*

**HYMN** *to Holy Mother St. Bridget,* *(pages 93 - 94).*

*Friday*

# COMPLINE

*Friday Compline is used each day in Lent from Ash Wednesday to Wednesday in Holy Week inclusive; except on Solemnities, such as the Annunciation, if they occur. (Lenten melodies: p. 494)*

**OPENING PRAYERS** *as before Sunday Compline, pages 95 - 96.*

**In sorrow but not despair,** TONE I

**Psalms 131, 132 & 133** *as on Sunday, pages 97 - 98.*

ANTIPHON

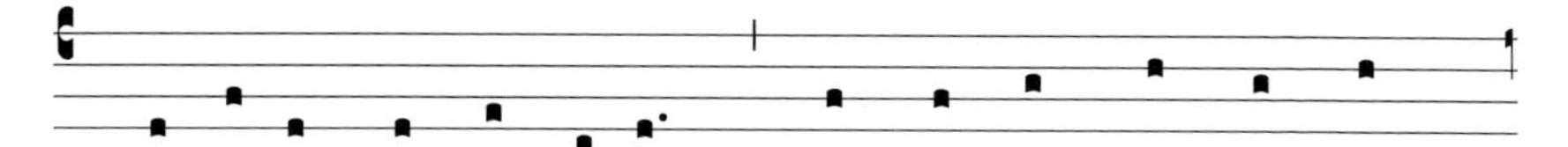

**In sorrow but not despair,** Mo - ther of Christ she stands

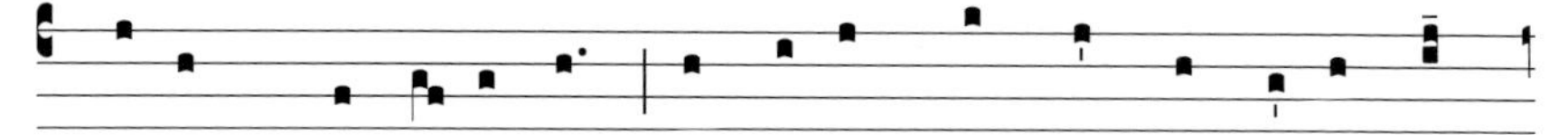

a-lone where all is dark: yet piercing her dark-ness ev-er shines

the light of faith, that he will rise a-gain; that God in his

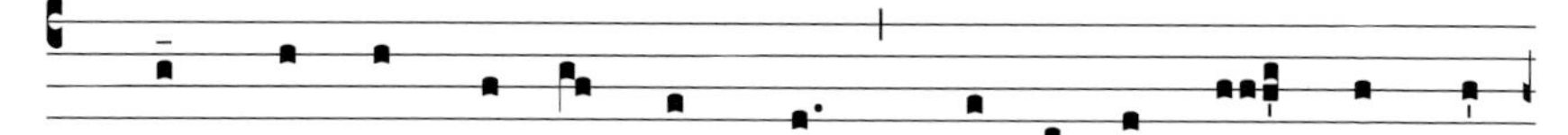

power will raise his Son from death and so pro-claim him Son

**READING** *as on Sunday, page 99.*

**SHORT RESPONSORY** *as on Sunday, pages 99 ff.*

## Hymn

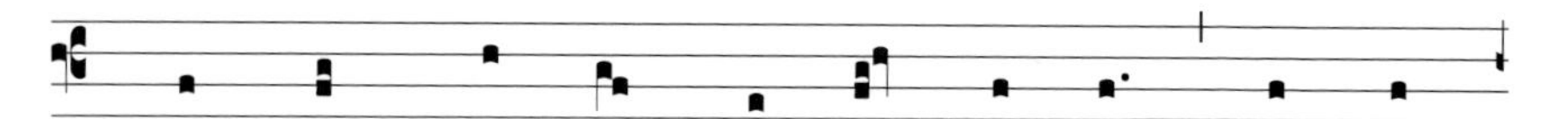

1. This Rose, more fair than earth - ly flowers, the Vir-
2. Heart - pierced she stands be - side her Son to see
3. Yet in her heart the words of Christ with- stand
4. Ma - ry, as once the Ark of old wel - comed
5. Pray Ma - ry Mo - ther full of grace, pray in
6. Christ Son of God we pray to you, and hon -

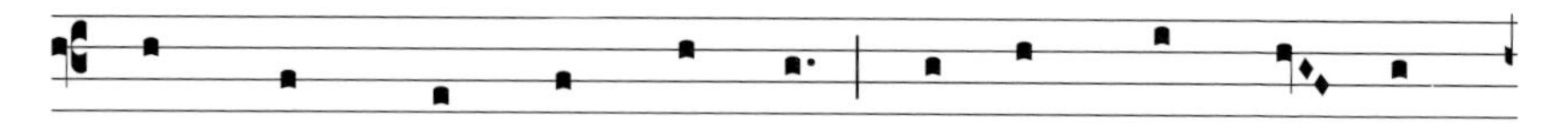

1. gin with her child new-born, hears in her joy sad
2. his death, sin's great price paid; this earth's re - dem-ption
3. the un - be - lief of men, bring to her sor - row
4. God's sign brought by a dove, we know through you God's
5. your love for all we need, pro- tect us from all
6. our you the Vir - gin's Son; we praise the Fa - ther,

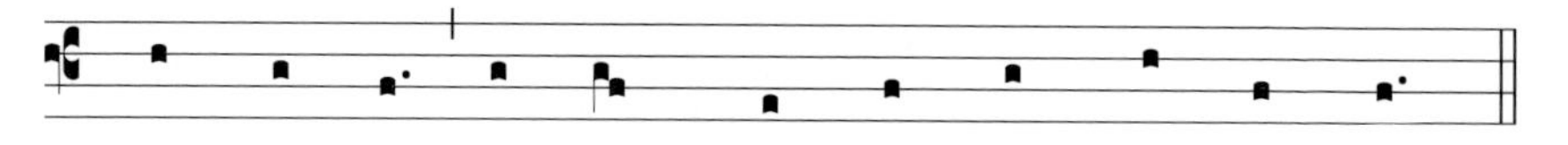

1. words fore-tell a pal - er rose, a pierc -ing thorn.
2. dear - ly won and earth's dread tomb where he is laid.
3. su - rest hope that he who died will rise a - gain.
4. sa - ving gifts, his truth, his mer - cy and his love.
5. dan - ger now and at our dy - ing in - ter - cede.
6. God, with you and with the Spi - rit, Three in One.

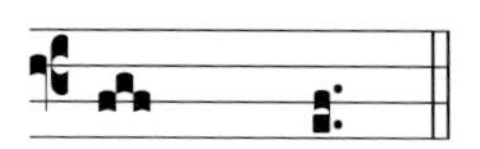

6. A - men.

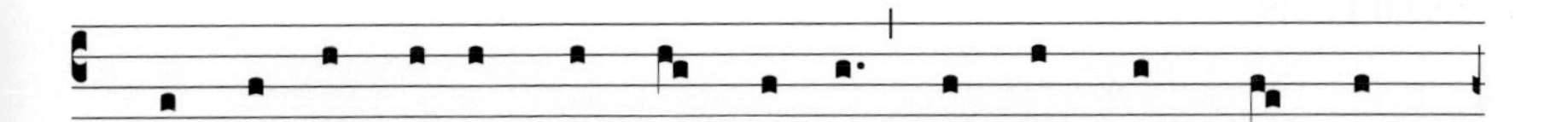

℣. In deepest sorrow she stood to see how life went down to

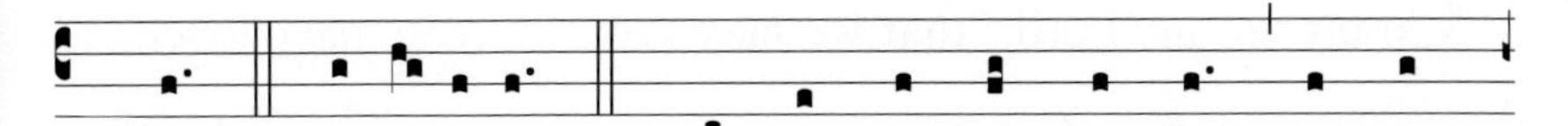

death. (Al-le-lu-ia) ℟. But from the tomb of death, life rose

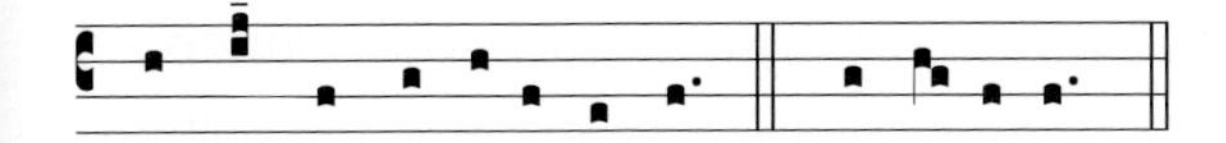

a-gain to her eternal joy. (Al-le-lu-ia)

## ANTIPHON

**Grant to us, Lord, that we may love** TONE I

## CANTICLE OF SIMEON *(Luke 2: 29 - 32)*

At last, all powerful Master you give leave
to your servant to go in peace,
according to your promise.

For my eyes have seen your salvation which you have prepared
for all nations.
The light to enlighten the gentiles and give glory to Israel, your people.

Give praise to the Father Almighty: to his Son, Jesus Christ, the Lord;
to the Spirit who dwells in our hearts, both now and forever. Amen.

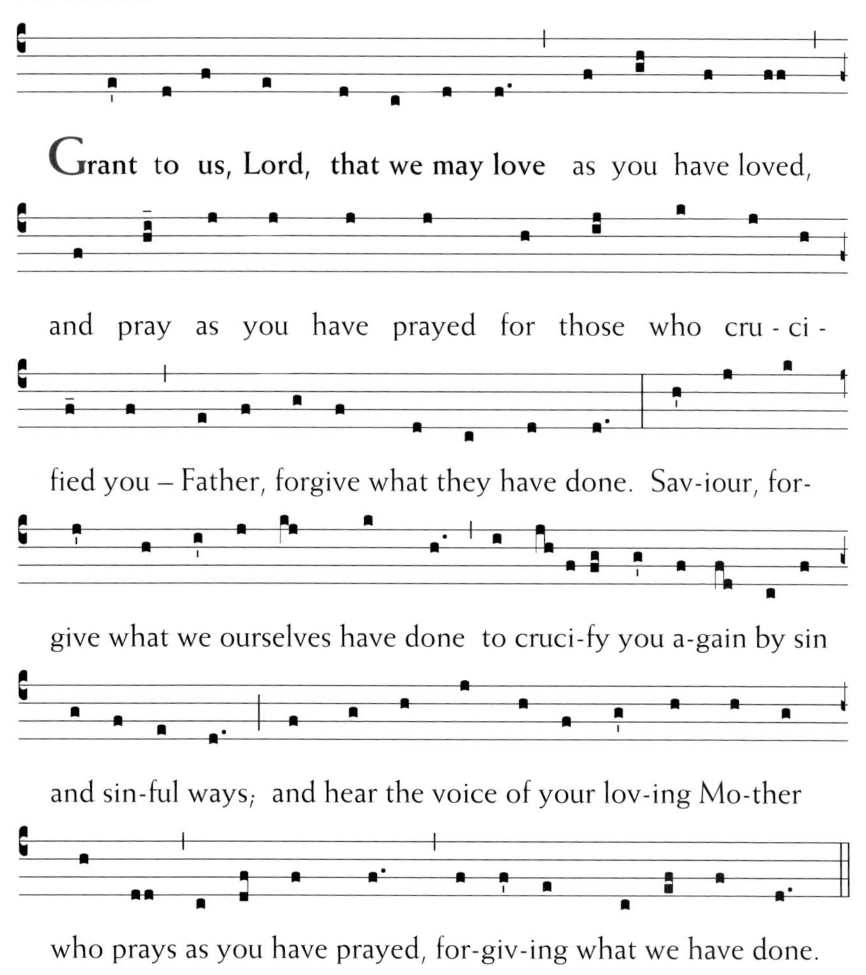


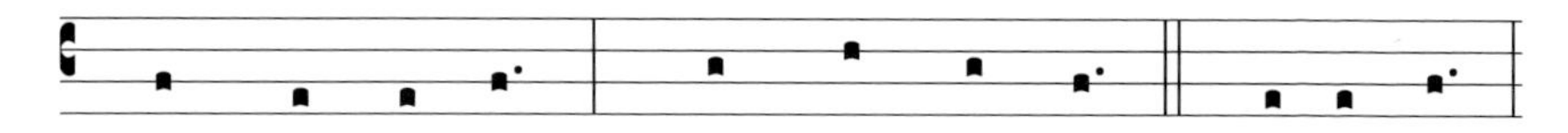

℣. Lord, hear my prayer. ℟. Lord, grant my prayer. ℣. Let us pray.

**PRAYER** *as on Sunday, page 104.*

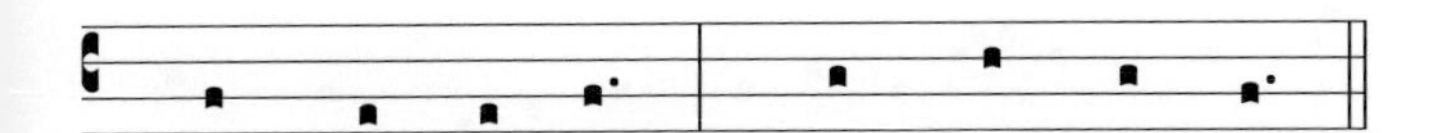

℣. Lord, hear my prayer. ℟. Lord, grant my prayer.

## Thanksgiving

℣. Glory, hon-our and praise to God. ℟. And our thanks to him.

*(with Alleluia)*

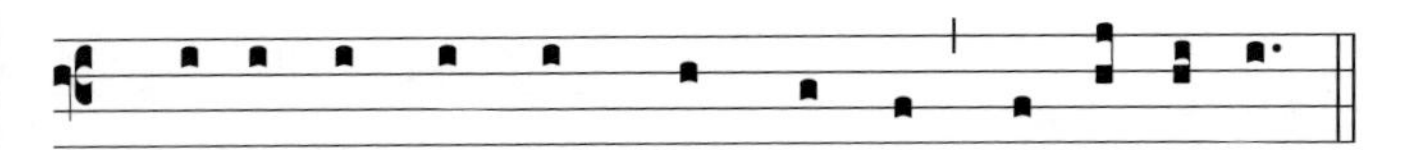

℣. Glory hon-our and praise to God, Al- le- lu- ia.

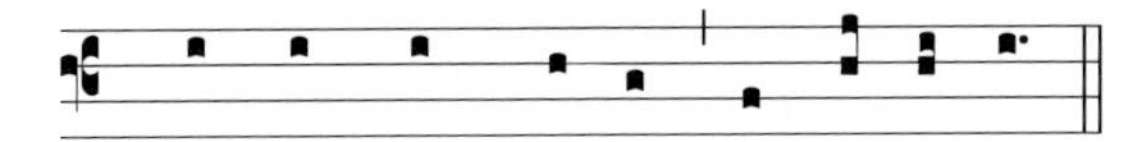

℟. And our thanks to him, Al- le- lu- ia.

℣. Mary, you are full of grace, the Lord is with you.
℟. Mary, you are most blessed of all women, for Jesus Christ is your Son. (Alleluia)

## Lauds of Our Lady

**Mary, we may call you Queen of earth,** for you are crowned

in heav'nly glo-ry Queen of heaven; highest hol-iest in God's

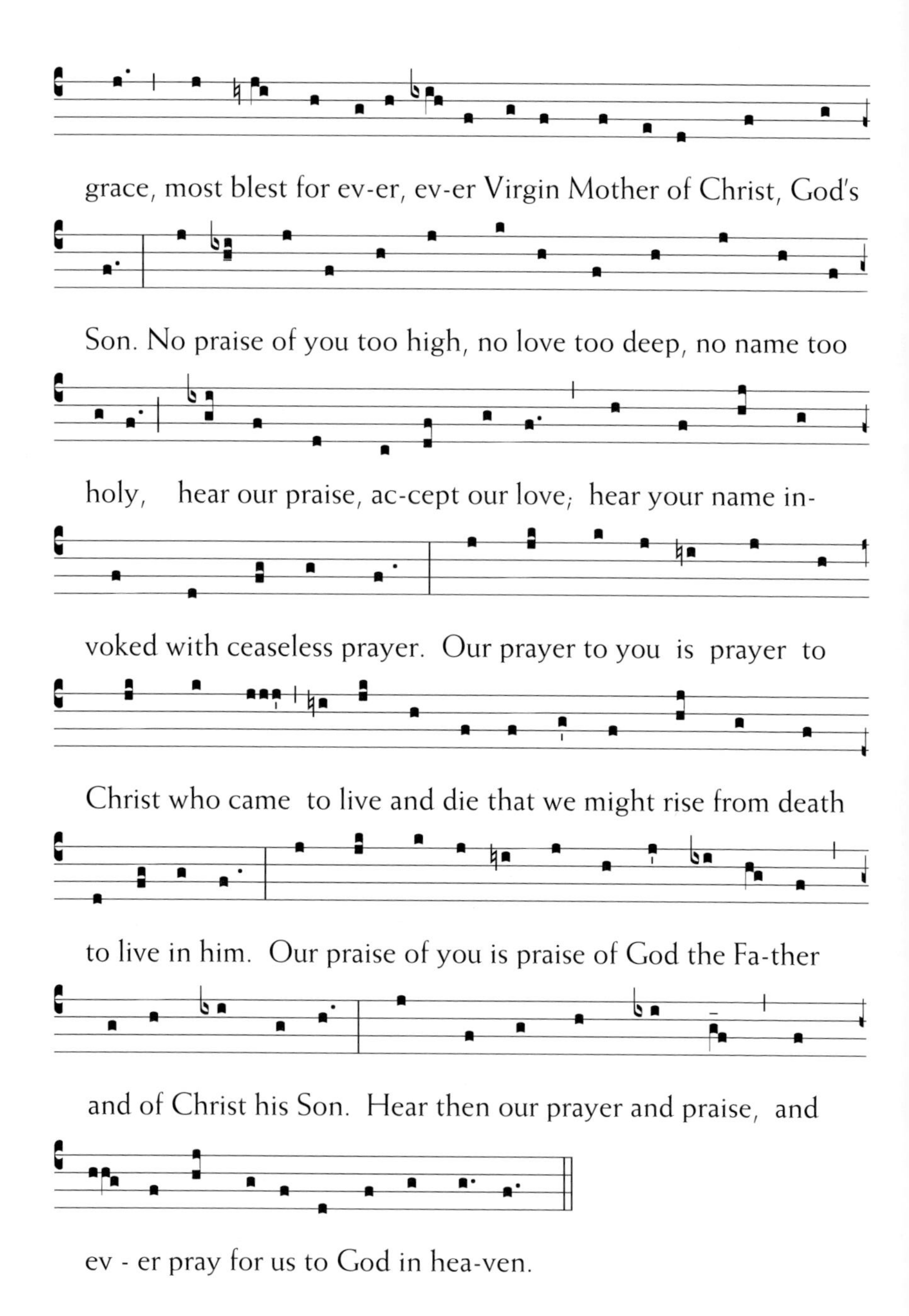


℣. Pray for us, holy Virgin Mary, Mother of God.
℟. That we may be made worthy of the promises of Jesus Christ.

℣. Let us pray.

## PRAYER

Forgive, we ask you Lord, the sins of your servants: and may we who of ourselves are unable to please you, be saved by the prayers of the Mother of your Son, Jesus Christ our Lord. ℟. Amen.

## CLOSING PRAYERS

'Mary, rejoice in God,' … *as on Sunday, page 107.*

*Illustration from the 1697 Landshut edition of the Bridgettine Breviary.*

*Saint Bridget received many divine revelations which spoke of the Blessed Virgin Mary, body and soul, assumed into heaven. (Revelations, Book 6, chapter 62)*

*Saturday*

# LAUDS

## OPENING PRAYERS

***(The first prayer of the day...)*** *(page 33).*

Open my mouth, O Lord ... *including Invitatory psalm (Ps. 94)*

## ANTIPHON

M**ary has entered into the glory of God.**

Psalms and Canticle as for Sunday Lauds *(pages 39 ff).*

M**ary has entered into the glory of God;**
the angels in heaven rejoice,
praising God for her glory.

## READING *as on Sunday, page 44.*

## HYMN

Christ would not let his Virgin-Mother know
the darkness and corruption of the grave,
from whose pure body he had willed to take
that flesh and blood which he would give to save.

How could he show on high those precious wounds,
his glorious manhood crowned, to heaven's joy,
yet leave that fount from which his manhood flowed
for death's decay to poison and destroy?

From earth Christ raised her to himself in heaven,
her sacred body ever glorified,
shrine of that soul where God had loved to dwell,
to be by her for ever magnified.

Praise God, creation, praise him, heaven and earth,
for all he is, and for himself alone;
and for the Virgin, glorious now in heaven –
see, in her glory, God's great love made known.

Pray Mary Virgin-Mother, … *Last two verses as on Sunday, page 44.*

℣. Bring me a rose from Jericho and I will plant it to grow in Jerusalem. (Alleluia)
℟. This rose is Mary, growing ever in beauty, to the glory of God and the joy of all angels. (Alleluia)

## ANTIPHON

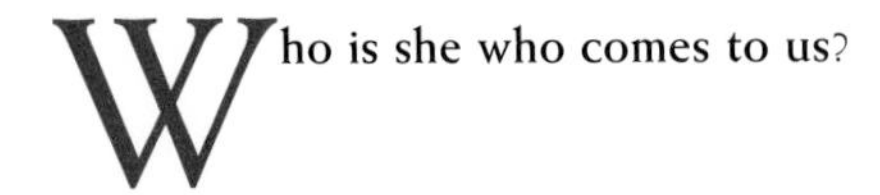

**Who is she who comes to us?**

## CANTICLE

Blessed be the Lord, the God of Israel! … *as on Sunday, page 45.*

**Who is she who comes to us,** fairer than dawn of purest light,
more radiant than the sun new-risen, lovelier than the moon at night,
more glorious than an army advancing at dawn?

℣. Lord hear my prayer. ℟. Lord grant my prayer. ℣. Let us pray.

## PRAYER

Grant us, your servants, …
*As on Sunday page 46 or according to the time of year. See pages 36ff.*

**ANTIPHON** to holy Mother Saint Bridget *as on Sunday, page 46.*
Bridget, loving servant of God, …

*or on ferial days:* Bridget, Saint and Patron, …

℣. and ℟. with Prayer *(page 47).*

℣. Lord hear my prayer. ℟. Lord grant my prayer.

## Thanksgiving

℣. Glory, honour and praise to Christ, the Son of God, and through him to God the Father, who for his Son has chosen a Virgin-Mother, Mary, most blest, now and for ever.
℟. Our thanks to God.

*(with Alleluia)*
℣. Glory, honour and praise to Christ, who has called his holy Mother into the joys of heaven for ever with him; for this earth could not hold one so blessed in grace. Alleluia, alleluia, alleluia.
℟. Our thanks to God. Alleluia, alleluia, alleluia.

## Closing Prayers *(page 37)*.

'Mary, rejoice in God,' …

*Saturday*

# TERCE

## OPENING PRAYERS

*(page 33).*

## HYMN

Virgin, your Son has willed and ever wills
all angels, men, and every thing;
so we may pray to you as Queen,
who in God's grace brought forth God's King.

Look from your throne in heaven to earth,
show for us all a Mother's care,
lead all to love and serve your Son,
who hears with love his Mother's prayer.

Pray Mary Mother, full of grace,
pray in your love for all we need;
protect us from all danger now,
and at our dying intercede.

Christ, Son of God, we pray to you,
and honour you, the Virgin's Son.
We praise the Father, God with you,
and with the Spirit, Three in One. Amen.

## ANTIPHON

**Mary, we think of you.**

### Psalm 122

To you have I lifted up my eyes, you who dwell in the heavens;
my eyes, like the eyes of slaves on the hand of their lords.

Like the eyes of a servant on the hand of her mistress,
so our eyes are on the Lord our God till he show us his mercy.

Have mercy on us, Lord, have mercy.
We are filled with contempt.

Indeed all too full is our soul
with the scorn of the rich, (with the proud man's disdain).

*Glory be...*

**Psalm 123**

"If the Lord had not been on our side,"
this is Israel's song.

"If the Lord had not been on our side when men rose against us,
then would they have swallowed us alive when their anger was kindled.

Then would the waters have engulfed us, the torrent gone over us;
over our head would have swept the raging waters."

Blessed be the Lord who did not give us a prey to their teeth!
Our life, like a bird, has escaped from the snare of the fowler.

Indeed the snare has been broken and we have escaped.
Our help is in the name of the Lord, who made heaven and earth.

*Glory be...*

**Psalm 124**

Those who put their trust in the Lord
are like Mount Sion, that cannot be shaken, that stands for ever.

Jerusalem! The mountains surround her,
so the Lord surrounds his people both now and for ever.

For the sceptre of the wicked shall not rest over the land of the just
for fear that the hands of the just should turn to evil.

Do good, Lord, to those who are good,
to the upright of heart;

but the crooked and those who do evil, drive them away!
On Israel, peace!

*Glory be...*

## ANTIPHON

Mary, **we think of you** and love you;
your loveliness is like the fragrance of summer,
like the sweet scent of fairest flowers.

## READING *(Eccles. 24: 9)*

In the eternal decree of God, I was present before his creating, and I shall be for ever with him, in the holiness of his heaven. ℟. Our thanks to God.

## SHORT RESPONSORY

℣. This is she who has crushed the Serpent's head. (Alleluia, Alleluia)
℟. *Repeat.*
℣. Envying the gifts of God to her race, this mortal enemy has waited for her, to wound her heel.
℟. But she has crushed the Serpent's head. (†℟. Alleluia, Alleluia)
℣. Glory to God, Father, Son and Holy Spirit.
℟. This is she who has crushed the Serpent's head. (Alleluia, Alleluia)
℣. Satan is cast down to hell for ever. (Alleluia)
℟. Mary who crushed the Serpent's head, is raised to eternal glory and joy. (Alleluia)

## CLOSING PRAYERS *(page 38)*.

---

† ***Response during Easter and on other special days where shown, as well as in brackets thus: (Alleluia). For style, see Sunday Terce on page 51.***

*Saturday*

# SEXT

## OPENING PRAYERS *(page 33).*

## HYMN

Virgin, your Son has willed and ever wills... *as at Saturday Terce, page 356.*

## ANTIPHON

**Mary, most bless-ed child of God.**

**Psalm 125**

When the Lord delivered Sion from bondage, it seemed like a dream.
Then was our mouth filled with laughter, on our lips there were songs.

The heathens themselves said: "What marvels the Lord worked for them!"
What marvels the Lord worked for us! Indeed we were glad.

Deliver us, O Lord, from our bondage as streams in dry land.
Those who are sowing in tears will sing when they reap.

They go out, they go out, full of tears, carrying seed for the sowing:
they come back, they come back, full of song, carrying their sheaves.

*Glory be...*

**Psalm 126**

If the Lord does not build the house, in vain do its builders labour;
if the Lord does not watch over the city, in vain does the watchman keep vigil.

In vain is your earlier rising, your going later to rest,

you who toil for the bread you eat: when he pours gifts on his beloved
while they slumber.

Truly sons are a gift from the Lord, a blessing, the fruit of the womb.
Indeed the sons of youth are like arrows in the hand of a warrior.

O the happiness of the man who has filled his quiver with these arrows!
He will have no cause for shame when he disputes with his foes in
the gateways.

*Glory be...*

**Psalm 127**

O blessed are those who fear the Lord and walk in his ways!
By the labour of your hands you shall eat. You will be happy and prosper;

your wife like a fruitful vine in the heart of your house;
your children like shoots of the olive, around your table.

Indeed thus shall be blessed the man who fears the Lord.
May the Lord bless you from Sion all the days of your life!

May you see your children's children in a happy Jerusalem!
On Israel, peace!

*Glory be...*

## ANTIPHON

**Mary, most bless-ed child of God,**
through you we have tasted
the fruit of life.

## READING *(Eccles. 24: 11)*

Jerusalem has been my dwelling and my resting-place:
there in the holy city, I have taken up my rule and my reign.
℟. Our thanks to God.

## Short Responsory

℣. Mary, who crushed the Serpent's head, is raised to eternal glory and joy. (Alleluia, Alleluia) ℟. *Repeat.*
℣. Satan is cast down to hell for ever.
℟. Mary is raised to eternal glory and joy. († ℟. Alleluia, Alleluia)
℣. Glory to God, Father, Son and Holy Spirit.
℟. Mary, who crushed the Serpent's head, is raised to eternal glory and joy. (Alleluia, Alleluia)
℣. Bring me a rose from Jericho, and I will plant it to grow in Jerusalem. (Alleluia)
℟. This rose is Mary, growing ever in beauty, to the glory of God, and the joy of all angels. (Alleluia)

*NOTE: If continuing immediately with None, omit the Opening Prayers and Hymn for None and start with the (short) Antiphon before the Psalms: as detailed in the Structure, page 26.*

## Closing Prayers *(page 38)*.

---

† ***Response during Easter and on other special days where shown, as well as in brackets thus: (Alleluia). For style, see Sunday Terce on page 51.***

*Saturday*

# NONE

**OPENING PRAYERS** *as before Sunday None, pages 55 - 56.*

**HYMN**

1. Vir-gin, your Son has willed and ev - er wills
2. Look from your throne in heav'n to earth,
3. Pray Ma - ry Mo - ther full of grace,
4. Christ Son of God we pray to you,

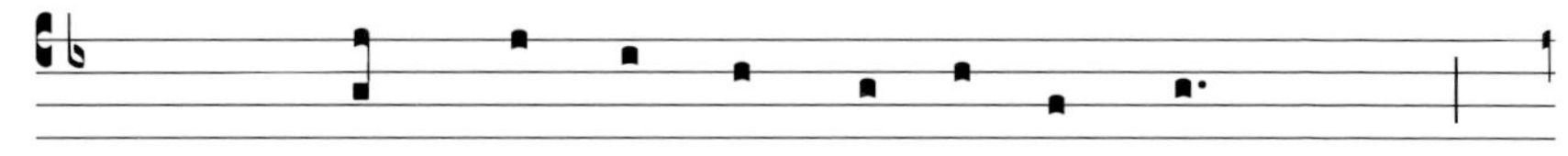

1 all an - gels, men, and ev - ry thing;
2. show for us all a Mo-ther's care,
3. pray in your love for all we need;
4. and hon- our you, the Vir -gin's Son;

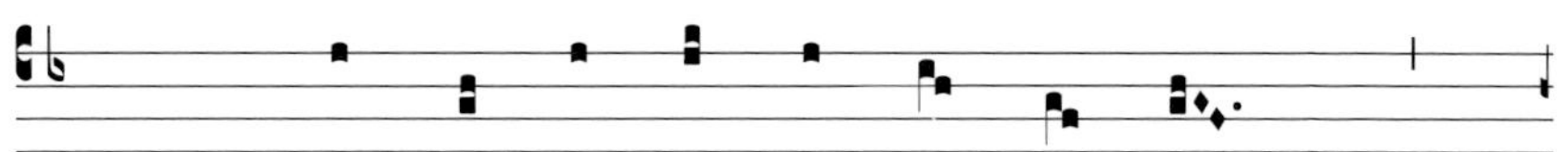

1. so we may pray to you as Queen,
2. lead all to love and serve your Son,
3 pro- tect us from all dan - ger now,
4. we praise the Fa - ther, God with you,

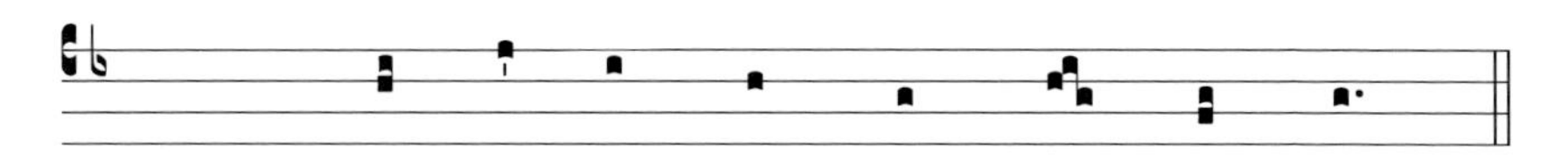

1. who in God's grace brought forth God's King.
2. who hears with love his Mo - ther's prayer.
3 and at our dy - ing in - ter - cede.
4. and with the Spi - rit, Three in One.

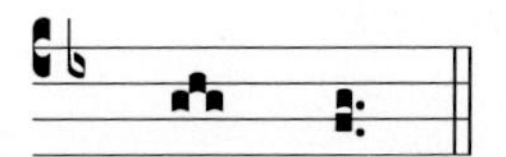

4. A - men.

ANTIPHON

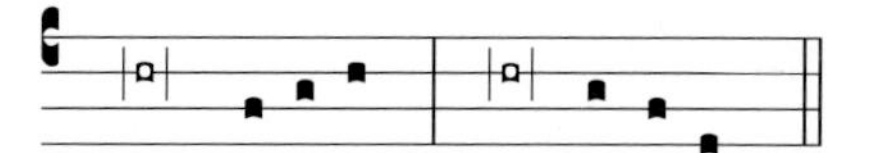

**Fairer than flowers of earth,** TONE I

**Psalm 128**

"They have pressed me hard from my youth," this is Israel's song.
"They have pressed me hard from my youth but could never destroy me.

They ploughed my back like ploughmen, drawing long furrows.
But the Lord who is just, has destroyed the yoke of the wicked."

Let them be shamed and routed, those who hate Sion!
Let them be like grass on the roof that withers before it flowers.

With that no reaper fill his arms,
no binder makes his sheaves

and those passing by will not say: "On you the Lord's blessing!"
"We bless you in the name of the Lord."

*Glory be...*

**Psalm129**

Out of the depths I cry to you, O Lord. Lord, hear my voice!
O let your ears be attentive to the voice of my pleading.

If you, O Lord, should mark our guilt, Lord, who would survive?
But with you is found forgiveness: for this we revere you.

My soul is waiting for the Lord. I count on his word.

My soul is longing for the Lord more than watchman for daybreak.

Let the watchman count on daybreak
and Israel on the Lord.

Because with the Lord there is mercy and fullness of redemption,
Israel indeed he will redeem from all its iniquity.

*Glory be…*

**Psalm 130**

O Lord, my heart is not proud nor haughty my eyes.
I have not gone after things too great nor marvels beyond me.

Truly I have set my soul in silence and peace.
A weaned child on its mother's breast, even so is my soul.

O Israel, hope in the Lord
both now and for ever.

*Glory be…*

## ANTIPHON

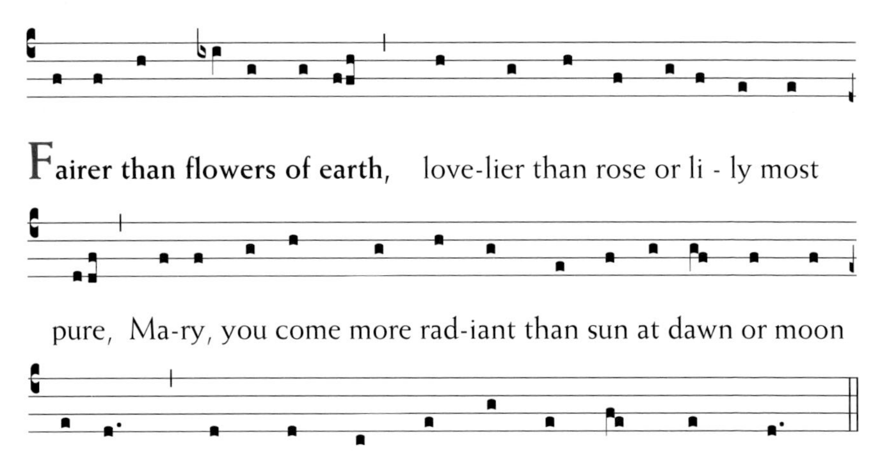

## Reading (*Eccles.* 24: 12)

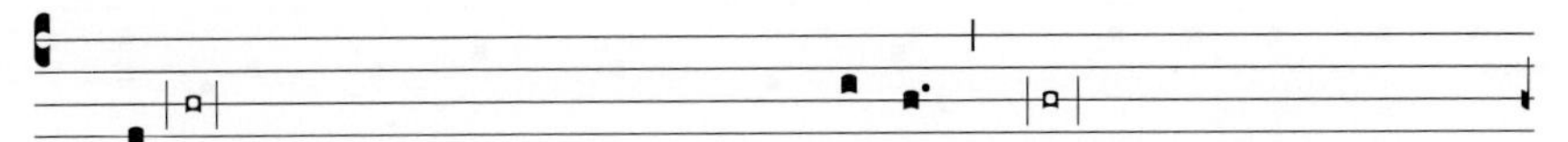

I have grown up among God's people: I will live for ever

in the land of the Lord. ℟. Our thanks to God.

## Short Responsory

℣. Bring me a rose from Je-ri-cho and I will plant it to grow in

Jerusalem, ℟. Bring me ... ℣. This rose is Ma-ry, growing ev-er

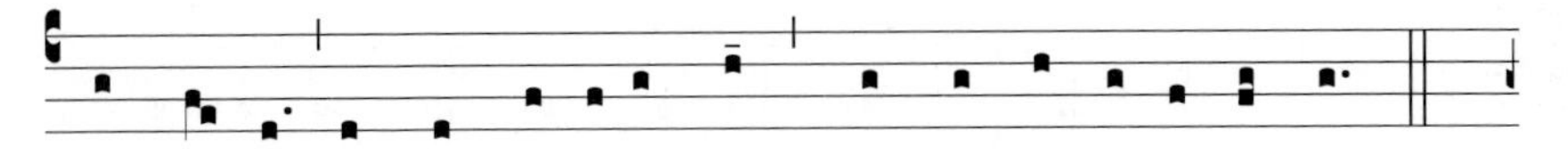

in beau-ty, to the glo-ry of God and the joy of all an-gels.

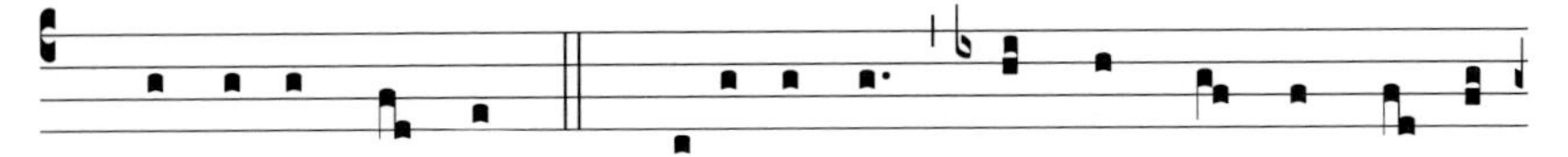

℟. And I will plant it... ℣. Glory to God, Fa-ther, Son and Ho-ly

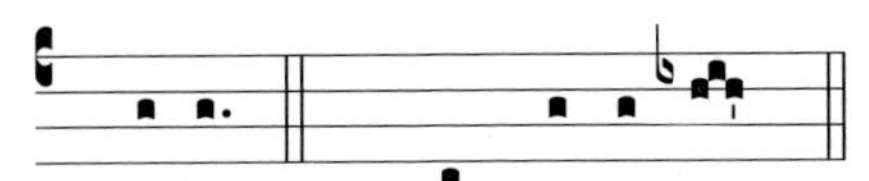

Spir-it. ℟. Bring me a rose...

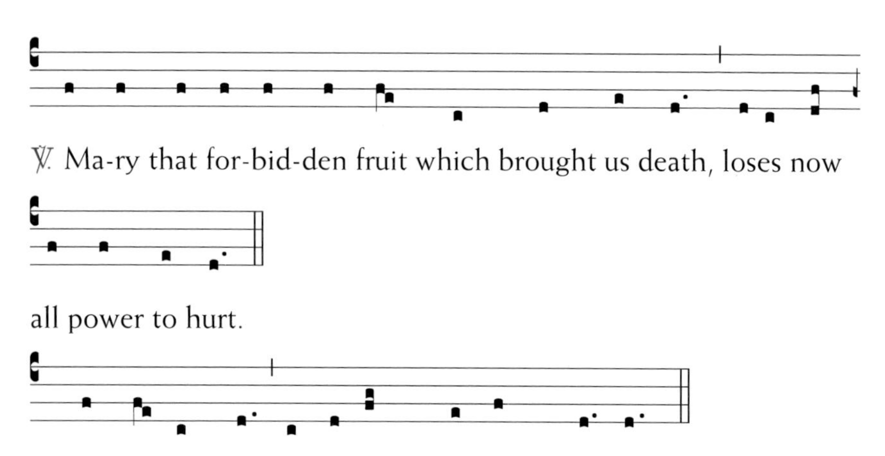


*(with Alleluia)*

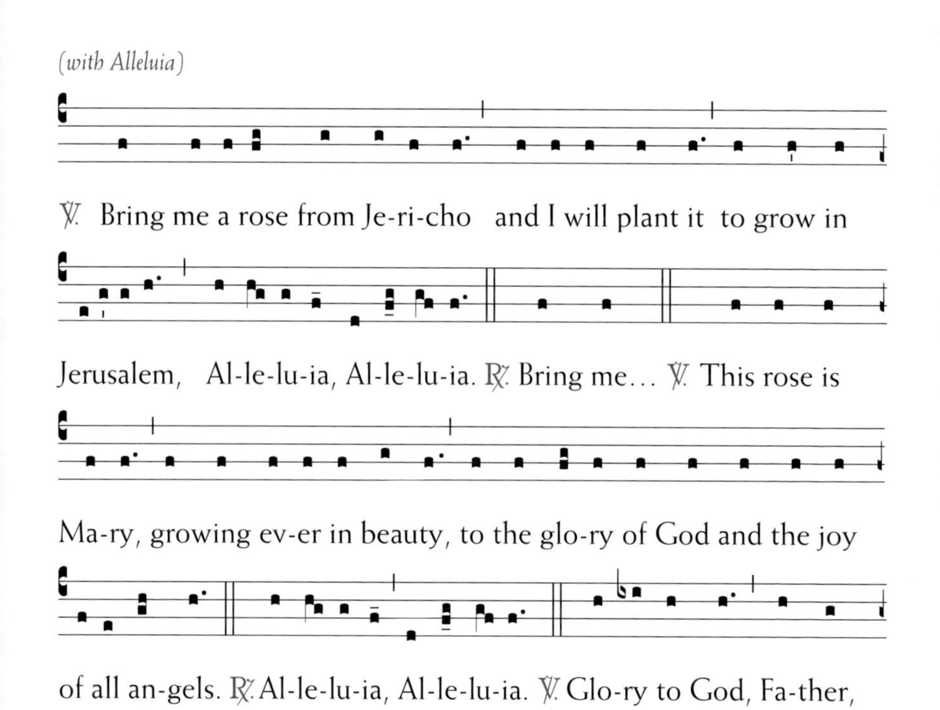

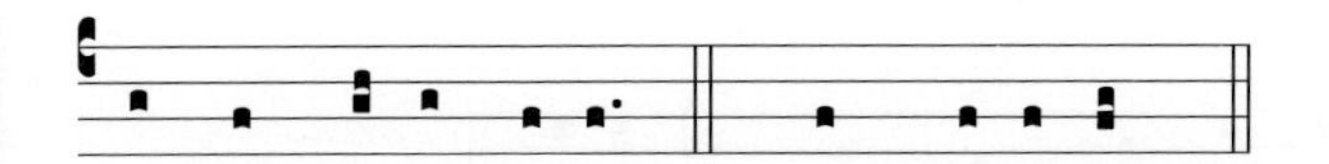

Son and Ho-ly Spir-it. ℟. Bring me a rose…

℣. Ma-ry that for-bid-den fruit which brought us death, loses now

all power to hurt, Al-le-lu-ia.

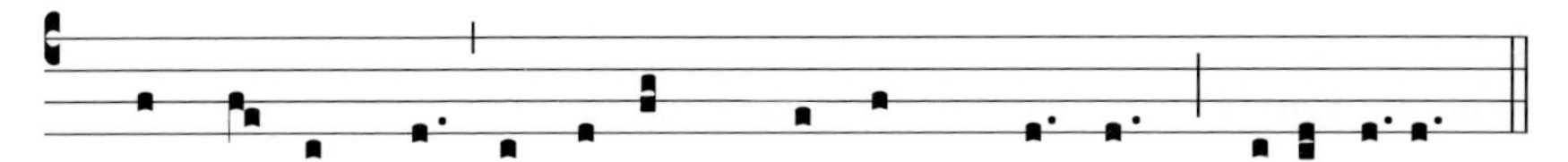

℟. And all this earth is refreshed by your sweetness, Al-le-lu-ia.

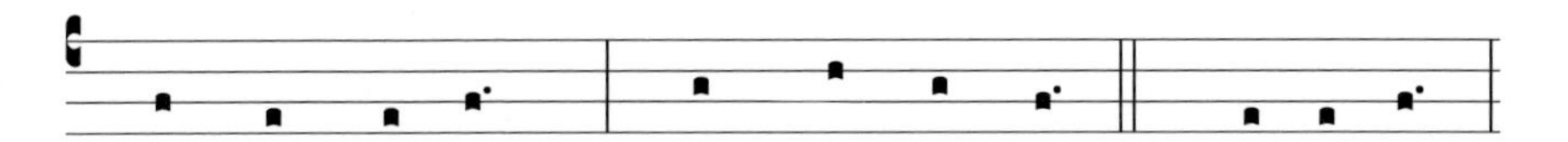

℣. Lord, hear my prayer. ℟. Lord, grant my prayer. ℣. Let us pray.

**Prayer** *(pages 36 - 37)*

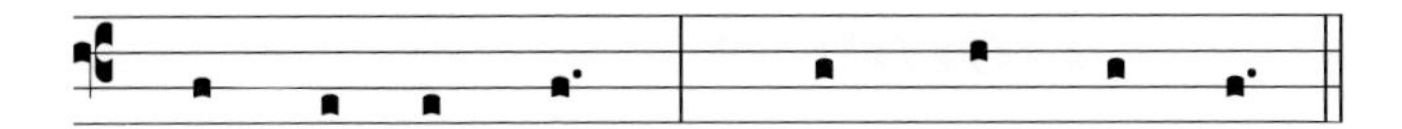

℣. Lord, hear my prayer. ℟. Lord, grant my prayer.

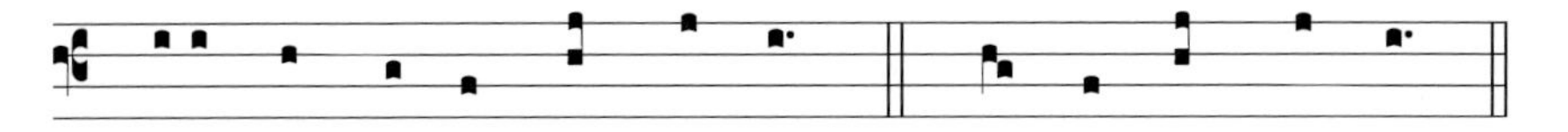

℣. Glory hon-our and praise to God. ℟. And our thanks to him.

*(with Alleluia)*

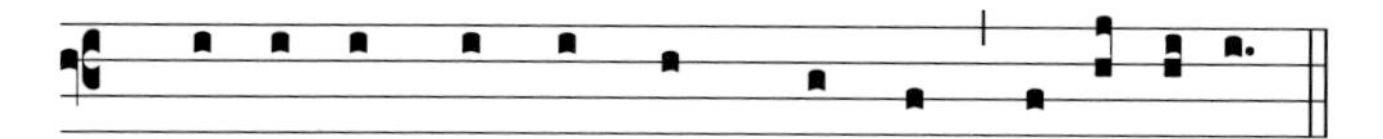

℣. Glory hon-our and praise to God, Al-le-lu-ia.

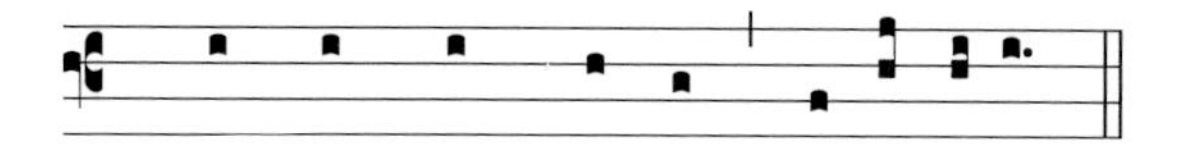

℟. And our thanks to him, Al-le-lu-ia.

## CLOSING PRAYERS

'Mary, rejoice...' *as on Sunday, pages 64ff.*

**LAUDS OF OUR LADY** *of the day, season or feast. (See daily after Compline)*
*With* ℣. & ℟. *and Prayer. Then* 'May the souls of our founders...' *and...*

**Psalm 129** 'Out of the depths...' *and two or three memorial prayers for the souls of the departed, as on Sunday, page 65 - 66.*

*Saturday*

# OFFICE OF READINGS (MATINS)

**OPENING PRAYERS** *(page 67).*

## HYMN

O glorious Queen, enthroned on high,
above the stars which light the sky,
Virgin by your Creator blessed,
you held him, fed him at your breast.

That which was lost by sin of Eve,
Mary, through Christ, you did retrieve,
bringing the light of heaven again
into this darkened world of men.

You were that Gate of heaven most bright
through which Christ came, true Light from Light.
Rejoice, all peoples, dearly bought
in that new life the Virgin brought.

Pray Mary Mother full of grace,
pray in your love for all we need;
protect us from all danger now,
and at our dying intercede.

Christ, Son of God, we pray to you
and honour you, the Virgin's Son;
we praise the Father, God with you
and with the Spirit, Three in One. Amen.

## ANTIPHON 1

**Holy Mother of God.**

**Psalm 8**

How great is your name, O Lord our God,
through all the earth!

Your majesty is praised above the heavens; on the lips of children and of babes you have found praise to foil your enemy, to silence the foe and the rebel.

When I see the heavens, the work of your hands, the moon and the stars which you arranged,
what is man that you should keep him in mind, mortal man that you care for him?

Yet you have made him little less than a god; with glory and honour you crowned him,
gave him power over the works of your hand, put all things under his feet.

All of them, sheep and cattle, yes, even the savage beasts,
birds of the air, and fish that make their way through the waters.

How great is your name, O Lord our God,
through all the earth!

*Glory be...*

## ANTIPHON 1

**Holy Mother of God,**
you are more glorious in the kingdom of God,
than all the angels of heaven.

## ANTIPHON 2

**Mary, you have opened the gate to heaven.**

**Psalm 18**

The heavens proclaim the glory of God, and the firmament shows forth the work of his hands.

Day unto day takes up the story and night unto night makes known
the message.

No speech, no word, no voice is heard
yet their span extends through all the earth, their words to the utmost bounds
of the world.

There he has placed a tent for the sun;
it comes forth like a bridegroom coming from his tent, rejoices like a
champion to run its course.

At the end of the sky is the rising of the sun; to the furthest end of the sky
is its course.
There is nothing concealed from its burning heat.

The law of the Lord is perfect, it revives the soul.
The rule of the Lord is to be trusted, it gives wisdom to the simple.

The precepts of the Lord are right, they gladden the heart.
The command of the Lord is clear, it gives light to the eyes.

The fear of the Lord is holy, abiding for ever.
The decrees of the Lord are truth and all of them just.

They are more to be desired than gold, than the purest of gold
and sweeter are they than honey, than honey from the comb.

So in them your servant finds instruction; great reward is in their keeping.
But who can detect all his errors? From hidden faults acquit me.

From presumption restrain your servant and let it not rule me.
Then shall I be blameless, clean from grave sin.

May the spoken words of my mouth, the thoughts of my heart,
win favour in your sight, O Lord, my rescuer, my rock!

*Glory be...*

## Antiphon 2

**Mary, you have opened the gate to heaven,**
and entered yourself in glory,
to the joy of the angels.

## Antiphon 3

**Beauty and joy have met in you.**

### Psalm 23

The Lord's is the earth and its fullness, the world and all its peoples.
It is he who set it on the seas; on the waters he made it firm.

Who shall climb the mountain of the Lord?
Who shall stand in his holy place?

The man with clean hands and pure heart, who desires not worthless things,
(who has not sworn so as to deceive his neighbour.)

He shall receive blessings from the Lord and reward from the God who
saves him.
Such are the men who seek him, seek the face of the God of Jacob.

O gates, lift high your heads; grow higher, ancient doors.
Let him enter, the king of glory!

Who is the king of glory?
The Lord, the mighty, the valiant, the Lord, the valiant in war.

O gates, lift high your heads; grow higher, ancient doors.
Let him enter, the king of glory!

Who is he, the king of glory?
He, the Lord of armies, he is the king of glory.

*Glory be...*

## ANTIPHON 3

**Beauty and joy have met in you;**
grace and glory are come together in you,
Mary, Mother of God.

℣. This is she who has crushed the Serpent's head. (Alleluia)
℟. Envying the gifts of God to her race, this mortal enemy has waited for her to wound her heel. (Alleluia)

Our Father...

## ABSOLUTION

God and father, holy and merciful Lord, take into account the prayer and holiness of Mary, the Virgin-Mother of God, and of all the saints and bring us back from death to life.
℟. Amen.

*Reader:* Lord, we ask for your blessing.

**Week One**
*Blessing, Reading and Response for Saturdays in Week Two start on page 524, and for Week Three on page 545.*

## BLESSSING

May Mary the Mother, highest and holiest of all creation, strengthen us in faith and holiness. ℟. Amen.

## READING

We read that the Queen of Sheba
made the long journey from her own lands in the south
to visit Solomon the King.
Her journey was not wasted,
for she found great delight in his words.
No gifts were too precious for her to give,
no praise too high,
and she departed in admiration of such great wisdom.

The Virgin Mary spent long hours in thought,
considering the course of events in this world,
and all the things that this world holds dear.
Nothing delighted or attracted her,
except the wisdom she had learned from God.
This was her desire and her search,
and she did not rest till she had found it in Christ.
In the Son of God she found wisdom infinitely greater than Solomon's.

The Queen of Sheba was overcome with wonder
as she contemplated the wisdom of Solomon.
Mary was overcome with sorrow as she pondered the loving wisdom of Christ,
who saw salvation in suffering,
and willed to save man from subjection to Satan
by his sufferings and cross.

When at last the sufferings of Christ were over,
Mary looked up from the depths of her sorrow,
ever offering herself and her will to God for his glory,
gifts most precious to him.
Gifts too of another kind,
for many were led to the truth of God by her faith.
No words or works of men were so powerful
to bring men to God.
Many lost faith when they saw Christ die.
She alone withstood the unbelief of men,
seeing in Christ her Son the Son of God,
over whose Godhead death could have no dominion.

When the third day came,
it brought bewilderment and anxiety to the disciples.
The women going to the tomb to anoint the body of Jesus
sought him and could not find him.
The Apostles were gathered together in their fear, guarding the doors.
Then, surely, though we are not told of this in the Gospels,
Mary spoke of the resurrection of her Son,
that he had truly risen from death,
that he was alive again in all his humanity,
no more subject to death,
risen to an eternal glory.

We read that Mary Magdalen and the Apostles were first to see the risen Christ.
But we may believe that Mary his Mother knew of his rising before all others,
and that she was the first to see him.
It was Mary in her lowliness who first gave praise and adoration to the risen
Christ.

When Christ ascended to the glory of his kingdom,
the Virgin Mary remained on earth.
We cannot know what her presence meant to so many.
Those who loved God were strengthened in their love;
those who had turned from him were brought back to his love.

The Apostles looked to her for guidance and counsel.
The Martyrs found in her, courage to face suffering and death.
The Confessors of the Faith were strengthened in their believing.
Virgins were drawn to her purity.
Widows were consoled by her sorrows.
Husbands and wives found in her a pattern of perfection.
All who heard and obeyed the word of God
found in Mary great comfort and help.

Whenever the Apostles came to her,
she was able to teach them about Christ,
and help them to understand.
The Martyrs rejoiced to suffer for Christ,
for he had suffered for all.
They remembered the long years of sorrow borne so patiently by Mary his
Mother,
and they bore their martyrdom even more readily.
The Confessors, meditating on Mary, learnt many things about the truths of the
Faith.
From her example, they learnt too the wise use of earthly things,
food, drink and sleep, work and rest,
and how to order their lives in all things
to the honour and glory of God.
Virgins learnt from Mary's example true chastity and modesty,
resistance to temptation, and perseverance in virtue.
They learnt too the wise use of their time,
how to avoid vanity and foolish talk,
and see all things in the light of true holiness.
Widows learnt from her, consolation in sorrow,
strength against temptation,

and humble submission to God's will.
With a mother's love,
Mary could never have wished for the death of her Son,
still less for the death of the Son of God.
Yet she willed in all things the will of God.
She chose for God's sake the humble acceptance of suffering and sorrow.

Husbands and wives learnt from Mary true love for each other, in body and in soul,
and the union of their wills, as of their flesh,
in all that the will of God demanded.
They learnt how she had united herself for ever with God by faith,
and never in any way shown resistance to his divine will.

℣. Have mercy, Lord, and help our understanding. ℟. Our thanks to God.

## RESPONSORY

**Mary, in you God's promise has been fulfilled,** and his word which you believed, has made you the Virgin-Mother of God. Glorious now in heaven, higher than all the angels of God, pray for us to your Son, Jesus Christ our Lord.
℣. Mary, you are full of grace, the Lord is with you.
℟. Pray for us to your Son, Jesus Christ our Lord.
℣. Glory to God, glory to Father, Son and Holy Spirit.
℟. Pray for us to your Son, Jesus Christ our Lord.

## TE DEUM *as on Sunday, page 75* or PSALM 50 *as on Friday, page 330.*

℣. Satan is cast down to hell for ever. (Alleluia)
℟. Mary who crushed the Serpent's head is raised to eternal glory and joy. (Alleluia)

## CLOSING PRAYERS *(page 38).*

*Saturday*

# VESPERS

**PRAYERS** before Vespers, *(pages 77 - 78)* and
**OPENING PRAYERS** – with music – *as at None, pages 55 - 56.*

**ANTIPHON**

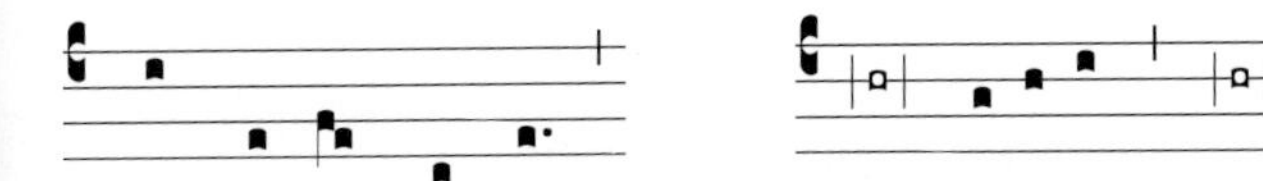

**Joy beyond all joy,** TONE IV

**Psalm 143**

Blessed be the Lord, my rock, who trains my arms for battle,
who prepares my hands for war.

He is my love, my fortress; he is my stronghold, my saviour,
my shield, my place of refuge. He brings peoples under my rule.

Lord, what is man that you care for him, mortal man, that you keep him
in mind;
man, who is merely a breath whose life fades like a passing shadow?

Lower your heavens and come down; touch the mountains; wreathe them
in smoke.
Flash your lightnings; rout the foe, shoot your arrows and put them to flight.

Reach down from heaven and save me;
draw me out from the mighty waters,

from the hands of alien foes whose mouths are filled with lies,
whose hands are raised in perjury.

To you, O God, will I sing a new song; I will play on the ten-stringed lute
to you who give kings their victory, who set David your servant free.

You set him free from the evil sword; you rescued him from alien foes
whose mouths were filled with lies, whose hands were raised in perjury.

Let our sons then flourish like saplings grown tall and strong from their youth;
our daughters graceful as columns, adorned as though for a palace.

Let our barns be filled to overflowing
with crops of every kind;

our sheep increasing by thousands, myriads of sheep in our fields,
our cattle heavy with young,

no ruined wall, no exile, no sound of weeping in our streets.
Happy the people with such blessings; happy the people whose God
is the Lord.

*Glory be...*

**Psalm 144**

I will give you glory, O God my king,
I will bless your name for ever.

I will bless you day after day and praise your name for ever.
The Lord is great, highly to be praised, his greatness cannot be measured.

Age to age shall proclaim your works, shall declare your mighty deeds,
shall speak of your splendour and glory, tell the tale of your wonderful works.

They will speak of your terrible deeds, recount your greatness and might.
They will recall your abundant goodness; age to age shall ring out your justice.

The Lord is kind and full of compassion, slow to anger, abounding in love.
How good is the Lord to all, compassionate to all his creatures.

All your creatures shall thank you, O Lord, and your friends shall repeat
their blessing.
They shall speak of the glory of your reign and declare your might, O God,

to make known to men your mighty deeds and the glorious splendour
of your reign.
Yours is an everlasting kingdom; your rule lasts from age to age.

The Lord is faithful in all his words and loving in all his deeds.
The Lord supports all who fall and raises all who are bowed down.

The eyes of all creatures look to you and you give them their food in due time.
You open wide your hand, grant the desires of all who live.

The Lord is just in all his ways and loving in all his deeds.
He is close to all who call him, who call on him from their hearts.

He grants the desires of those who fear him, he hears their cry and he
saves them.
The Lord protects all who love him; but the wicked he will utterly destroy.

Let me speak the praise of the Lord, let all mankind bless his holy name
for ever, for ages unending.

*Glory be...*

**Psalm 145**

My soul, give praise to the Lord; I will praise the Lord all my days,
make music to my God while I live.

Put no trust in princes, in mortal men in whom there is no help.
Take their breath, they return to clay and their plans that day come to nothing.

He is happy who is helped by Jacob's God, whose hope is in the Lord his God,
who alone made heaven and earth, the seas and all they contain.

It is he who keeps faith for ever, who is just to those who are oppressed.
It is he who gives bread to the hungry, the Lord, who sets prisoners free,

the Lord who gives sight to the blind, who raises up those who are
bowed down,
the Lord, who protects the stranger and upholds the widow and orphan.

It is the Lord who loves the just but thwarts the path of the wicked.
The Lord will reign for ever, Sion's God, from age to age.

*Glory be...*

**Psalm 146**

Praise the Lord for he is good; sing to our God for he is loving:
to him our praise is due.

The Lord builds up Jerusalem and brings back Israel's exiles,
he heals the broken-hearted, he binds up all their wounds.

He fixes the number of the stars; he calls each one by its name.
Our Lord is great and almighty; his wisdom can never be measured.

The Lord raises the lowly; he humbles the wicked to the dust.
Sing to the Lord giving thanks; sing psalms to our God with the harp.

He covers the heavens with clouds; he prepares the rain for the earth,
making mountains sprout with grass and with plants to serve man's needs.

He provides the beasts with their food
and young ravens that call upon him.

His delight is not in horses nor his pleasure in warriors' strength.
The Lord delights in those who revere him, in those who wait for his love.

*Glory be…*

**Psalm 147**

O praise the Lord, Jerusalem!
Sion, praise your God!

He has strengthened the bars of your gates, he has blessed the children
within you.
He established peace on your borders, he feeds you with finest wheat.

He sends out his word to the earth and swiftly runs his command.
He showers down snow, white as wool, he scatters hoar-frost like ashes.

He hurls down hailstones like crumbs. The waters are frozen at his touch;
he sends forth his word and it melts them: at the breath of his mouth
the waters flow.

He makes his word known to Jacob, to Israel his laws and decrees.
He has not dealt thus with other nations; he has not taught them his decrees.

*Glory be…*

---

## ANTIPHON

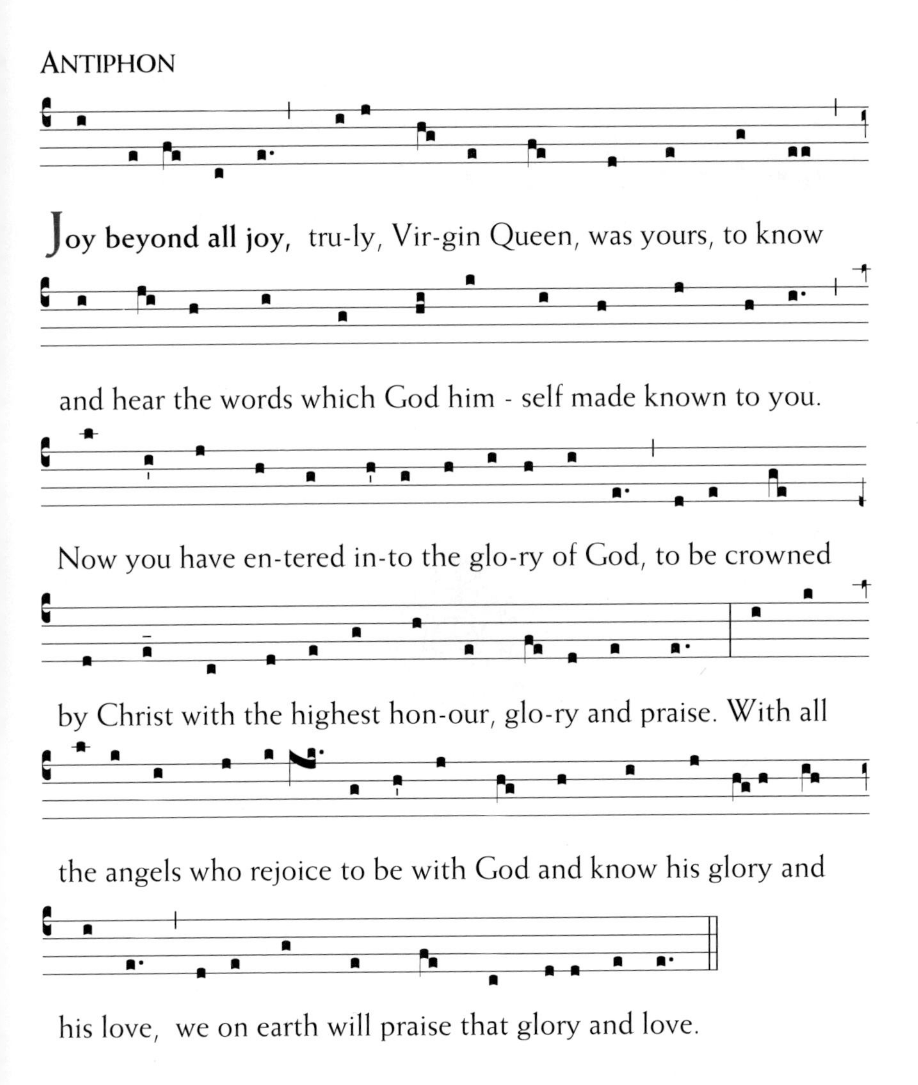

READING

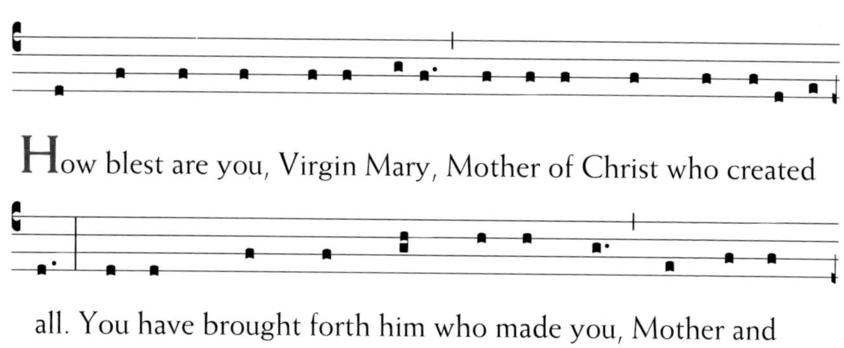


Virgin for ev-er. ℟. Our thanks to God.

## Hymn

1. Ma - ry, how love - ly the light of your glo - ry,
2. Blessed of all wo - men, both Vir - gin and Mo - ther
3. Pray for us, plead for us, ex - iles in dark- ness
4. Fa - ther, the prayer of your Son in - ter - ced - ing,

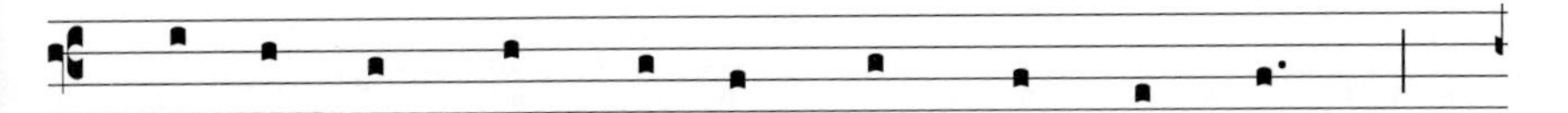

1. from Da - vid's house, roy- al daught - er, you come
2. fav - oured in grace for the Son whom you bore,
3. pray with us pray - ing to Christ in our needs,
4. wins for us life and light, for all our days,

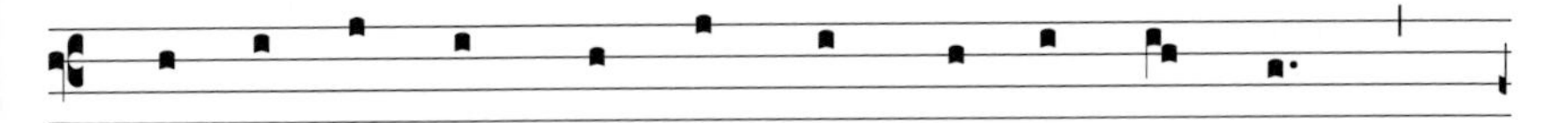

1. ho - li - er, high - er than an - gels in hea - ven,
2. Christ is your Son whom all peo - ples must wor- ship,
3. all power is giv - en him here and in hea - ven,
4. praise to you, Fa - ther, to Christ and your Spi - rit,

1. ho - li - est, high - est through all God has done.
2. Christ is your Son whom all an-gels a - dore.
3. Christ ev-er lives for us and in - ter-cedes.
4. glo - ry, e - ter - nal God, hon-our and praise. A - men.

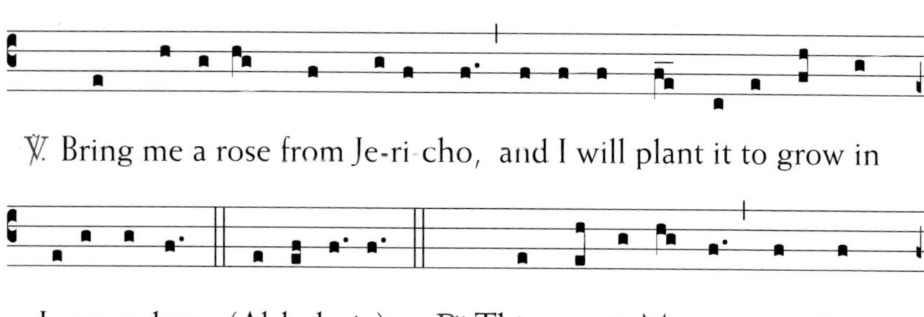

℣. Bring me a rose from Je-ri-cho, and I will plant it to grow in

Je-ru-sa-lem. (Al-le-lu-ia) ℟. This rose is Ma-ry, grow-ing

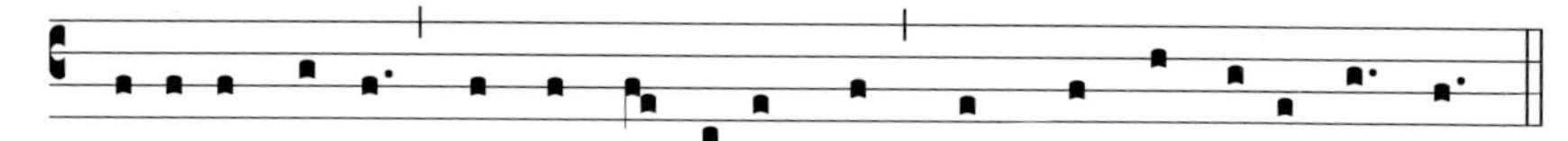

ever in beauty, to the glo-ry of God, and the joy of all an-gels.

(Al-le-lu-ia)

## ANTIPHON

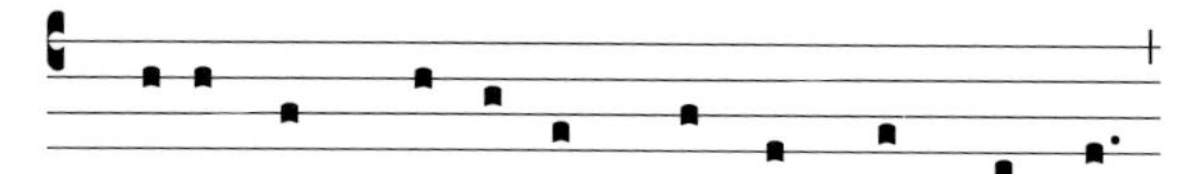

**Mary, the Spi-rit of God has come to you,**

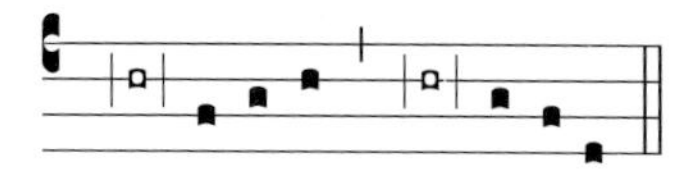

TONE I

## MAGNIFICAT *(Luke 1: 46 - 55)*

My soul glorifies the Lord,
my spirit rejoices in God,
my Saviour.

He looks on his servant in her nothingness; henceforth all ages
will call me blessed.
The Almighty works marvels for me. Holy his name!

His mercy is from age to age, on those who fear him.
He puts forth his arm in strength and scatters the proud-
hearted.

He casts the mighty from their thrones and raises the lowly.
He fills the starving with good things, sends the rich away empty.

He protects Israel, his servant, remembering his mercy,
the mercy promised to our fathers, to Abraham and his sons
for ever.

Praise the Father, the Son and the Holy Spirit,
both now and for ever, world without end.

ANTIPHON

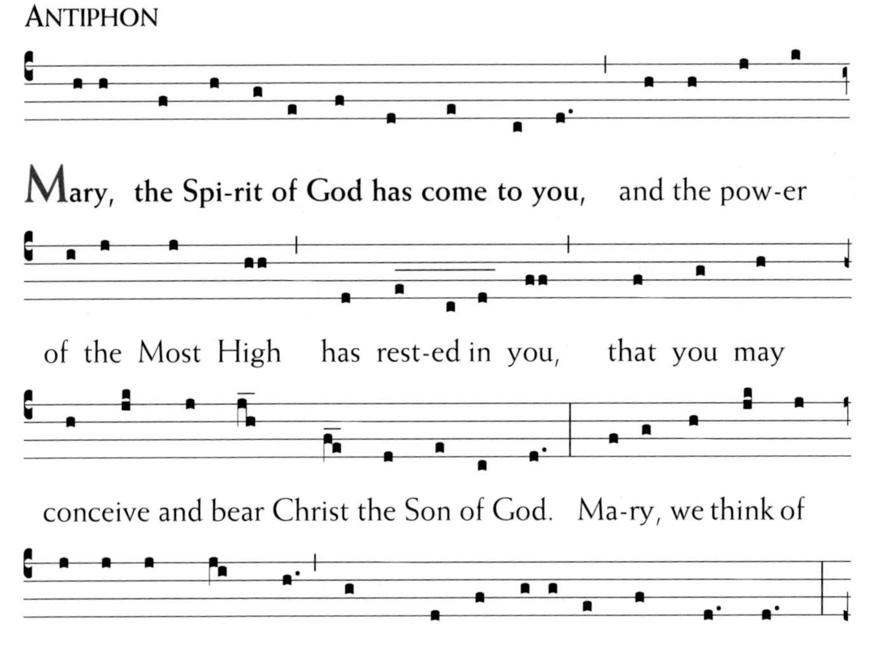

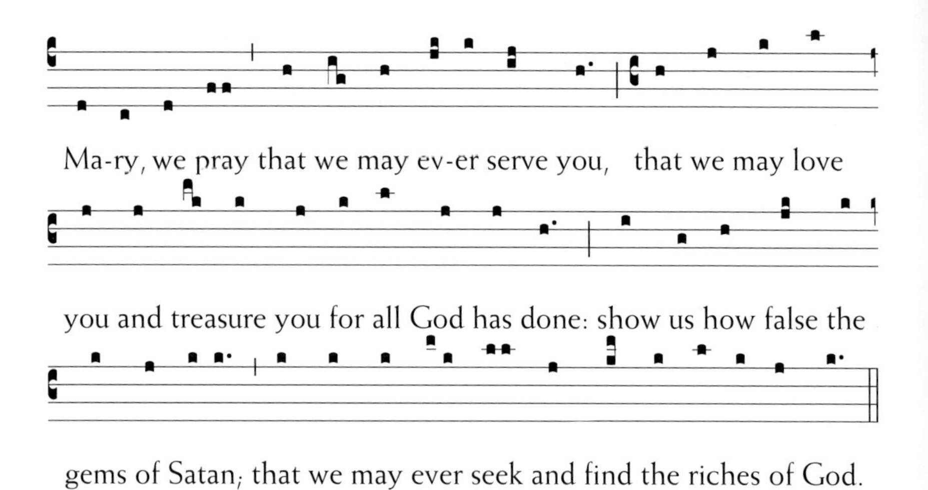


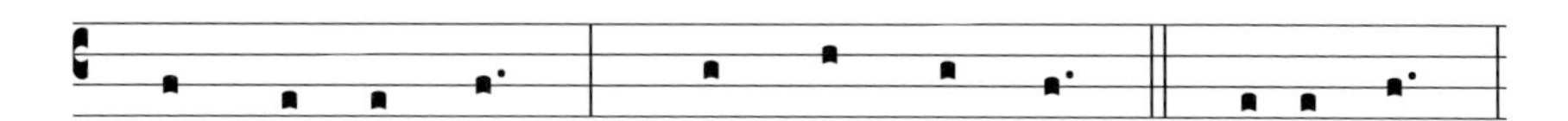

℣. Lord hear my prayer. ℟. Lord grant my prayer. ℣. Let us pray.

**PRAYER** *(pages 36 - 37)*

**ANTIPHON TO ST. BRIDGET & PRAYER** *(pages 88 - 90).*

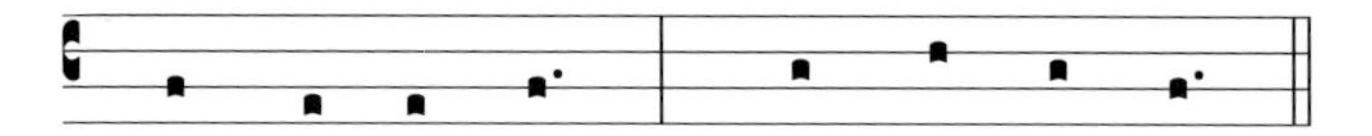

℣. Lord hear my prayer. ℟. Lord grant my prayer.

**THANKSGIVING**

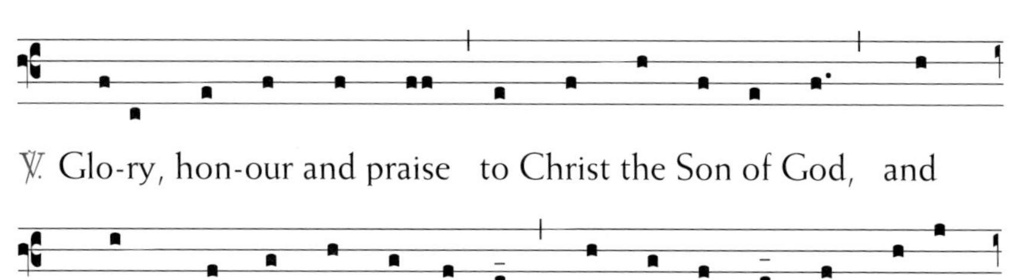


through him to God the Fa-ther who for his Son has chosen

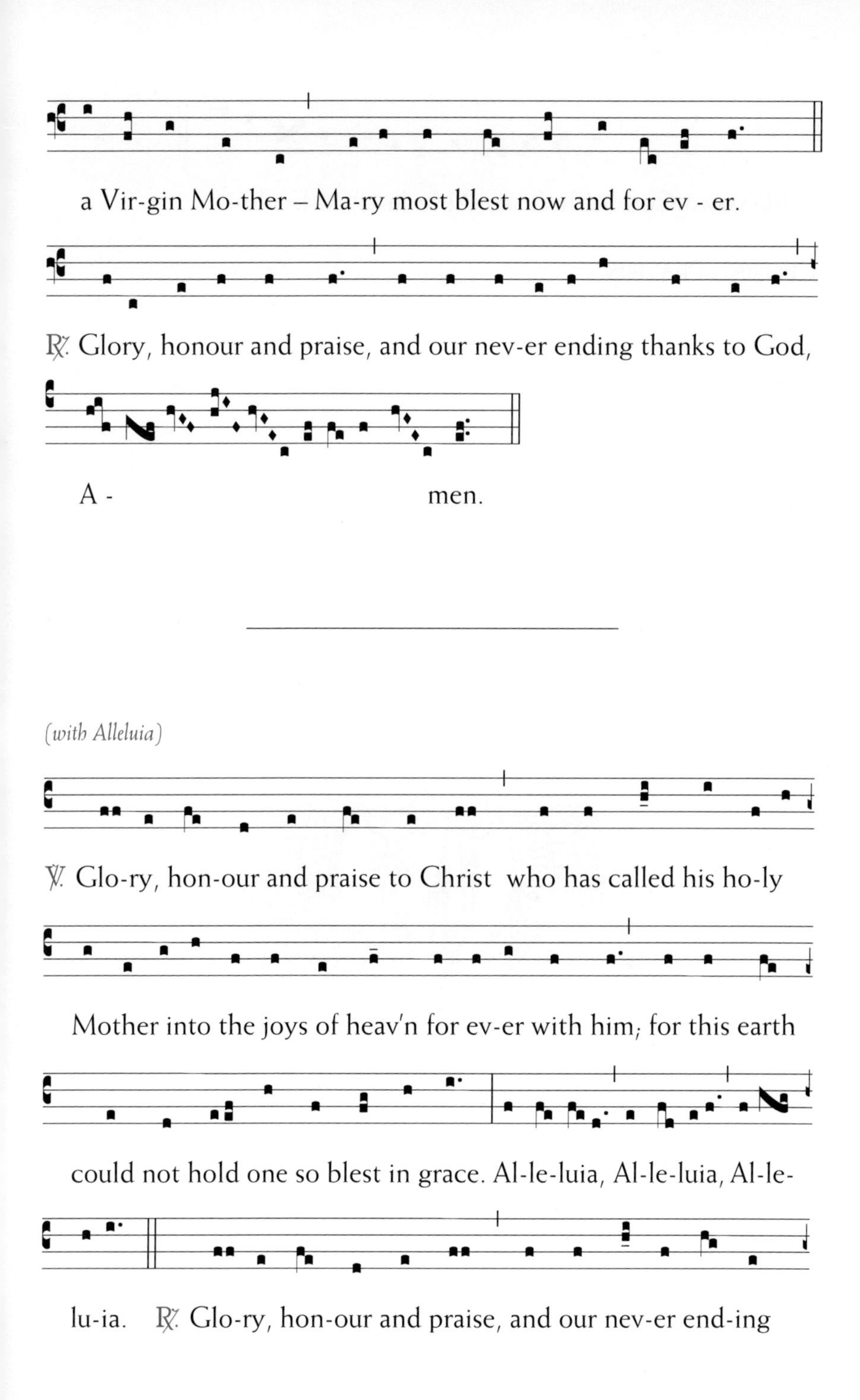
a Vir-gin Mo-ther – Ma-ry most blest now and for ev - er.
℟. Glory, honour and praise, and our nev-er ending thanks to God,
A - men.
(with Alleluia)
℣. Glo-ry, hon-our and praise to Christ who has called his ho-ly
Mother into the joys of heav'n for ev-er with him; for this earth
could not hold one so blest in grace. Al-le-luia, Al-le-luia, Al-le-
lu-ia. ℟. Glo-ry, hon-our and praise, and our nev-er end-ing

thanks to God. Al-le-lu-ia, Al-le-lu-ia, Al-le - lu-ia.

## Closing Prayers

'Mary, rejoice in God,' ... *with music (page 92) followed by...*

**HYMN** *to Holy Mother St. Bridget, (pages 93 - 94).*

*Saturday*

# COMPLINE

**OPENING PRAYERS** *as before Sunday Compline, pages 95 - 96.*

**ANTIPHON**

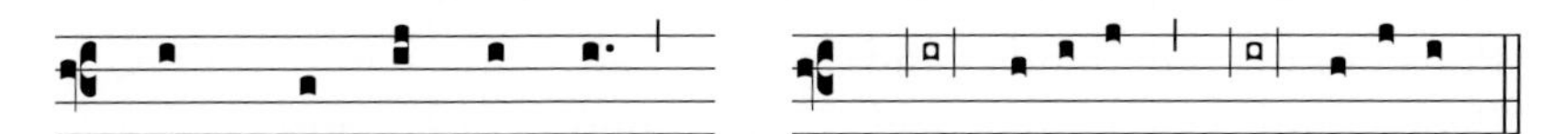

With great joy we sing TONE VII

**Psalms 131, 132 & 133** *as on Sunday pages 97 - 98.*

**ANTIPHON**

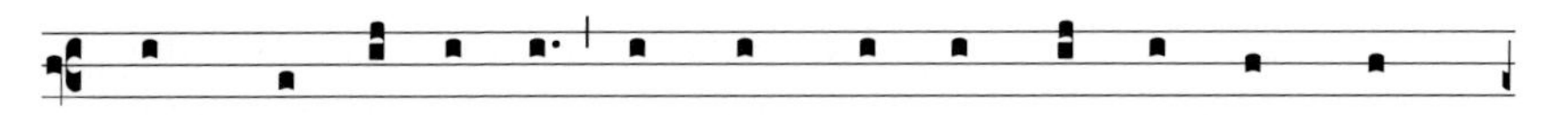

With great joy we sing in praise of the Vir - gin Ma - ry

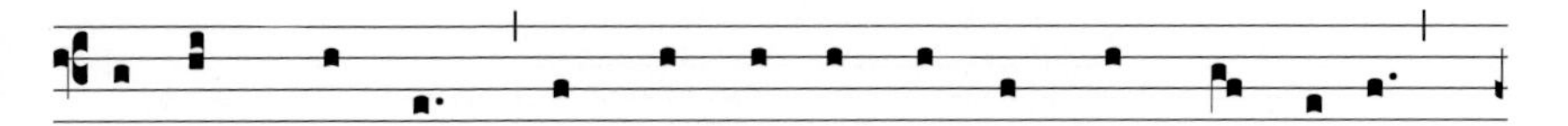

as-sumed to heav'n, and pray to her that she may pray for us

to Je-sus Christ the Lord.

**READING** *as on Sunday, page 99.*

**SHORT RESPONSORY** *as on Sunday, pages 99 ff.*

## Hymn

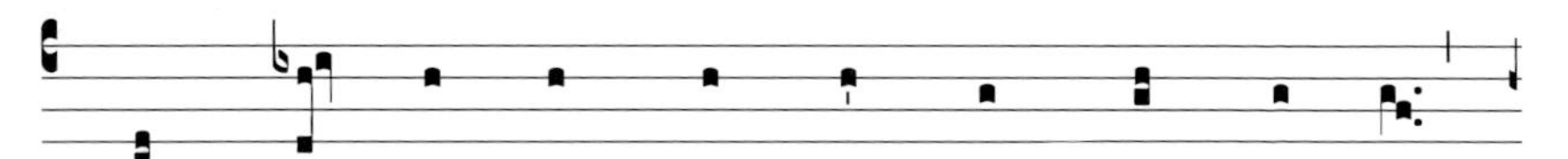

1. All things that are praise God by what they are,
2. To praise, and praise him for him - self a - lone,
3. Praise God, all an - gels made by him to be
4. Praise God, all earth - ly things which he has made,
5. Praise God, all lands and seas, all liv - ing things,
6. Praise God, all men and wo - men, young and old –
7. Praise him, the Fa - ther, Son and Spi - rit, God,

1. their be - ing speaks to us of God who is;
2. and for all things his power and love have done,
3. for ev - er in the ser - vice of his throne;
4. come, cold of win - ter, heat of sum - mer sun;
5. all trees and plants that he has made to grow;
6. cre - a - tion's high - est praise is yours to sing,
7. for all he is, for all that he has done,

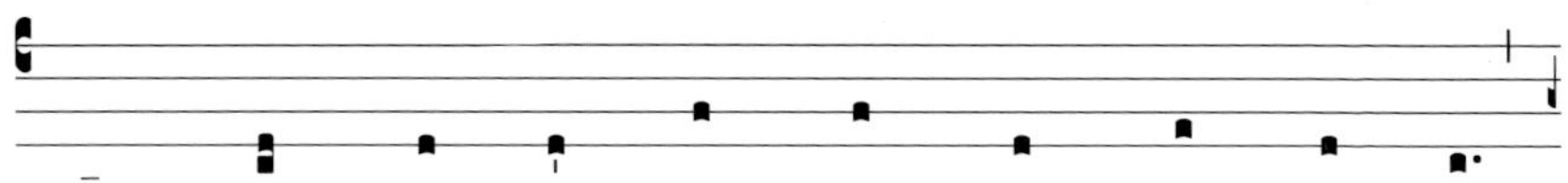

1. so we may call on them to praise his name,
2. but first for her, the Vir - gin, high - est blest,
3. shine, sun and moon, all stars whose light we see,
4. come, spring and au - tumn, change and change a - gain,
5. all birds and beasts, praise, each in your own way,
6. to hon - our God, to praise with ev - ery praise
7. but most for her, the Vir - gin ev - er blest,

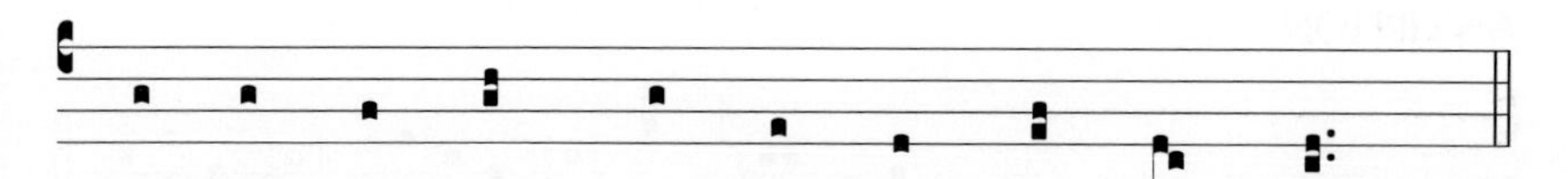

1. to give with us the hon - our that is his.
2. by his de - cree pre - des - tined for his Son.
3. and by your shi - ning make his great light known.
4. show in your chan - ging how his will is done.
5. his great - ness, which all things cre - a - ted show.
6. his be - ing, ev' - ry - where, in ev' - ry - thing.
7. by his de - cree the Mo - ther of his Son.

7. A - men.

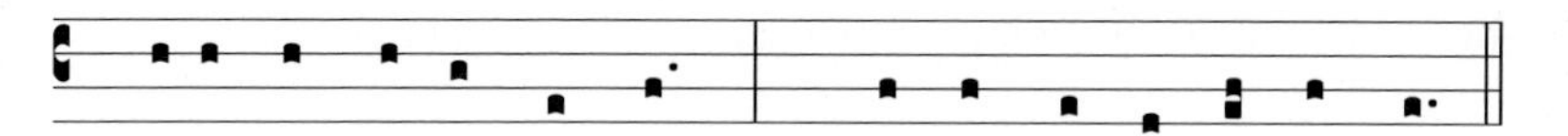

℣. I am the servant of God, ℟. To hear and o-bey his word.

*(with Alleluia)*

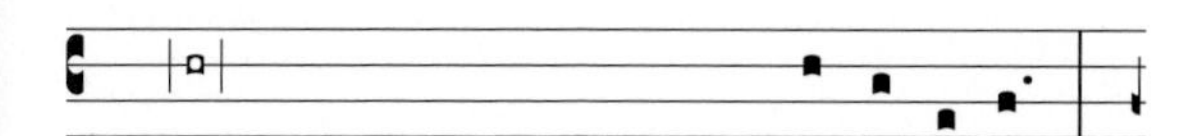

℣. I am the servant of God, Al-le-lu-ia.

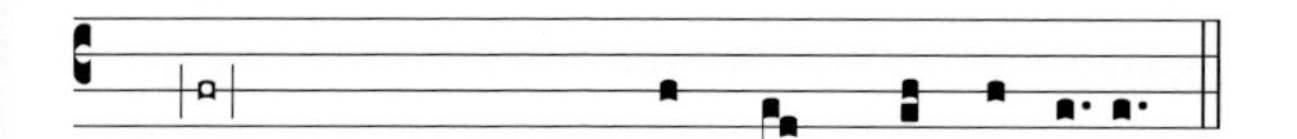

℟. To hear and obey his word, Al -le-lu-ia.

ANTIPHON

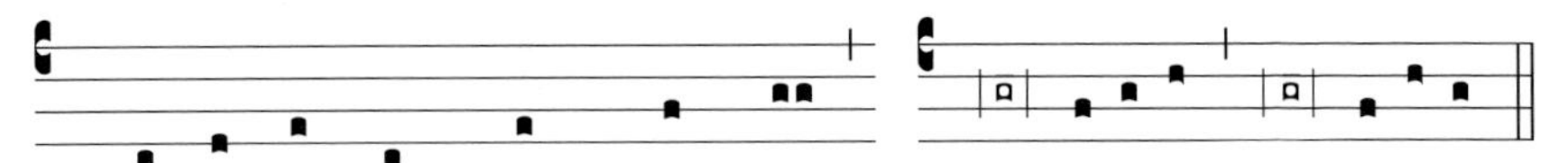

**Who is she who comes, more fair** ? TONE VII

CANTICLE OF SIMEON *(Luke 2: 29 - 32)*

At last, all powerful Master you give leave
to your servant to go in peace,
according to your promise.

For my eyes have seen your salvation which you have prepared
for all nations.
The light to enlighten the gentiles and give glory to Israel, your people.

Give praise to the Father Almighty: to his Son, Jesus Christ, the Lord;
to the Spirit who dwells in our hearts, both now and forever. Amen.

ANTIPHON

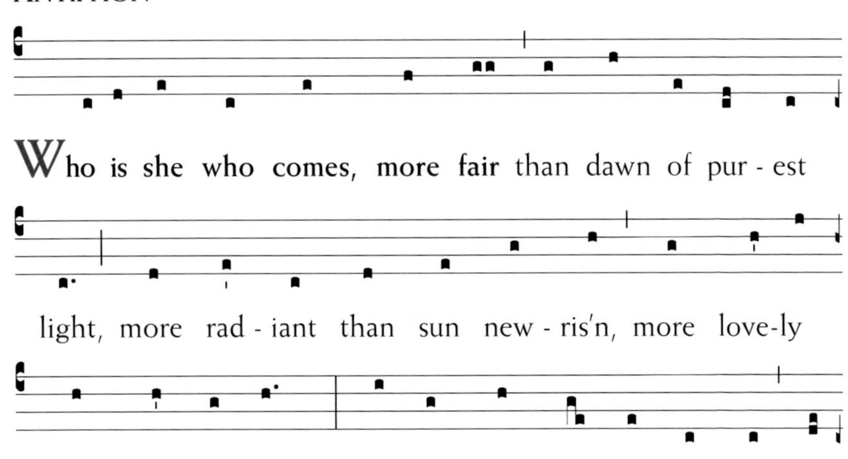

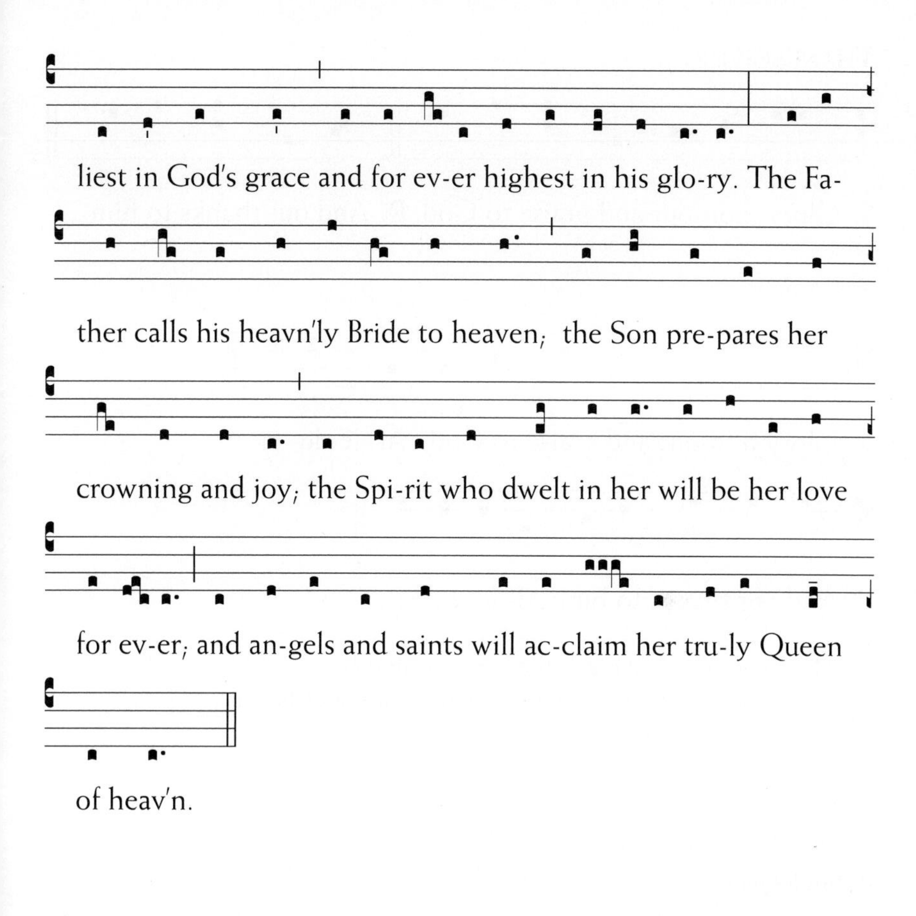

℣. Lord, hear my prayer. ℟. Lord, grant my prayer. ℣. Let us pray.

**PRAYER** *as on Sunday,* *page 104.*

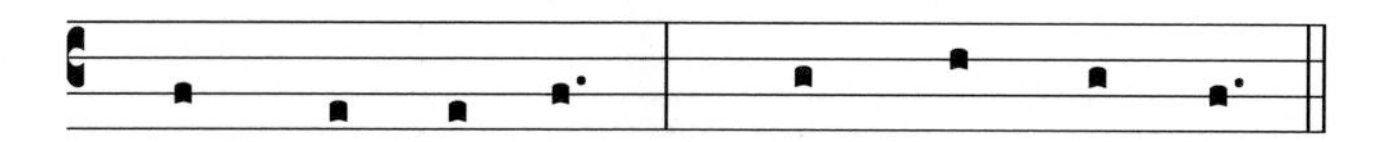

℣. Lord, hear my prayer. ℟. Lord, grant my prayer.

## Thanksgiving

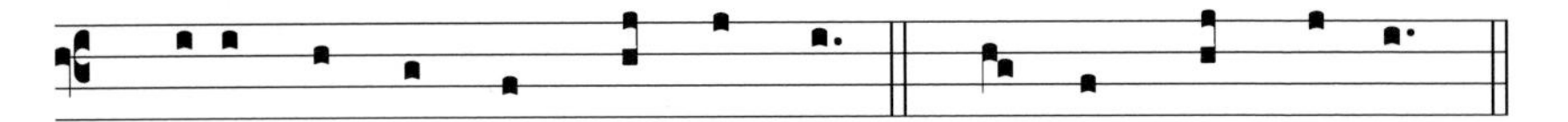

℣. Glory, hon-our and praise to God. ℟. And our thanks to him.

*(with Alleluia)*

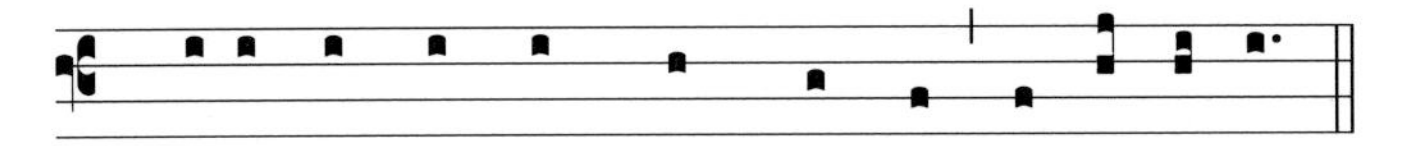

℣. Glory hon-our and praise to God, Al- le- lu- ia.

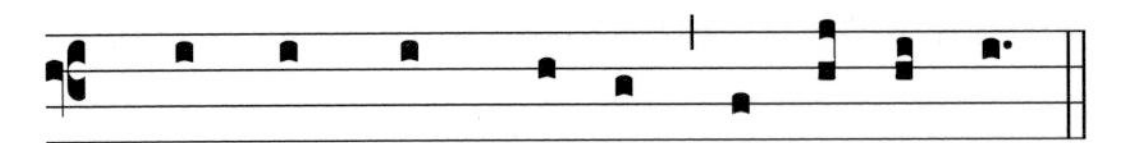

℟. And our thanks to him, Al- le- lu- ia.

℣. Mary, you are full of grace, the Lord is with you.
℟. Mary, you are most blessed of all women, for Jesus Christ is your Son. (Alleluia)

## Lauds of Our Lady
*(Salve Regina)*

**Virgin Ma-ry,** Queen of mer - cy we name you, for in your

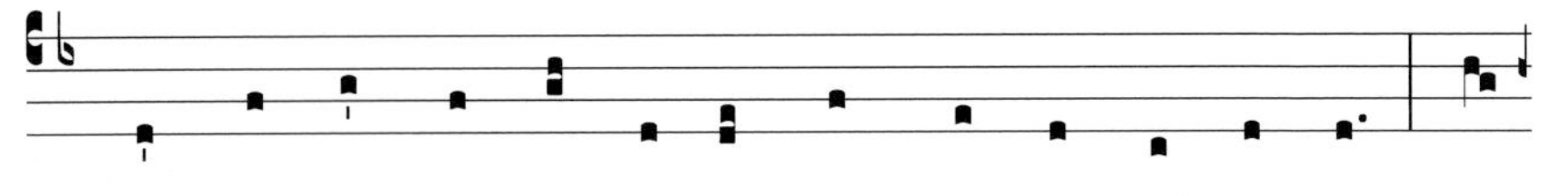

grace and love we find our life, our sweetness and our hope. Vir-

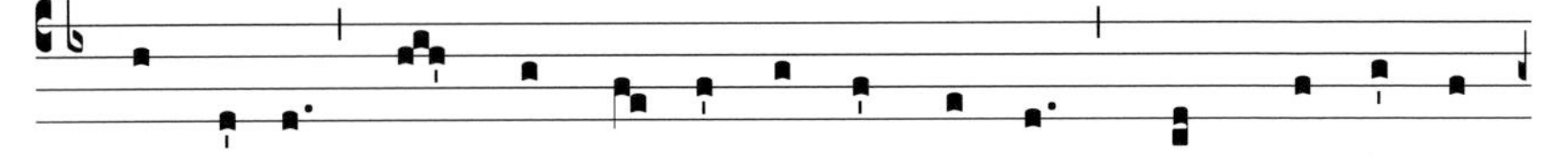

gin Ma-ry, Queen of mer-cy we pray to you – come and fill our

hearts with your sweet grace and love. Come to console our ex-
ile here; make light the bur-den of life's long distress. Queen of
mer - cy, hear our cry for help; see how we mourn and weep for
sor-row, and ev-er on earth must weep in sin and sin-ful-ness.
Vir-gin Mother of God, be our ad - vo - cate with God; in-ter-
cede for us; plead in your love for us for grace to heal our weakness, and in your pity help us in our sorrow and our need. Ma-ry
when death's last hour is near, come first your-self to lead us to

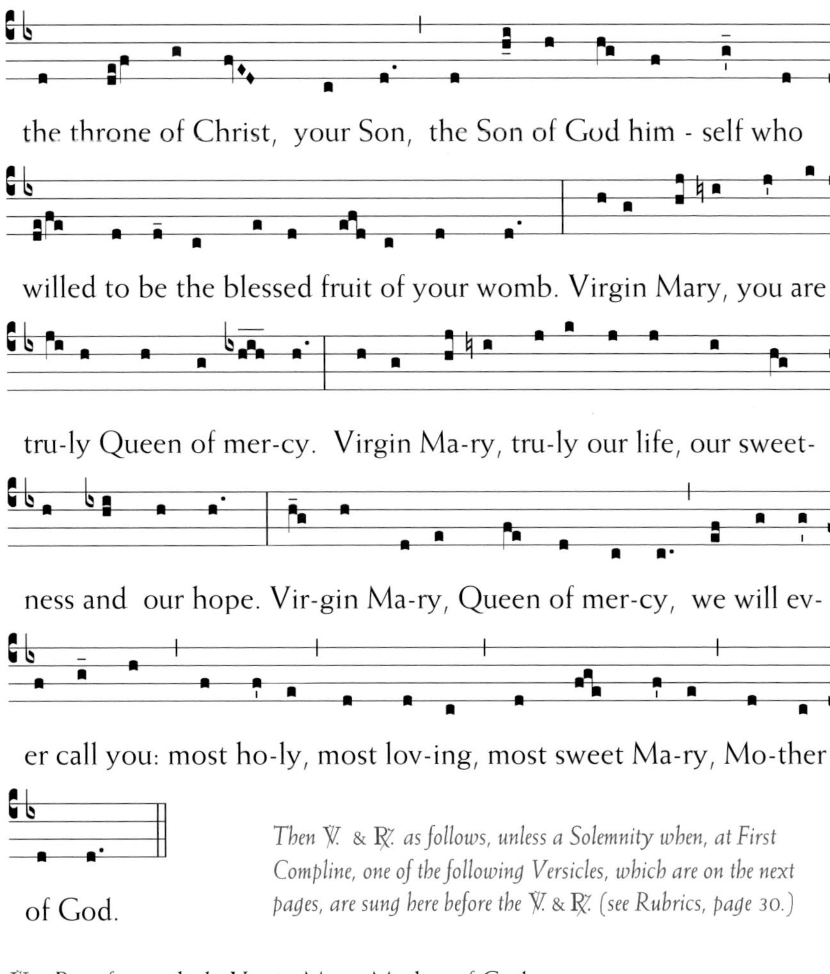


*Then ℣. & ℟. as follows, unless a Solemnity when, at First Compline, one of the following Versicles, which are on the next pages, are sung here before the ℣. & ℟. (see Rubrics, page 30.)*

℣. Pray for us, holy Virgin Mary, Mother of God.
℟. That we may be made worthy of the promises of Jesus Christ.
℣. Let us pray.

## PRAYER

Forgive, we ask you Lord, the sins of your servants: and may we who of ourselves are unable to please you, be saved by the prayers of the Mother of your Son, Jesus Christ our Lord. ℟. Amen.

**CLOSING PRAYERS** 'Mary, rejoice in God,' … *as on Sunday, page 107.*

*Saturday – Short Versicless and Responses after* Salve Regina.

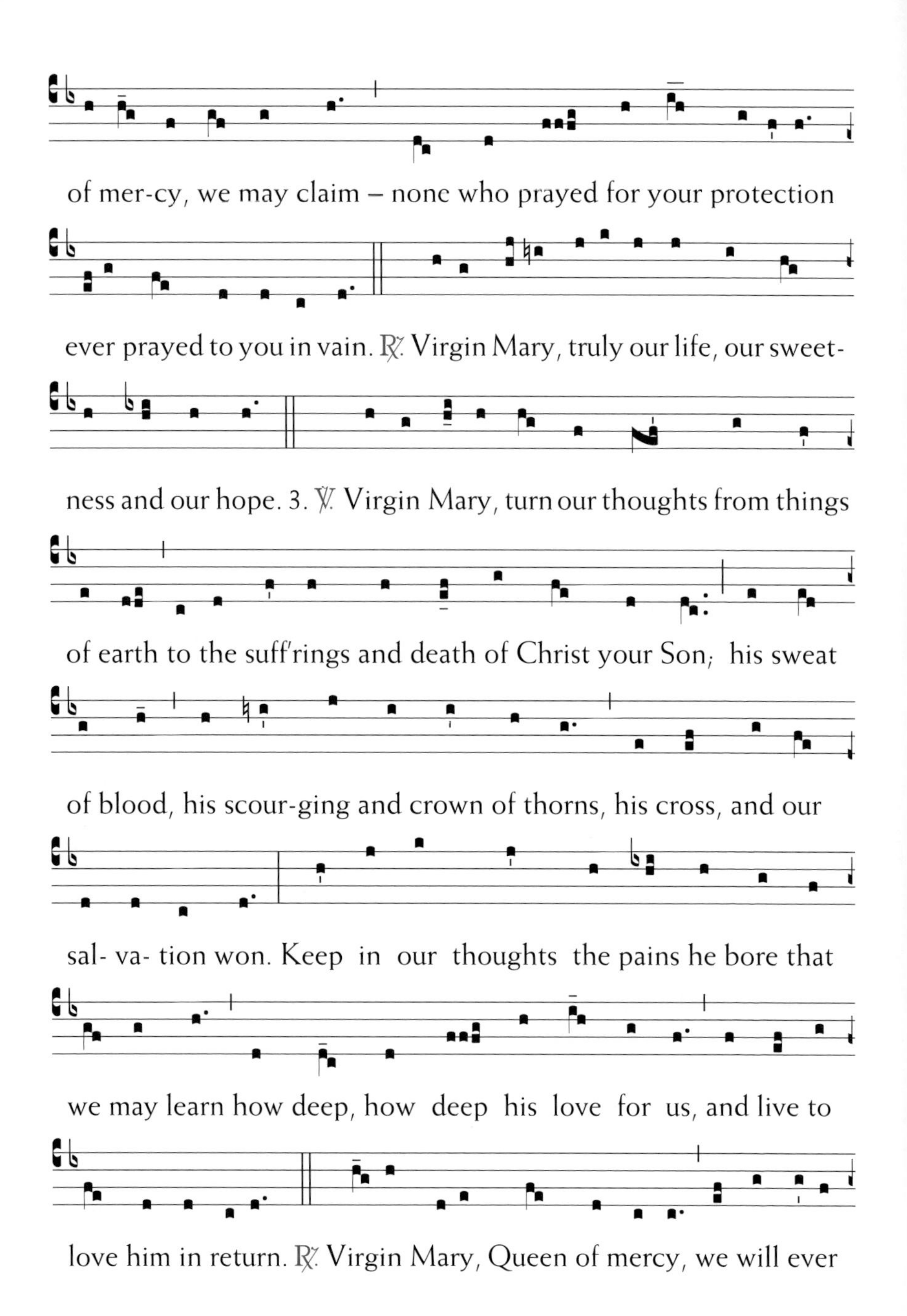
of mer-cy, we may claim – none who prayed for your protection
ever prayed to you in vain. ℟. Virgin Mary, truly our life, our sweetness and our hope. 3. ℣. Virgin Mary, turn our thoughts from things
of earth to the suff'rings and death of Christ your Son; his sweat
of blood, his scour-ging and crown of thorns, his cross, and our
sal- va- tion won. Keep in our thoughts the pains he bore that
we may learn how deep, how deep his love for us, and live to
love him in return. ℟. Virgin Mary, Queen of mercy, we will ever

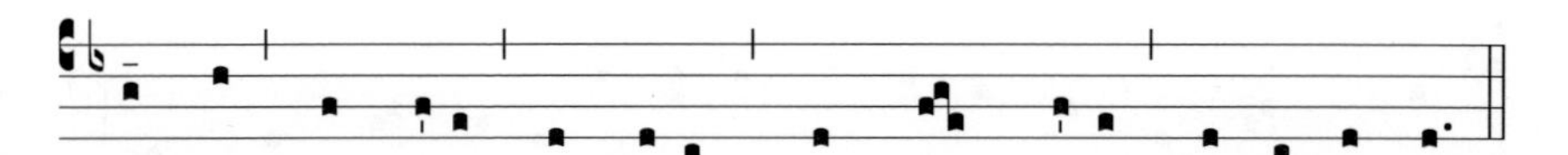

call you: most holy, most loving, most sweet Mary, Mother of God.

℣. Pray for us, holy Virgin Mary, Mother of God.
℟. That we may be made worthy of the promises of Jesus Christ.

℣. Let us pray.

Forgive, we ask you Lord, the sins of your servants: and may we who of ourselves are unable to please you, be saved by the prayers of the Mother of your Son, Jesus Christ our Lord. ℟. Amen.

**CLOSING PRAYERS** 'Mary, rejoice in God,' ... *as on Sunday,* *page 107.*

---

*Saturday – Long Versicles and Responses after* Salve Regina *(for special feasts).*

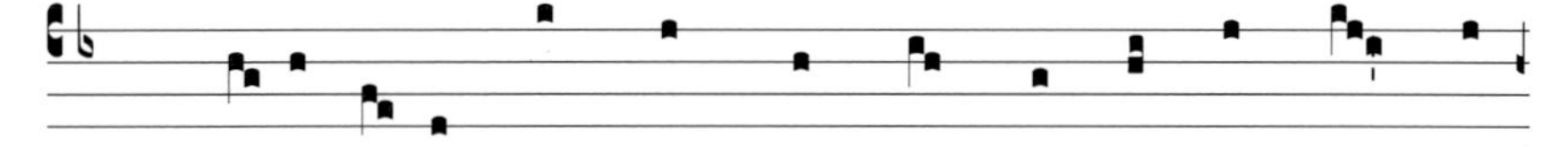

1. ℣. Virgin Ma-ry, we praise and love you, tru - ly Queen of

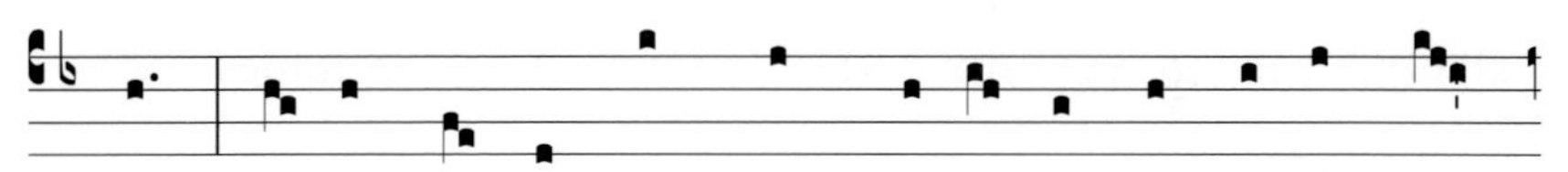

heav'n; highest, ho-liest, en-throned in glo-ry, near to the throne

of God. You are the fairest flower of heav'n, Rose of beau-ty, in

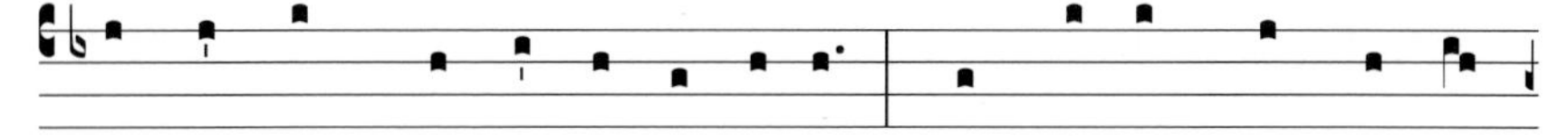

that gar-den where all are fair to see. Mo-ther of Christ our Sav-

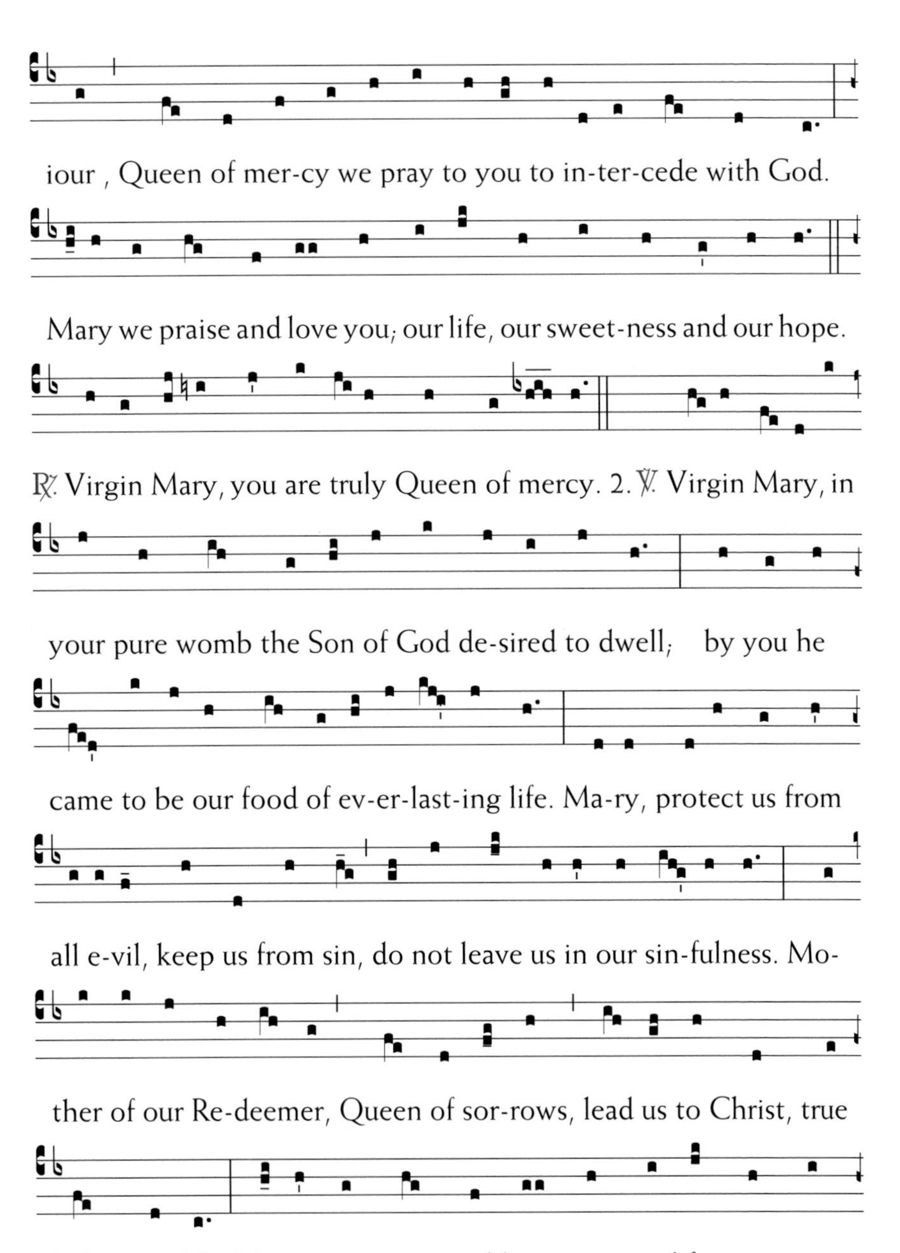
iour , Queen of mer-cy we pray to you to in-ter-cede with God.
Mary we praise and love you; our life, our sweet-ness and our hope.
℟. Virgin Mary, you are truly Queen of mercy. 2. ℣. Virgin Mary, in
your pure womb the Son of God de-sired to dwell; by you he
came to be our food of ev-er-last-ing life. Ma-ry, protect us from
all e-vil, keep us from sin, do not leave us in our sin-fulness. Mother of our Re-deemer, Queen of sor-rows, lead us to Christ, true
light, true life. Ma-ry, we praise and love you, our life, our sweet-

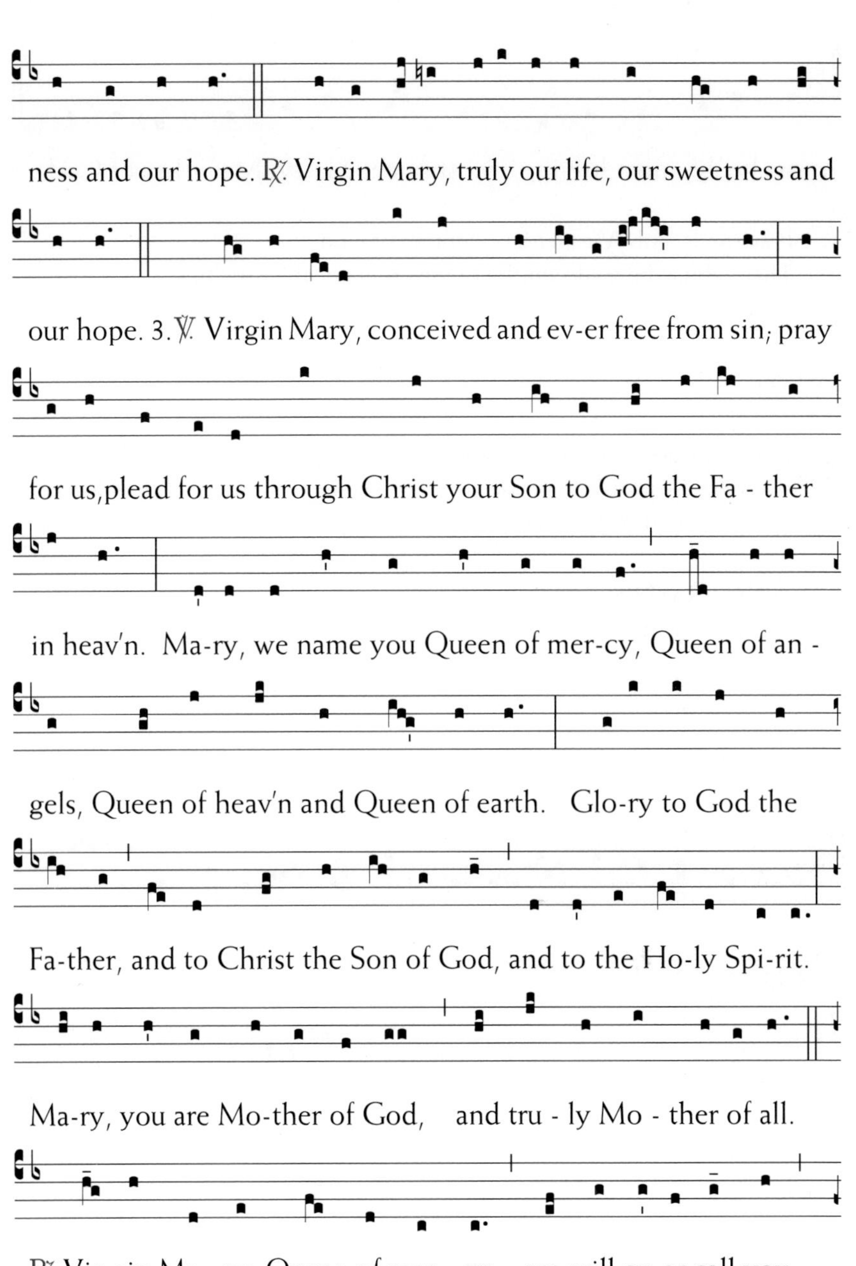
ness and our hope. ℟. Virgin Mary, truly our life, our sweetness and
our hope. 3. ℣. Virgin Mary, conceived and ev-er free from sin; pray
for us, plead for us through Christ your Son to God the Fa - ther
in heav'n. Ma-ry, we name you Queen of mer-cy, Queen of an -
gels, Queen of heav'n and Queen of earth. Glo-ry to God the
Fa-ther, and to Christ the Son of God, and to the Ho-ly Spi-rit.
Ma-ry, you are Mo-ther of God, and tru - ly Mo - ther of all.
℟. Vir-gin Ma - ry, Queen of mer - cy, we will ev-er call you

℣. Pray for us, holy Virgin Mary, Mother of God.
℟. That we may be made worthy of the promises of Jesus Christ.
℣. Let us pray.

## Prayer

Forgive, we ask you Lord, the sins of your servants: and may we who of ourselves are unable to please you, be saved by the prayers of the Mother of your Son, Jesus Christ our Lord. ℟. Amen.

## Closing Prayers

'Mary, rejoice in God,' … *as on Sunday, page 107.*

---

## Lauds of Our Lady

*During Easter – Regina Coeli (Queen of Heaven)*

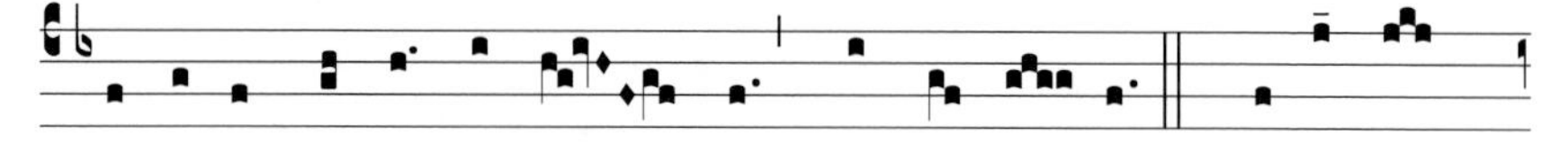


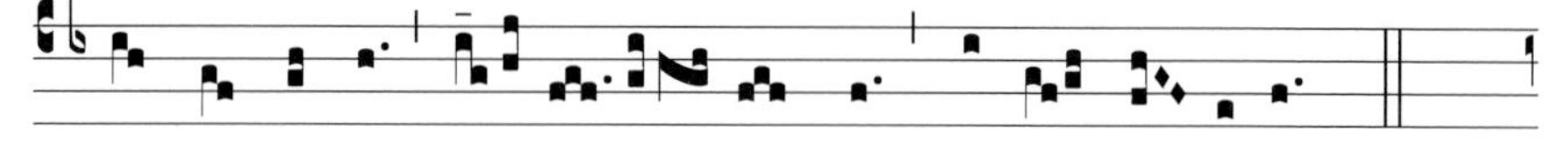

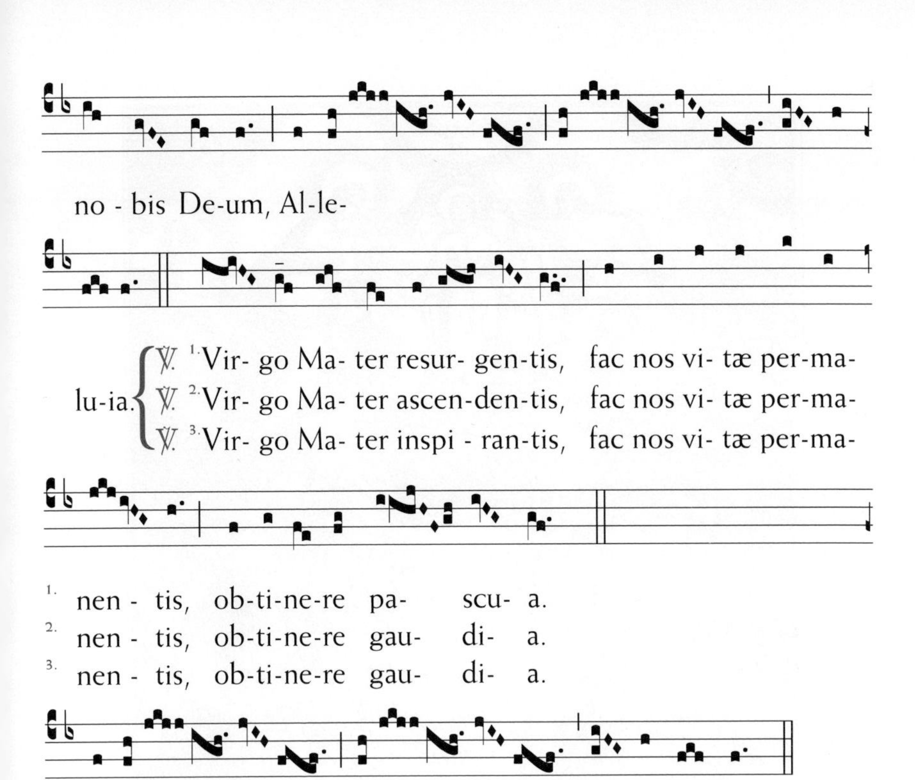


1. *At Easter.* 2. *At the Feast of the Ascension.* 3. *At Pentecost.*

℣. Speciosa facta es et suavis, Alleluia. [You are created fair and kind, Alleluia.]
℟. In deliciis tuis, sancta Dei genitrix, Alleluia. [In your grace, O holy Mother of God, Alleluia.]
℣. Let us pray.

## Prayer

Favourably regard at all times, Almighty Father, but especially when we celebrate the Paschal solemnities of your Son, our continual remembrance of Mary, the Virgin Mother of God. When your Son, Jesus Christ our Lord was hanging on the Cross, his loving Mother stood by, suffering too. Now she sits at his right hand as Queen of heaven, where he lives and reigns with you in the unity of the Holy Spirit, for ever and ever. ℟. Amen.

**Closing Prayers** 'Mary, rejoice in God,' … *as on Sunday, page 107.*

*Illustration from the 1697 Landshut edition of The Bridgettine Breviary.*

*Saint Bridget and Saint Katharine shown looking towards heaven and seeing the coronation of Mary as Queen of Heaven by God, Father and Son, with the Holy Spirit in the form of a dove hovering above. Reprinted in the 1908 Tournai edition.*

*Celebrations during the year*

# LITURGICAL CALENDAR

## SOLEMNITIES & FEASTS OF THE LORD *(See note on page 30).*

| | |
|---|---|
| **25th December** | The Nativity of the Lord, *solemnity.* |
| **2nd February** | The Presentation of the Lord, *feast.* [1] |
| **25th March** | The Annunciation of the Lord, *solemnity.* |

## SOLEMNITIES, FEASTS & MEMORIALS OF OUR LADY

*(See note on page 30).*

| | |
|---|---|
| **8th December** | The Immaculate Conception of the B. V. M., *solemnity.* |
| **1st January** | Mary, Mother of God, *solemnity.* |
| **11th February** | Our Lady of Lourdes, *memorial.* |
| **13th May** | Our Lady of Fatima, *memorial.* |
| **31st May** | The Visitation of Our Lady to St Elizabeth, *feast.* |
| *Saturday after Feast of the Most Sacred Heart of Jesus:* | The Immaculate Heart of Mary, *memorial.* |
| **16th July** | Our Lady of Mount Carmel, *memorial.* |
| **5th August** | Dedication of the Basilica of St Mary Major, *memorial.* *(Our Lady of Snows).* |
| **15th August** | The Assumption of the Blessed Virgin Mary, *solemnity.* |
| **22nd August** | The Queenship of the Blessed Virgin Mary, *memorial.* |
| **8th September** | The Nativity of the Blessed Virgin Mary, *feast.* |
| **12th September** | The Most Holy Name of Mary, *memorial.* |
| **15th September** | Our Lady of Sorrows, *memorial.* |
| **24th September** | Our Lady of Walsingham, *memorial.* |
| **7th October** | Our Lady of the Rosary, *memorial.* |
| **21st November** | Presentation of the Blessed Virgin Mary, *memorial.* |

## SOLEMNITIES, FEASTS & MEMORIALS OF THE BRIDGETTINE ORDER

*(See note on page 30).*

| | |
|---|---|
| **4th May** | St Richard Reynolds, *memorial.* |
| **27th June** | Holy Mother St Katharine, *memorial.* |
| **23rd July** | Holy Mother St Bridget, *solemnity.* [2] |
| **26th July** | St Anne & St Joachim, *memorial.* |
| **6th August** | The Transfiguration of the Lord *(Patronal Feast)* |
| **29th September** | Michael, Gabriel & Raphael, archangels, *feast.* |
| **2nd October** | The Holy Guardian Angels, *memorial.* |
| **23rd October** | Blessed Anne Mary & Blessed Mary Frances, *memorial.* |

## Other Offices

| | |
|---|---|
| **Easter Triduum** | The Prayer of the Church *(Roman Office)* |
| **2nd November** | All Souls' Day: The Prayer of the Church *(Roman Office)* |

## Office of the Dead

The Prayer of the Church *(Roman Office) especially on the following days, for…*

*Lord Fitzhugh* and all benefactors: first free day after The Baptism of the Lord.

Deceased parents of the monks and nuns of Syon: Shrove Tuesday.

Special benefactors: first free day after the Easter season – to include the parents, relatives and friends of our Founders.

Brothers and Sisters of the Chapter: first free day after 7th July.

*King Henry V*, Founder of Syon: August 31st – to include all the Kings, Queens and others who have governed England.

Confessors General & Abbesses of Syon: first free day after 8th September.

Professed Brothers and Sisters of Syon: prior to Advent.

On the funeral day, the 30th day after death and on the first anniversary of the death of a sister of the Syon community.

*For all other Solemnities, Feasts or Memorials we conform to the Diocesan Calendar.*

---

1. World Day of Prayer for the Consecrated Life.
2. *Solemnity* for our Bridgettine Order, otherwise *Feast* as a Patron of Europe.

*Solemnities and*

# FEASTS OF THE LORD

*February 2nd*

## THE PRESENTATION OF THE LORD

*(Feast)*

Christmas Office (as Thursday, *pages 248 ff*) and Christmas Prayer (*page 36*) with Alleluias. Lauds of Our Lady after None and Compline of the day occurring.

### READINGS

LAUDS, TERCE and VESPERS *(Malachi 3: 1)*

See, I will send my messenger, to prepare the way before me.
The Lord you are seeking will come at once to his holy temple,
the angel of the covenant you have so long desired.

SEXT *(Eccles. 24: 23)*

I am lovely as a vine;
sweet with flowers of holiness,
rich with the fruits of grace.

NONE *(Eccles. 24: 24, 25)*

I am the Mother of pure love, of fear, of knowledge and of holy hope.
In me is all grace of the way and of truth.
In me all hope of life and of strength.

*March 25th*

# THE ANNUNCIATION OF THE LORD

*(Solemnity)*

## FIRST VESPERS

### ANTIPHON *(For music, see pages 230, 234).*

W**e rejoice today in prayer and praise** to honour the Annunciation to the glorious Virgin Mary. For she alone was chosen by God to be both Mother and Virgin for ever.

### READING *(Isaiah 7: 14, 15).*

A Virgin shall be with child, and bear a son; and she shall name him Emmanuel. On curds and honey will he feed, until he knows how to refuse evil and choose good.

### RESPONSORY *(For music, see page 456).*

**This is no kingly town,** and she no royal child, yet here is glory and grace beyond compare. Here will come the Son of God himself, to dwell in her house, to find in her his joy and delight, and clothe himself with power.
℣. Now to his kingly home he returns in glory, there to crown her with everlasting honour, there to crown her Queen of all.
℟. Here will come...
℣. Glory to God, glory to Father, Son and Holy Spirit.
℟. Here will come...

## Hymn

The God whom earth and sea and sky
adore and praise and magnify,
who e'er their three-fold fabric reigns,
the Virgin's spotless womb contains.

The God whom sun and moon obey,
whom all things serve from day to day,
is borne upon a maiden's breast,
by fullest heavenly grace possessed.

How blest that Mother, in whose shrine,
the world's creator, Lord divine,
whose hand contains the earth and sky,
once deigned as in his ark to lie.

Blest in the message Gabriel brought,
blest by the work the Spirit wrought,
from whom the great desire of earth,
took human flesh and human birth.

Pray Mary Mother full of grace,
pray in your love, for all we need,
protect us from all danger now,
and at our dying intercede.

Christ, Son of God, we pray to you,
and honour you, the Virgin's Son;
we praise the Father, God with you,
and with the Spirit, Three in One. Amen.

℣. God has entered this world of ours, through the Virgin Mary. (Alleluia)
℟. To bring to heaven our fallen race. (Alleluia)

## Magnificat Antiphon *(For music, see pages 143 & 144).*

**Praise to Christ, the angels' creator and king.** He has chosen the Virgin Mary in her lowliness, and in his love has made her lovelier than all. Praise to Christ whose love has made her our Mother of love.

## MAGNIFICAT *(page 143)*.

## PRAYER

O Lord, you have willed that your word should take flesh in the womb of the blessed Virgin Mary at the message of an angel. We, your suppliants, believe her to be truly the Mother of God. Grant to us that we may be helped by her intercession with you, through our Lord Jesus Christ, your Son, who lives and reigns with you in the unity of the Holy Spirit, God for ever and ever. ℟. Amen.

## ANTIPHON TO ST BRIDGET

Bridget, your words to us... *(pages 88 - 90)*.

## THANKSGIVING *(For music, see page 281)*.

Glory, honour and praise we offer in humble prayer,
to Christ the Lord and creator of all, who was content to come
to us, a Virgin Mother's child.
℟. Glory, honour and praise, and our never ending thanks to God.

## THANKSGIVING *(During Easter – for music, see page 282)*.

Glory, honour and praise to Christ the Lord and Creator,
who was content to come to us, a Virgin Mother's child.
Alleluia, alleluia, alleluia.
℟. Glory, honour and praise, and our never ending thanks to God. Alleluia, alleluia, alleluia.

## CLOSING PRAYERS *(page 37 – for music, see page 92)*.

---

## COMPLINE as on WEDNESDAY *(page 241)*.

Lauds of Our Lady (*Salve Regina*) as on Saturday *(page 394)* with long versicles *(page 399)*. (Except during Easter: *Regina Coeli – page 402* with Prayer): also Closing Prayers *(page 107)*.

## LAUDS

### INVITATORY ANTIPHON

**Mary, you are full of grace;**
† the Lord is with you.

**Invitatory Psalm 94** *(page 34)*.

### ANTIPHON

**See what God has done,** the creator of man has come as man, born of a Virgin, not by the will of man, but by his eternal will, to show and share his divinity with man.

### READING *(Isaiah 7: 14, 15)*

A Virgin shall be with child, and bear a son; and she shall name him Emmanuel. On curds and honey will he feed, until he knows how to refuse evil and choose good.

---

### HYMN *(For music, see page 390)*

All things that are praise God by what they are,
their being speaks to us of God who is;
so we may call on them to praise his name,
to give with us the honour that is his.

To praise, and praise him for himself alone,
and for all things his power and love have done,
but first for her, the Virgin, highest blest,
by his decree predestined for his Son.

Praise God, all angels made by him to be
for ever in the service of his throne;
shine, sun and moon, all stars whose light we see,
and by your shining make his great light known.

Praise God, all earthly things which he has made,
come, cold of winter, heat of summer sun;
come, spring and autumn, change and change again,
show in your changing how his will is done.

Praise God, all lands and seas, all living things,
all trees and plants that he has made to grow;
all birds and beasts, praise, each in your own way,
his greatness, which all things created show.

Praise God, all men and women, young and old,
creation's highest praise is yours to sing,
to honour God, to praise with every praise,
his being, everywhere, in everything.

Praise him, the Father, Son and Spirit, God,
for all he is, for all that he has done,
but most for her, the Virgin, ever blest,
by his decree the Mother of his Son. Amen.

℣. From the Virgin's womb, Christ has come in joy. (Alleluia)
℟. And we have seen him, coming as a bridegroom to his bride. (Alleluia)

## CANTICLE ANTIPHON *(For music, see page 384 & 385)*

**Mary, the Spirit of God has come to you,** and the power of the Most High has rested in you, that you may conceive and bear Christ the Son of God. Mary, we think of you in your beauty, brightest jewel of all God's treasures. Mary, we pray that we may ever serve you, that we may love you and treasure you for all God has done. Show us how false the gems of Satan; that we may ever seek and find the riches of God.

## THE CANTICLE OF ZECHARIAH *(Luke 1: 68-79)*

*as at Sunday Lauds, page 45.*

**PRAYER** *as at First Vespers (page 410)* O Lord, you have willed…

## ANTIPHON TO ST BRIDGET

Bridget, loving servant of God... *(pages 46 - 47).*

## THANKSGIVING

℣. Glory, honour and praise to Christ, who to win our love, humbled himself, hiding his Godhead from our sight in the helplessness of a child, born of a lowly Virgin, and nourished at her breast. (Alleluia, alleluia, alleluia)

℟. Our thanks to God. (Alleluia, alleluia, alleluia)

## CLOSING PRAYERS *(page 37).*

---

# TERCE

## OPENING PRAYERS *(page 33).*

## HYMN *(For music, see page 258).*

Christ, Lord and King, in mercy come,
come take our hearts to be your own,
to love and serve you in all things,
to praise you for yourself alone.

Remember, Lord, that for our sake,
a sinless Virgin's child you came,
as man to men to save all men,
salvation we your own may claim.

Pray Mary Mother full of grace,
pray in your love for all we need,
protect us from all danger now,
and at our dying intercede.

Christ, Son of God, we pray to you,
and honour you, the Virgin's Son,
we praise the Father, God with you,
and with the Spirit, Three in One. Amen.

## ANTIPHON

**Now is the flower seen,** on that sweet branch.
Now are the heavens bright with that promised star.
Now has the Virgin brought forth her Son, the Saviour.
Glory and praise for ever, to you, our Lord and our God.

## READING *(Isaiah 7: 14, 15)*

A Virgin shall be with child, and bear a son; and she shall name him Emmanuel. On curds and honey will he feed, until he knows how to refuse evil and choose good.

## SHORT RESPONSORY

℣. God has entered this world of ours through the Virgin Mary.
(Alleluia, alleluia) ℟. *(Repeat)*
℣. To bring to heaven our fallen race.
℟. through the Virgin Mary. *(During Easter:* ℟. Alleluia, alleluia)
℣. Glory to God, Father, Son and Holy Spirit.
℟. God has entered...
℣. God himself has come down to the Virgin's womb, (Alleluia)
℟. There to clothe himself as man, with flesh to offer for us, and blood to shed for us. (Alleluia)

**PRAYER** as at FIRST VESPERS *(page 410)*.

**CLOSING PRAYERS** *(page 38)*.

---

## SEXT

**HYMN** as at TERCE *(page 413)*.

## ANTIPHON

**Mary**, you are full of grace,
the Lord is with you.

## READING *(Isaiah 11: 1, 2, 3)*

From the line of David he will come, and on him the Spirit of the Lord will rest, the Spirit of wisdom and understanding, counsel and strength, knowledge and holy fear of God.

## SHORT RESPONSORY

℣. God himself has come down to the Virgin's womb, there to clothe himself as man.(Alleluia, alleluia) ℟. *(Repeat)*
℣. With flesh to offer for us, and blood to shed for us.
℟. to clothe himself as man. (*During Easter:* ℟. Alleluia, Alleluia)
℣. Glory to God, Father, Son and Holy Spirit.
℟. God himself...
℣. From the Virgin's womb, Christ has come in joy. (Alleluia)
℟. And we have seen him, coming as a bridegroom to his bride. (Alleluia)

---

# NONE

## ANTIPHON

**Mary**, we name you woman most blest of all;
to you alone was given the Son of God himself
to be the blessed Fruit of your womb.

## READING *(Isaiah 45: 8)*

Lord, let your mercy come to us, like dew in the morning, like rain to refresh this earth. Let your saviour come from you, like the beauty of spring, to change our hearts with his holiness.

## SHORT RESPONSORY *(For music, see page 263)*

℣. From the Virgin's womb, Christ has come in joy. (Alleluia, alleluia)
℟. *(Repeat)*
℣. And we have seen him coming as a bridegroom to his bride.
℟. Christ has come in joy. (*During Easter:* ℟. Alleluia, alleluia)
℣. Glory to God, Father, Son and Holy Spirit.
℟. From the Virgin's...
℣. By choosing for himself a Mother on earth. (Alleluia)
℟. The Son of God makes known to all – his Father in heaven. (Alleluia)

**PRAYER** as at FIRST VESPERS *(page 410)*.

**CLOSING PRAYERS** *(page 64)*.

**LAUDS OF OUR LADY** – for the day or season,
with ℣. & ℟. and Prayer. Also...

**Psalm**
'Out of the depths ...' with Prayers *(page 65)*.

---

# OFFICE OF READINGS

**OPENING PRAYERS** *(page 67)*.

## HYMN

Mary, we name you by that shining star
which points the way to those who sail the sea,
for by your light we see the way to God
through life, through death, to joy eternally.

We name you with the names of fairest things,
yet earthly beauty fades before your grace;
draw us from earthly things, as God himself
was drawn to make with you his dwelling place.

Pray Mary Virgin-Mother, full of grace,
pray in your love for all, for all we need;
protect us from all sin and sinful ways,
and at our dying hour intercede.

Christ Jesus, Son of God, we pray to you
and praise you, naming you the Virgin's Son;
we ever praise the Father, God with you
and with the Holy Spirit, Three in One. Amen.

## Antiphon 1

**God in his goodness has heard our prayer**: and Mary has come to us in the fullness of his grace, beautiful as a bride, to bring forth to this world the truth of God. And in this light of truth, we see the hidden dangers of falsehood, and the foolishness of sin.

## Antiphon 2

**People of God, praise and honour the Son of God;** rejoice as the angels rejoiced, that he has come to us, the Virgin's Son, to save and protect us from those who like lions would seek us as their prey.

## Antiphon 3

**Jesus, we pray that all men may bless you and praise you,** and adore that divine decree, by which a Virgin became a Mother, and God became man , that all men might come by faith to inherit the joys of heaven.

℣. God has entered this world of ours, through the Virgin Mary. (Alleluia)
℟. To bring to heaven our fallen race. (Alleluia)
Our Father...

## Absolution

God and Father, holy and merciful Lord, take into account the prayer and holiness of Mary, the Virgin-Mother of God, and of all the saints and bring us back from death to life. ℟. Amen.

*Reader:* Lord, we ask for your blessing.

**BLESSING & READING** for Week One is on *page 271.*
*Reading for Thursdays in Week Two on page 519, and for Week Three on page 538.*

**RESPONSORY** *(For music, see page 456).*

**This is no kingly town,** and she no royal child, yet here is glory and grace beyond compare. Here will come the Son of God himself, to dwell in her house, to find in her his joy and delight, and clothe himself with power.
℣. Now to his kingly home he returns in glory, to crown her with everlasting honour, to crown her Queen of all.
℟. Here will come…
℣. Glory to God, glory to Father, Son and Holy Spirit.
℟. Here will come...

TE DEUM *as on Sunday, page 75 followed by…*
℣. God himself came down to the Virgin's womb. (Alleluia)
℟. There to clothe himself as man, with flesh to offer for us and blood to shed for us. (Alleluia)

**PRAYER** of the Solemnity as at First Vespers *(page 410).*

**CLOSING PRAYERS** *(page 38).*

---

## SECOND VESPERS

As on Thursday *(page 274)* except…

**READING** *(Isaiah 7: 14, 15)* A Virgin shall be with child…
as at First Vespers above *(page 408).*

**PRAYER** of the Solemnity as at First Vespers *(page 410).*

## SECOND COMPLINE

### ANTIPHON (*For music, see page 194*).

T**he Lord looked on her lowliness**, looked on her and loved her,
Mary, handmaid of God. This shall be his dwelling place,
the house of God; in her the Lord will delight for ever.

### READING AND SHORT RESPONSORY
*according to season, as on Sunday, pages 99 - 101.*

### HYMN (*For music, see page 284*).

The Father's Son will make on earth
the Virgin's womb his dwelling place.
The Father and the Spirit too
will ever be with her in grace.

Here Christ will clothe himself as man,
his Godhead's glory set aside,
and angels see him and acclaim
the bridegroom coming to his bride.

The Virgin will be ever blessed
as Virgin-Mother of her Lord
and as his heavenly bride bring forth
children of grace to heaven's reward.

Pray Mary Mother full of grace,
pray in your love for all we need.
Protect us from all danger now,
and at our dying intercede.

Christ, Son of God, we pray to you
and honour you the Virgin's Son;
we praise the Father, God with you,
and with the Spirit, Three in One. Amen.

℣. I am the servant of God. (Alleluia)
℟. To hear and obey his word. (Alleluia)

**CANTICLE ANTIPHON** *(For music, see page 196).*

Like the morning star, Mary, you herald the dawn of day, the coming of Christ, true light from light. May this light of God which you have brought, leave no night, no darkness in this world of ours, and take from us every shadow of death and sin.

**CANTICLE OF SIMEON** *(Luke 2: 29 – 32) as on Sunday, page103.*

℣. & ℟. and Prayer as on Sunday *(page 104)* then ℣. & ℟. with…

**THANKSGIVING** ('Glory, honour and praise...' etc.) *(page 105)*

℣. Mary, you are full of grace, the Lord is with you.
℟. Mary, you are most blessed of all women, for Jesus Christ is your Son. (Alleluia)

**LAUDS OF OUR LADY** – for the day or season,
with ℣. & ℟. and Prayer, then...

**CLOSING PRAYERS** 'Mary, rejoice in God…' *(sung twice) as on Sunday, page 107.*

---

*During Easter*

# THE ASCENSION OF THE LORD

*(Solemnity)*

Office of the day (Thursday or Sunday, according to local custom.)

**RESPONSORY** at First Vespers *(page 456).*

*August 6th*

# THE TRANSFIGURATION OF THE LORD *(Feast*)*

Office of the day occurring, with First Vespers only if on a Sunday.
* *PATRONAL FEAST of the Bridgettine Order.*

---

*Solemnities and*

# FEASTS OF OUR LADY

## COMMON OF OUR LADY: ON ALL SOLEMNITIES, FEASTS, MEMORIALS OR OPTIONAL MEMORIALS OF OUR LADY

Wednesday's Office with Alleluias (*page* 201) always with the Psalms of the Day occurring and the Canticle of the Three Children at Vespers.
*See Rubrics, page* 30.

### CANTICLE OF THE THREE CHILDREN *(Daniel 3:57-88,56)*

O all you works of the Lord, bless the Lord: praise and exalt him for ever.
You angels of the Lord, bless the Lord: and you the heavens, bless the Lord.

All you waters above the heavens, bless the Lord: all you powers of God,
bless the Lord.
Sun and moon, bless the Lord: stars of the sky, bless the Lord.

All rain and dew, bless the Lord: all winds of God, bless the Lord.
Fire and heat, bless the Lord: cold and heat, bless the Lord.

Mists and frost, bless the Lord: ice and cold, bless the Lord.
Ice and snow, bless the Lord: nights and days, bless the Lord.

Light and darkness, bless the Lord: thunderclouds and lightning,
bless the Lord.
O let the earth, bless the Lord: praise and exalt him for ever.

You mountains and hills, bless the Lord: all things that grow in the earth,
bless the Lord.
You fountains, bless the Lord: you seas and rivers, bless the Lord.

Great fish, and all that move in the waters, bless the Lord: all the birds
of heaven, bless the Lord.
All beasts wild and tame, bless the Lord: O children
of men, bless the Lord.

Let Israel bless the Lord: praise and exalt him for ever.
You priests of the Lord, bless the Lord: you servants of the Lord,
bless the Lord.

You spirits and souls of the just, bless the Lord: you holy and
humble of heart, bless the Lord.
Ananias, Azarias, Misael, bless the Lord: praise and exalt him for ever.

Let us praise the Father, Son, and Holy Spirit: let us praise and exalt
him for ever.
May you be blessed, O Lord, in the heavens: to you be highest glory
and praise for ever.

(No *Glory be...* or *Amen*)

## Readings

LAUDS, TERCE and VESPERS *(Eccles. 24:23)*

I am lovely as a vine,
sweet with flowers of holiness,
rich with the fruits of grace.

SEXT *(Eccles. 24:24, 25)*

I am the Mother of pure love, of fear and of holy hope.
In me is all grace of the way and of truth,
in me is all hope of life and of strength.

NONE *(Eccles. 24:26,27)*

Come to me all you that seek me;
feed on the sweet fruit I offer you, for my gifts are
far sweeter than honey, for your joy and delight.

## Prayer

Grant us, your servants, ...
*(page 36 – unless otherwise indicated for the season or feast)*

*December 8th*

# THE IMMACULATE CONCEPTION OF THE B.V.M. *(Solemnity)*

Wednesday's Office with Alleluias, except as shown below and the Canticle of the Three Children at First & Second Vespers *(see Common of Our Lady, page 422)*.

## FIRST and SECOND VESPERS

### ANTIPHON *(For music, see pages 230 &234).*

**We rejoice today in prayer and praise** to honour the Immaculate Conception of the glorious Virgin Mary. For she alone was chosen by God to be both Mother and Virgin for ever.

### READING at LAUDS, TERCE & VESPERS *(Proverbs 8: 22, 23)*

In the eternal decree of God, in his creating mind,
I was ever present to him,
before his creation came to be.

### RESPONSORY *(For music, see page 457).*

℟. *(at First Vespers only)* Mary, you are the Morning Star, which heralds the dawn today; for Christ is the Sun, whose rising brings light to all, that all may see and know the truth and love of God.
℣. Rejoice, rejoice, all you who love God; look and see how his light is come.
℟. for Christ is the Sun ...
℣. Glory to God, glory to Father, Son and Holy Spirit.
℟. for Christ is the Sun ...

### MAGNIFICAT ANTIPHON *(For music, see page 238).*

**Most holy Virgin**, your Immaculate Conception brings joy to all, and the light of hope to shine in our darkness. Mary, most blessed child of blessed line, you are the flower-bearing branch, whose flower is Christ your Son.

## Prayer

O God, you foretold the Immaculate Conception of the Blessed Virgin Mary to our first parents, by the prophecy of an angel. Grant us, your servants here present, that we may be saved through the prayers of the same Blessed Virgin whose Immaculate Conception we solemnly venerate each year: through our Lord Jesus Christ your Son, who lives and reigns with you in the unity of the Holy Spirit, for ever and ever. ℟. Amen.

## Thanksgiving *(For music, see pages 239 - 240).*

℣. Honour and praise to Christ the Son of God, for Mary his Virgin Mother, conceived and ever free from sin. Honour and praise to Christ who is Lord of all. Alleluia, alleluia, alleluia.
℟. Honour and praise and glory for ever, and never-ending thanks to God. Alleluia, alleluia, alleluia.

---

# FIRST and SECOND COMPLINE

## Lauds of Our Lady *for Advent. (see page 484).*

---

# LAUDS

## Invitatory Antiphon

The Immaculate Conception of Mary, Virgin Mother to be,
must be our praise and joy.
† Christ her Son and Lord must be the adoration of our hearts.

## Antiphon

**Of the seed of Abraham**, of the tribe of Juda,
of the royal house of David, the Virgin Mary is conceived
immaculate, to the joy of all heaven and earth.

## Reading *as at Vespers.*

## Antiphon

**Virgin-Mother of God**, your Immaculate Conception was news of great gladness for all this world, for soon would come, by your motherhood, Christ, the light of light, the truth of God, and God himself; to change our evil to good, our damnation to redemption, our hate to love, our curse to blessing, and by opposing death, our death to everlasting life.

## Canticle

Blessed be the Lord, the God of Israel! ... *as on Sunday, page 45.*

## Thanksgiving

℣. Glory, honour and praise to God for the Immaculate Conception of Mary, the Mother of Christ his Son. Alleluia, alleluia, alleluia.
℟. Our thanks to God. Alleluia, alleluia, alleluia.

---

# TERCE

## Reading *as at Vespers.*

---

# SEXT

## Antiphon

**Glory, glory to Christ**, for the
Immaculate Conception of Mary his Mother,
truly the Mother of God.

## Reading *(Proverbs 8: 24, 25)*

The mountains and hills, the valleys and deep places of earth,
had not yet come to be,
when I was conceived in the all-creating mind of God.

## NONE

**ANTIPHON** *(For music, see page 215 & 218).*

**Mary, in you God took delight**; all the angels of God rejoiced in your sinless conception; and we will ever bless you and praise you, and name you Mary, most blessed of all.

**READING** *(Proverbs 8: 34, 35)*

Blest are those who listen to me, blest are those who wait for me, who look for me each day. Blest are all who seek me, for they will find in me true life and salvation from God.

**RESPONSE** *after the Short Responsory – instead of 'There is joy in Heaven'.*

℣. The Immaculate Conception of Mary is ever the joy of heaven. Alleluia.
℟. The sinless Virgin has brought to our hearts a never-ending joy. Alleluia.

**LAUDS OF OUR LADY** *for Advent. (page 484).*

---

## OFFICE OF READINGS

**READING** *for Week 1 or 2 as appropriate.*
*Begin Week One on the First Sunday of Advent.*

**PRAYER** *as above, at Vespers.*

*January 1st*

# MARY, MOTHER OF GOD *(Solemnity)*

Thursday's Office (*pages 248 ff* – as at Christmas) with Alleluias and the Canticle of the Three Children at First & Second Vespers (*see Common of Our Lady, page 422*) and Lauds of Our Lady after None and Compline of Christmas (*with music, page 484*).

**RESPONSORY** *of Thursday at First Vespers. (For music, see page 458).*

---

*February 11th*

# OUR LADY OF LOURDES *(Memorial)*

Wednesday's Office (*pages 201 ff*) with Alleluias (*except in Lent*); Lauds of Our Lady after None or Compline, of the day or season and the Canticle of the Three Children at Vespers, *see Common of Our Lady, page 422.*

## READINGS

LAUDS, TERCE and VESPERS (*Cant. 2: 13, 14*)

Arise, my dearest, my lovely one and come to me.
Come, my dove, do not hide from me in your nest among the rocks.
Let me see you, let me hear your voice.

SEXT (*Proverbs. 8: 18, 19*)

I have true wealth and honour to give you; holiness and everlasting glory.
My gifts are sweeter than sweetest fruits,
more precious than silver or gold.

NONE *(Eccles. 24: 25, 26)*

I have truth for your minds, and strength to follow this truth;
I have life to give you, and life-giving help.
Come to me, all you who love me, and share in the gifts I give.

**PRAYER**

Lord of mercy, as we keep the memory of Mary, the Immaculate Mother of God, who appeared to Bernadette at Lourdes: grant us through her prayer, strength in our weakness and grace to rise up from our sins; through our Lord Jesus Christ your Son, who lives and reigns with you and the Holy Spirit, God, for ever and ever. ℟. Amen.

---

*May 13th*

# OUR LADY OF FATIMA *(Memorial)*

Wednesday's Office *(pages 201 ff)* with Alleluias and the Canticle of the Three Children at Vespers, *see Common of Our Lady, page 422;* with Lauds of Our Lady after None and Compline of the Easter season *(page 402).*

**READINGS** *as in the Common of Our Lady, page 423.*

**PRAYER**

Father, you who have given us the Mother of your Son to be our mother also; grant us that, by obeying the appeals of the Blessed Virgin Mary, we may always work through prayer and penance for the kingdom of Christ and attain eternal happiness. Through our Lord Jesus Christ your Son, who lives and reigns with you in the unity of the Holy Spirit, God for ever and ever. ℟. Amen.

***Lucia dos Santos*** *and her two cousins Francisco and Jacinto Marto, declared they had seen a vision of Our Lady at the Cova da Iria near the Portuguese town of Fatima on 13th May 1917. They were three young shepherds. They described a woman in white, shedding rays of brilliant white, standing on a cloud in an evergreen tree. She asked them to come back on the 13th of each month until October and to pray the Rosary every day. On subsequent visits the Lady asked that Russia be consecrated to her Immaculate Heart and that a Communion of reparation be made on the first Saturday of each month.* (from The Plymouth Diocesan Ordo.)

*May 31st*

# THE VISITATION OF OUR LADY

*to Saint Elizabeth (Feast)*

As on the Solemnity of the Annunciation *(page 411)* – but begin with Lauds – with Alleluias throughout and the Canticle of the Three Children at Vespers, *see Common of Our Lady, page 422;* with Lauds of Our Lady at None and Compline of the season or the day occurring.

## READINGS

LAUDS, TERCE & VESPERS *(Cant. 2: 8, 9)*

See how he comes, leaping on the mountains, bounding over the hills. My beloved is like a gazelle, like a young stag. See where he stands behind our wall. He looks in at the window, he peers through the lattice.

SEXT *(Cant. 2: 10, 11, 12)*

My beloved lifts up his voice, he says to me,
"Come then, my love, my lovely one, come.
For see, the winter is past, the rains are over and gone.
The flowers appear on the earth. The season of glad songs has come."

NONE *(Cant. 2: 13, 14)*

Come then, my love, my lovely-one, come.
My dove, hiding in the cleft of the rock, in the coverts of the cliff, show me your face, let me hear your voice; for your voice is sweet and your face is beautiful.

## PRAYER

Almighty, ever-living God, through the abundance of your love you inspired the Blessed Virgin Mary, when she was bearing your Son, to visit Elizabeth. Grant that, through this same visitation, we may be filled with heavenly gifts and be freed from all adversities, through our Lord Jesus Christ, your Son, who lives and reigns with you and the Holy Spirit, God, for ever and ever. ℟. Amen.

*Saturday after the Feast of the Most Sacred Heart of Jesus*

# THE IMMACULATE HEART OF MARY

*(Memorial)*

Wednesday's Office *(pages 201 ff)* *(pages 201 ff)* with Alleluias and with Lauds of Our Lady after None of the day occurring.

## READINGS

LAUDS & TERCE *(Eccles. 24: 14)*

In the eternal decree of God, I was present before his creating,
and I shall be for ever with him,
in the holiness of his heaven.

SEXT *(Eccles. 24: 15, 16)*

Jerusalem has been my dwelling and my resting-place; there in the holy city, I have taken up my rule and my reign. I have grown up among God's people, I will live for ever in the land of the Lord.

NONE *(Eccles. 24: 20)*

I am sweet as the scent of cinnamon and balsam,
fragrant as the fragrance of myrrh,
on the winds of summer.

## PRAYER

Almighty and everlasting God, in the Heart of the blessed Virgin Mary you prepared a dwelling worthy of the Holy Spirit; grant in your mercy, that we, who with devout minds celebrate the feast of that Immaculate Heart, may be able to live according to your own Heart. Through our Lord Jesus Christ your Son, who lives and reigns with you in the unity of the Holy Spirit, God for ever and ever. ℟. Amen.

*July 16th*

# OUR LADY OF MOUNT CARMEL

*(Memorial)*

Wednesday's Office *(pages 201 ff)* with Alleluias and the Canticle of the Three Children at Vespers, *see Common of Our Lady, page 422*; with Lauds of Our Lady after None and Compline of the day occurring.

**READINGS** *as in the Common of Our Lady, page 423.*

**PRAYER**

O God, you were pleased to honour the Order of Carmel with the particular title of Mary ever Virgin and your Mother; grant we pray you, that we who celebrate this day her commemoration by a solemn Office, may be shielded by her protection, and attain eternal joys. You who are God, living and reigning with the Father in the unity of the Holy Spirit, for ever and ever. ℟. Amen.

---

*August 5th*

# DEDICATION OF THE BASILICA OF ST. MARY MAJOR *(Our Lady of the Snows)* *(Memorial)*

Wednesday's Office *(pages 201 ff)* with Alleluias and the Canticle of the Three Children at Vespers, *see Common of Our Lady, page 422*; with Lauds of Our Lady after None and Compline of the day occurring.

**READINGS** *as in the Common of Our Lady, page 423.*

**PRAYER**

Grant us, your servants, we pray you, Lord God, to enjoy perpetual health of mind and body. By the glorious intercession of blessed Mary ever Virgin, may we be delivered from present sorrow and enjoy everlasting happiness: through our Lord Jesus Christ your Son, who lives and reigns with you in the unity of the Holy Spirit, God for ever and ever. ℟. Amen.

*August 15th*

# THE ASSUMPTION OF THE B.V.M.

*(Solemnity)*

Saturday's Office *(pages 353 ff)* with Alleluias and the Canticle of the Three Children at first and second Vespers, *see Common of Our Lady, page 422;* with Lauds of Our Lady after None and Compline.[1]

**RESPONSORY** at first Vespers *(For music, page 465).*

## READINGS

LAUDS, TERCE & VESPERS *(Eccles. 24: 17,18)*

See how I grow in beauty, tall as a cedar on Lebanon, fragrant as a cypress on Mount Sion, graceful as a palm tree, by the water's edge, lovely as a rose in the gardens of Jericho.

SEXT *(Cant. 4: 7, 8)*

Come to me, my love, come from your dwelling-place in the land of Lebanon; come in your purity and beauty, for you are dearer to me than all, and my love shall be your crown.

NONE *(Eccles. 24: 19,20)*

I am lovely as the olive tree growing in the fields, tall as the plane tree by the wayside; sweet as the scent of cinnamon and balsam, fragrant as the fragrance of myrrh on the winds of summer.

## PRAYER

Almighty, eternal God, you have raised the Immaculate Virgin Mary, Mother of your Son, body and soul into the glory of heaven. Enable us to direct our minds always to heavenly things, and to be found worthy to share in her glory: through our Lord Jesus Christ your Son, who lives and reigns with you in the unity of the Holy Spirit, God for ever and ever. ℟. Amen.

---

[1] *For Lauds of Our Lady at Compline: First Compline as on Saturday (pages 394 - 396) with long versicles (pages 399 - 402); None and Second Compline is of the day occurring.*

*August 22nd*

# THE QUEENSHIP OF THE B.V.M.

*(Memorial)*

Saturday's Office *(pages 353 ff)* with Alleluias and the Canticle of the Three Children at Vespers, *see Common of Our Lady, page 422*; with Lauds of Our Lady after None and Compline of the day occuring.

## READINGS

LAUDS, TERCE & VESPERS *(Eccles. 24: 5,6,7)*

I came forth from the mouth of the Most High
and I covered the earth like a mist.
I had my dwelling in the heights; and my throne in a pillar of cloud.

SEXT *(Eccles. 24: 9, 10)*

Over the waves of the sea and over the whole earth,
and over every people and nation,
I have held sway.

NONE *(Eccles. 24: 30, 31)*

Whoever listens to me will never have to blush;
who acts as I dictate will never sin;
and they will have life eternal.

## PRAYER

We ask you, Lord, to hear us on this solemn feast of Mary our Queen, and through the grace of her protection, may we obtain peace in this present life and glory in the life to come: through our Lord Jesus Christ your Son, who lives and reigns with you in the unity of the Holy Spirit, for ever and ever. ℟. Amen.

*September 8th*

# THE NATIVITY OF THE B.V.M. *(Feast)*

*(Our Lady's Birthday)*

Wednesday's Office *(pages 201 ff)* with Alleluias and the Canticle of the Three Children at Vespers, *see Common of Our Lady, page 422;* with Lauds of Our Lady after None and Compline of the day occurring.

**READINGS** *as in the Common of Our Lady, page 423.*

**PRAYER**

Grant to your servants, Lord, we pray, the gift of heavenly grace. As the childbearing of the Blessed Virgin was the beginning of their salvation, so may this feast in honour of her birthday bring them increase of peace: through our Lord Jesus Christ, your Son, who lives and reigns with you in the unity of the Holy Spirit, God for ever and ever. ℟. Amen.

---

*September 12th*

# THE HOLY NAME OF MARY *(Memorial)*

Wednesday's Office *(pages 201 ff)* with Alleluias and the Canticle of the Three Children at Vespers, *see Common of Our Lady, page 422;* with Lauds of Our Lady after None and Compline of the day occurring.

**READINGS** *as in the Common of Our Lady, page 423.*

**PRAYER**

Lord our God, when your Son was dying on the altar of the Cross, he gave us as our mother the one he had chosen to be his own Mother, the Blessed Virgin Mary. Grant that we who call upon the holy name of Mary our Mother, with confidence in her protection, may receive strength and comfort in all our needs: through our Lord Jesus Christ, your Son, who lives and reigns with you and the Holy Spirit, one God for ever and ever. ℟. Amen.

*September 15th*

# OUR LADY OF SORROWS *(Memorial)*

Friday's Office *(pages 291 ff)* with Alleluias and the Canticle of the Three Children at Vespers, *see Common of Our Lady, page 422;* with Lauds of Our Lady after None and Compline of the day occurring.

## READINGS

LAUDS, TERCE & VESPERS *(Lamentations. 2: 13)*

Who is like to you, daughter of Jerusalem, who so sorrowful and suffering? Who can console you, Virgin daughter of Sion or take away your sorrow? Far deeper than deepest ocean, the sorrow of your heart.

SEXT *(Lamentations. 1: 2)*

Weeping, weeping she mourns, long nights of sorrow;
alone she weeps,
for there is none to console her.

NONE *(Lamentations. 2: 18)*

There is none to take away her sorrow,
no consolation by day or night;
her tears will be the measure of her sorrow.

## PRAYER

Lord, at your Passion, a sword of sorrow pierced the most gracious soul of the Blessed Virgin Mary, your Mother, as Simeon had foretold. Grant in your mercy that we who reverently recall her sorrows, may reap the fruits of your Passion: you who live and reign with the Father in the unity of the Holy Spirit, God for ever and ever. ℟. Amen.

*September 24th*

# OUR LADY OF WALSINGHAM *(Memorial)*

Wednesday's Office *(pages 201 ff)* with Alleluias and the Canticle of the Three Children at Vespers, *see Common of Our Lady, page 422;* with Lauds of Our Lady after None and Compline of the day occurring.

**READINGS** *as in the Common of Our Lady, page 423.*

**PRAYER**

Grant us, your servants, ... *(page 36).*

---

***Today we celebrate*** *the memorial of Our Lady of Walsingham whose shrine in Norfolk was one of the great pilgrimage centres of medieval times. The lady of the manor of Walsingham, Richeldis de Faverches, was instructed by a vision of the Virgin Mary to build in her village an exact replica of the house in Nazareth in which the Annunciation had taken place. The vision occurred, according to tradition, in 1061, though a more likely date for the construction of the shrine is a hundred years later. The original house was destroyed at the Reformation, but during the 19th and early 20th centuries pilgrimage to Walsingham was revived both for Anglicans and for Catholics.* (from The Plymouth Diocesan Ordo.)

*Statue of Our Lady at Walsingham.*

*October 7th*

# OUR LADY OF THE ROSARY *(Memorial)*

Wednesday's Office *(pages 201 ff)* with Alleluias and the Canticle of the Three Children at Vespers, *see Common of Our Lady, page 422;* with Lauds of Our Lady after None and Compline of the day occurring.

## READINGS

### LAUDS, TERCE & VESPERS *(Eccles. 24: 25, 26)*

I have truth for your minds, and strength to follow this truth; I have life to give you, and life-giving help. I am like a rose tree growing near the waters, and the flowers are for your delight.

### SEXT *(Eccles. 39: 19)*

Come to me, hear and obey my words, and you shall be pleasing to God; like flowers you shall grow in beauty, spreading your fragrance around. Your words shall be praises of God, your works ever praising the works of God.

### NONE *(Eccles. 24: 17, 18)*

See how I grow in beauty; tall as a cedar on Lebanon, fragrant as a cypress on Mount Sion, graceful as a palm tree by the water's edge, lovely as a rose in the gardens of Jericho.

## PRAYER

O God, your only begotten Son has won for us the rewards of eternal salvation by his life, death and resurrection. Grant that we who meditate on these mysteries in the most holy Rosary of the Blessed Virgin Mary, may both imitate what they contain and receive what they promise: through our Lord Jesus Christ, your Son, who lives and reigns with you, in the unity of the Holy Spirit, God for ever and ever. ℟. Amen.

*November 21st*

# THE PRESENTATION OF THE B.V.M.

*(Memorial)*

Wednesday's Office *(pages 201 ff)* with Alleluias and the alternative Magnificat Antiphon *(page 238)* together with the Canticle of the Three Children at Vespers, *see Common of Our Lady, page 422;* with Lauds of Our Lady after None and Compline of the day occurring.

**READINGS** *as in the Common of Our Lady, page 423.*

## PRAYER

Lord God, you willed that the blessed Virgin Mary, dwelling place of your Holy Spirit, be presented in the temple this day. We ask for her prayers, that we may one day be presented in the temple of your glory: through our Lord Jesus Christ your Son, who lives and reigns with you in the unity of the Holy Spirit, God for ever and ever. ℟. Amen.

*Feasts and Memorials of –*

# SAINTS & MARTYRS OF THE ORDER

*May 4th*

## SAINT RICHARD REYNOLDS *Martyr, (memorial)*

**ANTIPHON** *before Antiphon to Holy Mother St Bridget at Lauds and Vespers.*

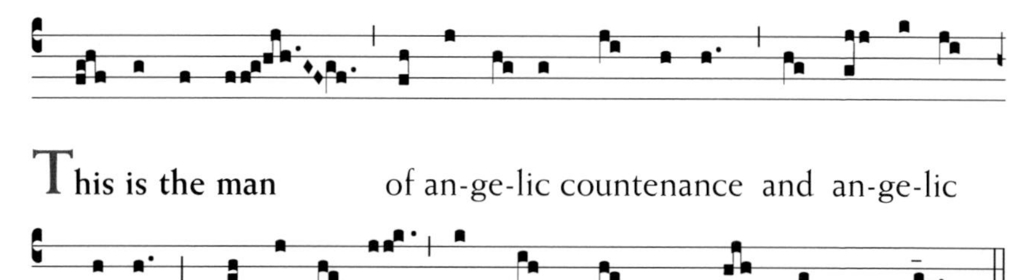


spi-rit, dear to all men, and filled with the spi - rit of God.

**RESPONSE**

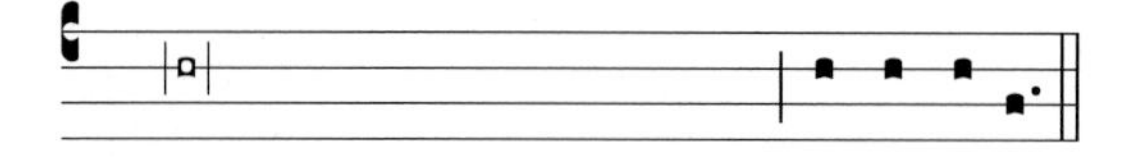

℣. Pray for us, Saint Richard, Al-le-lu-ia.

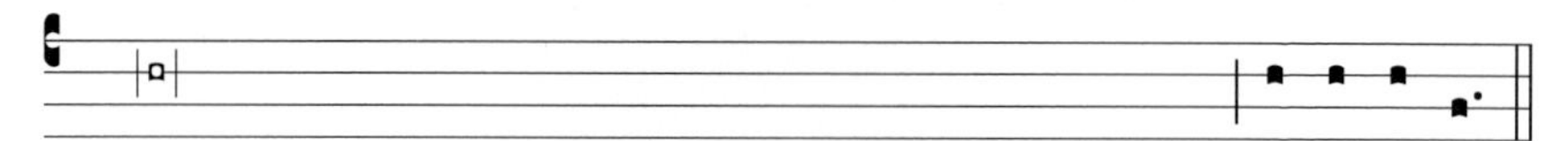

℟. That we may be made worthy of the grace of God, Al-le-lu-ia.

**PRAYER**

God, in your goodness, you have granted to St Richard a place among the illustrious martyrs of the Apostolic See; grant to us, through his example and intercession, that we may loyally live and holily die in faithful obedience to the same holy See, through Christ our Lord. ℟. Amen.

*The Angel of Syon ~*

# SAINT RICHARD REYNOLDS

*Bridgettine monk of Syon Abbey, martyred at Tyburn in defence of the Catholic faith on May 4th 1535. Canonised by Pope Paul VI, October 25th 1970.*

Richard Reynolds was born about 1487. The place of his birth is uncertain, but he was probably connected with the Reynolds family of Pinhoe, Devon. He was elected a Fellow of Corpus Christi College Cambridge in 1510, became a Bachelor of Divinity in 1513 and was appointed University preacher. On June 13th of the same year he made his profession as a Bridgettine monk at Syon Abbey, Isleworth.

His contemporaries describe him as one of the foremost preachers and scholars of his day, and a man of angelic countenance and angelic life. He was a personal friend of SS John Fisher and Thomas More.

Arrested and required to take the Oath of the King's Supremacy in spiritual matters, he refused, and was martyred with three Carthusian Priors and John Hale, the Vicar of Isleworth, on May 4th, 1535.

St Richard was the last of these five heroic protomartyrs of the Reformation to mount the scaffold.

As he watched the brutal sentence of being hanged, cut down alive, drawn and quartered, carried out on his companions, he encouraged them with the promise of a "happy banquet and supper in heaven for their sharp breakfast on earth."

*Saint Richard Reynolds.*

*June 25th*

# HOLY MOTHER SAINT KATHERINE

*(Memorial)*

**ANTIPHON** *before Antiphon to Holy Mother St Bridget at Lauds and Vespers.*

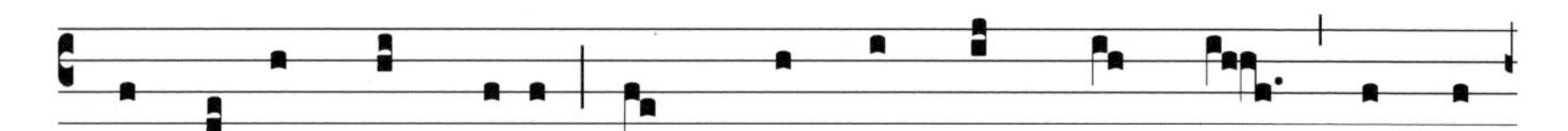

This is the wise virgin who, when the bridegroom came, had her

lamps rea - dy and went in with her Lord to the wedding feast.

**RESPONSE**

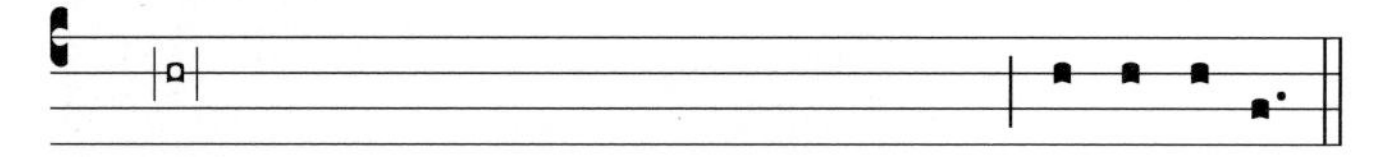

℣. Pray for us, holy Mother Katherine, Al-le-lu-ia.

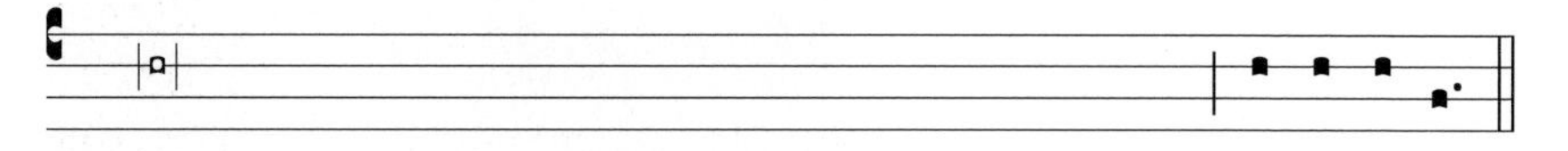

℟. That we may be made worthy of the grace of God, Al-le-lu-ia.

**PRAYER**

O God, you have adorned blessed Katherine in many ways with the privilege of outstanding chastity and the holiness of virtues, as an example to your faithful people. Give to us, your servants, by the intercession of her merits, purity of mind and body, so that we may obtain with you the happiness promised to us, through Christ our Lord. ℟. Amen.

*A life of chastity and obedience ~*

# HOLY MOTHER SAINT KATHERINE

Saint Katherine was born in 1331 or 1332, the fourth child of Bridget and Ulf Gudmarsson. When in 1341 Bridget and Ulf went on pilgrimage to Santiago de Compostela in Spain, Katherine and her sister Ingeborg were placed with the Cistercian Sisters in their convent in Närke.

*Saint Katherine.*

Ingeborg remained in the convent for the rest of her life but at twelve years of age, Katherine was given in marriage according to the wishes of her father, to Eggard van Kyren, who was perhaps ten years her senior. Ulf died in 1344 and when her mother went to Rome in 1349 to join the celebrations for the Holy Year of 1350, Katherine is said to have remarked: "I forgot how to smile," she missed her mother so much.

Katherine asked Eggard for permission to visit her mother, which he granted her, and she arrived in Rome in August 1350. She was destined not to return to Sweden until after her mother's death in 1373, as when the time came for her to return to Eggard, Bridget asked her to stay with her as her companion. Not long afterwards Eggard died and Katherine dedicated her life to Christ, who in a vision had said to Bridget: "I have decided that she shall remain with you, for I myself will care for her." *(Rev.VI.118).*

As a faithful companion, Katherine accompanied her mother on her visits to the churches of Rome and to the poor and sick of the city, and on her many pilgrimages in Italy; and finally was with her on Bridget's last pilgrimage which was to the Holy Land. In December 1373, following her mother's death on 23rd July of that year, Katherine, with her brother Birger and accompanied by Bishop Alfons, Prior Peter and Master Peter and others, took Bridget's remains to Vadstena, a journey lasting some seven months. For the next months Katherine was able to encourage and enlighten the fledgling community which had been set up at Vadstena, having shared her mother's life of humility, poverty and obedience for 24 years. But it was necessary to have confirmation of the Rule from the Pope and to begin, as soon as possible, the proceedings for the canonisation of Bridget. Soon after Easter 1375 Katherine returned to Rome.

Due to very many difficulties it was not until December 1378 that Bridget's Rule was sanctioned and February 1380 when the ordinances already published for the new Abbey at Vadstena were confirmed by Pope Urban VI. The canonisation process was hampered by the schism in the Church and did not take place until 1391. However, Katherine's main work was completed and on 15th March 1380 she began the return journey to Vadstena once again, arriving some four months later. In a letter dated 17th July 1380, Bishop Nicolaus Hermann calls her "the Abbess and Mother of the Abbey, first in precedence after her illustrious mother, the holy Bridget." Over the following months her health began to fail and she died on 24th March 1381 at the age of 49. She was never officially canonised but Pope Sixtus IV allowed her to be honoured as a saint in Scandinavia and Pope Innocent III extended this to the Bridgettine Order.

*July 23rd*

# HOLY MOTHER SAINT BRIDGET

*(Solemnity)*

Office of the day occurring with Alleluias.

*Holy Mother Saint Bridget.*

*July 26th*

# SAINT ANNE AND SAINT JOACHIM

*(Memorial)*

## READINGS

LAUDS, TERCE and VESPERS *(Proverbs 8: 22, 23)*

God created me when his purpose first unfolded, before the oldest of his works. From everlasting I was firmly set, from the beginning, before the earth came into being.

SEXT *(Proverbs 8: 24, 25)*

The deep was not, when I was born; there were no springs to gush with water. Before the mountains were settled I came to birth.

NONE *(Proverbs 8: 34, 35)*

Happy the man who listens to me, who day by day watches at my gates to guard the portals. For the man who finds me finds life; he will win favour from God.

**ANTIPHON** *before Antiphon to Holy Mother St Bridget at Lauds and Vespers.*

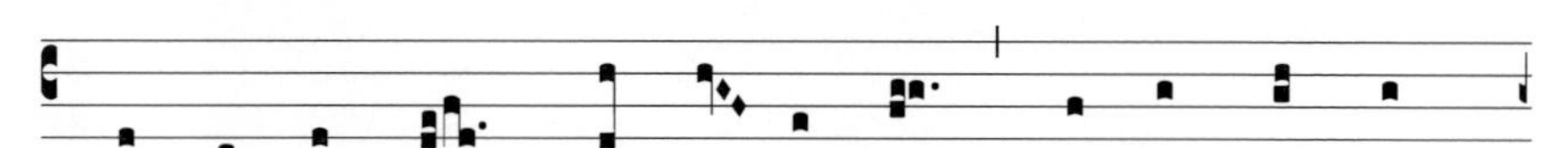

**Blest is the world, blest is the hour,** when a - mong its

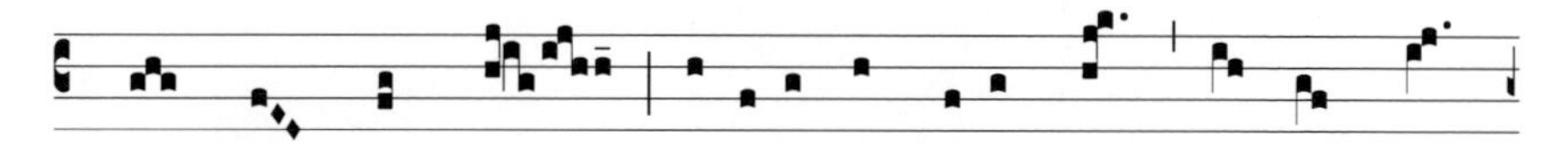

daughters stands A - nne, as if a beau-ti-ful light, gi - ving us

the first fruits of her vir-tue.

## Response

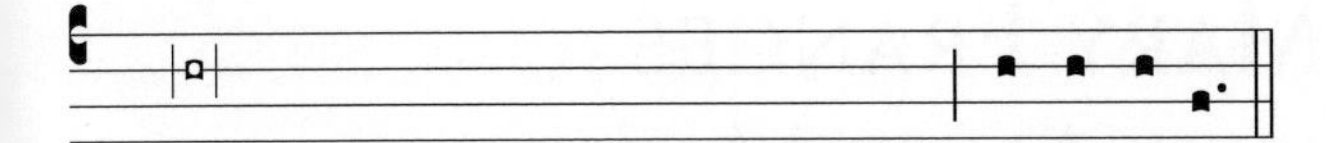

℣. Pray for us blessed Mother Anne, Al-le-lu-ia.

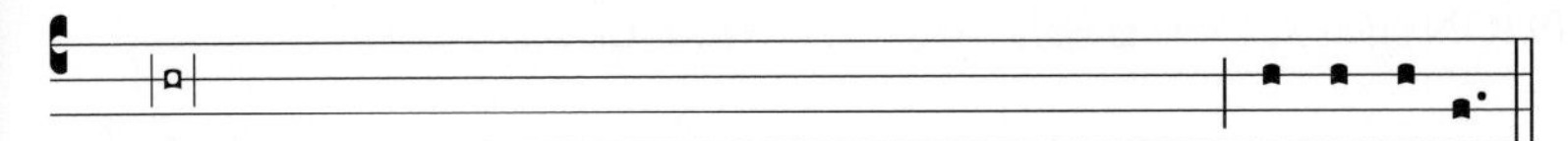

℟. That we may be made worthy of divine grace, Al-le-lu-ia.

## Prayer

O God, who bestowed such great grace on blessed Anne that she was made worthy to become the mother of Mary, the Mother of your only-begotten Son: graciously grant that we who celebrate her feast may be helped by her intercession. We ask this through Christ our Lord.
℟. Amen.

*October 23rd*

# BLESSED MARY FRANCES AND BLESSED ANNE MARY *Martyrs (memorial)*

**ANTIPHON** *before Antiphon to Holy Mother St Bridget at Lauds and Vespers.*

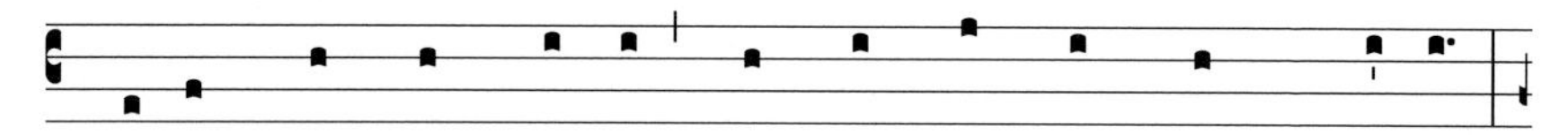

**Virgins wise and pru-dent**, wel-come the bridegroom's coming;

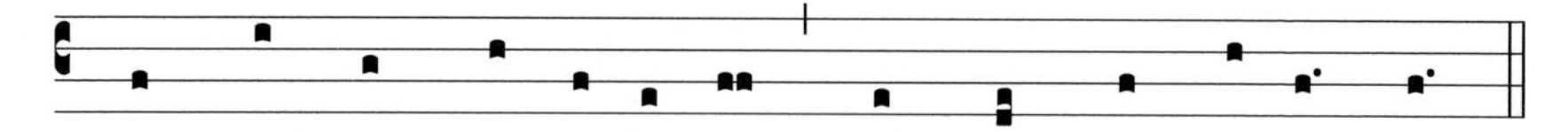

take your lamps and go to him with love and re-joi - cing.

## RESPONSE

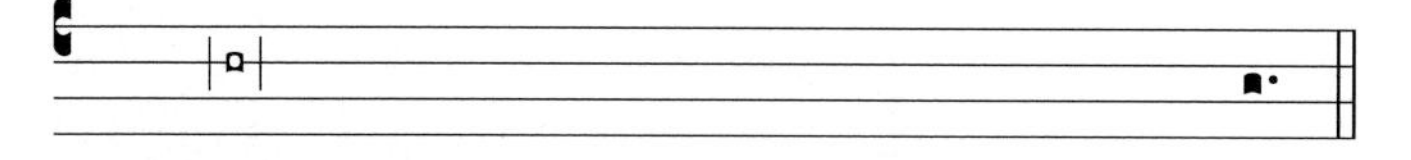

℣. After her shall virgins be brought to the King.

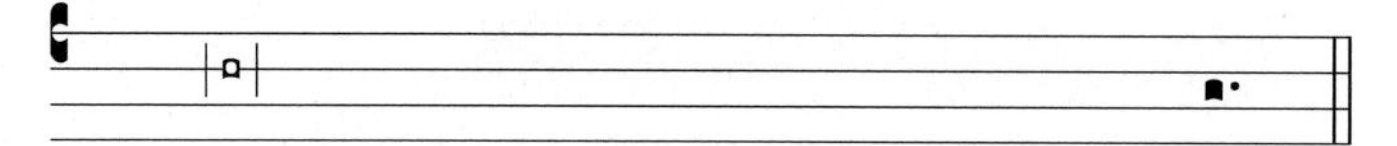

℟. Her neighbours shall be brought to you.

## PRAYER

Lord, we honour your martyrs Mary Frances and Anne Mary, who were faithful to Christ even to the point of shedding their blood for him. Increase our own faith and free us from our sins, and help us to follow their example of love. Through Christ our Lord. ℟. Amen.

# BLESSED MARY FRANCES AND BLESSED ANNE MARY

*Two Bridgettine Sisters, martyred by guillotine at Valenciennes in 1794 during the French Revolution. Beatified by Pope Benedict XV on June 13th, 1920.*

Today we commemorate two Bridgettine Sisters who died for their faith in 1794 during the French Revolution's 'Reign of Terror'. They were Sister Mary Frances who was born Marie Liévine LaCroix and Sister Anne Mary, born Marie Augustine Erraux. As young women they left their families to join the Bridgettine community at Valenciennes, a town in French Flanders near the border with Belgium. Here they lived a holy, peaceful life of devotion unaware of the crown of martyrdom which awaited them.

The Revolutionary Assembly confiscated all Church property in November 1789 and no longer recognised religious Orders. The Bridgettine convent at Valenciennes was suppressed in 1792 and destroyed in November 1793. The Sisters returned to their families awaiting better times. But, after spending several months with their families, these two Sisters sought refuge with the Ursuline Sisters who, after a period of exile at Mons in Belgium, had returned to their own convent in Valenciennes which had not been destroyed. At this time the town was safely in the hands of the Austrians, but it was surrendered to French revolutionary troops on 27th August 1794.

*Blessed Mary Frances (L) and Blessed Anne Mary.*[2]

On 1st September, the nuns were told to disperse but some of the Ursulines and our two Bridgettine Sisters remained, only to be arrested the same night. The convent itself became a prison for them and others, including several priests who would not take the State oath. On 17th October they heard that the Ursulines in other prisons had been guillotined. On 20th October one of the Ursulines wrote a letter telling of the joy in their hearts and that they were not afraid of death, adding: "Clotilde [the Superior], my sister, Sister Cordule, the two Bridgettines and myself are still here. All the priests have been executed."

Similarly, one of the Bridgettines wrote to her brother a few days before her martyrdom, returning to him a little money, asking that it be given to the poor. She wrote: "... I cannot express my gratitude at soon being allowed to shed my blood for the Faith and as a penance for my sins, and of soon quitting this prison for the eternal dwelling place. May God give me grace to persevere until the end ... I need that badly ... and love for Christ. May you all, you and my dear parents, be united as in one heart. With God's mercy, I hope to see you again in heaven. I pray for heaven's blessing to fall upon you. Your sister,
Sr. Anne-Marie." [1]

On 23rd October, now their feast day, the Sisters were summoned before the local tribunal and sent from there directly to the guillotine. On their way to martyrdom they sang the *Te Deum* and recited the Litany of our Blessed Lady and at the end forgave the guard of soldiers and their executioners. Sister Mary Frances and Sister Anne Mary were declared martyrs by decree of Pope Benedict XV on 6th July 1919 and beatified by him on 13th June 1920.

Blessed Mary Frances and Blessed Anne Mary, pray for us.

● ***Abridged from a sermon preached by the Very Rev. Canon Augustine Morford at Syon Abbey on October 23rd 1923.***
*(from 'The Poor Souls' Friend', January 1924)*

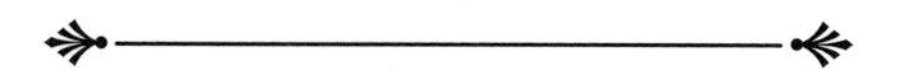

*1. 'Bridgettines' by Kirsten Stoffregen Pedersen, 2nd ed. 2003, p. 98. 2. Image courtesy of Special Collections, University of Exeter. All these illustrations of our saints and martyrs were drawn by Sister M. Stanislas Simmons, O.Ss.S. a sister of Syon, 1916 - 1968.*

*First Vespers*

# RESPONSORIES

*Responsories are sung or said after the Reading and before the Hymn on Solemnities and on Feasts of Our Lord falling on a Sunday; that is having First Vespers on the eve of the feast.*
*See Rubrics, page 29.*

## Sunday

### RESPONSORY I

*for The Most Holy Trinity and The Body & Blood of Christ (Corpus Christi).*

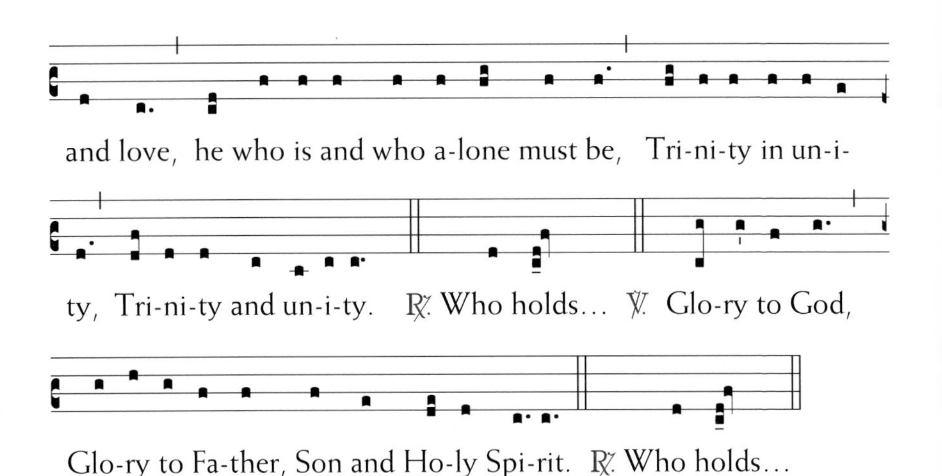

## Responsory III

*for Pentecost Sunday.*

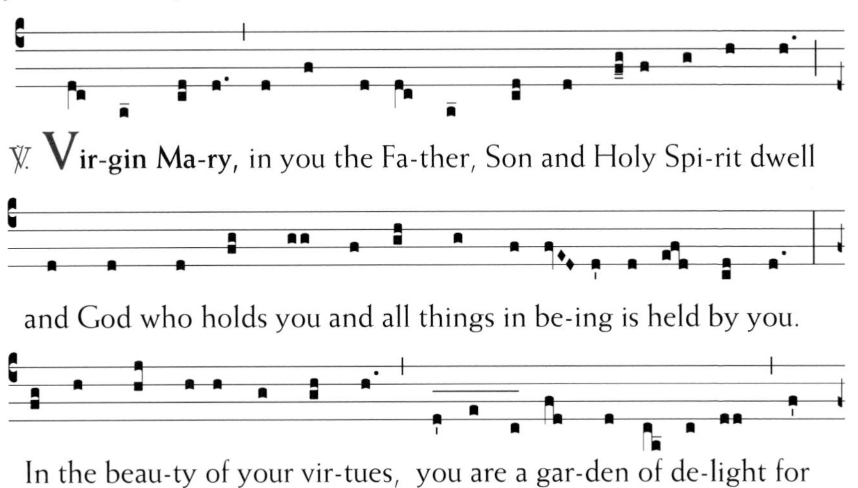

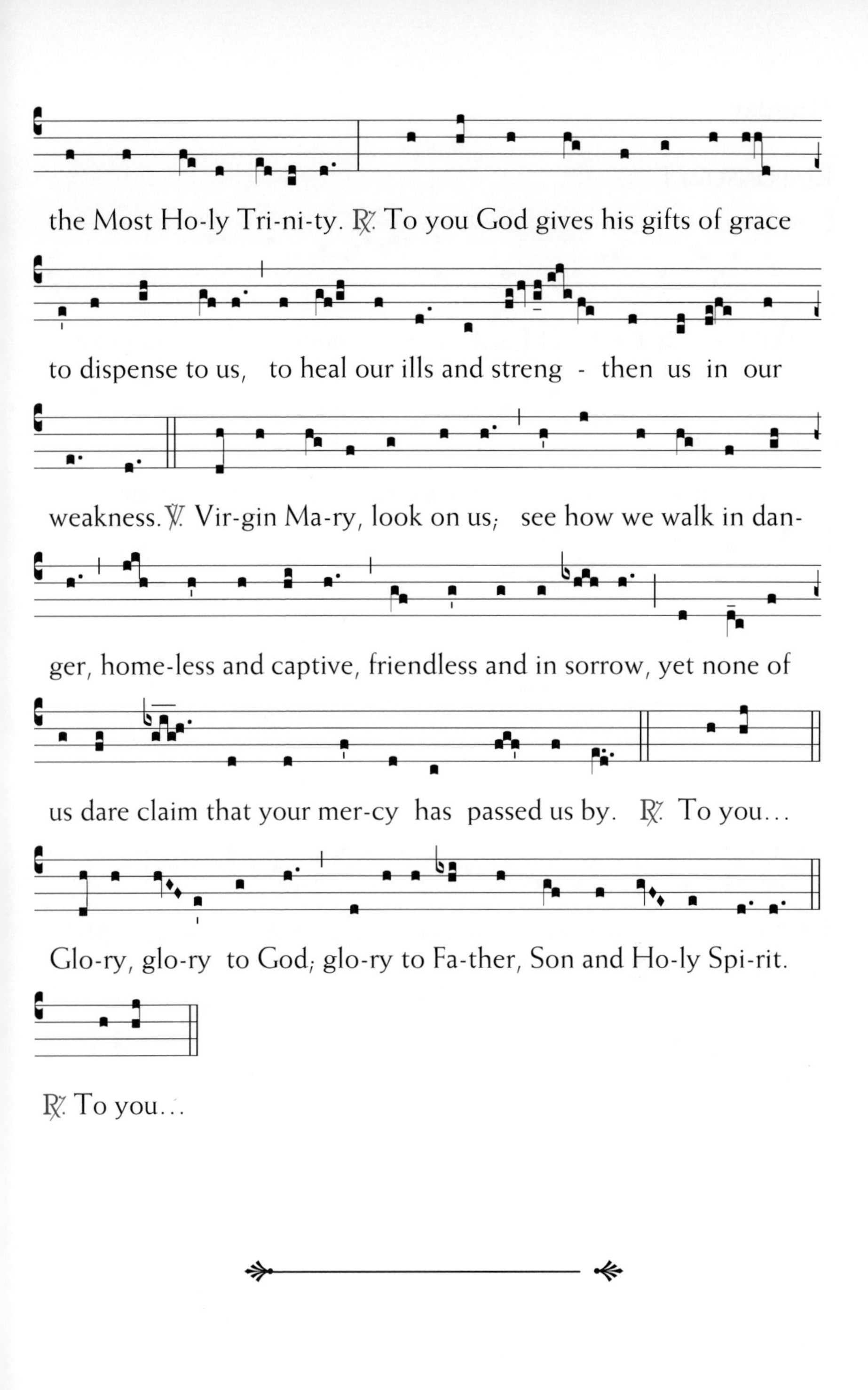
the Most Ho-ly Tri-ni-ty. ℟. To you God gives his gifts of grace
to dispense to us, to heal our ills and streng - then us in our
weakness. ℣. Vir-gin Ma-ry, look on us; see how we walk in danger, home-less and captive, friendless and in sorrow, yet none of
us dare claim that your mer-cy has passed us by. ℟. To you…
Glo-ry, glo-ry to God; glo-ry to Fa-ther, Son and Ho-ly Spi-rit.
℟. To you…

## Monday

### Responsory I

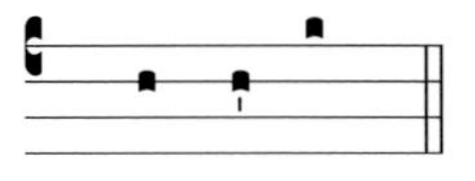

℟. "All honour...

## Responsory III

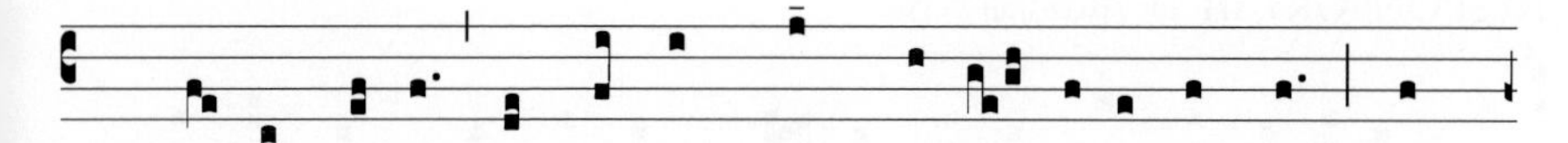

℣. **Vir-gin Ma-ry,** so dear to Christ, so ho - ly in his grace, we

pray to you, and will ev-er pray: ℟. Queen of heav'n, help us in

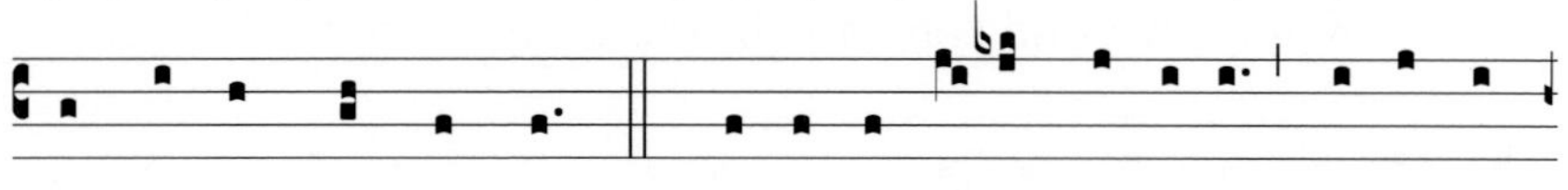

our sorrow and our need. ℣. We are so weak, so sinful; Ma-ry, we

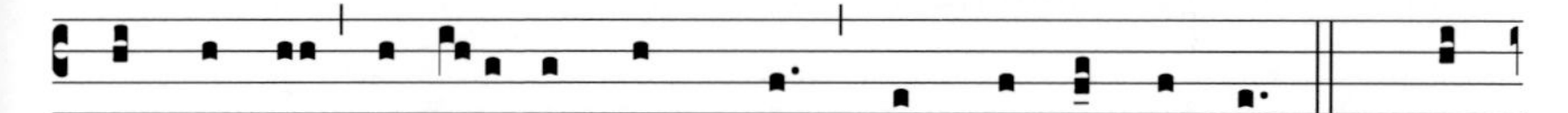

think of you so holy in God's grace, and we pray to you. ℟. Queen

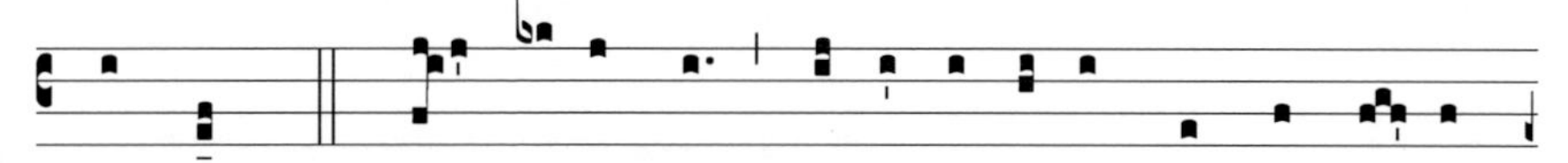

of heav'n... ℣. Glo - ry to God, glo-ry to Father, Son and Ho-ly

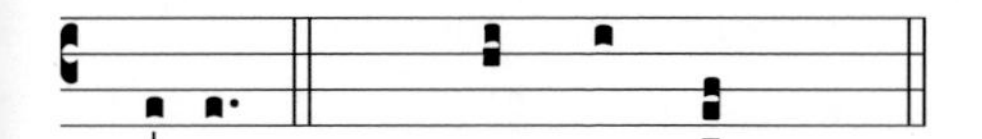

Spi-rit. ℟. Queen of heav'n...

**Tuesday**

RESPONSORY III *for Ascension Day.*

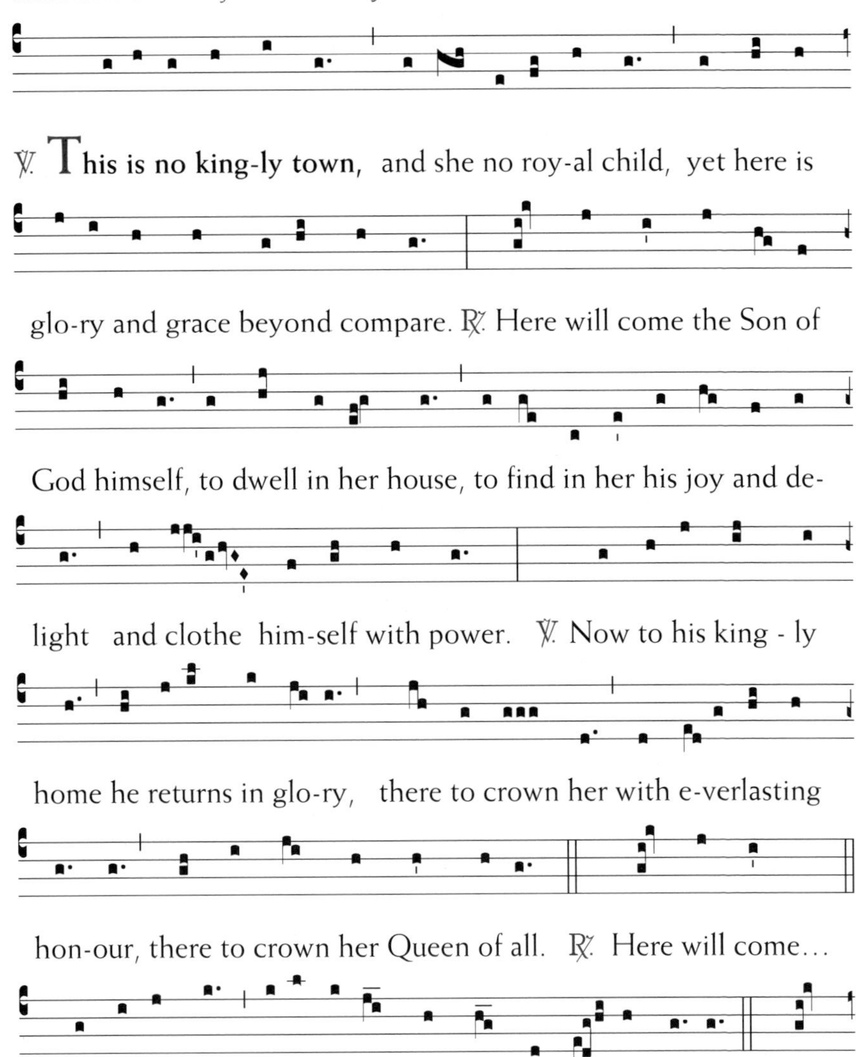


℣. Glo-ry to God, glory to Fa-ther, Son and Ho-ly Spi-rit. ℟. Here

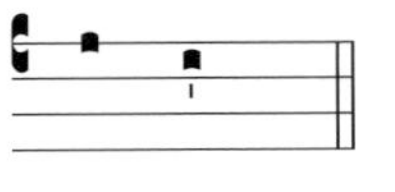

will come…

## Wednesday

### Responsory III

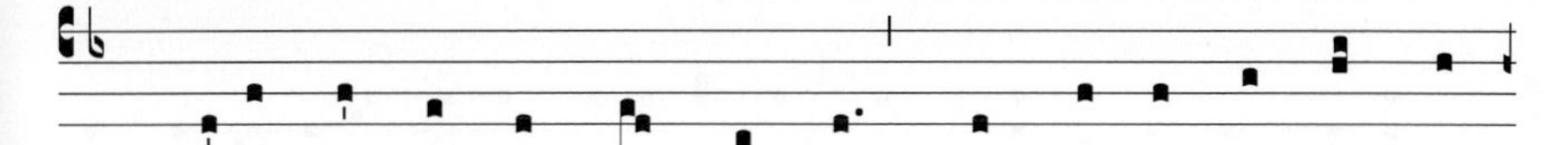

℣. **Ma-ry, you are the morn-ing star,** which heralds the dawn of

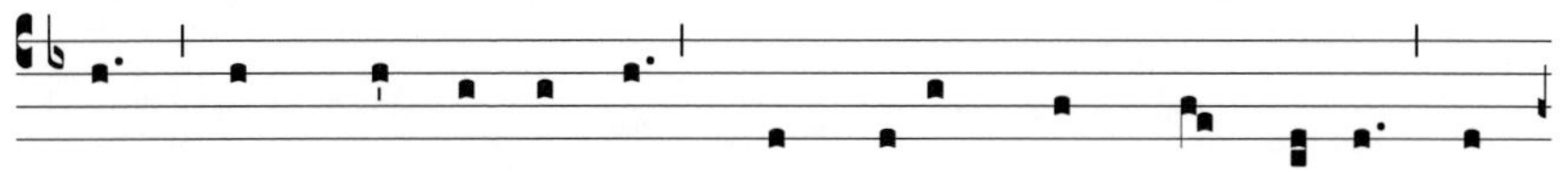

day, ℟. for Christ is the sun, whose rising brings light to all, that

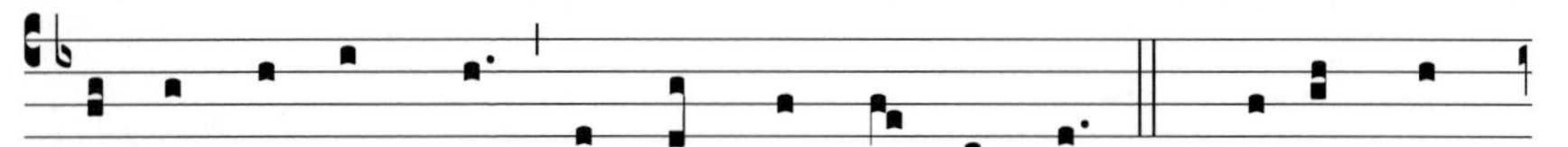

all may see and know the truth and love of God. ℣. Rejoice, re-

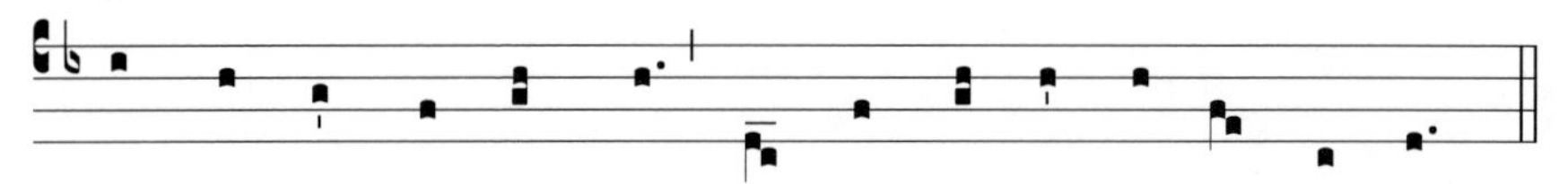

joice, all you who love God; look and see how his light is come.

℟. for Christ is the sun… ℣. Glo-ry to God, Fa-ther, Son and

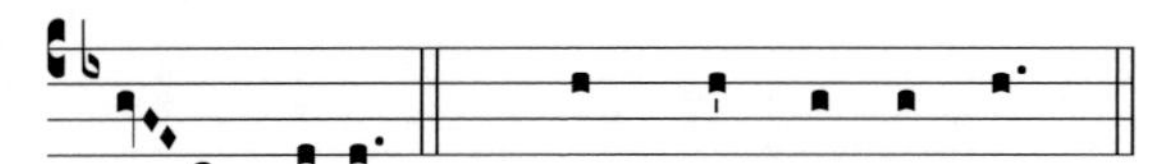

Ho-ly Spi-rit. ℟. for Christ is the sun…

## Thursday

### RESPONSORY I

*for the Solemnity of Mary, Mother of God (1st January).*

and borne him in your womb. ℣. Virgin Mary, you are most blest

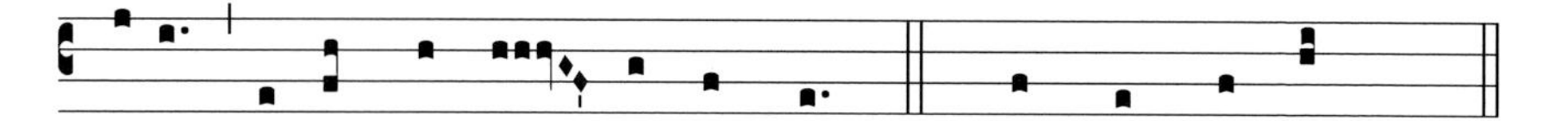

of all, for Je - sus Christ is your Son. ℟. No land, no world...

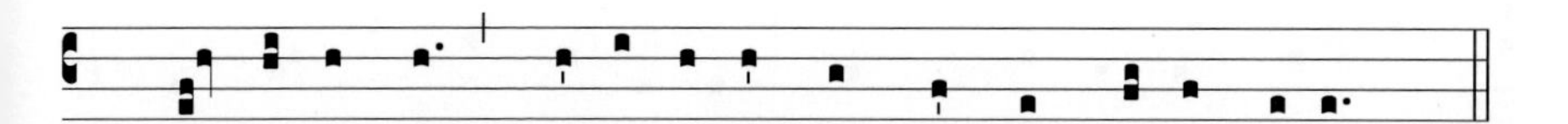

℣. Glo - ry to God, Glo-ry to Fa-ther, Son and Ho-ly Spi-rit.

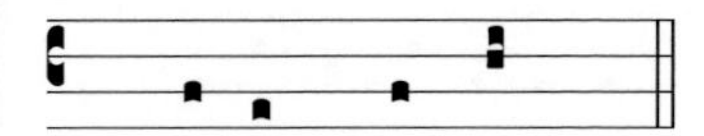

℟. No land, no world…

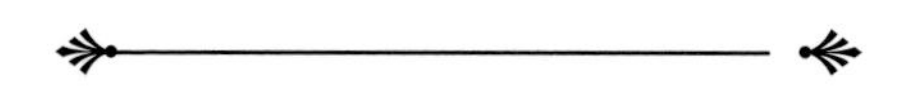

## Responsory II

*for Christmas Day.*

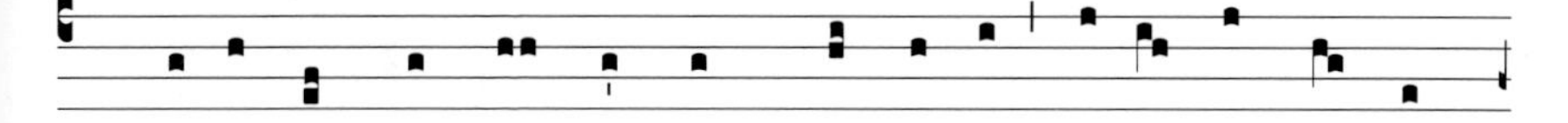

℣. **Every age shall call her most blest of all,** for all the wonders

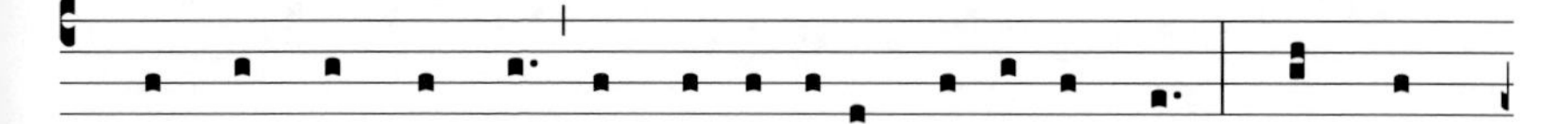

God has done for her, for she is truly Mother of God. She who

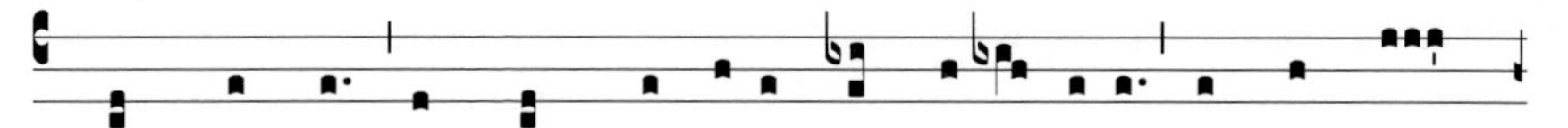

knew not man, in whom was ever pure virgin-i-ty, has con-ceived

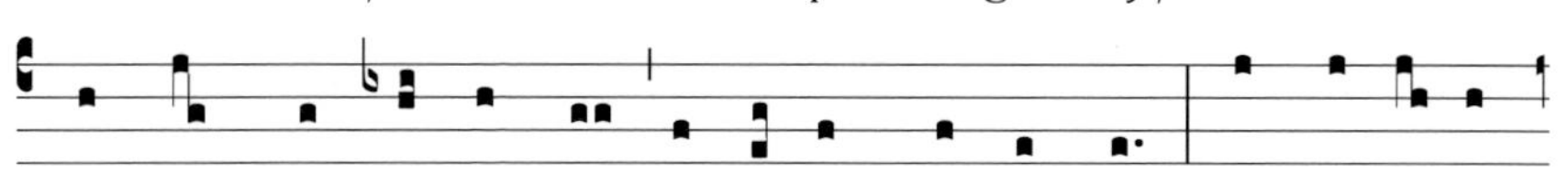

and borne the Son of God, in Virgin Motherhood. She has ev-er

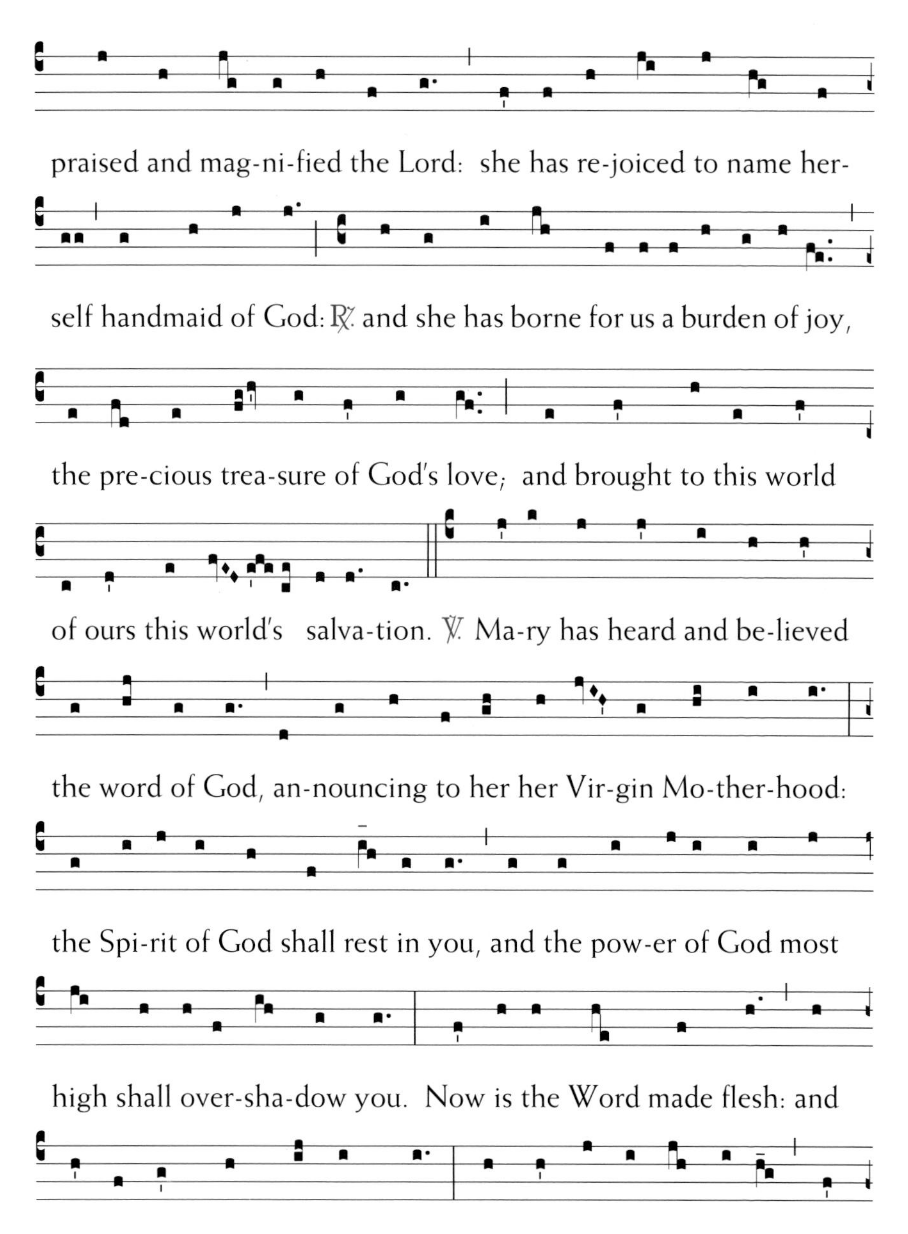
praised and mag-ni-fied the Lord: she has re-joiced to name her-
self handmaid of God: ℟. and she has borne for us a burden of joy,
the pre-cious trea-sure of God's love; and brought to this world
of ours this world's salva-tion. ℣. Ma-ry has heard and be-lieved
the word of God, an-nouncing to her her Vir-gin Mo-ther-hood:
the Spi-rit of God shall rest in you, and the pow-er of God most
high shall over-sha-dow you. Now is the Word made flesh: and
now is come the promised One. And she who is blest of all will

bring forth to the joy of all Christ her Lord and God. ℟. and she
has borne… ℣. Glory, glory to God the Fa-ther, who be-gets the
Son. Glory to Christ that on-ly Son, Lord and Cre-a-tor, e-qual
God. And to the Holy Spi-rit Lord and God, who with the Father and Son is ev-er one, from both pro-ceed-ing in love e- ter-
nal. Glo.......ry from all both now and ev-er. A-men. ℟. and
she has borne…

## RESPONSORY III

*for the Solemnity of The Epiphany.*

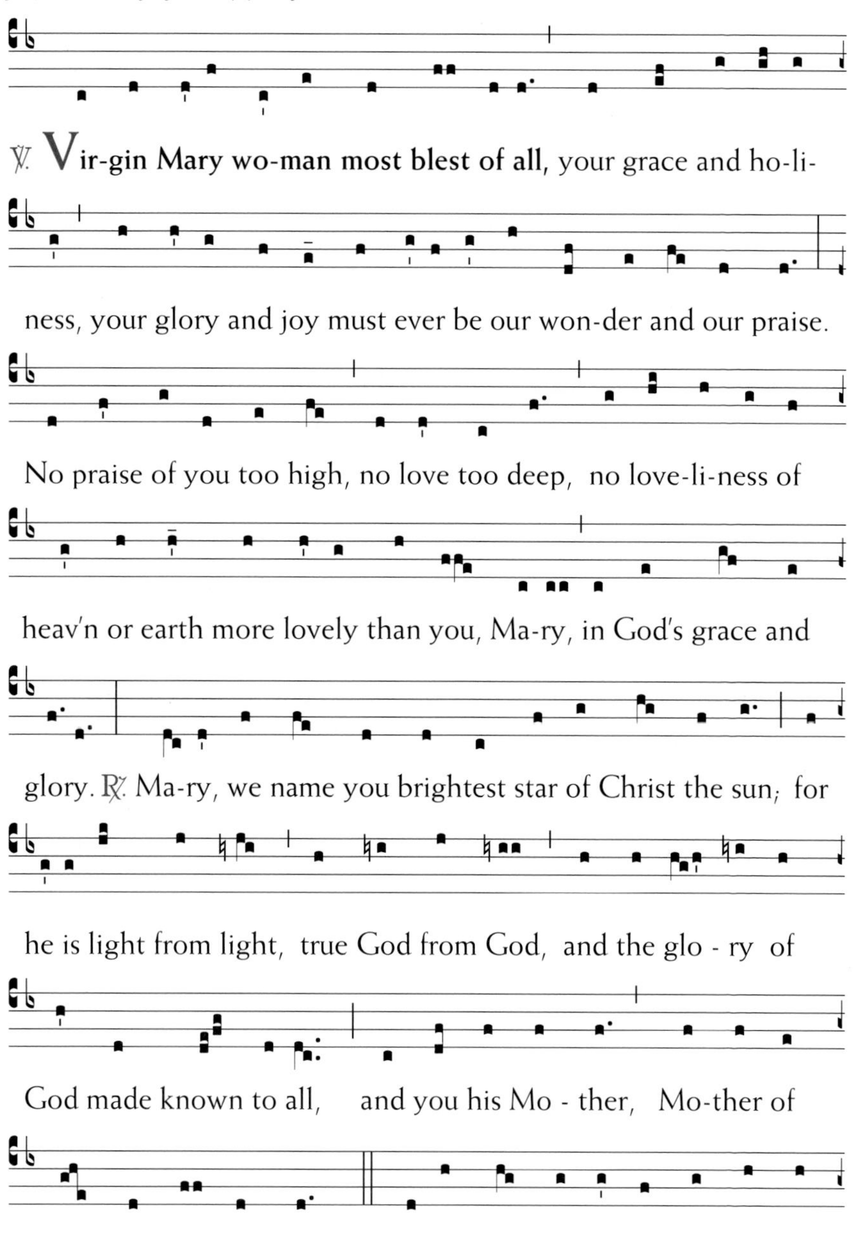

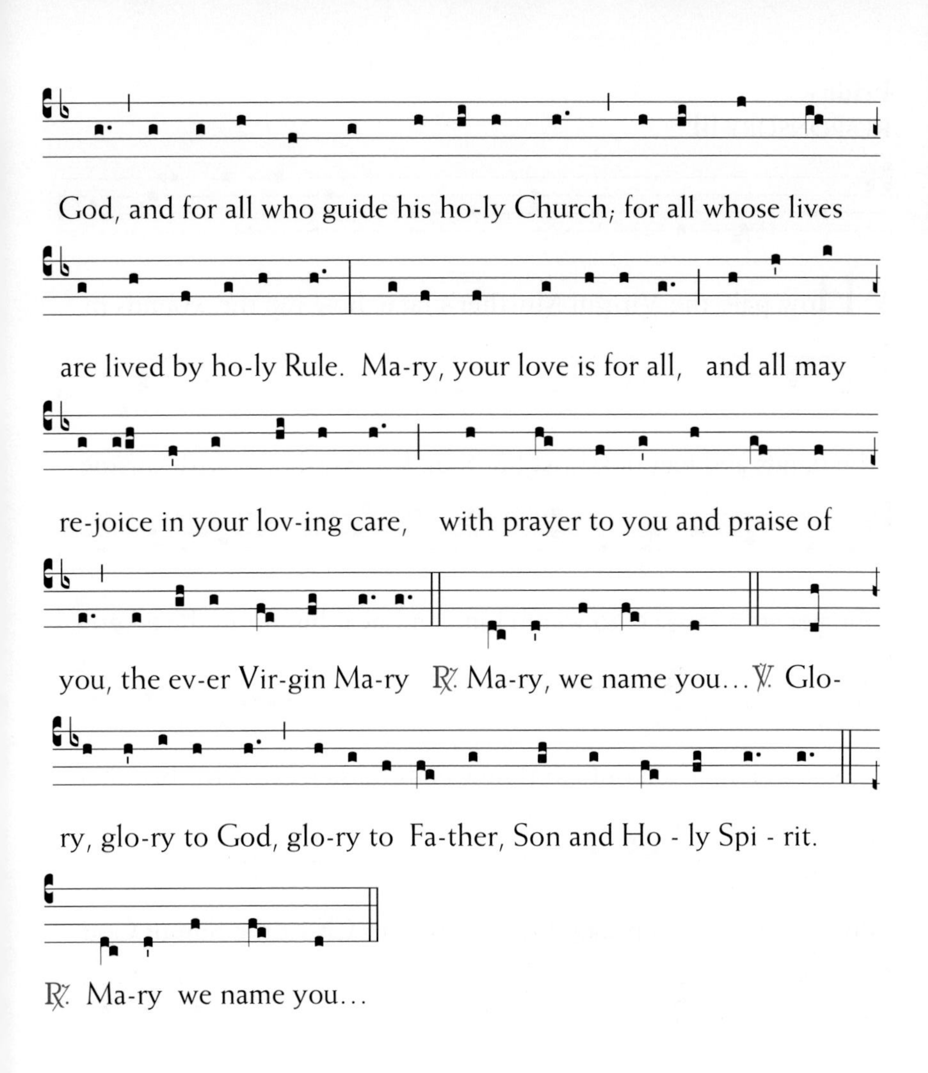
God, and for all who guide his ho-ly Church; for all whose lives
are lived by ho-ly Rule. Ma-ry, your love is for all, and all may
re-joice in your lov-ing care, with prayer to you and praise of
you, the ev-er Vir-gin Ma-ry ℟. Ma-ry, we name you… ℣. Glory, glo-ry to God, glo-ry to Fa-ther, Son and Ho - ly Spi - rit.
℟. Ma-ry we name you…

**Friday**

## RESPONSORY III

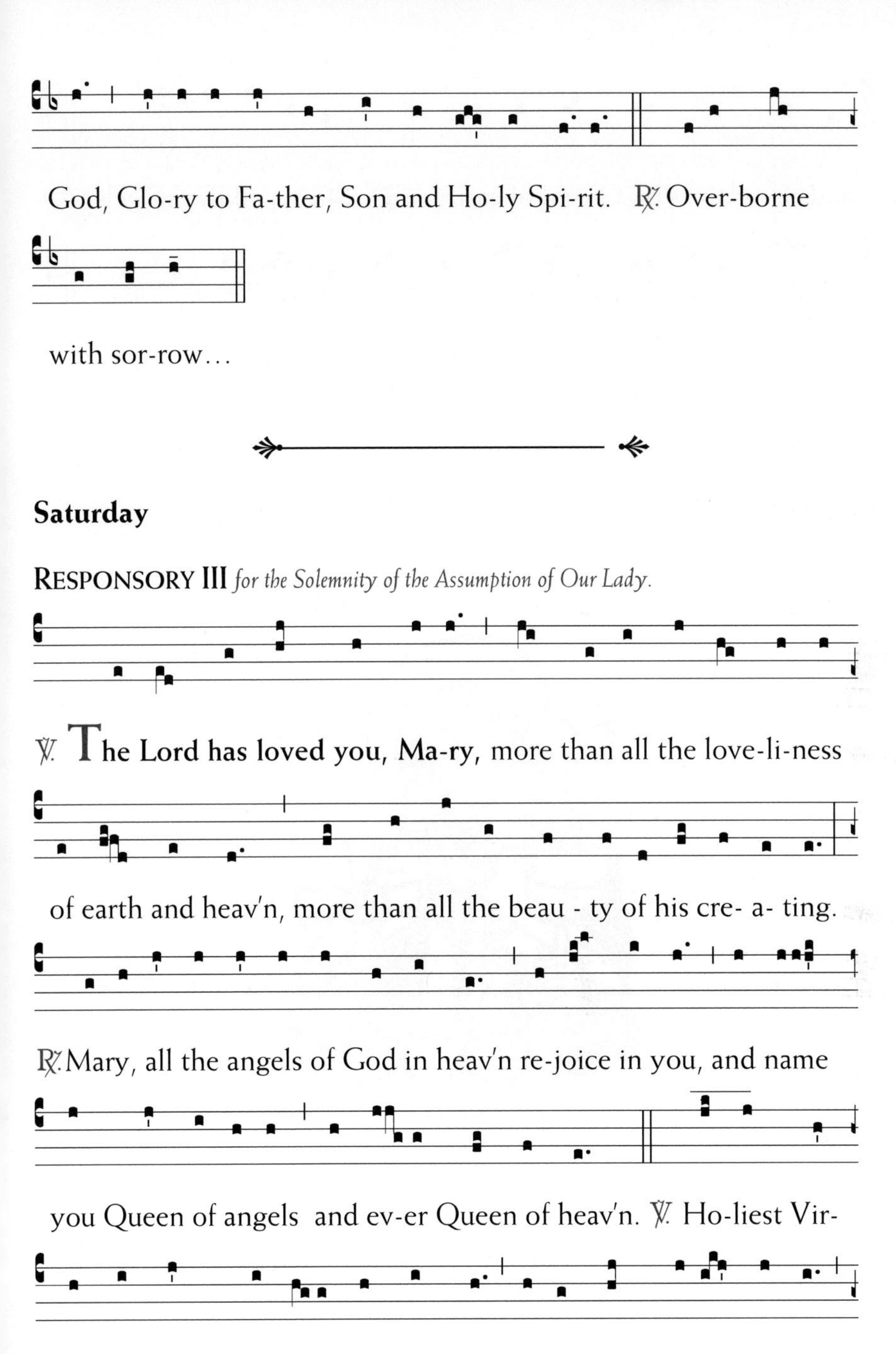
God, Glo-ry to Fa-ther, Son and Ho-ly Spi-rit. ℟. Over-borne
with sor-row…
Saturday
RESPONSORY III for the Solemnity of the Assumption of Our Lady.
℣. The Lord has loved you, Ma-ry, more than all the love-li-ness
of earth and heav'n, more than all the beau - ty of his cre- a- ting.
℟. Mary, all the angels of God in heav'n re-joice in you, and name
you Queen of angels and ev-er Queen of heav'n. ℣. Ho-liest Vir-
gin, conceived and ever free from sin, we on earth rejoice in you,

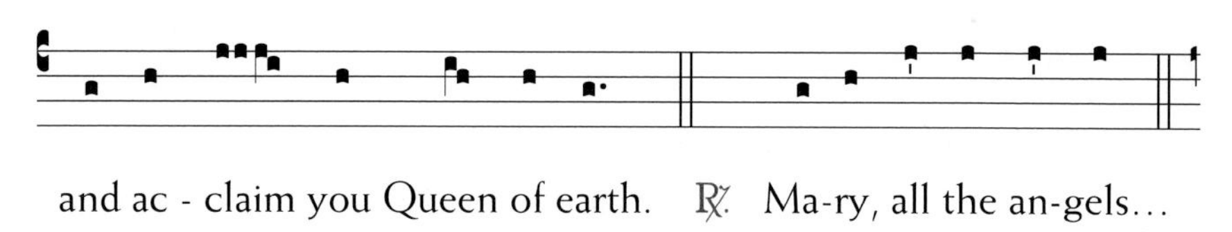

and ac - claim you Queen of earth. ℟. Ma-ry, all the an-gels...

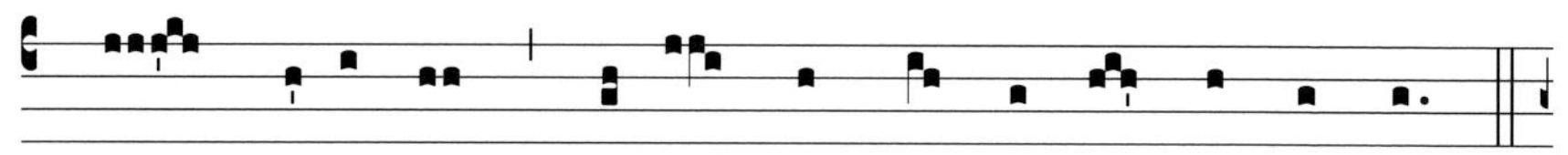

℣. Glo - ry to God, the Fa - ther, Son and Ho - ly Spi - rit.

℟. Ma-ry, all the an-gels...

*An early woodcut of Saint Bridget with a pilgrim's hat, purse and staff.*
*In the centre of the crucifix there is a representation of the figures of Mary,*
*the Mother of God and Saint John at the foot of the Cross.*
*This emblem can still to be seen on the rings worn by the Sisters.*

*During Advent*

# Melodies for Advent

**HYMN** *for Small Hours (Terce, Sext & None) each day:*

**Sunday**

1. God, One in Three, your light re-veals your - self to all men

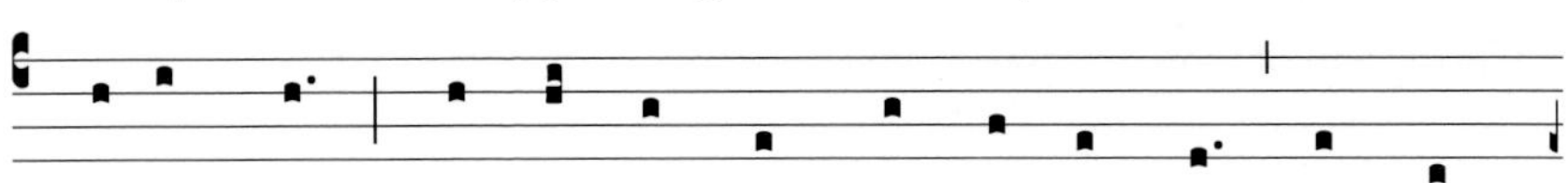

ev'-ry-where; this light is Christ, the Vir-gin's Son: hear now

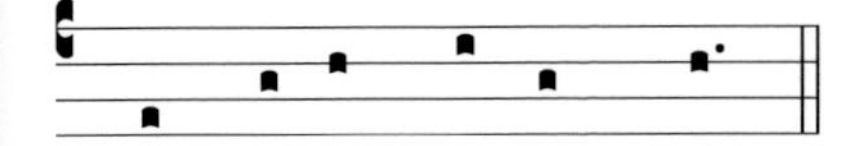

the Virgin-Mother's prayer.

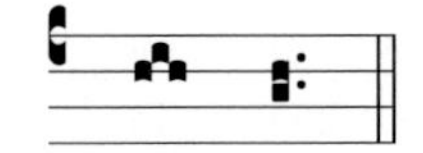

4. A - men.

2. For she who came by your decree
first sign of dawn in our dark night,
holds out to all men everywhere
her Son, your all-revealing Light.

3. Pray Mary Mother, full of grace,
pray in your love for all we need;
protect us from all danger now,
and at our dying intercede.

4. Christ, Son of God, we pray to you,
and honour you, the Virgin's Son.
We praise the Father, God with you,
and with the Spirit, Three in One. Amen.

## Monday

1. God made you, Mary in his grace,
creation's crown most blessed of all:
so we are blessed who find in you
strength and protection when we call.

2. Strength and correction when we fall,
and grace to drive all sin away,
new love to win God's love again,
your love and mercy as we pray.

3. Pray Mary Mother, full of grace...

4. Christ, Son of God, we pray to you...

## Tuesday

1. Come, Lord Creator Spirit, come,
inspire our hearts to tell again
that news your prophets once foretold,
God virgin-born and peace to men.

2. Come in our need as Advocate,
Consoler of our troubled days;
come for her sake whom you have made
Virgin and Mother by your grace.

3. Pray Mary Mother, full of grace...

4. Christ, Son of God, we pray to you...

## Wednesday

1. See how fierce flames of three-fold fire,
have wilted all fair things of earth;
see how a fountain springs on high,
and with fresh flowers the land gives birth.

2. O Virgin fountain of delights,
water our withered hearts and bless;
that they bedewed with heaven's grace,
may bring forth flowers of holiness.

3. Pray Mary Mother, full of grace…

4. Christ, Son of God, we pray to you...

## Thursday

1. Christ, Lord and King, in mercy come,
come, take our hearts to be your own;
to love and serve you in all things,
to praise you for yourself alone.

2. Remember, Lord, that for our sake,
a sinless Virgin's Child you came
as man to men to save all men,
salvation we your own may claim.

3. Pray Mary Mother, full of grace…

4. Christ, Son of God, we pray to you...

## Friday

1. Could there be joy so great as hers,
to be the Mother of God's Son?
Could there be sorrow deep as hers,
to see the evil men have done?

2. Mary, keep ever in our minds
your share in Christ's most bitter pain;
and through your sufferings make us know
how earth and earthly things are vain.

3. Jesus, keep ever in our hearts
your bitter death, that we may learn
the depths of your great love for men,
and ever love you in return.

4. Pray Mary Mother, full of grace...

5. Christ, Son of God, we pray to you...

## Saturday

1. [Vir-gin], your Son has willed and e-ver wills
all angels, men, and every thing;
so we may pray to you as Queen,
who in God's grace brought forth God's King.

2. Look from your throne in heaven to earth,
show for us all a Mother's care,
lead all to love and serve your Son,
who hears with love his Mother's prayer.

3. Pray Mary Mother, full of grace...

4. Christ, Son of God, we pray to you...

## Reading at Lauds, Terce & Vespers *(Isaiah 7: 14, 15)*

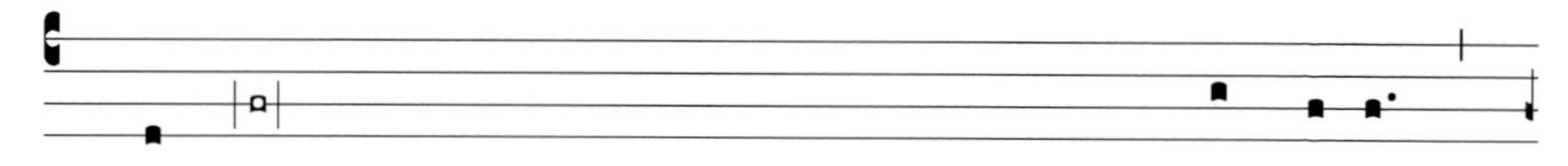

Be - hold, a vir - gin shall con - ceive and bring forth a son;

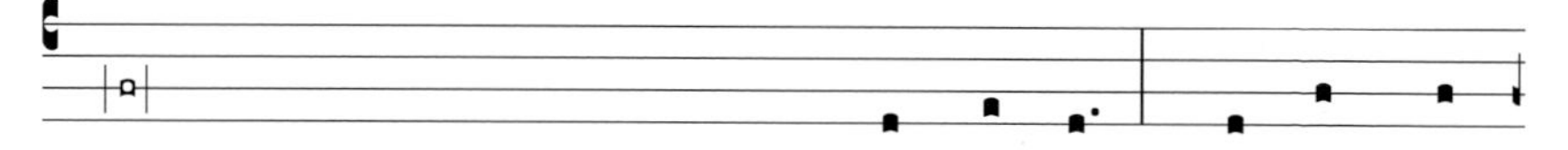

and his name shall be Emmanuel: God with us. On curds and

READING AT SEXT *(Isaiah 11: 1, 2)*

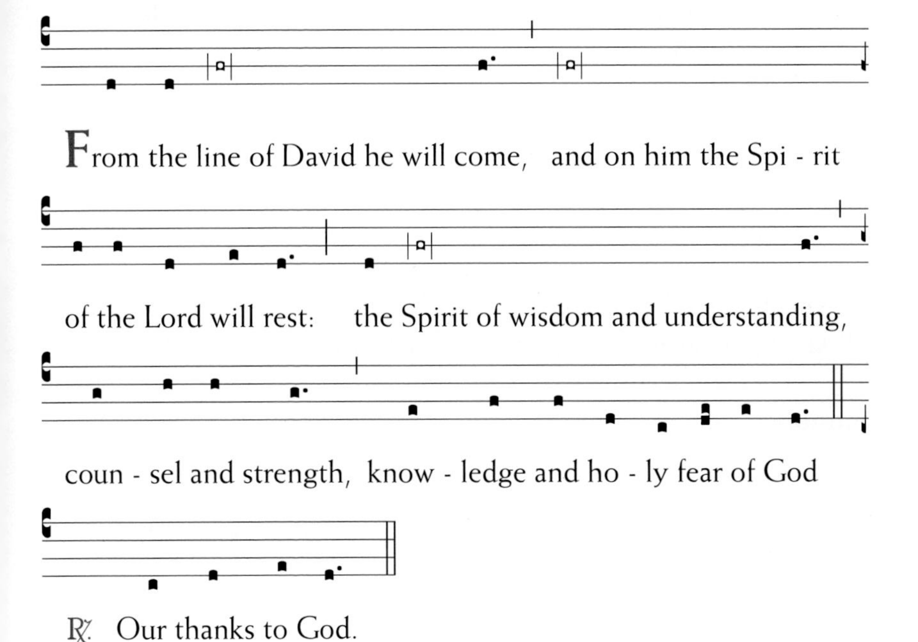

## READING AT NONE *(Isaiah 45: 8)*

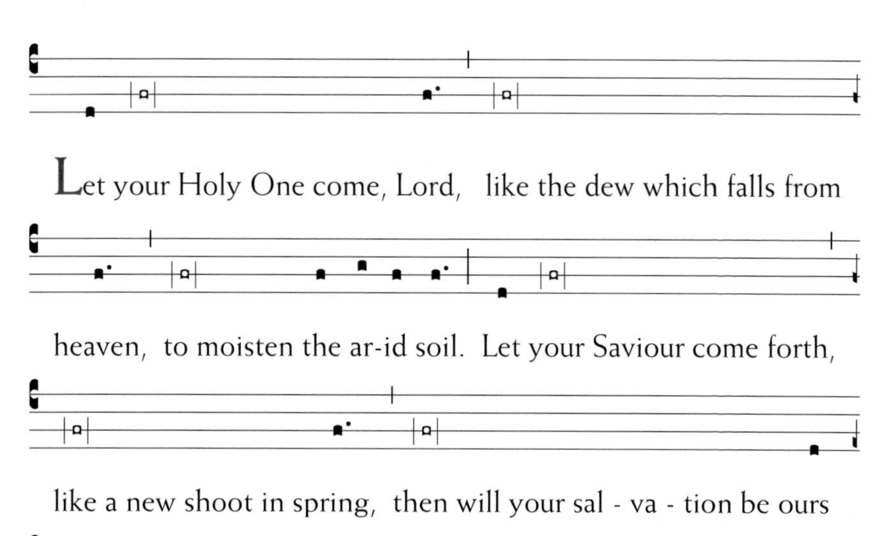


---

## HYMN AT VESPERS *on Sunday, Monday, Tuesday & Friday:*

**Sunday**

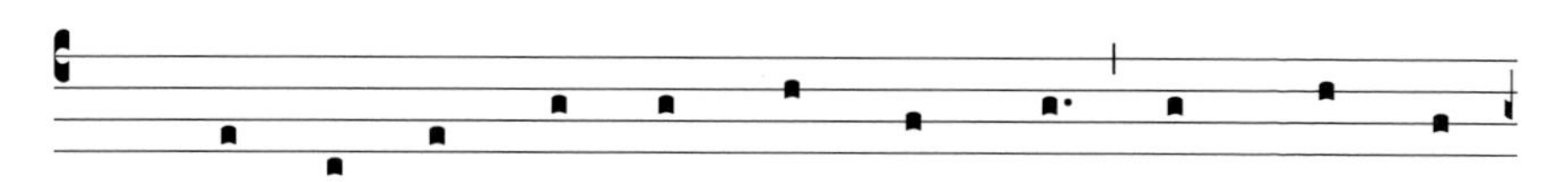

1. Christ, Son of God, true light from God, as eve - ning
2. We saw you, knew you, liv - ing here, Christ, Son of
3. Ma - ry we name you, bright-est Star, of Christ the
4. Guard us by night to rest in Christ, by day in
5. Pray Ma - ry Mo - ther full of grace, pray in your
6. Christ Son of God, we pray to you, and hon - our

1. comes to end our day, guard now our dark - ness
2. God, the Vir - gin's Son, as light from heav'n to
3. Sun, the light of light, shine now pro - claim the
4. ac - tion, thought and word, to do the will of
5. love for all we need, pro - tect us from all
6. you, the Vir - gin's Son; we praise the Fa - ther,

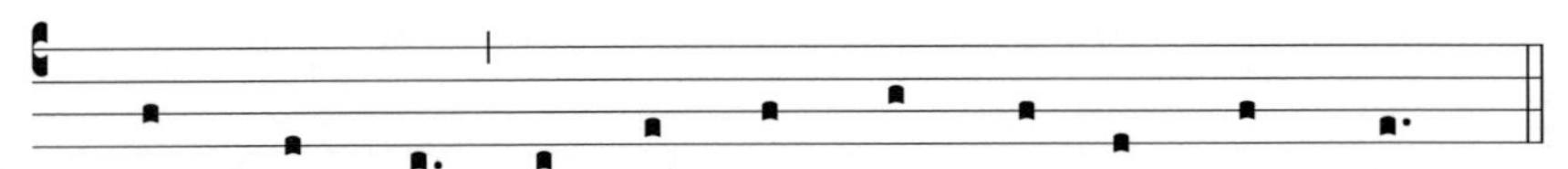

1. and our night, and guide our minds in love we pray.
2. be our life, as truth from God, to make God known.
3 dawn of day, pier- cing the clouds of sin's dark night.
4. Christ your Son, plea- sing to him who is our Lord.
5 dan - ger now and at our dy - ing in - ter - cede.
6. God with you and with the Spi - rit, Three in One.

6. A - men.

## Monday

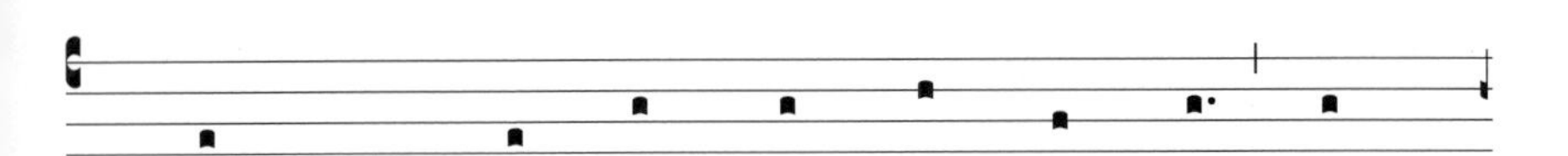

1. Christ, Lord Cre - a - tor, vir - gin born you
2. The an - gels and our - selves in pride a -
3. Re - pent - ant hearts you wel - come back, from
4. To all who do your ho - ly will, your
5. Grant, Lord, that we may come to you when
6. Pray Ma - ry Mo - ther full of grace, pray
7. Christ Son of God we pray to you, and

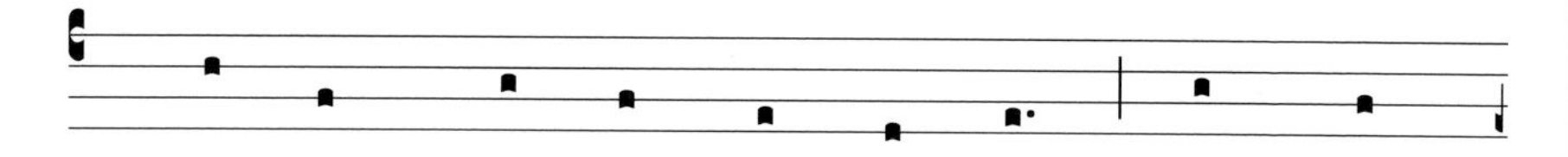

1. willed all things that are to be, you see
2. gainst your will and clear com-mands, ab - used
3. hard - ened hearts you turn a - way, you look
4. own true life is ours to share, make us
5. love is set a - part from pride, through Ma -
6. in your love for all we need; pro - tect
7. hon - our you, the Vir - gin's Son; we praise

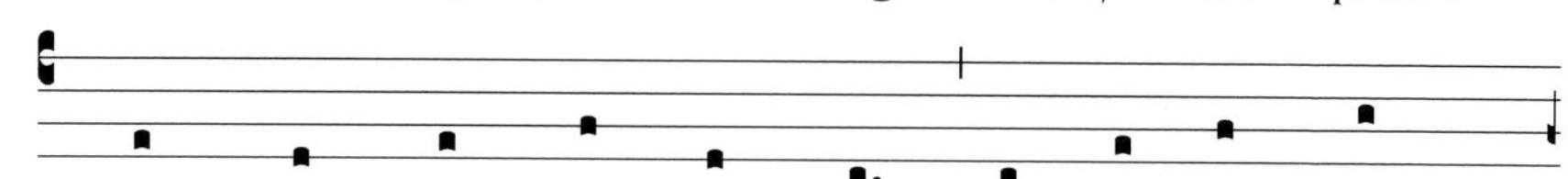

1. all things our hearts will choose yet in all things
2. your gift and so must bear the bur - den of
3 on those who look to you but not on those
4. o - bed - ient, quick to choose your will in all
5. ry's in - ter - ced - ing prayer call us for ev
6. us from all dan - ger now and at our dy-
7. the Fa - ther, God with you and with the Spi -

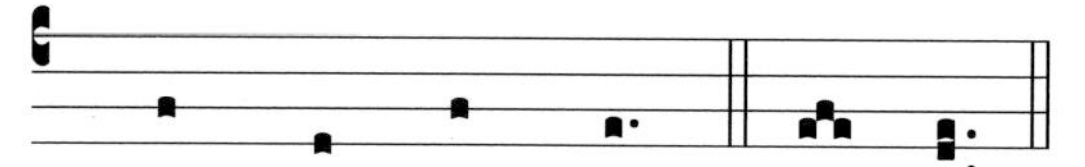

1. you leave us free.
2. your just de - mands.
3 who dis - o - bey.
4. things ev' - ry - where.
5. er to your side.
6. ing in - ter - cede.
7. rit, Three in One. A - men.

## Tuesday

1. Ma - ry, in you God took de - light, the
2. Pro - phets and pa - tri - archs made known your
3. Great joy to all that cho - sen race great
4. God's love which chose you for his Son, will
5. Pray Ma - ry Mo - ther full of grace, pray
6. Christ Son of God, we pray to you, and

1. an - gels praised you, yet to be, fore - told at
2. com - ing to God's cho - sen race, great joy to
3. joy to ev' - ry race to see the word of
4. ev - er Ma - ry, be our praise, your love for
5. in your love for all we need, pro - tect us
6. hon - our you, the Vir - gin's Son; we praise the

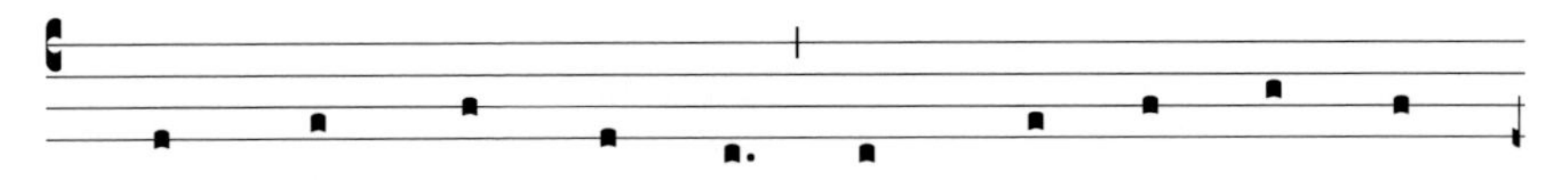

1. our first par - ents' fall man looked to you to
2. those whose child you were, to know and won - der
3. God ful - filled in you, God's Vir - gin Mo - ther
4. us, your prayer for us, will save us from our
5. from all dan - ger now, and at our dy - ing
6. Fa - ther God with you and with the Spi - rit

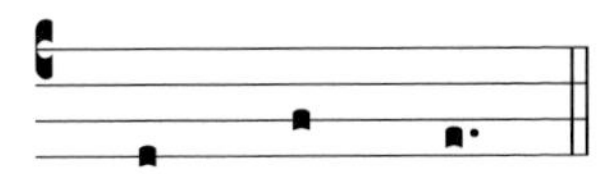

1. set man free.
2. at God's grace.
3 soon to be.

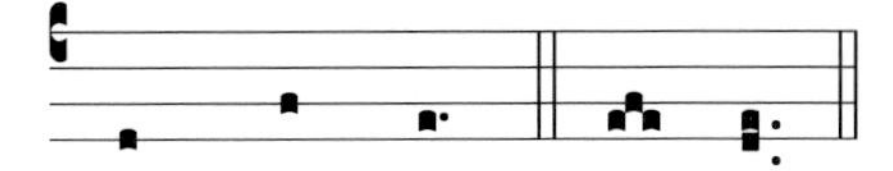

4. sin - ful ways.
5. in - ter - cede.
6. Three in One. A - men.

## Friday

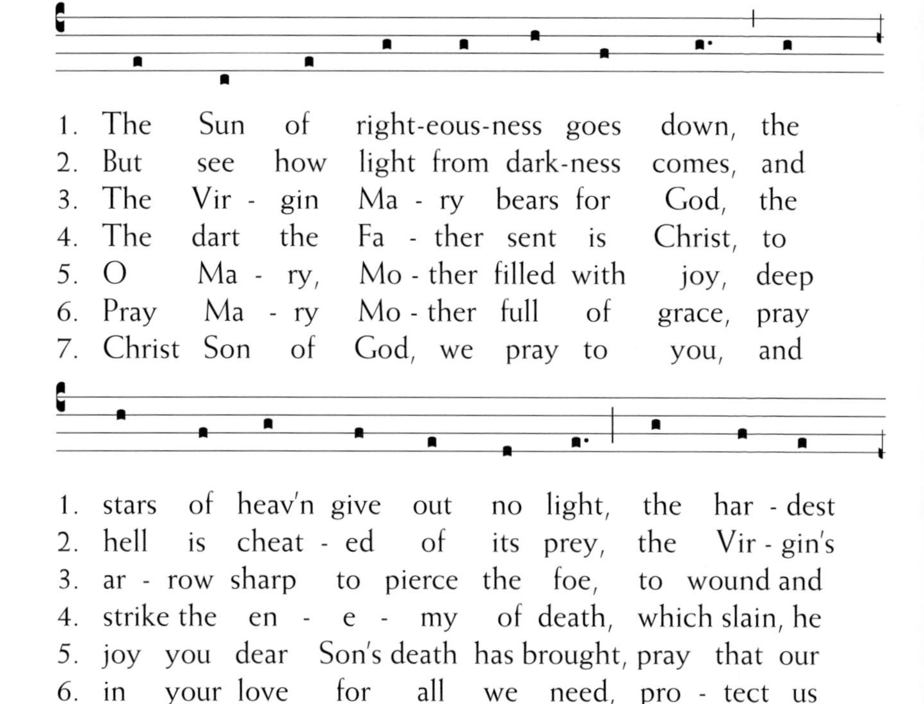


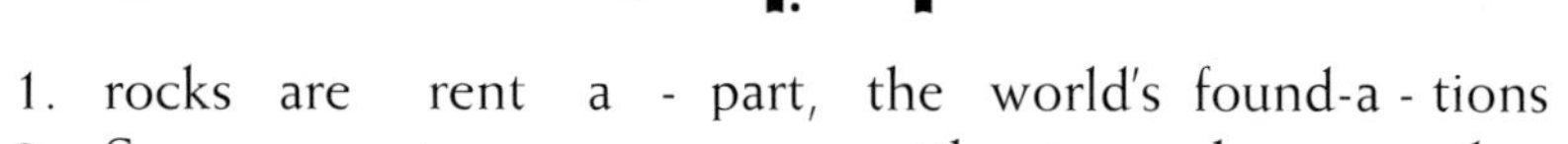

1. rocks are rent a - part, the world's found-a - tions
2. Son re - turns once more, with tro - phy won by
3. end his e - vil sway, which ev - er troub - les
4. gave us his own life, and liv - ing to his
5. hearts made free from sin, may flow - er with all
6. from all dan - ger now, and at our dy - ing
7. Fa - ther God with you and with the Spi - rit

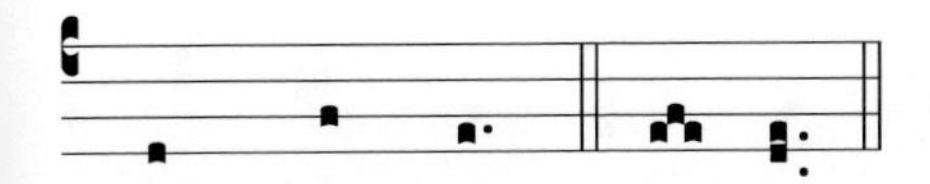

1. fail and shake.
2. his own blood.
3. all the world.
4. Fa - ther went.
5. vir - tues' grace.
6. in - ter - cede.
7. Three in One. A - men.

HYMN AT COMPLINE *for each day except Saturday:*

**Sunday**

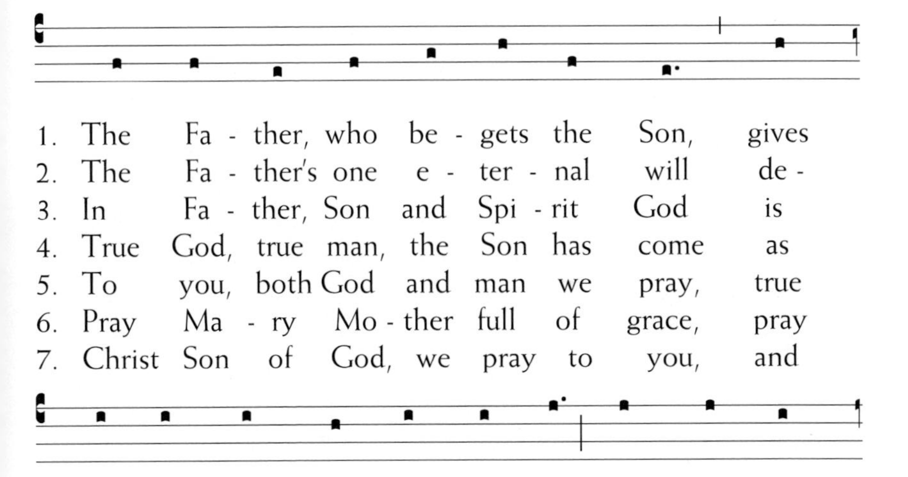


1. him the be - ing that is his; the Son and
2. crees that Ma - ry should be - come made rea - dy
3. U - ni - ty in Tri - ni - ty; in Ma - ry
4. man to men to make God known; the Vir - gin
5. God from God, God with us here; look on us,
6. in your love for all we need, pro - tect us
7. hon - our you, the Vir - gin's Son; we praise the

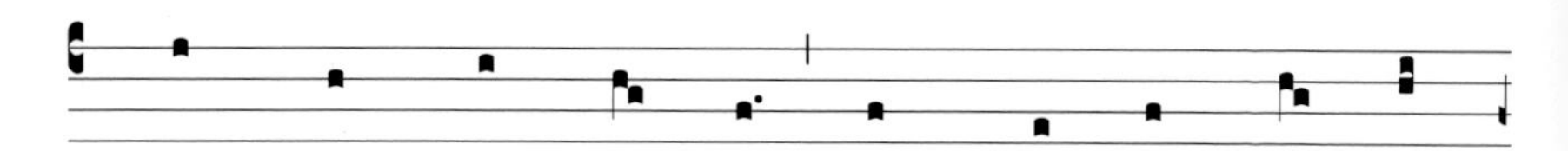

1. Fa - ther each in each, love with the love the
2. by his Spi - rit's power the Vir - gin Mo - ther
3. is true Moth - er - hood and yet most pure vir -
4. Mo - ther bears God's Son, the Son of God is
5. guide us in God's way and take from us all
6. from all dan - ger now, and at our dy - ing
7. Fa - ther God with you and with the Spi - rit

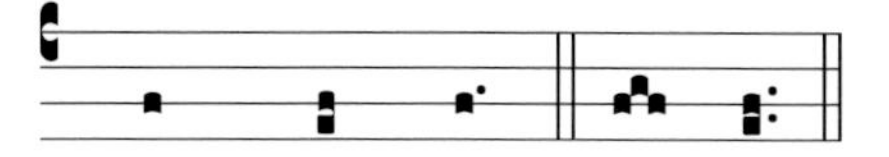

1. Spi - rit is.
2. of his Son.
3. gi - ni - ty.
4. hers a - lone.
5. sin and fear.
6. in - ter - cede.
7. Three in One. A - men.

---

**Monday**

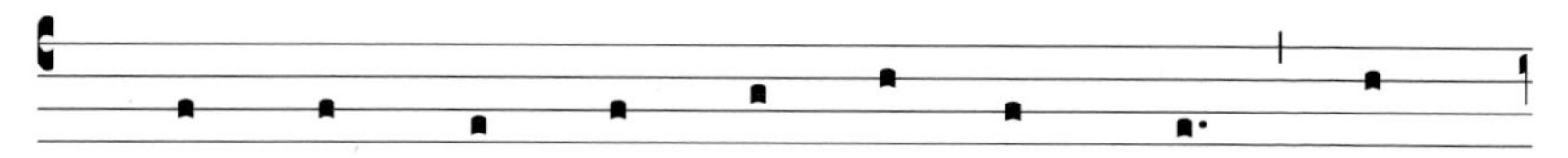

1. God's heaven is God him - self, who wills cre -
2. This, this is heaven, to be with God, in
3. Yet in God's time there came to earth a
4. We found a li - ly gro-wing here, a
5. Christ, seed of Ma - ry, flower of grace, grow
6. Pray Ma - ry Mo - ther full of grace, pray
7. Christ Son of God, we pray to you, and

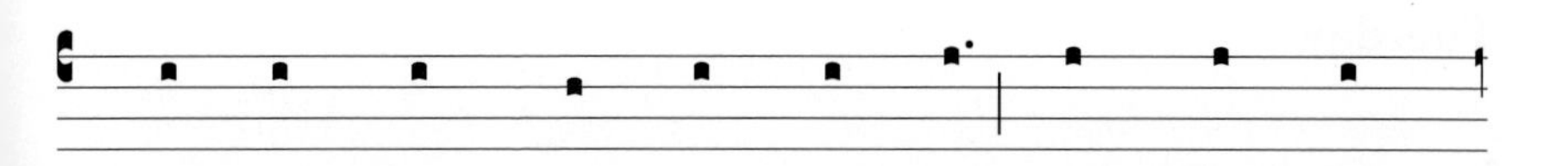

1. a - tion and cre - a - tion's praise, who brings forth
2. ev - er - las - ting joy with him, where flowers of
3. gent- ler breath, a sa - ving dew, to wa - ter
4. low- ly plant, to bloom a - lone, but not to
5. in earth's gar - den ev' - ry- where, grow in our
6. in your love for all we need, pro - tect us
7. hon - our you, the Vir - gin's Son; we praise the

1. beau - ty from his thought, and makes all ho - ly
2. grace and good-ness grow, not touched by earth's cold
3. and re - fresh all lands and make with sweet-ness
4. die – to live and bear the pre- cious seed which
5. hearts, bring forth in us, the fruits you look to
6. from all dan - ger now, and at our dy - ing
7. Fa - ther God with you and with the Spi - rit

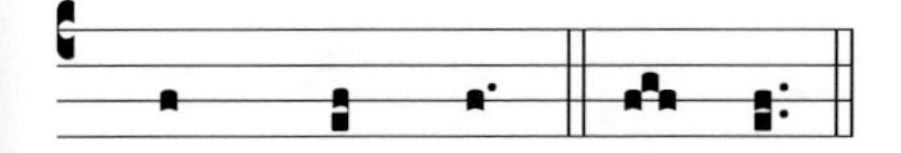

1. in his grace.
2. winds of sin.
3. all things new.
4. God had sown.
5. us to bear.
6. in - ter - cede.
7. Three in One. A - men.

**Tuesday**

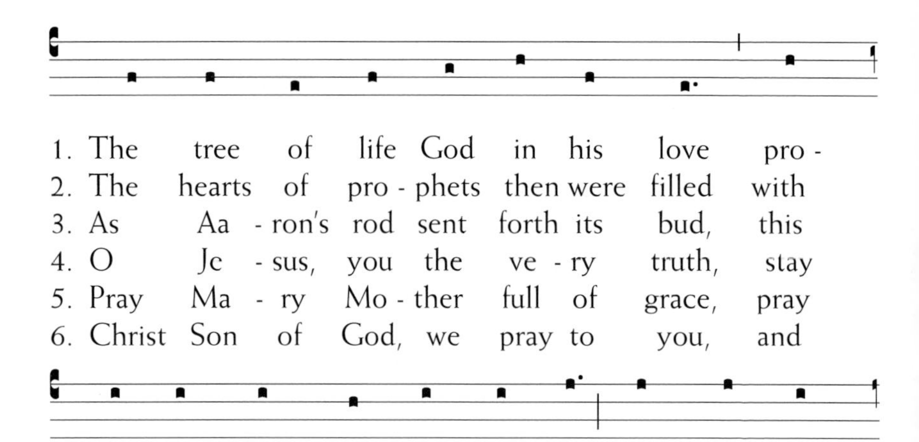


1. vi - ded for the hu - man race, the en - e -
2. sweet and sac - red flame to tell the mar - vel
3. mai - den should bring forth a fruit, and he would
4. with us now and e - ver- more, lest that same
5. in your love for all we need, pro - tect us
6. hon - our you, the Vir - gin's Son; we praise the

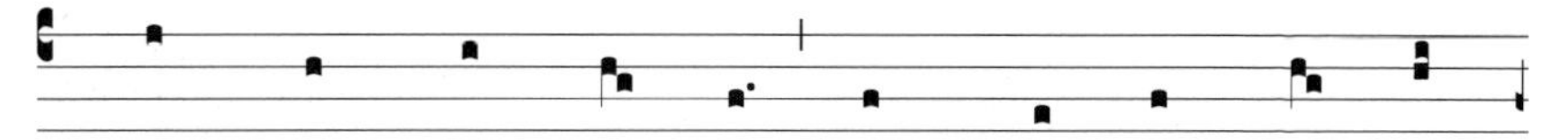

1. my by ly - ing words spread dead - ly poi - son
2. that was yet to come, a Vir - gin who would
3. bring a draught of life to those the e - ne -
4. fierce and ly - ing foe en - snare us by his
5. from all dan - ger now, and at our dy - ing
6. Fa - ther God with you and with the Spi - rit

1. in its place.
2. all ex - cel.
3. my had hurt.
4. craf - ty lore.
5. in - ter - cede.
6. Three in One. A - men.

## Wednesday

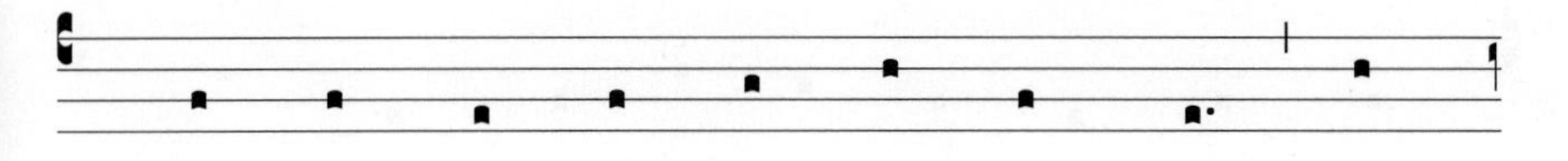

1. This is the gate through which Christ comes, the
2. This is the gate through which Christ comes, in -
3. This is the gate through which Christ comes, to
4. To all who hear him and be - lieve, Christ
5. Pray Ma - ry Mo - ther full of grace, pray
6. Christ Son of God, we pray to you, and

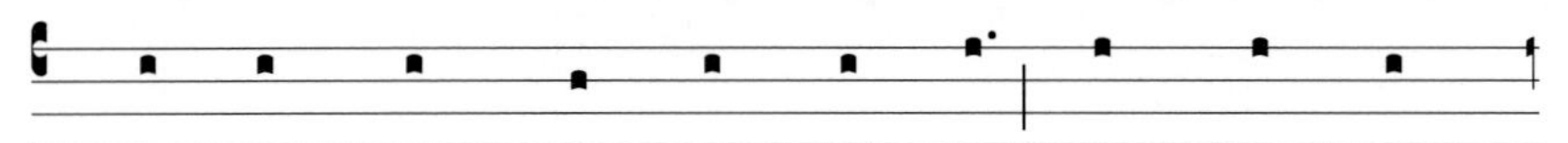

1. Vir - gin in her low - li - ness, made Vir - gin
2. to this sin - ful world of men, and he a -
3. die and rise as King and Lord, and call to
4. is the hope of life and rest, to her the
5. in your love for all we need, pro - tect us
6. hon - our you, the Vir - gin's Son; we praise the

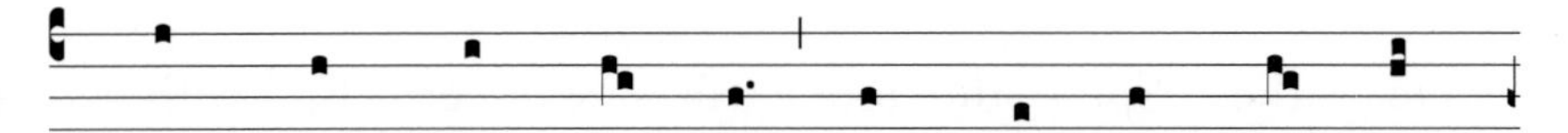

1. Mo - ther by God's will, in full - est grace and
2. lone of men has right to op - en and to
3. all to en - ter in to his new king - dom
4. gate through which he comes her glo - ry and her
5. from all dan - ger now, and at our dy - ing
6. Fa - ther God with you and with the Spi - rit

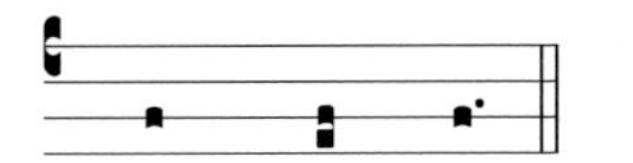

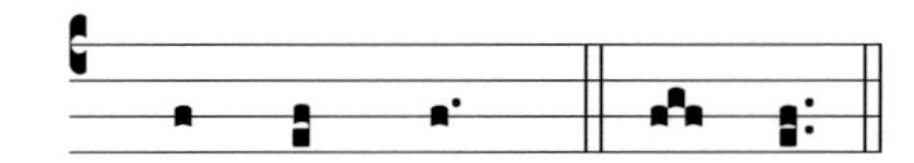

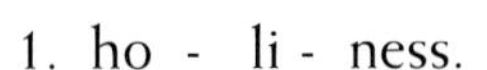

1. ho - li - ness.
2. close a - gain.
3. and re - ward.

4. joy most blessed.
5. in - ter - cede.
6. Three in One. A - men.

**Thursday**

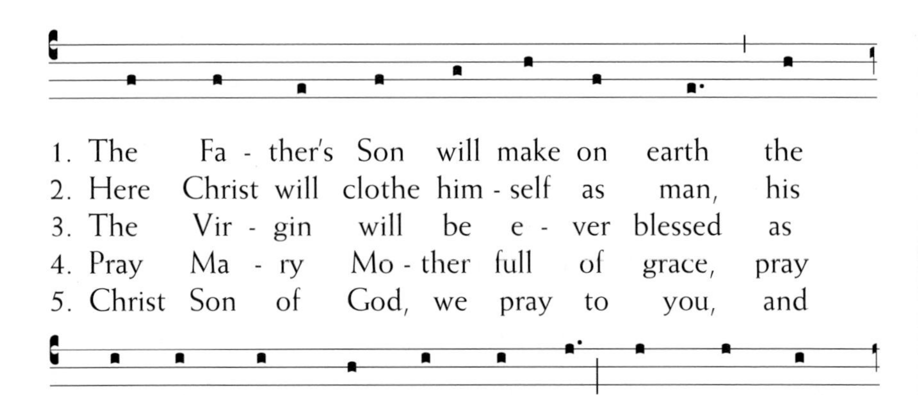

1. The Fa - ther's Son will make on earth the
2. Here Christ will clothe him - self as man, his
3. The Vir - gin will be e - ver blessed as
4. Pray Ma - ry Mo - ther full of grace, pray
5. Christ Son of God, we pray to you, and

1. Vir - gin's womb his dwel - ling place, the Fa - ther
2. God-head's glo - ry set a - side, and an - gels
3. Vir - gin Mo - ther of her Lord, and as his
4. in your love for all we need, pro - tect us
5. hon - our you, the Vir - gin's Son; we praise the

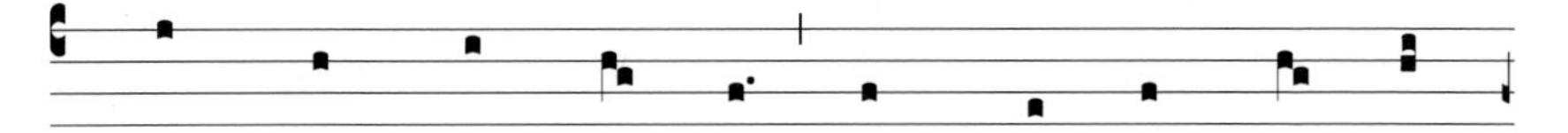

1. and the Spi - rit too will ev - er be with
2. see him and ac - claim the Bride-groom co - ming
3. heaven-ly bride bring forth child - ren of grace to
4. from all dan - ger now, and at our dy - ing
5. Fa - ther God with you and with the Spi - rit

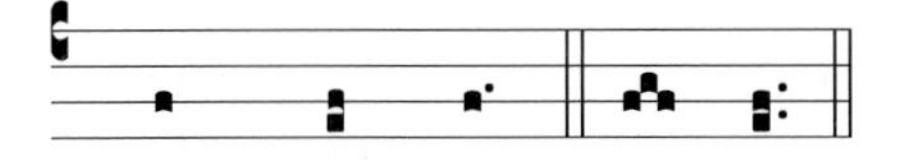

1. her in grace.
2. to his Bride.
3. heaven's re-ward.
4. in - ter - cede.
5. Three in One. A - men.

## Friday

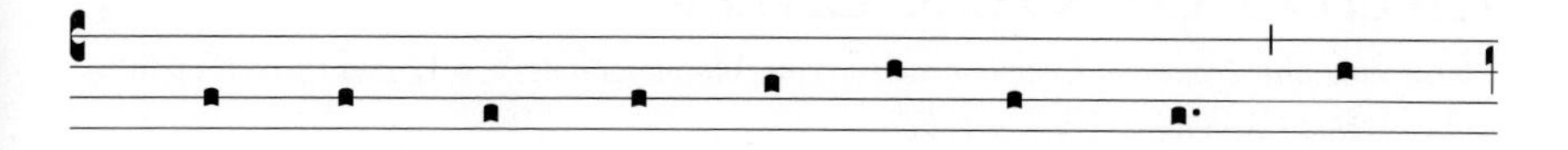

1. This Rose, more fair than earth - ly flowers, the
2. Heart-pierced she stands be - side her Son to
3. Yet in her heart the words of Christ with-
4. Ma - ry, as once the Ark of old wel-
5. Pray Ma - ry Mo - ther full of grace, pray
6. Christ Son of God, we pray to you, and

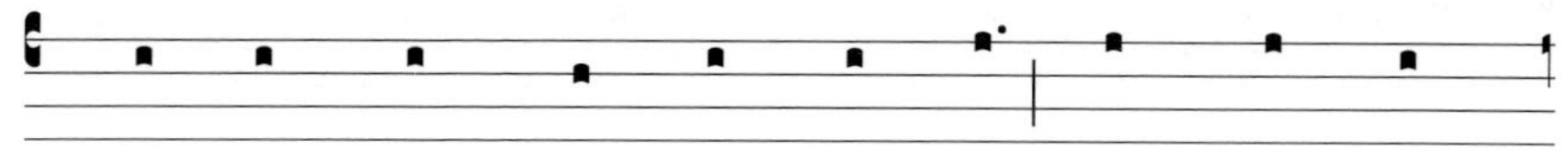

1. Vir - gin with her child new-born, hears in her
2. see his death, sin's great price paid; this earth's re -
3. stand the un - be - lief of men, bring to her
4. comed God's sign brought by a dove, we know through
5. in your love for all we need, pro - tect us
6. hon - our you, the Vir - gin's Son; we praise the

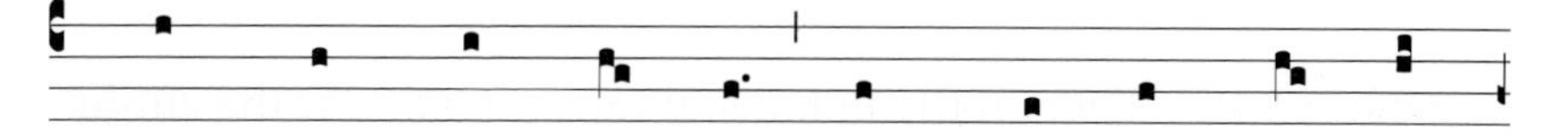

1. joy sad words fore- tell a pal - er rose, a
2. dem - ption dear - ly won and earth's dread tomb where
3. sor - row su - rest hope that he who died will
4. you God's sa - ving gifts, his truth, his mer - cy
5. from all dan - ger now, and at our dy - ing
6. Fa - ther God with you and with the Spi - rit

1. pierc- ing thorn.
2. he is laid.
3. rise a - gain.

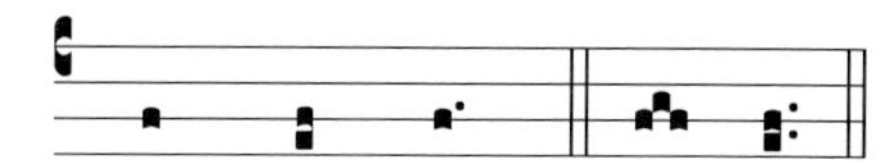

4. and his love.
5. in - ter - cede.
6. Three in One. A - men.

*Advent*

# LAUDS OF OUR LADY

*This is sung after None and Compline each day in Advent, with its ℣. & ℟. and Prayer, up to and including Compline on Christmas Eve.*

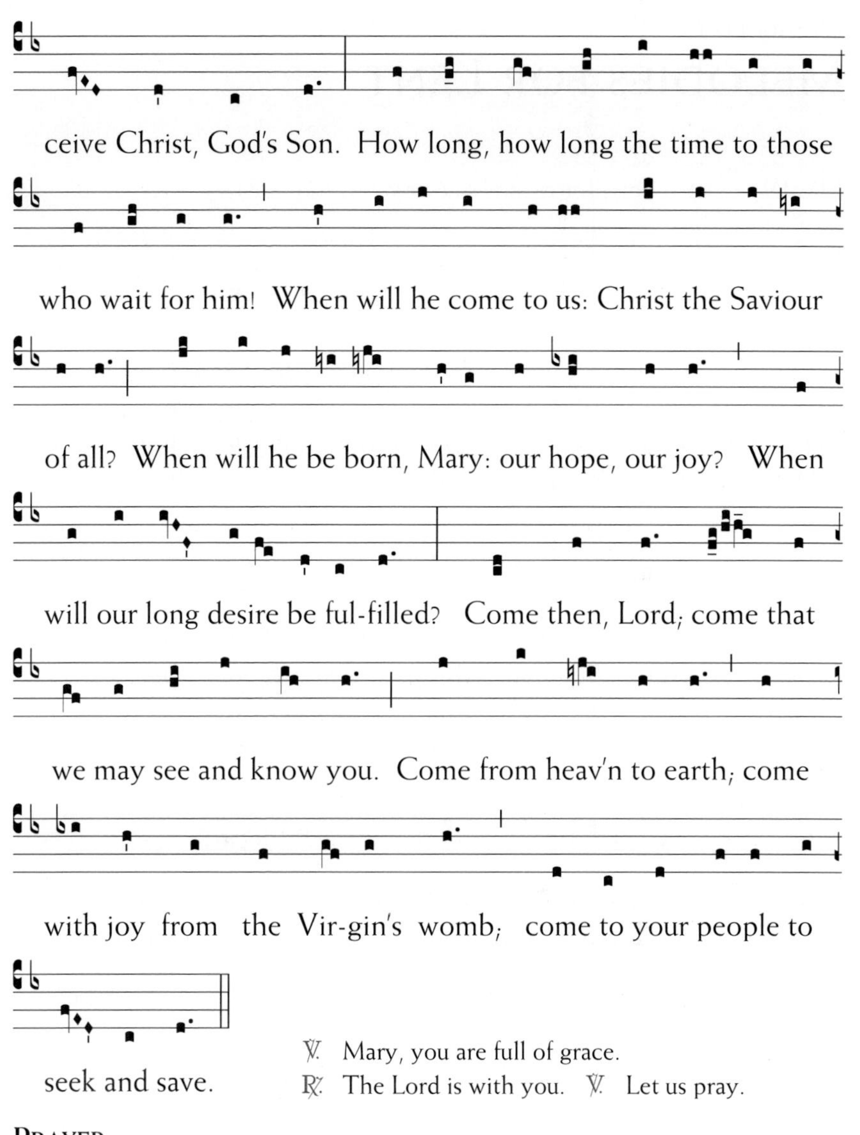


℣. Mary, you are full of grace.
℟. The Lord is with you. ℣. Let us pray.

## Prayer

O Lord, you have willed that your Word should take flesh in the womb of the blessed Virgin Mary at the message of an angel. We, your suppliants, believe her to be truly the Mother of God. Grant to us that we may be helped by her intercession with you. Through the same Jesus Christ, our Lord. ℟. Amen.

**Closing Prayers** 'Mary, rejoice in God…' *as on Sunday page 107.*

*During Lent*

# MELODIES FOR LENT

**HYMN** *for Vespers during Lent on Sunday, Monday, Tuesday & Friday.*

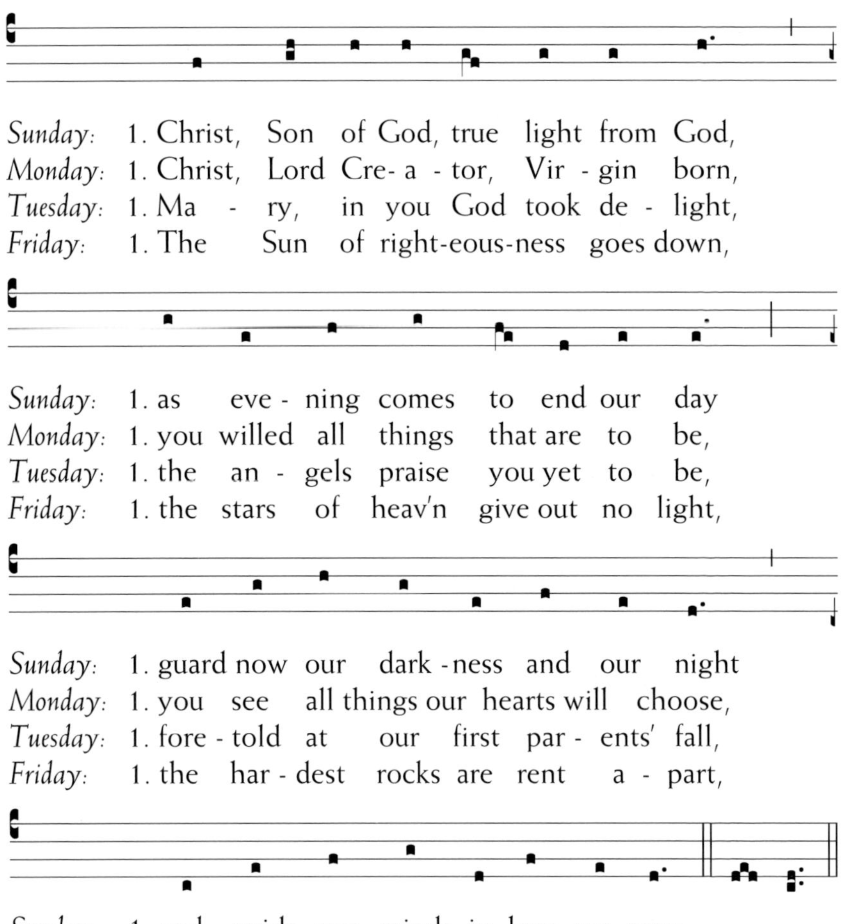

## Sunday

1. Christ, Son of God, true light from God,
as evening comes to end our day,
guard now our darkness and our night
and guide our minds in love we pray.

2. We saw you, knew you living here,
Christ, Son of God, the Virgin's Son,
as light from heav'n to be our life,
as truth from God, to make God known.

3. Mary we name you brightest Star,
of Christ the Sun, the light of light,
shine now proclaim the dawn of day,
piercing the clouds of sin's dark night.

4. Guard us by night to rest in Christ,
by day in action, thought and word,
to do the will of Christ your Son,
pleasing to him who is our Lord.

5. Pray Mary Mother, full of grace,
pray in your love for all we need;
protect us from all danger now,
and at our dying intercede.

6. Christ, Son of God, we pray to you,
and honour you, the Virgin's Son.
We praise the Father, God with you,
and with the Spirit, Three in One. Amen.

## Monday

1. Christ, Lord Creator, virgin born,
you willed all things that are to be,
you see all things our hearts will choose
yet in all things you leave us free.

2. The angels and ourselves in pride
against your will and clear commands,

abused your gift and so must bear
the burden of your just demands.

3. Repentant hearts you welcome back,
from hardened hearts you turn away,
you look on those who look to you
but not on those who disobey.

4. To all who do your holy will,
your own true life is ours to share;
make us obedient, quick to choose
your will in all things ev'rywhere.

5. Grant, Lord, that we may come to you
when love is set apart from pride,
through Mary's interceding prayer,
call us for ever to your side.

6. Pray Mary Mother, full of grace...

7. Christ, Son of God, we pray to you...

## Tuesday

1. Mary, in you God took delight,
the angels praised you, yet to be,
foretold at our first parents' fall
man looked to you to set man free.

2. Prophets and patriarchs made known
your coming to God's chosen race,
great joy to those whose child you were,
to know and wonder at God's grace.

3. Great joy to all that chosen race,
great joy to ev'ry race to see
the word of God fulfilled in you,
God's Virgin Mother soon to be.

4. God's love which chose you for his Son,
will ever Mary, be our praise,
your love for us, your prayer for us,
will save us from our sinful ways.

5. Pray Mary Mother, full of grace...

6. Christ, Son of God, we pray to you...

## Friday

1. The Sun of righteousness goes down,
the stars of heav'n give out no light,
the hardest rocks are rent apart,
the world's foundations fail and shake.

2. But see how light from darkness comes,
and hell is cheated of its prey,
the Virgin's Son returns once more,
with trophy won by his own blood.

3. The Virgin Mary bears for God,
the arrow sharp to pierce the foe,
to wound and end his evil sway,
which ever troubles all the world.

4. The dart the Father sent is Christ,
to strike the enemy of death,
which slain, he gave us his own life
and living to his Father went.

5. O Mary Mother full of joy,
deep joy your dear Son's death has brought,
pray that our hearts made free from sin
may flower with all virtue's grace.

6. Pray Mary Mother, full of grace...

7. Christ, Son of God, we pray to you...

**HYMN** *for Small Hours (Terce, Sext & None) each day during Lent.*

## Sunday

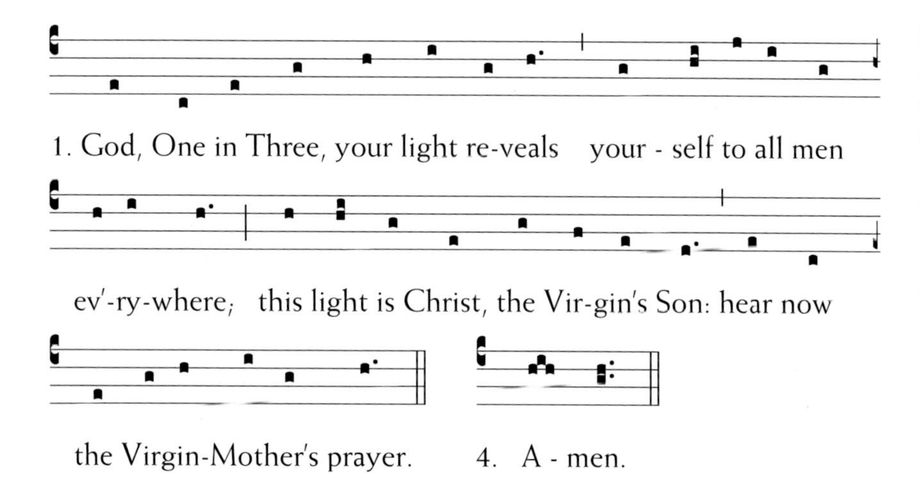


2. For she who came by your decree
first sign of dawn in our dark night,
holds out to all men everywhere
her Son, your all-revealing Light.

3. Pray Mary Mother, full of grace,
pray in your love for all we need;
protect us from all danger now,
and at our dying intercede.

4. Christ, Son of God, we pray to you,
and honour you, the Virgin's Son.
We praise the Father, God with you,
and with the Spirit, Three in One. Amen.

## Monday

1. God made you, Mary in his grace,
creation's crown most blessed of all:
so we are blessed who find in you
strength and protection when we call.

2. Strength and correction when we fall,
and grace to drive all sin away,
new love to win God's love again,
your love and mercy as we pray.

3. Pray Mary Mother, full of grace…

4. Christ, Son of God, we pray to you...

## Tuesday

1. Come, Lord Creator Spirit, come,
inspire our hearts to tell again
that news your prophets once foretold,
God virgin-born and peace to men.

2. Come in our need as Advocate,
Consoler of our troubled days;
come for her sake whom you have made
Virgin and Mother by your grace.

3. Pray Mary Mother, full of grace…

4. Christ, Son of God, we pray to you...

## Wednesday

1. See how fierce flames of three-fold fire,
have wilted all fair things of earth;
see how a fountain springs on high,
and with fresh flowers the land gives birth.

2. O Virgin fountain of delights,
water our withered hearts and bless;
that they bedewed with heaven's grace,
may bring forth flowers of holiness.

3. Pray Mary Mother, full of grace...

4. Christ, Son of God, we pray to you...

## Thursday

1. Christ, Lord and King, in mercy come,
come, take our hearts to be your own;
to love and serve you in all things,
to praise you for yourself alone.

2. Remember, Lord, that for our sake,
a sinless Virgin's Child you came
as man to men to save all men,
salvation we your own may claim.

3. Pray Mary Mother, full of grace...

4. Christ, Son of God, we pray to you...

## Friday

1. Could there be joy so great as hers,
to be the Mother of God's Son?
Could there be sorrow deep as hers,
to see the evil men have done?

2. Mary, keep ever in our minds
your share in Christ's most bitter pain;
and through your sufferings make us know
how earth and earthly things are vain.

3. Jesus, keep ever in our hearts
your bitter death, that we may learn
the depths of your great love for men,
and ever love you in return.

4. Pray Mary Mother, full of grace…

5. Christ, Son of God, we pray to you...

## Saturday

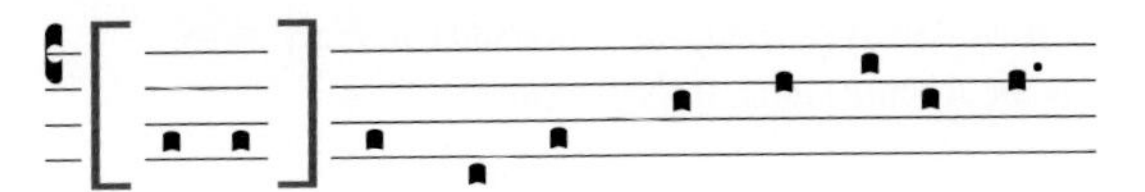

1. [Vir-gin], your Son has willed and e-ver wills
all angels, men, and every thing;
so we may pray to you as Queen,
who in God's grace brought forth God's King.

2. Look from your throne in heaven to earth,
show for us all a Mother's care,
lead all to love and serve your Son,
who hears with love his Mother's prayer.

3. Pray Mary Mother, full of grace…

4. Christ, Son of God, we pray to you...

*During Lent*

# COMPLINE

*This Lenten Compline is used each day from Ash Wednesday to Wednesday in Holy Week inclusive; except on Solemnities, such as the Annunciation, if they occur.*

**OPENING PRAYERS** *as before Sunday Compline (pages 95 - 96).*

**ANTIPHON** *(Short) as in Friday Compline (page 344).*

**Psalms 131, 132 & 133** *as on Sunday (pages 97 - 98).*

**ANTIPHON** *(In full) as in Friday Compline (page 344).*

**READING** *as on Sunday (page 99).*

## SHORT RESPONSORY

℣. There then they laid him, where no man had yet been laid,

there to sleep, to sleep a-while, and rest in the peace of God.

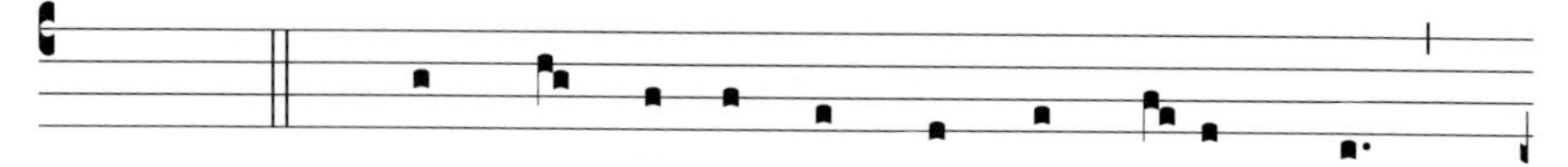

℟. *Repeat.* ℣. Christ chose for rest-ing place the Virgin's womb,

that from a Mo-ther he should come, yet leave the Mo-ther

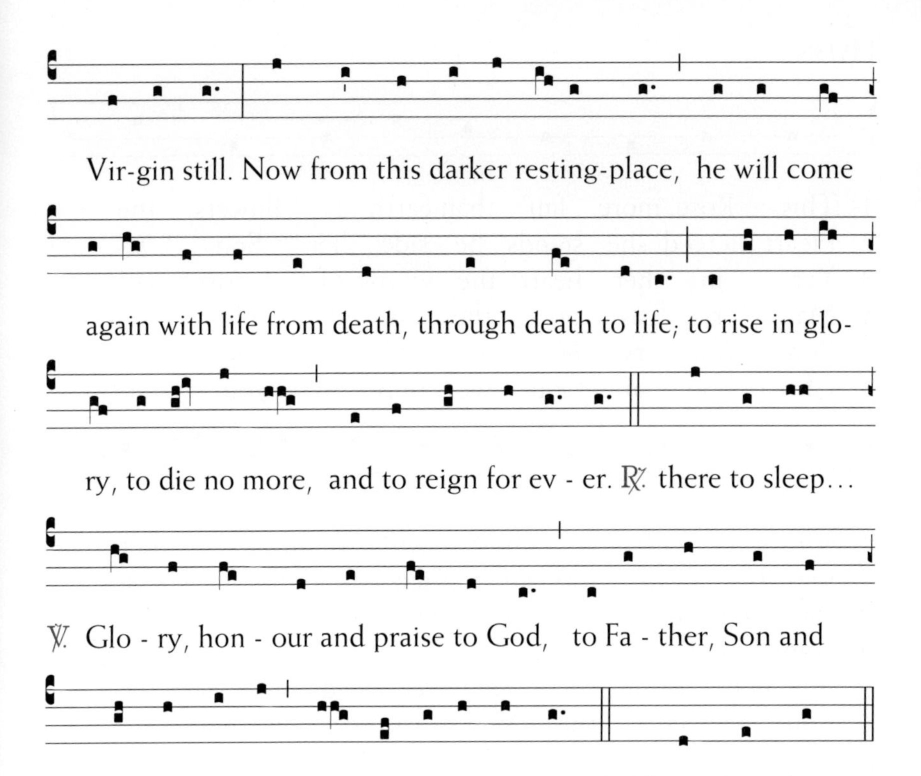
Vir-gin still. Now from this darker resting-place, he will come
again with life from death, through death to life; to rise in glo-
ry, to die no more, and to reign for ev - er. ℟. there to sleep…
℣. Glo - ry, hon - our and praise to God, to Fa - ther, Son and
Ho - ly Spi - rit, now and ev-er, A-men. ℟. There then they…

Rosa Mystica

## Hymn

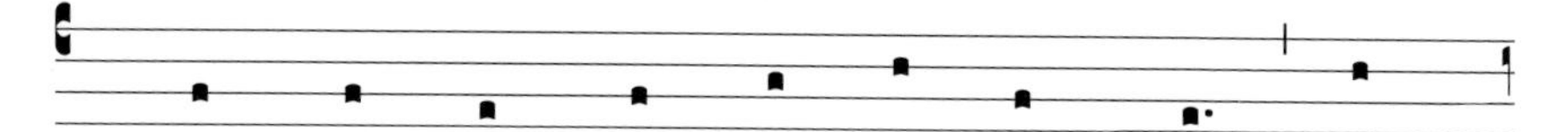

1. This Rose, more fair than earth - ly flowers, the
2. Heart-pierced she stands be - side her Son to
3. Yet in her heart the words of Christ with-
4. Ma - ry, as once the ark of old wel-
5. Pray Ma - ry Mo - ther full of grace, pray
6. Christ Son of God, we pray to you, and

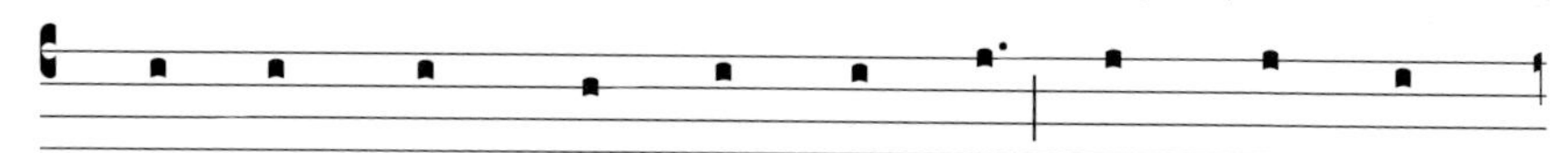

1. Vir - gin with her child new-born, hears in her
2. see his death, sin's great price paid, this earth's re -
3. stand the un - be - lief of men, bring to her
4. comed God's sign brought by a dove, we know through
5. in your love for all we need, pro - tect us
6. hon - our you, the Vir - gin's Son; we praise the

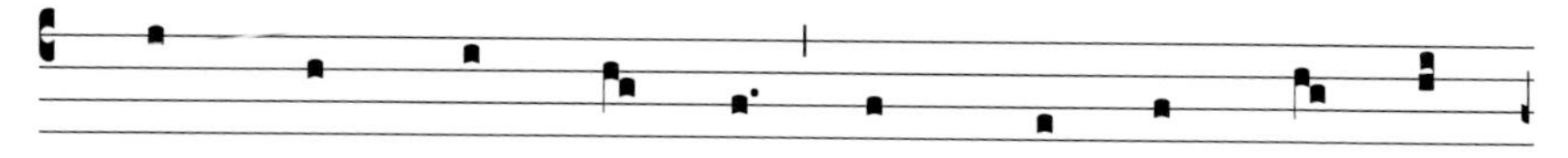

1. joy sad words fore- tell a pal - er rose, a
2. dem - ption dear - ly won and earth's dread tomb where
3. sor - row su - rest hope that he who died will
4. you God's sa - ving gifts, his truth, his mer - cy
5. from all dan - ger now, and at our dy - ing
6. Fa - ther God with you and with the Spi - rit

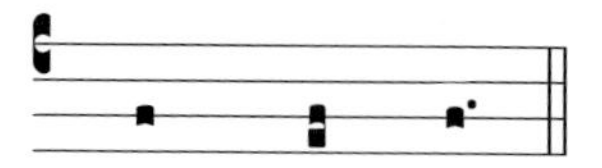

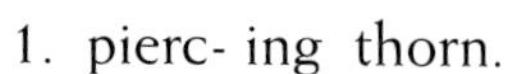

1. pierc- ing thorn.
2. he is laid.
3. rise a - gain.

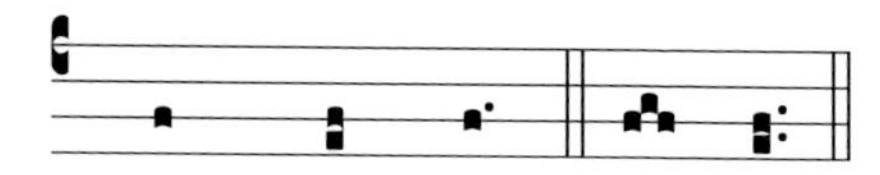

4. and his love.
5. in - ter - cede.
6. Three in One. A - men.

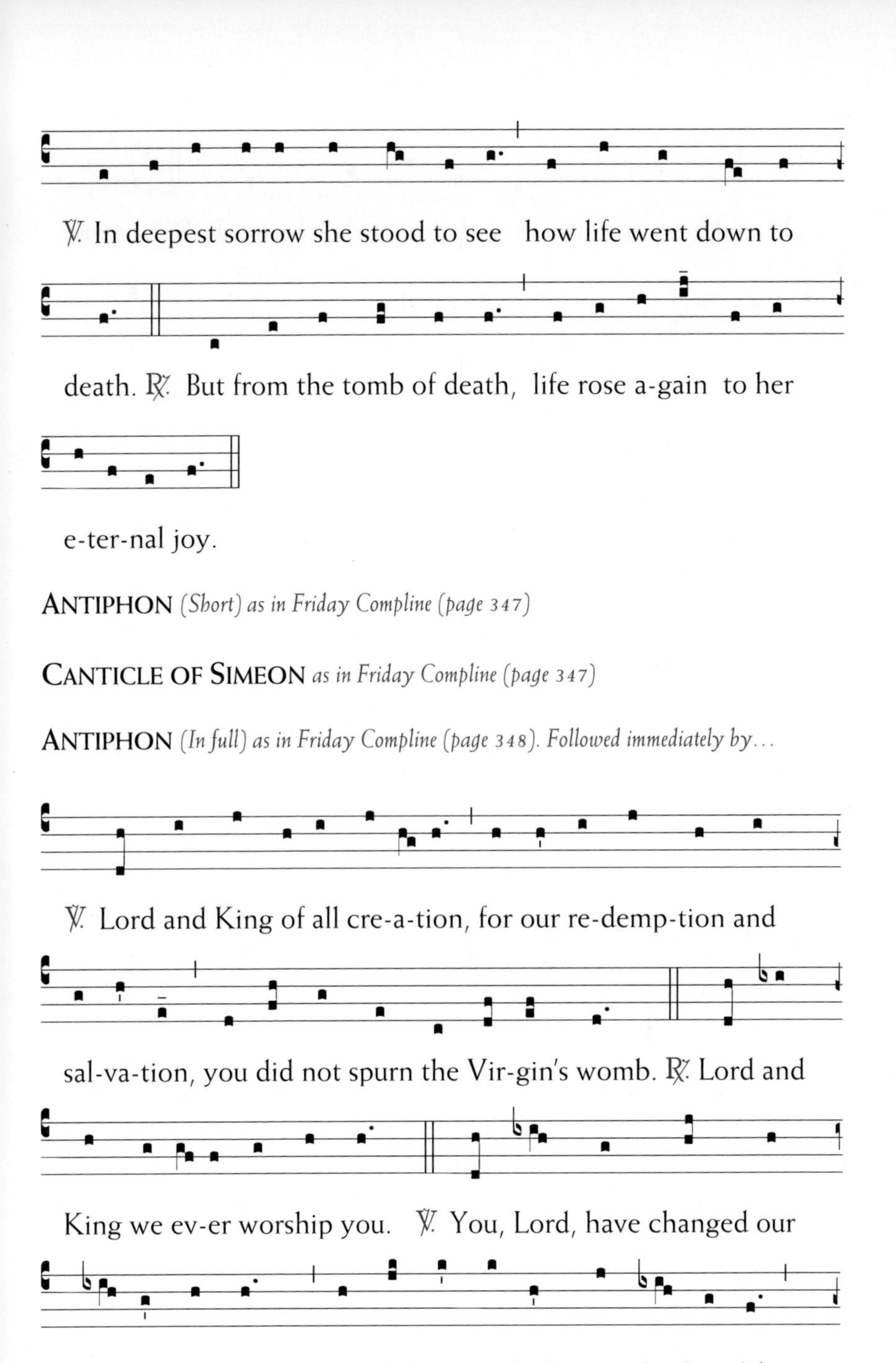
℣. In deepest sorrow she stood to see how life went down to
death. ℟. But from the tomb of death, life rose a-gain to her
e-ter-nal joy.
ANTIPHON (Short) as in Friday Compline (page 347)
CANTICLE OF SIMEON as in Friday Compline (page 347)
ANTIPHON (In full) as in Friday Compline (page 348). Followed immediately by…
℣. Lord and King of all cre-a-tion, for our re-demp-tion and
sal-va-tion, you did not spurn the Vir-gin's womb. ℟. Lord and
King we ev-er worship you. ℣. You, Lord, have changed our
weakness to strength, our darkness to light, our death to life;

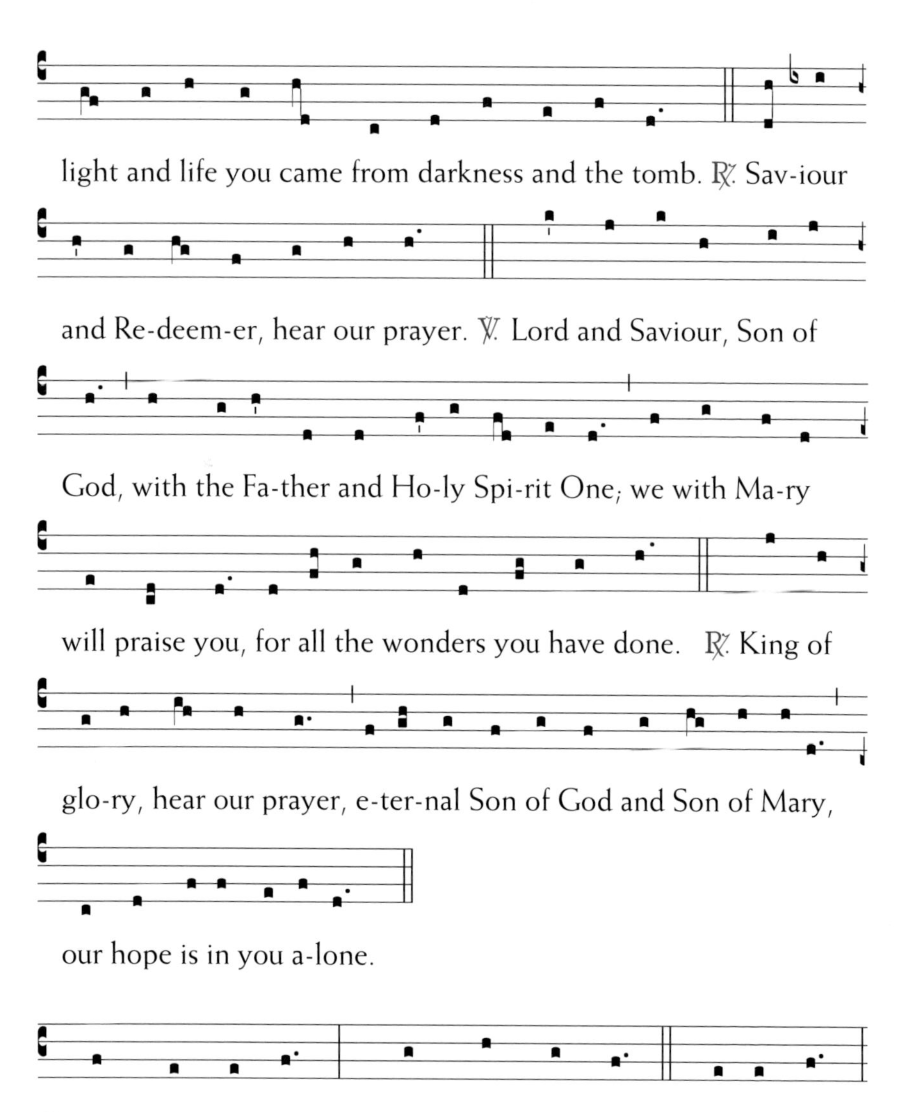


**PRAYER** *as on Sunday,* *page 104.*

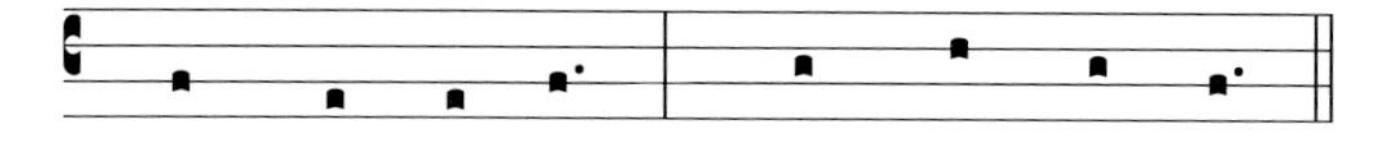

## THANKSGIVING

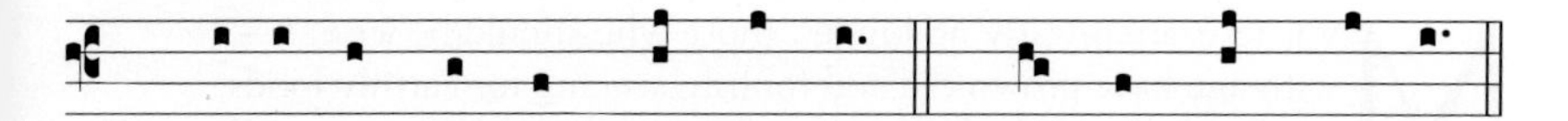

℣. Glo-ry, hon-our and praise to God. ℟. And our thanks to him.

℣. Mary, you are full of grace, the Lord is with you.
℟. Mary, you are most blessed of all women, for Jesus Christ is your Son.

**LAUDS OF OUR LADY** *of the day occurring until Passiontide then as on Friday* *(page 349).*

℣. Pray for us, holy Virgin Mary, Mother of God.
℟. That we may be made worthy of the promises of Jesus Christ.
℣. Let us pray.

## PRAYER

Forgive, we ask you Lord, the sins of your servants: and may we who of ourselves are unable to please you, be saved by the prayers of the Mother of your Son, Jesus Christ our Lord. ℟. Amen.

**CLOSING PRAYERS :** 'Mary, rejoice in God...' *as on Sunday, page 107.*

---

*Readings in*

# PASSIONTIDE

## READINGS IN PASSIONTIDE

*During Passiontide, Friday's Office is used every day.*

LAUDS *(Lamentations 17: 18, 19)*

My people, look on me and see my sorrow:
my children have let themselves be taken captive by sin;
my friends have turned from me when I called them.

TERCE *(Lamentations 1: 19)*

My priests are priestly no longer; those who should be wise with age have grown old and foolish, seeking for earthly foods, not heavenly wisdom.

SEXT *(Lamentations 1: 20)*

I the Virgin-Mother of Christ, pray to the Lord, my God. Look on me, Lord and God, and see how great is my suffering, how deep the sorrow of my heart. Could there be suffering and sorrow so deep as mine?

NONE *(Lamentations 1: 20, 21)*

The promised sword of sorrow has pierced my soul. Could there be consolation for sorrow so deep?

VESPERS *(Lamentations 1: 21, 22)*

Those who passed by mocked at me, and rejoiced at my suffering. Could there be sorrow so deep as mine?

## PRAYER DURING PASSIONTIDE

The most holy soul of your Mother, Mary, O Lord Jesus Christ, was pierced with a sword at the time of your Passion. May this blessed Virgin, we pray you, intercede for us with your mercy, now and at the hour of our death, you who are God, living and reigning with the Father, in the unity of the Holy Spirit, for ever and ever. ℟. Amen.

*During Pentecost*

# TERCE FOR PENTECOST

*(Sunday, Monday & Tuesday)*

**Sunday**

OPENING PRAYERS *(with music: pages 55 - 56).*

HYMN *for Terce, Sext and None on Pentecost Sunday.*

Come, Lord Creator Spirit, *(with music: page 166).*

ANTIPHON

TONE I

Ma-ry, Mother,

**Psalm 118** *(vv. 33 – 48),* **Psalm 118** *(vv. 49 – 64)* & **Psalm 118** *(vv. 65 – 80)*
*(See pages 48 to 50.)*

ANTIPHON

Ma-ry, **Mother,** help us to resist the attraction of foolish things,

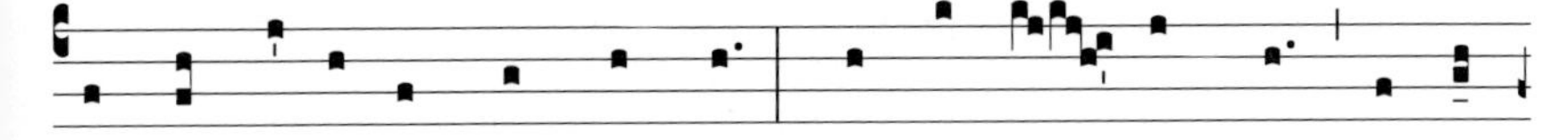

and seek only the things of God. Make us strong in Christ, to will

as you willed the things for which he made us.

**READING** *(Eccles. 24:9)*

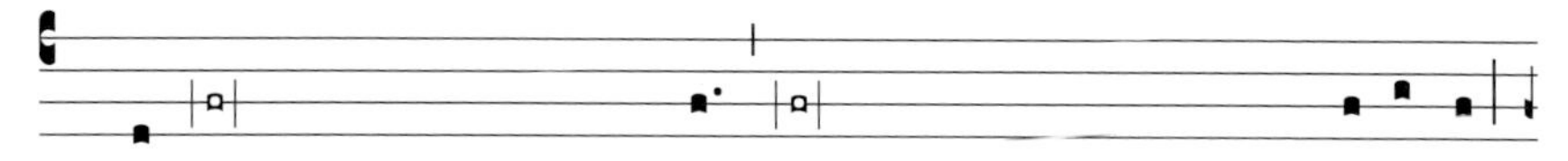

In the eternal decree of God, I was present before his cre-a-ting

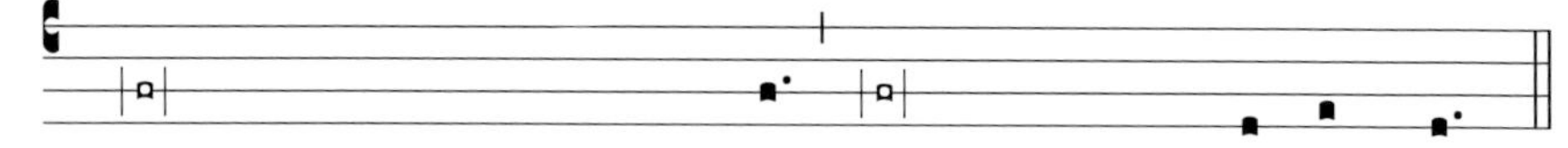

and I shall be for ever with him, in the ho-li-ness of his heaven.

℟. Our thanks to God.

**SHORT RESPONSORY**

Queen of heaven, we who pray to you, know the power of your

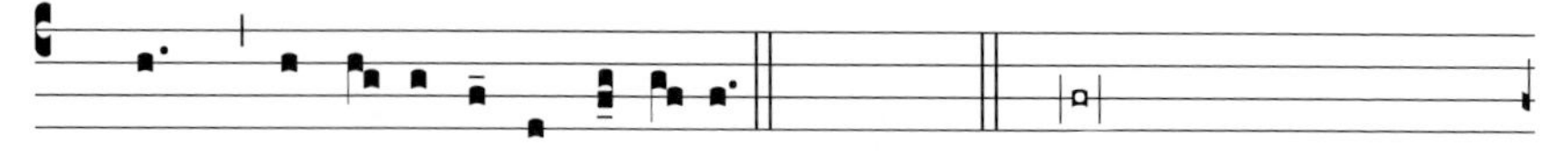

prayer. Al-le-lu-ia, Al-le-lu-ia. ℟. *Repeat.* ℣. Mary, your Son who

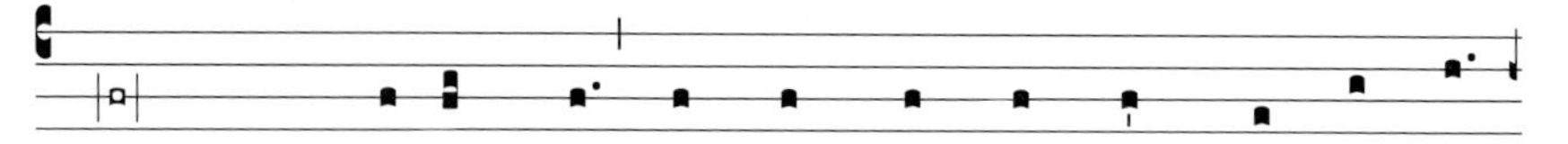

is truly God, obeyed you, and your word was power-ful with him.

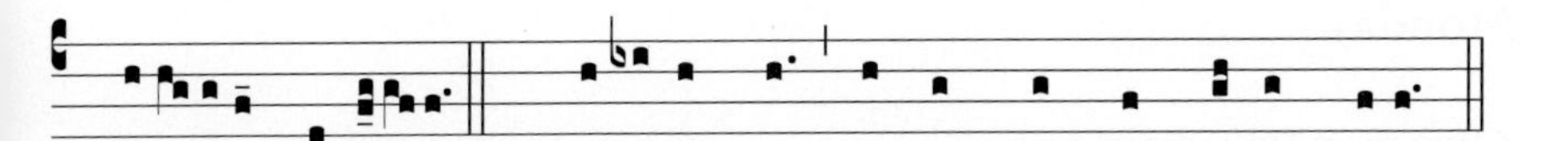

℟. Alleluia, Alleluia. ℣. Glory to God, Father, Son and Holy Spirit.

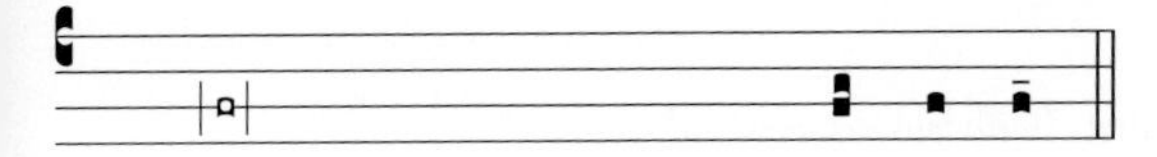

℟. Queen of heaven, we who pray to you…

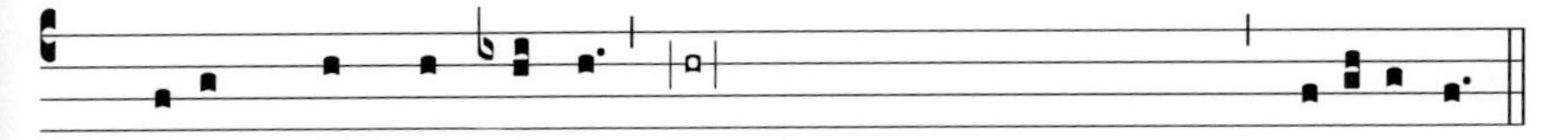

℣. Mary, Queen of heaven, do not leave us unprotected, Allelu-ia.

℟. Look on us in mer-cy and love, Al-le-lu-ia.

**CLOSING PRAYERS** *(page 38)*.

## Monday

OPENING PRAYERS *(with music: pages 55 - 56).*

HYMN

Come, Lord Creator Spirit, *(with music: page 166).*

ANTIPHON

**Ma-ry, your co-ming.**

**Psalm 13, Psalm 15 & Psalm 16**
*(See pages 111 to 114.)*

ANTIPHON

**Ma-ry, your coming** has brought to nothing the evil of Sa-tan,

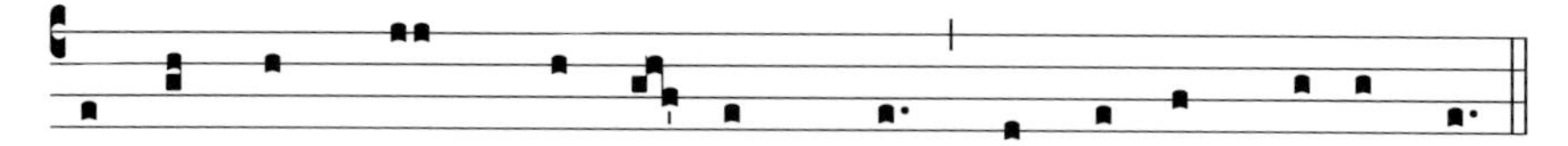

for you have crushed the ser-pent's head and re-stored us to grace.

READING *(Eccles. 24:9)*

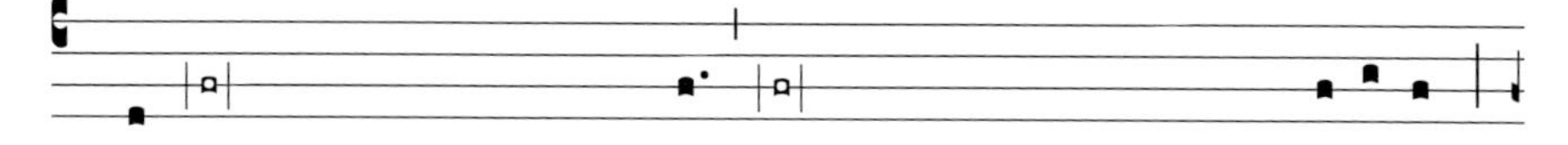

In the eternal decree of God, I was present before his creating

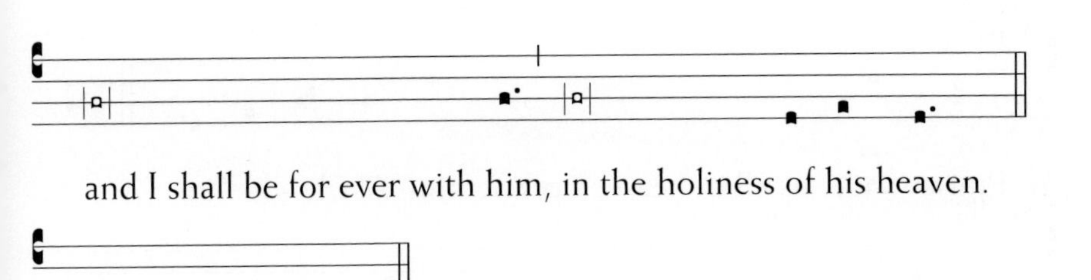

and I shall be for ever with him, in the holiness of his heaven.

℟. Our thanks to God.

## Short Responsory

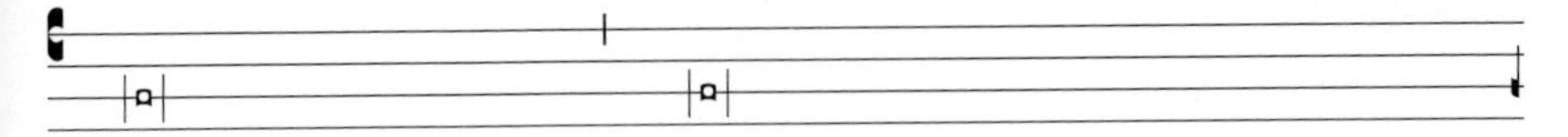

Mary, Queen of an-gels, ho-liest and high-est of all in hea-ven,

pray for us in our need, Al-le-lu-ia, Al-le-lu-ia. ℟. *Repeat.*

℣. Protect us from sin and the snares of Satan. ℟. Alleluia, Alleluia.

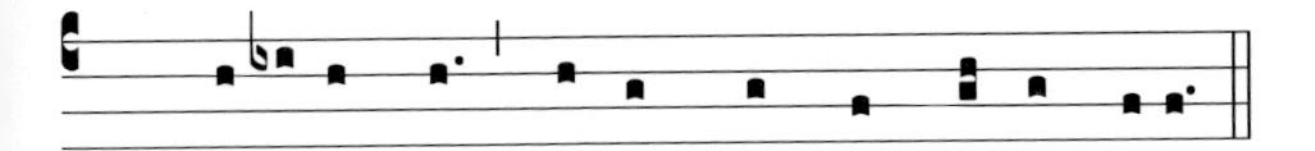

℣. Glory to God, Father, Son and Holy Spirit.

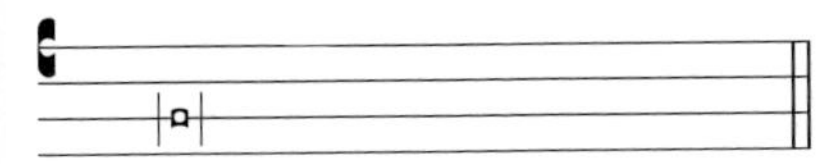

℟. Mary, Queen of angels…

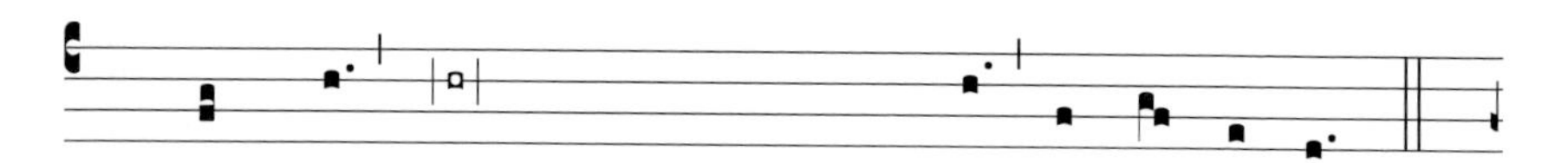

℣. Praise God, as all in hea-ven praise him, Al - le - lu - ia.

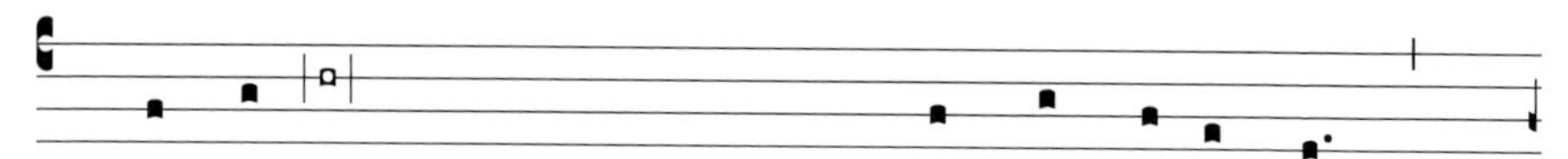

℟. For the holiness and glory of Mary the Mo-ther of God,

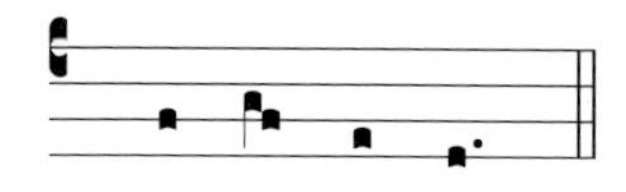

Al - le - lu - ia.

**CLOSING PRAYERS** *(page 38)*.

---

## Tuesday

**OPENING PRAYERS** *(with music: pages 55 - 56)*.

**HYMN**

Come, Lord Creator Spirit, *(with music: page 166)*.

**ANTIPHON**

**We know you, Lord,**

**Psalm 35**, **Psalm 36** *(vv. 1 – 15)* & **Psalm 36** *(vv. 16 – 40)*. *(See pages 157 to 160.)*

ANTIPHON

℟. Our thanks to God.

## Short Responsory

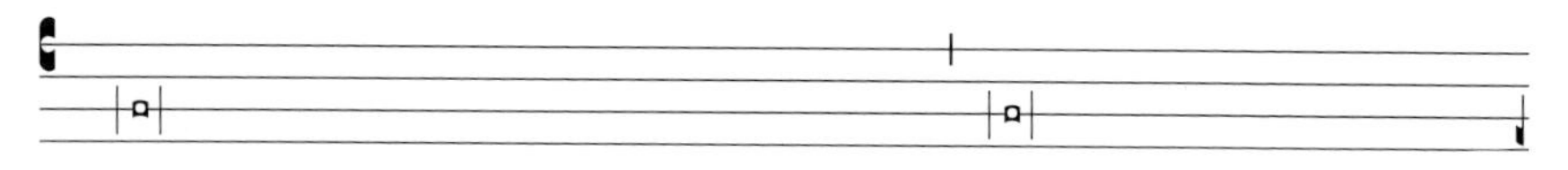

He who brought death into the world, was driven out into a

world of death, Al-le-lu-ia, Al-le-lu-ia. ℟. *Repeat.* ℣. Man was

ensnared into an exile with-out end. ℟. Al-le-lu-ia, Al-le-lu-ia.

℣. Glory to God, Father, Son and Holy Spirit. ℟. He who brought…

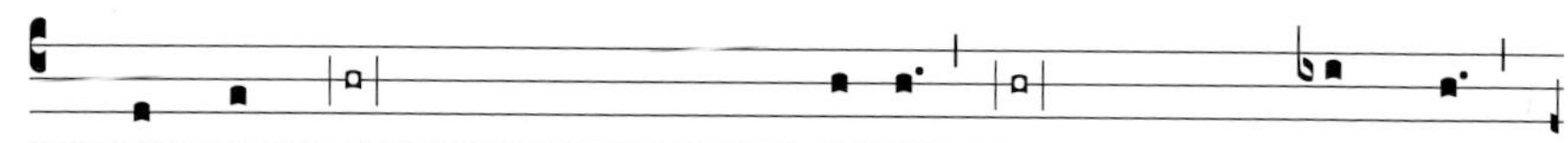

℣. She who was mother of all the liv-ing, the woman named Eve,

Al-le-lu-ia.

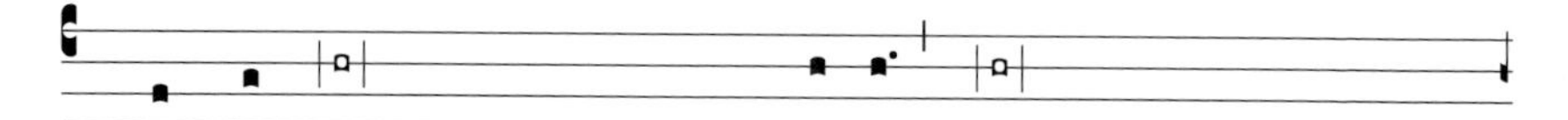

℟. En-ticed by the lying voice of Sa-tan, sub-jected her chil-dren

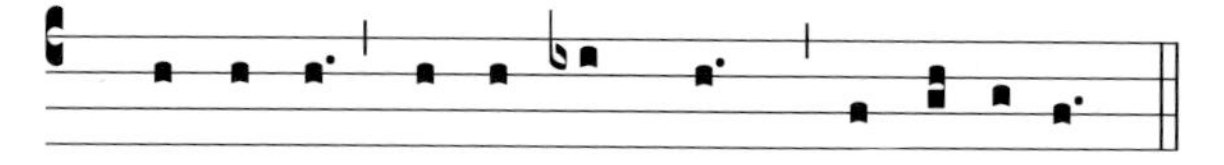

yet to be, to sin and death. Al-le-lu-ia.

## Closing Prayers *(page 38)*.

*Readings for Week Two*

# OFFICE OF READINGS (MATINS)

## SUNDAY

### BLESSING

Mother of Christ, change our weakness to strength, as once you changed the sorrow of this world to joy. ℟. Amen.

### READING

Mary, we know that you were ever in the mind of God,
before his creating brought you to be
the most perfect of all his creatures.
He knew you as Noe, before the flood,
knew the Ark he was to build,
and the way he was to build it.
The design of the Ark had been made known to him,
and he waited for the time when God would command him to set to work.
The design and perfection, Mary, of your glorious body,
the Ark of God,
was known to God before all time.
And he knew the time when he would bring it into being by his creating.
As Noe rejoiced at the thought of the Ark he was to build,
so God rejoiced, Mary, at the thought of you.
Noe's Ark would withstand the storms;
you, Mary, the Ark of God, would withstand,
in the strength of your holiness,
every attack of the hatred and sin of hell.

Noe's Ark was so built that no water could seep in,
a ship whose timbers were carefully protected both inside and out.
You, Mary, the Ark of God, would be so strong in God's grace,
anointed and protected by his Holy Spirit,
that no desire would ever enter your heart,
either for your own glory
or for the possession of earthly things.

Such desires, we know, are as displeasing to God
as the water which seeps into the keel of a ship,
and collecting there becomes stale and offensive.
Noe was pleased at the size and capacity of his Ark.
God rejoiced, Mary, in that holiness which would be yours,
in your love which would embrace all creatures,
and in your gentleness which would look with pity on sinners,
and hate only what was hateful to him.
But most of all,
he rejoiced in that ever increasing grace
which would fit you to bear in your womb
that which heaven and earth could not contain,
the person of God the Son,
to hold him and be truly his Mother.

Noe took pride, as every captain of a ship takes pride,
in the cleanliness and tidiness and brightness of the Ark.
God rejoiced, Mary, in your virginity,
for in you there would be no sin,
nor slightest stain of sin,
to taint your perfection.
Noe provided for himself and those with him,
all that was needed to survive the days ahead.
God chose you, Mary, for his Son,
that your body should provide for him a perfect human body.
Noe came from the Ark unchanged.
But from you, Mary, the Ark of God,
the Son of God came forth,
clothed with that pure flesh and blood
which he had taken from you.
When Noe left the Ark, its purpose was served,
it was empty and useless.
But when Christ came forth from your womb,
you were filled with every gift of the Holy Spirit,
growing ever in holiness,
not further now from Christ,
but nearer to him,
and dearer even than before,
united to him on earth and in heaven for ever.

## Responsory

Mary, through you the King of glory came to this world, to comfort us in our sickness and despair. Through you we are taken from this desolate plain of earth to the mountain of God, to be the living stones of the heavenly city.
℣. Set in our hearts true love for Christ, who came to us through you.
℟. Through you we are taken from this desolate plain of earth to the mountain of God, to be the living stones of the heavenly city.
℣. Glory to God, glory to Father, Son and Holy Spirit.
℟. Through you we are taken from this desolate plain of earth to the mountain of God, to be the living stones of the heavenly city.

**Te Deum** *as on Sunday, page 75* or **Psalm 50** *as on Friday, page 330.*
℣. Mary, Queen of heaven, do not leave us unprotected. (Alleluia)
℟. Look on us in mercy and love. (Alleluia)

## Closing Prayers *(page 38).*

# MONDAY

## Blessing

May Mary the Virgin-Mother make known to us our way to God, for she herself was the way of Christ to man. ℟. Amen.

## Reading

God's creation of the world and all it contains
took place in the instant of his will's expression;
and with that design and perfection foreseen by him.
Yet there remained still uncreated
another work of creation which would surpass what he had already done.
You, Mary, are, as it were, another world,
a world which God foresaw with greater joy,
a world the angels were more pleased to contemplate,
a world of more benefit to those of good will
than the whole earth and all it contains.

Mary, we may see in God's act of creation and in all created things
an image of your creating.

We read that it pleased God to separate the darkness from the light
when he created the earth.
How much more it pleased him to enlighten you from childhood.
The darkness, the time of your infancy,
was made light by your knowledge of God,
your understanding of God,
and the will to live for God
which day by day led you on
to a love surpassed only by the love of God.

The mental darkness of childhood,
without knowledge of God,
without reasoning power to guide,
is for us a time of defencelessness and danger.
But we know that for you, exempt from sin,
it was a time of purest innocence.

We read that it pleased God to make,
together with the stars, two lights:
the sun for daytime, the moon for the night.
It pleased God still more, Mary, to set in you
two heavenly lights, brighter and more beautiful than the sun or the moon:
the first, perfect obedience,
a radiant light for angels and men to admire,
guiding all who saw it to God himself, who is the light of eternal day;
the second, a most complete and trusting faith,
a light to men in the darkness of despair and unbelief
when your Son chose suffering and death,
a light to cast out all shadow of doubt and uncertainty
when he rose from the dead.

We read that it pleased God to create the stars.
The thoughts of your heart, Mary, were more pleasing to him.
We read that it pleased God to create the birds,
whose flight and song are a delight to men.
All the words which you spoke, Mary,
heard also in heaven to the joy of the angels,
were more pleasing still.

We read that God created the earth itself,
the dry land and the soil;
and flowering and fruit-bearing trees of many kinds.
Your life, Mary, your occupations and work,
were more pleasing to him,
for you would give nourishment, and life itself, to all,
and your love would make each act of your life
more beautiful to God and the angels
than the fairest of flowers are to men.
God created the plants, flowers, trees, and fruits,
minerals, metals, and precious stones;
he has made the earth rich with these things.
Yet he saw in you, Mary, even before your creating,
more qualities and virtues than in all earthly things.

We read that God's creation was pleasing to him,
and that he looked with joy on all he had done.
It pleased him still more to create you, Mary,
and he looked with greater joy on you,
even before your creating,
than on this earth and all earthly things.

That world and everything in it,
all would be destroyed.
Though created before you, Mary, it would not endure.
But you, by God's eternal decree,
were created to be for ever,
and to be for ever united to him in deepest love,
created in fullest grace,
responding to his grace in all things,
and so growing to the perfection of holiness.

## Responsory

A **garden where flowers ever bloom,** where every tree bears fruit, to nourish and delight. What garden is this? None other than the Virgin Mary, garden of delight, where the precious flowers are her grace and holiness, where the life-giving fruit is her Son.
℣. Truly the Virgin Mary is our garden of delight
℟. Where the life-giving fruit is her Son.
℣. Glory to God, glory to Father, Son and Holy Spirit.

℟. Where the life-giving fruit is her Son.

**Te Deum** *as on Sunday, page 75* or **Psalm 50** *as on Friday, page 330.*

℣. Praise God, as all in heaven praise him. (Alleluia)

℟. For the holiness and glory of Mary the Mother of God. (Alleluia)

**Closing Prayers** *(page 38).*

## TUESDAY

### Blessing

Virgin, in your love, help us, protect us, for temptation is ever near. ℟. Amen.

### Reading

Adam's punishment made him see the justice and mercy of God.
Throughout his life he feared to offend God
and was guided in all things by love for God.
This way of life he handed on to those who came after him.
With time they forgot God's justice and mercy.
With time they forgot God himself,
and that he was their Creator.
They believed only what pleased them,
immersing themselves in pleasure and sin.
So came the flood,
when God destroyed all men on earth,
saving only Noe and those with him in the Ark,
through whom he willed to people the earth again.
Once again men multiplied on the earth,
and once again they fell,
tempted away from God,
turning to the worship of false gods and idols.
God's mercy and fatherly love led him to intervene,
and he chose one who was a faithful follower of his law,
Abraham, to make a covenant with him and his descendants.
He fulfilled his desire for a son,
and Isaac was born.
And he promised that from his descendants,
Christ, his Son, would come.

It is possible that Abraham, by God's permission, foresaw many things.
We may think of him as having foreseen Mary, the Mother of Christ.
We may think of him rejoicing in her, and loving her more than Isaac his son.

It was not greed or ambition that led Abraham to acquire lands and wealth.
It was not for his own sake that he desired a son.
He was like a gardener of some great lord's estate.
He had planted a vine,
and planned to make cuttings from that vine,
and so in time make for his master a vineyard of great worth.
Like a good gardener,
he knew that each plant needed careful attention,
and proper feeding, if it was to bear good fruit.
One plant in particular he cherished,
watching its growth with great delight.
He knew that it would be the choicest of all the trees in his vineyard.
His master would love to rest in the shade beneath it,
praising its beauty and the sweetness of its fruit.

If Abraham was the gardener,
then the vine which he first planted was Isaac;
the cuttings of that vine his descendants;
the feeding of each plant the goods of this world
which Abraham acquired for the sake of Isaac and his race;
the most cherished tree,
that tree of beauty and sweetness,
was the Virgin Mary;
and the master for whom Abraham the gardener worked,
the owner of the vineyard,
was God himself,
who waited till the vineyard (the race of Isaac) was established,
and then, coming, saw with content,
the perfect vine in the midst of his vineyard,
the Virgin Mother of God.
The beauty of this tree was the perfect and sinless life of Mary;
the sweetness of the fruit, the acts of her life;
the shade of that tree, her virginal womb, overshadowed by the Spirit of God.

If Abraham then foresaw what was to be,
he rejoiced in his many descendants,
but most of all in that one of his descendants who,

as Virgin Mother,
was to bear the Son of God.

This faith and holy desire
Abraham handed on to Isaac, his son:
"Your oath," he had said to the servant sent for Isaac's wife,
"must be sworn on the One who is to come of my race."
Isaac too handed on this same faith and desire,
when he blessed his son Jacob.
And Jacob in blessing his twelve sons,
handed on this same faith and desire in his turn to Judah.

God so loved Mary, the Mother of his Son,
even before the creation of the world,
and before her creating,
that he gave to those he had specially chosen as his friends
some foreknowledge of her, for their consolation.
First to the angels,
then to Adam,
and then to the patriarchs,
the creation of Mary was a thing of wonder and joy.

## RESPONSORY

**Abraham rejoiced,** for God had said to him:
"Your descendants will outnumber the stars of heaven";
and from afar, he saw the day of Christ, heralded, Mary,
by your coming.
℣. Mary, we who are of that promised line, the people of God, must ever rejoice in you, for Christ your Son.
℟. As Abraham rejoiced, seeing the day of Christ, heralded, Mary,
by your coming.
℣. Glory to God, glory to Father, Son and Holy Spirit.
℟. As Abraham rejoiced, seeing the day of Christ, heralded, Mary,
by your coming.

**TE DEUM** *as on Sunday, page 75* or **PSALM 50** *as on Friday, page 330.*
℣. She who was Mother of all the living, the woman named Eve. (Alleluia)
℟. Enticed by the lying voice of Satan, subjected her children yet to be to sin and death. (Alleluia)

**CLOSING PRAYERS** *(page 38).*

## WEDNESDAY

### Blessing

Mary, we name you Morning Star; guide us on our way through life. ℟. Amen.

### Reading

That seed of life was ready,
and at God's chosen moment, life began
as he infused into it a living soul.

We see the bees in summer, busy seeking the flowers for honey;
led by instinct to their sweetness,
they seem often to wait for the buds to open.

God foresaw, as he foresees all things,
the birth of Mary, and he waited with joy as she lay
hidden in her mother's womb,
for he knew that none ever of those to be born
would equal her in holiness.
None would so make known to men his infinite love.
The infusing of Mary's soul in the womb of Blessed Anne
was more beautiful than the dawn of the most beautiful day.
As we so often long for the dawn,
so angels and men longed for her birth.
Where the nights are short in summer,
so that there is little darkness,
people do not notice the dawn;
they wait for the sun itself,
thinking of their crops and their fruits.
Where the nights are quite long, even in summer,
the dawn is watched for and welcomed,
not only for the coming of the sun to the fields,
but because men weary of the night and the darkness.

The angels in heaven did not await the coming of Mary
that they might see Christ,
for they were ever in the light of his presence;
they longed for her, so that the love of God might be made known in the world,
so that men who loved God might be strengthened in their love,

and then they, the angels, could go out to gather them
as an everlasting harvest for God.
But men, living in this world of sorrow and hardship,
desired the coming of Mary that they might see Christ their Saviour.
They longed for her coming, that they might learn from her perfect life
how man should live.
The Virgin Mary is foretold as the branch which would grow
from the root of the father of David,
to bear a flower on which the Spirit of God would rest.
In her mother's womb (how light Anne's burden!)
Mary was the tender branch which would soon come forth.
The flower that branch would bear was Christ.

He himself, from the moment of her assent to God's message,
was a richer and infinitely sweeter nourishment
than blessed Anne had given to her.
Though Mary was to him the food of life,
giving her own flesh and blood to be his,
that he might appear in true humanity,
he was to Mary her heavenly food,
that she might bear him as her child,
though he was truly the Son of God.

They were Mother and Son, Son and Mother,
yet this Son was truly the Son of God,
the only-begotten Son of the Father,
eternally with him,
eternally united with him and the Holy Spirit,
eternally the Person of the Son of God,
who with the Father and the Spirit lives in glory,
eternally One.

## Responsory

S**ee how as God had foretold**, the promised root takes hold of life,
and sends forth a branch; see on that branch a flower bloom,
caressed by the breath of the winds.
℣. That promised branch is Mary, the Virgin-Mother of God; her flower is Christ; ℟. And the caressing breath of the winds is the Spirit of God.
℣. Glory to God, glory to Father, Son and Holy Spirit.
℟. And the caressing breath of the winds is the Spirit of God.

**TE DEUM** *as on Sunday,* *page 75* or **PSALM 50** *as on Friday,* *page 330.*
℣. The prophets of God made known to us. (Alleluia)
℟. The Virgin who would come of a kingly line. (Alleluia)

CLOSING PRAYERS *(page 38).*

---

## THURSDAY

### BLESSING

May our sin and sinfulness be taken away by the help of Mary, whose grace and sinlessness were reverenced by the angel of God. ℟. Amen.

### READING

With our slow and clouded minds,
it is hard for us to appreciate that moment
when Mary first knew God
and gave herself to him.
His will became her one desire and her joy.
She saw how she owed everything to his creating;
but she knew that according to his plan,
her will was free,
to choose or refuse his will and his way.
She saw the blessings which God had already bestowed,
and for these alone she chose to love him in return,
and to love him for ever.
Soon she was to understand how much more he would do.
She learnt that he who created all would not rest content,
but would himself come to his creation
as redeemer of his creatures.
And this out of love alone.
She learnt that man's will,
free to choose good or evil,
could make satisfaction to God for sin,
or incur his anger by sin.

In that moment of understanding,
she chose once for all her course through life.

The captain of a ship knows what dangers lie ahead,
and he charts his voyage to avoid the storms.
He watches the ship's course,
and works out the distance sailed,
and the distance still to sail before arriving in port.
Every rope, every piece of equipment is in place and ready for use.
The cargo he carries must reach port as quickly as possible.
Every detail of the voyage must be worked out ahead.

Mary was like the captain of a ship.
As soon as she had understood God's will,
she set her course according to his commandments.
She was watchful at all times
that her attention should never be distracted from God.
She took care, when those around her spoke of their ambitions,
their successes or failures,
not to let herself become less devout in her service of God.
Anything contrary to God's law she knew at once as a danger
to be avoided at all cost.
With this self-training and discipline,
all that she did was good.
All that she said,
all that she listened to,
all that she gave her attention to,
was sensible and wise.

Her work was useful to herself and to others,
and each journey she made had some good reason.
The trials of life she accepted with patience and joy.
Her one thought was God.
Her one desire was to be for ever with him,
to offer to him in return for all he had done for her
all her love and her praise.

So perfect a life won her from God,
who is the giver of all good things,
the highest holiness and glory.
It is no wonder that God loved her
more than all other creatures.
She alone of all men and women
was ever sinless
and immune from sin.

How near she was to heaven
at that moment when the angel Gabriel greeted her:
Hail, full of grace!
How pure, how holy she was,
at that moment when the Father entrusted to her his only Son,
at her assenting:
Be it done unto me, according to thy word!

At that moment of time,
Divinity was united with humanity,
humanity with Divinity;
the Son of God was made man;
the Son of the Father become the Son of Mary.

## RESPONSORY

E**very age shall call her most blest of all,** for all the wonders God has done for her, for she is truly Mother of God. She who knew not man, in whom was ever pure virginity, has conceived and borne the Son of God, in Virgin-Motherhood. She has rejoiced to name herself handmaid of God; and she has borne for us a burden of joy, the precious treasure of God's love; and brought to this world of ours this world's salvation.
℣. Mary has heard and believed the word of God, announcing to her her Virgin-Motherhood: the Spirit of God shall rest in you, and the power of God most high shall over-shadow you. Now is the Word made flesh; and now is come the promised one, and she who is blest of all will bring forth, to the joy of all, Christ her Lord and God.
℟. She has borne for us a burden of joy, the precious treasure of God's love; and brought to this world of ours this world's salvation.
℣. Glory to God, glory to Father, Son and Holy Spirit.
℟. She has borne for us a burden of joy, the precious treasure of God's love; and brought to this world of ours this world's salvation.

**TE DEUM** *as on Sunday, page 75* or **PSALM 50** *as on Friday, page 330.*
℣. God himself came down to the Virgin's womb. (Alleluia)
℟. There to clothe himself as Man, with flesh to offer for us and blood to shed for us. (Alleluia)

CLOSING PRAYERS (*page 38*).

## FRIDAY

### Blessing

May Christ our Saviour, whose precious blood was the price of our sin, hear the prayer of his Virgin Mother, pleading for us. ℟. Amen.

### Reading

The prophets foretold many things about Christ.
They spoke of the death of the innocent one
and the pains he would suffer
to win for men on earth an eternal life with him in heaven.
They foretold and set in writing
that the Son of God, to save all men,
would be bound, scourged, mocked,
led out to be crucified,
and reviled as he hung on the Cross.
They knew that the immortal God would take man's mortal form.
They knew that he willed to suffer as man for man.

If the prophets foresaw these things,
would not Mary foresee them, even more clearly?
She was the Mother predestined for the Son of God.
How could she not have foreseen his sufferings
when he took flesh in her womb for this very purpose?
The presence of the Holy Spirit would enlighten her,
so that she knew better than the Prophets
the things which they, through the Holy Spirit, foretold.

At the moment of Christ's birth,
as she held him for the first time in her arms,
Mary foresaw the fulfilment of prophecy.
As she wrapped him in swaddling-clothes,
she foresaw the scourging of his flesh
which would make him a leper in the eyes of men.
The hands and feet of her Child brought the thought
of the nails which would pierce them.

The face of her Son, beautiful beyond the beauty of men,
was the face men would spit on.
His cheeks would feel the blows of their hatred.
His ears would hear the curses of their defiance.
His eyes would be blinded by the blood from the wounds in his head.
His mouth would taste the bitterness of gall.
His arms would be bound,
then stretched in agony on the Cross;
and his heart, empty at last of blood, would shrink in death.
No part of that sacred body would escape the bitterness
of that most bitter death.
And when all breathing ceased,
there would still be the soldier's sharp spear
to pierce his lifeless heart.

Mary rejoiced as no mother ever rejoiced
when her Son, the Son of God, was born,
true God, true man,
mortal in his humanity,
immortal in his Divinity.
But Mary knew sorrow deeper than the sorrows of all mothers,
foreseeing the Passion of her Son.
Her joy was beyond words,
but her joy brought with it a sorrow deeper
than all the sorrows of this world.
A mother's joy is complete when her child is born
and she sees it healthy and perfectly formed.
Her pain and anxiety are over.
Mary rejoiced at Christ's birth,
but she knew that no moment of her life would be free of sorrow.
The prophets foretold,
long before the coming of Christ,
his sufferings and death.
Simeon foretold,
in the presence of Mary and her Child,
the piercing of her heart by a sword of sorrow.

We know that the mind is more sensitive to pain even than the body.
We know that the soul of Mary, even before the death of her Son,
would feel that sword of sorrow more sharply
than all women on earth would feel the sufferings of childbearing.
Each day brought nearer the sufferings of Christ.

Each day brought nearer the piercing of Mary's heart.
It was the compassion of Christ alone
which enabled her, by his presence and his words,
to bear day by day such piercing sorrow.

## Responsory

E**ternal praise to you, Mary,** Mother of Christ, our everlasting joy; for though the sword of sorrow pierced your sinless soul, you spoke no word of bitterness or dissent, knowing how the sword of eternal death was turned aside from our weakness.
℣. This indeed was true love; and we may pray to you to teach us such love, the perfect love of Christ, who loved us unto death, and by the shedding of his precious blood, won back our sinfulness to the love of his heart;
℟. Knowing how the sword of eternal death was turned aside from our weakness.
℣. Glory to God, glory to Father, Son and Holy Spirit.
℟. Knowing how the sword of eternal death was turned aside from our weakness.

**Te Deum** *as on Sunday, page 75* or **Psalm 50** *as on Friday, page 330.*
℣. There by the Cross of Christ she stood in deepest sorrow, (Alleluia)
℟. To see how men could spit on him and shed in hatred his Precious Blood. (Alleluia)

## Closing Prayers *(page 38).*

---

# SATURDAY

## Blessing

May Christ the Son of the Virgin Mary, take from us our sin and sinfulness.
℟. Amen.

## Reading

We read in the Gospels these words of Christ:
the measure you give
shall be the measure you receive.

No one on earth can know the glory of Mary, the Mother of God.
She who on earth gave so much
receives now in heaven
a measure of glory beyond the whole of creation.

When it pleased Christ to call her from this earth,
there awaited her
all whom her holiness had helped.

God himself,
whose love had been made known only through her,
awaited her coming to adorn her with a glory surpassed only by his own.
She was raised to the highest place in heaven,
to be Queen,
not only of his earthly creation,
but Queen over the angels for ever.
The angels rejoiced in this Queen,
made for ever obedient to her by their love for her.
Those angels too who had fallen from God
were made subject to her;
no temptation of theirs could withstand her;
no one calling with love for her help
would be left unprotected;
the tempters would choose rather an increase of their misery
than the opposing of her power.

Of all creatures the most humble,
Mary is now the most glorious,
the most perfect in beauty,
and nearest to God himself.
As gold surpasses all other metals,
angels and men surpass all the creatures of God.
Gold needs the fire and the work of the goldsmith
before it can be fashioned into a work of beauty.

Mary, more perfect than all angels and men,
was fashioned by her own will,
in the fire of the Holy Spirit,
into a thing of the highest beauty.
A work of art wrought in gold needs the light to be seen;
in the light of the sun, it will be seen in all its perfection.

All that the Virgin Mary accomplished,
and the beauty of her soul,
could not be seen while she was living on earth.
Lit by the light of God himself in heaven,
she appeared in the fullness of beauty.
All heaven gave praise to her,
and to that beauty of soul with which her will had adorned her,
a beauty beyond the beauty of all creation,
near even to God's own perfection.

Mary is enthroned for ever,
on that throne placed near to the throne of God.
No one is nearer than she to the Father, the Son and the Holy Spirit.
The Father is in the Son,
the Son is in the Father,
the Holy Spirit is in the Father and the Son.
The Son, when he became man in the Virgin's womb,
was not thereby divided from the Father and the Holy Spirit.
He took our humanity,
not losing his Divinity,
as Mary acquired Motherhood
without loss to her Virginity.
God gave to Mary, therefore, a place near to himself,
so that she is ever with the Father, the Son and the Holy Spirit,
and ever associated with this blessed Trinity in all things.

Who could measure the joy in heaven
when God raised Mary from this earth?
Who will measure our joy
when, seeing God face to face,
we see too the glory of Mary?

The angels rejoicing in Mary glorify God.
The death of Christ has filled again the places made vacant in heaven.
The raising of Mary to heaven has increased even the blessedness of heaven.

To Adam and Eve,
to the patriarchs and prophets,
to all who died before Christ and were released by his death,
to all who have died since Christ's death and been taken to heaven,
Mary's entry into heaven is an everlasting joy and delight.

They praise God for her glory,
for the honour he has bestowed on her
as the one who bore in holiness
Christ, their Redeemer and Lord.

We may picture the apostles and many holy ones
around Mary as her last hour approached.
We know the reverence and honour they paid to her
at the moment of her death.

We believe that she died,
as all others die.
We believe that her Son,
the Son of God,
took her to himself,
and raised her, body and soul,
to live for ever in heaven.

## RESPONSORY

**Who is she who comes to us,** more radiant than sun new-risen, lovelier than Jerusalem? The daughters of Syon have looked on her and declared her most blest, truly the Queen of all.
℣. Who is she who comes to us, sweet as the scents of summer, on the warm winds of the desert?
℟. The daughters of Syon have looked on her and declared her most blest, truly the Queen of all.
℣. Glory to God, glory to Father, Son and Holy Spirit.
℟. The daughters of Syon have looked on her and declared her most blest, truly the Queen of all.

**TE DEUM** *as on Sunday, page 75* or **PSALM 50** *as on Friday, page 330.*
℣. Satan is cast down to hell for ever. (Alleluia)
℟. Mary who crushed the Serpent's head is raised to eternal glory and joy. (Alleluia)

**CLOSING PRAYERS** (*page 38*).

# OFFICE OF READINGS (MATINS)

## SUNDAY

### BLESSING

May Mary make us pleasing to God, as she was pleasing to him and worthy to be his resting-place on earth. ℟. Amen.

### READING

From the moment of God's promise,
through the long years of waiting,
Abraham loved the son who was to be his,
the child who would be called Isaac.
How much more did God love you, Virgin Mary,
whom he had foreseen from eternity,
and knew before your creating,
for he knew also the joy your birth would be to him.
Abraham did not know how his love for God would be tested and proved through his promised son.
But God knew with his divine knowledge
how through you, Mary, his great love for man would be made known.
Abraham knew that Isaac would be born of his union with Sarah,
a child conceived unexpectedly in their old age.
God knew that his Son would be conceived in you, Virgin Mary,
without the intervention of man,
and be born of you,
true Mother yet ever a virgin.
Abraham knew that his son once conceived
would grow without his help to become a person, independent of his father.
God knew that the sacred body of his Son,
formed in your womb,
would in a special way,
be for ever most intimately united with the Godhead.
This must be so, since the Son is ever in the Father,
the Father in the Son, equal yet one.

Abraham knew that he and his son must return to dust
in the corruption of death.
God would not allow your pure body, Mary, to see corruption,
for it was the flesh and blood of your body
which had been given to form the body of his Son.
Abraham built a house for the son who was to be born to him.
But God himself,
the blessed Trinity,
is the dwelling in which you, Mary, will abide for ever.

In a wonderful way, then,
your dwelling, Mary, was in God,
who surrounded you with his protecting love.
Yet God dwelt ever in you,
leading you to the highest holiness by his presence.
For his promised son,
Abraham prepared wheat, wine and oil,
three kinds of essential nourishment.

For you, Virgin Mary,
God himself was to be your eternal meal,
Father, Son and Holy Spirit, three yet one.
And through you he was to give himself to men
as the food of life.
So we may attribute this food of life in a way, to you, Mary,
since it is by you that it has come to us.
The three things which Abraham prepared
can be thought of as a sign of the action of the three Persons.
Oil cannot burn without a wick.
This can suggest to us
that the love of God the Father could not be made known on earth
without the humanity of the Son,
that humanity which he took from you, his Virgin Mother.
Wheat has to be made into flour, and then bread, for our daily use.
The Son of God,
though he is truly the food of angels,
could not be our food
without that flesh and blood which he took from your loving womb.
Wine cannot refresh us unless it is in something we can drink from.
The Holy Spirit could not be poured out upon us
without the humanity of your Son.
For the salvation which Christ's Passion and death accomplished

is the fount of all the delights and graces
bestowed by God on angels and on men.

## Responsory

Mary, in you the Father, Son and Holy Spirit dwell; God who holds you and all things in being is held by you. In the beauty of your virtues, you are a garden of delight for the most Holy Trinity.
To you God gives his gifts, to dispense to us, to heal our ills and strengthen our weakness.
℣. Mary, look on us; see how we walk in danger, homeless and captive, friendless and in sorrow, yet none of us can claim that your mercy has passed us by.
℟. To you God gives his gifts, to dispense to us, to heal our ills and strengthen our weakness.
℣. Glory to God, glory to Father, Son and Holy Spirit.
℟. To you God gives his gifts, to dispense to us, to heal our ills and strengthen our weakness.

**Te Deum** *as on Sunday, page 75* or **Psalm 50** *as on Friday, page 330.*
℣. Mary, Queen of heaven, do not leave us unprotected. (Alleluia)
℟. Look on us in mercy and love. (Alleluia)

## Closing Prayers *(page 38).*

# MONDAY

## Blessing

May Mary, whose holiness makes her Queen of heaven, ever keep us in mind and protect us from evil. ℟. Amen.

## Reading

God is the Creator of all beings,
and he is Being itself.
Nothing can be or come to be without God.
Therefore, this world and all things in it
owe their existence to him alone.
He is the Creator of all.
And Creator, last of all, of man.

To man he gave, as he had given to the angels,
the gift of free will.
He wished that by free choice
man would cling to what was good,
and so avoid a just punishment and earn a just reward.
Among men, little regard is paid to work done unwillingly,
under threat of punishment.
We honour work done willingly out of love,
and it is such work that deserves reward.

Without free will, angels and men would have served God,
but with little claim to reward.
It pleased God rather to leave them free,
making known what a reward obedience would win
and what punishment pride and disobedience would incur.

God created man, forming him from the dust of the earth.
He looked for man's love and obedient service,
that so the places of those angels who had disobeyed in their pride
and fallen from joy into misery, might be filled once more.
They should have received a crown of joy for their love and obedience.
Instead, they lost their reward,
hating not only the joy they had forfeited
but also those virtues which would have assured it to them.

A king is given a crown of gold,
calling all to honour him who wears it.
But there is a heavenly crown for each virtue,
calling even to men on earth to honour one who loves God,
calling to angels in heaven to rejoice,
calling to God to reward.

What of the crown of God himself?
In him all virtues reside,
surpassing in every way
every other possible good.
In him all is virtue.

Yet three special virtues stand out in what we know of God,
three crowns of incomparable glory.

First, that he created the angels.
(It was the envy of such glory that led some of them
into their pride and fall.)

Second, that he created man.
(The loss of God's glory was man's most grievous loss,
when in his folly he let himself be led into sin.)

Third, that he created you, Virgin Mary.

The fall of angels and of man did not lessen the virtue of God,
or take from his crown of glory.
They were created for God's honour, and they refused it, it is true,
just as they were created for their own glory, and yet forfeited it by sin.
The wisdom of God turned their sin into an even greater glory for himself.
For your creation, Mary, gave such glory to God,
that what was refused him by angels and men
was made good a thousand times over.

Virgin Mary, our Queen and our hope of salvation,
you may truly be called the crown of God's honour.
Through you he showed his divine virtue.
From you he won honour and glory greater than from all other creatures.
The angels knew, even before your creating,
that by your holiness and humility
you would overcome the pride of the Devil and his hatred for man.

They had seen how man had fallen into misery,
but in their contemplation of God,
they still rejoiced, knowing well what great things God would do, Mary, through your lowliness, when his creating brought you to be.

## Responsory

**Virgin Mary, so dear to Christ**; so holy through his grace,
we pray to you and will ever pray to you:
Queen of heaven, help us in our sorrow and our need.
℣. We are so weak, so sinful. We think of you, so holy through God's grace, and we pray to you:
℟. Queen of heaven, help us in our sorrow and our need.
℣. Glory to God, glory to Father, Son and Holy Spirit.

℟. Queen of heaven, help us in our sorrow and our need.

**Te Deum** *as on Sunday, page 75* or **Psalm 50** *as on Friday, page 330.*
℣. Praise God, as all in heaven praise him. (Alleluia)
℟. For the holiness and glory of Mary the Mother of God. (Alleluia)

**Closing Prayers** *(page 38).*

---

# TUESDAY

## Blessing

Mary, most loving Mother, take from our hearts the attraction of sin and sinful things. ℟. Amen.

## Reading

God is all love, and all loving;
infinite in love, and infinite in loving.
We may truly say, God is love.

He makes known his love to those who love,
and all things speak to them of the love of God.

See how great was his love for his people,
the people of Israel.
He delivered them from the Egyptians,
and led them out from captivity,
into a fruitful land,
that they might live there in peace and prosperity.
It was this prosperity that was envied by the Devil,
and in his hatred for all that was loved by God,
he tempted God's people,
and by his deceits, led them time and again into sin.

They had the law of Moses;
they were the people whom God had made his own,
through his covenant with Abraham;
yet they fell into idolatry and worshipped false gods.

God looked on them and found there among them
some who still served him with true faith and love,
following his law.
To strengthen these followers of his,
amid the dangers that surrounded them,
to confirm them in their faith and love,
he raised up among them the prophets,
men who came not only for the help of God's own,
but also to rescue those who had made themselves enemies of God.

In time, like the mountain streams which join,
and then join to other streams as they descend,
increasing ever in volume and power,
carrying all before them,
down at last to meet other waters
and in the lower lands form into the great rivers,
the Holy Spirit filled the hearts of his prophets,
and first one, then another,
then more raised their voices,
to speak as he inspired them,
till their sound filled the ears of many,
to comfort and console,
to call back and restore.

The sweetest sound of their voices was that news of joy
that God himself would be born of a Virgin,
to make amends for the evil which Satan, through Adam, had caused to man;
that he would redeem man,
and rescue him from his misery,
restoring to him eternal life.

Joy too, that God the Father so willed this redemption of man
that he would not spare even his only-begotten Son:
that the Son so willed to obey the Father,
that he would take to himself our human flesh:
that the Holy Spirit, though inseparable from the Father,
willed to be sent by the Son.

The prophets knew that the Son of God would come into this world,
to be light in our darkness,
brighter than the sun at dawn,

to proclaim God's justice and love.
But they knew he would not come unheralded.
As the morning star heralds the sun,
they foresaw that a star would rise in Israel,
fairest of all the stars,
in brightness and beauty surpassed only by the sun itself.

This star was the Virgin Mary,
who would be Mother of Christ,
her love surpassed only by the love of God,
her heart ever responding to the will of God.

This news was given by God to his prophets,
to console them in their labour of teaching,
and encourage them in their trials.

For they grieved at the pride and sinfulness of the people,
who neglected the law of Moses,
rejected God's love, and incurred his anger.
But they rejoiced, Mary, in you,
foreseeing that God, the giver of all law,
would receive back to his grace those who had sinned,
for the sake of your humility and holiness of life.
They grieved to see the Temple empty and desolate,
and the worship of God neglected.
They rejoiced, Mary, to foresee the creation of that holy temple,
your pure body, where God himself would love to reside.
They grieved at the destruction of the gates and the walls of the holy city,
broken by armies, invaded by sin.
They rejoiced, Mary, to foresee how you would stand firm, against all attack,
a strong citadel where Christ would arm himself,
the gate through which he would come forth to his conflict
with the Devil and his own.
To the prophets, as to the patriarchs,
your coming, Mary, was a thing of wonder and joy.

## Responsory

**This is no kingly town,** and she no royal child, yet here is glory and grace beyond compare. Here he will come, the Son of God himself, to dwell in her house, to find in her his joy and delight, and clothe himself with power.

℣. Now to his kingly home he returns in glory, to crown her with everlasting honour, to crown her Queen of all.
℟. Here he will come, the Son of God himself, to dwell in her house, to find in her his joy and delight, and clothe himself with power.
℣. Glory to God, glory to Father, Son and Holy Spirit.
℟. Here he will come, the Son of God himself, to dwell in her house, to find in her his joy and delight, and clothe himself with power.

**TE DEUM** *as on Sunday, page 75* **or PSALM 50** *as on Friday, page 330.*
℣. She who was Mother of all the living, the woman named Eve. (Alleluia)
℟. Enticed by the lying voice of Satan, subjected her children yet to be to sin and death. (Alleluia)

**CLOSING PRAYERS** *(page 38).*

---

## WEDNESDAY

### BLESSING

May the thought of Mary born to be the Mother of Christ, be joy to us on earth as in heaven. ℟. Amen.

### READING

In Father, Son and Holy Spirit, there is only the one divinity.
There is ever the one divine will.
A fire with three flames is but the one fire.
The three flames of love in God are the one love of his will,
burning to fulfil his one divine purpose.
The love of the Father was seen most brightly by the angels
when they knew his will to give his Son
for the redemption of man.
The love of the Son proceeding from the Father was seen most brightly
when the Son willed to deprive himself of his glory
and take the form of a slave.
The love of the Holy Spirit was seen most brightly
in that readiness to make known in many ways
the one will of the Three.

All heaven was ablaze with these flames of God's love,

to the delight of the angels.
Yet all heaven must wait;
must wait for the coming of Mary.
The redemption of man,
willed and foreseen by God,
could not take place without her.

A flame of divine love was to be kindled in Mary
which would rise up to God
and return so filled with his love
that no corner of this world would be left cold and in darkness.

When Mary was born, she was like a new lamp, all ready to be lit;
to be lit by God with a light burning like the three-fold flame of his own love.

The first flame of her love was her choice, for God's glory, to be ever a virgin.
So pleasing was this to the Father
that he willed to entrust to her his beloved Son,
that Son who is inseparable from the divinity of himself and the Holy Spirit.

The second flame of her love was her humility,
so pleasing to the Son that he willed to take from her a true human body,
and that humanity which was destined to be honoured in heaven above all things.

The third flame of her love was her obedience,
which brought to her from the Holy Spirit the fullness of grace.

It is true that these flames of Mary's love were not lit at the moment of her birth.
She was still, as other children, only a little one,
unaware of God's will.
Yet God took more pleasure in her than in all other beings.

She was like a sweet-sounding harp, not yet in tune;
but he whose treasure she was knew how lovely the music he would make with her.

It may be believed that Christ's knowledge was not lacking in anything due
when he was conceived in Mary's womb.
We may believe too
that Mary developed in understanding earlier than others.

Since the coming of Mary was such joy to God and the angels,
men too must rejoice,
and give glory and honour to God,
who chose her from all his creation by eternal decree
and willed that she should be born among sinners,
to bring forth in sinlessness
the Saviour of the world.

## Responsory

M**ary, you are the Morning Star,** which heralds the dawn of day;
for Christ is the Sun, whose rising brings light to all;
that all may see and know the truth and love of God.
℣. Rejoice, rejoice, all you who love God; look and see how his light is come.
℟. For Christ is the Sun, whose rising brings light to all;
that all may see and know the truth and love of God.
℣. Glory to God, glory to Father, Son and Holy Spirit.
℟. For Christ is the Sun, whose rising brings light to all;
that all may see and know the truth and love of God.

**Te Deum** *as on Sunday,* *page 75* or **Psalm 50** *as on Friday,* *page 330.*
℣. The prophets of God made known to us. (Alleluia)
℟. The Virgin who would come of a kingly line. (Alleluia)

## Closing Prayers (*page 38*).

---

# THURSDAY

## Blessing

With her dear Son may the Virgin Mary bless us. ℟. Amen.

## Reading

This union between God and man,
between Christ and the Virgin Mary,
only God can comprehend.
The Son of God, truly God, all present and present to all,
whose eternal dwelling in heaven is the blessed Trinity itself,

made for himself on earth
a dwelling-place in the womb of the Virgin Mary.

The Holy Spirit,
who is ever in the Father and in the Son,
rested in Mary,
filling her, both body and soul, with his presence.

The Son, who is ever with the Father and the Holy Spirit in heaven,
acquired for himself as man
a new dwelling on earth.

The Father too, with the Holy Spirit,
dwelt in a new way on earth,
in the humanity of the Son,
for the Father with the Holy Spirit must be ever in the Son.
The Son alone took flesh.
He alone took our humanity.
True God, he came as man to men,
withholding from the eyes of men his divinity
seen ever by the angels in heaven.

All who hold the true faith must rejoice unceasingly
at this union achieved through Mary.
The Son of God took in her womb true flesh and blood,
and true humanity,
not losing his divinity:
in divinity was humanity, in humanity divinity.
Christ did not lose his divinity,
nor Mary her virginity.

It would be utterly wrong to think
that God could not have done such a thing,
for all things are possible to God.
It would be equally wrong to think
that he would not have done such a thing for his own,
for this would deny the goodness of God.

If we believe then that God could and would do such a thing,
why do not all men love God with all their love?

Picture some king, honoured by all, with great power and possessions,
and someone dear to him suffering great insult and injury;
if the king took on himself the burden of his friend,
if he gave all his wealth to save him from poverty,
still more, if he offered his life for his friend,
would not this be the greatest love he could show?

But no love of men on earth could equal the love of God in heaven.
No love could equal that love which led God to condescend to our need,
and entrust himself to the womb of the Virgin Mary
and take there our humanity.

Mary is like that bush which Moses saw,
burning yet never consumed by the fire.
God himself was there, till Moses knew and obeyed his word.
And to him he made known his name:
I am who am,
the name of the eternal.

The Son of God dwelt in Mary,
till the span of time between conception and birth was completed.
At conception, he had taken, by his divinity,
full possession of Mary's pure body.
At birth he came forth,
with his divinity united for ever to true humanity.
But as the sweet perfume of the rose, leaves the rose still as lovely,
his coming forth was no lessening,
but truly a glorification of the virginity of Mary.

To God,
to the angels,
to Adam,
to the patriarchs and the prophets,
and to countless servants of God,
this burning bush, which was Mary,
brought joy beyond words.
Mary, in the fire of her love,
conceiving the Son of God.
The Son of God in obedience to the Father,
resting in her,
to be born, true man, true God,

of a mother and virgin, a Virgin-Mother.
To ourselves also, and to all our race,
this must bring great rejoicing and consolation.
The Son of God,
he who with the Father and the Spirit is the eternal God,
has taken our humanity, through the love of the Virgin Mary.
Her love embraces all things that belong to God.
We then may claim, and be sure of her intercession.
We can say truly
that man who deserved eternal death through sin
can acquire eternal life only through her.

From Mary, the Son of God came in perfect humanity,
to fight as man with Satan who had subjugated man.
To Mary, men must resort
for strength against Satan's temptings.

Mary is the gateway by which Christ entered into this world,
to open to man the gate of heaven.

Pray then,
pray then to Mary,
that at death she may come to us,
to secure for us
entry into the eternal kingdom
of Christ, her Son.

## Responsory

**Virgin Mary, woman most blest of all,** your grace and holiness, your glory and joy, must ever be our wonder and our praise. No praise of you too high, no love too deep, no loveliness of heaven or earth more lovely than you, Mary, in God's grace and glory. Mary, we name you brightest star of Christ the Sun; for he is Light from Light, true God from God, and the glory of God made known to all; and you – his mother, Mother of Christ our Lord and God.
℣. Mary, pray for all the people of God, and for all who guide his holy Church; for all whose lives are lived by holy Rule. Mary, your love is for all, and all may rejoice in your loving care, with prayer to you and praise of you, the ever-Virgin Mary.

℟. Mary, we name you brightest star of Christ the Sun; for he is Light from Light, true God from God, and the glory of God made known to all; and you – his mother, Mother of Christ our Lord and God.
℣. Glory to God, glory to Father, Son and Holy Spirit.
℟. Mary, we name you brightest star of Christ the Sun; for he is Light from Light, true God from God, and the glory of God made known to all; and you – his mother, Mother of Christ our Lord and God.

**TE DEUM** *as on Sunday, page 75* or **PSALM 50** *as on Friday, page 330.*
℣. God himself came down to the Virgin's womb. (Alleluia)
℟. There to clothe himself as Man, with flesh to offer for us and blood to shed for us. (Alleluia)

**CLOSING PRAYERS** *(page 38).*

---

## FRIDAY

### BLESSING

May the sufferings of the Virgin's Son, be our sure pleading with God the Father. ℟. Amen.

### READING

"You shall seek me and shall not find me."
These words of Christ were the sharp point of the sword of sorrow, entering into Mary's heart.
That sword pierced deeper at the betrayal of Judas,
and at the arrest of Christ, when he willed to be taken
by the enemies of justice and truth.
Deeper still at each insult offered to Christ,
with each suffering inflicted on him.
The sorrow of her heart overflowed into all the members of her body.
She saw how cruelly Christ was struck,
and more cruelly beaten and scourged.
She heard the sentence of death passed by the Jews.
She heard the cries of the people:
"Crucify him, away with him!"
She saw him led out, bound as a criminal, to a traitor's death.
She saw him struggling to carry his Cross,
dragged forward and whipped as he stumbled,

led like some wild beast
rather than a lamb to the slaughter.
As Isaias had foretold, he went meekly to death;
like the lamb that is led to the slaughterhouse,
like the sheep that is dumb before its shearers.
Christ was patient in his sufferings.
Mary endured patiently the sorrow of his sufferings.
She followed him, even to the place of death.
She saw the wounds of his scourging,
the crown of thorns,
his cheeks disfigured with blows,
his face covered with blood,
and she wept in sorrow.

She saw him stretched on the Cross,
and heard the blows of the hammer as the nails pierced his hands and feet.
So great was her suffering and sorrow that her strength almost failed her
as she stood by and watched.
She saw the vinegar and gall offered for his lips to taste,
and her own lips could not move in prayer.
She heard his cry:
"My God, My God, why hast thou forsaken me?"
and saw his head fall forward and his body become rigid
as he breathed forth his spirit.
She stood and saw how he died.
Then truly was her heart quite pierced by the sword of sorrow.

It was the strength God gave that alone saved her from dying in such sorrow.
To see her Son,
stripped and bleeding,
dying,
pierced by a lance,
mocked by those who stood by,
jeered at by soldiers,
deserted by all but a few of his chosen ones,
abandoned by so many whom he had won to justice and truth,
to see this most bitter death:
could there be sorrow so deep as hers?

We read that once, when the Ark of God fell into the hands of enemies,
the wife of one of God's priests died for sorrow.
How much greater was the sorrow of Mary,

for she saw the body of her Son,
which the Ark prefigured,
nailed to the wood of the Cross.
Her love for her Son was love for the Son of God,
greater than the loves of all men.
If the loss of the Ark could cause sorrow and death,
the death of Christ would have brought Mary to death
but for God's gift to support so grievous a sorrow.

By his death, Christ opened the gateway to heaven,
and won for his own their entry into joy.
Mary looked up from the depths of her sorrow,
as one coming back from the gates of death.
Her faith never faltered
that Christ would rise again,
and in this faith she could comfort many whose faith had failed.

They took him down from the Cross,
and wrapped him in fine linen with spices,
and laid him in the tomb.
Then all left.
Few still had faith that he would rise.

Little by little,
the sorrow of Mary's heart lightened,
and she felt the first sweetness of consolation.
The sufferings of her Son were at an end.
She knew that on the third day he would rise,
would rise with his humanity united again to his divinity,
would rise to everlasting honour and glory,
to suffer,
to die no more.

## Responsory

**How pale the Virgin-Mother's face;** how red the wounds in the hands and feet of her Son. Overborne by sorrow, she yet stood to see, to watch him, to hear his cry in the agony of death. Then only did the weight of her sorrow bear her down.
℣. How deep such love to bring to Christ, the Son of God and Lord of all, such suffering and pain, for the redemption of our sinful race, and pierce the sinless

Mother's heart with so sharp a sword of grief.
℟. Overborne by sorrow, she yet stood to see, to watch him, to hear his cry in the agony of death. Then only did the weight of her sorrow bear her down.
℣. Glory to God, glory to Father, Son and Holy Spirit.
℟. Overborne by sorrow, she yet stood to see, to watch him, to hear his cry in the agony of death. Then only did the weight of her sorrow bear her down.

**TE DEUM** *as on Sunday, page 75* or **PSALM 50** *as on Friday, page 330.*
℣. There by the Cross of Christ she stood in deepest sorrow, (Alleluia)
℟. To see how men could spit on him and shed in hatred his Precious Blood. (Alleluia)

**CLOSING PRAYERS** *(page 38).*

---

# SATURDAY

## BLESSING

May Mary, Queen of angels, lead us to the glory of heaven. ℟. Amen.

## READING

The Son of God, the Son of Mary,
Christ who is truth itself, has said to us:
return not evil for evil,
but return good for evil.
Will not he himself therefore,
for he is God,
return good for good,
and give great reward even for little?
He promises in the Gospel that for every good work
he will repay a hundredfold.

What then will be Mary's reward?
Her life was a life of countless good works,
a life entirely pleasing to God,
a life ever free from defect
and unmarred by sin.
In all things her will chose,
and every member of her body responded gladly to that command.

The justice of God has willed that we must rise,
body and soul, at the last day,
to be repaid for our works.
Body and soul we shall stand before God,
for in all things, body and soul act as one.

Christ's sinless body rose from the dead,
and is now and for ever united in glory with his divinity.
The sinless body of Mary, together with her soul,
was taken up by God after her death into heaven,
and she is honoured there, body and soul, for ever.
No mind of ours can comprehend
the perfection and glory which is Christ's as reward for his sufferings.
No mind of ours can comprehend
the glory which is Mary's, in body and soul, for her perfect obedience to God.

The holiness of Mary,
those virtues adorning her soul,
glorified God her Creator,
and she is crowned now in heaven with his reward for those virtues.

The good works of Mary,
accomplished by her perfect subjection of body to soul,
proclaim for ever her praise.
She has done all things as God willed,
and omitted nothing that God desired,
to win an eternal heavenly glory of both body and soul.
No soul, except Christ's, was so filled with holiness and merit
as the pure soul of Mary.
No body, except the sacred body of her Son,
was so worthy to be glorified for its purity and perfection
as the pure body of Mary.

The justice of God flashed forth
when he drove Adam from the garden of paradise
for tasting the forbidden fruit of the tree of knowledge.
The mercy of God entered sweetly into this world
when the Virgin Mary was born,
whom we may fittingly name the tree of life.
The justice of God drove out Adam and Eve into instant exile and misery,
for their disobeying.

The mercy of God gently invites and attracts to the glory of heaven,
all who seek life in obeying.
Mary, the tree of life, grew up in this world,
to the joy of the angels in heaven.
They longed for the fruit of this tree, which was Christ,
and they rejoiced, as they rejoiced in their own eternal happiness,
that the great love of God would be made known among men,
and their own heavenly ranks increased in number.
The angel Gabriel rejoiced to be sent with God's message to Mary,
and his greeting was spoken with great love for her.
When Mary, in the perfection of her holiness and humility, assented,
he rejoiced still more that the desire of all the angels
was soon to be fulfilled.

We believe and we know,
that Mary was assumed body and soul into heaven.
We and all our race should ever think of her,
and pray to her.
In the trials and sorrows of our days,
in the sinfulness of our hearts,
in the bitterness of life, overshadowed by the certain approach of death,
we should look to her,
and draw near to her with true sorrow for sin.

We have called her the tree of life.
To taste the fruit of the tree,
we must first part its branches,
and stretch out our hands through the leaves.
The tree of life is Mary,
the sweet fruit of this tree, Christ her Son.
We reach through the branches to pluck the fruit
when we greet Mary, as Gabriel did, with great love.
She offers us her sweet fruit to taste
when she sees our hearts no longer in sin,
but willing in all things the will of God.
Her intercession and prayer help us to receive
the most holy Body of Christ,
consecrated for us by the hands of men.
This is the food of true life,
the bread of angels,
and the nourishment of sinful men.
We, though we are sinful and sinning,

we are the desire of Christ.
His own blood has redeemed us,
and he has destined us for heaven,
to increase there the numbers of his loved ones.

With wise thought, therefore, and with care,
with all reverence and love, take him and eat.
Let Christ fulfil in you this desire of his heart.

May the wondrous intercession of the Virgin whose name is Mary
win for you this joy from her Son, Jesus Christ,
who, with the Father and the Holy Spirit,
lives and reigns,
God for ever. Amen.

## RESPONSORY

**The Lord has loved you, Mary,** more than all the loveliness of earth and heaven, more than all the beauty of his creating. Mary, the angels of God in heaven rejoice in you, and name you Queen of angels and ever Queen of heaven.
℣. Holiest Virgin, conceived and ever free from sin, we on earth rejoice in you and acclaim you, Queen of earth.
℟. Mary, the angels of God in heaven rejoice in you, and name you Queen of angels and ever Queen of heaven.
℣. Glory to God, glory to Father, Son and Holy Spirit.
℟. Mary, the angels of God in heaven rejoice in you, and name you Queen of angels and ever Queen of heaven.

## TE DEUM *as on Sunday, page 75* or PSALM 50 *as on Friday, page 330.*

℣. Satan is cast down to hell for ever. (Alleluia)
℟. Mary who crushed the Serpent's head is raised to eternal glory and joy. (Alleluia)

## CLOSING PRAYERS *(page 38).*

*APPENDIX 1*

# THE ABBESSES OF SYON (1420 – 2011)

NEWTON, MATILDA, a nun of the Benedictine Abbey of Barking, appointed by King Henry V's charter of the foundation of Syon Abbey in 1415.
In 1417 she was pensioned by the King and retired to a Reclusory attached to the Abbey of Barking.

NORTH, JOAN, canonically elected on 5th May, 1420 *(First Abbess)*.

MUSTON, MAUD.

ASHBY, MARGARET.

MUSTON, ELIZABETH.

GYBBES, ELIZABETH.

BROWNE, CONSTANCIA.

Monumental Brass of Agnes Jordan, Abbess of Syon.
From Denham Church, Buckinghamshire.

JORDAN, AGNES, *(Pictured)* Abbess at the dissolution of Syon monastery.
She died at Southlands near Denham on 29th January, 1546.

PALMER, CATHERINE, took some of the community into exile after its dissolution by Henry VIII, returned to old Syon in Queen Mary's reign, and led the community into its second exile upon the accession of Queen Elizabeth I.
She died at Mechlin on 19th December, 1576.

ROOKE, BRIDGET, was Abbess when the community moved from Mechlin to Rouen.

HART, ELIZABETH, Abbess at the time of the community's flight from Rouen to Lisbon.

PRESTON, ELIZABETH *(First triennial Abbess)*.

WISEMAN, ANNE.

WISEMAN, BARBARA.

CARNABY, MARY.

MENDANHA, BRIDGET, she died with the reputation of extraordinary sanctity and was the only Portuguese Abbess.

BROOKE, BARBARA,

SALISBURY, CLARE.

PENRICE, GRACE.

HARNAGE, ELLEN.

CARR, JANE.

SMITH, MARY.

SUTTON, URSULA.
MILES, CATHERINE, one of the four foundresses of the Bridgettines' convent for Portuguese subjects at Marvilla, Lisbon.
CARR, MARY.
SALISBURY, MARIANNE.
HARNAGE, MARY.
WALDEGRAVE, BRIDGET.
GRAHEMES, DOROTHY
YARD, MARY.
HACKETT, MARY.
MEADE, MARY.
HODGSON, ELIZABETH.
BALDWIN, CATHERINE.
HUDDLESTON, PLACIDA.
HILL, WINIFRED.
HACKETT, CONSTANCE.
BECKETT, BRIDGET.
HODGSON, MONICA.
CARTER, URSULA.
LOLLY, VICTORIA.
BRIDE, HELEN.
HALFORD, DOROTHY.
FARNES, ELIZABETH.
LOWE, ROSE.
LAKE, ANNE CATHERINE,
JENKINSON, MARY JOSEPH.
ECCLES, BERNARD.
SMITH, MAGDALEN.
STRINGFELLOW, BRIDGET.
BURCHALL, MARY CATHERINE.
CARTER, MARY JOSEPH, Abbess at the time of the community's return from exile in 1861.
RICHMOND, MARY LUCY.
ROPER, WINIFRED.
HEYS, MAGDALEN, Abbess when the community moved from Spettisbury to Chudleigh in 1887.
BUDD, MARY IGNATIUS, the last of the nuns professed in Lisbon.
JOCELYN, MARY TERESA *(became Perpetual Abbess in 1921).*
NEVIN, MARY MAGDALEN.
WALLACE, MARY PETER.
SMYTH, ANNA MARIA *(Last Abbess, 1976 - 2011)*

*From 'The English Bridgettines of Syon Abbey' by Canon John R. Fletcher, pages 165-7, 1933. With the names of the last three abbesses added.*

*Syon Abbey, South Brent, Devon, which closed in 2011.*

## APPENDIX 2 ~ *The travels of the Sisters at home and in exile.*

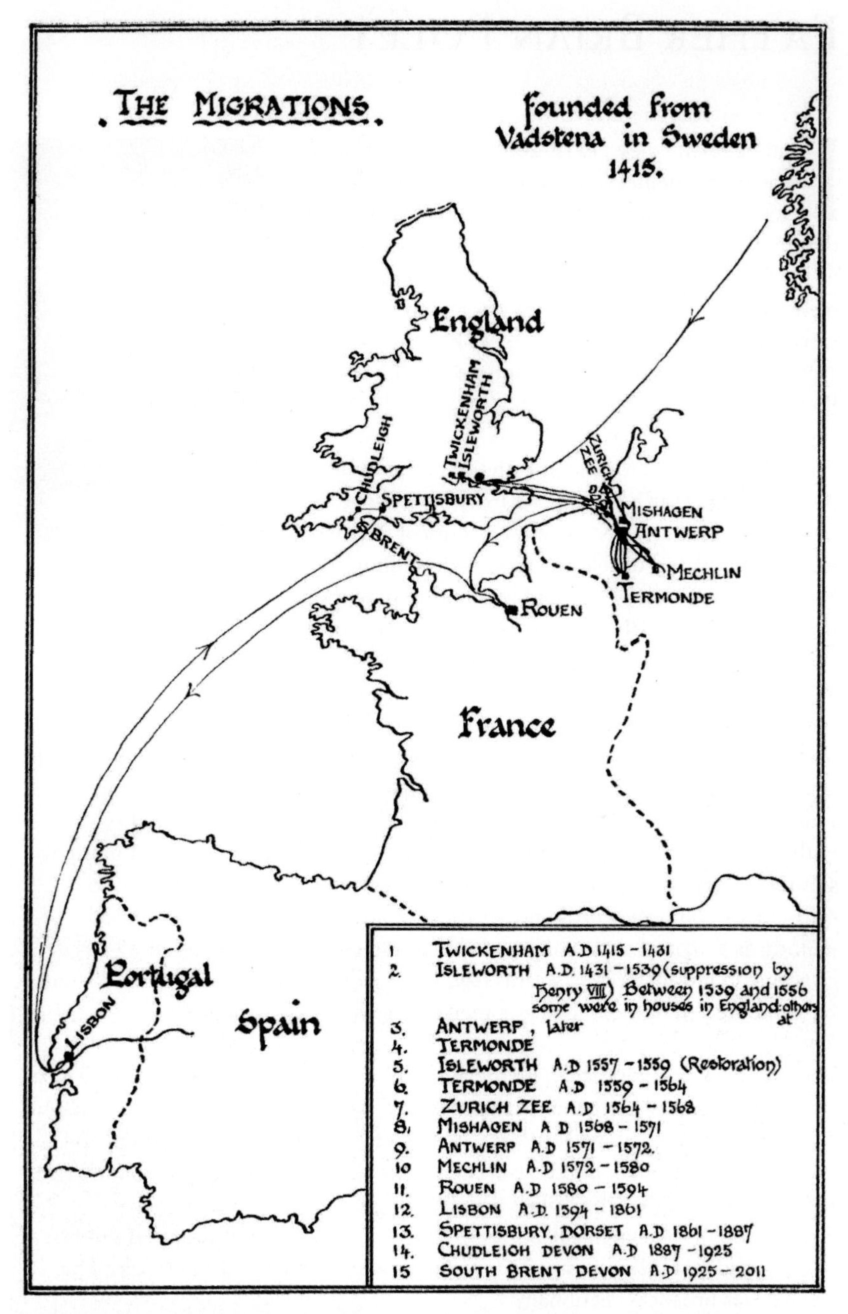


*Frontispiece from 'The English Bridgettines of Syon Abbey' by Canon John R. Fletcher, 1933.*

## *APPENDIX 3 ~ Biography: Bridgettine Office translated by*
# FATHER BRIAN FOLEY

Father Brian Foley (1919-2000), probably one of the most talented priests of the Archdiocese of Liverpool, shared his father's musical ability and enthusiasm from an early age. In their home parish of St Peter and St Paul in Great Crosby, Lancashire, the men's choir, of which his father was a member, was well-known for its ability to sing plainchant and other sacred music, inspired by the pronouncements of Pope St Pius X.

*Father Brian Foley.*

Brian Foley studied for the priesthood at the Liverpool Archdiocesan seminary, St Joseph's College, Upholland (1933-1945), where his musical talents were nurtured and developed to include singing classical sacred polyphony and learning to play the organ. He spoke of 'having to accompany the wonderful Hours of Prayer and Praise (as College Organist for the six years leading to ordination in 1945) as one of the greatest privileges of my life'. An assistant priest for twenty-six years, he served in various parishes of the Archdiocese, including the city of Liverpool itself. For a number of years he served as organist for diocesan celebrations. Life was always busy, but he had time for the parish choirs, many of which he founded. All of them benefitted from his wide repertoire, musical ability, enthusiasm and his sense of humour. He was able to simplify or adapt music to suit the ability of a 'stand-in' organist, or a very new group of singers; or to translate or compose words and set them to a familiar or newly composed melody as the need arose. Many of the young people inspired by him then, continue in music ministry to this day. For a number of years, in his spare time, he continued to play football as a member of the clergy team!

Looking back to 1960, when he moved to St James' Bootle, he wrote: 'The next six years proved to be the most exciting and lively time of all, with the two new recent Popes, the Second Vatican Council and the Beatles era beginning my involvement with the church's own choir and a wider group of Catholic singers with whom the BBC (the British Broadcasting Corporation) asked me to arrange the first Ecumenical 'Songs of Praise' ...to have seven hundred singers, from all the local churches united in song and prayer was a great thrill.' The service was broadcast nationally.

It was in the quieter years between 1966 and 1971 – when he became parish priest of St Bede's Clayton Green, near Preston – that he began work, which extended over four or five years, translating the Bridgettine Office, using the original music as far as possible for the antiphons and responsories. During that same time he was working on other projects of which he said, 'From the beginning of my writing, I wished to write words ... that contain teaching about the faith and spiritual life.' In 1968, a letter appeared in the Catholic press asking for new hymn texts. It was written by Geoffrey Laycock, principal lecturer in Music at Norwich, and Anthony Petti, lecturer in English at University College London. From their joint enterprise came the *New Catholic Hymnal* in 1971 (Faber Music Ltd, London).

'There are 14 of my texts in this book, and all of them have been used in later hymnals in England, USA, Australia and South Africa, some translated, one even into Japanese. I regard it as a privilege to have been set to music by [Sir] Lennox Berkeley, Edmund Rubbra, Herbert Howells, Colin Mawby and others ... it is a surprise to me to count the hymns I have written over the years, a hundred at least. More than a third of them are now in hymnals world-wide.' His book *Sacred Words – a lifetime of verses for meditation* was published in 1994 by Kevin Mayhew Ltd.

Brian Foley, a priest for over fifty-five years, and a writer of hymns for well over half of that time, began his jottings in the 1950's. 'I wanted something like the Latin hymns I learned to love through many years of the Divine Office,' he wrote and acknowledged that he was inspired by the nineteenth century hymn writer, Father F. W. Faber.

It is easy for the reader, and for those who celebrate the Bridgettine Office, to see that his aims and his spirituality are present in this most sensitive and thoughtful translation, and in the settings of so many beautiful and reflective responsories and antiphons. The many hours and the effort he expended so generously are a great gift to us and to the future, for the greater glory of God.

*Barbara M. Hunt, September 2001.*

*APPENDIX 4 ~ Syon Abbey on the Internet*

# WEBSITES WITH LINKS TO SYON

The Syon Abbey Society
http://syonabbeysociety.wordpress.com/
Syon Abbey Research Associates (SARA)
http://syonabbeysociety.wordpress.com/sara-bibliography/
Syon Park, Isleworth
www.syonpark.co.uk/history.asp
'The Lost Abbey of Syon'
http://www.syonpark.co.uk/downloads/syon_abbey.pdf
Musica Sacra (The Church Music Association of America)
http://musicasacra.com/
Short Breviaries by Theo Keller
http://www.gregorianbooks.com/gregorian/www/www.kellerbook.com/INDEX.HTM
Vadstena Abbey, Sweden
http://birgittaskloster.se/en /
The Bridgettine Sisters of Rome in UK
www.bridgettine.org
The Brigittine Monks in USA
www.brigittine.org
Blessed Sacrament Church, Exeter
http://www.blessedsacrament.org.uk/syon-abbey.html
Channel 4's Time Team at Syon (49 minutes – sign in or register)
http://www.channel4.com/programmes/time-team/4od#2933989
Syon Abbey Library at The University of Exeter
https://as.exeter.ac.uk/library/librariesandcollections/special/archives/rare/title_289481_en.html
British History Online – House of Bridgettines – Syon Abbey
http://www.british-history.ac.uk/report.aspx?compid=22119
Syon Abbey in Tudor times
http://www.tudorplace.com.ar/Documents/SyonAbbey.htm
Syon Abbey at Chudleigh
http://www.chudleighhistorygroup.com/convents.html
The Syon Cope at the V & A
http://collections.vam.ac.uk/item/O93171/the-syon-cope-cope-unknown/
Wikipedia online encyclopedia
http://en.wikipedia.org/wiki/Syon_Abbey

PLEASE NOTE that the contents of these websites are not the work or copyright of the Sisters of Syon.

*APPENDIX 5 ~ Vocations contacts.*

# THE BRIDGETTINES WORLD-WIDE

For centuries women and men have been attracted to the way of life in a Bridgettine community and to the Rule of St Bridget. If you wish to enquire about vocations to the Order of the Most Holy Saviour, you can be sure of a friendly welcome and someone who can provide all the information you may need. A number of websites and contacts are listed below.

Nowadays there are five distinct branches of the Order:

1. **Autonomous Abbeys** *(From about 1370 onwards)*
2. **Spanish Branch** *(1637)*
3. **The Bridgettine Sisters of Rome** *(1911)*
4. **The Brigittine Monks** *(1976)*
5. **Mexican Branch** *(1980)*

**1. Autonomous Abbeys** *(Originally founded c. 1370; Rule approved in 1378; officially enclosed in 1384).*

Vadstena Abbey – Sancta Birgittas Kloster, 'Pax Mariae', Myntbacken 2, S-592 3
Vadstena, Sweden. *Tel:* 0046 (0)143 109 43
*E-mails:* guesthouse@birgittaskloster.se or kloster@birgittaskloster.se
*Website in English:* http://birgittaskloster.se/en/ *(Re-founded from Uden in 1963)*
Syon Abbey *(1415)* – South Brent, Devon, England UK. *(Closed 2011)*
Altomünster Priory *(1497)* – Birgitta Kloster , St. Birgittenhof 7, Altomünste
Germany 85250. *Tel:* 0049 (0)8254 8255, (0)8254 8830.
Uden Abbey *(1437)* – Birgittinessenabdij 'Maria Refugie', Vorstenburg 1, 5
AZ Uden, The Netherlands. *Tel:* 0031 (0)4132 52535 *Website:* www.abdiju

**2. Spanish Branch** *(1637)*

This branch of the Order was established by the *Venerable Marina de Esco*
- 1633).
Valladolid *(1637)* – Monasterio del Santisimo Salvador de Santa Brigi
de Gijón 23, 47009 Valladolid, Spain. *Tel:* 0034 983 333687.
*This branch of the Bridgettines has houses in Spain, Mexico , Peru and Venezuela*

**3. The Bridgettine Sisters of Rome** *(1911)*

This branch of the Order was established by *Blessed Elisabeth Hessel*
1957). – Curia Generalizia: Piazza Farnese 96, Roma 00186 Italy
*Tel.* 0039 06 6889 2596 or 0039 06 6889 2497 *Fax.* 0039 06 68

*E-mail:* brigida@mclink.it *Website:* www.brigidine.org
*UK Website:* www.bridgettine.org

**4. The Brigittine Monks** *(1976)*
This branch was founded by *Brother Benedict Kirby (1929 - 1998).*
– The Brigittine Monks, Priory of Our Lady of Consolation, 23300 Walker Lane, Amity, Oregon 97101, USA.
*Tel:* 001 503 835 8080 *Fax.* 001 503 835 9662 *E-mail:* monks@brigittine.org
*Website:* www.brigittine.org

**5. Mexican Branch** *(1980)*
This branch is known as *The Misioneras del Santisimo Salvador y de Santa Brigida* and was founded in the 1980s by the Bridgettine Nuns of the Recollection, Mexico City. They have two houses: Mexico City *(1980)* and Venezuela (2002).

*International dialing codes shown are those for direct dialing from the U.K. Omit the Trunk Code where shown thus (0) unless dialing from within the country itself in which case omit the Country Code, for example (0046). To place a call via an international operator, call 155.*

*APPENDIX 6 ~ With thanks to…*

# ACKNOWLEDGEMENTS

Our Syon Abbey community had been using Fr Brian Foley's translation and musical adaptation of this Breviary for about twenty years when ***Sister M. Cecilia Coyle*** began to suggest to me that we should try to publish it and so offer it to others for their use. For many reasons I was unable to pursue this suggestion until ***Theo Keller*** wrote to me from America in the 1990s and persuaded me that, with his help, it could be done.

Theo, born on 1st January 1944, writing in 2002, was typically modest about his accomplishments. He described himself as 'a life-long pastoral musician and liturgical researcher,' adding: 'My primary career as an adult has been as a pastoral musician;' (He was a talented choirmaster in New York) 'secondly, I am a liturgical scholar, which has become my full-time work.' He added: 'I have been intrigued by these [breviary] texts for most of my life and even more by the people who produced them – used them – and by how the texts were (or are) used.'

As his gift to our community Theo, already seriously ill, typeset and produced the music pages in plainchant, using fonts developed and supplied by the Benedictine monks of *Saint Meinrad Archabbey*, Indiana, U.S.A. (www.saintmeinrad.org). It was also his suggestion to use the *Weiss* font throughout. Theo died before this edition could be published but his comments on the early drafts were: 'The work is beautiful. I know the [finished] book will be just as beautiful, if not more so.' My hope is that it fulfills his expectations and is a fitting tribute to a dear friend and Brother of our Chapter.

***Bishop Christopher Budd***, Bishop of Plymouth (1986 - 2014), responded very kindly – and promptly – to our request in 2001, to write the Foreword to this Breviary. In so doing, he approved its publication for private daily prayer. Neither he, nor any of us, had any idea that it would take so long to bring it to fruition. Thank you Bishop Budd for your unfailing help, support and encouragement throughout the time you were our Ordinary.

***Adrian Wardle,*** who designed, edited and produced this Breviary over a period of fifteen years, began his career in publishing in 1965. In 1980 he founded the *Westminster Cathedral Bulletin* magazine, now called *Oremus*. Later, having moved to Plymouth, in 1995 he launched *Catholic South West*, the monthly newspaper for the Diocese of Plymouth. His patience and forbearance, together with his knowledge accumulated over the years – and his most willing assistance – has been a constant source of encouragement, for which I express my great gratitude.

***Mary Cooper***, since her retirement from the teaching profession, has helped our Syon community in many practical ways. A Sister of the Chapter for about forty years, she has been involved with the preparation of this Breviary since its inception, especially by checking the hundreds of proof pages with a keen attention to detail. Thank you, Mary, for all your help.

***Dr Christine Faunch*** is Head of Heritage Collections at the University of Exeter. She and her team at the *Special Collections* department have been unfailingly helpful in searching out material which we have requested from Syon's archives. The medieval manuscripts, books and documents from our Abbey were deposited at the university over a number of years, up to the closure of Syon Abbey in 2011. I should like to include in my thanks ***Jessica Gardner*** and ***Charlotte Berry***, no longer with the department.

Indeed there are many others who in ways great and small have contributed to this work of love, especially: ***Roger Ellis, Ann Hutchison, James Carley, Barbara Hunt, Dom Sebastian Wolff OSB, Fr Kristian Paver, Fr Tim Lewis*** and ***Fr Peter Coxe.*** And last but not least, our new Bishop of Plymouth, the ***Rt. Rev. Mark O'Toole***. To these, and anyone I may have overlooked, my thanks and prayers are with you all.

Finally, I should like to thank my sisters of Syon for their encouragement and patience while waiting for the publication of this Breviary. Now that we are so few, may it be welcomed by others as their choice of daily prayer to the honour and praise of God.

**Sister Anne Smyth O.Ss.S.**
*Abbess of Syon, 1976 – 2011.*

---

**Picture credits**: Thanks to the following individuals and organisations for the use of their images: Front cover, Syon Abbey Mss (large) *'Horae'* (small) *'Antiphonale'* (Special Collections, University of Exeter); Back cover & p. 8 'Our Lady of Syon' (Buckfast Abbey), 1635 map (Collection of the Duke of Northumberland). Page 15 (Dr Jonathan Foyle). Page 17 (Channel 4's Time Team). Page 181 (Free Christ Images). Page 242 (Museum of Fine Arts, Houston). Page 449 (Special Collections, University of Exeter). Page 552 (Barbara M. Hunt). Endpapers, hardback only: Syon Mss *'Horae S. Trinitatis'* (Special Collections, University of Exeter).

*APPENDIX 7*
# BIBLIOGRAPHY


Andersson, A. Saint Bridget of Sweden, Patroness of Europe, *Catholic Truth Society (CTS) London, 1980. ISBN* 0-85183-296-2. ctsbooks.org

Andersson, A. The Mother of God & Saint Birgitta, *Vatican Polyglot Press, Rome 1983.*

Andersson, A. Catherine of Vadstena, *Vatican Polyglot Press, Rome 1983.*

Blunt, J. H. *(Ed.)* 'The Myroure of oure Ladye', by (?) Thomas Gascoigne, 1403-1458, *Early English Text Society, London, 1873.* Available online at archive.org/details/myroureourelady00abbegoog

Bridget, Saint Revelations of St Bridget: excerpts from her revelations. *Tan Books (Saint Benedict Press), 2009.* www.tanbooks.com *ISBN* 978-0-89555-233-4.

Collins, A. J. The Bridgettine Breviary of Syon Abbey; *The Henry Bradshaw Society, 1963.*

Cotton, Sister M. Bridget. In your midst I will leave a humble, lowly people. *Studies in St Birgitta and the Bridgettine Order, Vol. 2, 1993.*

De Hamel, C. Syon Abbey; *The Roxburghe Club, 1991.*

Ellis, R. The Spirituality of the English Bridgettines; *Analecta Cartusiana 68, Salzburg 1984.*

Fletcher, J. R. The Story of the English Bridgettines of Syon Abbey; *The Burleigh Press, 1933.*

Graf, Dom Ernest, OSB Revelations and prayers of St Bridget of Sweden, 1928.

Halborg, J. The Word of the Angel. *Peregrina Publishing Co. 1996. ISBN* 0-920669-47-6.

Hamilton, Adam, OSB The Angel of Syon, *Sands & Co, London, 1905.*

Hogg, J. St Birgitta's *Revelationes* reduced to a Book of Pious Instruction. From *'Vox Mystica': D. S. Brewer, 1995.*

Hutchison, A. 'The Myroure of oure Lady' a medieval guide for Contemplatives; *Studies in St Birgitta and the Bridgettine Order, Vol. 2, 1993.*

Johnston, F. R. Syon House (article) in: A History of the County of Middlesex Vol. III, *(Ed. Susan Reynolds), Oxford University Press, 1962. ISBN* 978-0-7129-1034-7. http://www.british-history.ac.uk/report.aspx?compid=22273&strquery=Religious Houses

| | |
|---|---|
| Johnston, F. R. | Saint Richard Reynolds, 1961 (*Syon Abbey booklet reprinted 2004*). |
| Johnston, F. R. | Syon Abbey – a short history of the English Bridgettines, *Eccles and District History Society, London, 1964.* |
| Jones, E. A. & Walsham, A. | Syon Abbey and its books, 2010; *ISBN* 978-1-84383-547-9 |
| Morris, B. | St Birgitta of Sweden, 1998. *ISBN* 0-85115-727-0 |
| Redpath, H. | God's Ambassadress, *Bruce Publishing Co., Milwaukee, 1947.* |
| Pedersen, K. S. Sander-Olsen, U. | Bridgettines, 2nd edition, 2003, *ISBN* 87-989457-1-8 |
| Nyberg, T. & Carlsen, P. S. | Birgitta Atlas, *Societas Birgitta Europa, 2013.* |
| Searby, D. and Morris, B. | 'The Revelations of St Birgitta of Sweden' (*Liber Caelestis*), *Oxford University Press, Vols. 1-3* 2006, 2008, 2012 (*4th Vol. due 2015*). |
| Syon Abbey | The Life of St Bridget, 1958 (*Syon Abbey booklet reprinted 1999*). |
| Syon Abbey | The Rule of Our Most Holy Saviour for Syon Abbey: being the XV Cent. Papal Bull of Pope Urban VI with additions by Dr John Joseph Keily, D. D., Bishop of Plymouth in 1914, available online at... https://archive.org/stream/ruleofourmosthol00briduoft/ruleofourmosthol00briduoft_djvu.txt |
| Syon Abbey | The Constitutions for Syon Abbey, updated and approved by *The Congregation for Religious & Secular Institutes, 1987.* |
| Thordeman, Bengt, *et al.* | Birgitta, a Swedish Saint: a series of lectures in October 1973 to celebrate the sixth centenary of her death. Introduced by Pope Paul VI. *Published in 1974 by the Swedish Embassy in Rome* (Ambassador, *Brynolf Eng*). |
| Yardley, Anne Bagnall | Bridgettine Spirituality and Musical Practices at Syon Abbey. *Studies in St Birgitta and the Bridgettine Order, Vol. 2, 1993.* |

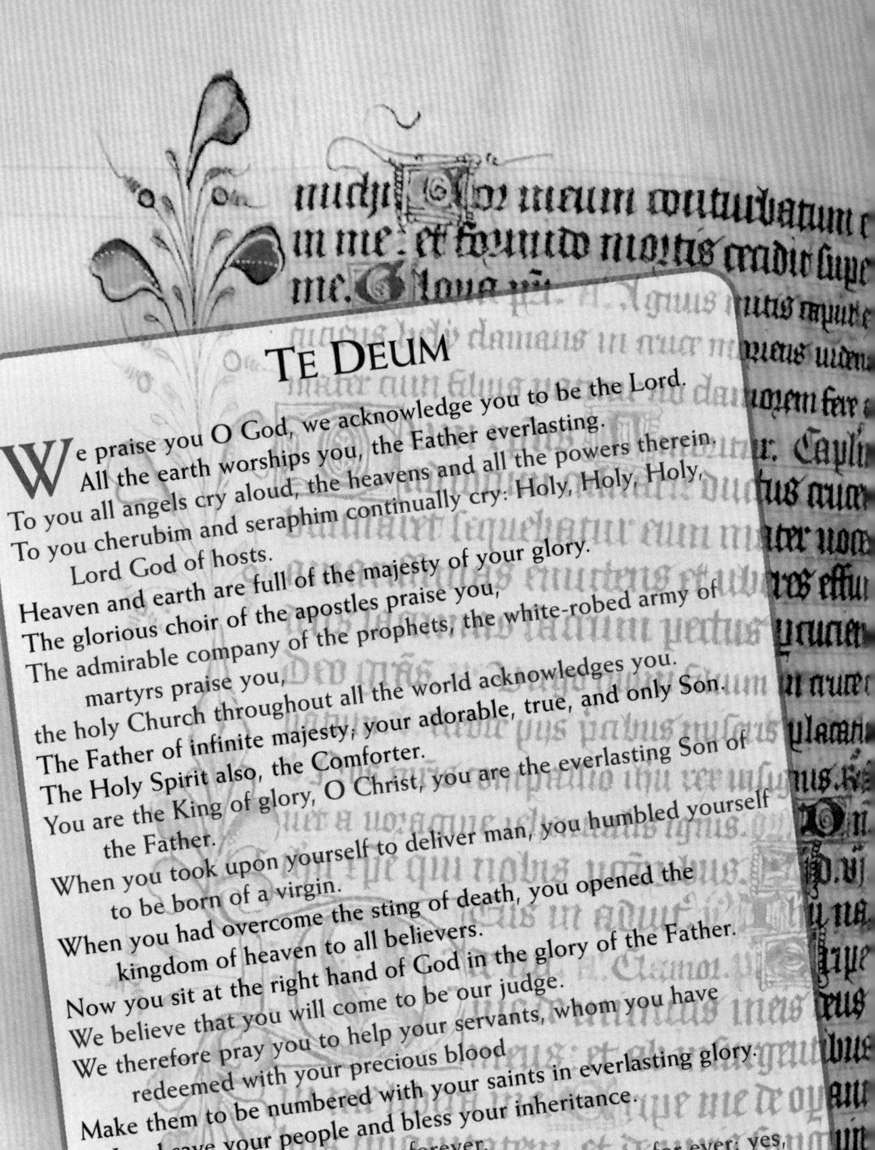

# Te Deum

We praise you O God, we acknowledge you to be the Lord.
All the earth worships you, the Father everlasting.
To you all angels cry aloud, the heavens and all the powers therein.
To you cherubim and seraphim continually cry: Holy, Holy, Holy,
Lord God of hosts.
Heaven and earth are full of the majesty of your glory.
The glorious choir of the apostles praise you,
The admirable company of the prophets, the white-robed army of
martyrs praise you,
the holy Church throughout all the world acknowledges you.
The Father of infinite majesty; your adorable, true, and only Son.
The Holy Spirit also, the Comforter.
You are the King of glory, O Christ, you are the everlasting Son of
the Father.
When you took upon yourself to deliver man, you humbled yourself
to be born of a virgin.
When you had overcome the sting of death, you opened the
kingdom of heaven to all believers.
Now you sit at the right hand of God in the glory of the Father.
We believe that you will come to be our judge.
We therefore pray you to help your servants, whom you have
redeemed with your precious blood
Make them to be numbered with your saints in everlasting glory.
O Lord save your people and bless your inheritance.
Govern them and lift them up forever.
Day by day we praise you, and we glorify your name for ever: yes,
for ever and ever.
Be pleased, O Lord, this day, to keep us free from sin.
Have mercy upon us, O Lord, have mercy upon us.
O Lord, let your mercy be shown to us, as we have hoped
in you.
In you, have I hoped, O Lord: I shall not be confounded for ever.

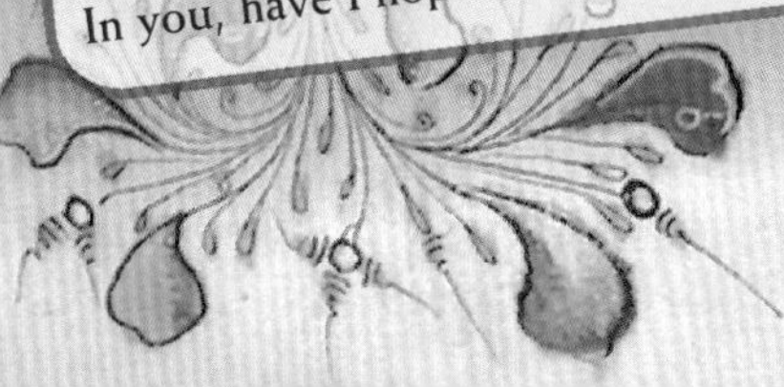